Middle-Income Trap

Zhijie Zheng

Middle-Income Trap

An Analysis Based on Economic Transformations and Social Governance

清華大學出版社
TSINGHUA UNIVERSITY PRESS

palgrave
macmillan

Zhijie Zheng
China Development Bank
Beijing, China

ISBN 978-981-15-7400-9 ISBN 978-981-15-7401-6 (eBook)
https://doi.org/10.1007/978-981-15-7401-6

Jointly published with Tsinghua University Press
The printed edition is not for sale in China Mainland. Customers from China Mainland please order the print book from Tsinghua University Press.

This Palgrave Macmillan imprint is published by the registered company Springer Nature Singapore Pte Ltd.
The registered company address is: 152 Beach Road, #21-01/04 Gateway East, Singapore 189721, Singapore

Foreword

The transformation of China over the past forty years from one of the poorest countries in Asia to the world's second largest economy is the most significant geopolitical event of our times. In the era of Reform and Opening-up, China has lifted 700 million people out of poverty—an unprecedented feat in human history. China's rise has redrawn the maps of commerce that defined the global trading system after World War II. Today its banks are among the largest financial institutions in the world; its leading internet companies stand with the world's most innovative and competitive. Chinese travelers can be found in numbers in the remotest corners of the globe, as well as in New York and Tokyo.

Success, however, can be its own worst enemy if a developing country remains bound to what has worked in the past and fails to adapt to new challenges brought about by development itself. Many emerging economics have failed to escape the "middle-income trap," while those that have averted it to achieve sustainable growth and join the ranks of high-income countries stand out precisely because they are the exceptions. According to the World Bank, only thirteen countries successfully made the transition between 1960 and 2008.

China's per capita income (in purchasing power parity terms) has grown from less than 1000 US dollars in 1990 to over $15,500 in 2016. In this remarkable achievement, however, it has essentially reached the level of $16,000 that many economists believe is the precipice of the middle-income trap. Indicators such as the deceleration of GDP growth from 10 to 6.5% in recent years have sparked discussion and focused policymakers on the question of how China can avert the stagnation experienced by so many other developing nations.

Given the urgency of the challenge, Mr. Zheng Zhijie's original and wide-ranging examination of the topic, The Middle-income Trap: An Analysis Based on Economic Transformations and Social Governance, could not be more timely or relevant. As the President of the China Development Bank (CDB), the largest finance development institution in the world with a mandate to support China's long-term development strategy, Mr. Zheng is in a singular position to understand the middle-income challenge in theory, policy, and practice. What comes through in these pages is not only President Zheng's deep technical expertise, but also his sense of professional and personal responsibility for the issues he explores. That combination makes it a book that should have profound influence on the debate about this vital question in the next phase of China's development.

The book's central insight is that for a country to transition successfully from middle income to high income, it must transform not only its economic system, but its social system as well. After a broad-ranging survey of the experiences of countries on four continents, President Zheng concludes that, "Historically, all countries that managed to escape the middle-income trap have undergone a series of comprehensive transformations in the economy, politics, society and culture before escaping the trap." He also finds that government plays a decisive role in determining whether or not a country makes the necessary changes to avoid the trap. This is particularly true in China, given the dominant role that government has played since ancient times through to the present day—in contrast to a country like the United States, in which the founders intentionally set out to restrict government's reach.

Regarding the economy, President Zheng argues that China's primary challenge is still to delineate the relationship between government and the market—the fundamental question for Chinese leaders since the late 1970s. There are still too many cases of large state-owned enterprises (SOEs) dependent on government planning and support. Local government leaders, meanwhile, rely far too much on capital investment to maintain the growth, tax revenues, and employment by which they are assessed and promoted. The same dynamic motivates them to protect inefficient SOEs through favorable policy, credit, and loans. Such actions distort the market incentives needed for sustainable growth. President Zheng argues that China needs to "further open up the market and remove barriers to allow the market to play a decisive role in resource allocation (and) create an equal competition environment," which in turn would "enable the government to play its role better." These insights are extremely important.

Given his decades of experience on the front lines of China's development work, President Zheng understands that meaningful change will inevitably face fierce resistance from those who are invested in the current system and can exert political influence. In case studies from Latin America and Southeast Asia, he draws cautionary lessons for China: economies controlled and dominated by interest groups sacrifice efficient markets and the broader good for the narrow benefits of the ruling class; in doing so, countries ruin their chance to achieve full modernization.

In the countries that failed, President Zheng observes that intense social conflict and the resulting damage to societal stability can be one of the major elements that block further progress. This is one reason China must transition from the growth-first orientation of previous decades, which has exacerbated income inequality, to one that narrows the wealth gap, expands the middle class, and devotes far greater resources to strengthening the social welfare system and safety net.

President Zheng goes on to argue that it is still not enough to execute the economic transformation successfully. Economic reform must be accompanied by an equally deep social transformation that strengthens the rule of law and brings about good governance. It requires the establishment of a legal system that enjoys the confidence of average citizens. Only by doing this can China "guarantee the lives and livelihoods of its people, handle social conflicts, and ensure long-term social stability and prosperity."

As with economic transformation, social transformation requires that government loosen its grip. The government should share responsibility with other stakeholders in managing civil affairs and ultimately let citizens govern their own affairs wherever possible. President Zheng contrasts this with the historical model, too much of which still persists, in which "social governance in China was limited by a fundamental problem with the government functioning as the sole governing body, while the powers of the market, society and the public were too weak, if not zero, leading to over-administration in social governance and low efficiency of social resource allocation."

Finally, President Zheng makes a persuasive case that education can be a great source of strength in helping China escape the middle-income trap. By any measure, China has had remarkable success in the daunting task of educating the largest population in the world. The effects can be seen from the efficient employees on the factory floors of Guangdong and Chongqing to colleges in the United States where over 300,000 Chinese currently study. In a highly competitive world, however, China cannot afford to be satisfied or complacent. Only education "can provide economic transformation and industrial upgrading…which, in turn, restructures productive forces, changes relations of production and, in the end, reshapes the economic base of a society."

Having known President Zheng for nearly 20 years, it comes as no surprise to me that he has written a book that is at once scholarly and deeply humane. It is a volume that will hold the interest of both experts and those concerned with an issue that will affect so many lives. It is also relevant for those of us based primarily outside China, because a world in which China averts the middle-income trap and joins the ranks of developed nations is much better than one in which it fails. We are all invested in China's success. If it can safely navigate this challenge, as it has in so many other cases, China will be an example for other nations who share the universal aspiration of providing a better life for their citizens.

John L. Thornton

John L. Thornton is Chairman of the Board of Trustees of the Brookings Institution, Executive Chairman of Barrick Gold Corporation and Professor and Director of the Global Leadership Program at China's Tsinghua University. He was President of Goldman Sachs. In 2008, he was awarded the Friendship Award of the People's Republic of China.

Preface

Escaping the Middle-Income Trap Requires Increasing Governance Capacities[1]

Socialism with Chinese characteristics has entered a new era; the main contradiction in our society has been transformed into a contradiction between the growing needs of the people and the inadequately balanced economic development. As China emerges as a middle-income country, its economic growth slows gradually. And it enters into a "new normal" characterized by medium or high speed growth. Xi Jinping, General Secretary of the CPC Central Committee, attaches great importance to issues such as how can China move on to the high-income stage, and how to stay in that stage, because escaping the middle-income trap, in its essence, is not an issue of quantity, but an issue of the quality of governance. Without modernized governance systems and capacities, countries may still come across development traps at the low-income stage. Although some countries have entered the high-income stage, they experience larger wealth gap, and intensified social conflicts, which makes it difficult to maintain sustainable development. Therefore, as we are at a critical juncture of escaping the middle-income trap, it's critical to review the lessons of

[1] This was an article originally published in the first edition of the August 11, 2016 issue of Study Times, a newspaper published by the Party School of the CPC Central Committee, and was edited as the foreword of this book.

success and failure learned by countries around the world in escaping the middle-income trap, enhance governance capacities, construct the legal system and roadmap for national economic governance in a comprehensive manner, and advance national governance on the track of rule of law.

I. Enhancing Economic Governance Capacities to Adapt to the Development Needs of the Economy

Reviewing the development path of our economy, it can be observed that the relationship between government and market continues to be an issue in the forty years of development since the reform. Although the economic boom requires the market to play a fundamental role in resource allocation, it is necessary to take further steps in escaping the middle-income trap, such as facilitating market-oriented reforms and invigorating the economy.

Further Reforming the Economic System to Transform Government Functions. In the Decision of the CCCPC on Some Major Issues Concerning Comprehensively Deepening the Reform made in the 18th The Third Plenary Session of the 18th CPC Central Committee, the reform of the economic system was recognized as the focus of all the efforts to deepen the all-round reform. And the core issue to be addressed is handling the relationship between government and market properly to allow market to play a decisive role in resources allocation, and enable the government to play its role better. The role and function of the government is to maintain the stability of the economy on the macro level, enhance and improve public services, safeguard fair competition, enhance market supervision, complement market failure, maintain the order of the market, promote sustainable development, and common prosperity.

Establishing a More Open Market to Eliminate Barriers to Market Entry. Due to historical reasons, the government and enterprises have been closely associated for a long time in China. In the early stage of building and refining the market economy mechanism, the functions of the government and those of the enterprise were not thoroughly separated. The operation system and management mindset were not completely changed. The access to some industries was not granted. And the government was still in control of the pricing of key resources, which lowered the efficiency of the economy. Some enterprises, especially large SOEs, were used to relying on government planning and support. Meanwhile, to increase tax revenue and assure employment, the local governments are highly motivated to rely on investment to drive economic growth, and support and protect some large enterprises through policy, credit and loans. Out of the concern for fiscal revenue and political track record, local governments were used to using administrative orders to restrict, reject, and hinder the involvement of non-local companies in the same industries in the market competition.

Further Opening Up the Market and Remove Market Barriers. Chinese economy is facing large downward pressure, yet still has great growth potential. However, some good investment opportunities are constrained by various market access policies, making these opportunities inaccessible for a large amount of social capital, thus taking a toll on the vigor and efficiency of the market. Therefore, we need to further open up the market, and remove market barriers to allow the market to play a decisive role in resource allocation, create an equal competition environment for social capital and unleash massive investment potential.

First, fully rolling out a negative list for market access to both international and domestic companies, and allowing the companies to engage in anything that is not prohibited by the law. Second, focusing on the development and opening-up of critical border areas such as pilot zones, state-level border ports, border cities, border, and cross-border economic cooperation zones. These areas are important platforms for our cooperation with neighboring countries and regions. Third, completing pricing mechanisms of critical sectors, and easing most of the control over the pricing in competitive sectors and segments. It is also necessary to strengthen government pricing mechanisms, facilitate the management of government-priced items through lists, and improve the openness and transparency of pricing activities by the government. We should also trust the market with the pricing of all items that can be priced by the market, combine power delegation with strict oversight, strengthen regulation in-process and afterwards, and improve the efficiency of regulation.

II. Improving Complementary Governance Capacities Between the Government and the Market with Balanced Roles Played

In the crucial stage of escaping the middle-income trap, to balance the roles of the government and the market with the latter playing a decisive role in the allocation of resources and the former doing complementary work, the key is to clarify the appropriate boundary between the government and the market, which depends on the identification of government acts. It is important to note that "taking economic development as the central task" does not imply that governments of all levels should be directly involved in business production or management. All governments should consistently stick to a "Three-No" principle of no intervention in microeconomic activities, no decision-making of business activities, and no introduction of investment for business entities, so as to gradually get rid of its business functions, giving back the leading role of resource allocation to the market, and avoiding directly promoting economic growth as a dominant force. In addition, efforts should be made to improve the government's functions of economic regulation and market supervision, and in the particular common cases where the governments fail to play their roles, to strengthen and improve their functions of social management and public service, with a view to filling the gaps in public goods supply as soon as possible, and gradually achieving balanced supply of basic public services.

From an objective point of view, it is reasonable for local governments to proactively involve themselves in the economic growth when the economy is underdeveloped, the industrialization has just started, and the market imperfect. In particular, it should be acknowledged that local governments have improved the business environment for business entities, especially for private entities, by taking pro-business measures in the competition for investments. However, a basic principle must be upheld by governments that they should not change the boundaries of rights or the amount of risks of related business entities, so as to avoid too much administrative intervention and ensure effective functioning of the market, keep the target of "distinct".

It is essential to note that against the backdrop of government acts being increasingly of micro level, similar to those of business entities, efforts should be made in particular to avoid an "ill-functioning market economy" created by marketization of powers during strong government intervention in forms of collusion of power and capital and exchange between powers and capitals, which may generate endogenous interest groups. These interest groups are different from the general ones fostered as a result of fair competitions during market development, as the former have stronger incentives to maintain the status quo and to curb Pareto-improving reforms. Since the endogenous interest groups have stronger capacities than the general ones and are able to exert greater political influences on the political decision-making process, they are therefore more likely to hinder the undergoing transition to a market economy and the withdrawal of deeply involved governments from the market, so as to maintain an inefficient yet balanced system for long. The harms of these interest groups can be seen in some countries (such as Latin American and Southeast Asian countries) where extremely powerful governments seeking profits are ubiquitous. These market economies controlled and dominated by the ruling elites have fallen into the trap of economic development, and failed to successfully achieve their modernization, from which we should learn lessons.

Meanwhile, we must develop accurate understanding of the modernization of governance capacities.

First, from the perspective of governing bodies, effective governance highlights governance of public affairs that involves multiple stakeholders. Previously, the social governance in China was limited by a fundamental problem, with the government functioning as the sole governing body, while the powers of the market, the society and the public being too weak, leading to over-administration in social governance and low efficiency of social resource allocation. The objectives of reforms include: from the perspective of the relationship between the government and the market, giving back the central role to the market so as to allow the market to play a decisive role in resource allocation, which is key to the modernization of governance capacities; and from the perspective of the relationship between the government and the society, putting the people in the center with a view to enabling them to function as a governing body in social governance and achieving self-governance, which is the impetus for the modernization of governance capacities.

Second, from the perspective of power operation, effective governance calls for a proper identification of government functions. The functions of other governing bodies previously practiced by the government should now be delegated to the market, business entities, and the society, with the boundaries of powers between the government and the market and between the government and the society clearly defined. On this basis, efforts should be made to adapt to the situation and requirements of economic and social development, and to promote the transition of government functions centered on creating favorable environments for development, providing high quality public services, and maintaining social fairness and justice.

Third, from the perspective of organizing structure, effective governance must be built on a scientific and reasonable government structure. The key is to optimize government functions, institutional settings and work processes, and to enhance an administrative mechanism with powers of decision-making, execution and supervision constraining and coordinating with each other that can be used to optimize processes, reduce costs, strengthen supervision, and improve efficiency.

III. Improving Capacities of Coordinated Fiscal and Monetary Governance and Properly Addressing Their Relationship

At the key stage of escaping the middle-income trap, to ensure the efficacy of fiscal and monetary policies, it is necessary for us to analyze the transmission mechanism of fiscal and monetary policies from the standpoint of economic structure. This type of analysis, which is distinct from the previous practice of analyzing the transmission mechanism itself, focuses the research on transmission mechanisms on the influence of economic structure on transmission effects, thus providing more targeted views on the selection of fiscal and monetary policy tools.

Improving people's livelihood is the focus of increasing fiscal expenditure. Increasing expenditure and decreasing taxation have always been the two threads of proactive fiscal policy operations. An important consideration as to why the main conduit of fiscal expansion is switched from increasing expenditure to decreasing taxation is that we need to seek balance between the two major goals of steady growth and structural readjustment.

Given that stabilizing the overall price level remains an important mission for us and due to further consideration that the two major goals of steady growth and structural readjustment must be compatible, we cannot revert to the old path of sacrificing economic structure in exchange for growth. This means that the focus of increasing expenditure needs to be shifted, at an opportune time, from investment to stimulating consumption demands.

To be more specific, as to the arrangements about increasing expenditure, aside from continuing to work on optimizing investment structure, the most important task is to stimulate terminal consumption by introducing and expanding a series of items of expenditure with the improvement of people's livelihood as the main thread. Important items include implementing the minimum wage system, increasing labor compensation for low-income workers, promoting farmers' income, basically realizing the full coverage of the new old-age pension system for rural residents and the old-age pension system for urban residents, improving the subsistence allowances for urban and rural residents, the treatment of certain recipients of special care, and the basic pensions for enterprise retirees, supporting the establishment of the mechanism to enable normal growth of the income of enterprise employees and ensure compensation payment, increasing the scale of fiscal aid to increase the income of rural and urban residents, especially middle and low-income residents, alleviating the burdens including education, medical care and housing of citizens with financial difficulties, and vigorously supporting the construction of affordable housing projects.

It can be expected that by focusing on structural tax reduction and taking the auxiliary measure of a series of expenditure-increasing operations with the improvement of people's livelihood as the main thread, coordination and interaction between revenue and expenditure can be realized and proactive fiscal operations in the future can lead to a path in line with domestic and international economic situations and coordinated with the entire layout of macroeconomic policies.

To increase demands, adjustments should be made to the fiscal system. Currently, the real challenge facing China's economy is the unbalanced inadequate and unsustainable nature of economic growth. The two major reasons are a marked lack of demand and the insufficient structural reform of the supply side. Prior to the global financial crisis, China's rapid economic growth was partly due to the strong external demands from the United States and Europe. However, such demands are gradually shrinking, leading to continuously decreasing rates of investments in the future. To resolve the issue of expanding demands and sustaining growth for the Chinese economy, the primary method should be adjusting China's fiscal system, which plays a positive role in compensating for the slowing investment growth and the weakened export market. What is unreasonable about China's financial budget is its limited scale and the inconsistency between the allocation methods of the revenues and expenditures of local and central governments. The socialist economy is characterized by its ability to possess and control all key resources and take the lead in all major strategic actions. China's total financial budget, however, accounts for only 28% of GDP, a proportion which is significantly lower than the figures of similar countries. The figure is 35% for upper middle-income countries and 40–50% for most economies of the OECD. According to the analysis in China 2030, published by the World Bank (WB). the percentage of social services and other consumption demands provided by China's financial budget in GDP ranked third to last when compared with similar countries. This explains why China's overall consumption ratio (for families and the government) is 10–15% lower than those of similar countries. The implementation of fiscal reforms can increase the expenditure of the government by 4% to 5% of its GDP. This way, sufficient demands can be ensured to sustain China's economic growth of 6–7% annually.

Orientation and Directions of Monetary Policies. The central bank will continue to implement robust monetary policies, while correctly addressing the relationship between stable economic development, structural adjustments, and inflation expectation management and sparing no efforts to safeguard the balance between economic growth, price stability, and risk prevention. The main directions in this regard are as follows.

First, facilitating the establishment of a regulated financial market and vigorously deepening the reforms of financial institutions. We need to deepen the reforms of large commercial banks and continuously improve corporate governance in all regards, gradually realizing a modern financial corporate system. Continuing to deepen internal management and risk prevention and management, and increasing innovation capacities and international competitiveness are also imperative.

Second, increasing the allocation efficiency of the financial system and improving the financial regulation and control mechanism to effectively advance interest rate liberalization and the reform of the RMB exchange rate formation mechanism. To achieve this, we should accelerate the formation of the system of benchmark market interest rates, increase the level of regulation and control over market interest rates by the central bank, and correctly guide financial institutions to perform risk-based pricing. Financial institutions should make good use of the right to floating rate pricing to conduct reasonable pricing and take the initiative to strengthen liability management and cost constraint, thus realizing scientific evaluation of interest risks, improving pricing mechanisms, actively safeguarding pricing order, and ultimately contributing to coordinated economic and financial development.

We should deepen reform and innovation of the RMB exchange rate formation mechanism and strengthen the two-way floating elasticity of RMB exchange rates, enabling the principle of market supply and demand to play a greater role in exchange rate formation so as to basically maintain the RMB exchange rate at reasonable and balanced levels. At the same time, we need to continue accelerating the development of the foreign exchange market, pushing forward the innovation of exchange rate risk management tools, paying close attention to the effect of changing international situations on capital flows, strengthening effective monitoring and control of international capital, coordinating the use of RMB in international trade, and actively expanding the channels of RMB outflow and inflow.

Third, vigorously supporting the economic restructuring and optimizing credit resource allocation to better serve the development of real economy, formation of synergy in the industrial industry. It is important to guide financial institutions to improve management and product innovation and explore proper credit management model, strengthen financial support to energy conservation and emission reduction as well as low carbon economy and cultivate a multi-level rural financial service system with various offerings under healthy competition to provide more financial support in boosting agricultural harvest, the income of farmers and development of the rural area. Efforts should be made to support projects affecting people's livelihood, including job creation, poverty relief, and education loans. More financial support should be provided for SMEs, especially micro and small businesses, key projects that bear importance on the big picture and can promote other sectors, and key national economy sectors such as technology, cultural industry, tourism, and strategic emerging industry. Also we should provide financial support and services that are in line with national policy to balance regional economic development, carry out tougher credit asset stock restructuring, implement differentiated housing credit policy, tighten supervision on indemnificatory housing, encourage construction of small and middle-sized commercial houses and first-time purchasing of commercial houses for living, and contain speculative property buying.

Fourth, guiding the steady and healthy growth of currency loans as well as aggregate financing to the real economy on all fronts; improving the micro-prudential policy framework and double-pillar regulation through bringing in various monetary policies so as to keep the market flow reasonable; continuing to let micro-prudential policy play its role in countercyclical regulation and adjust relevant factors in accordance with economic environment changes, shape of financial institutions, and implementation of credit and loan policies; guiding financial institutions to support the development of real economy in a targeted and flexible way. Regulating the mobility of banking system to make fluctuation in market interest stable through leveraging mobility managing tools such as central bank bills, reserve requirement ratio, reverse repos and sell repos, based on the global macroeconomic trend and the relation between monetary revenue and expenditure and between mobility supply and demand.

Five, upholding the stability of financial institution and guarding against systematic financial risks. Consolidating and improving the system of warning, preventing and evaluating systematic financial risks, not only to prevent the "black swan" incident, but also to prevent the "grey rhinoceros" event; strengthening the monitoring and evaluation of financial risks in different industries and markets as well as around the globe; guarding against the spreading of real economic risks and non-standard financial risks from certain areas, industries and enterprises to the financial system; Developing risk warning and dealing plans, and promoting deposit insurance schemes; implementing comprehensive measures to maintain financial stability so as to prevent any possible risks; deepening the macro-prudential policy reform; guiding the sound operation of financial institutions; strengthening the research into systematically important financial institutions supervision policies and encouraging innovation in order to put forward practical solutions. Urging financial institutions to strengthen internal control and risk management; continuing to strengthen the off-balance sheet business of financial institutions, local government financing and loans and real estate industry risk assessment, monitoring, and management.

IV. Strengthening Financial Governance and Increasing Marketization Level of Financial Sector

Among the changing financial landscape in the world, economic governance should focus on strengthening financial governance so as to escape the middle-income trap. Therefore, China's financial sector must understand major difficulties and challenges to achieve their strategic positioning in the globe.

The marketization level still has space to improve. Taking evolution of global financial system and historical experience of developed countries into account, we find that if a large developing country, such as China which shifts from planned economy to market economy, wants to have a place in the global financial landscape and achieve strategic positioning and leapfrog development in post financial crisis era, it requires a free and open macro financial environment. Therefore, in a relatively long period, China should continue to deepen financial reform, increase marketization level of financial sector, and overcome the following three obstacles.

Obstacle to interest rate liberalization needs to be overcome. Interest rate defines the basic price of financial products and services, and offers pricing baseline for many innovative financial products and derivatives, so it plays an important role in giving full play to the market's function of allocating resources. With interest rate liberalization, financial institutions can independently offer diversified financial products and services and compete to survive based on consumers' free choices, therefore balancing the supply and demand of differentiated financial products and services, helping enterprises accurately assess risks and set prices and optimizing capital allocation. In addition, interest rate liberalization ensures the development of an efficient and effective monetary transmission mechanism and reflects the needs of economic macro-control. Interest rate liberalization is a gradual process in China. Until now, China has removed restrictions on interest rate of deposit and loan denominated in foreign currencies, expanded the fluctuation range of interest rate for bank loans and deposits, applied market-oriented pricing for enterprise bond, financial bond, commercial bill and currency market transaction, and expanded the fluctuation range of interest rate of housing loans. However, China still falls short of the requirements of interest rate liberalization, so it must promote reform of interest rate liberalization in a well-planned, systematic, and determined manner.

Barrier to capital flow needs to be overcome. With steady progress in China's economic reform and gradual expansion of economic space, capital market has witnessed rapid development and its significance is increasing. Currently, China is playing a more and more important role in international economy, but its influence is still limited in international capital market. One key reason is that limited openness of its capital market restricts the inflow of international capital. Though capital flow regulation can effectively prevent relevant risks, it also prevents China from enjoying the benefits of optimizing resource allocation around the globe. If China wants to balance economic development and resource utilization, and increase its importance in global financial market, it should remove barrier to capital flow and support fair competition in market economy.

Obstacle to exchange rate should be reduced. According to "The Impossible Trinity" proposed by Krugman, free capital flow, independent currency policy, and stable exchange rate cannot be all realized in a single country. If China wants to allocate capital in global context and establish independent monetary policy, the trend is to promote marketization reform of exchange rate. More importantly, exchange rate regime reform can also offer good conditions for internationalization of RMB. In the future, China should further promote reform of RMB exchange rate formation mechanism, increase the flexibility of RMB exchange rate, improve anti-risk capacities during capital liberalization, and lay foundations for the strategic target of promoting RMB as a major international currency.

The financial structure needs to be further optimized. Banks are still dominant institutions in China's financial structure, marked by banks holding the vast majority share of the total financial assets; the indirect financing remaining dominant, though with direct financing increasing due to the development of the capital market; and the slow development of the insurance industry, trust industry and financial leasing industry, resulting in risks of social finance highly concentrated in banks. Excess monetary assets will undoubtedly reduce the availability and use of social finance and weaken businesses' abilities and motivations to innovative financing, resulting in businesses' increasing debt levels, which is harmful to the optimization of Chinese financial structure and the development of real economy. Moreover, massive financing resources are allocated to SOEs and large-scale enterprises, shutting the majority of SMEs and private companies out of organized financial markets with a result of different types of private financial markets popping up, which brings more challenges to both the stability of financial system and financial regulation.

The gap between urban and rural areas in finance needs to be narrowed. On one hand, rural and underdeveloped areas in China are less industrialized with less potential economic benefits, higher information costs and lack of sufficient collateral, and risk mitigation alternatives, where financial institutions are reluctant to operate, leading to "a market failure". On the other hand, due to the adverse selection and moral risks, funds that subsidized by the government and donated by NPOs are underused in these areas in practice, sometimes even with violations of contracts, which undermine the local capital circulation and lower the credit scores of rural and underdeveloped areas, leading to "a government failure." Those two "failures", in turn, will lead to siphon effects, resulting in the reverse flow of capital from rural to urban areas and from west to east regions, further impeding the development of local economy and the formation of a reasonable and balanced financial structure.

As a result, if China's financial sector wants to play a significant role in escaping the middle-income trap and achieve a strategic rise after international financial crises, we must try our best to address structural issues in the first place, then continue to optimize the internal structure of financial sector and build a national integrated financial market, driving the healthy development of China's financial system.

The significance of financial governance needs to be improved. It has turned out that countries all over the world will face huge challenges when transforming to high income countries from middle-income ones, during which financial governance is critical. The middle-income trap is largely the result of the economic instability of middle-income countries, which mainly stems from the frequent financial crises. Middle-income countries suffer financial crises frequently as a result of structural issues caused by the ongoing economic and social transformation. The key to escape the middle-income trap lies in how to avert financial crises. We should, politically, perform strong supporting reforms and prudential regulatory systems, develop policies to promote fiscal and financial reforms promptly and prudentially, and technologically, carry out macro-prudential regulation to maintain the stability of Chinese financial system and establish a mechanism for effective risk response and quick recovery. The key for China in the middle-income stage to escape the middle-income trap is to avert financial crises. And the key to preventing financial crises mainly lies in avoiding unhealthy and unsound financial liberalization and improper ways of managing enterprise debts.

V. Improving Social Governance Capacity to Accommodate the Demands of Social Development

The experience or lessons learned from the countries that have escaped or got lost in the middle-income trap indicate that economic and social transformation is indispensable for escaping the trap. Historically, all countries that managed to escape the middle-income trap have undergone a series of comprehensive transformation in economy, politics, society, and culture before escaping the trap. Xi Jinping, General Secretary of the CPC Central Committee, has proposed the strategy of comprehensively building a moderately prosperous society, deepening reform, advancing rule of law and strictly governing CPC, and the Decision adopted at the Third Plenary Session of the 18th CPC Central Committee suggests that efforts should be made to innovate and improve the social management methods, by "strengthening leadership by the CPC committee, giving full play to the leading role of the government and encouraging and supporting the participation of all sectors of the society, so as to achieve positive interaction between the government management on the one hand and social self-management and residents' self-management on the other." Against the new backdrop, what should we do to innovate and improve social governance methods and facilitate the government to play its leading roles? First and foremost, the government's capacity of social governance should be increased comprehensively.

First, increasing the leadership in social governance. We should give full play to the guiding and coordination roles of the government in social governance. Second, increasing the capacity of promoting cooperation between diverse entities. Besides the government, other entities should also take their responsibilities in social management to maintain social order and engage in social affairs. Third, increasing capacity of effectively preventing and resolving social conflicts. Efforts should be made to: (1) uphold the human-oriented philosophy and focus on solving universal issues related to people's livelihood; (2) take prevention as the main task and mediation as a priority and use multiple mediation methods to establish reasonable and efficient mechanisms for people's demands and expression, conflict resolution, interests coordination, psychological intervention, and rights protection, with the view to meeting the reasonable needs of all people; (3) complete the risk assessment mechanism for important decisions and social stability, and listen to people for decisions, projects, and programs involving interests of all people, to take all possible effects in consideration. Fourth, improving capacity of maintaining public security. Improving the government's capacity of maintaining public security is necessary for deepening the reform and facilitating development in the increasingly complicated global context. Fifth, improving capacity of self-transformation and development. An active and forward-looking transformation in the government is a precondition for ensuring a sound social governance system. To promote an active and forward-looking transformation, the government should: (1) review the changes in external contexts and demands of social development, to clarify its position as a rule maker of the society, a public service provider and a guardian of social orders; (2) use the think tank and external resources to conduct in-depth research on general rules and specific features in social governance and effectively integrate related resources to avoid "Tacitus trap"; (3) actively adjust and improve the governance models in alignment with the changes in environment and situations, to improve its capabilities in self-adjusting and self-reform.

According to the lessons learned and inspiration drawn from the economic and social transformation in developed countries, the US, UK, France, Germany, and other western countries have adopted different strategies in heading into the high-income stage. However, all of these countries have undergone comprehensive and deep economic and social transformation.

Industrialization in developed countries starts from the specialization of human resources. As labor force specializes, labor productivity rises, thus contributing greatly to the economic development. In a considerable time from now, it is imperative that the demographic dividend should be made full use of and counted upon. To that end, China has to bring about the integration of two powerful weapons—education and technology, to upgrade its capacity to create wealth and propel the wheel of society and civilization. The development and maturation of modern corporate system further spur the economic growth and industrial structural transformation in the western world. Developed countries have already shown that urbanization must be fostered on the foundation laid out by industrialization. On the whole, urbanization is impossible without industrialization.

However, when industrialization comes to a certain point, its effect on urbanization will be compromised and its role will be taken over by the emergence of the tertiary industry such as service industry.

Many researchers conclude that hostility among social strata, unequal distribution, political corruption, and social disorder are all consequences of the middle-income trap. But in reality, analysis on economic development and social problems in some Latin American, South Asian, and Eastern European countries that suffer from the trap indicates that except for lack of innovation and unsuccessful transformation, other factors like deformed social structure, dysfunctional network of interests, poor welfare system, and inefficient administration are pulling these countries into quagmires. In contrast, the development process of some European countries, the US, Japan, and South Korea shows that apart from industrial upgrading and social transformation, a sound welfare system, adjustment of social structure, and balanced political powers are the key to breaking into the high-income stage.

Experience from many countries makes it clear that both middle-income and high-income stages need the support of certain social conditions. Those that can enable high-speed growth in middle-income stage often fail to support economic development in high-income stage. We can learn from various lessons that in order to escape the middle-income trap, efforts must be made in both economic and social transformation.

It is a principle that also works for China. However, in the process of social transformation, China is confronted with multiple challenges that necessitate unprecedented efforts. The past 40 years show us a way out. That is to continue reform with confidence while keeping an open mind, seize opportunities, and make arrangements in a top-down fashion. Only in this way can we escape the middle-income trap quickly and efficiently.

Beijing, China

Zhijie Zheng

Introduction

Completing Economic and Social Transformation to Escape the Middle-Income Trap

Over the last 40 years, China has made remarkable economic achievements after adopting the Reform and Opening-up policies. The living standards, comprehensive national strength and international status of the country have been greatly improved. In 2016, China's GDP per capita reached USD 8123. According to the income group classification by the World Bank (WB), China has become an upper middle-income country (GDP per capita shall reach USD 3976~12275) after staying in the low-income and lower-middle-income groups for many years.

A research conducted by WB in 2007 reports that after entering the middle-income stage, a country will suffer from lack of growth drivers and incomplete new growth models, as well as challenges posed by developed and less-developed countries, which may lead to long-term economic stagnation and slower development—the so-called "middle-income trap". There is no doubt that with respect to this issue, China's academic community has varied opinions, and even totally different beliefs. For example, scholars argue over whether the concept of "middle-income trap" is valid or applicable for China. Nevertheless, the concept has great practical significance and value in understanding the current challenges faced by China's economic and social development.

As China has become a country in the middle-income stage, Chinese economy enters the "new normal" of medium-to-high speed growth, with its growth rate gradually slowing down. Currently, the growth rate of China's GDP has dropped from over 10 to 6.7%, and the Producer Price Index (PPI) has experienced negative growths for more than 40 consecutive months. Meanwhile, many social issues have emerged, such as aggravated environmental pollution, widening income gap, and high house price. Since the 18th National Congress of the CPC, Chinese Central Government has introduced various reforms in social, economic, financial, and industrial fields to achieve stable economic growth. Under such circumstances, it is of great significance to study the rationale of the middle-income trap in depth, summarize experiences and lessons learned from countries that escaped or got lost in the middle-income trap, and explore opportunities for escaping the middle-income trap, and how to perform successful transformation and upgrading in the future.

China Development Bank (CDB) has been devoted to the mission of "enhancing national competitiveness and improving people's livelihood", and makes great contribution to the economic and social development of China. Unlike other books on the middle-income trap, Middle-income Trap: An Analysis Based on Economic Transformations and Social Governance, a new book written by Zheng Zhijie, President of CDB, explores the essence of the middle-income trap from two major perspectives, namely "economic transformation" and "social transformation". First of all, this book analyzes the features of the economic growth pattern and economic transformation during the middle-income stage, from the perspectives of economic phenomena and economics. Then, it dives into how the social structure and institutions change and transform during the middle-income stage, from the perspectives of social phenomena and sociology. Finally, it reveals the essence of the middle-income trap: with the economic growth challenged by developed and less-developed economies, as well as the current social structure and governance system unsuitable for the new social development phase, a country in the middle-income stage will experience issues of both economic and social transformation, such as economic stagnation or recession and more intensified social conflicts. A country must perform both successful economic and social transformation in order to survive the middle-income trap. There is a causal relationship between the two types of transformation. They are also complementary to each other. Economic transformation makes changes to the social structure and relationships, thus requiring successful and reasonable social transformation and institutional reform, which would in turn promote further development of economic transformation.

Chapter 2 presents how various countries across the world escaped or got lost in the middle-income trap, demonstrating that a country must perform both successful economic and social transformation in order to survive the middle-income trap. Those that successfully escaped the middle-income trap are countries that introduced comprehensive reforms in economic, political, social, and cultural fields to avoid getting lost in the middle-income trap. Chapter 3 systematically outlines issues and challenges that China faces as a middle-income country. In the economic field, China's economic growth pattern is shifting from factor input to enhancing total factor productivity, which is restricted by institutions, environment, and international competitiveness. Analysis and comparison of China's current social features reveal that China is facing challenges that developed countries, developing countries, and countries in transition would face during social transformation, i.e., widening income gap and mounting social conflicts. Economic and social transformation requires changing some current ideas, transforming some existing models and systems, and phasing out some existing enterprises and sectors, which undoubtedly will encounter resistance. This book believes that rule of law can provide institutional guarantee for successful transformation, and identifies issues related to rule of law that hinder China's economic and social transformation, which distinguishes this book from other books on the middle-income trap.

Chapter 4 contains several sections, i.e., Accelerating Industrial Restructuring to Promote Economic Transformation, Advancing Market-Oriented Reform to Ensure Greater Economic Vitality, Promoting Innovation to Further Stimulate Development, Education: the Key to Escaping the Middle-income Trap, and Improving Economic Governance Capacity. Based on detailed data, this chapter analyzes opportunities and key areas for China to perform economic transformation and upgrading, makes recommendations for market-oriented and global approaches in fields including regional development, industry, finance, income, consumption, education, and technological innovation, and puts forward specific research strategies on the basis of strategies developed by Chinese Central Government, including the "One Belt, One Road" initiative and mixed ownership reform in state-owned enterprises. Given current social structure and social conflicts, Chapter 5 highlights the importance of reaching consensus on reforms based on fairness and justice. This book points out that, only through optimizing the national governance system to facilitate social transformation and development, reforming income distribution models, and improving livelihood, can we improve the social structure, ease social conflicts, and successfully perform social transformation, and achieving rule of law is the guarantee for successful economic and social transformation.

In the sixth chapter, China's participation in globalization and exploration of the country's development path are analyzed. Problems are discussed pertaining to participation in global governance, the direction of the global value chain and industrial restructuring, leaping over the middle-income trap and the government role's under the New Normal.

Solutions are then put forward. No one can ignore China's achievements since the Reform and Opening-up, including proposing the "Belt and Road Initiative" as a platform for world economic development, founding the Asian Infrastructure Investment Bank and co-founding the New Development Bank as supplements to the global financial system, pushing for more global cooperation in a number of areas and advocating a community of shared future for all mankind. It's undeniable that China has striven to lead and reshape a common civilization for all mankind that encompasses economic development, institutional innovation, globalization, and human values. Therefore, China's development is closely in line with the world's development as a whole. And not only will China succeed in crossing the middle-income trap, it will be trusted to offer economic opportunities and security for the world as a high-income country in the future.

As a banker, Mr. Zheng carries out in-depth study from perspectives of economic and social development instead of mere economics. This book compares the middle-income stage in various countries across the world, analyzes features and issues in China's economic and social development, and comprehensively explores approaches of reforms in China's economic, financial, social, and legal fields in the middle-income stage, which include changing economic growth patterns, facilitating reforms in social institutions, achieving rule of law, enhancing cultural and moral construction, and making use of development finance. This book is worth reading for demonstrating the broad vision, bold innovation, and pursuit for practice of Mr. Zheng. I believe it is beneficial for other economists and sociologists in this field, and will offer valuable references for China's economic and social development in the near future.

Li Yining

Contents

List of Figures

Chapter 1

Chapter 2

Chapter 3

Chapter 4

List of Tables

Chapter 4

CHAPTER 1

The Concept and Essence of Middle-Income Trap

Since the start of China's reform and opening-up in 1978, it has experienced nearly 40 years of rapid economic growth, with its gross domestic product (GDP) per capita crossing the $1000 mark in 2001, surpassing $3000 in 2008, exceeding $8000 in 2015 and reaching $8123 in 2016.[1] But in recent years, economic growth has slowed down markedly. This is not only a fact, but also a new normal of social consensus. Has China encountered a middle-income trap? Can the development problems encountered by China be explained by the current concept of a middle-income trap and related theoretical framework? And can a reasonable solution to crossing the middle-income stage be found? To answer these questions correctly, we must accurately grasp the essence of the concept of middle-income trap. To understand the essence of middle-income trap, the concept must be reinterpreted in a context that goes beyond the experience of a particular country and a purely economic perspective. This means that the middle-income trap is understood not only as a problem that some developing countries may encounter in their own development, but also as a problem that all countries may encounter in the middle-income stage; the middle-income trap will not only be defined from the perspective of economic growth, but also understood from the perspective of social development.

[1] Source: National Bureau of Statistics of the People's Republic of China.

Z. Zheng, *Middle-Income Trap*,
https://doi.org/10.1007/978-981-15-7401-6_1

1 Origin of the Concept of Middle-Income Trap

1.1 The Concept of Middle-Income Trap Was First Mentioned in World Bank Reports

In 2007, the World Bank published two reports on economic growth in East Asia, namely An East Asian Renaissance: Ideas for Economic Growth and East Asia & Pacific Update: 10 Years After the Crisis. In the reports, World Bank experts used economic stagnation in Latin America as a cautionary tale for the economic development of East Asia, and formally introduced the concept of middle-income trap. The World Bank used the concept of middle-income trap to describe the considerably long period of economic stagnation and slow economic development that developing countries fall into after entering the middle-income stage, and attributed the middle-income trap to the consequences of failure to transform the economy: the existing growth factors have been exhausted while new modes of growth have not been formed, resulting in bottlenecks in economic development. Some countries in Latin America and Southeast Asia are considered to be typical examples of countries that have fallen into the middle-income trap. Although there is still debate in the academic community as to whether the concept of middle-income trap is valid and whether it is of universal significance in describing the economic development of developing countries, it is an objective fact that some developing countries encounter development problems characterized by stagnation after entering the middle-income stage.

Historically, the economic development of Latin American countries has been characterized by slow growth. Relevant data show that in the early eighteenth century, the per capita income in North America was almost the same as that in Latin America, but since the beginning of the twenty-first century, the former has been five times the latter. If North America (especially the United States) is unmatched by any other region in its ability to sustain economic growth, making this comparison unfair, then the rapid economic development in East Asia in the twentieth century (especially in the second half) fully demonstrates that the development of Latin America is problematic. Most Latin American countries have joined the ranks of middle-income countries since the early 1970s, but in the 1980s, thanks to a debt crisis, the entire Latin American economy grew at an average annual rate of only 1.2%, and on top of that, currency depreciation and high inflation reduced the real GDP growth rate, with GDP per capita growing by only −1.9%. Especially in the 45-year period from 1963 to 2008, Argentina experienced 16 consecutive years of negative growth. Today, most countries in Latin America are still stuck in the middle-income stage. Most countries and regions in East Asia, on the other hand, made the leap from a middle-income country to a high-income country from the 1970s to the 1990s. Although East Asia was hit hard by the financial crisis in 1997, and many people also predicted that East Asian economies would repeat the fate of Latin America in the mid-1980s by falling into stagnation, but in the decade after 1998, the GDP of East Asian economies grew at an average annual rate of more than 9% and doubled. Since the 1950s, there has been a sharp contrast between Latin America and East Asia in economic development when compared to the United States in the same period. From 1950 to 1998, the ratio of the per capita income of East Asia to the per capita income of the United States rose from 8 to 16%, while in Latin America this figure dropped from 27 to 21%.[2] Compared with the rapid economic growth in East Asia, economic development in Latin America has almost stagnated or even regressed.

In the second half of the twentieth century, Southeast Asian countries generally experienced a period of rapid economic development. However, in the 10-year period around 2000, these countries experienced a sudden decline in economic growth and then stagnation. It was not until 2005 that the economic development of Southeast Asian countries returned to the 1995 level. Take Thailand for example. Since the 1960s, Thailand has implemented a "dual-track" economic development strategy characterized by equal emphasis on stimulating domestic demand and promoting foreign trade and investment, and has achieved rapid economic development. Since the 1990s, its economy has been growing at an average annual rate of about 8%. In 1995, Thailand's per capita income exceeded $2500. As a result, the World Bank designated Thailand as a middle-income country. But since 1996, Thailand's economic growth rate has dropped sharply to 6.9%, the lowest level in the past 13 years. Its current account deficits accounted for 8.3% of the GDP, and inflation rose to 6.2%. Another example is Malaysia, which experienced rapid economic growth from independence until the 1960s. By the 1980s, it had emerged from an agricultural society to become one of the "Tiger Cub Economies" that led the development of the

[2] Francis Fukuyama. Falling Behind: Explaining the Development Gap between Latin America and the United States, 2008.

region. But soon afterwards, due to the impact of the Asian financial crisis, its economic development also stagnated. Vietnam has witnessed rapid economic growth since its economic reform in the 1990s. In the last decade of the twentieth century, Vietnam's GDP grew at an average annual rate of 7.6%. Since the first half of 2007, Vietnam's inflation rate has continued to rise and its trade deficit has expanded rapidly. As a result, its sovereign credit rating was downgraded, its financial strength was weak, capital fled it, and its currency depreciated substantially.

1.2 *The World Bank's Description of the Middle-Income Trap*

According to the World Bank's 2017 standards, countries with a GDP per capita of less than \$1005 are low-income countries; countries with a GDP per capita of between \$1006 and \$3955 are lower-middle-income countries; countries with a GDP per capita of between \$3956 and \$12,235 are upper-middle-income countries; countries with a GDP per capita above \$12,276 are high-income countries. The concept of middle-income trap describes an important phenomenon in world economic development in the twentieth century where many countries can usually reach the middle-income stage quickly, but only a few countries can cross this stage, because the policy and institutional changes needed to achieve this leap are politically, technologically and socially more challenging.

The World Bank assigns the world's countries into three income groups: high, middle, and low. It can be seen that in the past half-century, countries in different income groups have been shown to differ greatly in economic development. As can be seen from Fig. 1, measured by GDP per capita, high-income countries have been on a generally smooth, coherent and linear trend in growth; in stark contrast, the economic development of middle-income countries was virtually stagnant before the twentieth century, and only since the beginning of the twenty-first century have they shown a trend similar to that in high-income countries half a century ago when they were in the initial stage of growth; the growth of low-income countries is still stagnant. In the past half-century, high-income countries, middle-income countries, and low-income countries have differed greatly in economic development. This difference is reflected in the following three aspects.

First, the absolute gap in economic development is quite large (see Table 1). In 1960, the GDP per capita of high-income countries was about \$1257; the GDP per capita of middle-income countries was about

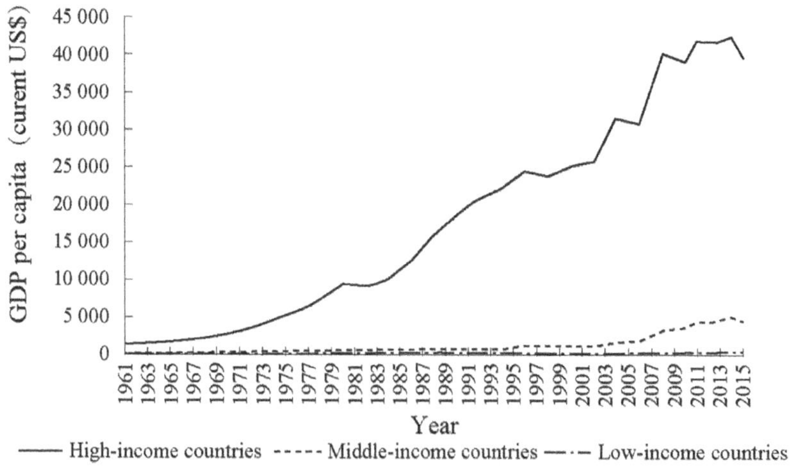

Fig. 1 GDP per capita of countries in different income groups worldwide over the years (*Source* World Bank website)

$133; the GDP per capita of low-income countries was about $93; and the GDP per capita of China was only $90. The GDP per capita of high-income countries was 9.5 times that of middle-income countries, and the GDP per capita of middle-income countries was 1.4 times that of low-income countries. In 2015, the GDP per capita of high-income countries was $39,577; the GDP per capita of middle-income countries was nearly $4668; and the GDP per capita of low-income countries was $616. The GDP per capita of high-income countries was 8.5 times that of middle-income countries, and the GDP per capita of middle-income countries was 7.6 times that of low-income countries. From 1960 to 2015, the GDP per capita gap between high-income countries and middle-income countries did not shrink significantly, and the GDP per capita gap between middle-income countries and low-income countries widened significantly.

Second, the economic development of middle-income countries and low-income countries is lagging far behind that of high-income countries (see Table 1). It was not until 1996 that the GDP per capita of middle-income countries reached the 1960 level of high-income countries, and it was not until 1970 that the GDP per capita of low-income countries reached the 1960 level of middle-income countries. Roughly speaking, based on the GDP per capita in 1960, middle-income countries

Table 1 GDP per capita of countries in different income groups (1960–2015) (USD)

Countries	*1960*	*1970*	*1975*	*1988*	*1996*	*2013*	*2015*
High-income countries	1257	2518	4716	14,654	22,092	39,116	39,577
Middle-income countries	133	195	376	710	1235	4814	4668
Low-income countries	93	133	237	276	264	722	616

Source World Bank website

are at least 36 years behind high-income countries, and low-income countries are at least 10 years behind middle-income countries in economic development. The GDP per capita of middle-income countries in 2015 was only equivalent to that of high-income countries in 1975, and the GDP per capita of low-income countries in 2015 was only equivalent to that of middle-income countries in 1988. Thus, based on the GDP per capita in 2015, middle-income countries are at least 40 years behind high-income countries, and low-income countries are at least 27 years behind middle-income countries in economic development. Therefore, from 1960 to 2015, the gap between middle-income countries and high-income countries widened from 36 years to 40 years, and the gap between low-income countries and middle-income countries widened from 10 years to 27 years.

Third, the economy of countries in different income groups grows at very different rates (see Table 1). From 1960 to 2015, the GDP per capita of high-income countries increased by 30.5 times, and the GDP per capita of middle-income countries increased by 34 times, while the GDP per capita of low-income countries increased by only 6 times. It took high-income countries about 15 years and middle-income countries 17 years to go from $1200 to $4800; it took middle-income countries 28 years (1960–1988) and low-income countries 43 years (1970–2013) to go from $133 to $722.

From the World Bank's statements on the concept of a middle-income trap, it can be seen that the concept is obviously presented using the development of high-income countries as a frame of reference. On this basis, the development of middle-income and low-income countries which pursue a vastly different path of development than high-income countries is considered problematic. The problems faced by middle-income countries are conceptualized as middle-income traps. As can be seen from Fig. 2, since the 1960s, growth in the GDP per capita of developed countries in Europe and America has shown a steady upward trend. In particular, the growth curve of the United States is the smoothest. Other countries have been on a steady upward trend on the whole except for some fluctuations. The significant fluctuations resulted primarily from the 2008 financial crisis and secondly from the 1997 Asian financial crisis.

Globally, after World War II, only a few countries and regions, such as Japan and the Four Asian Dragons (China Hong Kong, China Taiwan, Singapore and South Korea), successfully overcame this hurdle in a short period of time to become developed countries and regions (Fig. 3). Japan reached the lower-middle-income level in 1966 and made the leap from an upper-middle-income country to a high-income country from the early 1970s (1972, 1973) to the early 1980s (1981). China Hong Kong and Singapore entered the upper-middle-income stage in the late 1970s and the high-income stage in the late 1980s. China Taiwan entered the upper-middle-income stage in the mid-1980s and the high-income stage in the early 1990s. South Korea made this leap from the mid-late 1980s to the mid-1990s.

Latin American countries, such as Brazil, Argentina, Mexico, and Chile, joined the ranks of middle-income countries in the 1960s and

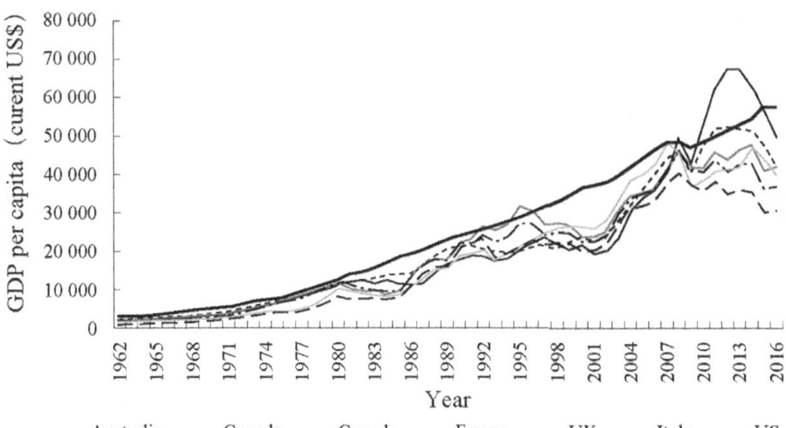

Fig. 2 GDP per capita of developed countries in Europe and America over the years (*Source* World Bank website)

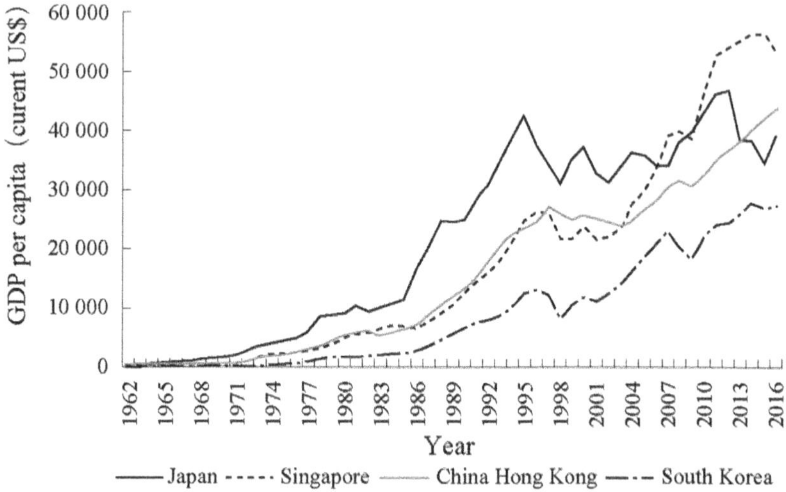

Fig. 3 GDP per capita of East Asian countries and regions over the years (*Source* World Bank website)

1970s. For the next half-century, these countries struggled and lingered in the middle-income stage. Only a few countries have recently made breakthroughs to join the high-income group (Fig. 4). For example, Argentina crossed the middle-income threshold of $1000 GDP per capita in the early 1960s, entered the middle-high-income stage in the mid-1980s, and reached the high-income threshold around 1998, but soon declined. In 2002, it even fell near the bottom end of the middle-income bracket before rebounding. It did not return to the 1998 level until 2008. After 2010, it grew steadily to join the ranks of high-income countries. Brazil entered the middle-income stage around 1975, entered the upper-middle-income stage in 1994, and struggled near the upper-middle-income threshold for the next 10 years, during which time it fell below the middle-income level in 2002; it did not achieve steady growth until around 2005; it crossed the high-income threshold in 2010. Mexico entered the middle-income stage in 1974, crossed the upper-middle-income line in 1981, but then declined, hovering at the lower-middle-income level, It crossed the upper-middle-income line in 1990, and then grew slowly until it reached the high-income threshold in 2013. Chile's GDP per capita surpassed the $1000 mark in 1971, and

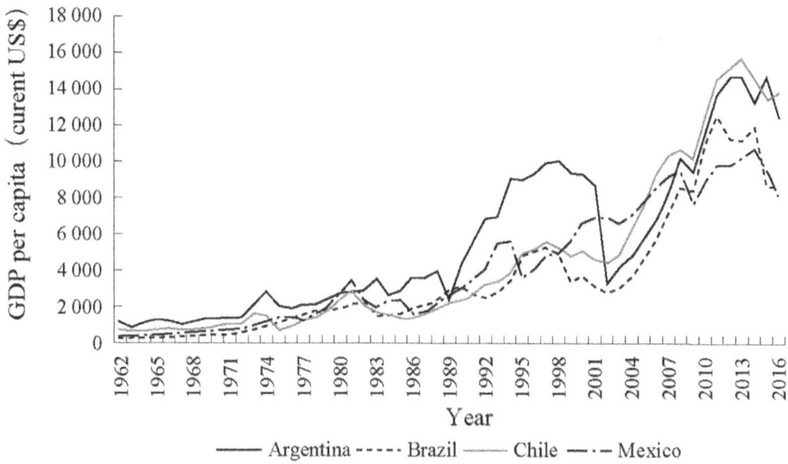

Fig. 4 GDP per capita of Latin American countries over the years (*Source* World Bank website)

had hovered around the low-middle-income line ever since; it crossed the $3000 mark in 1992 to enter the upper-middle-income stage; it entered the high-income stage in 2007.

In Southeast Asia, Malaysia entered the middle-income stage in 1977; it did not cross the upper-middle-income line until 1992; it reached the high-income level in 2011. Thailand entered the middle-income stage in 1988 and had grown steadily ever since; it touched the upper-middle-income line in 1996, but fell sharply after the 1997 financial crisis, and had been struggling in the lower-middle-income stage since then; it returned to the upper-middle-income level in 2006; as of 2016, Thailand's GDP per capita was $5908, falling short of $6000. The Philippines' GDP per capita surpassed the $1000 mark for the first time in 1995 and struggled around $1000 for the next 10 years; it began to grow slowly in 2005 and remained shy of the upper-middle-income threshold in 2016. Vietnam did not reach the lower-middle-income level until 2008; its GDP per capita in 2016 was only $2186. Indonesia entered the middle-income stage in 1995 and reached the upper-middle-income level in 2011 (Fig. 5).

In the course of development, why can some countries (regions) successfully overcome the middle-income trap, while others fall into the middle-income trap? What are the causes of the middle-income trap?

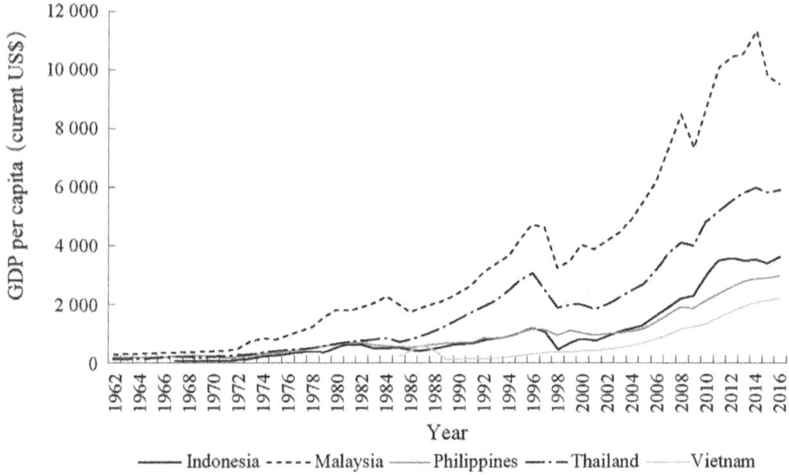

Fig. 5 GDP per capita of Southeast Asian countries over the years (*Source* World Bank website)

2 Economic Analysis of the Middle-Income Trap

2.1 Economic Phenomena of the Middle-Income Trap

An obvious economic indicator for countries that have fallen into the middle-income trap is economic stagnation, fluctuations, and even retrogression. Even with slow growth, they have been struggling to narrow the gap with high-income countries and raise their gross national income per capita to over $10,000. Meanwhile, contradictions accumulated in rapid development such as the widening gap between rich and poor, damage to resources and the environment, and the fragility of the financial system have come to the fore. Latin American countries and some Southeast Asian countries are typical examples of countries that have fallen into the middle-income trap. Income levels have been stagnant in some countries. For example, the Philippines' GDP per capita was $671 in 1980 and was only $2951 in 2016. Its per capita income, adjusted for inflation, has not changed much. In some countries, although income levels are rising, it is still difficult to narrow the gap with high-income countries. For example, Malaysia's GDP per capita was $1812 in 1980 and was only $10,804 in

2014. Argentina's GDP per capita was more than $1000 in 1964, rose to more than $8000 in the late 1990s, but fell to just over $2000 in 2002 and then rose to $12,873 in 2014. Mexico was an upper-middle-income country in 1973 with a GDP per capita of $10,000 and remained an upper-middle-income country 42 years later in 2015 with a GDP per capita of only $9476. There are many such countries in Latin America. Despite two or three decades of efforts and repeated attempts, they have not been able to steadily cross the $15,000 threshold (50% higher than the 2007 figure) for developed country status.

2.2 Challenges to Economic Development in the Middle-Income Stage

Most economic researchers are inclined to believe that: middle-income countries are in a relatively marginalized position in the world economic system and their dependence on developed countries imposes objective constraints on their economic growth, resulting in middle-income countries being subject to a "double squeeze" from developed countries and underdeveloped countries, possessing neither the advantages of the former in innovation nor the advantages of the latter in manpower in the world economic system. As a result, the economic growth of developing countries is "underpowered" and their economic growth is not only slower than that of developed countries, but also slower than that of underdeveloped countries. Economically, the challenges that middle-income countries face in economic development mainly include the following:

First, the loss of advantages in manpower. On the one hand, after entering the middle-income stage, a country will see its labor costs rise well above those of low-income and underdeveloped countries. On the other hand, the demographic dividend is disappearing, the population is aging, and manpower released from agriculture and other fields is decreasing.

Second, innovation capabilities are not strong, and there is no significant progress in reducing dependence on foreign technology. In the low-income stage, late-developing countries will make rapid technological progress by copying or imitating the technology of developed countries and through the transfer of technology from developed countries. In order to prevent competition, developed countries are reluctant to transfer core technologies to middle-income countries. If middle-income countries fail to develop robust innovation capabilities, they will not be able to master core technologies, can only stay at the low end of the industrial chain in international specialization and cannot complete industrial upgrading.

Third, resource and environmental constraints. Many low-income countries achieve rapid development by exporting mineral resources or attracting foreign investment at the expense of the environment. But as resource and environmental carrying capacity reaches its limit, this extensive mode of growth will be unsustainable.

Fourth, the squeeze on the international development environment. Developed countries want low-income countries to remain low-end processing bases in the industrial chain. Developed countries use the cheap labor and resources of low-income countries on the one hand, and prevent middle-income countries from competing with them on the other. Therefore, developed countries often use the say they have in international economic trade and financial transactions to develop rules and regulations that are favorable to themselves. For example, Western countries often raise trade barriers to limit developing countries, or control certain areas or industries in developing countries through financial means. Some developing countries have been taken advantage of by developed countries due to imperfect financial systems or monetary policy mistakes, which in some cases even triggered serious financial crises.

Fifth, imbalances in economic development, including imbalances between urban and rural development, imbalances in the industrial structure, and regional imbalances, as well as a widening income gap. This, coupled with the imperfection of the income distribution system, widens the income gap and exacerbates the divide between rich and poor, leading to a series of economic and social problems.

In 2011, the international economic community pointed out that the phenomenon of the middle-income traps is of universal significance. They further explained the concept of middle-income trap and believed that the middle-income trap is an objective problem that every country will encounter and be subject to in its development process, while stressing that falling into the middle-income trap is the consequence of a country's failure to effectively deal with objective constraints characterized by a "double squeeze."

2.3 *Transformation of the Mode of Economic Growth in the Middle-Income Stage*

From an economic point of view, low income and middle-income are two distinct stages of development. Different stages of development require different modes of growth. Historically, in the low-income stage, economic growth is factor-driven (cheap labor and capital, simple structure, and resource exports), while in the middle-income stage, a mode of productivity-driven growth is required. When a country moves from the low-income stage to the middle-income stage, if it cannot transform the mode of growth and still follows and maintains the development strategy for the low-income stage, then the successful experience in the low-income stage will inevitably turn into a barrier to development in the middle-income stage, the result of which is the loss of national competitiveness due to the lack of comparative advantages in the world economic system and ultimately prolonged economic stagnation. Economists use playing golf as a metaphor: the middle-income trap is an objective reality. Although not every golfer will fall into the trap, but the way each golfer plays is bound to be affected by the trap. Therefore, in the face of the middle-income trap, successful countries either avoid falling into the trap or jump out quickly after they have fallen into the trap, while failed country may be stuck in a quagmire and unable to jump out of the trap. Success or failure depends on whether a transformation of the mode of economic growth can be achieved.[3] And this transformation is the shift of economic growth from being factor-driven to improvements in total-factor productivity.

3 Sociological Analysis of the Middle-Income Trap

Sociology holds that the key to overcoming the middle-income trap is to achieve social transformation and establish a mode of social development that matches the middle-income stage. To find the answer, we need to answer the following sociological questions: What kind of problems does a country face in the economic, political, social, and cultural fields after

[3] Kharas H, Kohli H. What Is the Middle Income Trap, Why Do Countries Fall into It, and How Can It Be Avoided? *Global Journal of Emerging Market Economies*, 2011, 3 (3), 281–289.

entering the middle-income stage? What challenges does it face? How do interactions between these problems constitute an obstacle to the country's continued development and even lead to the country's development dilemma?

3.1 Social Phenomena of the Middle-Income Trap

The experience of countries around the world shows that after entering the middle-income stage, in addition to the possible stall of economic growth, there will be a series of social problems. Although different types of countries choose different development paths and face different social problems because they are at different historical stages or due to cultural and religious differences, comparative studies still show that almost all countries have experienced the following three social problems after entering the middle-income stage.

3.1.1 Worsening Social Fracture

The rapid growth before entering the middle-income stage usually leads to a widening gap between rich and poor. As the income gap widens, the whole society may be polarized, and the chasm between rich and poor will be difficult to bridge. This is the so-called "fractured" society. Due to the lack of a middle class and the lack of social mobility, the whole society has no buffers and lacks vitality. At this time, the legitimacy of the social structure will be directly questioned, and social problems will be easily exposed. For social problems, the most worrying scenario is the confrontation between rich and poor, and the resulting religious, racial, and other social conflicts and unrest.

Both developed countries such as the United Kingdom and the United States, and developing countries in Latin America and Southeast Asia have experienced a gradual widening of the gap between rich and poor in the middle-income stage. If the government cannot curb this trend in terms of the distribution pattern and welfare system, there will be a possibility that the gap between rich and poor will widen further. Lessons from Latin American and Southeast Asian countries show that the gap between rich and poor will lead to a confrontation between social classes and a fracture in the social fabric.

The fracturing of the social fabric is not only the result of a country falling into the middle-income trap, but also the reason why the country is unable to overcome the middle-income trap. An important reason why

Latin American countries have been trapped in the middle-income trap for a long time is that their social structure has not been successfully transformed after independence, which has perpetuated and amplified the fracture in their social fabric during the colonial period. A fractured social fabric leads to such a dilemma: if a pro-development strategy is chosen, social inequality will be further expanded, and the aggravation of inequality will lead to strong dissatisfaction among people on the lowest rung of society; if a specific social welfare policy is chosen, it will be financially unaffordable and unsustainable, and will eventually fail.

3.1.2 Intensifying Social Contradictions

Another typical manifestation of falling into the middle-income trap is a sharp confrontation between social classes, the piling up of social contradictions, and even an outbreak of contradictions and conflicts. Both developed and developing countries are not spared. Latin American countries and Southeast Asian countries are the most typical examples. The problem is mainly manifested in the form of ubiquitous corruption, rampant crime, widespread opportunism, a lack of social consensus, and antagonism between the elite and common people. Even the United States and the United Kingdom, which first entered the high-income stage, also experienced a period where social contradictions cropped up frequently. In the United States saw the "Gilded Age," an era of many problems masked by a thin gold gilding; the United Kingdom experienced the pessimistic and disappointing "British disease."

The outbreak of social contradictions is closely related to the mode of growth in the middle-income stage. Economic takeoff, poverty alleviation, and rapid income growth can effectively cover up domestic social contradictions and political problems, build a social consensus, and bring about social stability. As a result, it is very easy for these countries to develop a dependence on economic growth in the process of solving the problem of food and clothing, that is, economic growth becomes a panacea for social problems. But on the one hand, this kind of "solution" is not a real "solution" in the true sense of the word. We seldom see countries carry out large and thorough social transformation after they have shaken off poverty. The whole society's attention is focused on the rate of economic growth—so much so that social contradictions are ignored or masked. On the other hand, it is precisely because of the relative lack of progress in social transformation that it is easy to form and accumulate various new social problems, such as income gaps, corruption, interest groups, and other deep-seated contradictions, thus creating new, more differentiated social demands and giving rise to groups with different social demands. Generally speaking, the faster the economy grows, the faster the accumulation of these contradictions and problems, and the greater the dependence of the whole society on economic growth. Once economic growth slows down or stagnates, these contradictions will erupt.

3.1.3 *Deepening Psychological Crisis*

The middle-income trap manifests itself not only as a political and social crisis, but also as a crisis in social psychology in many countries. In the presence of a serious crisis in social psychology, any political or social reform measures may trigger greater social contradictions, which in turn will doom reform efforts. The psychological crisis in the middle-income trap is mainly divided into two types: one is relative deprivation that may occur during the period of high-speed economic growth in the middle-income stage; the other is the expectation gap that may occur during the period of economic stagnation or even recession.

Relative deprivation means that people judge whether life is improving not by comparing with their own lives in the past, but with people around them now. Although a person's income is growing, when the income of others is growing more significantly, the person will be dissatisfied because of relative deprivation. This type of crisis in social psychology is formed in the high-speed growth stage where the economy takes off, and is closely related to phenomena such as income increase and the enhancement of horizontal and vertical social mobility.

The expectation gap means that sustained growth in the middle-income stage will create a high expectation in the public's mind that "growth will not stop." Once the economy stagnates or even goes into reverse, the high expectation of the public will go unmet, and the huge gap between expectations and reality arising therefrom will lead to strong dissatisfaction and a lack of confidence among individuals or groups.

Whether it is "relative deprivation" or "expectation gap," this crisis mentality, once formed, will be strongly anti-social. At the social level, it is often manifested as general discontent or even hatred, as well as the spread of belligerent behavior. The emergence of a crisis in social psychology will have a great impact on national policy and cause the extreme polarization of policy, which in turn creates greater social contradictions and instability. This will also draw the country deeper into the middle-income trap, become an extreme form of the middle-income trap, and even bring about political and social unrest.

3.2 Challenges of Social Transformation in the Middle-Income Stage

Although different countries face the middle-income trap in different historical stages, take different paths to crossing the gap, and end up with different results, there is an unmistakable pattern in the challenges of social transformation they encounter in the middle-income stage. Generally speaking, to complete social transformation, we need to overcome a series of challenges. Through active structural and institutional adjustment, we can bridge social fractures, resolve social contradictions, and ease the psychological crisis, so as to enter the high-income stage smoothly.

First, the transition from the middle-income stage to the high-income stage means a major shift in lifestyle, value, and spending power. This transition can be seen as a shift from consumption based on daily necessities such as fuel, rice, cooking oil, and salt to consumption based on consumer durable goods such as automobiles and housing. In order to accomplish this transition, we need to achieve urbanization and middle-classization in terms of social structure.[4] On the one hand, society must be urbanized to a certain degree. Rural lifestyles can hardly support the consumption of large quantities of consumer durable goods, and the income of rural residents also cannot support payment for large quantities of consumer durable goods. On the other hand, the middle class must accounts for a considerable proportion of the urban population. The personal income and consumer preferences of the middle class make them the main consumer base for consumer durable goods. Only a society with a fairly large middle class can generate strong and lasting demand for consumer durable goods.

Second, the transition from the middle-income stage to the high-income stage means a major shift in the interest pattern and mode of governance. High-speed growth in the middle-income stage often leads to the increasingly unbalanced representation of interests and the accumulation of social contradictions, and may even cause a major outbreak of contradictions and conflicts. To complete the shift in the interest

[4] Sun Liping. Talk about China's Entering the Era of Consumer Durable Goods Again. *Economic Observer*, 2010-07-19.

pattern and mode of governance, we need to improve welfare and security and strengthen the governance system in terms of social institutions. On the one hand, only by establishing a relatively perfect welfare and security system can we expand spending power, balance the distribution pattern, improve the relationship between interest groups, narrow the gap between classes, and thus bridge the ever-expanding chasm between classes. On the other hand, only by continuously strengthening the social governance system can we safeguard the legitimate rights and interests of different groups through the institutionalization of interest articulation and participation in politics, strengthen capacity for social governance, prevent and resolve the accumulation of social contradictions, and ride out the period where social contradictions are likely to crop up frequently.

Third, the transition from the middle-income stage to the high-income stage also means a major shift in social psychology and social order. Once caught in the middle-income trap, a country may face a major crisis in the form of moral decline, loss of trust, and disorder in society as a whole. In order to accomplish this transition, we need to rebuild trust and morality. Only by rebuilding basic trust can we restore reasonable personal expectations and behavioral norms, reduce opportunism, reduce transaction costs, and stabilize social order. Only by rebuilding basic morality and supplementing it with an effective supervision mechanism can we establish correct values, truly punish evil and promote good, curb corruption, and prevent the whole society from descending into disorder.

The adjustment of the pattern of interests will unavoidably upset vested interests and original modes, and therefore will inevitably encounter great resistance; a perfect welfare and security system requires the support of a stronger economic foundation and the government's capacity for public administration; making gradual progress in rebuilding social trust and morality requires long-term unremitting efforts; the accumulation and intensification of social contradictions in the middle-income stage make it more difficult to deal with and resolve them and also test the wisdom and governing capacity of the government. Therefore, the complexity of social transformation in the middle-income stage is far greater than that in the low-income stage.

3.3 Social Transformation of Countries Around the World in the Middle-Income Stage

The problems encountered by different types of countries at their middle-income stages are different, as different countries face significantly different international environments and domestic economic, political, social, and cultural development patterns when they enter the middle-income stage. This also means that different countries have different priorities and processes for social transformation after entering the middle-income stage (see Fig. 6).

3.3.1 Developed Countries: Transformation of the Social Structure and Establishment of a Welfare System

The core challenge that developed countries, particularly the United Kingdom and the United States, faced in social transformation after entering the middle-income stage was how to form a social structure dominated by the middle class and a social security system based on universal welfare. Since the start of the twentieth century, the United States has also experienced problems such as the accumulation of social contradictions, the deterioration of class antagonism, and frequent turbulence in the economic cycle. The Great Depression of the 1930s was not only a prominent manifestation of social contradictions caused by this

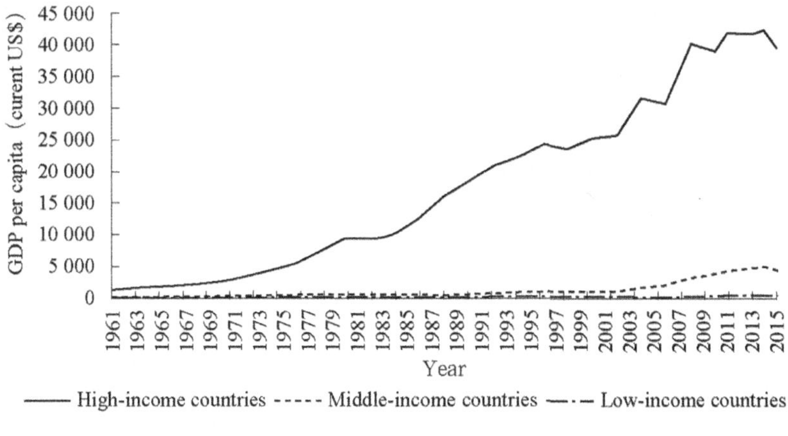

Fig. 6 The middle-income stage of countries in different income groups (*Source* World Bank website)

transformation, but also a turning point in the transformation of the social structure and the development of the welfare system. Thanks to policy adjustments in an array of areas such as employment, security and trade unions during Roosevelt's New Deal, the United States developed into an olive-shaped society with an absolute majority of the population being middle class after World War II, creating social conditions for economic transformation, and successfully completed the transition from liberal capitalism to monopoly capitalism. In the historical process of crossing the middle-income stage, developed countries like the United States realized the diffusion of power and the popularization of welfare, and thereby created a social structure dominated by the middle class by adjusting their industrial policies, labor policies and welfare policies without fundamentally changing their political and economic systems. In this way, they overcame the challenges of economic and social transformation in the middle-income stage, made the transition from monopoly capitalism to welfare capitalism, and, on this basis, entered the high-income stage.

3.3.2 Developing Countries: Governance Capabilities and Economic Modernization

The core challenge that developing countries (regions), particularly East Asian countries, face in social transformation after entering the middle-income stage is how to learn from the advanced experience of developed countries and achieve economic and political modernization by strengthening governance capabilities. Developing countries often have established basic social institutions by the time they enter the middle-income stage. The core task of overcoming the middle-income trap is to further complete economic and political modernization. Economic modernization consists mainly of the transition from the traditional mode of growth based on production factors to the economic mode of growth based on technological advances and increased productivity. The key to this transition lies in technological innovation and corresponding institutional innovation. By making full use of their advantages as latecomers and learning from the experience of European and American countries, and through policy adjustments, the Four Asian Dragons encouraged technological and institutional innovation, successfully coped with the technological squeeze from developed countries and the cost squeeze from low-income countries, and changed their mode of economic growth (see Fig. 7).

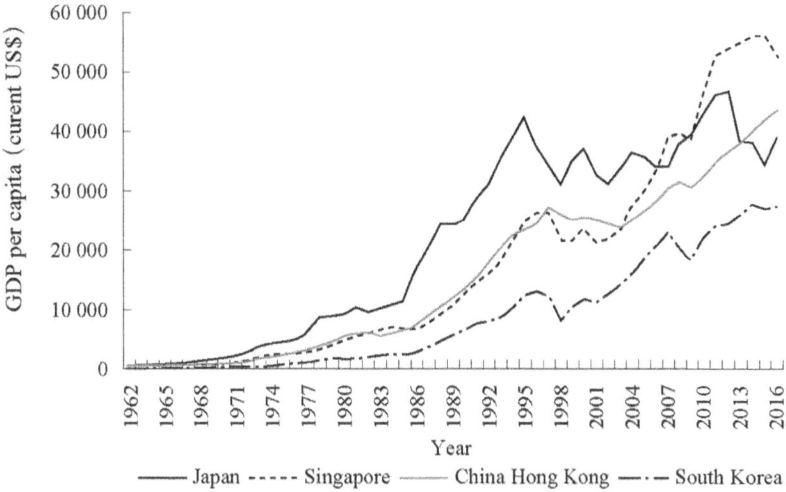

Fig. 7 GDP per capita of developed countries and regions in East Asia (*Source* World Bank website)

Latin American and Southeast Asian countries, which are also developing countries, also face the question of how to achieve economic and political modernization. However, due to insufficient technological innovation, uneven income distribution, unfavorable international markets, political corruption, and social unrest, these countries have failed not only to complete the upgrading from labor-intensive to capital-intensive and technology-intensive industries in time to effectively cope with the double economic squeeze, but also to curb the widening of the gap between rich and poor and the intensification of class contradictions in time. As a result, they have fallen into the middle-income trap and succumbed to prolonged economic stagnation and social crisis. The experience of East Asia and the lessons from Latin America show that the key for developing countries to get out of the middle-income trap lies in how to modernize their economies and politics in an all-round way (see Figs. 8 and 9).

3.3.3 *Countries in Transition: Change of Basic Institutions and Market and Economic Transformation*

Countries in transition, particularly the Soviet Union and the countries of Central and Eastern Europe, have basically completed the process

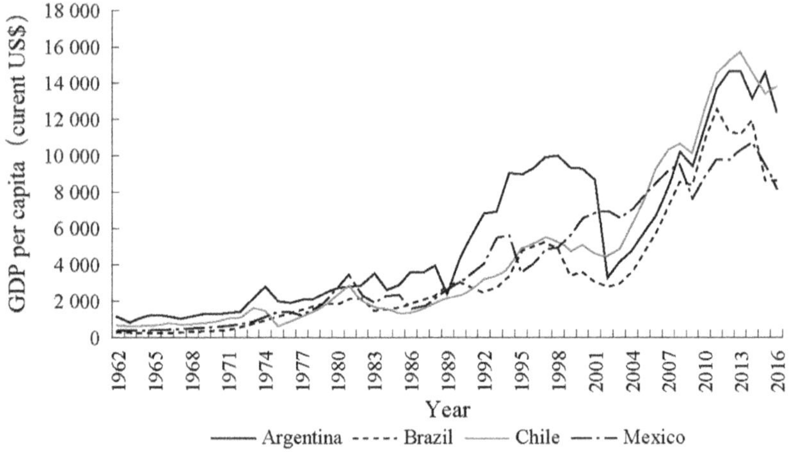

Fig. 8 GDP per capita of Latin American Countries (*Source* World Bank website)

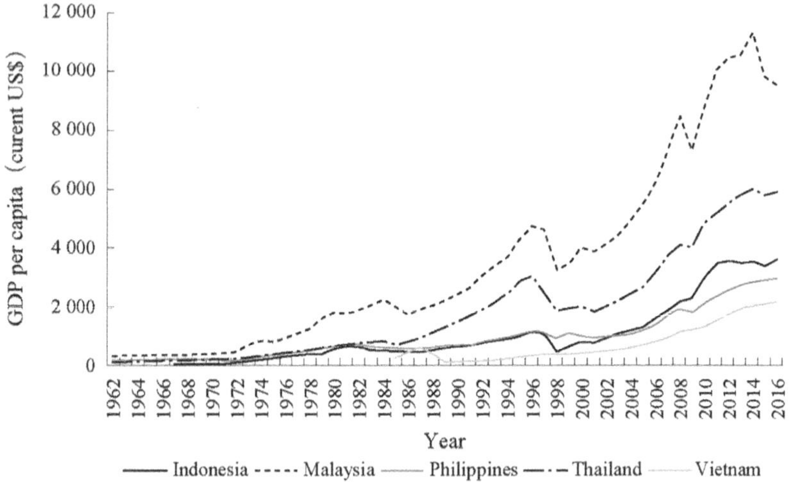

Fig. 9 GDP per capita of Southeast Asian countries (*Source* World Bank website)

of industrialization before entering the middle-income stage. At this stage, they are mainly faced with the transformation of "market-social system". After World War II, Eastern European countries transplanted the Soviet model and established an economic system characterized by an economic structure where the only form of ownership is public ownership and highly centralized command planning. This economic system once brought about a high rate of growth and enabled these countries to go neck-and-neck with developed Western countries until the mid-1960s. But after the 1970s, the socialist countries of Europe generally experienced a decline in economic growth, with their national economy facing great difficulties. After the drastic changes in Eastern Europe, these countries saw a comprehensive change of their political and economic systems, and carried out large-scale privatization of state property, at the heart of which were the democratization of politics and the marketization of the economy. The "rule of law" and "marketization" reforms that the Czech Republic, Poland, Hungary and other Central and Eastern European countries adhered to during the transformation process enabled them to finally overcome the middle-income trap, while in Russia, in the process of the "privatization of securities," due to the absence of democracy and the rule of law, a large number of insider transactions created a social-economic structure dominated by "bureaucrats-oligarchs," which resulted in a small number of people quickly amassing a fortune to become financial and industrial oligarchs and control the lifeline of the national economy, a sharp deterioration in the living standards of residents, and the intensification of social polarization between rich and poor (see Fig. 10).

Compared with developed and developing countries, countries in transition are the most exceptional in going through the middle-income stage in that their basic institutions undergo comprehensive changes. While there are many similarities between the social transformation of developed countries and the modernization process of developing countries, there are also important differences: developed countries and developing countries are in different positions in the world historical process and the international political and economic systems when they overcome the middle-income trap. When developed countries go through the middle-income stage, they have to grope their way forward as there are no historical precedents. But at the same time, owing their position at the core of the world system, they face little pressure in industrial transformation and upgrading, have ample room to address the costs of

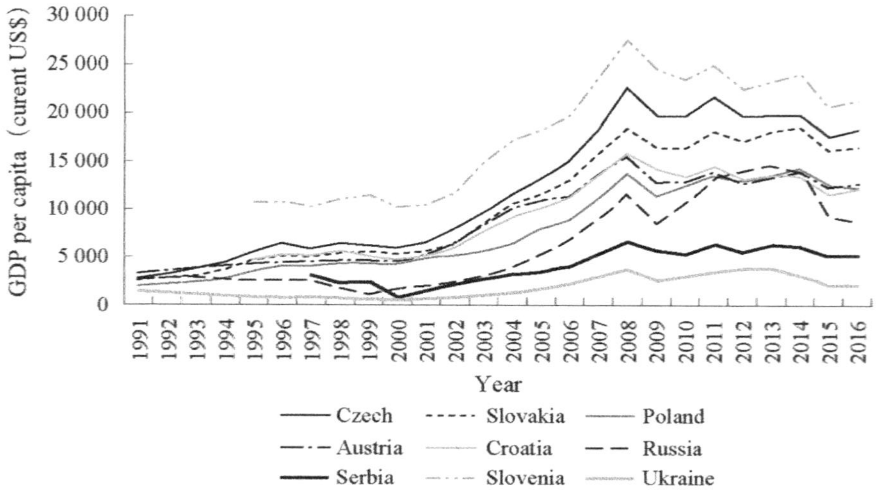

Fig. 10 GDP per capita of countries in transition (*Source* World Bank website)

economic and social transformation, and can even shift and reduce the social and economic costs of transformation at home through overseas markets. When developing countries overcome the middle-income trap, they mostly follow the example of developed countries by directly learning from and even copying the institutions and experience of developed countries. But at the same time, developing countries are in most cases not at the core of the world system, so they face greater pressure in industrial transformation and upgrading, and have less room to address the economic and social costs of transformation.

4 The Essence of the Middle-Income Trap: An Economic and Social Transformation Problem

The essence of the middle-income trap is the dual dilemma of economic transformation and social transformation that a country is facing after it has moved from the low-income stage to the middle-income stage.

4.1 Overcoming the Middle-Income Trap Requires Economic Transformation

As mentioned earlier, middle-income countries will face the problems of "double squeeze" and "underpowered," and encounter a series of challenges such as the gradual disappearance of the demographic dividend and environmental and resource constraints. To break through the "double squeeze" and cultivate new driving forces for economic growth, we must carry out economic transformation. There are two main sources of economic growth: one is factor accumulation and the other is increases in total factor productivity. After an economy has entered the middle-income stage, the mode of development that replies on large quantities of factors of production and expansion is no longer sustainable. It is imperative to effectively promote the transformation and upgrading of the economic structure, and achieve economic growth by increasing total factor productivity. First, optimize the demand structure. Get rid of the growth cycle that relies too much on investment and exports, root economic development in domestic demand, and create a situation where economic growth is driven evenly by consumption, investment, and exports. Second, optimize the industrial structure. Accelerate industrial innovation-driven transformation, service-oriented transformation, and domestic demand-led and consumption-driven transformation; actively encourage indigenous innovation, master core technologies, and cultivate new industries with independent intellectual property rights. Third, optimize the input structure of factors. Accelerate the formation of human capital, improve the spillover effect of technological progress and institutional reform on economic growth, and thereby enhance the country's position in the global division of labor for industrial production and the interest pattern.

4.2 Overcoming the Middle-Income Trap Requires Social Transformation

After experiencing rapid economic growth and an increase in income, countries that have entered the middle-income stage will suffer from endless social contradictions resulting from a widening income gap and increasing social polarization if effective social reforms are not carried out in time. Middle-income countries will face increasingly serious social fragmentation, intensifying social contradictions, growing psychological crisis and other social development problems, and even an outbreak of contradictions and conflicts. Meanwhile, the middle-income stage will see an increase in people's income as a whole, but the income gap is widening, and the transition from the era of necessities to the era of consumer durable goods puts forward new requirements for a country's social structure and social institutions, such as the growth of the middle class, improvement in the social security and welfare systems, a legal system and market system that encourage innovation, etc. In order to achieve such a transformation of the social structure and social institutions, it is necessary to make all-round and in-depth changes to the relationship between interest groups, distribution patterns, and even moral trust and governance capabilities. Therefore, in order to successfully cross the middle-income stage, it is necessary to make in-depth changes in society. Only by basing such changes on a consensus about fairness, justice, and moral construction, and advancing such changes in a manner that coordinates efforts to adjust income distribution and strengthen safeguards for people's livelihood and moral and cultural construction can we overcome social development challenges in the middle-income stage.

4.3 *The Middle-Income Trap Can Only Be Overcome Through Successful Economic and Social Transformation*

From the perspective of economic transformation, economics holds that whether a country can overcome the middle-income trap depends on whether it can successfully transform its mode of economic growth in the middle-income stage. Sociology, on the other hand, holds that in order to overcome the middle-income trap, it is necessary to establish a social structure and social institutions that are compatible with the middle-income stage, and solve growing social contradictions, starting with social transformation. In fact, the phenomenon of the middle-income stage and the economic and social problems in the stage as analyzed from the point of view of economics and sociology are all objective realities. The main characteristics of countries caught in the middle-income trap that are generally recognized by the academic community include: economic slowdown or stagnation, chaotic democracy, polarization between rich and poor, rampant corruption, excessive urbanization, shortage of social and public services, employment difficulties, social unrest, lack of faith, the fragility of the financial system, etc. There are both economic and social problems. Countries may have all or some the above economic and social problems in the middle-income stage to varying degrees, depending on their original economic and social foundations. But generally speaking, it is common to face the economic and social transformation problem in the middle-income stage.

Historically, the process of industrialization and modernization in developed countries has often been accompanied by social transformation. Economic transformation and social transformation have a mutual cause-and-effect relationship and promote each other. Economic transformation changes the social structure and social relations, and therefore requires the corresponding social transformation and institutional change; the success of social transformation and the rationality of institutional change, in turn, further promote the in-depth development of economic transformation. Therefore, in order to overcome the middle-income trap, middle-income countries must carry out a successful dual transformation of the economy and society. On the one hand, change the mode of economic growth to achieve industrial upgrading, break through the double squeeze and gain new impetus for growth; on the other hand, actively eliminate accumulated social contradictions, optimize the social structure, improve various institutions, establish a social system adapted to the new stage, and provide an institutional guarantee for economic development through social transformation. In economic transformation, the shift of economic growth from being factor-driven to improvements in total-factor productivity in particular requires strong reforms of social institutions in areas such as the land system, the household registration system, the financial system, income distribution, and the elimination of monopoly. In social transformation, improving social security and welfare, increasing public services, strengthening environmental protection governance, etc. also depend on the transformation and upgrading of the economy.

Therefore, the essence of the middle-income trap is the phenomena of economic stagnation or recession and the intensification of social contradictions caused by a "double squeeze" on economic growth in the middle-income stage coupled with the inadaptability of the original social structure and governance mode to the new stage of social development. To overcome the middle-income trap, we must successfully complete the transformation of the mode of economic growth from being factor-driven to improvements in total-factor productivity in the middle-income stage. Meanwhile, we should actively promote social transformation, optimize the social structure, eliminate social contradictions, and straighten out social relations to provide a stable social environment and institutional guarantee for economic transformation.

5 Summary

In 2007, the World Bank put forward the concept of middle-income trap to describe the considerably long period of economic stagnation and slow economic development that developing countries fall into after entering the middle-income stage, and attributed the middle-income trap to the consequences of failure to transform the economy: the existing growth factors have been exhausted while new modes of growth have not been formed, resulting in bottlenecks in economic development. Some countries in Latin America and Southeast Asia are considered to be typical examples of countries that have fallen into the middle-income trap. Although there is still debate in the academic community as to whether the concept of middle-income trap is valid and whether it is of universal significance in describing the economic development of developing countries, it is an objective fact that some developing countries encounter development problems characterized by stagnation after entering the middle-income stage.

The essence of the middle-income trap is the dilemma of economic and social transformation that a country is facing after it has moved from the low-income stage to the middle-income stage. The key to overcoming the middle-income trap lies in how to achieve the dual transformation of the economy and society, and establish a mode of economic growth, a social structure and social institutions that are compatible with the middle-income stage.

All over the world, entering the middle-income stage means the transition from the era of necessities to the era of consumer durable goods, which requires completely different social conditions and institutional foundations. Without targeted adjustment, this transition will be unable to be completed, leading to economic slowdown or even stagnation, and potentially a full-blown development dilemma. Different types of countries will encounter different types of problems during this transitional phase. To solve these problems and enter the high-income stage, different types of countries also need different paths and methods. Crossing the Middle-Income stage means transforming from liberal capitalism to welfare capitalism for developed countries; for developing countries, it means the modernization process centered on economic marketization and governance modernization; for countries in transition, it means the comprehensive institutional transformation from a traditional planned economy to market-society. After entering the middle-income stage, China also faces the dual challenges of economic transformation and social transformation.

Economics describes the middle-income trap as a "barrier." For any country, the middle-income trap is not just a "barrier," but a long-term and complex system problem composed of many "barriers." Overcoming the Middle-Income trap is not the process of jumping over a "barrier," but a comprehensive and continuous "hurdling" process throughout the middle-income stage. Therefore, the middle-income trap is a series of problems that are constantly unfolding in the process. This needs to be understood in the following ways.

First, the middle-income trap runs through the entire middle-income stage of a country.

Second, the problems faced by each country in the middle-income stage are asynchronous The problems faced by a country in overcoming the middle-income trap do not appear immediately and simultaneously at the moment of entering the middle-income stage, nor do they disappear immediately and completely at the moment of joining the ranks of high-income countries. These problems do not appear or disappear at the same time, but in sequence.

Third, the middle-income trap is stage-specific. The problems that each country encounters in different areas are distinctly stage-specific, that is, the main problems that each country encounters at different stages are different.

Fourth, in the economic, political, social, and cultural realms, the formation, appearance, intensification, mitigation, and disappearance of each specific problem are also a long and complex process.

Fifth, problems are not separated from each other, but interact with each other. This also means that there may be a superposition of different problems at the same stage; there may be continuity and connectivity between different problems at different stages.

Falling into the middle-income trap does not mean absolute stagnation. There are also some room and possibilities for development in the trap. It is also an indisputable fact that the economies of countries that have fallen into the trap are still developing. Development in the trap, on the one hand, manifests itself as slow growth, with the existing mode of economic growth being unsustainable, often is based on an inefficient mode of growth characterized by high input and low output, and comes with huge social costs and irreversible environmental costs, so it is abnormal economic growth; on the other hand, it also manifests itself as the abnormal development of society. The imbalance and asynchrony of development between the economic realm and the social, political, and cultural realms have resulted in increasingly fierce contradictions and conflicts. It is becoming increasingly difficult for the traditional mode of social development to gain recognition, and the existing social institutions are increasingly becoming a constraint on and an obstacle to development.

Historically, all countries that have successfully coped with the middle-income trap, without exception, have avoided or overcome the middle-income trap through comprehensive economic, political, social, and cultural changes. This also proves that the essence of the middle-income trap is not just a matter of economic growth. Successfully overcoming the middle-income trap requires not only in-depth economic transformation, but also comprehensive social transformation.

CHAPTER 2

Types of Middle-Income Countries and Lessons Learned from Their Experience

Crossing the middle-income trap requires not only a successful economic transformation, but also a successful social transformation. In the process of developing from the middle-income stage to the high-income stage, all countries will face enormous challenges of economic and social transformation, and different types of countries will encounter different problems in their respective middle-income stages. The middle-income trap problem is closely related to the economic, social, political, cultural, and other structural and institutional characteristics of various countries. Therefore, comparing and summarizing the successes and failures of different countries in overcoming the middle-income trap is of great significance in terms of providing precedents for China to learn from in completing economic and social transformation and successfully overcoming the middle-income trap.

1 Developed Countries Such as Europe and the United States

Developed countries, particularly Europe and the United States, have maintained their economic growth successfully for quite a long time, and were the first to grow into high-income countries, and their experience is worth learning from.

Z. Zheng, *Middle-Income Trap*,
https://doi.org/10.1007/978-981-15-7401-6_2

1.1 The Process and Experience of Overcoming the Middle-Income Trap in the United States

1.1.1 Economic Transformation in the United States

While completing the First Industrial Revolution at the end of the nineteenth century, the United States ushered in the Second Industrial Revolution, leading to the phenomenal growth of its economy. From 1869–1898, coal production in the United States increased by 800%, the length of railroads increased by 567%, and real wages increased by 53% in 30 years. In 1860, the United States ranked fourth in terms of industrial output among major capitalist countries, with its industrial output less than half of that of Britain. In 1890, the industrial output of the United States catapulted to the top spot in the world rankings, accounting for nearly one-third of the world's total industrial output.[1] From 1920 to 1929, the United States accounted for 48.5% of industrial output in the capitalist world, surpassing Britain, Germany, and France combined by 79%, making it the leading world power.[2]

The United States owed the strong and sustained growth of its economy mainly to technological advances, institutional innovation, industrial structural adjustment, and urbanization.

Technological Advances

Many studies have shown that technological advances, rather than capital accumulation, was the main cause of economic growth in the later stages of industrialization in the United States. After calculating the growth of total factor productivity in the non-agricultural private sector in the United States in the first half of the twentieth century (1909–1949), Solow (1957) concluded that technological advances accounted for 87.5% of the increase in output per man-hour in this stage, and the remaining 12.5% was attributable to capital growth. With the development of industrialization, investment in education in the United States grew exponentially. By 1916, Americans were spending about eight times as much on primary and secondary education as they did in 1870. In 1870, there were 563 colleges and universities in the United States. By 1910 that

[1] Liu Xuyi, Yang Shengmao. *The General History of the United States*. Beijing: People's Publishing House, 2008.

[2] Huang An'nian. *20th Century U.S. History*. Shijiazhuang: Hebei People's Publishing House, 1988.

figure reached nearly 1000, with a total of more than 330,000 students enrolled. During this period, the total number of students enrolled in all 16 universities in France was about 40,000. The United States increased investment in education mainly through the following measures: first, increasing education funding; second, levying a special tax in each state to supplement school funds; third, allocating a large amount of public land for education. By the end of the nineteenth century, the federal government had allocated about 150 million acres of land for national education, equal to France, Switzerland and Belgium combined.

Institutional Innovation

The development and maturation of the modern corporate system was also an important reason for the lasting prosperity of the US economy. The establishment of the legal status of corporations laid the foundation for the rise of corporations. The legal status of corporations was established in 1819 by Chief Justice of the Supreme Court John Marshall in the Dartmouth College v. Woodward case. In Marshall's interpretation, a corporation was considered to be a legal person that could live forever under law. This characteristic gives corporations an advantage that sole proprietorships or partnerships do not have. Limited liability is another advantage of corporations over sole proprietorships and partnerships. In 1830, Massachusetts passed a general limited liability statute, and by 1860, the principle of limited liability had become universally applicable in every state. The generalization of limited liability has been one of the reasons for the rapid spread of corporations in the United States.

The rise and explosive growth of corporations have undoubtedly contributed to the rapid development of US industries and the US economy. It first provided a solution to fundraising problems during the economic takeoff period at the start of the industrial revolution in the United States, encouraged the expansion of corporations and production, and contributed directly to the improvement of corporate management. Fundraising, technological advances and scientific management are the three major factors behind the economic takeoff of any country, two of which were effectively created by the rise of corporations.

But as corporations grew and expended, corporations increasingly showed their true colors by pursuing profit maximization and gradually evolved into tools for desperately seeking to expand private business opportunities without regard to public interests. The control of the national economy by big corporations increasingly exacerbated conflicts between the public and corporations, and the public demanded that the government bring big corporations under control. In 1890 and 1914, Congress separately enacted the Sherman Act and the Clayton Act, which outlawed corporations that restricted competition or attempted to monopolize, and their practices such as price discrimination, tying arrangements, exclusive dealing contracts, the acquisition of stocks of competing corporations and interlocking directorates between big corporations. The enactment of antitrust laws marked the Federal Government's control of private companies in the strict sense of the word.

Industrial Structural Adjustment

Between 1783 and 1860, agriculture was the dominant sector in the United States, and transportation and industry mainly served agriculture. Up until around 1832, about four-fifths of the population in the United States was still engaged in agriculture. After 1832, this proportion declined rapidly.

American manufacturing emerged during the Second War of Independence in 1812, helped by the boycott of British imports. But up until 1850, American manufacturing was still dominated by cottage industries and handicraft workshops that hired apprentices. The Civil War, which began in 1860, brought the Industrial Revolution to the United States, enabling the factory system to take root in the United States. The Civil War ended with the victory of industrial capital in the North, the abolition of slavery and the creation of a unified market. As a result, the United States rapidly rose to become the world's largest industrial power. In 1900, the rural population of the United States accounted for 51.7% of the total population, and by 1910 that figure had dropped to 45.3%.

The maturation of the industrial economy gradually turned the United States into a society where the service sector was the largest sector. At the end of World War II, America's manufacturing output accounted for about 30% of GNP. That figure then declined year by year, to 29.6% in 1947, 30.1% in 1970 and 16.0% in 1997. In 1929, 57.5% of the non-agricultural population was employed in the service sector in the United States. That figure rose to 71.5% in 1979. In 1995, the output of the service sector accounted for 72% of GNP.

Urbanization

The United States is a highly urbanized country, which began the transition from a rural society to an urban society as early as the nineteenth century. With the start of industrialization and the expansion of the domestic market, the number of cities increased rapidly and the size of cities has gradually expanded. The spatial structure of cities also changed dramatically, from a compact and dense structure to a multi-center and decentralized structure.

After the end of the Civil War (1865–1920), the industrialization and urbanization of the United States accelerated. At this stage, the American Manufacturing Belt was formed and urbanization accelerated. During this period, with the maturation of its industrial economy, the United States successfully transformed itself from an agrarian society to an industrial society. As industrialization moved west, a manufacturing belt was formed in the Northeast and Midwest around the Great Lakes. Urbanization made the swiftest progress at this stage, with the proportion of urban population rising from 19.8% in 1860 to 51.2% in 1920, which marked the basic completion of urbanization.

The Transportation Revolution further expanded the geographical scope of urbanization. The improvement of the railroad network, especially the construction of a railroad traversing the United States from east to west, strengthened economic links between the East and the West. People, material, and capital begun to flow from east to west, pushing industrialization and urbanization westward. By the time of the outbreak of World War I, the urban structure of the United States had reached its final shape: high-rise buildings were located in the city center, which was divided by function into areas where financial, retail, legal and other industries were relatively concentrated; residential areas developed outwards; the city developed in a multi-centered manner. Regional imbalances in industrialization and urbanization began to improve as East-West and North-South links strengthened. While centralized urbanization remained dominant, suburbanization had begun to appear. Due to the availability of raw materials, transportation costs, transaction costs, economies of scale, and other reasons, a large number of people and industrial activities were still concentrated in the city center, and through continuous competition and mergers, the concentration of industries was getting higher and higher.

1.1.2 Social Transformation in the United States

Emergence of the Progressive Movement

In the late nineteenth century and early twentieth century, while the US economy was growing at a high speed, a series of serious social problems emerged, mainly manifested in the widening gap between rich and poor (the wealthiest 2% of households owned one-third of the nation's wealth), poor production conditions (Of the 700,000 railroad workers in the United States, 1972 were killed and more than 20,000 were injured on the job), the intensification of labor–management conflicts (hundreds of people died in the 1887 railroad strike), a surge in the number of criminal cases (from 1880 to 1890, the incarceration rate in the United States rose by 50%; from 1881 to 1898, the number of homicides in Chicago increased from 1266 to 7480), and the unchecked spread of the idea of "survival of the fittest."[3]

Thus, the Progressive Era in the United States began. The theme of the progressive era can be summarized as "democracy in politics, freedom in markets and development in society." Politically, the Progressive Movement opposed official corruption, and the circulation of newspapers and magazines surged, setting off the "Muckraking Movement," which focused on reporting urban oligarchy and collusion between government and business and exposed a large number of corrupt officials and cases of collusion between government and business in preparing public opinion for social reform. At the same time, it actively called for greater political participation, with women gaining the right to vote, and senators being directly elected by voters. Economically, a series of progressive movements were launched to combat oligopoly, improve food safety, shorten working hours, and raise workers' wages. On the social level, the super-rich began to give back to society, setting up foundations like Rockefeller and Carnegie; the status of women was elevated; social participation by various groups was more active than ever.

Establishment of a Social Welfare System

Roosevelt's New Deal began the establishment of a social security and welfare system. The American distribution model is divided into two parts, delimited by the Great Depression (1929–1933): The model prior to the Great Depression was characterized by the strong position of

[3] Liu Xuyi, Yang Shengmao. *The General History of the United States*. Beijing: People's Publishing House, 2008.

capital, a tilt of distribution toward capital, the weak role that the government played in redistribution, and very limited tax collection and social security funding. After the Great Depression, the distribution model changed greatly. The main characteristics of the new distribution model can be summarized as follows: Income recipients became more equal in status, with distribution tilted slightly toward ordinary workers; the government played a greater role in redistribution, with the income gap shrinking. The government's adjustment of labor policy and other measures enabled trade unions to grow, giving an unprecedented boost to the status of ordinary workers. The expansion of trade union power and an increase in the voice of the working class tilted income distribution at this stage toward the working class.

In addition, after the crisis, the US government began to assume the function of improving income distribution and increased tax collection and social security funding. The US social security program started during the New Deal and developed rapidly, with federal spending on social security as a percentage of the federal budget reaching 22.6% in 1950.

Two-Way Movement of Executive Powers

First, executive powers were decentralized and devolved in the United States.

During the 100 years from 1870 to 1970, the United States saw a significant degree of decentralization and devolution of powers, including the universalization of suffrage, the improvement of the representative system (direct election of senators), etc. Economic oligarchs and urban gangsters that emerged during the Gilded Age could no longer manipulate public affairs as freely as they did in the past. When society changes from an elite-dominated structure to a more flat structure dominated by the middle class, the devolution of powers creates a strong demand for the institutionalization of political participation among members of the middle class, which in turn leads to a virtuous cycle of interaction between the market, the state, and society. This transformation is essentially a social transformation centered on political modernization.

Second, on the other hand, in the past 100 years, there had also been a distinct trend toward the centralization and concentration of powers in the United States. Compared with the Federal Government of 1870, the Federal Government of 1970 had grown tremendously in size and authority, as well as in capacity and complexity, and had become an unprecedented behemoth in American history. This historic process by which the Federal Government was continuously strengthened meant not only a marked and sustained decline in the status of state governments in policy-making and resource allocation, but also a continuous decrease in political and social participation by ordinary people, the cornerstone of a liberal democracy, after World War II, at least in terms of general election turnout and the number of members and frequency of activities of associations. The realization of the causal chain between the centralization of powers and the progress of society requires a set of institutional conditions.

1.1.3 Experience of the United States and Inspiration Drawn Therefrom

From the perspective of the economic system, the history of the United States was generally considered to have undergone two major transformations: the first one was a transition from liberal capitalism to monopolistic capitalism, mainly during the Gilded Age (1870–1900) and the Progressive Era (1900–1920); the second one was a transition from monopolistic capitalism to welfare capitalism, mainly during the "Roosevelt's New Deal" period from 1930 until the start of World War II. A series of efforts to build a "Great Society" initiated by President Johnson in 1965 could be seen as the final completion of this phase. Both of these two major transformations could be seen as an effort by the United States to transition from the era of necessities to the era of consumer durable goods. The first major transformation laid the economic foundation for the transition from the era of necessities to the era of consumer durable goods, and the second major transformation laid the social foundation for the transition from the era of necessities to the era of consumer durable goods.

Specifically, the history of the United States could be roughly divided into three stages that corresponded to the two major transformations mentioned above: the first stage occurred in the Gilded Age (1870–1900), during which the economy grew rapidly driven by technological innovation and industrial revolution, and with that, the industrial structure and social structure changed dramatically, resulting in a widening gap between rich and poor and an increase in social conflicts, which coupled with rampant administrative, judicial and legislative corruption catapulted American society into a full-blown credit crisis. By this time the United States had shown a tendency to transition from the era of necessities to the era of consumer durable goods. The second stage occurred in the Progressive Era from 1900 until the start of World War I, during which monopoly capitalism was established, the economy continued to grow, and financial oligarchs controlled the lifeline of the economy. Economically, this stage saw opposition to trusts and an emphasis on free competition; politically, it saw the expansion of participation and a crackdown on corruption; socially, it saw an active push for progressive movements. At this stage, there were already adequate food and clothing in American society, the era of necessities had come to an end, and the growth of the national economy could no longer be sustained by demand for necessities alone. The third stage was the New Deal after 1932, during which the government reined in capital, safeguarded people's livelihood and expanded participation through more thorough institutional adjustment and more comprehensive social construction, and seized the window of adjustment occasioned by World War II, thus achieving rapid economic growth and the formation of a middle-class society after the war. At this stage, people realized that entering the era of consumer durable goods required certain social conditions. "Roosevelt's New Deal" could be seen as an effort to achieve the social conditions required for the era of consumer durable goods through policy adjustment. At this stage, the United States truly became a middle-class society with the social conditions required to transition from the era of necessities to the era of consumer durable goods.

The experience of the United States tells us that overcoming the middle-income trap requires not only economic transformation, but also social transformation, and the two complement each other and are both indispensable.

1.2 The Process and Experience of Overcoming the Middle-Income Trap in Britain

Britain was the first country in the world to undergo industrialization and urbanization. Its development path is unique. Its experience in economic and social transformation is worth in-depth analysis and reflection.

1.2.1 Britain's Economic Transformation

Because Britain was the first country to industrialize, the adjustment of its industrial structure was slower than emerging countries: In 1820, industrial output exceeded agricultural output; around 1851, Britain's industrial labor force outstripped agricultural labor force; it was not until the eve of World War I, 150 years after the industrial revolution began in Britain, that the tertiary sector surpassed the secondary sector in both output and labor force.

After World War II, the British economy developed rapidly. Although the proportion of the secondary sector was slowly declining, during the 10 years from the early 1970s to the early 1980s, the secondary sector accounted for about 40% of GDP. Thereafter, Britain's economic development saw a turning point. At that time, Britain began to optimize and upgrade its industrial structure on a large scale, mainly by vigorously developing new industries such as finance, market intermediary services, real estate, patents, copyright, trademarks, and design, so as to accelerate the development of the service sector and improving its position among the three sectors. By the mid-1980s, Britain's service sector had accounted for more than 60% of GDP. Since then, this proportion had been increasing.

As Britain carried out excessive nationalization reform after World War II to nationalize industries of strategic importance to the country and society such as rail transport, coal mines, and shipbuilding, the proportion of the state-owned economy in GDP rose to 12% in the late 1970s, with the proportion of state ownership in industries such as postal service, telecommunications, electricity, gas, railroads, shipbuilding, and steel being as high as 75% or higher. The result was: The government became functionally inflexible and intervened in the economy excessively, and the consequent lack of a competition mechanism resulted in unreasonable allocation of resources, overstaffing, and poor enterprise management. For this reason, in 1979, Britain started structural adjustment and reform with a focus on "reducing the share of state ownership," with a view to improving the economic efficiency of enterprises, establishing a national innovation system, and enhancing the competitiveness of the national economy. Policy approaches that were effective fall mainly into the following three categories.

First, the reform of the shareholding system, which was divided into two types: (1) shareholding by insiders: the employees of a state-owned enterprise were allowed to hold shares in the enterprise so as to change the ownership of the enterprise from state ownership to private ownership or mixed ownership. (2) shareholding by outsiders: a joint venture was created through shareholding by outsiders. This on the one hand expanded the funding channels of the enterprise, and on the other hand obligated the management to respect the rights of shareholders, helped introduce the market mechanism, and reduced and prevented excessive administrative intervention by the government.

Second, transforming the administrative or service functions performed by the central or local governments into administrative or service functions performed by private individuals by agreement. This approach was very effective for institutions and companies under government departments, replaced government directives with market regulations, and greatly improved efficiency and service quality while reducing costs.

Third, the "state-owned + private" bundle mode of investment For the construction and maintenance of some infrastructure and the operation and management of some institutions that required a large investment with a long payback period and for which the government couldn't raise enough funds to meet the operational needs, private investment, operation, and management could be introduced on the basis of state ownership under this bundle mode to improve profits.

Structural adjustment resulted in more flexibility for enterprises in favor of a shift toward competitive and profitable industries, accelerating the shake-up of industries and technologies that was aimed at selecting the superior and eliminating the inferior. British GDP by industry in 1998: agriculture 2%, industry 31% (manufacturing 21%), services 67%. Structural adjustment dealt a heavy blow to state-owned enterprises with low economic efficiency. Emerging industries and competitive industries, by contrast, gained opportunities for development, such as the telecommunications industry, the computer industry, and the corresponding service and consulting industries, which developed rapidly during this period. After undergoing training, people who had been laid off found new employment in emerging industries. These industries became more competitive internationally through market competition and gradually expanded from the domestic market to the international market. International competition in turn promoted further innovation and upgrading in domestic industries. This virtuous circle caused the industrial structure of Britain to be continuously optimized and adjusted.

1.2.2 Social Transformation in Britain

The "British disease" began in the 1920s, when the civilian sector, which had shrunk during World War I, was expected to recover and grow after the war, but the economic crisis made it impossible. Due to a narrow domestic market and difficulties of exporting, the coal, cotton, and shipbuilding industries remained stagnant throughout the 1920s after the economic crisis of 1920. At the same time, an upsurge in working-class struggle in Britain also had had a negative impact on the British economy since then.

In the early days of the "British Disease," Britain's economic power weakened, the economy was stagnant for a long time, class tensions intensified at home, and Britain's grip over the Empire was not as strong as before. Then came the economic crisis of the 1930s on top of the long period of economic stagnation in the 1920s. Through international trade and finance, Britain was soon affected by the economic crisis in the United States. External shocks and impacts intensified the existing contradictions in the British economy. Since the first quarter of 1930, both the index of industrial production and the import and export trade indexes had declined significantly, and unemployment had soared. By the third quarter of 1932, the economic crisis in Britain had reached its worst point, with the number of unemployed people reaching 3 million and the unemployment rate hitting 23%.

The British economy was worsened by the economic crisis of the 1930s and World War II. After World War II, Britain's control over its colonies was much weakened. After the war, from 1945 to 1951, as the competitiveness of exports hadn't improved and it was impossible for exports to grow quickly, Britain's trade deficit grew in spite of loans and capital from the United States. In 1949, the British government announced a 30.5% devaluation of the pound.

During the postwar period, Britain pursued Keynesianism and intervened in the economy with fiscal and monetary policies. The result of Keynesianism was that, on the one hand, it created a brief boom for Britain, with the British economy showing "two lows and one high" (low unemployment rate, low inflation rate, and high growth rate) from 1951 to 1964; on the other hand, in the long run, Keynesianism also brought disaster to Britain. Government spending was too big to be covered by revenue. Consequently, businesses were overwhelmed with tax burdens and monetary policy was repeatedly eased. The knock-on effects were stagnant production, rebounding unemployment, soaring prices, and runaway inflation. Although Britain's GDP per capita exceeded $15,000 in 1965, a serious sterling crisis occurred in 1967, which further weakened Britain's position in international trade and finance. In the 1970s, Britain entered a period of economic stagnation, maintaining the lowest economic growth rate, the highest inflation rate, and the highest trade deficit among all developed capitalist countries.

In the 1970s, the then Labor government was faced with a comprehensive predicament of soaring prices, stagnant production, and high unemployment. Beginning in 1979, Thatcher's government pushed for a liberal economy, overhauled government regulation, reduced inflation, and kept prices stable, launching the British monetarist experiment. The reforms led to seven years of economic growth, a significant balance of payments surplus, and an improvement in the status of the government. Meanwhile, the government encouraged industry and improved efficiency, flexibility, and market competitiveness through microeconomic policies.

Thatcher's government, by curbing inflation, weakened the powers of trade unions, attracted investment, and achieved economic growth. Britain emerged from the economic crisis in 1988–1989. But Thatcher's government lost the election for hurting the interests of the middle and lower classes.

Since then, the Blair, Brown, and Cameron governments which took into account the interests of the middle and lower classes, had interpreted Britain's change and innovation in the "Third Way," seeking a balance between "development and justice" and "rights and obligations," and approaching globalization from a posture of reform, modernization, and cooperation. As Blair said, "The Third Way is a serious reappraisal. It is neither laissez-faire nor one of state interference. It seeks to take the essential values of the center and center-left and apply them to a world of fundamental social and economic change; and to do so free from outdated ideology." The Third Way has enabled Britain to maintain good economic growth, even though it has failed to balance economic development and social justice as well as in the case of Germany in terms of social reform.

1.2.3 Experience of Britain and Inspiration Drawn Therefrom

Britain was the first country to start the industrial revolution and also the first welfare state. But in the later stage of industrialization, Britain caught the "British disease": low rate of capital investment at home, poor management of corporate nationalization, market rigidity, and overloaded social security system. By reforming the traditional modern Keynesian policy of "big government and small society," Thatcher's government adopted a monetarist economic policy: restraining the issuance and circulation of currency, tightening monetary policy and controlling inflation; reducing public spending and cutting taxes; controlling the scale of the social security system and gradually eliminating the drawbacks of implementing a welfare state system through reform; promoting corporate privatization and tapping into the vitality of free market mechanisms. Britain helped drive the privatization of state-owned enterprises in Western countries in the 1980s. Thatcher's government gradually promoted the sale of state-owned enterprises, transferred people employed by the state to the private sector, and transferred the assets of state-owned enterprises to private enterprises in the form of shares. The development of Britain shows that during the period of social transformation, both economic structural adjustment and the accumulation of social contradictions are at their peak. Promoting technological advances, and driving the optimization and adjustment of the industrial structure with technological advances as the engine, reforming the market mechanism and the foreign trade system and at the same time, through institutional reform, matching the social security system with the actual level of economic development while promoting social justice to effectively avoid the "welfare trap" is a basic condition for a country to successfully emerge from the late stage of industrialization as a high-income country.

1.3 The Process and Experience of Overcoming the Middle-Income Trap in France

France is one of the world's major developed countries, with its GDP ranking among the highest in the world. In 2016, its GDP per capita reached $36,855. Compared with other major developed countries such as the United States, Britain and Germany, France's economic development process and path are quite unique.

1.3.1 Economic Transformation in France

France was the largest feudal autocracy in Europe during the Middle Ages. From the sixteenth to eighteenth century, French society experienced the rapid development of mercantilism and handicraft industries. Although feudal autocracy began to decline from its peak and the commodity economy had developed greatly, the basic political institutions and relations of production of a feudal society remained absolutely dominant in the whole society. The long-term existence of the small-scale peasant economy was one of the important characteristics of the French national economy.

From the end of the French Revolution to 1870, it was a period of great development for French industry, and the Industrial Revolution was almost complete. The development of French industry during this period could be divided into three stages: the first stage was from 1795 to 1815, that is, from the end of the French Revolution to the end of Napoleon's dictatorship. This stage laid the groundwork for French's modern industry. The second stage was the reign of the Bourbon and Orleans dynasties from 1815 to 1848. During this period, France was socially stable and was gradually recovering from the wounds of war, and the Industrial Revolution began on a large scale in France. The third stage was the Second Empire period from 1848 to 1870, which was the final stage of the French Industrial Revolution. The production of coal and pig iron tripled and steel production increased by sevenfold in 20 years. In the 1950s and 1960s, the French national economy experienced an unprecedented period of great development, with the national income doubling and the gross industrial output tripling. At this point, the Industrial Revolution was almost complete, and France officially joined the ranks of industrialized countries.

In the mid and late 1950s, especially after De Gaulle came to power, the French economy entered a golden age. From 1961 to 1974, before the outbreak of the oil crisis, the French economy grew exponentially at an average rate of 5.5% per year, second only to Japan (8.3%) and higher than other major developed countries in the same period such as the United States, Germany and Britain (4.2, 4.2, and 3.4%). In addition to strong US aid, the French economy was able to achieve rapid growth in this period mainly for the following reasons.

First, France's robust industrial base before World War II laid a solid foundation for the rapid economic recovery after the war. The global recession that began in the 1920s and World War II had wreaked havoc on France's economy, but France had long been one of the world's leading industrialized countries before the war, with a strong industrial base in areas such as machinery, motors, chemicals, metallurgy, automobile manufacturing, and aviation, and had been the most important agricultural powerhouse in Europe, with a high degree of agricultural mechanization and high agricultural labor productivity. For this reason, when the war ended and stability was restored to society, a robust industrial and agricultural production base provided the most important guarantee and precondition for the rapid recovery of the French economy.

Secondly, the founding of the European Economic Community (EEC) gave strong impetus to France's economic growth. France was the most active European country in advocating and promoting regional economic integration. After the founding of the EEC, trade between France and other EEC member states expanded rapidly. From 1970 to 1975, French's trade with other EEC member states accounted for about 50% of its total trade, which was twice as high as in 1960. In particular, France was a major exporter of agricultural products in the EEC. The common agricultural policy adopted by the EEC and guaranteed minimum prices for agricultural products had played an important role in promoting the agricultural production and exports of France, a major agricultural producer.

Third, the implementation of indicative planning. Unlike other Western countries, France had maintained a high proportion of state-owned enterprises in the national economy for a long time (in 1982, the proportion of workers employed by state-owned enterprises in France exceeded 20%). From 1947 to 1975, France carried out a total of six plans to regulate its economy and establish development priorities and planning indicators for each stage. Although France's economic plans were not mandatory and binding on the specific operation of enterprises, but played an indicative and guiding role, by implementing a proper method combining indicative planning and market regulation, French avoided aimless production by enterprises, which had played a role in promoting the steady and rapid development of the economy and the implementation of the national economic strategy.

Finally, investment in scientific research and education was increased, and technological advances made outstanding contributions to economic growth. In the late 1950s, France adopted a series of policies in order to emerge from a state of relative technological backwardness, including overhauling the scientific research management system, emphasizing the close integration of basic research with applied research, and scientific research with industrial application, increasing investment in scientific research, etc. Compared with 1959, investment in scientific research in France increased by more than 3.6 times in 1969, and funding for scientific research as a share of GDP also rose from 1.15 to 2.0%. The French Secretary of State for Higher Education and Research once estimated that the French economy grew at an average annual rate of 5.1% after World War II, of which 2.6% was the result of technological advances.

After World War II, France also attached great importance to the development of education and the cultivation of talents. In 1950, investment in education as a share of the national income of France was 2.4%. In 1970, that figure surged to 5.8%, surpassing the Federal Republic of Germany (5.7%) and the United Kingdom (5.2%), and second only to the United States (8.6%). During this period, France made great efforts to develop higher education and vocational education, and cultivated a large number of engineering and management personnel.

After more than 20 years of rapid economic growth after World War II, by 1975, France had been greatly strengthened economically and vaulted into a world-leading position in terms of comprehensive strength, re-emerging as a major political power and economically developed country in the world. World Bank data shows that the GDP of France at constant prices more than doubled from 1960 to 1975. In 1975, the GDP of France surpassed that of Britain, was lower than that of the United States, Japan, and Germany, and ranked fourth in the world. In 1975, the GDP per capita of France at constant prices surpassed that of Germany, was slightly lower than that of Britain, and was about 70% of that of the United States and Japan. Overall, the French economy did well during this period.

1.3.2 Social Transformation in France

Income inequality in French is low compared to other developed countries. The Gini coefficient of France was 0.327 in 1995 and 0.323 in 2014, below the warning level of 0.4. According to a sample survey conducted by the Statistical Office of the European Union, in 2001, the ratio of total income received by the 20% of the population with the highest income (top quintile) to that received by the 20% of the population with the lowest income (lowest quintile) in France was 4.0, 0.5 lower than 4.5 in 1995, while the average level of EU countries over the same period was 4.4. France was at a lower level than the Eurozone and all other European countries.

From a national accounts point of view, the macro composition of household income in France in 2001 was as follows: household income (mainly wages and subsidies) was 568 billion euros; operating income was 229 billion euros; transfer income was 290 billion euros; the total disposable income of residents calculated by subtracting 137 billion euros in personal income tax and property tax expenditures was 949 billion euros. The total net worth of French residents was 5.643 trillion euros, including 1.728 trillion euros in private housing. In addition, the ratio of the total value of residents' property to the total value of national property in French was 84.8%.

In recent years, growth in household income in France has slowed down due to an economic downturn. Since the beginning of the twenty-first century, due to weak economic recovery in the Eurozone as a whole, France's economic growth has slowed down gradually, with its real GDP growth rate dropping from 3.8% in 2000 to 1.2% in 2016. Job gains were rare in France's labor market. In 2016, the number of people employed was 20.66 million, growing by −0.11%, which was 2.6 percentage points lower than in 2000. Meanwhile, the unemployment rate remained high, reaching 9.97% in 2016, higher than the average of 8.19% for all European countries. Growth in household income in France had slowed down accordingly, mainly in terms of wage growth: the average monthly wage of French employees in 2013 was 2905 euros, a mere 1.39-fold increase over 2000, while the average monthly wage in 1990 increased by 2.24 folds over 1980. The poverty rate among French residents was 7% in 1997; the absolute number of people living in poverty was 1.63 million, 900,000 fewer than in 1970; the poverty rate was 8.7 percentage points lower. The poverty line for French residents was 528 euros a month, up 307 euros from 1970.

Equity in income distribution consists of equity in initial income distribution and equity in income redistribution, and France's income distribution policy represents an effort in both respects.

With regard to equity in initial income distribution: First, the French government has developed and implemented a system of wage guidance for the whole society. The main purpose of the system is to divide the whole society into two major sectors, namely, the public sector and the private sector. For the private sector, the state does not intervene directly, but implements indirect management and regulation by guiding and controlling minimum wages and industry-specific wage levels. Minimum wages are determined by the state based on factors such as price indexes, the employment situation, economic development, and the living standards of low-income people, and are adjusted appropriately according to the circumstances every year to ensure the basic livelihood of workers. For the public sector, wage management is mainly aimed at civil servants in government organs and state-owned enterprises, for whom the government develops the corresponding welfare system and pay scale.

Secondly, the French government adopts an active employment policy to ensure the full employment of residents. Labor supply-side measures to increase employment include: In order to increase youth employment, the government provides on-the-job training and different types of career change training for young people, and young people are eligible for reductions or exemptions from social charges; for people with disabilities and long-term unemployed people, the government attempts to provide internship opportunities and training on new skills; for women, the government has developed the Equal Remuneration Convention to ensure professional equality; for self-employed persons, the government subsidizes expenses incurred by long-term unemployed people before starting their own businesses, subsidizes home-based processing businesses, and grants reductions or exemptions from social charges to sole proprietorships that hire employees. Labor demand-side measures to increase employment include reducing working hours and implementing a time-based working system. For example, the implementation of the 35-hour working week can regulate the supply and demand structure of the labor market, increase the income of low-income people, and reduce the unemployment rate.

With regard to equity in income redistribution: First, the social security system implemented in France focuses on the protection of low-income groups. France is a state with high welfare benefits, providing its residents social security support that covers childbirth, old age, sickness, funerals, housing, unemployment, etc. There are five basic elements to the French social security system, namely, old-age pension, unemployment, medical care, family allowances, and accidents at work. According to French regulations, all salaried persons or students at the typical age for sitting the baccalauréat in France must participate in Social Security. Family allowances are the most wide-ranging branch of social security in France. It covers many items and is regarded as a reflection of the high level of welfare in France.

Second, the French government mainly relies on the personal income tax system and property tax system to regulate the income gap. France implements a progressive tax system for all income earners, that is, income amounts are subject to different income brackets. Meanwhile, after deducting household and other expenses according to the circumstances of each person and his or her household, tax liability for the household (with or without children) is then calculated based on the number of parts (shares) it is divided into. In addition to personal income tax, the government also regulates residents' existing assets through taxation. The main types of taxes include property appreciation tax, property transfer tax, and solidarity tax on wealth.

Third, France implements a universal system of social charges, which takes a certain proportion of people's wages, pensions, and other income. In addition to salaried employees, their employers are also required to pay their share of social charges. Even the unemployed shall pay social charges at a lower rate.

Fourth, the French government's subsidies to agriculture and farmers have become an important part of France's wealth redistribution system. These subsidies fall into the three categories of production, circulation, and life. Since the 1960s, the French agricultural subsidy policy has undergone the evolution process of subsidizing according to product prices, directly subsidizing according to the scale of production, and directly subsidizing according to the rural environment, development, the quality of agricultural products and the living conditions of animals.

1.3.3 Experience of France and Inspiration Drawn Therefrom

Among Western countries, France's economy is closest to the socialist market economy of China, so the experience of France and lessons learnt therefrom are the most useful to us.

First, the modern history of innovation in France shows that the indigenous innovation capability in science and technology is the decisive factor in the development of a country's science and technology undertakings and the core of national competitiveness. France has been very active in innovation in the field of basic scientific research. Although the original public scientific research system in France has been criticized, it is suitable for basic science that pursues free exploration. Strong basic science has laid a solid foundation for France's capacity for scientific research and innovation, paving the way for its rise in the future.

Second, missing opportunities for technological innovation will put the economic development of the whole country in a passive position, as evidenced by the lessons that France has learned from its failure to catch up with the last wave of technological innovation led by information technology in the 1990s. In response, the French government has changed its strategy with a view to the future of the country, prioritized scientific research and innovation over reform and development, strengthened strategic planning, and taken a series of important measures to strengthen the foundation, promote innovation, and seize the "commanding heights." France is making progress in deepening the reform of its scientific and technological system. The government's measures for reform in the field of science and technology are gradually producing results, with new progress being made on multiple fronts and new bright spots appearing in some fields. China should draw lessons from France's mistakes. Even though China's scientific and technological strength is growing and our level of development has caught up with that of the developed countries, we should avoid similar mistakes in our national strategy for technological innovation and development, which will causes losses through passive development.

Finally, indigenous innovation is France's strategic choice in history and should be China's only strategic choice. After the founding of the Fifth Republic in 1958, France began to change its development strategy, abandoned the postwar policy of dependence on the United States, and pursued Gaullist agenda which emphasized independence. Especially in the field of science and technology, France insisted on independence and improved its innovation capability. As a result, France ushered in its second glorious period in history. Core technologies cannot be bought. Western powers have realized that in the process of their development, not to mention China as an Eastern power. Therefore, sticking the development path of indigenous innovation should also be China's strategic choice.

1.4 The Process and Experience of Overcoming the Middle-Income Trap in Germany

1.4.1 Economic Transformation in Germany

Germany's Path to Economic Development

Germany's industrial revolution spanned the entire nineteenth century. Compared with Britain, the Germany's industrial revolution started late and developed rapidly. In the 1950s and 1960s, its industry developed much faster than countries like Britain and France. From 1870 to 1914, Germany went through the Second Industrial Revolution. Relying on its advantages in key industries (in particular steel, chemistry, and electricity) and core technologies during this period, Germany accelerated industrialization and entered the era of cluster innovation, with relevant industries expanding continuously and the increase in employment tending to be concentrated in new industries, especially hydropower, gas, printing, and chemicals. By the time World War I broke out, the German organic chemical industry had accounted for more than half of all employment and investment in the chemical industry. From organic chemicals new directions and products were constantly derived.

The German economy took a series of heavy blows from World War I, the First economic Crisis, and World War II. The Marshall Plan and the Schumann Plan revived the German economy and put it on the development path to the social market economy. In the late 1950s, Germany entered the economic takeoff stage. Its GDP per capita in constant 2005 US dollars exceeded $16,000 in 1970 and $25,000 in 1987. This stage was the main period during which Germany emerged from the late stage of industrialization as a high-income welfare state and also a critical period during which its path to the social market economy gradually matured, reflecting its positive institutional factors, such as respect for scientific and technological innovation and education, as well as the optimization of the industrial structure, the adjustment of foreign policy, the gradual correction of market mechanisms, the development of the idea of attaching equal importance to "equity and efficiency" and the pursuit of social harmony and equilibrium spearheaded by it.

Industrial Upgrading and Technological Innovation

Before World War I, Germany's primary, secondary, and tertiary sectors accounted for 25, 40, and 35% of its GNP, respectively. The characteristics of a modern industrial structure began to develop. Since then, Germany had been confronted with the trauma of World War I and World War II, weak demand in the international heavy and chemical products market, the impact of the oil crisis, and competition with the United States and Japan on heavy industrial products and with emerging countries on bulk commodities. In response to various shocks in different periods, Germany constantly adjusted its development strategy and upgraded its industrial structure. The measures it took were mainly as follows:

(1) Promoting industrial structural adjustment through trade liberalization policies

During the post-World War II reconstruction period, Germany acceded to the GATT. The Marshall Plan and the Schumann Plan also put Germany's industry on a fast track to recovery. From 1950s to early

1970s, Germany's pursuit of trade liberalization accelerated growth in Germany's exports of goods which was positively correlated with industrial development. Germany's industry began to grow rapidly against the backdrop of continued expansion of foreign trade, and exports rose sharply. During this period, Germany further transformed toward heavy and chemical industries. In 1970, Germany's heavy industry accounted for 74% of its total industrial output.

(2) Establishing its industrial position through centralized R&D

Since the 1970s, Germany's industrial structure had faced new transformational pressures and challenges due to weak demand in the international heavy and chemical products market and the impact of the oil crisis. Even as Germany began to phase out oil refining, steel, shipbuilding, and other traditional energy-intensive, material-intensive and low value-added heavy industries by supporting technological R&D and innovation for chemicals, automobiles, aircraft and other high value-added heavy and chemical industries that consume less energy and materials, its tertiary sector as a percentage of GDP was rising.

(3) Combating economic recession with high and new technology, and implementing strategies such as the green transformation of industries.

In the 1990s, Germany faced a recession at home, and internationally, it faced a huge challenge posed by high value-added products from the United States and Japan and competition with cheap goods from emerging countries. In response, the German government began to prioritize, develop, and invest in micro technology, biotechnology, and other high-tech industries, promoted the industrialization of high and new technology, and developed high and new technology and upgraded the industrial structure through profit orientation, structural reform, and global operations, so as to combat inflation and economic recession at home and develop an international competitive advantage in the new round of industrial transformation.

(4) Supporting Technological Innovation by Small- and Medium-sized Enterprises (SMEs)

Germany's approach to promoting industrial transformation was an organic combination of government policies and market mechanisms, and was focused on SMEs (mostly private enterprises). The federal government and state governments formulated various policies and measures in accordance with the principle of market competition to guide the development of enterprises and the reasonable combination of scientific research forces in society without directly interfering in the technological and economic activities of enterprises. Meanwhile, at the government level (including the federal and state levels), clear strategies and plans for the development of science and technology had been formulated to encourage enterprises and scientific research units to develop in areas of technology prioritized by the state for development.

1.4.2 *Social Transformation in Germany*

When Germany crossed the middle-income stage, an important social transformation was the establishment of an income distribution system that took into account both efficiency and equity.

Before World War II, Germany's Gini coefficient once exceeded 0.4. 4. By the 1970s, Germany's path to the social market economy had matured. Income inequality was reduced through various policy tools. The Gini coefficient gradually declined and was generally at or below 0.3. Income distribution was relatively even in Germany. When GDP per capita was $3000, $6000 and $10,000, labor compensation as a share of GDP was 48.7, 53.1 and 55.4%, respectively. Since the 1980s, there has been a clear synergy between growth in household income and economic development in European developed countries, including Germany. In Germany, labor compensation as a share of GDP is between 50 and 55% during the primary distribution phase; in the redistribution phase, the disposable income of residents accounts for about 70% of GDP. This means that through redistribution adjustment, the total income of residents has increased significantly, reflecting the inclusiveness and equalization of income.

Germany's income distribution system follows the principle of giving priority to efficiency and giving consideration to equity, that is, primary distribution emphasizes efficiency, while redistribution emphasizes equity. The main measures it takes to effectively intervene in income distribution include the following.

Promoting Employment by Adjusting Labor-Management Relations

After World War II, Germany gradually formed a set of social operation mechanisms and enterprise organization systems for regulating and dealing with labor-management relations. A relatively stable "social partnership" was formed between labor and management, which mainly followed the following principles: First, the principle of labor and management autonomy, that is, labor and management enjoy the right of autonomy over wages and reach a wage agreement through negotiations; second, the principle of joint decision-making, that is, employees participate in the decision-making and management of the enterprises, an supervisory board and works council are set up within the enterprise, with the works council representing the interests of employees and supervising the enterprise's implementation of laws, regulations, the labor agreement and other agreements with the enterprise designed to safeguard the rights and interests of employees; third, the principle of mediation of labor-management disputes, that is, labor-management disputes are resolved mainly through negotiations between labor and management, and the government or any other social group will mediate or arbitrate on the principle of neutrality and fairness when negotiations are deadlocked.

Regulating Through Taxes

Germany's long-standing high-tax system has played a crucial role in narrowing the income gap. The most widely levied tax in Germany's current tax system is personal income tax, which accounts for more than 40% of the total tax revenue and is levied on all persons who receive taxable income. Germany adopts a progressive tax system, which works on the principle that the higher the income level, the higher a tax rate you pay. Low-income earners pay less or no taxes. This kind of income distribution policy has played a positive role in narrowing the income gap and easing social contradictions. For example, Germany's Gini coefficient is 0.44 before tax and 0.28 after tax. The vast majority of German residents belong to the middle-income group. This "olive-shaped" social structure is also an important factor behind the stable development of German society.

Promoting Regional Balance in Economic Development Through Fiscal Means

After World War II, in order to solve the problem of regional imbalances in economic development, Germany formulated policies, laws, and regulations on balanced regional development. The Basic Law and other relevant laws stipulate that the federal government and state governments are obliged to maintain the balanced development of the economy as a whole when implementing financial assistance; economic development must ensure that people in all regions enjoy the same living conditions. On this basis, Germany implements a policy measure aimed at achieving fiscal balance under the guidance of the principle of "social justice." It is a balanced policy dominated by horizontal fiscal transfer payments between states, supplemented by vertical fiscal transfer payments from the federal government.

Improving the Social Security System

After World War II, with the establishment of the social market economy system, the social security system was restored and further developed and improved. At present, Germany is one of the most developed welfare states in the world, and its social welfare covers more than 90% of the residents. The social security system has become a shock absorber and safety net for social development. Germany's social security system is dominated by social insurance, including statutory endowment insurance, medical insurance, unemployment insurance, employment injury insurance, and nursing insurance. In addition to social insurance, there are social assistance and family allowances. Among them, social assistance is the last barrier of the social security system, that is, the government ensures the basic livelihoods of the poorest people through social assistance. Under the Social Assistance Act, every resident who is unable to help himself or herself and cannot get help can ask the government for social assistance.

1.4.3 Experience of Germany and Inspiration Drawn Therefrom

Germany's development experience shows that if economic growth relies more on technological advances and industrial upgrading, while maintaining the continuous growth of the total economic output, dynamic adjustments should be made to the economic structure, the distribution of benefits, the social and economic composition, the organizational form and so on. Meanwhile, external dependence will deepen with economic development. In addition, as the economy develops, internal social pressures will increase, so how to maintain the balanced development of society becomes an important issue. Germany's development path and system design at this stage are worth learning from.

Establishment of a Sound Economic Law System

Germany suffered a terrible defeat in World War II. The war devastated the social productivity of the Federal Republic of Germany. But today Germany is one of the most economically developed, efficient and orderly countries in the world.

An important reason for this "German economic miracle" was that the German government had enacted a large number of economic laws and regulations in various periods to reform, adjust, and manage the national economy. These laws and regulations covered a wide range of areas, forming a huge economic law system. The development of a sound economic law system compatible with the social market economy was not only a great boost to the economic takeoff of Germany, but also an important symbol and evaluation indicator of Germany's status as a country under the rule of law. Germany had a reputation as a "country with an economy under the rule of law," which was closely related to its strong economic strength and good economic order. In the decades after World War II, Germany continuously promoted and stabilized this social market economic order, and gradually formed a "German model," which attracted extensive attention. The initiation and deepening of German economic and social legislation was due to this emerging economic model. Germany was the first country to implement social welfare. Bismarck pioneered the national social insurance system. He once bluntly stated, "A person who is looking forward to a pension is the most law-abiding and also the easiest to rule." He saw social insurance as "an investment to eliminate revolution." Regardless of the original intention and essence of Bismarck's creation of a national social insurance system, this system had objectively improved the lives of employees and played a very positive role in developing the economy, stabilizing society, and easing contradictions. After World War II, with the formation and development of the German social market economy system, laws and systems related to social security were continuously improved.

Decentralized Dual-Track Vocational Education

Germany had not only established the world's first-class comprehensive university, but also built the best technical and business education system. As a result, the levels of educational attainment and technological literacy of workers at all levels had improved. Guilds played an irreplaceable role in the vocational education system. Guilds motivated rural labor force in cities to actively participate in relevant vocational training and learn the necessary skills related to their own occupations in order to adapt to career transitions and improve their social status in cities, and played an active role in training and supplying skilled workers. In addition, guilds created an honest business attitude and climate, motivated their members to adapt as quickly as possible to the unprecedented high demands imposed on them by industrialization, and encouraged their members to receive a higher level of education. This diversified education system provided citizens with a large number of development opportunities, promoted technological advances in industries, helped prevent the aimless and ineffective pursuit of higher education, and laid the foundation for the diversification of career choices.

A Stable and Flexible Public Finance System

Germany's public finance was permeated by a strong concept of equilibrium: First, the source of tax revenue was relatively balanced, with relatively equal proportions of direct and indirect taxes. A relatively balanced tax system could help public finance to provide stable tax revenue, which became a potential ace up Germany's sleeve as it coped with the recession. Second, raise the energy tax and resource tax. This not only provided the government with a stable source of revenue, but more importantly advanced energy conservation and environmental protection, and promoted the development of an environmentally friendly society. Third, people-oriented transfer payments. Transfer payments were made according to the actual social development needs of various places. Especially transfer payments could be made directly between so-called poor states and rich states without going through the central government.

Joint Decision-Making and Multi-Layered Governance Mechanism

The "joint decision-making + supervisory board" mechanism gradually formed in the process of industrialization in Germany organically integrated workers with enterprise management decision-making, so as to enhance the enthusiasm of workers, ease labor-management relations and avoid vicious labor-management conflicts. Multi-layered governance was key to achieving social equilibrium and decentralization in Germany. Although a multi-layered and multi-dimensional coordination mechanism will slow things down, the sufficient debate and communication provided by it guarantee the operability of policies and public acceptability to a large extent. Moreover, it helps solve negative externalities associated with policies (such as unfairness to stakeholders caused by policies), maximizes the balanced distribution of resources and public goods and services, allows the rights and interests of different stakeholders to be fully represented, and minimizes the damage to social justice caused by policy mistakes so as to effectively avoid social conflicts.

Necessary Welfare System

The social security system is a core element of the maintenance of social equilibrium. Governments and enterprises should provide basic housing and medical insurance for all workers, so that workers can concentrate on their work, which will indirectly improve economic efficiency. The German approach to this issue is worth learning from: German companies pay more attention to the long-term interests of companies, rather than the immediate interests of shareholders. Companies operate more for the benefit of employees than for shareholders, and attach importance to skills training and quality-oriented education for employees.

1.5 Experience of Economic and Social Transformation in Developed Countries and Inspiration Drawn Therefrom

Western developed countries, in particular the United States, Britain, France, and Germany, have taken different paths and strategies for entering the high-income stage. But they have all undergone comprehensive and profound economic and social transformation. The historical process of Western developed countries offers the following inspiration for China in overcoming the middle-income trap.

1.5.1 Transform the Mode of Economic Development and Enhance the Role of Technological Innovation and Human Capital

The successful experience of developed countries in Europe and America shows that to enter the high-income stage, a country first needs to change its mode of economic development, enhance the role of technological innovation and human capital, and take practical measures to ensure that SMEs and large enterprises participate in market competition and cooperation on an equal footing under the same market conditions as fully equal participants in the whole market economy. In the past 40 years of China's reform and opening-up, on the one hand, rapid economic development has been supported by an increase in resource inputs and an increase in investment, namely an increase in the number of factors; on the other hand, change in the structure of factor use and the opening-up to the outside world have greatly increased total factor productivity, which coupled with the government's ability to mobilize resources and coordinate has boosted economic growth. These factors have contributed to China's relatively smooth economic growth and relatively high economic growth rate over the past 40 years. But by the turn of the century, these advantages had gradually diminished; especially the unlimited supply of rural surplus labor had changed. To achieve the sustainable growth of the Chinese economy, we must change the way of economic development and enhance the role of technological advances and human capital in driving economic growth.

1.5.2 Attach Importance to Education, Update Concepts, and Create More "Talent Dividends"

The industrialization of developed countries is first manifested in human specialization. The specialized qualities of labor force and the improvement of labor productivity play a prominent role in the process of economic growth. In the long run, we should continue to make good use of the "demographic dividend" and place greater emphasis on relying on the "talent dividend." To this end, we must rely on education and science and technology, and organically combine the two to greatly enhance China's ability to create wealth and promote the progress of social civilization. Although the level of education in China has improved significantly in all aspects, there remains a prominent problem, namely a woeful inadequacy in our ability to cultivate innovative talent, which greatly affects the release of the "talent dividend." Attaching importance to education, updating the concept of talent cultivation, especially establishing the concept of all-round development, the concept of diverse talent and systematic training, and promoting the close integration of teaching, scientific research, and practice are important prerequisites for cultivating innovative talent.

1.5.3 Create a Fair and Just Competitive Environment for the Development of Enterprises

The development and maturation of modern company systems have contributed to the rapid economic development and industrial structural adjustment of Western developed countries. Driven by the accelerating process of global economic integration and the expanding scale of urbanization, China's national economic development agenda has put forward more comprehensive and systematic requirements for the development of various industries. We need to be soberly aware that the development of enterprises requires the government to create a fair and just competition environment. As far as the development of China's market economy at the present stage is concerned, in the process of participating in market competition, equal participants in the market economy are often treated differently in terms of financing, taxation and government support due to objective factors such as the nature of operation and management and the organizational size of the enterprise. Practical measures should be taken to ensure that SMEs and large enterprises participate in market competition and cooperation on an equal footing under the same market conditions as equal participants.

1.5.4 Provide Lasting Impetus for Urbanization Through Dynamic Adjustment of the Industrial Structure

The experience of Western developed countries has proved that urbanization must be based on industrialization. Generally speaking, there will be no urbanization without industrialization, but after industrialization have reached a certain stage, the role of industrialization in promoting urbanization will gradually weakens, and the rise of tertiary industries such as the service industry will accelerate the development of urbanization. The rate of industrialization in the United States began to decline after the 1950s, but the rate of urbanization continued to rise, indicating that the service industry gradually became the main driving force for urbanization in the United States after the 1950s. In the early stage of industrialization, the aggregation effect formed by industrial development has a direct driving effect on the improvement of urbanization rate. In the early stage of industrialization, the agglomeration effect of industrial development has a direct effect on increasing the rate of urbanization; when industrialization approaches and enters the middle stage, the role of industrial structure transformation and upgrading exceeds the role of the agglomeration effect, the rising proportion of employment in non-agricultural sectors leads to an increase of the rate of urbanization, and the increase in the proportion of employment in non-agricultural sectors is driven primarily by the growth of the service sector rather than the industrial sector. For China, the dynamic adjustment of the urban industrial structure is not blindly pursuing the upgrading of the industrial structure, but must adapt to local conditions and take full account of the employment needs of rural population in cities.

1.5.5 Effectively Alleviate the Pressure Brought by a Widening Gap in Per Capita Income in the Future

Judging from the evolution of income distribution in similar stages in developed countries such as the United States, China will face the severe challenge of a widening income gap for some time to come. On the one hand, due to a huge labor force and the huge differences in resource endowments between regions, the transfer of the industrial structure and the adjustment of the income gap in China are significantly more difficult than in the United States; on the other hand, change in the gap in per capita income in China is to a large extent caused by various factors and can be alleviated by institutional measures, that is to say, the government and society have plenty of leeway to take reasonable measures to prevent the income gap from expanding. Analysis shows that economic development does not necessarily result in the income gap rising first and then falling.

In addition, transportation infrastructure such as highways and railways is also very important for promoting the economic development of backward areas. At present, with regard to highway construction, some areas have the tendency to emphasize the construction of expressways and urban roads while neglecting the construction of rural highways. This should be changed. Marketization itself does not lead to widening income gap. The widening income gap is largely due to the distorted distribution of resources and income inequality caused by institutional imperfection, irregularities committed by the government, and corruption in the process of marketization. Therefore, it is necessary to build a fair, standardized and transparent institutional framework to support the market system and to form a public supervision system to restrain the government through government reform, so as to protect the interests of the public from being infringed in economic development.

2 Japan, South Korea, and Other East Asian Countries (Regions)

East Asian countries and regions, including Japan, South Korea, China Taiwan, and China Hong Kong, have not experienced an obvious middle-income trap in their development. Many studies suggest that these economies have also undergone a long process of obvious industrial upgrading, that is, the transition from labor-intensive industries to capital-intensive and technology-intensive industries, but unlike some other countries in the world, these economies have not been trapped in economic stagnation, political instability, and social unrest, but have crossed this potential "trap" relatively successfully. So, for these East Asian economies, the big question is what helped them avoid this potential problem.

2.1 The Process and Experience of Overcoming the Middle-Income Trap in Japan

Japan is a typical economy that transitioned from a low-income country to a middle-income country and then successfully joined the ranks of high-income countries. For more than 30 years after the end of World War II, the Japanese economy recovered quickly, and then grew rapidly for more than 20 years. The reason why Japan could successfully overcome the middle-income trap was that on the one hand, it had successfully transformed and upgraded its mode of economic development and industries, especially it had made the shift from imitation to indigenous innovation; on the other hand, it had achieved a well-balanced distribution of benefits and curbed the widening income gap to provide a relatively stable social environment for overcoming the middle-income trap (see Tables 1 and 2).

2.1.1 Economic Transformation in Japan

From the early 1950s to the 1980s, Japan transformed and upgraded from light industry to heavy industry to the tertiary sector in time, and completed the shift from "founding the nation on trade" to "founding the nation on technology" to "founding the nation on culture," laying a

Table 1 Japan's annual GDP growth rate from 1945 to 2016 (%)

Indicator	*1945–1950*	*1951–1955*	*1956–1960*	*1961–1965*	*1966–1970*	*1971–1980*	*1981–1985*	*1986–1999*	*2000–2009*	*2010–2016*
Annual GDP growth rate(%)	9.9	8.7	8.5	9.8	11.6	4.5	4.3	8.3	0.6	–0.18

Source ce.cn

Table 2 Japan's GDP per capita from 1945 to 2016 (current US$)

Indicator	*1945*	*1950*	*1955*	*1960*	*1965*	*1970*	*1980*	*1985*	*1986*	*1990*	*2000*	*2010*	*2016*
GDP per capita (current US$)	89	113	209	431	890	1940	9308	11,466	16,882	25,124	37,292	43,118	38,894

Source ce.cn

material and cultural foundation for successfully overcoming the middle-income trap. According to the actual needs of economic and social development and changes in the international environment after World War II, Japan had carried out three major industrial structural adjustments.

For nearly 20 years after 1955, Japan established the strategy of "founding the nation on trade," with heavy industry leading and driving the development of related industries. In the 1950s, fiber was Japan's main export. In the 1970s, Japan's general machinery, precision instruments, semiconductors and power equipment contributed the most to total factor productivity, the share of machinery in exports rose sharply, the rapid rise of automobile manufacturing led to the rapid growth of heavy industries and chemical industries such as steel and petrochemicals, and the mechanical and electronic industries gradually became Japan's most internationally competitive industries.

In the 1970s, the proportion of heavy industry in Japan dropped significantly as Japan accelerated the implementation of industrial structural adjustment centered on the "greenization" of industries, and actively built a resource-saving and environmentally friendly economic structure. The oil crisis of the 1970s further accelerated the adjustment of Japan's industrial structure, with the proportion of heavy industry decreasing significantly, and knowledge-intensive industries such as computers and aerospace gradually becoming the leading industries. Japan began to accelerate the implementation of industrial structural adjustment centered on the "greenization" of industries, and actively build a resource-saving and environmentally friendly economic structure. Especially starting in the 1970s, Japan adjusted its industrial structure by first tackling hyperinflation, developed new energy, carried out the "enterprise energy consumption slimming" campaign, and vigorously developed energy-saving technologies, new energy technologies, and oil replacement technologies. Japan put forward the Sunlight Plan and the Moonlight Plan in 1974 and 1978, respectively. The former was a plan to develop new energy sources such as solar energy, coal energy, geothermal energy, and hydrogen energy, and the latter was aimed at strengthening the research and development of energy-saving technologies, improving energy conversion efficiency, and recycling, and utilizing unused energy. Meanwhile, Japan set up the Ministry of the Environment, strengthened environmental legislation, and clarified its intention to promote the transformation from energy-intensive industries to energy-saving industries in an effort to break through resource and energy constraints on economic growth and ease the pressure caused by environmental pollution.

Starting in the 1980s, the center of gravity Japan's industrial structure once again shifted to final consumption. Thanks to a push by the government, the proportion of the tertiary sector, which was developing in the direction of cultural creativity, increased rapidly, and the service industry became the leading industry for Japan's economic growth. In 1995, the Conference on the Promotion of Japanese Cultural Policy issued an important report entitled "Founding the Nation on New Culture: Several Important Strategies for the Revitalization of Culture," which put forward the strategic policy of "founding the nation on culture" in the twenty-first century. In 2001, the gross output of Japan's cultural industry accounted for 18.3% of GDP, and the cultural industry became Japan's second largest pillar industry after manufacturing.

Meanwhile, in order to solve the problem of insufficient internal driving force, since the 1980s, Japan had accelerated the pace of fostering its indigenous innovation capability. The Japanese government not only designed a set of strategies to foster Japan's indigenous innovation capability from a national perspective, but also supported private sector R&D activities in terms of policy measures and platform building, vigorously supported the building of indigenous innovation platforms, and effectively improved the conversion rate of technological achievements. In the early 1980s, Japan's Ministry of International Trade and Industry put forward the strategic slogan "founding the nation on technology," and Japan's Ministry of Science and Technology put forward the strategic slogan "founding the nation on science and technology" in an attempt to develop Japan into a science and technology power in the world, indicating that Japan's technological progress had gone from the "era of imitation" to the "innovation stage" in the real sense of the word. Through the implementation of preferential policies such as preferential tax measures, subsidies, commission fees, and low-interest financing, the Japanese government increased support for enterprise R&D and vigorously supported private sector R&D in policy. The combination of "industry, government and academia" was a successful mode whereby Japan caught up with Europe and the United States through the introduction, assimilation, improvement, and development of industrial technologies. Meanwhile, the Japanese government also enacted laws to promote the establishment of "innovation center"-type science and technology parks and accelerate the transition to the era of the electronics industry, intensified the cultivation of strategic high-tech industries, and worked hard to foster indigenous innovation capability.

2.1.2 *Social Transformation in Japan*

In the early 1960s, the Japanese economy entered a "depression" stage. In order to solve the problems of over-reliance on investment-led growth, the imminent exhaustion of the demographic dividend, and insufficient personal consumption, Japan formulated the Income Doubling Plan. First, through farmland reform, accelerated the process of building water conservancy works on an extensive scale, making extensive use of chemical fertilizers, and mechanizing, raised the prices of agricultural products, improved agricultural productivity, and increased farmers' income. Second, recognized the important role of SMEs in the national economy by establishing a minimum wage, created a system for division of labor between large and small enterprises, established a system for division of labor and cooperation in society whereby large and small enterprises coordinated closely with each other, promoted the development of SMEs, reduced the wage gap and raised the overall wage level. Finally, adjusted and redistributed by implementing effective education policies. The popularization of basic education and secondary education effectively increased the accumulation of human capital and raised the income level. In addition, three national comprehensive development plans were formulated in 1961, 1969, and 1977 in an attempt to achieve balanced development between regions and between urban and rural areas. Since the Income Doubling Plan was launched in 1960, the purchasing power of Japanese citizens had enhanced, and private investment had increased. It took Japan only seven years to double its national income and significantly enlarge the ranks of middle-income earners to eventually develop into a modern middle-class society with "100 million middle-class people."

Meanwhile, as it developed into a high-income country, Japan drew on the experience of Europe and the United States with regard to welfare systems to build a social welfare system suitable for its own national conditions. In the 1960s, Japan established a social security system consisting of the five components of annuity, medical care, employment, industrial accident, and nursing. Since the 1980s, Japan had focused on the implementation of the four basic security programs of income, medical care, education, and residence. Before the bubble economy of the 1980s arrived, Japan had basically completed the development of a social security system and a social welfare system, and accumulated enough strength to counter the deeper and longer recession that followed.

2.1.3 Experience of Japan and Inspiration Drawn Therefrom

The role of the Japanese government in avoiding the trap is an important guarantee for the smooth realization of industrial upgrading. Many studies have found that the smooth adjustment of Japan's industrial structure was closely related to industrial policies that coordinated the Japanese government with large consortia large enterprises.

According to the new growth theory (Becker, 1970), although the material-human capital endowment possessed by the Japanese economy before World War II was destroyed by the exogenous shock of World War II, leading to a sharp decline in material capital, human capital was largely spared. Therefore, the economic rise after World War II was actually a process of returning to the track of economic development with the help of the high level of human capital preserved. The Wartime Origin Theory[4] holds that Japan's rapid postwar economic rise was due to the state-enterprise system established during the war and the corresponding material-human capital mobilization structure. The mobilization form inherited from the wartime system had shaped the special form of Japan's postwar economic development, which was very different from free market capitalism, and was embodied in the strong control exerted by the state over economic development. Such a centralized state-led market development mechanism guaranteed Japan's ability to concentrate resources and energy to develop its economy rapidly after World War II. The logistics and production system created during the war to serve the military industry had produced considerable thrust since it was converted to civilian use. The Postwar Formation Theory[5] holds that one of the great efforts after the war was to settle accounts with big capitalists for colluding with militarism, cut the link between the state and enterprises, and break up the monopolistic zaibatsu. Of course, this effort was not thorough, but it was the process of abandoning the

[4] [Japan] Tetsuji Okazaki, Masahiro Okuno-Fujiwara. *Contemporary Japanese Economic System and Its Historical Origins*. Tokyo: Nikkei, Inc., 1993; Yukio Noguchi The 1940 System.

[5] [Japan] Juro Hashimoto. *Japanese Economy After World War II*. Tokyo: Iwanami Shorten, 1995.

wartime system that had injected vitality into Japan's economic development. Researchers believe that the Japanese economy also benefited from Japan's status as an occupied country after World War II. For example, the occupying powers led by the United States carried out a series of tax and legal reforms, which helped Japan establish a scientific and effective institutional basis; during the Korean War, the United States exported a lot of materials and technology to Japan at low prices, and helped drive the development of Japan's processing industry. Under the guidance of the state, Japan has established an export-oriented economy and integrated into the global market well.

2.2 *The Process and Experience of Overcoming the Middle-Income Trap in South Korea*

In the 1950s, South Korea was a poor country. Since then, due to the smooth transformation of its economic and social structure, South Korea had experienced more than 30 years of rapid economic growth, quickly growing from a middle-income country into a high-income country. From 1961 to 1994, the South Korean economy grew at an average annual rate of 8.4%, with the average annual growth rate from 1980 to 1990 being 9% (see Table 3). Rapid economic growth had led to continuous growth in South Korea's national income per capita.

2.2.1 *Economic Transformation in South Korea*

Since the 1980s, the global economic landscape had changed dramatically, with Western countries, affected by the energy crisis, resorting to trade protectionism, which had greatly impacted South Korea's export-oriented economy. Meanwhile, Western countries had begun a new round of technological revolution with a big push for the transformation and upgrading

Table 3 GDP per capita in South Korea from 1953 to 1995 (current US$)

Indicator	*1953*	*1961*	*1970*	*1977*	*1980*	*1990*	*1995*	*2000*	*2005*	*2016*
GDP per capita (current US$)	67	100	270	1000	2330	5770	11,468	11,948	18,657	27,539

Source ce.cn

of the industrial structure. The South Korean government recognized the need to shift its mode of development in time, from an export-oriented, labor-intensive economy to an innovative economy. Some of the very distinctive practices are as follows: First, attaching importance to top-level design. In the early 1980s, South Korea established the strategy of "founding the nation on science and technology" in an attempt to transform and upgrade traditional industries by using advanced technologies and develop knowledge-intensive industries. In 1985, South Korea promulgated the Industrial Development Law, which emphasized the role of the market in industrial development and economic operations, and greatly unleashed market forces, creating a good external environment for the optimization and upgrading of the industrial structure. Since the 1990s, South Korea had further deepened its strategy of "founding the nation on science and technology," increased support for its high-tech industries, and gradually shifted from imitative innovation to indigenous innovation. In 1998, South Korea put forward the "Design Korea" strategy under which South Korea would vigorously develop the cultural and creative industries to transform from a manufacturing-oriented country to a design innovation-oriented country. Under the guidance of top-level design, South Korea's indigenous innovation capability had been greatly enhanced, with brands like Samsung and LG becoming world-famous brands. Second, increasing investment in R&D. Since the 1980s, South Korea had increased its investment in R&D year by year, with investment in R&D growing by more than 10% annually.

2.2.2 *Social Transformation in South Korea*

The New Village Movement narrowed the gap between urban and rural areas. In the early 1970s, the South Korean economy began to take off, but the gap between urban and rural areas remained large. In 1970, 80% of South Korean farmers lived in huts, relied on oil lamps for light at night, and had two meals a day, and more than half of the countryside was not accessible by car. In April of the same year, the then President Park Chung-hee launched the "New Village Movement." The government provided steel and cement to encourage farmers to participate in rural economic and social development and improve rural production and living environment. The New Village Movement improved infrastructure in rural South Korea, boosted agricultural development, increased farmers' income, and changed the spiritual outlook of rural areas and farmers.

Meanwhile, it prevented "city disease" brought by a sudden influx of farmers into cities, and played an important role in narrowing the gap between urban and rural areas and promoting urban–rural integration.

Reduce the income gap through tax reform. In the mid-to-late 1970s, South Korea introduced a more thorough comprehensive personal income tax system, under which savings and investment income were taxed at different rates.

Attach importance to education and promote the equalization of educational services. Korea began to implement a multi-level human resources development strategy in the 1960s. This strategy was reflected not only in the fact that South Korea was ranked among the highest in the world for average years of schooling, the percentage of the population who have received education and enrollment rates in secondary schools after compulsory education, but also in the popularization of higher education and the development of postgraduate education. "South Korea's economic growth is achieved by heavy investment in human capital. Its investment in education is the highest among developing countries, and its high school graduation rate is the second highest in the world, behind only the United States" (Song, Byung-Nak, 1994). While attaching importance to the education and training system, South Korea attached great importance to investment in R&D. In 1995, South Korea's per capita spending on R&D was as high as $80,420; that figure reached $88,678 in 2000 and $120,370 in 2006. South Korea's spending on R&D accounted for 3.47% of its GDP in 2007, totaling $33.7 billion. This emphasis on multi-level training and investment in R&D has enabled South Korea to lead the world in terms of value added in high-tech industries as a proportion of manufacturing value added in the past 20 years. It was the improvement of the education and training system and the emphasis on investment in R&D that provided the basis for the transformation and upgrading of industries to high-grade, precision and advanced industries.

2.2.3 *Experience of South Korea and Inspiration Drawn Therefrom*

The role of the South Korean government's industrial policy in helping the South Korean economy avoid the middle-income trap has been heeded by scholars. Researchers believe that South Korea's development is due to three government initiatives. First, promote the optimization and upgrading of the industrial structure, "found the nation on science and technology," and vigorously develop knowledge-intensive industries. These include reforming the economic system, strengthening the role of market mechanisms in the economic system, passing the Industrial Development Law, adjusting industrial policy, focusing on cultivating industries' capacity for technological innovation, passing the Law on the Promotion of Technology Research and Development, and introducing a series of policies to protect the domestic market and expand exports. Second, adjust the pattern of income distribution. Specific measures include adjusting the pattern of primary distribution through tax policy adjustment, adjusting the pattern of redistribution through social security measures, and narrowing the gap between urban and rural areas through the "New Community Movement" (or New Village Movement). Third, improve the quality of human capital as a whole. Specific measures include actively mobilizing all sectors of society to increase investment in education, mobilizing non-governmental actors to enhance the operational vitality of all types of schools, and giving priority to the development of basic education under the leadership of the government. Researchers focus more on initiatives at the public policy level, pointing out that South Korea's approach was not to change the industrial structure or enhance innovation capability, but to respond appropriately in terms of public policy by giving full play to a series of social equalization policies that were in line with economic development, such as employment, education, taxation, and social security, so as to achieve rapid and equitable development. Specifically, first, in terms of employment policy, as South Korea entered the middle-income stage, its employment policy shifted from cultivating labor force to promoting equity. Second, at the education policy level, the South Korean government achieved the goal of changing the economic plan and catered to changing market demands through the continuous change of education policy. Third, at the tax policy level, the South Korean government reduced the tax burden on low- and middle-income workers, and raised tax rates on high-income earners to ensure relatively fair distribution. Fourth, at the social security level, the fruits of economic growth were distributed to all social strata as social security exerted its redistributive effects.

2.3 Experience of Economic and Social Transformation in East Asian Countries and Inspiration Drawn Therefrom

2.3.1 Robust Rule of Law Safeguards Economic and Social Transformation and Development

The Rule of Law Helps Build a Powerful Nation in Science and Technology

Japan established the importance of science and technology in law. The Japanese constitution promulgated in 1946 placed a premium on scientific and technological advances. Since the 1980s, the Japanese government has enacted laws to promote the establishment of "innovation center"-type science and technology parks and speed up the progress toward the era of the electronics industry, increased efforts to develop strategic high-tech industries, and vigorously cultivated the indigenous innovation capability. In 1995, Japan promulgated the Basic Law on Science and Technology, followed by the Science and Technology Basic Plan (three versions) to meticulously lay out the direction and priorities for scientific and technological development. In 1986, the Japanese government enacted the Research Exchange Promotion Law, which greatly promoted the flow of scientific and technological personnel and technology transfer among governments, research institutions, universities, and private enterprises. The number of school-enterprise cooperative research projects supported under this framework was huge. Meanwhile, the Law on the Promotion of Technology Transfer from Universities to Industry has made great contributions to the patenting, practicalization, and commercialization of scientific research results. In the 1990s, on the basis of "bringism" and promoting technological progress, Japan paid more attention to basic and pioneering research, carried out independent technological innovation, enacted the Science and Technology Basic Law, and put forward the strategy of "founding the nation on technological creation," which later evolved into the strategy of "founding the nation on scientific and technological creation." As a result, Japan quickly caught up and overtook in terms of science and technology.

The South Korean government set up the Ministry of Science and Technology in 1967, and immediately thereafter enacted the Science and Technology Promotion Law. In the 1970s, the South Korean government enacted the Law on the Promotion of Technology Development, and established the system of industrial technology development in an effort to develop high and new technologies such as iron and steel, machinery and electronics. In the early 1980s, South Korea established the strategy of "founding the nation on science and technology," and formulated specific systems and regulations to support and encourage the development of science and technology. During this period, the Law on Financial Support for New Technologies and the Law on Financial Support for New Technology Businesses were enacted successively. The Law on the Promotion of Technology Transfer and the Special Law on Scientific and Technological Innovation enacted by the South Korean government have guaranteed the establishment and operation of the Korea Technology Transfer Center in law. On the basis of ensuring profits for innovators, they have encouraged and promoted the transfer and diffusion of technologies, and provided a legal safeguard for the research and development, transfer, and industrialization of technologies.[6] A sound system of laws on science and technology, and laws and regulations protecting scientific and technological personnel and scientific and technological innovations put scientific and technological innovation on a firm legal basis to become a "protective umbrella" for scientific and technological innovations.

The Rule of Law Helps Economic Development

Before the land reform in South Korea, high rents not only caused tensions between landlords and tenants, but also severely farmers' enthusiasm for production, resulting in a continuous decline in land productivity. For this reason, the South Korean government promulgated the Land Reform Act, under which the old tenancy relationship was abolished, an owner-peasant system was implemented on the principle of "land to the tiller," and land was sold directly to tenant farmers through non-gratuitous confiscation and allocation.[7] The land reform brought smallholder farmers under the feudal social system into the capitalist market economy, successfully completed the institutional change of rural society, and promoted the development of the productive forces of rural society. The Japanese government implemented similar measures. The Agricultural Land Adjustment Act of 1938 stipulated that the government should buy the land of landlords and sell it to peasants. Japan proceeded

[6] Li Yixue, Wang Jun. Experience of South Korea in Promoting the Industrialization of Achievements with Independent Intellectual Property Rights, 2007 (12): 68.

[7] [Japan] Yuhei Ogawa, et al. *Analysis of South Korea's Economy*. Translated by Zhao Fengbin Beijing: China Prospect Publishing House, 1989.

to embark on agricultural land reform, which abolished the feudal agricultural land system, created owner-peasants, and improved the tenancy relationship.

In the early days of its economic development, in order to support the country's five-year economic development plan, South Korea created a government-led financial system, and amended the central bank act to place the central bank under the Ministry of Finance, and transfer the functions and powers of the financial policy authority from the central bank to the government, laying the foundation for the development finance system. However, as the economy developed, the drawbacks of this government-led financial system were gradually exposed. Against the background of a rising call for reform at home and pressure from the international community, the South Korean financial system launched reform with a focus on privatization, liberalization, and internationalization, which reduced the government's administrative intervention, abolished the Interim Measures on Financial Institutions, replaced interventions with indirect regulatory approaches such as open market policy and the payment reserve system, and gradually marketized regulatory measures,[8] so as to institutionally guarantee the independence and autonomy of financial institutions. In 1985, South Korea promulgated the Industrial Development Law, which emphasized the role of the market in industrial development and economic operations, and greatly unleashed market forces, creating a good external environment for the optimization and upgrading of the industrial structure.

The Rule of Law Promotes Social Equity

After decades of continuous development and improvement, Japan's social security system has grown into a relatively complete social security system. There are relatively well-established laws and regulations corresponding to each part of the social security system. A sound legal system provides a legal basis for the social security system and guarantees the standardized implementation thereof. After World War II, under the guidance of the US occupying forces, in response to a dire situation where one-third of the citizens were in need of relief, the Japanese government promulgated the Life Protection Law in 1946 based on the principle of equality of citizens in terms of the right to subsistence, stipulating that it

[8]Fang Fang. Reform of South Korea's Financial System and Inspiration Drawn Therefrom. *Teaching and Research*, 2006 (5): 59.

was the responsibility of the state to ensure a minimum standard of living for all citizens. Since then, the Japanese government had promulgated the Child Welfare Act (1948) and the Welfare of Disabled Persons Act (1949). The period was known as the "Three Law Era" for social welfare. In the process of urbanization, Japan established a unified social security system to prevent the income gap from widening. The National Health Insurance Act and the National Pension Act were promulgated in 1959 and implemented in 1961. By the 1960s, a rural social security system based on rural public health care and old-age security had taken shape and begun to spread rapidly. In 1985, the Japanese government amended the National Pension Act to make the national pension basic old-age insurance for all citizens. It can be seen from Japan's social security system that the soundness and standardization of its laws and regulations to a large extent to ensure the effective implementation of its social security system.

The South Korean government implemented the Minimum Wage Act beginning in 1988. Since the 1980s, South Korea's Gini coefficient had decreased significantly. South Korea's Gini coefficient decreased from 0.39 in 1980 to 0.26 in 1991, as the distribution of income was equalized. The South Korean government regulated trade practices to ensure fairness, and took legal measures to restrict market monopolies and curb corruption. The South Korean government promulgated the Monopoly Regulation and Fair Trade Act in 1980 and the systemically feasible Anti-Corruption Act in 2001. These laws and institutions have played an important role in combating economic monopolies and political corruption.

The Rule of Law Fosters Educational Talents

Japan suffered tremendously during World War II and its economy was in tatters. Japan began the reform of its original education system, which mainly involved significant reforms of educational ideas, the educational structure, and educational content. Subsequently, Japan's economy achieved relatively rapid development, and various types of education were adjusted and reformed accordingly. In 1947, the Japanese government officially promulgated the Fundamental Law of Education, which was regarded as the fundamental law for educational reforms in Japan. The law changed the original six-year compulsory education system to a nine-year compulsory education system. Japan also attached great importance to vocational and technical education, requiring that the content of vocational education be diversified to meet the needs of Japan's economic development. In the late 1960s, the Vocational Training Law was comprehensively revised, and a set of relatively sound vocational and technical education systems was formed in Japan. The development of vocational education cultivated the necessary talents for Japan's economic development and further promoted the Japanese economy's takeoff.

The Constitution of the Republic of Korea and the Education Act promulgated in South Korea after World War II outlined a complete and standardized democratic education system, laying the legal foundation for the development of South Korea's education system in the future.

In 1951, the Education Act was amended to explicitly stipulate that industrial courses shall make up a certain percentage of the curriculum of middle and higher schools. The Industrial Education Revitalization Act enacted in 1963 established the legal status of industrial education. The Vocational Training Act promulgated by the South Korean Government in 1967, and the Industrial Education Revitalization Plan and the Industrial Education Revitalization Act promulgated in the 1970s promoted the development of vocational education. A multi-level, multi-disciplinary vocational education system that combined vocational school education with pre-employment training and corporate training had been formed for South Korea's vocational education, laying the foundation for the accumulation of human factors for economic development.

2.3.2 *Traditional Culture Is Conducive to Social Stability and Economic Development*

The cultural traditions of East Asian countries have also played an important role in avoiding the middle-income trap. Japan and the Four Asian Dragons belong to the typical Confucian cultural circle. Some characteristics of Confucian culture play an important role in technological innovation, the popularization of education, government policy, high savings rates, and social psychology, and are conducive to maintaining social stability and adjusting and calming social psychology when economic growth slows down.

The role that Japan's unique Oriental culture played in promoting economic development first caught the attention of Western scholars. When Westerners observe the Japanese economy and society, they often emphasize the differences between the heritage of the Japanese society and that of Western societies, and attribute the miracle of Japan's rapid economic development to such differences. The Japanese spirit as embodied their tradition, such as advocating cooperation rather than competition, advocating groups rather than individuals, praising the professional spirit of working hard and pursuing excellence, and elitism in national administration, accounts for some characteristics of Japan's economic development, such as lifelong employment, equality of distribution within companies, trade unions' preference for cooperation over confrontation, dedication and extreme attention to quality control. Researchers believe that it is the characteristics in these social fields that make capitalism appear different in Japan than in the West and bring overall competitiveness to Japanese companies.

Some South Korean scholars believe that the reason why the level of education of the labor force in East Asian countries is significantly higher than that in developing countries with the same income level is mainly because they are influenced by the Confucian cultural tradition. The Confucian civilization in East Asia has a long history and has never been interrupted. The dissemination of knowledge accumulated by it in East Asia has enhanced the ability of the people of all countries in East Asia to participate in industrialization. This understanding is based on Max Weber's study of the relations between religious ethics and economic growth, but its specific mechanism of action has not yet been clearly explained.

2.3.3 Other Favorable Factors

In East Asia, Japan was the first economy to join the club of high-income countries. Some studies suggest that Japan's economic success is largely due to its post-World War II economic structure and socio-political conditions. Among them, the post-World War II state-enterprise system and a good material-human capital mobilization structure are the key factors. Meanwhile, under the influence of the occupying powers led by the United States, a series of political and social reforms in taxation and law helped Japan establish a scientific and effective institutional basis, and the international economic and trade environment after World War II was also conducive to Japan's development and industrial upgrading.

In comparison, other regions, including South Korea, China Taiwan, and China Hong Kong, are latecomer economies. In South Korea and China Taiwan, a social wealth distribution system with land reform as the main starting point effectively narrowed the gap between rich and poor, and inhibited the rise of special interest groups in society, laying the social foundation for high savings and high investment-to-GDP ratios. Meanwhile, the government played a very significant role, as reflected in the fact that the government coordinated private sector investment through industrial policy to lend strong support to the development of new industries, especially knowledge-intensive industries. This is also the most important factor behind the smooth development of Singapore. The rapid development of China Hong Kong is mainly due to its unique geographical location and special system of political governance. In addition, the common factor in the economic development of most East Asian regions is the influence of East Asian culture.

In short, the important factors in the "East Asian experience" are politics, the rule of law, culture, education, and good industrial policies, of which the first two are more fundamental and critical. A government that is stable and has the right coordination capabilities seems to be the key to overcoming the middle-income trap. The so-called "right coordination capabilities" means that the government itself has formed a relatively benign governance structure. On the one hand, it can intervene in the unequal distribution of social wealth, and can implement strong education and industrial policies; on the other hand, it will not become a force that arbitrarily interferes with and influences economic growth.

3 Indonesia, the Philippines, and Other Southeast Asian Countries

In Asia, the fastest growing regions are concentrated in East and Southeast Asia. Regarding the middle-income trap issue we are discussing, this region can be divided into two major categories: ASEAN countries and East Asian countries. ASEAN countries mainly include Indonesia, the Philippines, Malaysia, Thailand, Vietnam, and Singapore, which can be classified as the Tiger Cub Economies; East Asian countries (regions) mainly include Japan and the Four Asian Dragons, namely South Korea, Singapore, China Taiwan, and China Hong Kong. These two sets of countries and regions have both experienced economic transformation and social transformation in the process of economic takeoff and rapid economic growth. Compared with countries like Japan, South Korea, and Singapore, Indonesia, the Philippines, Thailand, and other Southeast Asian countries have generally fallen into the middle-income trap.

3.1 *Reasons Why Indonesia Have Fallen into the Middle-Income Trap*

3.1.1 *Indonesia's Economic Trajectory Since Its Independence*

Since independence in 1945, Indonesia has made tremendous achievements, in that its national income has been rising and poverty rate has been declining, and its economic structure which was dominated by agriculture has gradually evolved into an economic structure dominated by industry and services. Indonesia's economy has gone through four stages: the recovery stage from 1945 to 1955, the import substitution stage from 1956 to 1966, the export-oriented stage from 1967 to 1998, and the structural adjustment stage after the Asian Financial Crisis of 1997. From 1965 to 1989, Indonesia's GDP per capita grew at an average annual rate of 4.4%, from $50 to $1200, representing an increase of more than 300% and close to the threshold for middle-income countries. Its GDP grew at an average annual rate of 4.7% between 1990 and 1999. Its economy grew slower than the Four Asian Dragons and China, but faster than most countries.[9]

The Asian Financial Crisis of 1997 dealt a heavy blow to Indonesia, plunging its economy into a severe recession. The value of Indonesia's currency nosedived, and its stock and property markets collapsed. Its GDP per capita dropped from $1050 in 1996 to $435 in 1998. Indonesia rejoined the ranks of the world's poorest countries, ranking 23rd among the world's poorest countries at that time. The gap between rich and poor in Indonesian society had also caused serious social problems, with ethnic conflicts intertwined with religious conflicts, culminating in serious anti-Chinese riots in May 1998. After the Asian financial crisis, the Indonesian government carried out a series of policy measures to adjust the economic structure, including reforming the banking system, adjusting investment policies, improving the investment environment, adjusting the mode of economic development, adjusting regional imbalances in economic development, and adjusting and upgrading the industrial structure. These reforms have helped maintain economic stability and prevented the economy from declining further. Meanwhile, Indonesia is also committed

[9] Lai Liyun. The Achievements and Drawbacks of Indonesia's Economic Development from 1945 to 1998. *Journal of Guangxi University* (Philosophy and Social Sciences Edition), 2006 (2): 171–173.

to changing its economic development path to restore growth vitality to its economy. In recent years, its GDP growth rate has been maintained at around 5%. According to World Bank data for 2017, Indonesia's GDP has reached $932.3 billion, ranking 16th in the world.[10] Nevertheless, according to statistics released by the Indonesian Bureau of Statistics, its GDP per capita in 2016 was $3570, still at the level of middle-income countries.

3.1.2 Major Problems in Indonesia's Economic Development

As the world's fourth most populous country, Indonesia has abundant natural resources and a large supply of cheap labor, giving it great potential for economic development. Meanwhile, there are still some major problems in Indonesia's economic development, including chronic unemployment and poverty, uneven regional development, incomplete market-oriented reform of the financial system, an unreasonable economic structure, and so on.

Unemployment Is Intertwined with Poverty, and Regional Development Is Uneven

From 1976 to 2000, Indonesia's unemployment rate rose from 2.5 to 6.0%. The figure does not include hidden unemployment. In 2006, the number of unemployed persons was 10.93 million and the unemployment rate was 10.5%. The high unemployment rate has hampered efforts to alleviate poverty in Indonesia, where nearly half of the population lives on less than $2 a day. In terms of regional development, Java accounts for only 6% of the land area of Indonesia, but it accounts for 56% of Indonesia's GDP and 63.1% of foreign investment, and its GDP per capita is 6–8 times that of other regions.

The Market-Oriented Reform of the Financial System Is Not Complete

Government investment plays a leading role in economic development. Banks were in the hands of the government. Most of the loans that the government had issued without regard to market demand became non-performing loans, and then the government resorted to printing money

[10] World Bank WDI Database.

to make up for bad debt, resulting in fiscal deficits and hyperinflation. This once brought Indonesia's economy to the brink of collapse. Although interest rate liberalization reform was carried out later, too much freedom in markets and an unsound regulatory system led to a credit glut and high bad debt levels. An unsound financial system has been an important reason why Southeast Asia is prone to economic crisis.

The Industrial Structure Is Unreasonable and Exports Are Undiversified

Indonesia's pillar industries are mostly export-oriented labor-intensive processing industries, while the development of high-tech industries, basic industries, and service industries is relatively backward. It is deficient in indigenous innovation capability and basically depends on imports for high-tech key equipment. Its service industries as a percentage of GDP are low. The upgrading of Indonesia's industrial structure has been in a relatively stagnant state since 2005. Industry and manufacturing, which dominate the national economy, have been developing slowly. The phenomenon of "deindustrialization" has begun to appear in Indonesia. Such "premature deindustrialization" has had a negative impact on Indonesia's economic growth.[11]

Despite the challenges, the Indonesian Government is moving forward with infrastructure construction, improving the investment environment, simplifying administrative procedures, and actively responding to the impact of a complex international environment. It is hoped that through a series of adjustments of the economic structure, Indonesia will achieve an annual economic growth rate of 7–8%, and attain a GDP per capita of $13,000–$15,000 by 2030,[12] so as to overcome the middle-income trap.

[11] Huang Guangfeng, Lu Zehui. Analysis of the Stages of Industrialization of Indonesia Since Its Independence and the Characteristics of Its Policies. *Productivity Research,* 2014 (6): 102–106.

[12] Wu Chongbo. Analysis and Prospects of the Rising Indonesian Economy. *Southeast Asian Affairs*, 2012 (3): 1–9.

3.2 Reasons Why the Philippines Has Fallen into the Middle-Income Trap

3.2.1 The Philippines' Economic Trajectory Since the End of the War

The Philippines was the first developing country in Asia to embark on the path of industrialization. Prior to the 1960s, the Philippines was one of the most advanced countries in the Asia-Pacific region, with its economic strength second only to Japan's and greater than that of other Asia-Pacific countries. In 1978, the Philippines joined the ranks of middle-income countries. However, since the 1980s, the Philippine economy had entered a period of prolonged stagnation, with an average growth rate of only 1.7% over a 10-year period, which was lower than the average of middle-income countries. Throughout the 1990s, the per capita GDP growth rate of the Philippines was less than 3%. In recent years, as economic and trade relations between China and ASEAN improves, economic growth in the Philippines has picked up pace. In 2016, the Philippine economy grew by 6.9%, ranking 11th in the world, but its GDP per capita was only $2951, still the lowest among the four ASEAN countries.

The Philippines is one of the world's largest labor exporters, with more than 10 million overseas workers, accounting for about 10% of the country's population. Successive governments have regarded overseas employment and remittances from overseas Filipino workers an important factor in social and economic stability. Remittances from overseas workers drive domestic consumption in the Philippines and are an important factor in contributing to the country's economic growth. According to data from the central bank of the Philippines, the total amount of cash remittances from overseas Filipino workers in 2013 was equivalent to 8.5% of its GDP. The then Aquino government proposed to create jobs at home during its tenure, so that the people no longer had to go abroad to find employment, and were no longer forced to make seeking a livelihood abroad their first choice. However, low investment as a percentage of GDP has been a major obstacle to economic development and transformation in the Philippines, and is also the main cause of high unemployment in the Philippines. One of the major challenges facing the Philippine economy for some time to come is how to translate high economic growth into jobs to help further reduce poverty and support inclusive growth.[13]

3.2.2 *Major Constraints on the Economic Development of the Philippines*

The structural contradictions in economy, politics, and systems accumulated over a long period of time in the Philippines have severely constrained the economic development of the Philippines.

The Land System Has Led to Polarization Between Rich and Poor and a Protracted Rebellion

The Philippines inherited the manorial system of the Spanish colonial era, with large amounts of land still concentrated in the hands of a few people, and several land reforms have had little effect. With the improvement of production technology, the popularization and application of agricultural machinery have reduced the demand for agricultural workers, leaving a large number of rural people in limbo. Some of them have become Filipino domestic workers and the urban poor, while others have formed armed anti-government forces. Despite the rapid economic development in the Philippines and Aquino III's pursuit of a "cash transfer program" aiming to reduce poverty, a FAO report pointed out that the number of hungry people in the Philippines in 2010–2012 was 5.4% higher than that in 1990–1992.[14] Peace talks between the government and armed anti-government forces such as the Moro National Liberation Front, the Communist Party of the Philippines, and the Abu Sayyaf Group remain stalled. The absence of a stable political environment makes it impossible to attract tourists and investment and difficult to achieve sustainable economic development.

[13] Shen Hongfang, Feng Chi. The Philippine Economy: Growth Without Development. *Asia-Pacific Economic Review*, 2014 (3): 72–76.

[14] Chen Qinghong. A Brief Look at the Philippines' Economic Takeoff. *International Study Reference*, 2013 (1): 28–32.

The Absence of the Rule of Law Has Led to Political Turmoil and Widespread Corruption

The Philippines is a democracy in Southeast Asia. After Marcos stepped down in 1986, democratic elections and the rotation of ruling parties were reinstated in the Philippines. But every election has been plagued by problems such as vote-buying, cheating, and violence. Mass demonstrations forced President Estrada to step down in 2001; there was a failed coup attempt against President Mrs. Arroyo in 2006. Political turmoil has left everyone in Philippine society feeling insecure and hit the economy hard. Corruption in the Philippine government, among local officials and in private institutions is deep-rooted and very serious. About 40% of the national budget funds of the Philippines are embezzled every year.[15] The Philippines ranked 94th out of 177 countries and territories on the 2013 Corruption Perceptions Index published by the NGO Transparency International.[16] The root cause of political turmoil and rampant corruption in the Philippines is the absence of the rule of law. The Philippines has enacted many anti-corruption laws, but they exist in name only and have not been implemented.

3.3 *Reasons Why Thailand Have Fallen into the Middle-Income Trap*

3.3.1 *Thailand's Economic Trajectory Since the End of World War II*

Thailand was still an agricultural country in the late 1940s. Since the 1950s, the Thai government has begun to implement an industrialization plan, which was marked by the creation of a state-run economy. In 1959, the National Economic and Social Development Board was established to oversee the implementation of Thailand's five-year plan.

During the two five-year economic development plan periods of 1961–1971, Thailand set a record high of 8.4% for annual economic growth and a record high of 11% for industrial growth through the development of an import-substituting economy. This period was known as the "Thai

[15] Huang Jiwei, Quan Yi. Reasons Why ASEAN Countries Have Fallen into the Middle-Income Trap and Lessons Learned. *Contemporary Economy & Management*, 2014 (7): 92–97.

[16] Huang Yaodong. The Philippines: 2014 Review and 2015 Outlook. *Around Southeast Asia*, 2015 (3): 20–24.

Industrial Revolution" period. After the signing of the Plaza Accord in September 1985, the US dollar depreciated significantly, while the currencies of Japan and the then Four Asian Dragons appreciated to varying degrees, which made the comparative advantages of these countries and regions in terms of low value-added manufactured goods disappear. As a result, Thailand received a lot of investment in labor-intensive industries. In 1987, Thailand attracted \$182 million in foreign direct investment, which increased to \$2.402 billion in 1990. The massive inflow of foreign capital had contributed to the rapid development of Thailand's economy. The average annual GDP growth rate of Thailand reached 11.6% in 1987–1990 and 9% in 1991–1995. Thailand's strong growth momentum had earned Thailand a reputation as an "East Asian Tiger."

In the late 1990s, despite being hit hard by the Asian financial crisis, the Thai economy grew at an average annual rate of 8–9% in the 10 years after 1995, making it one of the fastest growing economies in the world. In 1996, Thailand joined the ranks of middle-income countries. According to World Bank data, Thailand's GDP per capita in 2015 was \$5815.

3.3.2 Major Constraints on the Economic Development of Thailand

Political Turmoil Affects the Normal Operation of the Government and Seriously Hinders Economic Development

Since Thaksin was ousted in a military coup in 2006, the Red Shirts who supported Thaksin and the Yellow Shirts who opposed Thaksin had each staged anti-government rallies over a protracted period of time, causing social rifts, frequent violent and bloody clashes and a large number of casualties.

It was not until August 2011 when Thaksin's younger sister Yingla was elected Prime Minister of Thailand that the five-year-long political turmoil basically ended. However, the good times did not last long. In December 2013, Thailand's anti-government group the People's Committee took to the streets again, demanding the complete eradication of the "Thaksin regime." Yingluck announced the dissolution of Parliament and the holding of national elections in a failed attempt to solve the political crisis. The prolonged political unrest has had a huge negative impact on Thailand's economy. From 2006 to 2016, Thailand's GDP grew at an average annual rate of only 6.5%.

The Gap Between Rich and Poor Is Wide, and the Middle Class Is Weak

Thailand's economic development is very uneven geographically. The development of other cities and regions is backward compared to Bangkok, which is the economic and political center, and the gap between Bangkok and these places is widening. As a result, a small number of people are very wealthy and most people are living in poverty. Of the 10 provinces with the highest average monthly income in Thailand, nine are in Bangkok and the central region surrounding it, while all of the 10 provinces with the lowest monthly average income are in the north and northeast regions. 9.6% of the Thai population are living in poverty. That figure is 0.5 and 3.3% for Bangkok and the central region, and as high as 16.8 and 12% for the north and northeast regions. The middle class has not yet formed an independent political force. Since the democratization of Thailand in 1932, its ruling elite has been divided into three main factions: military, civilians, and royalists. In the absence of a strong middle class, the division and struggle between civilians and military have led to constant coups and political turmoil in the process of political development in Thailand.

3.4 Lessons from Southeast Asian Countries Falling into the Middle-Income Trap

Southeast Asian countries such as Indonesia, the Philippines, and Thailand have both commonalities and some differences in economic development. Among them, the Philippines was the first country to achieve economic takeoff; Thailand was the last country to achieve economic takeoff; Indonesia was somewhere in between. Chronologically, the Philippines joined the ranks of middle-income countries in the mid-1970s, and Indonesia and Thailand joined the ranks of middle-income countries in the early 1980s. Their economic takeoffs were mostly achieved through industrialization. Among them, the Philippines and Indonesia began to stagnate after reaching the middle-income level. The Philippines' gross national income (GNI) grew by only 1.69% in 1980–1990 and grew at an average annual rate of 2.94% in the 1990, which, when combined with a population growth rate of 2%, led to a GDP per capita that was actually stagnant or even declining. This state continued until the end of the first decade of the twenty-first century. Therefore, although the Philippines was the first to achieve an economic takeoff, it is the slowest growing economy among the four ASEAN countries and also has the lowest GNI per capita. Indonesia also experienced economic stagnation after it joined the ranks of middle-income countries, and was dealt a further blow in the Asian Financial Crisis of 1997. It was not until 2004 that its economy began to show signs of recovery. Its level of development is only better than that of the Philippines among the four ASEAN countries. Thailand's economy took off later, but it grew faster. After reaching the middle-income level, Thailand's economy continued to grow at a relatively high rate for 10 years, until the Asian Financial Crisis of 1997. Since then, it had entered a 6-year recession, which lasted until 2004 when recovery began. The following lessons and inspiration can be drawn from the characteristics of the economic and social transformation of Indonesia, the Philippines, and Thailand after they became middle-income countries.

3.4.1 A Relative Shortage of Technological Innovation and Relative Shortage of Talents Makes Industrial Transformation Difficult to Achieve

Compared with East Asian countries, although Indonesia, the Philippines, and Thailand have experienced a long or short period of rapid economic growth, the growth of their total factor productivity (TFP) has not been fast enough. From 1970 to 1994, the rate of TFP growth in the Philippines remained negative, and that in Indonesia never exceeded 1%. The rate of TFP growth in Thailand was higher than that in both countries, most of the time between 1 and 2%. The rate of TFP growth is an important measure of economic growth driven by technological innovation. The shortcomings of ASEAN economies in this respect are visible. So far, there have been no significant improvements in this regard. In 2007, Thailand's R&D expenditure as a percentage of GDP stood at 0.21%; that figure was 0.11% for the Philippines and only 0.08% for Indonesia (2009 data). Thailand had 315 R&D personnel per million population (2006 data); that figure was 90 for Indonesia (2009 data) and only 78 for the Philippines.

3.4.2 Severe Income Inequality Is One of the Main Manifestations of the Middle-Income Trap

While causing a general increase in income across the whole of society, economic takeoff has widened the income gap. In countries such as the Philippines, Thailand, and Malaysia, income inequality is a prominent feature, and will increase when the economy stagnates. Its manifestations vary from country to country. Income inequality in Thailand is mainly reflected in differences between regions and between urban and rural areas. With economic growth, Thailand has been divided into two geographically distinct halves: one is the rich industrialized capital region; the other is the poverty-stricken agricultural hinterland.[17] The gap between urban and rural areas is mainly related to Thailand's economic development strategy. Thailand's import substitution strategy and export-oriented development strategy ignores the development of rural areas and agriculture, and supports the development of cities at the expense of agriculture. As a result, the income level of the rural population is significantly lower than that of the urban population. According to World Bank statistics, in 2009, the Gini coefficient of Thailand was 0.4, that of Philippines was 0.43 and that of Malaysia was 0.462, all above the international warning level of 0.4. Income inequality interacts with economic stagnation, resulting in social and political crises.

3.4.3 Corruption and Political Instability Make Southeast Asian Countries Sink Deeper and Deeper into the Trap

Short and rapid economic takeoff hasn't given rise to a middle class in countries such as Indonesia, the Philippines, and Thailand, and national governments emerging from colonial rule have failed to establish a mature constitutional system. The resulting lack of constraints on government power has led to widespread corruption in ASEAN countries. The interaction between corruption and social inequality has greatly increased political turmoil and social chaos in various countries. Indonesia is one of the most corrupt countries in the world. The lack of an effective legal supervision mechanism is the fundamental cause of widespread corruption in Indonesia. In the Suharto era, which was known for its authoritarian rule, the military dominated Indonesia's politics for a long time and was above the law; during the period of democratic transition when the Megawati government was in power, the power of local governments expanded, but they lacked the ability to govern, and the supervision mechanism existed in name only. Among ASEAN countries, the Philippines have a relatively mature democratic electoral system and ruling party rotation system, but almost every election is dogged by scandals such as

[17] Xiao Sanhua. Thailand's Regional Development Strategy. *Southeast Asian Studies*, 1995 (1): 15–17.

vote-buying and cheating, and related violence. Social contradictions in Indonesia are often manifested in extreme anti-Chinese incidents. Thailand is the best example among these countries when it comes to political and social unrest Since the beginning of the twenty-first century, conflicts among political forces such as the Red Shirts, the Yellow Shirts, and the military have been raging, leading to many violent bloodsheds, which has greatly affected foreign investment in Thailand and the development of tourism, one of the pillar industries of Thailand.

3.4.4 A Double Squeeze in the International Competitive Environment Is Not Conducive to Southeast Asian Countries Getting Out of the Trap

The economic takeoff of Southeast Asian countries in the 1970s was related to the international environment at that time. In this era, the rapid economic growth in Europe and the United States boosted global demand for primary products, which was very favorable to export-oriented ASEAN countries. In the 1980s, expansionary investment in Southeast Asia by SMEs in relatively advanced Japan, South Korea, and China Taiwan also contributed to the economic growth of ASEAN countries during this period. But in the late 1990s, the Asian financial crisis and the rise of the Chinese economy subjected ASEAN countries to a tremendous squeeze. China's development has greatly reduced the chances of ASEAN countries relying on traditional industries to maintain economic growth, and their domestic political and social environment is not conducive to economic transformation, further dimming ASEAN countries' prospects of getting out of the trap.

In short, the middle-income trap in Indonesia, Philippines, and other Southeast Asian countries is reflected in the slowdown of economic growth caused by a failure to bring about industrial upgrading and social transformation, which leads to political and social instability, which in turn prevents the successful completion of industrial upgrading. It can be seen that economic structural adjustment and industrial upgrading are the only way for any economy to overcome the middle-income trap. In this process, changes in political and non-governmental actors and their impact on economic transformation are decisive factors in overcoming the middle-income trap.

4 Mexico, Argentina, Brazil, and Other Latin American Countries

Overall economic growth in Latin American countries has been extremely slow in the past half century. From 1950s to 1970s, their GDP grew by an average of 2–3% annually, higher than developed regions of the world, but far behind emerging industrial countries and regions in East Asia (such as Japan, Korea, China, Hong Kong, etc.). In the 1980s, their growth fell into negative territory their annual average growth rates rebounded to more than 1% in the 1990s and fell to 0.2% in the twenty-first century. It was during this period that Latin American countries saw themselves fall further behind developed countries and emerging developed countries in economic development as they were stuck in the vicious cycle of sluggish growth and weak development.

In the study of national development, Latin American countries have become typical negative examples and are important subjects of discussion in academic research and development strategy selection. When discussing the reasons for the stagnation of Latin American countries, the existing literature points to factors such as institutional problems, ethnic and cultural divisions, political instability, development strategy mistakes, and overspending on social welfare. These factors all provide more or less reasonable explanations for Latin America's "growth in the trap." Careful analysis shows that the theoretical levels of these explanations are different. But they follow a clear line of thought: fractures in the social fabric lead to the predicament of the institutional environment, which ultimately leads to economic stagnation; long-term stagnation in turn creates more social and political problems and worsens the institutional environment for economic growth, leading to the hopeless vicious cycle of "slow growth in the trap."

4.1 Reasons Why Mexico Has Fallen into the Middle-Income Trap

From the end of World War II until the mid-1970s, Mexico's economic growth remained basically at 6%, culminating in it joining the ranks of middle-income countries, which was known as the "Mexican miracle." Since the 1980s, Mexico's economic growth has been unstable, with its economic growth hovering around 3%, and its GDP per capita and other indicators hardly achieving any growth.

4.1.1 Legacy of the "Import Substitution" Industrialization Model

Mexico had been committed to economic independence since its political independence in the nineteenth century. However, due to the profound influence of the colonial economy, Mexico's national economic development was highly dependent on the export of primary products as it had not fundamentally broken free from the bondage of the colonial economy. The world economic crisis of the early 1930s hit Mexico's economy hard, forcing it to gradually abandon its "export-led" mode of development in favor of the import substitution industrialization strategy. That is to say, it would manufacture its own goods. Under this model, Mexico freed itself from the "low-income trap" and became a middle-income country in the mid-late 1970s. Since then, the negative consequences of this model have become more and more obvious.

Excessive External Debt

In order to pursue industrialization, Mexico borrowed heavily from foreign countries, but its debt-servicing capacity was insufficient. In order to pay its external debt, it had to pursue further industrialization. Therefore, Mexico's industrialization required continuous financial input from the government, which led to excessive debt and forced it to borrow again, a vicious circle that evolved into the debt crisis of 1982.

Large Gap Between Rich and Poor and Between Urban and Rural Areas

Due to the widening gap between rich and poor, ordinary Mexicans were unable to enjoy the fruits of industrialization and wealth growth. They were generally pessimistic about the prospects of industrialization and modernization in Mexico. Feelings of being abandoned and treated unfairly permeated the whole society, resulting in frequent outbreaks of violence. Various social contradictions were unprecedentedly intensified.

4.1.2 Legacy of Neoliberal Economic Reforms

The debt crisis of 1982 forced Mexico to change its mode of economic growth. The main approach to reform was to adopt the neoliberal ideas, that is, to open Mexico's economy to the world economy. In 1986, Mexico joined the World Trade Organization (WTO). In 1988, Mexico opened its markets, actively participated in international competition, and signed the North American Free Trade Agreement with Canada and the

United States. But instead of getting Mexico out of the predicament, neoliberal reforms made Mexico sink ever deeper into the middle-income trap.

Excessive Openness Led to Imbalances in National Economic Security

Under the banner of neoliberalism, Mexico actively participated in economic globalization. It lowered tariffs and gradually removed trade barriers. As a result, foreign capital, especially speculative capital from the United States, flooded its markets, which directly led to the bankruptcy of its SMEs and a high unemployment rate.

Excessive Privatization

In 1990, some state-owned enterprises in Mexico were privatized, and many of them were acquired by foreign investors, but this did not increase the capital stock of Mexico. The only change was the change of ownership of capital, and a large amount of state-owned assets were lost in the process. In addition, mass privatization had also reduced the resources directly controlled by the government, leaving it with inadequate financial resources to address livelihood issues such as education and training, employment, transportation, and social security.

Loss of Innovation Capability

Innovation is the source of a country's sustainable development. But Mexico grew its economy, not through technological innovation and solved its development dilemma by simply selling its natural resources cheaply and opening its markets. The result was that it drank poison to quench its thirst, its economy was gradually sapped of vitality and the country's overall innovation capability was lost.

Productivity Setback

From 1980 to 2016, Mexico's GDP per capita grew slowly. The ratio of Mexico's per capita GDP to the GDP per capita of the United States has been fluctuating and has never surpassed the value before the debt crisis of 1982. It can be concluded that Mexico's economy has basically not grown and its productivity has fallen sharply (see Fig. 1).

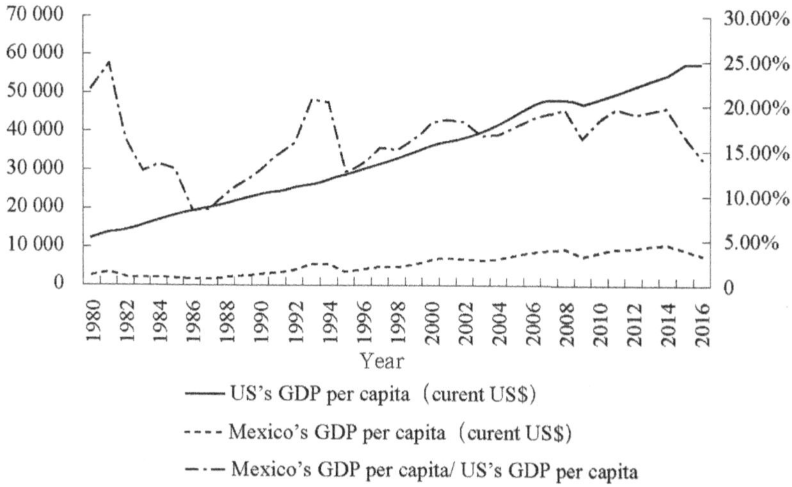

Fig. 1 Mexico vs. United States by GDP per capita 1980–2016 (*Source* ce.cn)

4.2 *Reasons Why Argentina Has Fallen into the Middle-Income Trap*

Argentina, with its superior geographical conditions and abundant natural resources, was one of the world's top ten economic powers in the early twentieth century. It reached the middle-income level in the early 1970s. But after three to four decades of ups and downs, its GDP per capita did not exceed $10,000 until 2010 and reached $12,449 in 2016. It has been caught in the middle-income trap for a long time.

4.2.1 *There Were Many Contradictions Between Government Regulation and Market Mechanisms*

From the end of World War II until the 1980s, Argentina's military government chose the path of direct state intervention in the economy to achieve about 30 years of steady growth under the import substitution industrialization model. But the high level of government intervention had engendered inherent defects in economic development, such as the decline of agriculture, prominent contradictions between regions and industries, weak innovation capability, and corruption. As Argentina's economy got into trouble, the military junta collapsed and democracy was restored. Faced with all kinds of problems stemming from "government failure," Argentina turned from the extreme of state interventionism to the extreme of radical liberalism. The role and executive capacity of the government had been weakened by the impact of the powerful neoliberalism. Mass privatization, trade liberalization, and deregulation had become the new order of the day. But the level of maturity of markets grown up under a centralized economy was very low, which coupled with the complete relaxation of government controls and the absence of an effective market self-regulation mechanism and market order had resulted in a series of serious consequences, such as an increased fiscal burden, foreign capital monopolies over markets, prominent financial risks, aggravated inequity in distribution, larger current account deficits, and a worsening of the balance of payments, Meanwhile, most of the domestic enterprises which were still in their infancy found it difficult to withstand the fierce impact of foreign enterprises and foreign products brought in by the hasty opening-up. As a result, a large number of domestic enterprises have gone bankrupt or been acquired, and the national economy has stagnated, with no real recovery in sight so far. This is due to the economic turmoil caused by the lack of reasonable coordination between government regulation and market mechanisms.

4.2.2 *Fiscal Mismanagement Led to a Government Debt Crisis*

A bloated civil service, complex fiscal relations between the central government and local governments, an unreasonable taxation system, massive tax evasion, and a heavy debt burden had contributed to Argentina's huge fiscal deficit. The Argentine government had to fill the growing fiscal hole with huge external loans. Throughout the 1980s, debt service accounted for more than 50% of exports each year. Total external debt as a percentage of total exports reached an all-time high of 717% in 1987. High external debt overwhelmed its debt-servicing capacity. After the outbreak of the economic crisis in 2001, the Argentine government had to announce a temporary suspension of the payment of $132.1 billion of government debt. As a result, the country's credit was severely impaired, which further exacerbated capital flight and worsened its economic woes.

4.2.3 *A Pegged Exchange Rate Regime Was Blindly Implemented*

Since the beginning of the 1990s, in order to cope with high inflation and exchange rate volatility, the Argentine government introduced a currency board, under which it pegged the value of the domestic currency to that of the US dollar and prohibited issuing more of the domestic currency without acquiring US dollar reserves in an amount equal to the domestic currency issue. This move reined in runaway currency (peso) issuance, with inflation falling from 3079.5% in 1989 to 1.6% in 1994. However, the implementation of a pegged exchange rate regime must be backed by sufficient foreign exchange reserves. But Argentina's low export-earning capacity, continuous fiscal deficits, and rigid exchange rate regime had hamstrung the government's efforts to carry out macro-control using tools such as exchange rates and monetary policy, resulting in a large increase in debt and the depletion of foreign exchange reserves. As a result, the pegged exchange rate regime collapsed and its external debt is denominated in US dollars ballooned. Eventually, investors lost confidence and a large amount of foreign capital fled, forming a vicious circle.

4.2.4 *The Economic Lifeline of the Country Fell into the Hands of Foreign Capital*

After coming to power in 1989, the Menem government vigorously pursued a policy of trade liberalization by dramatically reducing import tariffs and quantitative restrictions, and suspending the implementation of export duty relief, subsidies and other incentives. This caused foreign capital and enterprises to flock in, crushing and acquiring a large number of Argentine enterprises, which dealt a heavy blow to national industries. What's more serious is that the complete opening up of the real economy and the virtual economy has allowed foreign capital to control the entire banking and financial system, control the basic sectors of the national economy and service industries, control the production and distribution of all energy sources except nuclear power, such as oil, coal, hydropower and thermal power, and control he mining industry and a large amount of land resources. It can be said that the country's economic sovereignty has been basically lost.

4.3 *Reasons Why Brazil Has Fallen into the Middle-Income Trap*

After Brazil's GDP grew rapidly between 1968 and 1973 at an average annual rate of more than 10%, its GDP per capita surpassed $1000 in 1974, catapulting it into the ranks of middle-income countries. Since then, however, Brazil has been lingering in the middle-income stage and has not been able to join the ranks of high-income countries. After 2002, Brazil's economy began a new round of rapid development, but it was not until 2010 that its GDP per capita exceeded $10,000, which fell to $8650 in 2016, still below the level for high-income countries. Brazil's lingering in the middle-income stage for nearly 40 years has brought many problems to its economy and society, seriously hampering efforts to improve people's standard of living.

4.3.1 *The Development Strategy Has Not Been Transformed in Time According to the Stage of Economic Development*

The Industrial Structure Has Long Been Out of Balance

The emphasis had been on industrial investment for so long as to cause the industrial structure to get out of balance. The oil crisis of the 1970s further exacerbated structural contradictions. Brazil began to implement an "import substitution" strategy in the 1930s in order to protect the development of national industries and strengthen its economic independence and autonomy. The "import substitution" led to rapid industrialization in Brazil. In the late 1970s, a relatively complete industrial system was established, with a complete range of basic industrial sectors. However, because Brazil had long pursued an import substitution strategy, it had neglected export markets. Meanwhile, Brazil had protected backward industries to a considerable extent, resulting in backward industrial technology, outdated technology and equipment, poor product quality, and high costs. This made it difficult for Brazil to participate in international market competition, and was not conducive to the further development of industrialization. The long-standing emphasis on industrial investment had also caused the industrial structure to get out balance: the primary sector was weak; the internal structure of the secondary sector was unreasonable as it lacked infrastructure support internally and depended heavily on external funds and resources; due to the rapid expansion of the informal sector, the tertiary sector had difficulty developing as a whole in a planned way, let alone replacing the secondary sector as a driving force for economic growth. This structural contradiction was further aggravated after the oil crisis of the 1970s.

The Mode of Development Was Not Changed in Time

In the 1970s, the world industrial structure began to be optimized and upgraded. Brazil still pursued "import substitution" and failed to change its mode of development in time. The energy crisis of the 1970s plunged Western countries into economic depression. As a result, Western countries began a new round of trade protectionism, leading to the deterioration of the international trade environment. Meanwhile, information technology based on microelectronics technology was spreading quickly, the new technological revolution was sweeping the world, high-tech industries were mushrooming, and the world industrial structure was undergoing optimization and upgrading In the face of challenges and opportunities at home and abroad, Brazil still "resorted to borrowing to finance its development," continued to promote import substitution for durable goods and capital goods, and failed to change its mode of development in time, missing the opportunity to optimize and upgrade its industrial structure.

Over-Reliance on Foreign Investment Caused the Decline of Domestic Industries

In the 1990s, Brazil pursued neoliberal policies, liberalized its economy, and mainly relied on foreign investment for development in an attempt to stabilize and modernize its economy. Although efforts to liberalize trade and attract foreign investment went well at first, in the late 1990s Brazil suffered the following consequences: a huge deficit in its balance of payments accounts; economic stability based on exchange rate overvaluation came with a very high and irrecoverable cost—structural growth in imports, which made it impossible for local enterprises to resist cheap imported products, components, and spare parts; they were increasingly replacing domestically produced products, and domestic production was mostly destroyed by them; international competitiveness came mainly from large-scale and low value-added commodity production sectors, the main commodities sectors were raw materials sectors (agriculture, natural resources, and energy-intensive sectors), and the level of industrial transformation was relatively low. The neoliberal reforms of the 1990s brought about only the deindustrialization of Brazil.

4.3.2 Technological Advancements and Innovations Have Not Received the Support and Attention They Deserve for a Long Time

An Economic Recession Made It Financially Impossible to Invest in R&D

When the energy crisis of the late 1970s forced the world industrial structure to start optimizing and upgrading, Brazil's economy began to weaken. In the 1980s, Brazil's investment decreased dramatically, which made it difficult for Brazil to introduce the new technologies it needed.

Continued financial difficulties and external pressures also brought the reform of major state-owned technology R&D centers to a standstill. Faced with difficulties caused by foreign exchange and inflation crises time and again, the government had been unable to make the necessary coordination or consistent adjustments. Brazil's R&D intensity was low, always hovering below 1%.

Multinational Corporations Aggressively Acquired Local Enterprises, Further Weakening Local Innovation Capability
In the 1990s, influenced by the trend toward neoliberalism started by the Washington Consensus, the Brazilian government began to slash public budgets. As a result, investment in R&D shrank sharply, and local excellent R&D institutions were abandoned. Meanwhile, multinational corporations aggressively acquired and reorganized local Brazilian enterprises, further weakening local Brazilian local enterprises' capacity for technological innovation. Under these circumstances, Brazil had been unable to create and foster the necessary conditions to promote the rise of emerging industrial clusters with microelectronics as the core, and then achieve a new round of capital accumulation driven by technological innovation.

Institutions Hindered the Application of Scientific and Technological Achievements and Enterprise Innovation
Prior to 2004, Brazilian law prohibited the government from directly financing innovations by companies and did not allow companies to hire university researchers, hindering not only the application of new scientific and technological achievements to the economy, but also the innovative development of SMEs.

4.3.3 Unreasonable Income Distribution Has Led to Social Polarization

Equitable development is not only conducive to improving income distribution and creating more balanced development, but can also ease social contradictions and conflicts, thus contributing to sustainable economic development. After Latin American countries have entered the middle-income stage, the extreme disparity between rich and poor and social polarization caused by the rapidly expanding income gap forced their ruling parties to adopt populist distribution policies and promise generous welfare benefits to alleviate social pressure. But the government's financial resources could not sustain a financially draining welfare policy, eventually leading to high inflation and capital flight. This caused violent social unrest, and even regime change, which had a serious impact on economic development. When opposition parties come to power, they also had no ability and courage to get rid of the vicious circle. Frequent changes of government went hand in hand with hyperinflation, resulting in persistent polarization. In the 1970s, the Gini coefficient of Latin American countries ranged from 0.44 to 0.66. Brazil's Gini coefficient was still as high as 0.64 in the late 1990s. With income polarization comes an increase in inequity of educational opportunity, which perpetuates the cycle of poverty and makes it a stubborn disease that is difficult to suppress.

4.4 *Experience of Overcoming the Middle-Income Trap in Chile*

Chile's development offers a success story of breaking away from the middle-income trap. Chile was basically on the same starting line as most Latin American countries and even below the average level of Latin America from 1950 to 1973. But after 1973, Chile entered a period of rapid economic growth that eventually made it a high-income country in Latin America.

Before 1973, Chile was very similar to other major Latin American economies in terms of course and level of development. Thanks to their abundant resources, after a century of development, by 1950, Latin American countries had attained the highest GDP per capita among developing countries, and had developed some favorable conditions for industrialization to take off. But over the next 50 years, Latin America as a whole with the exception of Chile grew slowly, never able to overcome the middle-income trap.

Chile grew at a rather slow rate between 1950 and 1973, both lower than that of major Latin American economies and below the average level of Latin American countries. At this stage, it can be said that the country fell into the middle-income trap. However, since 1973, the situation has been reversed, with Chile's growth rate significantly higher than that of major Latin American economies and the average level. The gap between Chile and other Latin American countries has further widened since 1998, and Chile has become one of the highest income countries in the region.

4.4.1 The Main Reasons Why Chile Fell into the Middle-Income Trap Between 1950 and 1973

Failure to Change the "Import Substitution" Strategy at the Right Time

Like other Latin American countries, Chile fell into the middle-income trap mainly because of wrong development strategies, especially the "import substitution" industrialization strategy implemented after the 1930s. At that time, major Western countries fell into the Great Depression and adopted extensive trade protection measures. The subsequent World War II led to the interruption of imports from Western countries, prompting Latin American countries to generally adopt the "import substitution" industrialization strategy. This development strategy stimulated economic growth to a certain extent at first, with industrial production and the number of workers growing rapidly, but its drawbacks soon became apparent.

The "import substitution" strategy violated the principle of comparative advantage, and the efficiency of related industries was low and improved very slowly. As a result, the price of domestic products is significantly higher than that of imported products. Domestic products could only be protected through trade barriers such as high tariffs, which increased domestic inflationary pressures. Because Chile's industrial sector was incomplete, many key components and equipment needed to be imported. In order to reduce the import cost of these products, it had to adopt the policy of overvaluing the exchange rate, which hit the export sector and caused a deterioration in the balance of payments. To keep its balance of payments in equilibrium, Chile incurred a large external debt, sowing the seeds of a debt crisis. In fact, China Taiwan and South Korea, which have successfully overcome the middle-income trap, also implemented an "import substitution" strategy for a short period of time, which also led to the rise of inflation and a deterioration in the balance of payments, but they quickly switched to an export-oriented strategy.

Land Reform Had Been Prevented by Powerful Interests

Due to the instability of the government's political power at the time, Chile failed to adjust its policy quickly. Land concentration was also an important reason for the large gap between rich and poor in Chile. 80% of land was owned by hacendados who made up 10% of the population. In order not to offend hacendados, the land reform had to be shelved. In order to ease employment pressure, the Chilean government increased public expenditure and the number of public servants dramatically, resulting in a deterioration of the financial situation. The Chilean government then had to pursue a policy of deficit monetization, which caused hyperinflation. By the early 1970s, the Chilean economy was in trouble and social contradictions were very prominent.

4.4.2 The New Chilean Government Comprehensively Established Market Mechanisms in the 1970s

In September 1973, the Chilean military launched a coup and established a military dictatorship headed by Pinochet. The new government believes that at the micro level, it is necessary to comprehensively establish market mechanisms, promote exports and open up to the outside world in accordance with the principle of comparative advantage, and replace dependence on the state with entrepreneurship, the government should refrain from extensive intervention in the economy, and its sole responsibility was to guard the market economy as a "night watchman." As a result, the average import tariff was reduced from 70% in 1974 to 10% in 1980, the privatization of state-owned enterprises was accelerated, extremely relaxed foreign investment laws were passed, and the taxation and exchange rate regimes were comprehensively reformed. At the macro level, the Chilean government implemented "shock therapy" for the economy, cutting public spending by a quarter, sharply raising interest rates and reducing the money supply.

Establish a Fiscal and Tax System Suitable for National Conditions in the Context of Financial Globalization

The new Chilean government made a useful exploration of fiscal and taxation policies suitable for Chile's national conditions in the context of financial globalization. By moderately restricting public expenditure, establishing stabilization funds, and maintaining a structural surplus in public finances, the country gradually formed a relatively sound and responsible fiscal policy. In order to encourage the export of products, Chile also set up special export credit, established export credit funds, offered favorable terms for loans, and encouraged manufacturers to invest in the production of goods for export through tax breaks. Since the 1990s, Chile has maintained investment at about 27–28% of GDP. This was a key factor driving its economic growth.

Adjust Exchange Rate Policy According to National Conditions and Gradually Increase Exchange Rate Flexibility

In the 1980s, in order to strengthen internal competition and promote exports, the Chilean government adopted a crawling peg that allowed the exchange rate to gradually adjust according to changes in the rate of inflation in Chile and other countries. Since then, peso exchange rates had become market-oriented and more flexible. The successful exchange rate reform in Chile from 1985 to 1990 has resulted in a depreciation of the real effective exchange rate for the peso. Since the 1990s, a large influx of foreign capital, especially short-term private capital, had put increasing upward pressure on the country's currency. In view of the fact that most of the capital inflows were denominated in US dollar, Chile made important adjustments to its exchange rate policy, gradually increasing exchange rate flexibility and pegging its currency to a basket of currencies instead of the US dollar alone.

Lend Strong Support to the Development of SMEs

Chile attaches great importance to the development of SMEs, and has established a relatively complete policy system for supporting SMEs and the related institutional framework. Chile's policy system for supporting SMEs consists of several components: opening up special financing channels for SMEs and providing investment loans to SMEs; establishing a technical assistance fund for SMEs to help SMEs pay for the costs of hiring consultants and solve various problems encountered in their operations; implementing a tax rebate system, under which enterprises in the non-traditional export sector can receive a refund equivalent to a certain percentage of the FOB price of their exports; implementing R&D assistance for SMEs. Chile established a national technology and production fund in 1991 to support the R&D activities of SMEs.

After a series of reforms, Chile's economy took on a new look. First, the inflation problem had been gradually resolved, with the inflation rate dropping from triple digits in the early 1970s to a single digit in 1981. Secondly, the export structure and export profits have improved significantly: in the 1960s, copper exports accounted for 90% of total exports, and that figure dropped to less than 50% in the 1980s as agricultural, forestry and fishery products and related processed products had become Chile's comparatively advantageous products; the privatization of state-owned enterprises had fostered a large number of competitive private enterprises and entrepreneurs; external debt had fallen sharply, while foreign direct investment had soared, and most foreign direct investment had gone to production.

Chile has always adhered to market-oriented and export-oriented economic policies. Despite the impact of Mexico's debt crisis in 1994, East Asia's financial crisis in 1997, and Argentina's debt crisis in 2001, Chile has been able to adjust rapidly every time to maintain macro stability and economic growth, gradually pulling ahead of other Latin American countries. In 2016, Chile's GDP per capita reached $15, 0196, ranking first among Latin American countries.

4.5 Experience of Latin American Countries in the Middle-Income Stage and Lessons Learnt Therefrom

Latin America in the past half century has basically been in the stage of "growth in the trap." They are mired in various social and economic problems, but that's not to say they have stopped developing, but are developing slowly—so slowly that they have fallen far behind other fast-growing regions. After more than 50 years of accumulation, they have been left far behind by regions that were comparable to or even inferior to their level of development, and become typical examples of countries that have fallen into the "trap." And there remains no prospect of them leaping out of the "trap."

The economic and social reasons why Latin American countries have been stuck in the middle-income trap for a long time mainly include the fracturing of the social structure, serious institutional inertia, inadequate state capacity, and deficiencies in legal protection.

4.5.1 Fracturing of the Social Structure

The colonial history of Latin America has shaped the special social structure of Latin America. It is characterized by a great divide between the upper and lower classes. The middle class is small and weak. Such a social structure was formed during the colonial era. Even in the process of social and historical development after the independence of Latin America, it has not been fundamentally changed and has been a drag on Latin America's development.

Latin America's Social Structure During the Colonial Era

The Spanish and Portuguese colonization of Latin America was violent and bloody. In the process of establishing their colonies to plunder resources and wealth, the colonists brutally conquered, expelled, and even slaughtered Indians throughout Latin America. In addition, the Portuguese imported black slaves from Africa to make up for the shortage of labor. The social structure polarized between colonists and the colonized has been a historical legacy haunting the development of Latin America.

In various regions of Latin America, differences in the colonial process have resulted in significant differences in the demographic structure of subsequent societies. In Central America, due to the existence of the highly civilized and highly organized Aztec Empire and Inca Empire, the colonists directly completed another conquest in the region, forming a social structure polarized between colonists and Indians. In the Portuguese colonies, because Indians were few and mostly in the early stage of civil society, they could not be used as colonized labor, and the colonists had to bring black slaves from Africa. Further south, in places such as Argentina and Uruguay, the colonists simply killed or drove out Indians who were few in number, and did not import black slaves from Africa, but relied on white European immigrants to establish colonies.

Latin America's population consists mainly of colonial rulers (whites from colonizing countries, known as "peninsulars"), native whites (known as "creoles"), mixed-race people, Indians, and black slaves. "peninsulars" exercised power on behalf of colonizers and occupied the main resources; "creoles" could own land and other property, but had little political power; mixed-race people, though free in status, could not hold public office or own land; Indians and black slaves were slave laborers. Whether it was conquered Indians, trafficked African slaves, or penniless European immigrants to South America, they were at the bottom of Latin America's colonial social structure and had no political and economic resources.

In particular, such a tear in the social fabric was formed along distinct racial and color lines. These physiologically distinct lines have permeated into various fields such as politics, economy, and culture, reinforcing each other and forming an enduring and hard to break social structure.

The Social Structure of Latin America After Independence

In the early nineteenth century, countries in Latin America began their national independence movements. In nearly half a century, the colonial rule of Spain and Portugal basically collapsed, and Latin American countries gained independence. This great wave of national independence and liberation movements was mostly led by creoles who owned land and other assets. Discontented with the colonial rule and privileges of "peninsulars," they intended to get rid of colonial rule through national independence movements.

From the perspective of the social structure, the national independence of Latin American countries was very limited. National independence was a major historical change in Latin American countries, but it had not changed the pre-independence social structure. The result of independence and liberation was that "creoles" replaced "peninsulars" as the ruling class, while Indians, black slaves, and even mixed-race people had not achieved any substantial improvement in social and economic status.

After independence, Latin America, being economically committed to modernization and catching up with Western developed countries, experienced the export-oriented, import substitution, and later free market economic development models. From independence in the 1820s until the world economic crisis in the late 1920s, the export-oriented economic model brought handsome profits to white hacendados and mine owners who exported agricultural products, raw materials, and minerals to foreign countries, while the income of people at the bottom of society had not really improved. Although the import substitution and free market economic models after the 1930s brought success, all kinds of internal and external troubles eventually led to the "pendulum"-style ups and downs of economic development (such as the debt crisis in the 1980s). Each cycle of ups and downs in economic development was usually accompanied by hyperinflation, massive unemployment, and huge loss of national wealth. Such a cycle is reflected in the social structure as an increase in the number of poor people, the widening of the gap between rich and poor, and an intensification of social contradictions.

In the process of modernization, the population structure of Latin American countries has also undergone great changes. On the one hand, the proportion of Indians has fallen sharply, white immigrants have flooded in, and the proportion of people of mixed European and American Indian descent has risen sharply.

But all these economic developments and demographic changes have not changed the polarized social structure of colonial times. On the one hand, in the social structure of Latin America, elite status has always been a privilege reserved for the descendants of white colonists. They own a lot of land, monopolize the economic lifeline, wield state power, and dominate the cultural landscape. More importantly, they close channels of social mobility in order to maintain their special class privileges. On the other hand, the vast majority of mixed-race people and the descendants of Indians and black slaves are trapped on the bottom rung of society's ladder. They haven't had their fair share of the real fruits of national independence and economic development, and lack the opportunities and channels to rise to the middle class.

Current Social Structure in Latin America

In the more than 200 years since Latin America gained national independence and autonomy from European colonial rule, the social structure of Latin American countries has been polarized, shaped like a "pyramid."

In the last 10 years of the twentieth century, the occupational hierarchy of the eight major Latin American countries (generally Argentina, Bolivia, Brazil, Chile, Colombia, Mexico, Peru, and Venezuela, if not specified, the same below) consisted of the upper class (employers, managers, and professionals), the middle class (technicians and administrative employees), the top of the lower class (commercial workers, factory workers, craftsmen, and drivers) and the bottom of the lower class (private service providers and agricultural workers).

Only a quarter of the Latin American working population had a middle- or upper-class job, while nearly three-quarters of the workforce was at the lower end of the occupational hierarchy. The differences between the lower class and the other two classes were remarkable.

In the last 10 years of the twentieth century, the proportion of the working population of the upper class remained basically unchanged, the proportion of the middle class declined slightly, and the proportion of the lower class rose slightly. On the plus side, the education level of all classes had improved, and the education level of the lower-class employees had improved the most. On the minus side, the education level of the upper and middle classes was much higher than that of the lower class, with the average length of education for the upper and middle classes being twice that of the lower class. In terms of relative income (expressed as a multiple of poverty line income), employees in the upper and middle classes who made up 25% of the workforce saw an increase in the 10-year period, while employees in the lower class who made up 75% of the workforce saw a decrease.

In terms of the class structure of eight Latin American countries including Brazil and Chile in 2000, Latin America had relatively high institutional costs, and many industries had formed large informal underground economies. Employees in the informal sector often do heavier work in worse working conditions, but receive less pay.

At that time, Latin American countries had a ruling class which made up a small proportion of the population (mostly less than 10%) and a petty bourgeoisie which also made up a small proportion of the population (mostly less than 10%). The two classes combined made up less than 20% of the population in all countries except Venezuela.

By contrast, more than 80% of the population in these countries (more than 75% in the case of Venezuela) belonged to the proletariat. More worrying was that a considerable proportion of them were employed in the informal sector without any government or institutional supervision, and the proportion of these workers was much higher than that of those employed in the formal sector.

The income gap in Latin America has always been far ahead of the rest of the world. The social structure of Latin America is shaped like a pyramid with a huge base and a tiny top. It consists of two opposite social classes: the rich and powerful at the top and people who are living a hand-to-mouth existence on the bottom rung of society. These two social classes are at odds with each other in terms of interests, making social conflicts inevitable and even leading to political unrest.

Such a social structure evidently bears the hallmarks of Colonial Latin America. Such path dependence has prevented Latin America from effectively changing such a fractured structure in social, political, economic, and cultural changes since its independence nearly 200 years ago. Under this structure, social inequality is manifested in all aspects of politics, economy, society, and culture, and is intertwined with social development policies and strategies, forming a unique development path for Latin American countries. With regard to consequences, a fractured social structure has an inescapable negative impact on the institutional environment for economic development and national governance capability. The whole society also exhibits the drawbacks of political instability, frequent changes in policies, great ups and downs in economic fluctuations, and stagnation in development.

4.5.2 *Institutional Predicament*

A fractured social structure has led to an institutional predicament in political and economic development, which makes it difficult for Latin American countries to choose an appropriate development strategy, resulting in an institutional predicament in the economic and social development of Latin American countries.

Institutional Inertia of Elite Control

In Latin American countries, the elite who hold the political and economic lifeline control the choice of development strategies. They invariably choose specific policies and measures that pose no threat to their dominant position in order to maintain their rent-seeking activities aiming to obtain economic income and their monopoly of political power. Any structural change aimed at reducing the power and interests of the ruling elite cannot be truly implemented. This is the institutional inertia of Latin American countries. It can be seen that if the elite of Latin America countries want to maintain institutions through which they can concentrate wealth in their hands, they will inevitably block any reform in primary distribution so as to continue to get the lion's share of the benefits, perpetuating the extremely high level of social inequality.

In fact, the elite has raked in more wealth under the three economic development models since Latin America's independence. In the early stages of development led by the export of primary goods, the real beneficiaries were hacendados and mine owners; in the stages of import substitution industrialization, the biggest beneficiaries were capitalists who expanded their operations, estancieros who shifted from agricultural production to industrial production, and import agents; in the stages of liberalization, multinational corporations and big capitalists profited most from the process of marketization and privatization.

Although, needless to say, people at the bottom have also benefited from economic development, the speed at which they advance is obviously far slower than the speed of economic development and still slower than the speed at which the rich and powerful accumulate additional wealth. This will inevitably lead to the further polarization of the social structure.

The most striking feature of Latin American countries is that a high proportion of national income is concentrated in the hands of the elite (the richest 10% of the population), ranging from approximately 1/3 in Bolivia to approximately 1/2 in Chile. The same indicator is just over 1/5 in Japan and South Korea which has achieved successful transformation.

Meanwhile, a considerable proportion of employees in these Latin American countries are forced to work in the informal sector which offers no labor protection and social security, low wages, and no room for development, from 1/5 in Chile to 2/3 in Bolivia. Only 1/9 of employees work in the informal sector in Japan and 1/4 in South Korea.

The differences in innovation and education between Latin America and East Asia are even more pronounced, with the former investing far less in innovation and education that could contribute to structural change. Obviously, Western developed countries and East Asian countries Japan and South Korea have completed this structural transformation process through appropriate and effective development strategies to eventually embark on a more developed stage.

Brazil which spends the most on R&D among Latin American countries spends less than 1% of its GDP on R&D, and Peru which spends the least on R&D spends only 0.1% of it GDP on R&D, far below the average level of 2% in developed countries, and still lower than East Asian countries that have achieved successful transformation. In keeping with this, Latin American countries are not spending enough on education. In Chile, the best educated country, just over 1/3 of the adult population (25 years or older) has completed secondary education, while in Venezuela, the least educated country, only less than 1/10 of the adult population has completed secondary education. Almost half of the adult population in Japan and South Korea have completed secondary education.

High Levels of "Social Welfare" Spending

In discussions of Latin American countries' choices of development strategies, high "public welfare" expenditures are often cited as a major constraint contributing to the institutional predicament. The excessive social pressure caused by persistent high social inequality made the government turn to "populism" in secondary distribution, and spend most of the public money on social welfare for consumption, while public infrastructure spending was woefully inadequate, making it difficult to improve the investment environment. Such a "welfare catch-up" has become an obstacle to economic development.

All of the eight major Latin American countries discussed repeatedly above have experienced typical "populist" governments, and some "populist" policies have continued to this day.

In the 1980s, Latin American countries were at a relatively low level in social spending. But by the late 1980s, Latin American countries were rethinking their social policies, realizing that wage subsidies had only benefited the urban middle class. As a result, Latin American countries adjusted their "populist policies," increasing spending on education and health and including a large number of poor people among recipients of social welfare support.

Since the 1990s, Latin American countries have seen a huge leap in social spending, from an average of about 5% in the 1980s to more than 10% in the 1990s to 13.8% in 2001. Social welfare spending has been a squeeze on public expenditure in Latin America. In the early 1990s, social spending in Latin American countries accounted for an average of 41.8% of public expenditure, which rose to 47.8% in the late 1990s. In some of these countries (such as Argentina, Brazil, Chile, etc.), that proportion even reached more than 60% in the late 1990s.

However, "populist" policies have not been effective enough to achieve the original goal of raising workers' wages and benefits and improving social welfare. Income inequality in major Latin American countries remains the most serious decades after the introduction of policies designed to reduce the income gap in these countries in the early twenty-first century.

Instead of reducing the income gap, excessive "social spending" under the guidance of "populist" policies has led to a huge development trap: not only increasing the financial burden, but also dampening growth. Under such policies, the cycle of macroeconomic development can usually be divided into the following four stages.[18] Stage 1: The policies yield initial results, with output, real wages, and employment remaining at a high level, and there are no serious inflation and shortage of commodities. Stage 2: Growth hits a bottleneck, with the expansion of domestic demand and insufficient foreign exchange reserves leading to a serious shortage of commodities. Inflation is rising, wages are soaring and the fiscal deficit is worsening. Stage 3: There is an overall shortage of commodities, inflation is running high, capital is flowing out, money is in short supply, real wages have declined substantially, the financial position is unsustainable, and the government is on the verge of bankruptcy. Stage 4: the new government comes into power and implements orthodox

[18] Dornbusch, R, Edwards S. Macroeconomic Populism in Latin America (No. w2986). National Bureau of Economic Research, 1989.

stabilization policies. Real wages have fallen to low levels before the "populist" policies were implemented and will remain at low levels for a considerable period of time. Such "populist" policies in their final stages often lead to economic chaos, social unrest, and even political turmoil.

"Populist" policies resulting from a polarized social structure are doomed to be unsustainable. However, the weight of such a social structure forces the new government to make the same commitments and implement the same "populist" policies. It was in this "pendulum"-like cycle that Latin American countries fell into the "development trap" from which they have difficulty escaping.

Disorderly Urbanization, the Informal Sector and Distorted Efficiency Mechanisms

Throughout the twentieth century, Latin America experienced rapid population growth. After World War II, its population growth rate increased further, with the average annual population growth rate rising from 1.9 to 2.9%.

This population growth process was accompanied by a faster urbanization process. After the import substitution industrialization development strategy was implemented in the 1930s, a large amount of surplus labor began to appear in rural Latin America. This portion of the rural population could only move to cities. This inevitably led to rapid urbanization in Latin America. After World War II, Latin America's urban population grew three times faster than its rural population.

Since the late 1920s, the proportion of urban population in Latin America has risen rapidly, over 40% in 1950, over 60% in 1975, and over 75% in 2000, making it the second most urbanized region after Europe and North America.

It should be pointed out that the rapid urbanization of Latin America took place in the context of incomplete industrialization and unsuccessful economic development. The industrialization level of Latin American countries was only about 30%. Such a level of economic development could hardly support such a high level of urbanization.

As a result, a large number of farmers who had flooded into cities simply could not find decent jobs. Many of these new urban migrants were unemployed or had to find employment in the informal sector. These new migrants had formed a huge urban underclass, which not only led to urban poverty, but also caused a lot of social problems related to urban slums. At the same time, the urban poor had further exacerbated the gap between rich and poor in society, sowing the seeds of political unrest. These groups became the most important political forces supporting "populist" policies.

In the context of high social inequality and a "welfare catch-up," barriers to institutional reform were getting higher and higher, the efficiency mechanisms of factor markets were distorted, and it was difficult to improve production efficiency, giving rise to the informal economy. This further prevented efforts to formulate policies and correct efficiency mechanisms, plunging development into a predicament.

In "The Other Path," Peruvian economist Hernando De Soto describes the procedural difference between opening a small factory in the United States and Peru. In 1983, his research team submitted an application to open a garment factory to the relevant departments in Tampa, Florida, and Lima, Peru, respectively. In Tampa, the entire application process took two hours. In Lima, it took the research team a total of 289 days to complete the application process without paying bribes. The difference here lies in institutional barriers, which make the whole society much less efficient.

4.5.3 Incompetent Governance

The polarized social structure of Latin American countries confronts the government with a dilemma in national governance. The government often cannot strike a balance between development and equity, and is caught between a rock and a hard place when making policy choices, which may eventually lead to frequent change of government and political unrest. This shows incompetent governance by Latin American governments in a particular social structure: The government can neither completely side with the rich and powerful to become an oligarchy nor completely become a sustainable "populist" government.

Whether it's during the period of development led by the export of primary goods, the period of import substitution industrialization, or the period of liberalization that began in the 1980s, Latin American governments needed to rely on the elite to promote development, so that policy-making preferences are controlled to some extent by the elite. Accordingly, most of the benefits of economic development go to the elite. This is why over the past 100 years, social inequality in Latin American countries has been rising, and has been at the highest level in the world.

Common people also benefit from economic development. But once the economy stagnates (such as the world crises of the 1930s and 1980s), the cost is usually borne by them. This is why during the interval between the failure of an economic model and the implementation of the next economic development model, Latin American countries always experience intense social conflicts, political unrest, and even a profound social revolution.

The aforementioned excessive "social spending" and its consequences are also manifestations of the weak governance capability of Latin American governments. In order to avoid fierce social conflicts and appease people at the bottom, Latin American governments usually increase the share of social welfare spending in public spending. Because these plans are politically expedient, often no regard is paid to financial capacity and expenditure often exceeds government revenue.

Of course, such "populist" policies cannot be sustained for long. Finally, when the policy of excessive social spending fails, the government has to step down in the face of the loss of credibility with people at the bottom and accusations of misusing resources to restrict development. Faced with a social structure with great masses of people at the bottom, the new government first has to appease people at the bottom who have been hurt by economic fluctuations. In such a particular environment, its national governance capability is tied up and cannot be used at all.

In the 1930s, after the failure of the model of development led by the export of primary goods, some major Latin American countries (such as Argentina, Brazil, Mexico, etc.) basically experienced violent social revolutions and even military interventions in politics before gradually stabilized. Since the 1990s, the democratic systems of most Latin American countries have been further consolidated, but the political demands of people at the bottom are inevitably competing in the economic and social fields.

In summary, the predicament of Latin America is largely due to the fact that the post-independence social structure has not been transformed successfully, continuing and amplifying fractures in the social structure of the colonial period. This particular historical heritage and development trajectory present Latin American countries with a dilemma in the process of formulating development strategies: strategies that promote development will further increase social inequality, and any economic stagnation will incur more fierce resistance from people at the bottom; policies that promote social welfare are financially unsupportable and therefore are unsustainable and will eventually fail.

Such a polarized social structure has also led to serious deficiencies in the national governance capability of Latin American countries. In the face of the elite who control the political and economic lifeline of the country—they get the lion's share of the benefits in primary distribution, the government is unable to make any change, because that means the collapse of the economy; nor is the government able to compel people at the bottom to make sacrifices, because that means political unrest. Latin American governments have been struggling to deal with such a dilemma, let alone to make institutional changes.

Correspondingly, in the urbanization process, Latin American countries were unable to control the situation and guide and bring order to the flow of farmers into cities. Consequently, urbanization was competed in a short period of time, which resulted in the high level of inequality between social classes and class antagonism being directly manifested in cities and led to the rise of social pressure and the intensification of social conflicts, killing any chance for institutional change.

4.5.4 Deficiencies in Legal Protection

Some countries in Latin America that have been caught in the middle-income trap are facing serious problems in the operation of laws and regulations and deficiencies in legal protection. These problems have greatly hindered the process of overcoming the middle-income trap.

Deficiencies in Legal Protection Hinder Economic Development

In Brazil, for example, despite the many reforms from the 1990s to the beginning of the twenty-first century, barriers to competition still exist in the Brazilian economy. In particular, there are several prominent problems in the business environment: high costs, regulatory complexity, and problems in the operation of laws and regulations all contribute to deficiencies in legal protection. Defects in the operation of the legal system lead to the legal uncertainty of various contracts. For Brazil, reform should focus on improving its business environment, with particular emphasis on reducing regulatory complexity and strengthening the protection of contracts by law, replacing the rule of man with the rule of law, and restoring the role of the market in resource allocation as the best way to ensure equity and combat corruption.

Legal Prohibition Hinders Enterprise Innovation
Before 2004, Brazilian law prohibited the government from directly funding corporate innovations, and did not allow companies to hire university researchers. This not only weakened the capacity of innovating entities, institutionally constrained interactions and connections between innovating entities, and hindered the application of new scientific and technological achievements to the economy, but also obstructed the innovation and development of SMEs. The Brazilian government has come to realize the innovation-related institutional deficiencies, claiming that there are contradictions and obstacles in Brazil that prevent the effective industrialization of research findings, which has seriously affected Brazil's international competitiveness. In recent years, Brazil has introduced a series of laws and policies to promote cooperation between universities and enterprises, with a view to applying research findings to the economic and social fields. But this contradiction has its roots in history. Institutional deficiencies can hardly be reversed overnight. Barriers to enterprise innovation have also retarded Brazil's economic development.

5 The Soviet Union and Eastern European Countries in Transition

Although the concept of middle-income trap was invented mainly in connection with Latin American countries, if the GDP per capita of $3000–10,000 is regarded as a landmark stage of economic growth, former socialist countries such as the Soviet Union and Eastern Europe also faced the question of whether they could cross such a landmark stage in the process of development and transformation. Since former socialist countries such as the Soviet Union and Eastern Europe and China have both undergone the process of economic and social transformation from "totalitarian" states to market-oriented social reconstruction, the experiences of the Soviet Union and the socialist countries of Eastern Europe offer more useful precedents for China.

5.1 *Economic and Social Dilemma Before the Drastic Changes in Eastern Europe*

5.1.1 *Market-Oriented Reform and Economic Involution in the Soviet Union and Eastern Europe*

After the Second World War, Eastern European countries transplanted the Soviet model and established an economic system characterized by an economic structure where the only form of ownership was public ownership, highly centralized command planning, a one-sided emphasis on the development of heavy industry, and convergent political and social structures. Although it played a certain historical role in the early stage, the disadvantages of this rigid model became increasingly apparent. After the death of Stalin in 1953, especially after the 20th Congress of the Communist Party of the Soviet Union and the Hungarian incident in 1956, Eastern European countries, led by Yugoslavia, began the first wave of reform, forming classic models such as the Yugoslav model and the Hungarian model, as opposed to the single Soviet model.

Yugoslavia was the first to embark on a path of reform. After 1945, Yugoslavia completed the socialist transformation by basically copying the Soviet model. Since 1948, the relations between the Soviet Union and Yugoslavia broke down, and Yugoslavia began to reform in order to seek survival and development. In June 1950, Yugoslavia enacted the Basic Law on the Management of State Enterprises and Higher Economic Associations by Work Collectives, announcing the implementation of workers' self-management, namely the management of factories through management committees elected by workers themselves. In 1952, Yugoslavia replaced highly centralized national command planning with social planning based on autonomy to guide the development of enterprises. In Hungary, after coming to power in the wake of the Hungarian Revolution of 1956, Kadar began to implement partial reforms in 1957. Economic reforms include slowing down the development of heavy industry, reducing command planning targets, expanding corporate autonomy, implementing a corporate profit sharing system, and raising employees' wages; political reforms include pursuing democratic centralism and strengthening the rule of law. Poland's reforms are equally representative. After returning to power in 1956, Gomulka opposed the blind imitation of the Soviet Union and proposed the "Polish road" to socialist construction for the second time. Economically, Poland expanded corporate autonomy, allowed workers' self-management, disbanded most agricultural cooperatives, recognized the law of value, abandoned the policy of giving priority to the development of heavy industry, and raised the prices of agricultural products. Politically, Poland advocated expanding parliamentary powers and improving relations with other political parties, social groups and churches. After Khrushchev came to power, the Soviet Union took some reform measures beginning with agriculture. While adhering to highly centralized management by the state, the Soviet Union expanded corporate autonomy and made use of market mechanisms to a limited extent. In August 1954, the Soviet Union began to expand the power of corporate leadership, and reduced planning targets set by the state for enterprises by 52%.

In the 1960s and 1970s, in response to the economic crisis, the Soviet Union and the socialist countries of Eastern Europe launched the second round of reforms. In the Soviet Union, after coming to power in 1964, Brezhnev introduced a new economic system, focused on the improvement of planning, strengthened economic accounting, and established a material incentive mechanism in an effort to improve labor productivity. In October 1965, the Soviet Union announced that it would "combine centralized and planned leadership with the operational initiative of the enterprise and all employees, with strengthening economic leverage and material incentives for the development of production and with full economic accounting," with "the dominant role of centralized and planned leadership in the development of the economy as the starting point." Hungary's economic reform came into full swing in 1968, with the goal of "organically combining the centralized management of the planned development of the national economy with commodity relations and the positive role of the market on the basis of socialist ownership of means of production" to "establish an organic unity of planning and the market." Yugoslavia introduced "New Economic Measures" in the mid-1960s, and adopted a series of financial measures to alleviate the economic crisis. Meanwhile, Yugoslavia promoted intra-party democracy and expanded the scope of autonomy from factories and enterprises to state organs and public institutions. In early 1964, Czechoslovakia issued the principles of the economic reform program formulated by a committee headed by Czech economist Ota Šik, declaring that it would expand corporate power and make more use of market mechanisms to develop its economy. In October of that year, the Czech Communist Party issued a statement that it decided to try out a "new economic management system" in some enterprises and replace the "management system based on central instructions and administrative means" with "a complete set of economic management systems"; increase labor productivity and develop production by "expanding the rights and responsibilities of enterprises, and giving full play to the initiative of working people and enterprises."

These reforms overcame the disadvantages of the Stalin model to a certain extent, and continued the trend of economic growth in the Soviet Union and the socialist countries of Eastern Europe after the war. Data shows that from 1950 to 1965, the Soviet Union and the socialist countries of Eastern Europe maintained a relatively high growth rate, with annual growth rates ranging from 6 to 10%, comparable to Western capitalist countries in the same period (see Fig. 4).

But the economic system reforms of the Soviet Union and Eastern Europe were not complete, and basically belonged to the category of "technical reforms." Although the reforms of countries such as Yugoslavia and Hungary emphasized the role of the market to varying degrees, they had not fundamentally gone beyond the basic framework of a planned economy. Yugoslavia's made "workers' self-management" the goal of its reform and remained critical of the concept of "market economy." Hungary's economic reform emphasized "indirect administrative coordination." The Soviet Union was more conservative, denying the existence of different models in the economic system, and making a big push for administrative "joint ventures" dominated by rules and regulations. Due to the obstruction of domestic and foreign anti-reform forces, the reforms of various countries actually met many difficulties and setbacks. In Czechoslovakia, for example, after reformist Dubček came to power in early 1968, he pushed for more radical economic reform and political pluralism, but this led to a backlash from conservative forces at home and abroad. The Czech reforms were halted by Soviet military intervention.

After 1965, socialist countries (including the Soviet Union and China) generally began to experience problems in their economies. In the 1970s, economic development in the Soviet Union and Eastern European countries began to slow down. Especially in the late 1970s, their economies slowed significantly, but were still growing at a low rate. From 1976 to 1980, the average GDP growth rate of the Soviet Union and Eastern European countries was only just over 4%. After 1980, although the Soviet Union and many Eastern European countries were still pushing forward reforms, they failed to reverse the general trend of economic slowdown. No matter what economic model they adopted, all Eastern

European countries except the German Democratic Republic experienced a major economic downturn in varying degrees. The Polish economy even experienced negative growth (see Table 4).

In the 1980s, in the face of worsening economic conditions, countries including Yugoslavia, Hungary, and Poland launched the third round of reforms and achieved some partial success, but they failed to fundamentally reverse the overall economic decline. In the late 1980s and especially in the early 1990s, the Soviet Union and Eastern Europe slumped into full-scale recession, with their main economic indicators all registering a negative reading, indicating a serious economic crisis. According to estimates by some scholars, the average annual growth rate of Eastern European countries was −0.8% from 1973 to 1992, while that of Western European countries was 1.8% in the same period. As a result, the gap between Eastern and Western Europe expanded from 1:2 to 1:4.

On the whole, since the 1970s, GDP per capita growth in the Soviet Union and the socialist countries of Eastern Europe had been seriously "involute." From 1965 to 1990, the GDP per capita of the seven major countries of Eastern Europe was just over $6000 at its best, while that of the Soviet Union never exceeded $7500 (see Fig. 2). Although originally, the concept of middle-income trap was not intended primarily to describe

Table 4 Growth rates of national income in the Soviet Union and some Eastern European countries

Country	*1971–1975*	*1976–1980*	*1981–1985*	*Increase over the previous year (%)*				
				1986	*1988*	*1988*	*1989*	*1990*
Soviet Union	5.7	4.3	3.2	1.7	1.7	4.1	2.4	−4.7
Bulgaria	7.8	6.1	3.7	5	10.8	6	−0.4	−10
Hungary	6.3	2.8	1.3	0.9	3.7	0.5	1.2	−3
Former Democratic Republic of Germany[a]	5.4	4.1	4.5	4	3.8	3	2	–
Poland	9.8	1.2	−0.8	5	2	4	0	−13
Romania	11.4	7	4.4	7.2	5.3	2.8	−9.9	−10
Czechoslovakia	5.5	3.7	1.7	1.8	2.7	2.5	1.7	−3.1

[a]The German Democratic Republic joined the Federal Republic of Germany on October 3, 1990

Source Chen Xiuying. Economic Statistics of Eastern European Countries. *World Economy*, 1991 (5)

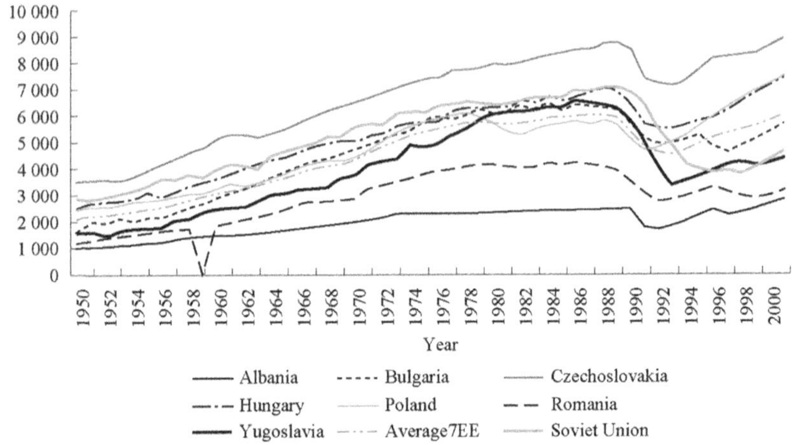

Fig. 2 Per capita GDP of the former Soviet Union and the socialist countries of Eastern Europe (1950–2002) (1990 international $) (*Source* Angus Maddison. *The World Economy: Historical Statistics*. OECD Publishing, 2003)

these countries in transition, but these manifestations are very similar to the manifestations of the middle-income trap in some developing countries at the economic level.

5.1.2 *The Challenge of Shifting from "Extensive Growth" to "Intensive Growth"*

The predicament of the Soviet Union and Eastern European countries was related to the shift from extensive growth to intensive growth. The shift from "extensive growth" to "intensive growth" is an important dimension of many scholars' portrayal of the economic transformation of the Soviet Union and the socialist countries of Eastern Europe. Similar to the Great Depression of capitalist countries in the 1920s and 1930s, the economic depression of socialist countries in the 1970s and 1980s could be seen as a structural crisis from "extensive growth" to "intensive growth."[19]

[19] Szelenyi, Ivan. "Eastern Europe In an Epoch of Transition: Toward a Socialist Mixed Economy?" In *Remaking the Economic Institutions of Socialism: China and Eastern Europe* (1989): 208–232. [Hungary] Kornai. *The Socialist System—The Political Economy of Communism*.Beijing: Central Compilation & Translation Press, 2007.

Conceptually, the so-called "extensive growth" is mainly based on an increase in the supplies of factors of production such as labor, capital, and land. The extensive mode of development is subject to the law of diminishing marginal returns, characterized by being driven by quantity at the expense of quality, and inefficient. The so-called intensive growth is mainly due to an increase in comprehensive productivity and the optimal combination of factors of production; i.e., an increase in labor productivity and the more efficient use of capital and other means of production. Such growth is generally attributed to technological innovation and well-established laws and regulations. Intensive growth will result in sustained improvements in people's income and welfare, and will continue even when the population is declining.

In the late 1960s, as surplus agricultural labor was absorbed into the industrial sector, the "extensive growth" marked by industrialization or capital accumulation in the Soviet Union and the socialist countries of Eastern Europe had to come to an end. This change called for a change in the centralized economic management system. There is a contradiction between the prescriptive nature of planning and the difficulty of planning personal consumption. The old command economy made some sense in the "extensive growth" stage of socialist countries where industrial production was centrally planned, but in the transition to "intensive growth," it had difficulty adapting in the face millions of consumers. More importantly, the shift to the "intensive growth" model needs to be achieved by improving productivity and developing new technologies and must be conditioned on economic and social structural adjustment, including a series of changes such as increasing the real income of residents, expanding the production of consumer goods and transitioning to a mass consumer society. However, due to inherent defects such as "soft budget constraints" and "shortage economy" in the command planning economic system, the economic transformation of the Soviet Union and the socialist countries of Eastern Europe had been beset with difficulties, as summarized below.

First, demand was woefully inadequate. As Kornai pointed out, under the socialist system of the Soviet Union and Eastern Europe, the "forced growth" model was implemented. Resources were highly monopolized by the state; heavy industry and large enterprises were given priority; the level of investment was high, but the level of consumption was low; investment was given priority over consumption; consumption was always the least considered factor in macro-distribution; the public was asked to abandon or postpone current consumption and make sacrifices; in some areas, especially education, health, and environmental protection, public demand was woefully ignored and opportunities for reform were missed. Meanwhile, there is a serious shortage of consumer goods, the level of personal consumption lagged far behind that of capitalist countries, and domestic demand was insufficient. Although the overall level of consumption had increased, the growth rate of consumption lagged far behind the growth rate of GDP.

Second, there was huge overinvestment and investment efficiency was low. Under the socialist system, "expansion impulse," "soft budget constraints" and "investment hunger" are inherent characteristics. The rate of growth of investment in fixed assets in the Soviet Union and the socialist countries of Eastern Europe had been higher than in capitalist countries. However, under the "forced growth" model, the investment-led system had been continuing the extensive mode of growth. Although the growth rate was high in certain periods, the comprehensive productivity of factors was low, and the contribution of factor productivity to economic growth was far lower than in capitalist countries in the same period (see Table 5). Since the 1980s, capital productivity in the Soviet Union and the socialist countries of Eastern Europe had fallen into negative territory (see Table 6). The Soviet Union and the socialist countries of Eastern Europe consumed twice or three times as much energy per product as market economy countries.

Third, soft budget constraints and lack of market competition discouraged technological innovation by enterprises. Bureaucracy not only hindered technological innovation, but also impaired daily production efficiency. Almost all technological advances were replicates of technological innovation in capitalist countries, and even such imitative technological advances were very accidental.

Demand was inadequate, innovation was limited, and resources were over-consumed in inefficient investment. Although high economic growth could be achieved in the early stages, this "forced growth" model forced people to "cut back on clothing and food" and was too costly to sustain for a long time. Sooner or later, the rate of economic growth would gradually decline as the potential of various resources was exhausted (In Eastern Europe this was mainly manifested as a depletion of surplus labor).

Table 5 Contribution of factor productivity to production growth: international comparison

	Country	*Period*	*Average annual rate of change*		*Contribution to output growth*
			Output	*Factor productivity*	
Socialist countries	Czechoslovakia	1960–1975	3.0	1.0	0.33
		1976–1980	2.2	0.7	0.29
		1981–1988	1.4	0.1	0.07
	Poland	1960–1975	5.1	2.4	0.47
		1976–1980	0.7	−0.6	–
		1981–1988	0.8	0.2	0.40
	Soviet Union	1960–1975	4.6	1.2	0.26
		1976–1980	2.3	0.5	0.22
		1981–1988	1.9	0.5	0.13
Capitalist countries	France	1960–1973	5.8	3.9	0.67
		1973–1979	2.8	1.7	0.65
		1979–1988	1.9	1.5	0.75
	Japan	1960–1973	10.8	6.6	0.61
		1973–1979	3.6	1.8	0.43
		1979–1988	4.1	1.8	0.43
	United Kingdom	1960–1973	2.9	2.2	0.76
		1973–1979	1.5	0.5	0.60
		1979–1988	2.2	1.9	0.95

Source [Hungary] Kornai. *The Socialist System—The Political Economy of Communism*. Beijing: Central Compilation and Translation Press, 2007

5.1.3 Overall Economic, Social and Political Crises

After World War II, despite the continuous reform measures taken by the Soviet Union and the socialist countries of Eastern Europe in the process of economic development and even bold explorations such as those made by Yugoslavia, they still failed to fundamentally achieve economic growth or cope with the many challenges brought about by phased transitions in economic growth. In fact, although the highly centralized planning system and the forced mode of growth would inevitably cause economic inefficiency, it is difficult to fully understand the nature of the difficulties facing this transformation without taking into account the social structure and political system.

Under a totalitarian system, resources are highly monopolized by the state, consumption is squeezed in the development strategy, and the social

Table 6 Extensive growth in the Soviet Union and Eastern Europe in the 1980s (average annual percent change) %

Country	*Labor productivity*		*Capital productivity*	
	1981–1985	*1986–1989*	*1981–1985*	*1986–1989*
Bulgaria	3.5	4.0	−2.9	−2.2
Czechoslovakia	1.1	2.1	−3.6	−2.1
German Democratic Republic	4.3	3.5	0.2	−1.3
Hungary	2.1	2.9a	−2.2	−0.8b
Poland	−0.1	4.5	−3.4	−1.2
Romania	4.2	4.5a	−4.2	−1.2b
Soviet Union	2.7	3.3	−3. 1	−2.3

Note a stands for 1986–1988 and b for 1986–1987
Source M Knell, C Rider. *Socialist Economies in Transition: Appraisals of the Market Mechanism.* Edward Elgar Publishing Limited, 1992

base for expanding domestic demand is excluded in the social structure. Under a redistribution system, the privileged class monopolizes all kinds of superior resources and opportunities, the income of ordinary social classes is generally low, there is a lack of a sizable middle-income class, and domestic demand is woeful inadequate. The preference of the state for state-owned enterprises squeezes out the living space of the private economy and seriously affects the indigenous innovation capability. These problems are important factors that result in the absence of the necessary socio-economic base for economic transformation.

Meanwhile, due to the lack of an effective institutional interest articulation mechanism caused by limitations of the political system, it is difficult to form checks and balances on special interest groups, and promoting in-depth economic and social reform has become an impossible task. In Poland, for example, conservative forces in the bureaucratic machinery strongly opposed any change that could jeopardize the way established organizations control society and economy. They tried to limit the direction and pace of social and economic change through the party apparatus.[20] Gomulka' reforms stalled in 1959 because of resistance from conservative forces at home and abroad.

[20] [Poland] Brus. *The Economics and Politics of Socialism.* Translated by He Zuo. Beijing: China Social Sciences Press, 1981.

In sharp contrast, when the Soviet Union and the socialist countries of Eastern Europe got bogged down in these problems, developed-market economies are gradually moving toward an "era of mass consumption" through a series of institutional changes. In the United States, through the reforms of the Roosevelt and Kennedy administrations, a social democratic welfare system had been established, which helped the United States through the economic crisis and ensured sustained economic growth.

With macroeconomic contradictions intensifying, the economy stagnating, and people's income and living standards in decline, the Soviet Union and Eastern European countries had encountered major economic and social crises. Calls for change had been growing, and protests were erupting. In the face of various crises, the legitimacy of the socialist regimes of the Soviet Union and Eastern Europe was challenged.

5.2 *Development Path and Consequences After the Transformation of the Soviet Union and Eastern Europe*

Economically, the drastic changes in Eastern Europe can be seen as a response to the failure of economic transition. Among countries belonging to the former socialist camp, according to the World Bank's 2011 classification criteria, countries like the Czech Republic, Hungary, Poland, Russia have joined the ranks of high-income economies, but how to consolidate their positions as high-income countries is still an important issue. The economies of some countries are still in danger of falling back into the middle-income trap. In addition to factors such as resource endowment and country size, this difference can be largely attributed to the path dependence of the pre-socialist period and the transformation process.

Central and eastern European countries such as the Czech Republic, Poland, and Hungary have not seen much social unrest during their transformation. These countries all reformed their political systems before undergoing economic transformation. Their common characteristics are marketization, stabilization, and privatization. In economic reform, state-owned property rights were fairly equitably privatized through the "democratic division of property," which focused on the legitimacy and fairness of transactions. Although the negotiation process between multiple interest groups was rather tortuous and increased transaction costs, it ensured the fairness and transparency of the privatization process and laid the foundation for the legalization of property rights. In Russia, the lack of democracy led to the abortion of the "privatization of securities" and the formation of financial-industrial oligarchies through insider transactions. The ways to privatize state-owned assets in these countries in transition could be divided into three categories: the first was to distribute them to common people in a manner that was equitable, at least formally; the second was to auction them in an open and competitive manner, which led to the influx of powerful foreign capital; the third was insider trading. The Czech Republic and Poland belonged to the first category, Hungary the second, and Russia the third.

5.2.1 Transformation of the Czech Republic

The transformation of the Czech Republic was characterized by the smooth development of "mass privatization" promoted by its original democratic tradition. The Czech Republic was the only former Eastern European country with a well-developed and stable parliamentary democracy before World War II. Under the dual influence of the concept of democratic participation and supervision and the concept of leftist equality, Czech political circles and the Czech people concurred that Czech industry was built through the cooperation of all citizens and that universal social compensation was necessary, so "universal shareholding" should be implemented through the distribution of investment vouchers in the privatization process. As Czech politician Klaus put it, "Find the original owner on the basis of equity at the starting point and the ultimate private owner on the basis of fair rules."[21] Therefore, mass privatization based on the privatization of securities characterized by the equality of opportunities and equity at the starting point went relatively smoothly. Oligarchic and under-the-table property right reform was unacceptable to the people. Privatization based on democracy and the rule of law had effectively suppressed oligarchic and under-the-table property right reform, and to a large extent reduced income inequality caused by capital possession.

The Czech Republic has planned for privatization with great care. In May 1992, the then Czechoslovak Federation began a campaign to privatize securities. The first tranche of transactions lasted for 14 months and the second tranche for seven months. All the transactions were completed on schedule and occurred at rather regular intervals, while in the case of

[21] Jin Yan. *From "Eastern Europe" to "New Europe": 20 Years of Transition in Review*. Beijing: Peking University Press, 2011.

Russia, there were repeated delays, the progress was slow, and transactions did not took place until the very last minute before the invalidation of securities. The listing of enterprises through the conversion of assets into shares was carried out in accordance with unified government regulations, and there was no bargaining with "insiders." Unlike Russia which distributed securities for free, the Czech Republic imposed a registration fee to exclude non-citizens, so as to reduce short selling and speculation by citizens.

Another important institutional innovation in the Czech privatization process was the establishment of hundreds of privatization investment funds aimed at solving the problem of "governance vacuum" arising from highly dispersed ownership after mass privatization. Investment funds were used to counterbalance corporate insiders in order to protect the interests of minority shareholders, effectively preventing the phenomenon of "swapping privatized securities for alcohol" in Russia. By investing in privatized securities in investment funds, Czech citizens became shareholders of the funds and receive dividends from the investment returns of the funds. According to the statistics of the Ministry of Privatization in Czech Republic, the average Czech citizen received more than $5000 in assets, and each asset generated an average of $300 a year in the years of privatization (both assets and earnings are measured in terms of purchasing power).[22]

The privatization process in the Czech Republic which was declared complete in 1996 brought equal benefits to the vast majority of citizens. The fairness of "all people are shareholders" was conducive to improving the legitimacy of the regime. The Czech Republic, which bottomed out economically in late 1992, was the second eastern European country after Poland to recover economically. This provided favorable social and economic conditions for the transformation of the Czech Republic in terms of the rule of law, the control of government expenditure, economic freedom and market openness (see Fig. 3).

5.2.2 *Transformation of Poland*

The transformation of Poland was characterized by its strong union power. Trade unions in Poland were the main driving force for the drastic changes. With the support of "Workers' President" Wałęsa, trade unions

[22] Jin Yan, Qin Hui. Czech Republic: After Equity at the Starting Point. *Reform*, 2001 (2): 112–127.

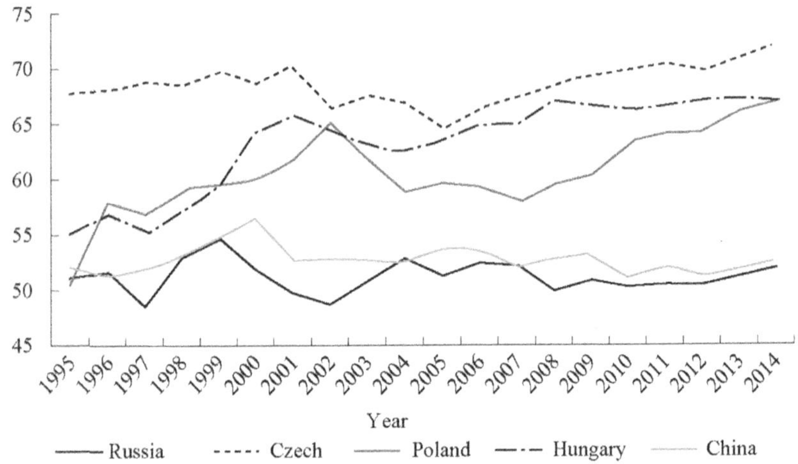

Fig. 3 Russia, Jet, Poland, Hungary and China as measured by the Index of Economic Freedom (1995–2014) (*Source* World Bank website)

continued to grow and develop. Trade unions' voice was conducive to the fairness of the transition process and eliminating the disadvantage of "privatization in favor of the rich and powerful," and did more good than harm to the transition in the long run. The privatization process in Poland was slow because of powerful trade unions. Mass movements launched by independent trade unions under the former system were aimed at corruption and the embezzlement of public property. Therefore, during the reign of the first non-communist government after the Polish upheaval, the process of privatization of state-owned enterprises did not accelerate, but slowed down.[23] After repeated consultations, a committee composed of the government, representatives of the three major trade unions, enterprises and foreign experts adopted the first privatization program accepted by all parties in 1994. By the time the first phase of restructuring was completed in 1996, it was already the seventh year after the Polish upheaval. Powerful trade unions subjected holders of private capital who intended to enter enterprises to complicated negotiations with trade unions. Although the tug-of-war between the two sides increased

[23] Jin Yan. Poland's Achievements and Experience in Economic Transition and the Lessons It Has Learnt. *International Economic Review*, 2003 (2): 20–29.

the cost of the transition, it guaranteed the interests of ordinary workers in the privatization process. In the privatization process in Poland, about 15% of the state-owned assets were given to enterprise employees for free. Some enterprises converted assets into shares and allowed their employees to purchase the shares at a discount or in installments. This is "employee ownership" with Polish characteristics.

Although in the case of both Russia and Poland, insiders were in control, the biggest difference with Russia was that in the case of Poland, "insiders" were shareholders, and transactions between them were "free transactions." Small shareholders passed responsibility when they sold their shares; large shareholders took over responsibility when they took possession of shares. In the case of Russia, "insiders" were in fact the powerful who were regarded by the authorities as reliable people on their own side. Instead of dealing with independent small shareholders, they "traded" with the state, taking profits from the state's treasury and leaving the burden to the state. Poland's transition process was highly democratized and subject to the rule of law and strong oversight. Among countries in transition in Eastern Europe, Poland was least affected by institutional corruption and power rent-seeking activities, let alone serious capital flight similar to that in Russia.

5.2.3 *Transformation of Hungary*

The transformation of Hungary was based on earlier economic reforms and was characterized by "sale only and no sharing" and opening up to foreign investment. Starting in 1965, Hungary, taking advantage of the liberal environment for open discussion of economic freedom in the Soviet economic circles, launched an experiment with marketization, which saw the cancelation of planning targets set by the state for enterprises, and the expansion of the autonomy of enterprises. In the subsequent 20 years of reform, the contracting system and the leasing system were widely implemented in commerce, the handicrafts sector, the service sector, and SMEs, making it easy for people to accept the market economy and laying a broad social foundation for the subsequent economic transition. Hungary had developed well-established economic laws and regulations in previous economic reforms, so it was one of the Eastern European countries with a legal system most akin to that in the West. Meanwhile, it had cultivated a batch of professional brokers who were familiar with the market economy.

Hungarian governments before the drastic changes in Eastern Europe left behind the highest debt per capita in Europe. The new government launched a public auction of state-owned assets that needed to be monetized urgently. Most of the high bidders were foreign companies, so the auction became a "big auction open to foreign players." Sectors such as energy, power, military, banking, and media had undergone several rounds of "privatization campaigns." Of the 1857 large state-owned enterprises throughout the country, 1299 had been auctioned off, only 10 were retained and the rest had been closed down, suspended, merged or switched to other lines of production. Thanks to a robust supervision mechanism under the democratic system, the auction took place without any irregularities, with foreign bidders actively participating in the competition and state-owned assets sold at a good price. As a result, the state's treasury saw a significant increase in revenue from "privatization" (revenue from privatization in 1995, the second year of the Socialist administration, reached 4.439 billion forints, more than the previous five years combined). Competitive bidding for the purchase of state-owned assets brought a lot of foreign investment to Hungary. In 1996, Hungary received $14.3 billion in foreign investment, accounting for half of the total foreign investment in Eastern Europe.[24] Substantial revenue from privatization stabilized Hungary's finances and enabled Hungary to survive crises during the transition period and cope with social security, debt, and other burdens during the transition period. The inflow of foreign capital also contributed to the revival of Hungary's economy.

This approach primed the Hungarian market for integration into the international market once and for all. As buyers of Hungarian enterprises already had customer relations and marketing networks in place, Hungarian enterprises did not have to start from scratch and fight hard in the international market like many private enterprises in Eastern Europe. Multinational corporations had played a prominent role in promoting the economic transformation of Hungary. Many multinational corporations had set up research institutes or R&D centers in Hungary, bringing

[24] Jin Yan, Qin Hui. *Economic Transition and Social Justice*. Zhengzhou: Henan People's Publishing House, 2002.

advanced processes and technologies as well as internationally competitive products.[25] Hungary experienced a very difficult period in the early stages of the transition. It was not until the late 1990s that its economy got on a growth trajectory. But by which time, the economic structure and legal system required for a market economy had been formed.

5.2.4 *Transformation of Russia*

Although Russia's transformation also followed the path of the "privatization of securities," due to the absence of democracy and the rule of law, a large number of insider transactions created a social-economic structure dominated by bureaucrats-oligarchs. Russia's oligopoly was born out of the state monopoly of the past, and oligarchy originated from the centralized system of the past. State capital operating under market conditions was controlled by bureaucrats and used for personal gain and enrichment due to an insufficient level of democracy in the country. Russia's financial and industrial oligarchy was formed not through the sale and concentration of privatized securities, but by the use of state power to transfer the assets (good assets) which the authorities were unwilling to "share" with the people directly into the hands of the rich and powerful in the context of the transition from democratic politics to "new authoritarianism".[26]

Both the Czech Republic and Russia shared state-owned assets, at least in form, by distributing securities to their citizens, so they are often compared with each other. The difference is that Russian interest groups resisted the privatization of securities: Financially there was a need to replace sharing with sale, insiders wanted to divide the spoils among themselves, and oligarchs wanted to seize public assets directly by power and did not want to achieve this through the time-consuming and laborious process of trading and amassing privatized securities, leading to the actual abortion of mass privatization. And the better the assets and the more profitable enterprises were, the more reluctant they were to sell to the public and the more willing they were to divide the spoils among insiders. As a result, when the privatization of securities ended, most of the controlling interests in Russia's "privatized" enterprises were in the

[25] Wang Yueping. On Industrial Structural Adjustment in Regions Undergoing Economic Transformation—A Report on the Study of Industrial Structural Adjustment in Germany and Hungary. *Macroeconomics*, 2000 (4): 59–63.

[26] Li Xin. Understanding of the Two Transformations of the Russian Economy. *Academic Journal of Russian Studies*, 2014 (1): 34–47.

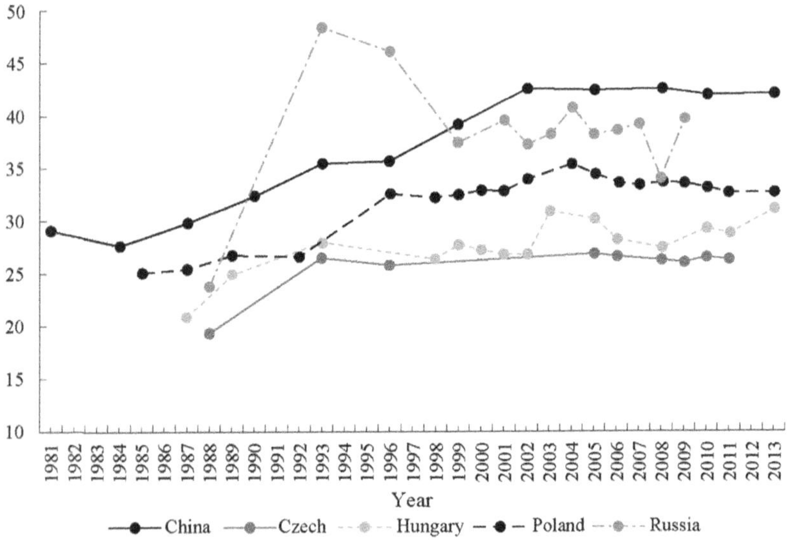

Fig. 4 Gini coefficients of Czechoslovakia, Hungary, Poland and Russia (1981–2013) (*Source* World Bank website)

hands of insiders. According to a survey by the Russian government, in 1994, 65% of the equity interests in these enterprises were owned by insiders, 13% were in the hands of the state; only 21% were owned by external natural and legal persons.[27] Czech citizens, on the other hand, held 80–90% of the property rights of enterprises directly and indirectly.

As state-owned enterprises were transferred for little or no compensation, a few people quickly amassed a fortune to become financial and industrial oligarchs who controlled the lifeline of the country's economy. People's living standards had deteriorated drastically, and polarization between rich and poor had intensified (Fig. 4). Meanwhile, Russia's economic model, which was heavily dependent on the export of energy raw materials, had prevented the smooth transformation of Russia's industrial structure. Its economic structure had become more deformed. It had

[27] Tian Chunsheng. "Insider Control" and Interest Groups—An Empirical Analysis of the Corporate Governance Structure of China and Russia. *Comparative Economic & Social Systems*, 2002(5): 18–25.

failed to transition from an extensive economy to an intensive economy. Its economy was very susceptible to volatility in the international raw material market. Russia's energy-dependent economy puts it at risk of returning to the middle-income trap.

Compared with Russia, the Czech Republic, Poland, Hungary and other Central and Eastern European countries, although their paths of economic transition were different, had allocated property rights in a highly creditable manner, carried out bankruptcy reorganization under market conditions so as to select the superior and eliminate the inferior, and achieved pretty good results in attracting foreign investment, economic growth, social security and controlling polarization between rich and poor.[28] In short, it was the "rule of law" and "marketization" reforms that Central and Eastern European countries insisted on in the process of transformation that enabled them to eventually get out of the middle-income trap.

5.3 Development Path of Russia in the Later Stages of Industrialization

We can examine the development path of the Russian economy in the later stages of industrialization from the following five angles.

5.3.1 Technological Advances and Innovation Capability

Russia has inherited a huge amount of scientific and technological assets from the Soviet Union; the average level of education of its citizens is high; it has a strong potential for scientific and technological innovation. According to the World Development Indicators, in 2007, the proportion of persons who had received higher education in the Russian workforce was as high as 52.5%, which is not only much higher than in developing countries, but also much higher than in many developed countries such as Japan, Britain, France, and Germany (40, 31.8, 29.3, and 24.1%, respectively), second only to the United States (61.1%), and Russia had the highest level of human capital reserves in the world. Russia has far more scientific researchers, engineers, and technicians per million people than any other emerging economy, and no less than most developed countries.

[28] Jin Yan, Qin Hui. *A Decade of Vicissitudes: Economic and Social Transition and Ideological Change in Eastern European Countries*. Shanghai: Shanghai Joint Publishing, 2004.

Unfortunately, due to long-standing institutional and policy constraints, Russia's abundant scientific and technological factors of production have not been well-developed and utilized, and have not been translated into real innovation capability.

First, because the Soviet Union's R&D strategy and thoughts on innovation were mainly oriented toward the defense industry, despite inheriting the abundant scientific and technological factors of the Soviet Union, Russia has not fundamentally weaned itself off the extensive economic development path characterized by long-term dependence on massive investment in physical capital and one-sided pursuit of economic growth, and has ignored the role of scientific and technological innovation in improving production efficiency and quality. Although Russia has a large pool of human capital, its spending on R&D is not high compared with other countries. In 2005, Russia's spending on R&D as a percentage of GDP was higher than that of Brazil and India, but lower than that of China, and the gap with developed countries was more significant; developed countries such as Japan, the United States, and Germany spent more than 2–3 times on R&D as much as Russia. Since investment in R&D was limited and mainly concentrated in the defense sector, from 1998 to 2008, Russia's exports of high-tech products other than military products were almost negligible. The role of high-tech industries in promoting Russia's economic growth is also very limited. In 2008, the proportion of high-tech industries in its GDP was only 3%. Deficiencies in capacity for technological innovation and the backwardness of high-tech industries not only have an unfavorable effect on the long-term development of the Russian economy, but also restrict Russia's economic structural adjustment and economic transformation.

Second, although successive Russian governments have recognized the importance of upgrading the capacity for technological innovation and changing the mode of development for economic growth, and have adopted many policy measures to promote technological advances and enhance innovation capability, such as the establishment of "technological innovation zones" as part of the national innovation strategy, and innovation platforms such as special economic zones and science parks have emerged one after another. But Russia's existing innovation mechanism still has the disadvantages of the Soviet model, such as dependence on the government, state-owned enterprises, and research institutions as core driver of innovation. The R&D capabilities and innovation capability of private enterprises involved in market competition are, on the whole, limited; there is no enterprise spontaneous incentive mechanism driven by market competition, and the market competition mechanism for R&D is far from being established; a non-enterprise spontaneous research and innovation mechanism makes it difficult to directly connect the results of technological development with enterprises that apply technologies, which is not conducive to technological spillovers and diffusion in different sectors. In addition, the government's over-regulation of innovative enterprises, corruption, the lack of strong financial support due to financial strain, a massive loss of technological talent, a regional imbalance in the distribution of innovative R&D capabilities all hinder the improvement of Russia's capacity for technological innovation in varying degrees.

5.3.2 Industrial Structural Adjustment

Russia's industrial structure is a continuation and extension of the deformed industrial structure of the Soviet Union. Under the guidance of the policy of giving priority to the development of heavy and chemical industries, the Soviet Union formed an industrial structure where the secondary sector dominated by heavy and chemical industries was too large, and the agricultural and service sectors were relatively backward. After the collapse of the Soviet Union in 1991, Russia entered a period of massive industrial structural adjustment. After more than 20 years of adjustment, Russia's industrial structure mainly exhibits the following characteristics: on the one hand, in terms of the overall industrial structure, Russia's tertiary sector has developed rapidly, and the overall agriculture/industry/services ratio is close to the level of developed countries and seems reasonable; on the other hand, the proportions of industries within the three sectors are still very unreasonable, the heavy industry/light industry structure remains deformed, the dominant industries are still the basic industries formed during the industrialization period, and in particular, resources, raw materials, and energy now account for greater proportions of the industrial sector. Instead of being significantly upgraded, the industrial structure has retrogressed.

It should be recognized that the overall industrial structure of Russia has undergone positive changes since the collapse of the Soviet Union. Not only has the relationship between the three sectors has been preliminarily adjusted, but also the industrial structure has become more advanced: In terms of the composition of GDP by sector, the proportion of the output of the primary sector has declined the most, from 16.8% in

1989 before the collapse of the Soviet Union to 4.0% in 2010; overall, the proportion of the secondary sector in GDP has declined steadily, from 50.2% in 1989 to 32.6% in 2003, and has been hovering around 36% since then, but compared with the Soviet era, the proportion of the industrial sector in the national economy has dropped sharply, from more than half in the past to slightly over 1/3 now; the proportion of the tertiary sector has increased significantly, from 33.0% in 1989 to 61.7% in 2009. Despite fluctuations in varying degrees during and after this period, the dominant position of the service sector in the national economy (about 60%) has been established. The proportion is already close to the level of developed countries (75% in the United States, 60–70% in the United Kingdom, France, Germany, and Japan).

Nevertheless, the internal structure of Russian industries has become increasingly unreasonable. Instead of being upgraded and going high-end, Russian industries have retrogressed. This is mainly manifested by the fact that instead of being corrected, the over-reliance of industry on energy and raw material processing has worsened. In terms of structural distribution, Russia's energy and raw materials sectors, such as electric power, fuel, non-ferrous and ferrous metals, and forests and timber account for half of the total industrial output. Statistics show that the proportion of Russia's fuel and power sectors, especially the oil extraction industry, has been on the rise since 1995; although the proportion of the machinery manufacturing and metal processing sectors in industry has increased, they only account for about one-fifth of the total industrial output, and their current output is only 68% of the 1990 level; the proportion of light industry, which was small, has declined further, and its output in 2004 was only 14% of the 1990 level; the proportion of some labor-intensive industries, such as textile, sewing and leather boot manufacturing, has declined compared with 1990; the proportion of high-processing industries such as the chemical and petrochemical industries has not changed significantly; basic industries have been growing significantly faster than processing industries. According to the World Development Indicators, from 1992 to 2010, especially from 1992 to 2000, natural resource rents as a percentage of GDP in Russia increased significantly, reaching an all-time high of 42.5% in 2000. Although it has declined since then, it was still 20% by 2010, far higher than the level in the early 1990s. Within the tertiary sector, the commercial and public catering industries have developed rapidly, while the transportation industry has developed relatively slowly and has decreased continuously as a percentage of GDP. High-tech industries have developed relatively slowly, account for a very small proportion of the economy, and have grown little. Since the economic transition, Russia's tertiary sector has developed rapidly. But because such development took place in the context of a severe social and economic crisis and economic transition, there are inevitably some structural contradictions, mainly as follows: Parts that serve the market, such as trade services, financial credit services, and consulting and auditing services, have grown rapidly, while areas such as education, science, health, and culture, which are important to a post-industrial society, have shrunk as a percentage of GDP, from 11% in 1990 to 6% in 2004.

Russia's industrial structural adjustment since its transition has a positive effect on its economic growth. Especially the industrial structure dominated by energy and raw materials has played an important role in preventing economic collapse and promoting economic recovery, but it is also a serious constraint on current and future economic growth. First, it has deprived Russia of the effect of promoting economic growth through structural optimization for quite a long time. Sustained and rapid economic growth is based on the continuous optimization of the industrial structure, which can be explained by the efficient allocation of resources and the formation of coordinated industrial relations. But it is difficult for Russia's current economic growth to gain momentum from either. Meanwhile, economic growth supported by the fuel and energy sectors is fragile. The energy and fuel sectors are vulnerable to drastic fluctuations in the international market, and are typical sectors prone to "big ups and downs." Second, it increases the difficulty of future industrial structural adjustment in Russia. Under the existing structure, a virtuous circle among industries has not been established. Weak light industry and agriculture cannot expand the space for the further development of heavy industry, and the latter cannot promote the development of the former without the support of the former. Third, the high profits of the energy and raw materials sectors have attracted a lot of capital and technology. For example, in 2000 and 2001, oil extraction alone accounted for 33% of the industrial investment, and the metallurgical, natural gas, and electric power sectors accounted for 13, 11, and 10%, respectively. When large amounts of economic resources are tied up in these industrial sectors, the development of other industrial sectors including education, science, and high-tech industries will inevitably be restrained. This will adversely affect not only the efficiency of Russia's economic growth, but also the accelerated transformation of its industrial structure. Finally, it condemns Russia to the lower end of the chain of international specialization. In the context of economic globalization, in addition to institutional transition, Russia must face the issue of how to integrate into the global economy, and seize the commanding heights in the new international specialization. An underdeveloped and low-level industrial structure determines that Russia mainly participates in international specialization in a vertical way. As a result, Russia has been marginalized in the world market in that it has to share limited benefits with many less developed countries, mainly in the world's primary goods market. This is not only inconsistent with the current level and trend of world economic development, but also dims the prospects of Russia using the international market to develop its own economy.

5.3.3 Income Distribution and Income Disparity

Social equity became a subject of universal interest and theoretical research in Russia in the early 1990s. The enormous economic and social transformation has brought the issues of poverty and income distribution in Russia to the fore. In the more than 20 years since Russia's transformation, incomes in Russia rose fast as the economy improved. Russia has made a lot of efforts to eradicate poverty and narrow the income gap, and achieved certain results. However, poverty and income inequality remain an acute issue in Russia. It has become an important issue in Russian society that is the most difficult to resolve and must be resolved.

In the 23 years from 1992 to 2015, real wages in Russia fell first and then rose: Before 1999, real wages decreased every year except 1997 which saw a 5% increase; from 2000 to 2015, real wages increased every year except 2008 which saw a 3% decrease, with an increase of 4.7% in 2015. Actual retirement pensions were declining from 1992 to 1999, and have been growing since then, with an increase of 11% in 2009 and 35% in 2010. Real minimum wages were declining from 1992 to 1999, and have also been growing since then, with an increase of 68.6% in 2009, 7.4% in 2015, and 25.7% in 2016. Changes in real wages, pensions, and minimum wages in Russia are roughly in line with economic trends.

Generally speaking, the main criterion for judging whether the primary distribution of national income is fair is the distribution rate, namely, the share of labor compensation in GDP. The higher the distribution rate, the fairer primary distribution is. The primary distribution rate of national income in developed countries is mostly 60%, with that in the United States as high as 70%. From 1991 to 2011, the primary distribution rate of national income in Russia rose from 34.9 to 35.7%, reaching a high of 37.9% in 2009 and a low of 29.1% in 2000, and ranging from 31 to 35% in other years. In 2011, it was only 0.8% higher than before the economic transition (1991). Even with the inclusion of hidden compensation, the distribution rate does not meet the standard of countries with a mature market economy (the highest was only 52.6% in 2009). The low proportion of labor compensation in the primary distribution of national income indicates that the economic status of workers has declined relatively, resulting in an imbalance between consumption and investment, which is not conducive to economic and social development.

In terms of income disparity, the Gini coefficient during the Soviet era was generally around 0.25. Since the economic transition, Russia's Gini coefficient has risen from 0.238 in 1988 to 0.417 in 2012. Income disparity is quite obvious and above the international warning level for income disparity. Judging by the income disparity coefficient calculated using the quintile approach, income disparity was decreasing in the Soviet era. The income disparity coefficient was 4.7 times in 1970 and dropped to 2.6 times in 1991. Since the economic transition, income disparity in Russia has been growing, with the income disparity coefficient increasing from 2.6 times in 1991 to 9.1 times in 2011. Judging by the income disparity coefficient calculated using the docile approach, the income disparity between the highest income group and the lowest income group was narrowing in the Soviet era, generally between 2 and 5 times. The gap has widened sharply since 1991. It was 8 times in 1992 and rose to 16.1 times in 2011. This ratio is above Russia's national economic security warning level (8 times), and also well above the internationally recognized warning level of 10 times.

Polarization between rich and poor in Russia is mainly manifested in the widening gap between regions, between urban and rural areas and between different sectors of the economy. People in poor areas earn one-third less than people in rich areas; poor areas have 30% more pensioners than rich areas. The income disparity between different sectors of the economy is also widening. In particular, the income of workers in the energy sector such as oil, and in the financial sector is much higher than that of workers in other sectors. The salary level of civil servants is relatively low. An average civil servant makes only a few hundred dollars a month, which is several to more than ten times lower than the average income of private sector employees. In the course of Russia's institutional change, many wealthy people started by acquiring state-owned enterprises, and made their fortunes by buying at low prices and selling at high prices. With oil and gas prices soaring in recent years, they have had the opportunity to grow their wealth again.

The main reasons for the continuous widening of income disparity during the period of economic transition from the Soviet Union to Russia were as follows.

Russia Pursued a Path of Radical Transformation

By adopting the so-called "shock therapy" advocated by Sachs and others, Russia quickly transformed its economy and society in all its aspects. Rapid privatization was one of the most important steps and also one of the core measures. After privatization, most of the enterprises which formerly operated under "soft budget constraints" had to directly face competitive pressure from the market. In order to survive and be efficient, enterprises must minimize their own costs and take measures to motivate workers, so it became a matter of course to adopt a wage differentiation policy. The direct result of this policy was income polarization. This phenomenon cannot be seen in black-and-white terms. A reasonable degree of income disparity is beneficial to economic growth. This is something that all countries in transition must face and is the inevitable result of the introduction of market mechanisms.

A New Situation for Soft Budget Constraints Further Increased Income Disparity

Soft budget constraints were supposed to no longer have any effect and be replaced by hard budget constraints, but the fact was that in the process of Russia's transformation, a considerable number of enterprises operated without hard budget constraints. Soft budget constraints in the transition period even had a worse impact on the economy than soft budget constraints under the planned economy, because under the planned economy there were administrative controls to check the unethical behavior of managers. In the case of radical transition, the market economy cannot immediately form an effective supervision mechanism. This makes the principal–agent problem worse.

The Widening of Income Inequality in Russia Was Related to the Rapid Expansion of Monopoly Power in Russia

A prominent feature of Russia's transformation was the creation of a large number of wealthy upstarts. These wealthy upstarts were inextricably linked to monopoly power. They spared no effort to seek political gains and at one point interfered with politics as oligarchs. After Putin came to power, he fought hard against oligarchy. But as Berezovsky said, "it is impossible for Russia to get rid of oligarchy." These wealthy upstarts made their riches by seizing state assets in seemingly legitimate ways during privatization. First, the existence of wealthy upstarts had led to a sharp increase in income disparity; second, the monopolies they controlled made big profits by seeking preferential policies that were advantageous to them, their staff earned much more than people in ordinary industries. Such income disparity was realized under unfair conditions and therefore was particularly detrimental to social development.

Some Government Actions Led to the Further Widening of Income Disparity

Interest groups that controlled monopolies could only realize their own interests by obtaining government policy support in various ways, Loopholes in government policies and rent-seeking behavior encouraged monopoly power. Transfer payments can not only redress regional imbalances in development, but also directly regulate income gaps between individuals. In contrast to taxation, transfer payments increase personal disposable income, but they target selected groups and are a kind of "redistribution" of income. Russia's social security system was far from perfect. Without a sound social security system, it would be difficult to address widening income inequality. In addition, although a progressive income tax was implemented in Russia, the government failed to perform its regulatory functions effectively, which diluted the effect of the function designed to reduce the gap between rich and poor, and indirectly increased the income gap.

Income Differences Within the Normal Range Caused by Economic Development

According to scholars such as Kuznets, there is an "inverted U" relationship between income disparity and the level of economic development. According to this hypothesis, in the initial stage of economic development, the widening of income inequality may be reasonable. But this theory is only a hypothesis, and scholars' opinions diverge on whether this hypothesis is true or not.

5.3.4 *Development of Urbanization*

In 1900, Russia was still an agricultural country, with only 15% of its population living in cities, and the level of urbanization in Western countries was 2.5 times higher than that in Russia. 20 years later, despite the fact that Russia had suffered a considerable loss of human life in World War I, the ratio remained unchanged. In the following years, with the large-scale industrialization of the Soviet Union, Russia underwent rapid urbanization. By 1980, the level of urbanization in the Soviet Union had approached that in developed countries, much higher than that in third world countries. Measured by the proportion of urban population, the level of urbanization in Russia is close to that in developed countries. According to the World Development Indicators, the proportion of urban population in Russia rose from 53.7% in 1960 to 74% in 2012 (in 2012, the proportion of urban population in the United States was 82.6%; that proportion was 91.7% in Japan, 74% in Germany, 76.8% in Britain, and 86.3% in France).

When it comes to the process of urbanization in Russia, it is necessary to point out the influence of the Soviet Union on the level of urbanization in Russia. As we all know, the Soviet Union had made remarkable achievements in urbanization. Of the more than 1000 cities in Russia, more than 600 were established after 1917. From 1926 to 1939, the Soviet Union implemented compulsory industrialization and collectivization. During this period, cities developed greatly. Large cities developed the fastest and small cities developed the slowest, indicating that the Soviet Union had gradually transitioned from the early stages of urbanization to the polarization stage. This process continued until 1940. World War II disrupted the process of urbanization in the Soviet Union. In the 1950s, with the rapid recovery of the economy, the Soviet Union resumed the normal process of urbanization. It was not until the 1960s and 1970s that urbanization slowly recovered to the pre-war level. Thereafter, the pace of urbanization began to slow down. Urbanization in the Soviet Union since the 1980s had been developing at a slow pace. This indicates that urbanization is bound to slow down after reaching a certain level. But on the other hand, the Soviet Union attached too much importance to the development of urban industry, especially heavy industry, while ignoring support for and the development of the secondary and tertiary sectors, which obviously hampered the further development of urbanization in the Soviet Union. Although its level of urbanization was relatively high, it lagged far behind Western developed countries in terms of the quality of urban life. During this period, which lasted until the collapse of the Soviet Union, the level of urbanization rose and remained at around 73%.

Since 1992, both rural and urban population in Russia have experienced a process of negative growth, with urban population declining even faster. During the urban crisis of 1991–1992, food shortages and soaring prices caused a mass exodus of people from cities in a short period of time. Rural areas absorbed large numbers of Russians from other former Soviet republics, and some residents from eastern and northern Russian cities moved to the countryside in traditional Russian regions. Another specific factor contributing to the decline of urban population was administrative redivision: hundreds of semi-urbanized towns demanded a return to rural status, so that their residents could pay less for utilities and public transport and own large areas of private land. These factors conspired to cause population growth in rural areas and a decrease in total population in semi-urbanized areas. Big cities had also experienced a population decline.

Before the economic transition, there had been a net flow of migrants from rural Russia for a long time. According to classical urbanization theory, migration from rural to urban areas is always the dominant flow. Generally, only in wartime can a reverse flow occur. But what happened in Russia in the 1990s was an exception. For the first time in peacetime, urban residents migrated to the countryside in Russia. But as Russia's economy gradually recovered, this process lasted only a very short period of time. Migration from rural to urban areas became the dominant flow again, and migrants from former Soviet republics also moved their homes from the countryside to cities.

Prior to the collapse of the Soviet Union, Russia slowly transitioned to the early mature stages of urbanization, with the rate of net migration from rural areas slowly transitioning from very high to very low; the rate of migration into large- and medium-sized cities was very high at first and began to decline slowly after reaching a certain level. The recession in the early 1990s pushed the development of all city groups back to the early stages of urban development. As mentioned earlier, from 1992 to 1994, the countryside and small towns became popular destinations for migrants, attracting large numbers of Russians from large cities and former Soviet republics. Migrants from other Soviet republics were often forced to settle first in the countryside and small towns. But surveys showed that these settlers were not faring well in the countryside and small towns, and many of them demanded to leave.

In summary, Russia's urbanization has stagnated since the early 1990s, and its level of urbanization has once dropped to the level of developing countries. Continued recession and social unrest have led to a dramatic increase in the mortality rate of urban population in Russia, and young couples are reluctant to have children, which in turn has caused the problems of negative population growth and aging. Western developed countries are facing the same problems. But the phenomenon of counterurbanization in Russia in recent years is different from the counterurbanization stage experienced by Western countries. The process of urbanization in Russia had been going well until it was disturbed by more than a decade of unrest. It was not until recent years that Russia's urbanization regained some momentum as its economy recovered. But it will take some time before Russia reaches the mature stage of urbanization in Western developed countries.

5.3.5 *Russia's Opening-Up*

From 1949 to 1991, the Soviet Union's foreign economic and trade relations were conducted within the framework of Comecon. Within the framework of Comecon, trade among member states was conducted in a planned way in accordance with "five-year plans" agreements established at Comecon meetings. Annual trade between member states was arranged according to memoranda on bilateral trade with the goal of implementing "five-year agreements." Prices in trade among member states were calculated in "transferable rubles." Such prices were very different from prices on world markets. In some categories of commodity trade, the price difference was quite prominent. For example, in the trade of energy products among Comecon members, the prices of energy products were calculated based on a moving average of world prices for the preceding five years and then converted into "transferable rubles" at the cross rate. Generally speaking, the prices of energy products in intra-Comecon trade were much lower than prices on world markets, while the prices of manufactured goods were generally higher than those on world markets. Since the Soviet Union exported mainly petroleum and raw material products to other Comecon members and imported mainly manufactured goods, it was at a disadvantage regarding terms of trade. In a sense, such a disadvantage was a kind of "aid" or "subsidy" from the Soviet Union to other Comecon members.

Russia's foreign trade environment underwent profound changes following the dissolution of Comecon in 1991. In Russia's trade with other CIS countries and other former Comecon members, prices were gradually aligned with prices on world markets, and payment and settlement switched to hard currencies.

Foreign Trade

After the collapse of the Soviet Union in 1991, Russia began comprehensive economic structural adjustment. The development of its foreign trade mainly underwent the following three stages.

The first stage is 1991–1992. In 1992, Russia began to implement a radical economic transition, causing a substantial decline in production, serious inflation, and a sharp drop in foreign trade. At constant prices, the total volume of its foreign trade in 1991 and 1992 decreased by 30 and 28.7%, respectively, from the previous year. The sharp decline in imports and exports was an important signal of an economic crisis at home, and was the inevitable result of the failure of state-owned foreign trade institutions and the absence of well- developed private foreign trade institutions after the economic transition. On November 15, 1991, Russia passed the Decree on the Liberalization of Foreign Economic Activity in the Russian Federation, which marked the abolition of the trade monopoly system and the beginning of a new round of reforms to liberalize foreign trade in Russia. The major steps taken by Russia on the road to foreign trade liberalization had created equal conditions for fair competition among enterprises participating in foreign trade activities, thus becoming one of the important factors for the normal development of foreign trade activities and playing a certain role in promoting Russia's economic development.

The second stage is 1993–1999. Since 1993, the rate of decline in Russia's production has diminished, inflation has slowed down, and some sectors suited to the market economy have begun to form and develop. By 1997, the economy had stopped falling and the GDP had grown for the first time. The commercial sector was active and the financial market was relatively stable. At constant prices, the total volume of its foreign trade in 1994 increased by 9.5% compared with the previous year. In spite of the rapid growth of trade in this period, by 1999, the total volume of its foreign trade had still failed to return to the pre-economic transition level. Especially its imports fluctuated significantly. In 1999, Russia's imports stood at only $54.1 billion, the lowest level since the transition and a decrease of over 85% compared with 1991.

The third stage is 2000–present. As a result of the smooth implementation of a series of policies since Putin came into power, Russia's foreign trade has entered a period of rapid development: At constant prices, Russia's exports have generally maintained rapid growth except during the 2008 financial crisis, growing from $103.1 billion in 2000 to $343.9 billion in 2015 at an average annual rate of 9.0%; its imports grew from $44.9 billion in 2000 to $192.8 billion in 2015 at an average annual rate of 19.6%; Russia maintained a trade surplus from 2000 to 2015, and the average annual trade surplus exceeding $100 billion after 2005 and peaking at $213.3 billion in 2013.

Foreign Direct Investment

Russia's use of foreign direct investment (FDI) is also divided into two distinct stages: Before 2003, FDI net inflows into Russia were small and fluctuated greatly; FDI inflows into Russia were no more than $10 billion each year from 1992 to 2003, reaching a high of $7.9 billion in 2003 and a low of just $690 million in 1993. Since 2004, Russia's use of FDI has improved markedly. FDI inflows exceeded $10 billion for the first time in 2004, reaching $15.4 billion, and peaked at $74.8 billion in 2008. FDI inflows into Russia dropped sharply in 2009 thanks to the financial crisis. In 2009, FDI net inflows were $36.6 billion, down more than 100% year-on-year. Since then, FDI inflows have gradually picked up, with FDI net inflows reaching $55.1 billion in 2011, the highest level in recent years.

Overall, Russia's use of foreign capital accounts for a small proportion of the national economy, falls behind most emerging economies in terms of scale, and has undergone significant ups and downs. This has much to do with Russia's long-standing poor business climate. According to the World Bank's Ease of Doing Business Index, Russia ranked 112 out of 185 countries in the world in 2012, among the most difficult countries to do business (China ranked 91). This is blamed mainly on strict market regulation by the Russian government. It not only strictly controls high-profit monopoly industries such as resource exploitation, banking, telecommunications, and tobacco, but also strictly regulates downstream industries associated with these industries, creating high barriers to entry for foreign investors. The government over-regulates prices, excludes foreign investors from entering monopoly high-profit industries, and overprotects and blindly supports state-owned enterprises. This limits the incentive mechanism for Russian companies to participate in market competition through technological innovation, distorts the efficiency of resource allocation, and leads to the waste and loss of a lot of social resources.

Problems such as the difficulty of obtaining an entry permit for starting a business in Russia, inadequate protection of investors' interests, the difficulty of conducting cross-border trade settlement, and the difficulty of obtaining access to tax incentives have worsened Russia's business climate in varying degrees. Business managers need to invest a lot of energy to communicate and negotiate with government departments, which makes it difficult for a large number of SMEs in Russia to survive. The fact that business activities are not frequent enough also greatly hampers the improvement of the competitiveness of the Russian economy.

Trade Structure

The level of opening-up is reflected not only in foreign trade and the use of foreign capital, but also in a country's trade structure and competitiveness. The trade structure is a reflection of the production structure. Russia is no exception in this regard. Statistics show that the share of manufactured goods in Russia's exports has not increased, but has gradually declined. The share of exports of manufactured goods fell to less than 20% in 2005. High-tech products account for about 50% of exports of manufactured goods, and high-tech exports mainly consist of arms; IT products account for less than 0.5% of total exports. Meanwhile, exports of primary products such as fuel, minerals, and metals account for an absolutely dominant share, with the proportion of fuel exports reaching a high of 66.7% in 2009. Primary products account for more than 70% of total exports.

Contrary to the structural characteristics of exports, the share of manufactured goods in Russia's imports rose from 45.3% in 1996 to 80.5% in 2011. The share of Russia's imports of IT products and food is also much higher than the corresponding share of exports. The share of imports of primary products generally does not exceed 5%.

Compared with other emerging market countries, Russia's export structure is significantly resource-intensive. This feature shows no signs of changing and is becoming more prominent. In the case of Brazil which is endowed with equally abundant resources as Russia, the share of exports of primary products such as mineral resources reached a high of 19.3% in 2011, and the share of exports of manufactured goods averaged more than 40% from 1980 to 2011 on an annualized basis, reaching a high of over 58% in 2001; in the case of India, the share of exports of manufactured goods averaged more than 70% from 1990 to 2011 on an annualized basis, and the share of fuel imports exceeds 30%. The feature is more obvious compared with changes in China's trade structure. The share of China's exports of manufactured goods increased gradually from 47.6% in 1984 to 93.3% in 2011; the share of high-tech exports has averaged more than 25% since 2000 on an annualized basis; IT products account for more than 95% of high-tech exports; the share of China's fuel and ore imports rose from about 6% in 1984 to more than 31% in 2011.

Russia's economic development has long relied on exports of natural resources and primary products. This defect has a number of causes. First, frequent fluctuations in the prices of energy and raw materials on world markets will have a significant negative impact on the economy in that they cause serious disruption to the steady and sustainable development of the economy, and the cost of big ups and downs in economic growth is enormous; Second, the elasticity of demand for natural resources and low value-added primary products is generally small, and large-scale sustained exports are likely to cause a deterioration in terms of trade and plunge the country into the trap of immiserizing growth, that is, with the continuous expansion of exports of primary products, export earnings deteriorate instead of improving, condemning the economy to low-level redundant development, and the lack of innovation, competition and other sustained driving forces of economic growth make economic growth unsustainable; finally, to make matters worse, the heavy reliance on energy exports for economic growth will lead to the shift of factors of production from other industries to the energy sector, triggering a reduction in the output of other industries, which in turn leads to a continuous appreciation of the real exchange rate, resulting in a substantial increase in imports in the industrial sector, further undermining the development of the non-energy sector, exacerbating the structural and proportional imbalances of industries, and causing the so-called "Dutch disease" in the process of economic development.

5.4 *Experience of the Soviet Union and Eastern European Countries in Transition in the Middle-Income Stage and Lessons Learnt Therefrom*

The economic development of the Soviet Union and Russia over the past few decades and the lessons learnt therefrom are rich in content and of great significance in terms of providing precedents for the Chinese economy to learn from, which is in a critical period for economic transformation, to learn from. Especially because China's economic development is has been heavily influenced by the Soviet Union for a long time, it has the distinctive characteristics of extensive development. Based on an analysis of the development experience of the Soviet Union and Russia, we believe that China's future economic development and transformation should focus on the following areas.

5.4.1 *Promote Technological Advances and Improve Capacity for Technological Innovation*

Although the Soviet Union and Russia also attach great importance to investment in education and scientific research, have a well-educated population, and possess abundant human capital and a solid foundation for scientific research, due to long-standing institutional obstacles, their scientific research and technological innovation are mainly government-driven. Scientific research and technological innovation are centered on the defense sector, the role of the market is ignored, no attention is paid to improving the quality of economic development by strengthening technological and innovation capability, the industrial structure is over-reliant on the resources and energy sectors, and industrial competitiveness has not been improved for a long time. Russia has paid a heavy price in its economic development for this.

Like Russia, for a long time, China has focused too much on quantitative expansion and ignored qualitative enhancement in its economic development. In terms of basic sciences and education, China is not only considerably behind developed countries, but also has lagged behind Russia for a long time. With the rapid growth of China's economy, China's investment in scientific research investment and higher education has developed fast in recent years. Although the gap with developed countries in terms of the relative proportion of investment in scientific research and the absolute number of people who have received higher education has narrowed significantly, the problems of low input–output efficiency for scientific research, overall quality needing to be improved, higher education being out of touch with market demand and a lack of progress in the development of vocational education still persist. In terms of the scientific research management system and incentive mechanism, there is no substantial difference between China's scientific research management system and that of the Soviet Union and Russia, the government is still the main driver of scientific research and technological innovation, and the number of technological development and innovation activities carried out by enterprises on their own initiative driven by market competition is still very limited.

Therefore, with regard to the scientific research and innovation incentive mechanism, China needs to actively learn from the experience of developed countries, establish scientific management, assessment, and supervision methods, focus on improving the quality of scientific research, put an end to administrative interference in institutions of higher learning and research institutes, and resolutely reverse the tendency to take a short-sighted view and put quantity over quality in scientific research management and assessment to provide a reasonable and relaxed research environment with orderly competition for researchers. Meanwhile, we should also provide an innovation-friendly environment for enterprises, especially small- and medium-sized private enterprises that have a strong inclination for market competition, encourage enterprises to participate in international market competition through technological innovation, and reduce government interference in enterprises' activities.

5.4.2 *Vigorously Develop Modern Service Industries, Optimize the Structure and Promote Upgrading*

A gradual increase in the proportion of service industries in the national economy and the corresponding decline in the proportion of the agricultural and industrial sectors are a general rule that the economy must follow as it is modernized and goes high-end. Although the development of many emerging economies (including Russia and China) generally exhibits the above characteristics, there are still two outstanding issues.

First, in general, the proportion of service industries in the national economy is still low compared with high-income countries, while the proportion of the industrial sector in the national economy remains high for a long time. Especially in the middle-income stage, the rate of increase in the proportion of services in the national economy is slow. Due to the rapid expansion of the energy and industrial sectors, there has been a tendency of re-industrialization in Russia in recent years, which is contrary to the law of economic development. This not only hinders the development of service industries, but also squeezes out room for the development of the manufacturing sector.

Second, the internal structure of the development of service industries is unreasonable. Traditional labor- and capital-intensive service industries such as tourism, catering, and accommodation, project contracting and transportation account for a predominant proportion, while the development of knowledge- and technology-intensive service industries such as information, finance, insurance, consultation, legal services, and scientific and technological services is lagging behind.

Modern service industries are characterized by high human capital content, high technology content, and high added value. The rapid development of modern service industries will not only directly lead to the rationalization of the entire industrial structure and optimize the industrial structure, but also play a significant role in driving and transforming the manufacturing sector due to a close correlation between modern service industries and the manufacturing sector. Worldwide there has been a growing trend of servitization and informationization in the manufacturing sector. Only by relying on modern service industries for support and transforming traditional manufacturing industries with modern service industries can we enhance the core competitiveness of the manufacturing sector and promote the competitiveness of the whole sector.

5.4.3 *Narrow the Three Inequality's to Create a Good and Stable Development Environment*

Income inequality in Russia expanded dramatically after the collapse of the Soviet Union. Interest groups embezzled state-owned assets and monopolized the state's energy and resources sectors through rapid privatization, leading to division and antagonism between social classes and causing serious social contradictions. It is also because of the long-term monopoly by interest groups that Russia's economic structural adjustment has often been retarded, the industrial structure has long been deformed, there have been major economic ups and downs, and Russia has been repeatedly frustrated in the process of developing a road map to modernization.

Like the Soviet Union during the period of industrialization and Russia during a period of development of more than 20 years, China also faces the problem of income inequality that has been expanding since the reform and opening-up, and compared with Russia, income inequality in China seems to be more serious. According to sample surveys conducted by the National Bureau of Statistics and some scholars, the Gini coefficient in China has approached or exceeded 0.5, well above the World Bank's warning level for income distribution. Meanwhile, compared with Russia, China's income inequality is more complex. In addition to income inequality between urban and rural households, China also has to solve the problem of widening regional inequity and wealth inequality in urban areas. The problem of imbalances in economic development is more prominent than Russia. Although China's national income per capita already reached $7800 in 2015, income inequality has not yet narrowed. There is still no sign of income inequality narrowing. The continued widening of income inequality has become the thorniest issue in China's economic development. In the next 10 years, if income inequality continues to expand, not only will economic growth be unsustainable, but contradictions between social classes will also intensify, thereby destroying the harmonious environment for economic development. China is also likely to fall into the middle-income trap, repeating the economic mistakes of Latin American countries.

The continued widening of income inequality has become a very serious problem threatening the long-term development of China's economy. We must make up our minds to narrow income inequality between urban and rural households, regional inequity and wealth inequality in urban areas as soon as possible. According to Cai Fang, a scholar who has studied income inequality in China for a long time, the leading cause of the deterioration of China's income inequality is the serious inequality of property income. We should approach the issue of income inequality from three angles: increment, stock and income flow. First, to solve incrementally formed inequality, we should focus on institutionally putting an end to intervention by public authorities in the development of land and mineral resources really based on the law and through standardized procedures. Second, to solve the unreasonable stock of individual or group assets, we should focus on regulating excessively high incomes through taxation. To this end, taxes such as inheritance tax and property tax aimed at regulating income distribution should be introduced as soon as possible. Meanwhile, encouraging and promoting employee stock ownership also has an equalizing effect on asset ownership. Third, to solve the income flow arising from unequal possession of resources, we should focus on regulating through legal means.

Meanwhile, long-term institutional building should be carried out in the following areas. First, a substantial reduction in wage inequality requires the development and improvement of a series of labor market systems including labor laws and regulations, such as minimum wages, trade unions, and collective bargaining. Second, policies for improving income distribution should be substantially adjusted, that is, while continuing to implement policies that promote equality of results, we should put more effort into eliminating the influence of special interest groups on income distribution policies, so as to free the distribution, possession, and use of resources from the interference of power and achieve equality of opportunity. This requires reforming the government's decision-making mechanism to make it more democratic, fair, and transparent. Thirdly, more inclusive and equal development of education is the fundamental way to narrow income inequality and prevent the intergenerational transmission of poverty. Finally, the government's efforts to improve income distribution must focus on creating the right balance between economic growth and redistributive policies. Meanwhile, we should prevent the arbitrariness of policies and avoid hurting employment, reasonable consumption, and capital accumulation and investor enthusiasm.

5.4.4 Vigorously Promote the Process of Urbanization and Promote Industrialization and Agricultural Modernization Through Urbanization

The Soviet Union basically completed the process of urbanization in the early stages of industrialization, so the level of urbanization in Russia is much higher than that in China. The key to accelerating the urbanization process in China lies in the urbanization of people. First, we need to build more equitable systems. Promoting urbanization and the creation of equitable systems first involves the reform of the household registration system and the establishment of a system for ensuring equal employment opportunity. Meanwhile, the management system of cities and towns should be more democratic. We should make the relevant decisions of cities and towns as negotiation-based and open as possible, so that more urban residents have the opportunity to participate in and discuss politics and express their demands. Second, we should take the development of modern agriculture as an important driving force. Industry is the economic driver of cities and towns. Without industry, urbanization will be without substance. We should attach great importance to the important role of modern agriculture and industry in promoting the process of urbanization in China. Specifically, the following should be considered with respect to China's urbanization.

First, China's urbanization cannot follow the old road of developed countries or Russia, because it has a different historical starting point. Urbanization in Western developed countries started with technological revolution and industrial revolution, and ran basically in parallel with industrialization. Industrialization promoted urbanization, and urbanization further promoted industrialization. China's urbanization does not have the same historical starting point as developed countries. Therefore, China has to find its own road to urbanization.

Second, China's urbanization cannot follow the road to failure of some developing countries. China needs to draw lessons from the failure of urbanization in developing countries, and promote urbanization based on coordination between urban and rural areas and between industry and agriculture. The reason why over-urbanization occurred in some developing countries, such as some Latin American countries was because they failed to foster positive interaction and a virtuous circle between agricultural development and urbanization, failed to actively promote agricultural modernization, wrongly equated industrialization with modernization, and blindly pursued industrialization without improving agricultural productivity, resulting in a population explosion in urban areas, inadequate food supply, the exacerbation of urban poverty, and the stagnation of domestic purchasing power. Facts have proved that the acceleration of urbanization in Latin American countries on the basis of relatively stagnant agriculture not only made rural areas increasingly poor in development, but also led to urban poverty and crisis, resulting in urbanization going astray.

Third, China's urbanization needs to conform to China's national conditions. As a country with a large population, China needs to achieve an organic unity of development and stability. Building modern agriculture is key to achieving an organic unity of development and stability. Building modern agriculture can effectively guarantee the supply of food, which is an important foundation for national stability. Modern agriculture in turn lays a solid foundation for industrialization. From the point of view of demand, the development of modern agriculture can provide broader market demand space for industrialization; from the point of view of supply, modern agriculture can provide more stable raw material supply channels and lower supply costs for industrialization.

5.4.5 *Comprehensively Improve the Level of Opening-Up*

The process of Russia's opening-up has two main characteristics: first, the volume of foreign trade fluctuates significantly, and the import and export structure is undiversified, dominated by energy, resources, and arms; second, the investment and business climate is poor. Russia has strict restrictions on foreign investment, and the scale of foreign direct investment is generally small. Russia's opening-up bears the hallmarks of extensive growth. Opening-up has not significantly promoted Russia's industrial structural adjustment and economic transformation. On the contrary, it is the long-term dependence on exports of energy and resources products that has led to the severe contraction of Russia's manufacturing industry. Meanwhile, fluctuations in the prices of energy and basic resources products on world markets has directly led to the dramatic ups and downs of the Russian economy.

Compared with Russia, the overall level of China's opening-up is much higher. Especially in the past 40 years, China's opening-up has played an extremely important and positive role in promoting domestic technological progress, enhancing industrial competitiveness, optimizing the industrial structure, and accelerating the process of industrialization and urbanization, with great achievements made.

But there's no avoiding the fact that the level of China's opening-up still has huge room for improvement. We need correct the problem of "putting quantity over quality" when it comes to foreign trade and foreign investment, and improve the effect and quality of foreign trade and foreign investment. Meanwhile, we should encourage Chinese enterprises to go overseas, improve the international competitiveness of Chinese products and enterprises, and switch from relying mainly on labor cost advantages to relying on core technologies and brands in international competition.

6 Summary

Many studies have suggested that phenomena such as class antagonism, unequal distribution, political corruption, and anomie are the social consequences of a country falling into the middle-income trap. But in fact, an analysis of the economic development and social problems of countries caught in the middle-income trap such as Latin American countries, South Asian countries, the Soviet Union, and Eastern European countries shows that the reasons for these countries falling into the middle-income trap lie in a deformed social structure, unbalanced interests, scanty welfare benefits, and administrative inefficiencies, besides inadequate innovation and poorly executed transformation. The experience of developed countries in Europe and the United States, Japan, and South Korea also shows that successful entry into the high-income stage, in addition to economic transformation such as industrial upgrading and transformation, also requires social transformation such as the improvement of the welfare system, the adjustment of the social structure and the balance of political power. The experience of various countries shows that the middle-income stage requires different social conditions than the high-income stage, and social conditions that can support rapid economic growth in the middle-income stage often cannot support economic growth in the high-income stage. Therefore, the middle-income trap is not only an economic transformation issue, but also a social transformation issue.

The experience of some countries in the world in their encounter with the middle-income trap and the lessons learnt therefrom provide useful insights for China to overcome the middle-income trap.

The successful experience of developed countries in Europe and the United States shows that to enter the high-income stage, a country first has to change its mode of economic development, enhance the role of technological innovation and human capital in driving growth, and create more "talent dividends"; take practical measures to ensure that SMEs and large enterprises, as fully equal participants in the whole market economy, participate in market competition and cooperation equally under the same market conditions; effectively ease pressure that will cause the further widening of the per capita income gap to lay a good foundation for the formation of a stable social structure dominated by the middle class.

The successful experience of East Asian countries and regions such as Japan and South Korea shows that overcoming the middle-income trap requires a balanced government structure, extensive basic education, and accurate and flexible industrial policies. A government that is stable and has the appropriate coordination capacity is the key to overcoming the middle-income trap. The so-called appropriate coordination capacity means that the government has formed a relatively sound governance structure, can interfere with the unequal distribution of social wealth, and can implement strong education and industrial policies. Meanwhile, the Confucian cultural tradition in East Asia has also played an important role in overcoming the middle-income trap. Some characteristics of Confucian culture play an important role in technological innovation, the popularization of education, government policy, high savings rates, and social psychology, and are conducive to maintaining social stability and adjusting and calming social psychology when economic growth slows down.

Lessons learnt from Southeast Asian countries such as Indonesia and the Philippines falling into the middle-income trap are mainly reflected in social corruption and government ineffectiveness. Short and rapid economic takeoff hasn't given rise to a middle class in countries such as Indonesia, the Philippines, and Thailand, and national governments emerging from colonial rule have failed to establish a mature constitutional system. The resulting lack of constraints on government power has led to widespread corruption in Southeast Asian countries. The interaction between corruption and social inequality has increased political turmoil and social chaos in various countries, making sustained economic growth impossible.

Latin American countries such as Brazil, Argentina, and Mexico, as typical examples of countries that have been stuck in the middle-income trap for a long time, tell us that they are unable to achieve industrial upgrading and transformation in the face of a double squeeze in economic transformation, and also face a fractured social structure, the institutional inertia of elite control and an incompetent government in social transformation. First, a fractured social structure means a huge gap between rich and poor and the consequent intense antagonism between the elite and the public. High social tensions lead to the proliferation of populism in secondary distribution. Most of the public money is spent on social welfare for consumption, while public infrastructure spending is woefully inadequate, making it difficult to improve the investment environment. Second, the institutional inertia of elite control means that in these countries, the elite who hold the political and economic lifeline control the choice of development strategies. They invariably choose specific policies and measures that pose no threat to their dominant position in order to maintain their rent-seeking activities aiming to obtain economic income and their monopoly of political power. Therefore, any structural change aimed at reducing the power and interests of the ruling elite cannot be truly implemented. Finally, an incompetent government means that the government is unable to make any change, because that means the collapse of the economy; nor is the government able to compel people at the bottom to make sacrifices, because that means political unrest. Latin American governments have been struggling to deal with such a dilemma, let alone to promote economic and social transformation.

The experience of countries in transition such as the Soviet Union and Eastern European countries and the lessons learnt therefrom show that the key to successfully overcoming the middle-income trap lies in whether comprehensive and profound social transformation can be effectively advanced. Countries that have completed social transformation can expand political participation, balance interests and improve the social structure, thus providing solid social conditions for successful economic transformation. Countries that are unsuccessful and incomplete in social transformation will get into a predicament where power is not subject to checks and balances, capital constraints are absent, and social contradictions are increasingly intensified, which will eventually lead to weak economic growth and a descent into the middle-income trap.

CHAPTER 3

Problems and Challenges China Faces in the Middle-Income Stage

The report to 18th CPC National Congress made it clear that speeding up the transformation of the mode of economic development was an important measure to implement the inherent requirements of the scientific concept of development and promote scientific development, and that technological advances and innovation should be taken as an important underpinning for speeding up the transformation of the mode of economic development. We should further implement the strategy of rejuvenating the country through science and education and the strategy of strengthening the country through talent, give full play to the role of science and technology as primary productive forces and talents as primary resources, improve the level of education modernization, enhance indigenous innovation capability, expand the ranks of innovative talents, push for a shift toward relying mainly on technological advances, the improvement of the quality of the workforce, and innovation in management for development, and accelerate the building of an innovation-driven country. At present, China is in the critical stage of overcoming the middle-income trap and transforming the economy in an all-round way, and the existing mode of economic growth is facing many challenges. The key to economic transformation is to transform the mode of economic growth and achieve sustainable economic development. This chapter first summarizes the experience of major economies in overcoming the middle-income trap, and then comprehensively analyzes and summarizes the challenges to sustainable development in China, China's

Z. Zheng, *Middle-Income Trap*,
https://doi.org/10.1007/978-981-15-7401-6_3

economic situation and development stages, China's industries, systems of ownership, regional structure and economic growth, important areas of development, problems and challenges in China's economic transformation, problems and challenges in China's social transformation, and the weak points China has in terms of the rule of law in overcoming the middle-income trap.

1 Challenges to China's Sustainable Economic Development

Over the past 40 years of China's reform and opening-up, China has made tremendous achievements in all aspects of economic and social development, but we should also be soberly aware that China is still at the primary stage of socialism and is still the largest developing country, overcoming the middle-income trap and the road of development. On the one hand, socio-economic and political problems have not been fundamentally solved because of rapid economic development. On the other hand, China is facing tremendous challenges in overcoming the middle-income trap, and at the core of the issue is the sustainability of development. Scholars at home and abroad have done a lot of research on the main challenges and problems facing the sustainability of China's development path, which can be mainly summarized as follows.

1.1 *Restrictions that Unbalanced Economic Development Has Created on Sustainable Economic Growth*

For a long time, the two main driving forces for China's rapid economic growth have been large-scale investment and rapid growth in exports.

1.1.1 Investment

From the point of view of internal demand that drives economic growth, there are significant differences between China and other major economies, which are mainly manifested in the tendency to overly rely on investment. Table 1 gives a comparison of the changes in investment, consumption, and savings rates between China and other major economies over the past 30 years. The data in the table show that in 2010, China's fixed capital formation accounted for 45.7% of GDP, which

Table 1 Comparison of the changes in investment, consumption and savings rates between China and other major economies (1980–2015)

Country	*1980*	*1990*	*2000*	*2010*	*2015*
Gross fixed capital formation as a percentage of GDP (%)					
China	29.09	25.86	34.11	45.73	43.76
Brazil	22.90	20.66	16.80	19.46	18.09
India	17.92	23.82	22.83	31.74	29.26
Russia	–	28.70	16.86	21.23	20.75
South Korea	32.22	37.08	29.96	28.27	29.31
Japan	31.55	31.96	25.21	19.99	23.43
United States	20.42	17.45	20.02	14.44	19.83
Britain	18.70	20.38	17.13	14.91	16.93
Germany	24.23	22.81	21.47	17.44	19.91
Consumer spending as a percentage of GDP (%)					
China	50.29	46.73	46.69	34.58	37.14
Brazil	69.71	59.30	64.34	59.64	63.84
India	74.86	64.61	64.07	55.95	59.09
Russia	–	48.87	46.19	51.48	52.09
South Korea	63.64	51.75	54.62	52.69	49.11
Japan	54.77	53.31	56.52	59.26	56.56
United States	63.44	66.62	69.00	70.85	68.14
Britain	58.22	62.07	65.50	64.20	65.04
Germany	58.43	57.65	58.36	57.41	53.94
Gross savings as a percentage of GDP (%)					
China	–	39.50	36.83	52.38	48.89
Brazil	17.87	18.92	13.96	17.53	14.43
India	16.98	23.11	25.10	34.61	30.59
Russia	–	–	36.15	26.69	30.44
South Korea	23.05	36.80	33.01	31.92	35.88
Japan	31.05	33.93	27.81	23.48	23.59
United States	19.09	15.07	17.86	11.67	17.45
Britain	18.01	15.10	14.42	12.40	15.59
Germany	19.65	22.99	20.18	23.52	26.81

was more than 2–3 times as much as major developed countries and much higher than other emerging market economies and countries in transition.

From 1980 to 2010, other major economies (except India) saw a gradual decline in fixed capital formation as a percentage of GDP, while China experienced a rapid increase. Especially in the decade following 1990, China's investment-to-GDP ratio remained at a high level of more than 40%.

Compared with the development of other major economies, China is very special in terms of both the level of the investment-to-GDP ratio and the length of time the level was maintained. There are two main reasons for China's sustained high investment-to-GDP ratio: On the one hand, it is determined by the reality of China's long-standing high savings rate. The data in Table 1 show that there is a high degree of consistency between changes in China's savings rate and investment-to-GDP ratio. In 2015, China's gross savings rate reached 48.89%, far higher than that of major developed countries and emerging market economies. On the other hand, compared with other countries, the Chinese government is more capable of intervening in the process of modernization. Its leading role is largely reflected in a strong impulse to invest. The GDP competition mechanism of local governments also plays an important role.

Although large-scale investment plays a very important role in improving infrastructure in the process of China's modernization and is also a process that China's economic development must go through, in recent years, investment in China has been increasingly concentrated in real estate and related industries that offer a high rate of return. On the one hand, this increases the risk of a realestate bubble. On the other hand, rising real estate prices severely squeeze out consumer demand and consumption space, resulting in a steady rise in savings rates and a rapid decline in the relative proportion of consumer spending.

The statistics in Table 1 show that consumer spending as a percentage of GDP in China declined from 50.29% in 1980 to 37.14% in 2015. Especially since 2000, consumer demand as a percentage of GDP has fallen fastest. Compared with other major economies, China's consumer demand was very low. Consumer spending as a percentage of GDP in major developed countries ranged from 55 to 70% and remained relatively stable. Although Brazil, India, and South Korea, which, like China, were emerging economies and countries in transition, also saw some decline in consumer spending as a percentage of GDP over the same period, consumer spending as a percentage of GDP in these countries still exceeded 50% until 2015.

Judging by the economic development history of various countries, relying on sustained large-scale investment to drive economic growth is not sustainable. First, sustained high levels of investment will inevitably lead to a decrease in the marginal return on capital, and it is an objective economic law that the stimulating effect of investment on the economy will decrease progressively. Second, a large portion of China's investment goes to real estate and related industries. Although the sustained and rapid growth of the real estate industry will boost economic growth in the short term, in the long run, the real estate industry cannot improve capacity for technological innovation, nor will it help enhance the competitiveness of industries. Only technological advances and human capital accumulation are the lasting driving forces for long-term economic growth.

Moreover, the real estate and related industries are typical highly polluting industries. The dozens of industries closely related to real estate are all energy-intensive, highly polluting, and carbon-intensive industries. The rapid and excessive growth of the real estate industry has strengthened the development space of these low-end extensive industries. Especially in the past 10 years, China has paid a huge environmental price for this. More importantly, the rapid growth of the real estate industry severely squeezes out consumer demand, resulting in the over-reliance of China's economic growth on investment expansion, chronically slow growth in consumer demand and increasingly weak economic momentum. Therefore, gradually getting rid of the mode of economic growth that relies too much on investment as a driving force in the long term and raising the level of consumer demand has become one of the important tasks related to transforming the mode of economic development. Over the years, especially since 2012, progress has been made on these issues.

1.1.2 Foreign Trade and Foreign Investment

From the point of view of external demand and factors that drive economic growth, thanks to cheap labor, a massive market, relatively sound infrastructure and huge human capital reserves, China has become the most successful country in the world in terms of developing foreign trade and attracting foreign direct investment, so it is a model in this regard. In more than 30 years, China has made a meteoric rise from an almost completely closed society to the world's most important trading power, and from a backward agricultural society to a manufacturing center in the world, becoming a veritable "factory of the world." Obviously, foreign trade and an influx of foreign investment have played a vital role in China's rapid economic growth over the past 30 years.

Table 2 gives a comparison of foreign trade and net inflows of foreign direct investment (FDI) between China and other major economies at different time points from 1980 to 2016. The data in the table show that compared with other major economies, China's foreign trade and

Table 2 Comparison of export-oriented economic development between China and other major economies (Billion $)

Country	*1980*	*1990*	*2000*	*2010*	*2016*
Gross exports					
China	51	67	300	1500	2198
Brazil	21	42	81	150	218
India	14	23	73	270	–
Russia	–	210	180	320	332
South Korea	18	49	210	500	605
Japan	180	310	490	750	809
United States	350	600	1200	1700	2212
Britain	–	290	510	670	740
Germany	280	460	840	1400	1604
Gross imports					
China	39	55	280	1200	1950
Brazil	37	36	94	210	218
India	14	26	86	340	467
Russia	–	190	72	250	264
South Korea	27	76	210	430	500
Japan	190	350	500	590	–
United States	350	670	1600	2100	–
Britain	–	290	530	700	785
Germany	300	450	820	1200	1330
Gross FDI net inflow					
China	–	3.5	38	240	171
Brazil	1.9	0.99	33	53	79
India	0.079	0.24	3.6	27	–
Russia	–	–	2.7	43	33
South Korea	0.006	0.79	9.3	1.1	11
Japan	0.28	1.8	8.2	1.1	35
United States	17	49	320	270	425
Britain	10	34	120	61	300
Germany	0.34	3.0	210	28	52

net inflows of foreign direct investment have expanded at an astonishing rate. The total volume of China's foreign trade in 2015 (measured in constant 2005 US dollars) was about 50 times that of 1980. Over the same period, trade grew by an equally impressive 26 times in South Korea and 32 times in India, compared with 5–7 times in the traditional trading powers of the United States and Germany. Especially since 2000 and its accession to the World Trade Organization, China's foreign trade has expanded at an average annual rate of more than 20%, making China the world's fastest expanding country in world trade. As trade was expanding rapidly, multinational corporations were making big inroads into the Chinese market. China attracted $136 billion (Constant Prices, US Dollars) in foreign direct investment in 2015, second only to the United States ($380 billion) and on a par with the seven other major economies. As of 2015, China has absorbed more than $1 trillion in foreign direct investment. Not only is the total amount of foreign capital absorbed the highest among developing countries, but its net inflow of foreign capital is also growing much faster than major developed countries and other emerging economies.

Although China's long-term adherence to opening-up and the path of export-oriented economic development has played a vital role in promoting the sustained and rapid growth of the Chinese economy, the mode of economic growth, which relies too much on trade expansion and massive foreign direct investment, has become increasingly difficult to sustain.

First, the rapid expansion of China's foreign trade is based on cheap factors of production such as labor and land. In recent years, with a sharp rise in the prices of labor and other factors of production, the "demographic dividend" effect has gradually weakened, and there has been less and less room to compete solely on price in international markets.

Second, since the outbreak of the 2008 financial crisis, the global economy has entered a period of difficult and slow recovery and adjustment. External demand has dropped significantly, and China's exports, constrained by the external economic environment, can hardly achieve rapid expansion again.

Third, over the past 30 years or more, especially in the past 20 years, China's rapid export expansion has led to a sharp increase in trade surplus, which has not only triggered frequent trade frictions between China and many other countries, but also put tremendous upward pressure on the RMB. Since the reform of the RMB exchange rate formation mechanism in 2005, the RMB has appreciated by more than 30%, and the profit margin of Chinese enterprises competing in international markets is getting lower and lower.

Fourth, although China's large-scale attraction of foreign direct investment has produced many beneficial effects on economic development, the large number of multinational corporations that have flocked to China are mainly engaged in low-end processing trade activities by transferring backward industries to China. On the one hand, Chinese enterprises make little profit from processing trade, and multinational corporations hardly transfer core technologies and therefore play a limited role in promoting the upgrading of domestic industries. On the other hand, for a long time, in order to encourage foreign investment, local governments have adopted many policies and measures on supernational treatment for foreign direct investment. Although the entry of a large number of low-end, energy-intensive, and highly polluting industries into the Chinese market has played a positive role in local economic development and employment, the large number of foreign-funded enterprises in China mainly use China's cheap factors of production to engage in export processing trade, which has brought tremendous pressure on China's resource and environmental carrying capacity.

In summary, for a long time, while great achievements have been made in the development of China's export-oriented economy, it has brought a series of challenges. Especially in recent years, as the economic environment at home and abroad has changed, it has become unrealistic to rely solely on the rapid expansion of exports to promote economic growth. China's foreign trade must undergo a comprehensive transformation from focusing on quantitative expansion to relying on improving product quality, mastering core technologies and fostering indigenous innovation capability. Meanwhile, China's policy on the use of foreign capital also needs to be transformed, from attracting foreign capital in a proactive and all-round manner to using foreign capital in emerging high-tech fields in a targeted manner and improving the international competitiveness of Chinese enterprises, and from focusing on introducing foreign capital to comprehensively exploiting foreign markets and encouraging Chinese enterprises to compete in international markets through direct investment. In the past five years, China's export-oriented economic structure has undergone considerable changes, and its export structure has been optimized.

1.2 Face the Challenge of Escaping the Middle-Income Trap

In the first and second chapters of this book, we conclude that the characteristics of countries that have failed to overcome the middle-income trap are: decline in or stagnation of economic growth, polarization between rich and poor, corruption, abnormal development caused by overurbanization, shortage of public services, employment difficulties, social unrest, and fragile financial system.

Therefore, all countries have to face the problem of how to overcome the "middle-income trap" in the late stages of industrialization or after entering the middle-income stage. The development of emerging economies over the past 60 years shows that although all countries will experience a rapid expansion of income inequality at the takeoff stage of economic development, only countries that can solve the problem of income inequality satisfactorily in the middle-income stage can successfully complete industrialization and join the ranks of high-income developed countries. Widening income inequality will not only hinder economic growth, but also cause a series of social problems, which will lead to a prolonged period of stagnation of economic and social development, and even serious regression, sacrificing previous achievements in economic development.

Countries around the world have different choices when faced with the middle-income trap. Developed countries use their first-mover advantage to overcome the middle-income trap by leading technological advances and using global resources cheaply. Newly industrialized countries and regions have also achieved the goal of overcoming the middle-income trap through export-oriented development strategies, industrial transfers from developed countries and industrial upgrading. Countries and regions that are internationally recognized as having succeeded in the leap from middle-income to high-income are Japan and the "Four Asian Dragons" (China Hong Kong, China Taiwan, South Korea and Singapore). It took Japan and South Korea about 12 years to grow from a middle-income country into a high-income country. Compared with the relatively long process of industrial revolution in Western developed countries, the experience of Japan and South Korea is worth learning. Although some Latin American countries joined the ranks of middle-income countries in the 1970s, they eventually fell into the middle-income trap because they failed to properly handle issues such as development strategies, income inequality, and economic relations with foreign countries. Some of them are still in a state of fluctuation or stagnation.

In 2009, China's GDP per capita reached $3600, its GDP ranked third in the world, and its population of 1.3 billion people began to enter the middle-income stage of development. How to overcome the middle-income trap as development accelerates is a challenge that China must face. The different characteristics and history of economic development in different countries show that only countries that can iron out the many imbalances in economic development, narrow the income gap and improve production efficiency and the quality of education, and are good at institutional and technological innovation can cross the middle-income stage to successfully join the ranks of developed countries.

The pattern of income distribution in China has undergone dramatic changes in recent years, and has deviated considerably from the original income inequality. According to estimates by the World Bank and some Chinese scholars, by 2015, China's Gini coefficient has risen to 0.462, second only to Brazil's 0.56 and South Africa's 0.63, with income inequality surpassing that of Russia and India, and with a clear trend toward Latin Americanization or Southeast Asianization. The long-term deterioration of income distribution is one of the main reasons why many countries fall into the development trap after they become middle-income countries. As can be seen from the composition of GDP calculated by the income approach, China's income structure has changed greatly since 2003, that is, the share of labor compensation remained at around 52% for 25 years, and then dropped to 40% in 2007 in just three or four years. The reason why income inequality in developed countries is low is that the share of labor compensation is more than 55%, and the share of operating surplus is appropriate, standing at about 20%.

It's a different story for countries that have been stuck in the middle-income trap for a long time. In these countries, the share of labor compensation is less than 40%, and in some cases it has been only 20–30% for a long time, while the share of operating surplus is relatively high, standing at about 50%. A large capital share of income is the root cause of income inequality. As far as East Asian countries are concerned, Thailand and the Philippines are typical Latin Americanized countries, Japan is similar to developed countries in Europe and America, and South Korea is in the middle. The problem of a low labor share of income in South Korea has improved significantly in the 1980s, which is one of the important reasons why it has avoided falling into the middle-income trap.

Income inequality, especially if not improved over a long period of time, will lead to social instability and inhibit consumption, which will have a huge impact on economic growth, that is, a country's growth will face the huge obstacle of insufficient consumption after reaching the middle-income level. Both prolonged lack of progress in urbanization and regional inequality will produce a demand trap. At this stage, policies to narrow the growth gap will not only receive more support from the public, but also promote new developments, because they will drive the expansion of consumer demand, thus correcting the imbalance between investment and consumption.

1.3 Transform the Mode of Economic Development and Promote Technological Advances and Upgrading in Industries

An important reason why countries at the middle-income stage are vulnerable to falling into the growth trap is that the industrial development of middle-income countries is often between mature industries dominated by low-income countries and emerging high-tech industries dominated by high-income countries, and subject to a double squeeze from fierce market competition posed by low-income countries and the technological advantages of emerging industries in high-income countries. In other words, industrial upgrading is of great significance for middle-income countries to escape the middle-income trap, and if sustained high economic growth cannot bring about a steady increase in their industrial competitiveness and technological levels, they will inevitably fall into the middle-income trap.

If China continues down its current development path without making any fundamental strategic changes, it will be caught in a dilemma due to insufficient incentives for innovation and slow technological progress. On the one hand, the competitiveness of labor-intensive industries will gradually disappear due to the rising cost of domestic factors and pressure from competitors in low-income countries; on the other hand, it is difficult for capital-intensive industries to develop strong international market competitiveness under competitive pressure from multinational corporations and when it is difficult to establish their own effective incentive mechanisms. Although China's situation is not as bad as countries that have fallen into the middle-income trap, inadequate indigenous innovation capability in capital-intensive industries and the lack of core technological advantages and competitiveness are undoubtedly a key factor affecting the stability and quality of future economic growth.

To get out of this situation, we need to effectively regulate and control China's real estate industry. The real estate industry plays a very small role in promoting industrial competitiveness and technological innovation, but it consumes a lot of social resources. We should create a good environment for the survival of and innovation in emerging high-tech industries, especially strategic heavy and chemical industries and high-tech industries, so that operators in these industries will not be distracted from innovation by opportunities to make huge profits in a short period of time. Meanwhile, the state should increase policy incentives for indigenous innovation activities, use macroeconomic policies to encourage and support enterprises improving production efficiency, eliminate outdated capacity, technologies and equipment, and gradually improve product quality and indigenous innovation capability.

1.4 The Macroallocation of the Factors of Production Is Inefficient

China's economic growth internally relies too much on investment expansion (largely on real estate investment) and externally relies too much on the rapid expansion of exports backed by cheap factors of production. Both the real estate industry and large-scale exports of low-cost products mean that economic growth is over-reliant on energy- and resource-intensive industries. Meanwhile, the real estate industry and industries based on the large-scale low-cost expansion of exports play a very limited role in technological advances, the improvement of indigenous innovation capability and the enhancement of industrial competitiveness, and also have very limited requirements for the upgrading of downstream industries. Therefore, long-term dependence on large-scale real estate investment and the rapid expansion of exports based on cheap factors of production not only faces growing resource constraints, but also comes at an unbearable ecological and environmental cost. Meanwhile, it will also hinder the normal development of emerging industries, resulting in slow industrial upgrading and difficulty to make big breakthroughs in technological advances and indigenous innovation capability, which has a serious negative impact on the long-term and sustainable development of the economy.

Over the past 10-plus years, China's real estate industry has overdeveloped, which not only affects the efficiency of the macroallocation of resources of the economy, but also may lead to a major financial or economic crisis, that is, there is the risk of a hyper-bubble in real estate. Both the experience of countries that joined the ranks of middle-income countries earlier (South American countries) and the experience of countries that joined the ranks of middle-income countries later (some Southeast Asian countries) show that it is difficult to avoid a real estate bubble. This is undoubtedly an important reason why they have fallen into financial or economic crisis. Therefore, after a country or region reaches the middle-income level, resisting the temptation of real estate is the key to avoiding a financial or economic crisis. The successful experience of Japan, South Korea and China Taiwan is worth learning. South Korea did the best job in this regard. In 1975, South Korea began to implement a heavy industry strategy. At that time, real estate speculation began to rear its head. Bearing in mind the big picture of enhancing the competitiveness of the heavy and chemical industries, the South Korean government adopted a restrictive policy to avoid creating a real estate bubble. Thailand's fall into a development trap is directly linked to a severe real estate bubble that occurred in 1990s.

Here is an important question: Is a real estate bubble always fatal? The answer is No. This depends mainly on when and the degree to which the real estate bubble occurs, that is, at which stage of economic growth it occurs. Japan's real estate bubble occurred after the completion of industrialization and modernization. South Korea basically avoided the problem of a hyper-bubble in real estate. Southeast Asian countries experienced a real estate bubble just as they reached the middle-income level. In the case of China, a real estate bubble may occur before it reaches the upper-middle-income level. However, the earlier the real estate bubble occurs, the greater the relative harm; the later, the lesser the relative harm. In the case of Japan, the bubble is a "result bubble," while in the case of Southeast Asia and China, it may be a "process bubbles." "Result bubble" is not a big problem, while "process bubble" may destroy the whole long-term high growth mechanism, thus plunging the country into the middle-income trap. To avoid falling into the middle-income trap, to a large extent, is to avoid a hyper-bubble in real estate, especially a bubble economy during the strategic transition period of development.

In summary, the current development path cannot be sustained in the new internal and external economic environment. China's economic growth is internally dependent on real estate investment and externally dependent on exports. In the new international and domestic economic situation, China is facing great challenges. In particular, the global financial crisis of 2008 will completely change the traditional mode of economic growth, that is, the situation of US economic growth will depend on overconsumption and the bubble of financial markets. In particular, the 2008 financial crisis will completely change the traditional mode of economic growth, that is, the reliance of US economic growth on overconsumption and the bubblization of financial markets will change significantly, the government will strengthen financial regulation, and consumer behavior will depend mainly on income growth rather than asset bubble expansion. Therefore, it can be foreseen that without overconsumption, the US economy will return to normal during the crisis and remain normal for a long time thereafter. This will make it impossible absorb China's excess capacity formed by high investment, and force it to turn to domestic demand and international capacity cooperation. This is an inevitable law, but also a major opportunity to change the original development path. But the growth of domestic demand will be severely constrained by a series of unreasonable results associated with high growth in the previous period (widening income inequality and long-term failure to improve it, inadequate consumer incentives, overspending on real estate, slow improvement of industrial competitiveness, etc.), while the impulse of Chinese governments at all levels to invest remains strong, which will worsen China's economic situation. The only way out for future economic growth is to change the current imperfect mode of development as soon as possible, reshape the international competitiveness of Chinese industries, enhance the indigenous innovation capability of Chinese industries, and foster new areas of economic growth.

2 China's Economic Situation and Development Stage

With the development of China's economy, China's gross domestic product (GDP) in 2016 reached 74.41 trillion Yuan, ranking second in the world, after the United States. With a GDP per capita is 54,000 Yuan, or about $8123, China has joined the ranks of upper-middle-income countries. Meanwhile, China's GDP grew by 6.7% year-on-year in 2016, down 0.2% from 2015, and economic growth slowed down further. China's economy has moved from high-speed growth to the "L-shaped new normal" of medium-high-speed growth. So, after China enters the upper-middle-income stage, how will its economy develop? What problems and constraints does economic growth face? What are the bottlenecks in social development? In the face of these problems and challenges, it is necessary for us to review the evolution of China's economic development strategy and policy.

2.1 Review of the Evolution of China's Economic Development Strategy and Policy

After World War II, many countries summarized the experience of industrialization and proposed different economic development models such as "import substitution development strategy" and "export substitution development strategy." The United Nations also formulated international development strategies for the three decades of the 1960s, 1970s, and 1980s, making the concept of "development strategy" spread worldwide. The so-called economic development strategy refers to general ideas about the development of the national economy that are overarching, long-term, and fundamental in nature, and overall plans, guidelines, and policies implemented in connection therewith. It is the overall plan and strategy of the state for economic development, generally including the main objectives to be achieved by the economic system over a long period of time, as well as major policies and measures taken to achieve these objectives, or an overarching and long-term guideline for economic development.[1] In 1958, Albert O. Hirschman, an American development economist, published the book the Strategy of Economic Development, which first put forward the important concept of "economic development strategy." Due to the popularity of the system of modern theories after the war, the concept of an economic development strategy gradually evolved from a reference to the strategy of economic growth in all countries to a reference to a strategy for developing countries' transition from a backward economy to a modern economy. For this reason, in China, in the late 1970s, some scholars began to invoke the concept of "development strategy" and conducted special studies on it. After the launch of reform and opening-up, with China's transition from a planned economy to a market economy, not only an economic development strategy was clearly put forward, but it also became the focus of the Party and the government's efforts to govern the country and manage state affairs.

Since the founding of the People's Republic of China, China's economic development strategy has undergone several major adjustments and changes. Especially since the establishment of the socialist market economic system, the economic development strategy has promoted

[1] Li Chengxun. *Science of Economic Development Strategy*. Beijing: Intellectual Property Publishing House, 2009.

China's economic and social development and transformation alongside fiscal, monetary, and financial policies.

The economic strategy of the People's Republic of China can be roughly divided into two stages: before and after the launch of reform and opening-up in 1978. The two stages are distinctly different from each other, as one is the planned economy stage and the other is the market economy stage. Although the transition between these two stages was a long process, from the point of view of the way in which the economy is organized, the economic strategy before 1978 (1949–1978) generally negated the role of the market and adopted a planned and centralized resource allocation method, and the position of the market gradually strengthened after 1978. However, it must be made clear that one thing remained unchanged throughout process, that is, the basic socialist economic system had not changed in any fundamental way. In other words, the state-owned economy's hold on the lifeline of social and economic development, and the core and dominant position of socialist public ownership remained unchanged. The evolution of China's economic strategy is highly consistent with the pace of China's economic development, reflecting the interaction between economic development and the economic strategy. Of course, the two stages before and after 1978 can be subdivided into different stages.[2]

As far as the specific evolution process of China's economic strategy is concerned, because during different periods, China faced different domestic and foreign environments and was influenced by various historical factors, China's economic development strategy took on different characteristics.[3] After the founding of the People's Republic of China, the economic strategy was first aligned with the overall development goal of transitioning from New Democracy to socialism, so the basic thinking behind the economic development strategy in this period was to fully realize a publicly owned economy, vigorously develop industry, especially heavy industry, and lay the groundwork for a socialist economy. After 1956, with the establishment of the basic socialist economic system, developing the socialist economy in an all-round way became the core of the economic strategy of this period. But this period was in a process of

[2] Zhi K. New Advances in Research on Modern Chinese Economic History. *Contemporary China History Studies*, 2002 (2): 96–102.

[3] Zhi K. New Advances in Research on Modern Chinese Economic History. *Contemporary China History Studies*, 2002 (2): 96–102.

continuous exploration, during which the development strategy experienced two major setbacks, and major social and economic problems were surfacing. During this period, the economic strategy was characterized by an emphasis on the development of industry and the strengthening of economic planning and concentration. Under the guidance of this strategy, on the one hand, the level of industrialization in China continuously improved; on the other hand, the highly centralized planned or command economy has led to a gradual decline in the capacity and efficiency of social and economic organizations. During this period, the society as a whole was relatively poor, but social distribution was relatively reasonable. In addition, due to the adoption of a socialist planned economic system similar to that of the Soviet Union, it was difficult to integrate into the world economic system, so the external development of the economy was basically at a standstill. After 1978, the reform and opening-up strategy is not only a national development strategy, but also can be understood narrowly as an economic strategy. This transformation is of epoch-making significance in the history of China's economic development and overall social development. Reform and opening-up, first of all, is economic reform and opening-up. Since then, economic development has become the center of social development. This process can be roughly divided into three stages: 1978–1992, 1992–2001, and 2001–present. Among them, 1978–1992 was the specific exploration stage of the economic strategy under the reform and opening-up strategy. The basic thinking behind the economic strategy at this stage was to surrender part of the profits and delegate powers, and comprehensively enhance the enthusiasm of various social and economic factors. However, due to the lack of development experience, the economic development strategy of this period had the shortcomings of both a planned economy and a market economy. The concept of overall public ownership in a planned economy was combined with the distribution problems of a market economy, spelling trouble for economic development. Then, after Deng Xiaoping's Southern Tour of 1992, the general thinking behind the economic development strategy was to further emancipate the mind, integrate the advantages of a market economy and a planned economy, and creatively put forward the concept of a socialist market economy - that is to say, to maintain the basic socialist economic system and give full play to the role of the market, but carry out strong macro-control. By 2001 or so, a socialist market economy had taken shape after two big strides: the reform of the fiscal dual-track system and the reform of state-owned enterprises. After 2001, China joined the WTO on the basis of adhering to reform and opening-up in its economic development strategy. In the face the situation at home and abroad, driving the economy by consumption, investment and exports became the basic development thinking. China's economy rapidly developed into the world's second largest. However, there were various problems with this economic development strategy, such as the wasting of resources, environmental problems, and distribution problems, which were becoming increasingly serious. Although overall social development strategies related to the economic development strategy such as sustainable development and the scientific outlook on development were put forward in this period or earlier, an unsound legal system and other problems increasingly affected economic development. After the 18th CPC National Congress, the economic development strategy was further improved. On the one hand, comprehensively deepening the reform became a basic task; in terms of ruling the country by law, economic development was required to be subject to the rule of law in all aspects. On the other hand, opening-up gradually "went out," and the "Belt and Road" strategy was put forward. Meanwhile, comprehensive innovation became the motive force that drove economic development. After decades of exploration, the economic development strategy has been improved in an all-round way.

2.1.1 Evolution of China's Economic Development Strategy

Strategy for Building a Planned Economic System (1949–1978)

In fact, for a long time after the founding of the People's Republic of China, China did not explicitly and specifically mention any national economic development strategy. But the general lines, general tasks, general guidelines, and general policies put forward in different periods actually implied an economic development strategy.

China's first economic development strategy after the founding of the People's Republic of China could basically be called a "strategy for building a planned economic system." "Industrialization and three transformations" was as the path to practicing the economic development strategy. After the founding of the People's Republic of China in October 1949, the Party led the people of all ethnic groups in quickly restoring the national economy that was severely damaged in the old China and embarking on the great journey of transforming from New Democracy to socialism. At the end of 1952, the CPC Central Committee, in accordance with comrade Mao Zedong's proposal, put forward the Party's general line during the transition period, pointing out the tasks, ways and steps during the transition from New Democracy to socialism in China. Its essence was to change the relations of production, solve issues surrounding ownership of the means of production and create conditions for the further liberation and development of productive forces. On June 15, 1953, at the enlarged meeting of the Political Bureau of the CPC Central Committee, Mao Zedong made a relatively complete statement on the Party's general line and tasks during the transition period for the first time: to basically realize the industrialization of the country and the socialist transformation of agriculture, handicrafts and capitalist industry and commerce over a fairly long historical period.

The "general line for the transition period" was the first national economic development strategy after the founding of the People's Republic of China. Its most remarkable feature was that socialist industrialization and socialist transformation were carried out simultaneously, with industrialization as the main body and the three transformations as the two wings, and the two adapting to each other, promoting each other and developing harmoniously. The general line aimed to solve the ownership issue by changing capitalist private ownership of means of production to socialist public ownership of means of production. The great significance of this economic development strategy lies in: first, expanding the socialist public sector of the economy; second, basically establishing a planned economic system. This system lasted until the beginning of reform and opening-up. As some studies have pointed out, "From the founding of the People's Republic of China to the beginning of reform and opening-up, China basically adopted a catch-up development strategy that gave priority to the development of heavy industry as its economic development strategy. This strategy and the traditional planned economic system serving it were not suitable for China's resource endowment structure, resulting in the distortion of resource allocation and the general inefficiency of the economy. China had not achieved the expected goal of catching up with Western developed countries."[4]

[4] Lu Wenpeng. Learning, Path Dependence and Later-Mover Disadvantages: Adjustment of China's Economic Development Strategy. *Economic Review*, 2003 (01).

Strategy for Building a Market Economy with Chinese Characteristics (1979–2008)

The Cultural Revolution which lasted 10 years brought China's economy and society to the brink of collapse. In 1978, the Third Plenary Session of the 11th CPC Central Committee decided to shift the focus of the Party's work to socialist modernization, and made the great historical choice of reform and opening-up, kicking off a new historical period of China's economic and social development.

On the economic development strategy, the Third Plenary Session of the 11th CPC Central Committee initiated a new process of rural reform. When discussing the national economic plan for 1979 and 1980, the plenary session put forward the requirement that attention should be paid to solving major imbalances in the national economy and maintaining an overall balance. The plenary session also discussed agriculture, believing that agriculture as the foundation of the national economy was still very weak overall, and only by vigorously restoring and accelerating the development of agricultural production could the country's standard of living be improved. The plenary session put forward a series of policies and measures for the development of agriculture, and agreed to send documents such as the Decision of the CPC Central Committee on A Number of Issues Concerning Accelerating Agricultural Development (Draft) to provinces, municipalities and autonomous regions for discussion and trial implementation. This document was revised and enriched before it was officially released, followed by the formulation, issuance, and implementation of some important agricultural documents, which gave a strong impetus to the process of rural economic and social reform.[5]

The success of the rural economic system reform centered on the "household responsibility system" provided important experience for the state's reform of the urban planned economic system. Since 1984, the reform of urban economic system kicked into full gear. The focus of the reform of the urban economic system was the reform of state-owned enterprises, which proceeded mainly along three lines: first, develop the economy in which the only form of ownership is public ownership into an economy in which public ownership is dominant and multiple forms of ownership coexist; second, implement the separation of government functions from enterprise management for state-owned enterprises, gradually

[5] Xinhua: The Third Plenary Session of the 11th CPC Central Committee (1978). http://news.xinhuanet.com/ziliao/2003-01/20/content_697755.htm.

expand enterprises' autonomy in production and management, and implement the management responsibility system; third, implement a system in which distribution according to work done is dominant and multiple modes of distribution coexist.

On the basis of exploration during a decade of reform, the 14th CPC National Congress put forward the great strategy of establishing a socialist market economic system in 1993, pointing out that the reform of state-owned enterprises should go from the delegation of powers, the surrender of part of the profits and policy adjustment to the stage of mechanism transformation and institutional innovation pursuant to the requirements for establishing a socialist market economic system. In an useful exploratory effort to establish a modern enterprise system, pilot programs on the establishment of a modern enterprise system were carried out at a large number of state-owned enterprises, with them undergoing reform aimed at introducing the corporate system and shareholding system in state-owned enterprises.[6]

Generally speaking, we can call China's economic development strategy over the past 40 years of reform and opening-up, which has gone from the delegation of powers, the surrender of part of the profits and the fiscal responsibility system to the development of a planned commodity economy to the development of a socialist market economy with Chinese characteristics, a "strategy for building a socialist market economic system." Under this strategy, the household responsibility system, township enterprises and rural industrialization, small-town development models, and regional economic development models (represented by the Wenzhou model, the southern Jiangsu model and the Pearl River model) became the main implementation paths for the strategy for building a rural market economic system; the delegation of powers, the surrender of part of the profits, the restructuring of state-owned enterprises, the separation of government functions from enterprise management, and the creation of a modern enterprise system became important operational paths for the strategy for building an urban market economic system.

The reform of economic and social systems initiated by the Third Plenary Session of the 11th CPC Central Committee was carried out under the principle of progressive reform that was described as "crossing

[6]Fu Xiaodong, Yu Jing. 30 Years of Urban Economic Development and Institutional Reform in China. *China Urban Economy*, 2009 (1).

the river by feeling the stones," and took place in the favorable circumstance of international specialization in the fields of economy and industry brought about by a new round of globalization. By relying on its unique resource and labor endowment, building a market economic system, and joining the WTO, China quickly found its niche in the new global division of labor—the creation of an export-oriented economic system. The "three plus one trading mix" became the core business model of companies in coastal areas. This model took full advantage of the large amount of cheap labor released by China's rural reform, catapulting China to become the "factory of the world" and the world's second largest economy. For this reason, Lin Yifu and Cai Fang referred to China's economic development strategy during this period a "comparative advantage strategy."[7]

Economic Transformation and Upgrading Strategy Oriented Toward Global Competition (2009–Present)

The global financial crisis of 2008 was a wake-up call for the export-oriented Chinese economy. Global trade disputes continue to intensify and escalate, the achievements of WTO are negligible, and the profit model of China's economic system is facing major challenges to deep transformation. The factor dividend, demographic dividend, and globalization dividend which have sustained China's rapid economic growth for a long time are losing momentum. The ultra-high-speed growth of exports driven mainly by low costs has gradually returned to normal growth. The extensive mode of growth maintained by substantially increasing the input of resources and capital has come to an end. The Chinese economy still has a long way to go before it can achieve high-quality and high-efficiency economic growth in the face of many external environmental variables, greater resource and environmental constraints and rising costs of factors of production.

Against this background, during the 12th Five-Year Plan period, the state set 24 major targets in the 12th Five-Year Plan for national economic development, including 12 anticipated targets and 12 binding targets, to help adjust the economic structure and change the mode of economic

[7] Lin Yifu, Cai Fang, Li Zhou. *China's Miracle: Development Strategy and Economic Reform*. Shanghai: Shanghai Joint Publishing, Shanghai People's Publishing House, 1994.

development. These targets mainly focused on the economic structure, science, and technology education, resources and the environment, fostering domestic demand, and improving people's livelihood.[8]

In order to cope with the various crises and challenges brought about by the new economic normal, the new generation of leadership is working on a global strategy for economic transformation and upgrading. From the perspective of Western industrial and capital powers, particularly the United States, the establishment of various multilateral strategic cooperation platforms, the founding of the New Development Bank and the Asian Infrastructure Investment Bank, and the launch of the Belt and Road Initiative, and planning for a Free Trade Area of the Asia-Pacific (FTAAP) all boil down to an attempt to challenge the US-led institutionalized financial and trade system. The international hype surrounding the "China's Marshall Plan" is in fact an attempt to push China to the forefront of strategic competition with the United States early.

In fact, as an important part of the strategic transformation of economic development, China's move to build itself into a global industrial and capital power by devising various constructive strategic measures is an inevitable trend of China's economic development strategy. The rise of high-end manufacturing represented by high-speed rail in the global value chain is changing the stereotype that Chinese manufacturing is characterized by OEM (original equipment manufacturer) manufacturing. The continuous improvement of the competitiveness of innovative Chinese companies such as Huawei, Alibaba, and Tencent in international markets is an important indicator that Chinese companies have won international respect. The acceptance of Alibaba by American investors shows that Chinese companies can make a difference in international capital markets. With the acceleration of the liberalization of cross-border renminbi flows, the New Development Bank and the BRICS Contingent Reserve Fund may create a basket of reserve currencies including the renminbi in the future. If the renminbi becomes the monetary capital of the New Development Bank, combined with the China Development Bank, the Export-Import Bank of China and the Asian Infrastructure

[8] Central government portal website. The 12th Five-Year Plan for National Economic and Social Development [EB/OL]. http://www.gov.cn/2011lh/content_1825838_2.htm.

Investment Bank, it will significantly promote the economic development of developing countries.[9] All this, of course, also shows that China's future economic development strategy must go beyond the framework of the international economic and financial order dominated by the United States to actively build a new global economic and financial order.

If we follow the thinking of economists, we can call the economic transformation and upgrading strategy oriented toward global competition a "competitive advantage strategy." In today's increasingly globalized international economic landscape, the construction of such a competitive advantage-based economic development strategy goes far beyond the horizon of labor and resource endowment in traditional economic development, relying more and more on the close support and cooperation of industrial strategy, geopolitics, diplomatic strategy, as well as supporting systems such as modern fiscal, monetary, and financial systems.

2.1.2 Evolution of China's Monetary, Fiscal and Financial Policies

In a narrow sense, China's monetary policy is part of China's economic development strategy, so its evolution is consistent with China's economic development strategy. However, due to the particularity and independence of monetary policy itself, especially its unique significance to the contemporary market economic system, the evolution of China's monetary policy has different characteristics.

China's monetary policy can also be roughly divided into two stages: Before 1978, China's monetary policy was monetary policy for a planned economy. Because money was ideologically associated with the comprehensive criticism and negation of capital, monetary policy was suppressed in an all-round way during this period and the whole social credit system was undiversified and inelastic. The monetary strategy of this period did not exist in the strict sense. The state had absolute control over money, and money virtually had little market function. After 1978, China's economy changed from a highly centralized planned economy to a market-oriented economy, the role of money began to become increasingly important, the social credit system became market-oriented, and the

[9] Zhang Yugui. Seek A Fundamental Breakthrough in the Strategic Transformation of the Economy [EB/OL], xinhuanet.com. http://news.xinhuanet.com/fortune/2014-11/10/c_127195384.htm. 2014-11-10.

state gradually switched from controlling to regulating the social credit system.

After 1979, the People's Bank of China first transformed itself from a national bank to a central bank. Before the socialist market economy was established, China's monetary policy was still focused on the creation of a national basic credit system. Meanwhile, in order to adapt to the opening-up strategy, attempts to reform national monetary policy were mainly directed at the outside world principally for the purpose of creating a favorable credit environment for opening-up. This way of thinking was also conducive to exploring the experience of building a monetary system, and gradually applying the experience to domestic monetary policy, so as to avoid the risks brought about by drastic reforms at home.

After 1993, with the establishment of the socialist market economic system, China's monetary policy became an important tool for the state to regulate the market. During this period, the central bank system was gradually established and perfected, and the People's Bank of China truly became a vehicle for implementing monetary policy. Meanwhile, market-oriented reform of state-owned banks was carried out, a number of policy banks were established, the regulatory system was perfected, and the CBRC was founded. It could be seen that a social credit system with the market economy as its core had been basically established. At this stage, monetary policy has become a key tool to stimulate and regulate economic development. Through interest rate regulation and the comprehensive monitoring and regulation of inflation and deflation, currency circulation was stabilized.

Unlike China's economic development strategy, China's monetary policy reform lags behind the overall economic development. The change of the thinking behind monetary policy often lags behind the economic development strategy. This is because the use of monetary policy requires professional team practice. On the other hand, the use of monetary policy is a double-edged sword, and improper use often leads to a serious economic crisis, so monetary policy must be pursued with caution, especially for China, which lacks experience in the use of monetary policy.

In the era of the planned economy, it could be said that there was fiscal policy but no monetary policy and financial policy. After the launch of reform and opening-up, with the gradual establishment of the socialist market economic system, in addition to financial policy, monetary, and financial policy increasingly became an important support for the economic development strategy. Deng Xiaoping once pointed out:

"Finance is very important, because it is the core of the modern economy. Handling financial affairs well is the key to success in this sphere".[10] This argument succinctly clarifies the core position and importance of finance in the construction of a modern economic development strategy. The process from the economic development model dominated by an inflexible fiscal policy under the planned economic system to the building of a modern financial system in which fiscal policy and monetary and financial policy complement each other under the market economic system with Chinese characteristics marks the gradual maturation of China's modern financial policy. In the future economic transformation and upgrading strategy oriented toward global competition, innovation in the financial system and the systematic construction of financial policy will become an important support for the implementation of the economic development strategy, and even have a direct bearing on the success or failure of the economic development strategy.

Fiscal Policy and Its Operation Under the Planned Economic System (1953–1980)

Under the catch-up economic development strategy in the era of the planned economic system, in order to concentrate financial and material resources to do great things, the state directly regulated and comprehensively intervened in the national economy mainly through the fiscal policy of "unified collection and allocation of funds by the state" and "state monopoly over purchase and marketing."

The period from the founding of the People's Republic of China to 1953 was a recovery period for China's national economy. The Chinese economy was facing serious difficulties. On the one hand, the Kuomintang had left behind a mess with production paralyzed, workers unemployed and inflation running out of control. On the other hand, fiscal revenue had few sources and were difficult to concentrate, while the expenditure was huge, resulting in imbalances in the national budget. Under such circumstances, in order to heal the wounds of war, resume production, develop the economy and stabilize society as soon as possible, the central government must concentrate financial and material resources, so it implemented a highly centralized fiscal system where the collection and allocation of funds was under the unified control of the state. The

[10] General Office of the People's Bank of China. *An Anthology of Policy and Regulation Documents*. Beijing: China Financial Publishing House, 2008.

core essence of this system was that the power to manage the national budget and the power to decide on institutions were concentrated in the central government, and all revenue and expenditure items, revenue- and expenditure-related measures, the scope of revenues and expenditures, and revenue- and expenditure-related standards were formulated by the central government in a unified manner; financial resources were concentrated in the central government, and budgetary revenues and expenditures were subject to unified control and distribution by the central government, that is, local revenues were concentrated in the central government, local expenditures must be examined and approved by the central government, funds required to cover local expenditures were allocated level by level, and there was basically no relationship between fiscal revenue and expenditure.

After "industrialization and three transformations," China established a catch-up economic development strategy centered on heavy industry. In order to implement this strategy smoothly, China gradually established a system of state monopoly over purchase and marketing for the allocation of materials. The system of state monopoly over purchase and marketing was initially intended to solve the problem of food shortage. According to the National Bureau of Statistics, the total urban population increased from 57.65 million in 1949 to 82.49 million in 1954, an increase of 43% in five years.[11] With the development of industrial construction, the urban population continued to increase substantially, worsening the food supply situation. The food panel at the National Conference on Finance and Economics in June 1953 pointed out that the problem was very big, there were not many solutions, and this was a bit difficult to sustain.[12] In the face of the sharp contradiction of food shortages, Mao Zedong asked the Central Financial and Economic Affairs Commission to come up with a solution. Chen Yun, the then head of the Central Financial and Economic Affairs Commission, worked out eight solutions, of which the solution of state monopoly over purchase and marketing was finally chosen. On the evening of October 2, 1953, Mao Zedong chaired the enlarged meeting of the Political Bureau of the CPC Central Committee, at which he listened to Chen Yun's report and

[11] *China Statistical Yearbook of 1984*. Beijing: China Statistics Press, 1984: 81.

[12] *A Review of a Number of Major Decisions and Events (Volume I)*. Beijing: Party School of the Central Committee of the CPC Press, 1993: 255–256.

adopted Chen Yun's suggestion. On October 16, the Political Bureau of the CPC Central Committee discussed and passed the Resolution of the CPC Central Committee on the Planned Purchase and Planned Supply of Grain. After that, the Government Administration Council (the predecessor of the State Council) issued relevant orders and implementation measures. From then on, "all purchases and supplies, purchase standards and supply standards, and purchase prices and supply prices must be uniformly regulated or approved by the central government".[13] At that time, state monopoly over purchase and marketing was not only a means to solve the problem of food shortages in cities, but also laid a solid foundation for the establishment of a planned economic system and the carrying out of the industrialization strategy.

The Gradual Establishment of a Modern Financial System After the Launch of Reform and Opening-Up (1980–2008)

After the launch of reform and opening-up, with the transition of the economic system, a modern financial system marked by the establishment of the central bank system, the reform of the commercial bank system, and the establishment and development of a securities market was gradually established.

In 1984, the People's Bank of China specially exercised the functions of the central bank, and China formally established a modern central bank system, marking the beginning of the practice of monetary policy in the real sense of the term in China. Generally speaking, in these nearly 30 years, China's monetary policy before 1997 was primarily focused on combating inflation and therefore curbed demand; monetary policy after 1997 aimed primarily at combating deflation and promoting economic growth and therefore expanded demand.

After the establishment of the central bank, the focus of the reform of the financial system was to speed up the reform of China's commercial bank system. Professor Liu Hongru believed that in order to establish a socialist market economic system, there must be a new financial system which was compatible with it, and central to the new financial system was the reform of commercial banks. Without the reform of the commercial bank system, it would be difficult to deepen the reform of the

[13] Editorial Committee on Party Literature of the CPC Central Committee. *The Selected Works of Chen Yun (Volume II)*. Beijing: People's Publishing House, 1995: 208.

financial system.[14] Since the beginning of reform and opening-up, great achievements have been made in China's banking reform and development. China's banking system has formed a multi-level and multi-form landscape where five state-controlled banks, 12 joint-stock banks, 147 local commercial banks, several village and town banks, and some foreign banks coexist and compete with each other. A banking landscape characterized by gradually opening-up and all-round competition has gradually formed.[15]

In addition, the establishment and development of a securities market had been an important task in the building of a modern financial system since the start of reform and opening-up. China has managed its economy under a highly centralized planning system for a long time, forming a pattern of "big budgetary allocations and small banks," that is, investments are mostly made with budgetary allocations. With the establishment of a modern banking system, China has gradually strengthened the functions of banks, and credit funds had come to dominate the landscape. But economic development at different levels requires the diversification of forms of finance and the introduction of the market mechanism into the financial market to achieve financial securitization. A securities market should be established and developed, so as to make enterprises fundraisers, financial institutions intermediaries, and financing market-oriented. This model will revolutionize China's fiscal, planning, and financial systems. Therefore, the securities market is an important part of the financial market, occupies an important position in the financial market system, and plays a tremendous role in promoting the reform of China's economic system as a whole. For more than 20 years since the early 1990s, China's securities market has gradually matured, with regulation gradually improved and the market size growing significantly. The securities industry has become an important industry in China's national economy, and has made significant contributions to promoting national economic growth.

[14] Jin Xiaobin. The Thinking Behind and Focus of the Reform of China's Commercial Bank System—Interview with Professor Liu Hongru. *Zhejiang Finance*, 1998 (01).

[15] Hu Xueqin, Chen Yong. Development and Change of China's Banking Industry since the Start of Reform and Opening-up 30 Years Ago. *Chin Finance*, 2008 (17).

Financial Development Strategy Oriented Toward a New Global Financial Order (2009–Present)

For example, since the Shanghai Stock Exchange and the Shenzhen Stock Exchange officially started operations more than 20 years ago, China's securities market has grown from nothing into the world's second largest securities market with more than 2600 listed companies and a market value of more than 36 trillion Yuan. But there is still a long way to go before the strategic objective of building an international financial center is achieved. This is mainly reflected by the fact that the degree of marketization is low, administrative or non-market forces play a significant role in allocating resources, the level of internationalization is low, information disclosure and market transparency are yet to be improved, there is a lot of speculation, and the investment function is inadequate. The underlying causes of these problems are mainly cognitive errors, design deviations, unclear policies and imperfect laws.

Research suggests that in order to build big power finance that matches China's status as a big power, we need to correctly understand the function of the securities market, deeply appreciate the strategic significance of developing the securities market, and push ahead with the market-oriented reform and the strategy for the internationalization of the securities market. We should amend the contents of relevant laws and regulations concerning the approval of stock issuance; focus on pushing for the reform of the issuance system, the adjustment of rules governing mergers, acquisitions and restructuring, and the strict implementation of the delisting mechanism; clarify the order of capital market opening; clarify the sequence in which the capital market is opened up.[16]

2.2 *Development of China's Economy*

2.2.1 *China's Economy Has Maintained a High Growth Rate for Nearly 40 Years*

China's economy grew 6.7% year-on-year to 74.41 trillion Yuan in 2016. From 1978 to 2016, China's economy maintained a medium-high growth rate. Over the past 10 years, despite the impact of the global

[16] National People's Congress. A Securities Market That Matches the Status of a Big Power Must Be Established [EB/OL]. caijing.com.cn, http://www.ctjin.com/ziben/caijing/pinglun/2014-12-30/57347.html. 2014-12-30.

financial crisis, China has maintained high growth, achieving the miracle of ranking first worldwide on indicators such as the economic growth rate, output of major industrial products, grain yield, total imports and exports, and foreign exchange reserves.

The demographic structure and reform dividend are the fundamental factors driving China's high economic growth. The two major demographic trends in China, namely, the "demographic dividend" and "urban-rural transfer," have contributed to economic growth in two ways. On the one hand, producers increasingly outnumber consumers, the supply capacity of the economy is increasing relative to the current consumer demand, and the savings rate is rising. On the other hand, a large number of rural surplus laborers are moving to cities and towns and competing with each other, which inhibits the rise of wages, tilts income distribution in favor of businesses, and increases corporate savings. In addition, the aggregation effect of cities improves labor skills and boosts labor productivity.

Over the past 40 years, China's economic growth has experienced three distinct acceleration periods. These three acceleration periods were linked to three major institutional reforms, reflecting changes in the economic system and organizational form brought about by reform, as well as changes in the competitive environment brought about by opening-up. The first rise occurred in the early 1980s, when the rural reform centered on the household responsibility system was carried out, significantly increasing the efficiency of agricultural production. The second rise occurred in the early 1990s, when Deng Xiaoping made his Southern Tour, the reform goal of building a socialist market economic system was established, and the reform and opening-up efforts were intensified. The third rise occurred in the early twenty-first century, when China's accession to the World Trade Organization (WTO) greatly improved the level of opening-up and increased total factor productivity in two ways: first, with the expansion of imports and exports and increases in foreign investment, Chinese companies participated fully in global competition, which improved production efficiency in terms of technology and management; second, the expansion of exports created favorable conditions for the transfer of rural surplus labor.

2.2.2 *The Quality of Economic Growth Is Low and the Problem Is Prominent*

Economic growth has two dimensions: quantity and quality. Quantitatively, economic growth is an increase in total economic output, i.e., GDP or GDP per capita; qualitatively, economic growth is the improvement of the economic structure and an increase in efficiency. As far as China's economic growth is concerned, the total economic output is already the second largest in the world, but the problem of low quality is prominent.

Let's examine the issue from the perspective of investment, consumption, and exports. First, investment is the main driving force behind China's rapid economic growth. We should fully recognize the historical role that investment has played in China's catch-up development, making up for historical debts and weaknesses, and supporting employment. Meanwhile, in recent years, the marginal contribution of investment to growth and the rate of return on investment have fallen in China. For example, every 1% increase in investment in previous years could boost GDP growth by about 0.8%, but by 2016, that figure had dropped to about 0.3%.

Second, consumption as a share of GDP is still small. In modern society, consumption is supposed to be the dominant factor in promoting economic development. However, for a long time, due to reasons such as an imperfect social security system and uncertainty about future income, China's household savings rate has been high while its consumption-to-GDP ratio has been low. This is one of the important reasons for the idling of massive amounts of capacity and the overstocking of commodities, and also forces China to rely on investment expansion to sustain growth.

Third, exports mainly rely on labor-intensive, low-tech, and low-value-added products. Exports are mainly at the low end of the global value chain, creating a situation in which China's resources amount to a subsidy for the global economy. In addition, because foreign capital makes up a large proportion in some important industries with high-profit margins in China, although China's export volume is high, earnings are low.

2.3 China's Mode of Economic Growth and Constraints on Its Transformation

2.3.1 China's Mode of Economic Growth Is in Transition

China reached the Lewis turning point (a point of transition from a labor surplus to a labor shortage) in 2008, with its economic development entering a stage of slow economic growth caused by a labor shortage and reversed transmission of the pressure for economic structural adjustment. Crossing the Lewis turning point makes it urgent for the Chinese economy to transform from "factor-driven" to "productivity-driven." From 2002 to 2013, the contribution of total factor productivity was only 29%, and 60.3% of China's economic growth was achieved by capital investment. But with the disappearance of the demographic dividend, the limitation of resource and environmental carrying capacity, and rising public debt, the extensive mode of growth relying mainly on factor inputs has become unsustainable. China has entered a stage where progress needs to be made simultaneously in solving "development problems" and "post-development problems." There is an urgent need to harness the institutional dividend through reform to build new driving forces for development.

From an international and historical perspective, China's rapid economic growth in the past 40 years is typical late-mover catch-up growth. China's catch-up growth process is not yet over. The current stage-specific transformation is stage-specific transformation in the process of late-mover catch-up growth. With regard to China's economic development during this period, the academic community has reached two basic common understandings in recent years: first, China's economic fundamentals are changing, the traditional growth momentum is weakening, the potential growth rate is falling, and it is impossible to return to the past near double-digit high growth; second, although the potential growth rate of the Chinese economy has declined, it will not slip to the low level of 2–3% in developed countries at once, but instead the Chinese economy has the potential to achieve medium-to-high-speed growth in a certain period of time. However, it should be noted that the potential growth rate is only a growth possibility depending on factors such as the stage of economic development, the development gap with developed countries and the size of the late-mover advantage, and it can only be realized through hard work. There are three aspects of international experience that illustrate this point: First, there are many countries or regions in the world at the low-income level of development that are very poor, and their late-mover advantages and growth potentials are great, but they have been unable to achieve rapid growth for a long time; second, although economies that have successfully achieved catch-up growth, including Japan, South Korea, and China Taiwan, have similar late-mover advantages or growth potentials at similar stages of development, their medium-to long-term average growth rates are quite different; third, although countries or regions that are not so successful in catching up experienced rapid growth in the early stages of development, they stagnated when reaching the middle-income stage, falling into the middle-income trap. These lessons are worth learning. It can be seen that the current transformation of China's economy from high-speed growth to medium-to-high-speed growth does not only mean a change in the speed of growth, but also means a major shift in growth momentum and the mode of growth. Medium-to-high-speed growth cannot be achieved automatically by continuing the old mode of growth, but needs to be pursued through the deepening of reform and policy adjustment. If we cannot truly build an institutional and policy environment that adapts to changes in the stage of development and is conducive to the transformation of the mode of growth, then not only will the medium-to-high-speed growth potential not be realized, but the economy may slip into the low-speed range and even fall into the middle-income trap.[17]

Therefore, at present, China should make it clearer that reform in the "deep-water zone" and "critical stage" is the biggest dividend. While keeping the economy basically stable and overall risks under control, we should lose no time in carrying out various reforms and accelerate the formation of a quality- and efficiency-oriented intensive mode of growth that suits the new environment and new stage. Meanwhile, we should speed up the cultivation and development of new industries, new formats, new business models, and new areas of growth to promote the transformation of the mode of economic growth.

[17] Zhang Kuojun. Theory of People's Importance. *People's Daily*, 2015-07-13.

2.3.2 *We Face Constraints in Transforming the Mode of Economic Growth*

Changing the mode of economic growth is an extremely arduous and complex task, and there are many constraints that need to be overcome. The four main constraints are as follows.

The Transformation of the Mode of Economic Growth Is Influenced by Views That Regard GDP as a Performance Metric for Officials

In the past, governments and leading cadres in some regions have used the GDP growth rate as a measure of their performance. In pursuit of political achievements, various localities and departments competed on GDP, putting the economic growth rate in the first place, so the transformation of the mode of economic growth existed in name only. GDP is a universal measure of economic development throughout the world, so there is nothing wrong in using it as a measure. The problem is that views that see GDP as a core metric of officials' performance without regard to resources, the environment and people's livelihood have big limitations. Such views on officials' performance only care about the speed of economic development, ignore the quality of economic development, cannot correctly evaluate the state of economic development or guide scientific development decision-making, and only encourage hasty expansion, the launch of flashy projects and the pursuit of scale. In the end, the criteria for evaluating the performance of leading cadres are distorted. Often the result is that people who have killed the goose that lays the golden egg by destroying the environment and depleting resources are encouraged and promoted, while people who care about the cost of development, try their best to protect the environment, and endeavor to increase the happiness of the people are denigrated and marginalized. Therefore, to change the mode of economic growth, we first have to change views that see GDP as a core metric of officials' performance.

There are several reasons why GDP is seen as a core metric of officials' performance. The first reason is the guiding effects of performance evaluation. In some areas, taking economic development as the central task is one-sidedly understood as focusing exclusively on economic development, and GDP is almost the only criterion for the promotion, demotion, dismissal or retention of cadres. The result is "economic development at the expense of the environment." The second reason is the current fiscal system. Under the current fiscal system, local governments mainly rely on corporate taxation for revenues. If local GDP growth is slow or negative, the local fiscal situation will be unsustainable. This forces local governments to pursue GDP growth. The third reason is inadequately implemented market-oriented reform. If market-oriented reform has been adequately implemented, the market has the final say on GDP numbers, and the government can only make predictions and cannot fundamentally change the GDP number for a year, views that see GDP as a core metric of officials' performance will be baseless.

It is impossible to change views on officials' performance overnight. First, the change of views on officials' performance involves how to objectively evaluate the performance of leading cadres. The establishment of a system of indicators for evaluation, the determination of evaluation methods and procedures, in-depth investigation and research, the necessary transparency and openness, the collection and filtering of all kinds of information, etc., are all the basic tasks that must be done in connection with the evaluation of officials' performance, and these tasks are very complicated. Secondly, the change of views on officials' performance is related to the consideration of and trade-offs between various interests. The adjustment of views on officials' performance often involves the readjustment of interests. It is difficult to properly handle and balance various interests. Finally, the change of views on officials' performance is also a process of continuous institutional innovation, change, and improvement, and institutional change is a difficult historical process.

The Transformation of the Mode of Economic Growth Is Constrained by Limited Capacity for Technological Innovation

Science and technology are primary productive forces and also the most fundamental factor determining the mode of economic development. Technological innovation can transform scientific and technological achievements into real productive forces, and achieve economic growth with a minimum of resources, labor, and pollutant emissions. It is the key to the transformation of the mode of economic development from "extensive" to "intensive." Technological innovation is also the key to the optimization and upgrading of the industrial structure. Technological innovation can improve the technological content and intensiveness of the economy, and is the main direction of the development of the secondary sector. A substantial increase in the productivity of the secondary sector will create huge space for the development of the tertiary sector and promote the coordinated development of the secondary and tertiary sectors.

Since the start of reform and opening-up, the conditions for technological innovation in China have improved and the level of innovation has increased continuously. But on the whole, China's capacity for technological innovation is still weak, and the gap with developed countries remains large, which has become a bottleneck in accelerating the transformation of the mode of economic development. The weakness of China's capacity for technological innovation is mainly manifested in the following aspects.

First, enterprises' innovation capability is low. Since the start of reform and opening-up, a number of enterprises with relatively strong innovation capability have emerged in China. But on the whole, Chinese enterprises' capacity for technological innovation is far from being adequate to accelerate the transformation of the mode of economic growth and upgrade the industrial structure. In 1995, the proportion of large- and medium-sized industrial enterprises in China with scientific and technological activities was 56.9%, which dropped to 37.1% in 2008. The proportion of enterprises with scientific and technological institutions was 39.8%, which dropped to 24.7% in 2008. Three-quarters of enterprises have not set up scientific and technological institutions, and enterprises' scientific and technological activities are declining. Moreover, the proportion of expenditure on the assimilation of imported technologies by enterprises is very low. In 2008, the ratio of expenditure on the assimilation of imported technologies by Chinese enterprises to spending on technology imports was only 0.24:1, while in Japan and South Korea., the ratio of expenditure on the assimilation of imported technologies to spending on technology imports ranged from 3:1 to 10:1.[18] The above data show that the development of the vast majority of enterprises in China is still not mainly dependent on the improvement of capacity for technological innovation. If the innovation capability of enterprises as microeconomic agents does not improve and the mode of development does not change, it will be difficult to fundamentally change the mode of development of the entire macro-economy.

Second, the level of transformation and industrialization of scientific and technological achievements is low. China's ability to transform scientific and technological achievements still needs to be greatly improved.

[18] Sun Fuquan, Chen Baoming, Peng Chunyan. Break Through Constraints That Limited Innovation Capability. *Study Times*, 2011-05-16.

According to a research report by the Ministry of Education, there are 6000–8000 scientific and technological achievements made by Chinese universities every year, and less than 1/10 of the achievements are transformed and industrialized. At present, more than 30,000 scientific and technological achievements are made by Chinese researchers every year, and more than 10,000 provincial and ministerial scientific and technological achievements and more than 20,000 patents are obtained every year. The popularization rate of scientific and technological achievements is about 15%. Very few of them have been applied on a large scale and yielded considerable economic benefits. Technological innovations, if not transformed and industrialized, will have no effect on productivity and economic development and therefore cannot support China in accelerating the transformation of its mode of economic development.

Third, China is dependent on other countries for critical technologies. For a long time, China's policy for the advancement of industrial technologies has been mainly "market for technology." China has become so accustomed to technological advances through introduction and imitation that it is oblivious to the need for indigenous innovation. As a result, China has become dependent on other countries for critical technologies. Due to the lack of core technologies, Chinese enterprises are always at the lower end of the global manufacturing industrial chain, the added value of their products is very low, their costs and profits are extremely rigid. Statistics show that foreign investors in China's automotive industry contribute 30% of the capital and own 50% of the shares, but take 70% of the profits, while Chinese capital can only get 30% of the profits.

According to statistics, for every iPod made in China, Apple takes 94% of the profits. The reason lies in Apple's technology. What Chinese companies do is simply putting the parts together and then packaging them for sale. OEM manufacturing makes up the bulk of the business of China's export-oriented SMEs. Without effective breakthroughs in key technologies, China's industrial upgrading, the development of emerging industries and the transformation of its mode of economic growth will face bottlenecks.

The Transformation of the Mode of Economic Growth Is Constrained by Institutions and Mechanisms

Institutions are fundamental, overarching, and long-term in nature, and are the basis for the transformation of the mode of economic growth. Although significant historical achievements have been made in China's reform and opening-up, the task of institutional and mechanism reform has not been completed. The reform is still in a critical period, and the requirements for changing the mode of economic development are far from being met. This is mainly manifested in the following four aspects.

First, the market mechanism is imperfect. The prices of factors of production in China, including labor, means of production, land, currency, energy, resources, and environmental protection, are all distorted. The market is underdeveloped and the price formation mechanism is subject to excessive administrative intervention. For example, land, as one of the main factors of production, is mostly in the hands of the government and has become the main source of government revenue and a means of attracting investment. It is often the case that a government has approved the use of land for decades to come, and the result is to encourage enterprises to expand. The prices of water, coal, electricity, oil, and other energy resources have not been liberalized, and the overall price level is too low to reflect their scarcity. Under China's current mining system, the cost of obtaining mining rights is very low, resulting in a serious disconnection between prices and costs, which causes a lot of waste in use.

Second, market entities are unqualified. The strategic adjustment of China's state-owned economy is not yet in complete; state-owned enterprises are major players in markets; state-owned capital still account for a high proportion in general areas of competition and is still employed on a large scale; the reform of some monopoly industries is still lagging behind. Because of the limitation of property rights, the operation and management of state-owned enterprises have not been fully marketized, and the capacity for technological innovation and resource allocation efficiency of enterprises are low. In addition, the government plays an important role in the economy and often interferes directly with economic activities. Due to a non-standardized government investment decision-making mechanism and an imperfect investment accountability system, decision-makers are not responsible for the consequences of their decisions. Under the current assessment system, governments pursue political achievements and government officials are busy attracting investment and launching projects and would even go so far as to bring in projects that cause serious pollution to the local environment, while areas that really need government attention, such as education, health care, and agriculture, are under-invested. This has resulted in not only a high investment-to-GDP ratio, but also a distorted investment structure and inefficient resource allocation in China.

Third, the reform of the fiscal, taxation, and financial system is lagging behind. Firstly, the reform of resource tax and fee system is lagging behind. The low resource tax policy adopted to subsidize state-owned enterprises is still in effect even though resource prices are rising. Second, financial reform is also seriously lagging behind. Interest rates are mainly determined by the central bank, have not been marketized and therefore cannot accurately reflect supply and demand in the capital market. Interest rates are low, and the allocation of credit funds is often subject to administrative intervention. The low cost of credit funds also induces enterprises to expand their operations.

Fourth, the social management mechanism is imperfect. The labor market system and employment service system are not yet perfect. The order of primary distribution is not yet standardized, the adjustment function of redistribution is limited, and the widening income divide has not been fundamentally reversed; the social security system lags far behind economic and social development, the coverage is narrow, the level of security is low, and the division between urban and rural areas, regions and industries makes social security connection difficult; a public service supply mechanism for pluralistic participation and equal competition has not yet been formed; the social management system is not yet adapted to profound changes in the social structure; a dual system that has created an urban–rural divide hinders the rational allocation and free flow of public resources and factors of production between urban and rural areas.

The Transformation of the Mode of Economic Growth Is Constrained by the Actual Conditions for Economic Development

The transformation of China's mode of economic development is also constrained by the actual conditions for economic development in many ways.

First, it is constrained by the stage of economic development. At present, China's relatively extensive mode of economic development is closely related to the stage of China's economic development. China is in the mid-to-late stages of industrialization where household demand for housing, automobiles, telecommunication products, etc., is expanding rapidly, which drives the rapid development of material- and energy-intensive heavy and chemical industries such as steel, cement, building materials, and chemicals. China is still in a period of accelerated urbanization. The construction of urban infrastructure, highways, railways, etc., on a large scale makes it inevitable that China's current economic development will be material-intensive. Meanwhile, China's economy started at a low level. China still lags considerably behind developed countries in terms of technology and management, making it difficult to completely avoid a relatively extensive mode of economic development.

First, it is constrained by the resource endowment. For example, China's coal resources are relatively abundant, and oil and other resources are relatively scarce, which makes it more difficult for China to adjust its current energy structure and curb environmental pollution. In 2010, raw coal accounted for 70.9% of China's energy consumption. This was due to the fact that raw coal accounted for 76.8% of China's energy production. More than half of China's coal is used for power generation, with about 78% of the installed electricity generation capacity coming from coal-fired thermal power units and 84% of the electricity generated from coal, so the power structure is dominated by coal. It is calculated that every ton of coal burned produces 4.12 tons of carbon dioxide gas, 30 and 70% more than oil and natural gas. Even more serious is the fact that the massive exploitation and consumption of coal have brought about ecological damage and water pollution, which has greatly increased the difficulty of transforming the mode of economic growth.

Third, it is constrained by regional differences in development. China is a vast country with different regions varying significantly in the speed and level of economic development. Eastern provinces that have a better foundation and started earlier in development have a much higher level of development than central and western regions that are relatively backward. In 2016, China had 12 cities with a GDP of over one trillion Yuan, including nine in the central and eastern regions, namely, Shanghai, Beijing, Guangzhou, Shenzhen, Tianjin, Suzhou, Hangzhou, Nanjing, and Qingdao. In 2010, the eastern region accounted for 53% of the total GDP, while the western region accounted for only 18.7%. The eastern region accounts for about 50% of the investment in the second and tertiary sectors and fixed assets in China, and 87.6% of China's imports and exports, far exceeding the central, western, and northeastern regions combined. Regional economic development is extremely uneven, and economic, social, and environmental conditions vary widely by region, making the transformation of the mode of economic development more complex and arduous.

3 China's Industrial, Ownership, and Regional Structures and Economic Growth

This section uses empirical data dating back to the start of China's reform and opening-up to empirically examine the effect of the reform with the market system as the objective of institutional change on the allocation of resources. In this way, we try to explain what kind of value orientation the market system should embody under existing technological conditions for production, so as to rationalize the economic structure through the market. A model-based empirical analysis of the industrial structure and ownership structure of China's economy and the interaction between the industrial structure and ownership structure shows that the economic structure cannot be rationalized by adjusting the industrial structure or ownership structure alone, and when the economic structure is adjusted through the market, the value orientation of the market system will play a key role. A comparative analysis of economic structural adjustment through the market under different value orientations of the market system reveals that the market can rationalize the economic structure only when an institutional environment in which the state-owned economy does not compete with the people (capital and labor) for interests is formed, and the value orientation of the market system focuses on protecting the interests of capital while taking into account the interests of labor.

The economic structure mainly refers to the ownership structure and industrial structure of an economy. Under certain technological conditions, the owners of factors of production put these factors into different industries through profit-seeking behavior in the market, thus forming a certain industrial structure. Because factors have different owners, such as the state or private persons, profit-seeking behavior in the market, the purposes for which factors are used and the organizational forms of factors are different, which shows from another angle that the ownership structure has a strong bearing on the industrial structure. In addition, the industrial structure determines the mode of production of the economy in a certain sense, and the mode of production has a bearing on the production efficiency of factors and the market exchange of factors, so the industrial structure has some bearing on the ownership structure of the economy. When studying economic structural adjustment, people tend to dwell on whether structural adjustment should be led by the government or driven by the market. The theoretical circles generally advocate that economic structural adjustment should be driven by the market. However, in the real economy, the value orientation of the market system is changeable, e.g., either efficiency or equity, so the economic structure depends on the market system. Based on existing technological conditions for production, this study tries to explain what kind of value orientation of the market system can enable the market to rationalize the economic structure.

The value orientation of the market system varies with the degree of market development. For example, in the early stages of a market economy, the market system almost only protects capital in pursuing profits in the market, the whole market system is arranged around how to maximize the interests of capital, labor is employed by capital, and the whole market system seldom considers the interests of labor. The value orientation of such a market system is completely inclined to protect the interests of capital. With the development of the market economy, labor forms organizations, and groups that protect their own interests in the market economy, such as trade unions. As part of the market system, these organizations and groups also play a certain role in the exchange and allocation of factors. In such a market economy, it is impossible for the market system to only protect the interests of capital, and it also needs to take into account the interests of labor. Therefore, in a relatively advanced market economy, the market system protects the interests of capital while taking into account the interests of labor. The value orientation of the market system determines the market operation mechanism, which in turn determines the economic structure chosen by the market. This section will discuss economic structural adjustment through the market under different value orientations of the market system, and present a comparative study of the resulting economic structures.

We attempt to study changes in the industrial structure and ownership structure of the Chinese economy and the interaction between the industrial structure and ownership structure from a new angle, and use such interaction to illustrate that under different market systems, through the optimization and adjustment of the industrial structure and ownership structure, different economic structures will be formed, thus explaining the effect of the value orientation of the market system on economic structural adjustment. Meanwhile, a comparative analysis of economic structures formed by market choices under different value orientations shows that only when the interests of capital and labor are protected, and only under a market system where the interests of capital are slightly more protected than the interests of labor can the economic structure adjusted through the market mechanism be an industrial structure that meets the needs of industrialization and an ownership structure that meets the needs of an advanced market economy.

Under existing technological conditions for production, a model-based empirical analysis of the industrial structure and ownership structure of the Chinese economy and the effect of the interaction between the industrial structure and ownership structure on the economy and an optimized analysis of the effect of such interaction show that under the existing ownership structure, regardless of the market system, the Chinese economy cannot be industrialized through market regulation, nor can the market expand; when the ownership structure is adjusted through the market under the existing industrial structure, if the value orientation of the market system is to protect the interests of capital only, the market will prefer the non-state-owned sector which makes up a larger share of the economy; when the market system reflects the protection of the interests of labor, the market will prefer the state-owned sector over the non-state-owned sector, but at this point, no matter whether the value orientation of the market system is to protect the interests of capital only or take into account the interests of labor at the same time, the economy cannot maximize the size of the economy or market through the ownership structure chosen by the market. The analysis also shows that under the existing industrial structure, although the growth of the private sector can increase the interests of capital seven times, the interests of labor account for only 1/2 of the state-owned sector. Therefore, the market system is more inclined toward the interests of capital and encourages capital to pursue profits in the market. Then capital, whether state-owned capital or private capital, will choose the private sector in line with their own interests. At this point the method of ownership adjustment chosen by the market is to privatize state-owned capital, which not only greatly boosts the private sector, but also develops the state-owned sector in tandem, so as to maximize the return on capital. But this method of adjustment will reduce the increase in the income received by labor by nearly half, which will inevitably increase the income gap between owners of capital and owners of labor. All in all, the economic structure cannot be rationalized by adjusting the industrial structure or ownership structure alone. Therefore, the economic structure can only be rationalized by adjusting the ownership structure and industrial structure in a coordinated way.

When the economic structure is adjusted through the market, the value orientation of the market system will play a key role. When the value orientation of the market system favors labor, or protects the interests of labor more than or as much as it does for the interests of capital, then the ownership structure chosen through the market is mainly an individual economy that is completely and absolutely privatized but has a low degree of organization; when the value orientation of the market system focuses on protecting the interests of capital while taking into account the interests of labor, then the ownership structure chosen through the market is mainly composed of a private economy with a certain degree of organization. This shows that the market will not choose the state-owned economy purely from the point of view of factors' interests, but considering the scale of the economy, the state-owned economy plays a very important role in the construction of the form of market organization (including economic infrastructure). Therefore, when using the market to regulate the ownership structure, we need to leverage the role of the state-owned economy in the form of market organization.

3.1 Structural Characteristics of Regional Differences and Sustained Growth of China's Economy

Significant regional differences in economic development in a country are often regarded as an important manifestation of economic duality and an important indicator of underdevelopment. But for China's economic growth at the present stage, the existence of such regional differences and the ensuing possibility of gradient advancement are, in a certain sense, precisely an important resource and unique development endowment enabling China to achieve sustained high-speed growth. Since the start of reform and opening-up, China's economy has maintained high-speed growth for 31 years, with an average annual GDP growth rate of over 9%. By 2010, China's GDP per capita had exceeded the average level of middle-income developing countries.

In economic history, no newly industrialized country has been able to sustain high-speed growth for 31 years. It is based on this reality that Western scholars have put forward the "22-year limit on growth theory" concerning the high-speed growth of newly industrialized countries in Asia. After nearly 40 years of reform and opening-up and economic growth, the economy of China's less developed regions has undergone profound changes, with progress made in many aspects such as economic system reform and infrastructure construction. Although the development of these regions still lags significantly behind the level of China's coastal developed regions and even lags behind the national average, if these regions further strengthen the development of human resources and infrastructure construction and at the same time capitalize on their advantage in terms of labor costs, natural resources, etc., they may become a new driving force for the next round of high-speed economic growth. The high-speed growth of China's economy in the past 40 years was mainly driven by the relatively developed coastal regions of eastern China. A small country without significant regional differences or a region with homogeneous economic development may experience a decline in growth and even stagnation after nearly 40 years of high-speed growth, while in the case of China, a big developing country that is heterogeneous and unbalanced and has significant regional differences, the objective development gap between regions is likely to form a driving force for gradient or high-speed advancement, thus making it possible for China's economy to develop at a higher speed for a longer period of time. This is where China has an edge over many newly industrialized countries in terms of sustained high-speed growth. This advantage stems from China's objective regional differences that constitute a developmental resource and endowment.

3.2 *Regional Differences in Development Level and Growth Rates and Gradient Advancement*

Generally speaking, GDP per capita is an important indicator of the level of economic development of a region, and the average annual growth rate of GDP reflects the economic vitality of a region. The two reflect the level of economic development of a region from a static and dynamic point of view, respectively. The static level is the result of dynamic growth, and dynamic growth is based on the static level. According to the current level of GDP per capita and the average annual growth rate of Chinese regions in recent years, the regions can be classified by dynamic and static level into the following categories.

1. Economically developed regions that statically have the highest GDP per capita and dynamically have the fastest growth

   The economic triangle with Shanghai, Guangdong, and Beijing as its vertices, including the Yangtze River Delta (Shanghai, Zhejiang, and Jiangsu), the Pearl River Delta (Guangdong and Fujian), and the Beijing-Tianjin region. From a static point of view, these regions rank the highest in terms of GDP per capita in China; from a dynamic point of view, these regions have been the fastest growing regions since the start of reform and opening-up.

2. Fairly economically developed regions that statically have a fairly high GDP per capita, dynamically have a fairly high growth rate, and are well above the national average on both metrics

   These regions include Shandong, Hebei and other regions around the Bohai Bay. Because they are located in coastal regions and close to the Beijing-Tianjin region, and have a good industrial foundation, they have a strong geographical advantage in future economic development and opening-up. Although their GDP per capita at the present stage is not as good as that of economically developed regions, but is significantly higher than the national average, and their average annual growth rate in recent years is also significantly higher than the national average growth rate for the same period.

3. Northeast China which statically has a fairly high GDP per capita, but dynamically is generally close to the national average in terms of the growth rate in recent years

   The three northeastern provinces have abundant resources and a good industrial foundation. Their GDP per capita has been at a high level, but their economic growth has been mediocre since the start of reform and opening-up. In recent years, the promulgation of the national "Plan of Revitalizing Northeast China" has provided conditions for the accelerated growth of the region in the future.

4. Chinese inland regions that statically have a moderate GDP per capita and dynamically have a moderate growth rate

   These regions include Henan, Shanxi, Hunan, Hubei, Jiangxi, Anhui, Sichuan, and Shaanxi.

5. Regions inhabited by ethnic minorities that have a relatively low GDP per capita, but have grown particularly rapidly in recent years

   These regions include Tibet, Ningxia, Qinghai, and Inner Mongolia. Due to various historical, realistic, natural, and social reasons, these regions have long been economically poor in China, with a relatively low GDP per capita. But in recent years, due to the State's strong support, the economy of these regions has developed particularly fast at a rate above the national average for the same period.

6. Remote regions with the lowest GDP per capita and GDP growth rate in China

   These regions include Guizhou, Yunnan, Gansu, and Guangxi.

   In short, regional imbalances in development in China, a big developing country in the accelerated phase of industrialization, whether they are regional differences in level of economic development and economic growth rate, regional differences in the height of the industrial structure, or regional differences in the characteristics of changes in investment and consumer demand, pose a great challenge to China's modernization, but they are also an important developmental condition and resource enabling China to maintain high-speed growth for a longer period of time than developed countries and small developing countries in general. The question is whether we can truly transform the potential advantage in terms of sustainable development stemming from this developmental resource and imbalance into wealth and a real development miracle by formulating the right development strategy, economic system, and economic policy.

3.3 Regional Economic Structure and Balanced Development in China

We studied and analyzed the impact of the economic structure of the three economic zones of eastern, central, and Western China on the economy. The findings show that a primary market economic structure conducive to absorbing capital and labor has taken shape in the eastern economic zone, the economic structure of the central economic zone is distinctly characterized by deindustrialization, and the Western economic zone is characterized by an agriculturalized economic structure.

The analysis shows that these economic structural characteristics are not conducive to the expansion of the overall economic scale of various regions, that is, they are not conducive to promoting the deepening of specialization and social division of labor in various regions, and to the formation of a high-level market economic system. In view of the regional differences in economic structure, the study holds that in order to promote regional balance in economic development, the government must play a guiding role by intervening instead of relying solely on market regulation. In guiding the economic structural adjustment of various regions, the government should emphasize the development of a mixed ownership economy and individual economy, and in the eastern region, it should emphasize the development of tertiary industries, especially commercial and financial tertiary industries; in the central region, it should emphasize the development of secondary industries, especially industrialization; and in the western region, it should emphasize the development of tertiary industries, especially tertiary industries related to environmental protection, tourism, culture, technology, and defense. Moreover, such economic structural adjustment must also be accompanied by a planned transfer of labor from the Western economic zone to the eastern economic zone and the central economic zone.

Economic growth and income distribution or balanced development is often discussed by economists under the topic of "efficiency and equity." However, it is meaningless to simply analyze economic efficiency and equity independently of a certain level of economic development, because the answer to the question of whether efficiency should be prioritized over equality or vice versa varies depending on the level of economic development. According to an economic analysis by Reberto Perotti (1993), there is an inverted U-shaped relation between levels of inequality and levels of income. He pointed out that in the real world of economics, a poor and backward country would have difficulty starting the pace of economic development if it adopted an egalitarian policy; on the contrary, if an unequal income distribution policy was adopted, the economy would be more likely to achieve high-speed growth in the initial stage. However, when a country reaches a certain (or higher) level of economic development, unequal income distribution or unbalanced economic development will impede further economic development. China's economic development level has reached the per capita income of $1000, and the next goal is to attain the well-off level of $3000. It has become increasingly important to balance regional development and narrow the income gap between factors. However, it is not easy for China to fully achieve balanced regional economic development. The reason is simple: Such differences in the level of economic development are not simply about the aggregate, and are based on differences in economic structure and resource conditions. Therefore, in order to understand balanced regional economic development, we must first analyze and explain the basis of such regional differences in economic structure.

Under certain technological and resource conditions, an economy will form a certain industrial structure through specialization and division of labor in society in a certain factor ownership environment. Kuznets

(1949) believed that industrial structure, in a certain sense, determined the mode of economic growth. As early as 1949, when discussing the measurement of national income, Kuznets pointed out that the national income of a country must be measured from the perspective of the industrial structure, and the industrial structure of an economy was determined by its mode of production. To this end, Kuznets (1957) compared empirical data from 50 countries and found that the growth of the manufacturing sector would be accompanied by an increase in per capita income. Therefore, people think it is necessary to study and analyze economic growth from the perspective of the industrial structure. To this end, Chenery (1960), starting with an analysis of the determinants of sector growth, used empirical data from 51 countries to show that when the size of the economy of a country in the process of industrialization changes, the service and agricultural sectors change the least, while the manufacturing sector grows the most, whereupon he proposed a mode of industrial growth, believing that this mode of industrialization could optimize the allocation of resources. Many economists have illustrated the mode of industrialization of economic growth from different perspectives using empirical data from different countries (Beason and Weinstein, 1996; Lee, 1981; Sacks, 1972; Ueno, 1972). But some economists (Gregory and Griffin, 1974) found that there were plenty of economic facts that contradicted Chenery's mode of economic growth. They showed through empirical data that when per capita income was very high, the rapid growth of the service sector would reduce the scale elasticity of the manufacturing sector. However, these studies have ignored a very important influencing factor, that is, under certain technological conditions and a certain industrial structure, different types of factor ownership will also have an important impact on the mode of economic growth. Some scholars have performed an empirical analysis of the interaction between the industrial structure and ownership structure in China's economic structure, which shows that in the Chinese economy which is undergoing market-oriented transformation, the economic structure cannot achieve a state that meets the reasonable needs of sound economic growth by adjusting the industrial structure or factor ownership structure alone. This also explains why both the factor ownership structure and industrial structure in China's economic structure are not compatible with the current level of development of production technology. Therefore, only by coordinating the ownership structure and industrial structure in the economic structure, can the economic structure be adjusted to a state that is most favorable to economic growth. This shows from another angle that in analyzing China's economic growth, ignoring coordination between the ownership structure and industrial structure will result in a cognitive bias, so only by taking both the ownership structure and industrial structure as control variables can we correctly understand the influence of the economic structure on China's economic growth.

We explain regional differences in economic structure from the point of view of the contribution of the regional economic structure, especially the industrial structure and factor ownership structure, to regional economic growth, and thus illustrate the development strategy of balancing regional economic development and narrowing the income gap between factors, especially the Western economic development strategy.

3.3.1 *Influence of the Economic Structure of the Eastern Region on the Economy*

From the analysis of the influence of the economic structure of China's eastern economic zone on the economy, it can be seen that in the current economic structure, raising the share of the tertiary sector in the industrial structure, and at the same time increasing the proportion of the employees of mixed ownership enterprises and self-employed individuals in the workforce can deepen specialization and division of labor in society in the economic zone, thus greatly expanding the overall size of the economy. However, under the current factor ownership structure, any increase in the share of the tertiary sector will improve the productivity of capital and reduce the productivity of labor, and the distribution of market-oriented factors is based on the productivity of factors. This means that in a market economy, any increase in the share of the tertiary sector will increase income derived from capital and reduce income derived from labor. Under the current industrial structure, any increase in the proportion of self-employed individuals in the workforce will reduce the productivity of capital, and thus reduce income derived from capital.

Therefore, under market-oriented conditions, if the economic structure is adjusted entirely by the profit-making behavior of the owners of capital and the owners of labor, there will be no economic structural adjustment in the eastern economic zone that is conducive to the improvement of specialization and division of labor in society, namely, increasing the proportion of the employees of mixed ownership enterprises and self-employed individuals in the workforce and the share of the tertiary sector. However, since any increase in the proportion of the employees of private enterprises in the workforce can increase income derived from capital and labor, if the economic structure of the eastern region is adjusted solely through the market behavior of factor owners, there will be a tendency of privatization in the economy, and the privatization of the economy will be accompanied by large amounts of capital and labor inputs. In other words, privatization in the eastern region will help attract funds and labor from outside the region to boost economic growth. However, such privatization is not conducive to specialization and division of labor in society, that is, it cannot expand the overall size of the economy. Therefore, the economic privatization in the eastern region will not improve and perfect the market system as one might imagine. On the contrary, it will hinder the formation of a higher level market system marked by deep specialization and division of labor in society. What the market realizes in economic structure adjustment is only a low-level and simple form of market organization that can attract large amounts of capital and labor inputs.

3.3.2 *Influence of the Economic Structure of the Central Region on the Economy*

From a qualitative point of view, in the eastern economic zone, under the established factor ownership structure, any increase in the share of the primary sector will reduce the overall size of the economy, but at the same time improve the productivity of capital and labor; any increase in the share of the secondary sector will reduce the overall size of the economy and improve the productivity of capital, but will reduce the productivity of labor, only the impact on the overall size of the economy is statistically insignificant; any increase in the share of the tertiary sector will reduce the overall size of the economy, but at the same time improve the productivity of capital and labor. In the central region, under the established industrial structure, any increase in the proportion of the employees of state-owned enterprises in the workforce will reduce the overall size of the economy, but at the same time improve the productivity of capital and labor, only the impact on the productivity of capital is statistically insignificant; any increase in the proportion of the employees of private enterprises in the workforce will reduce the overall size of the economy, but will improve the productivity of capital and labor, only the impact on the overall size of the economy and the productivity of labor is statistically insignificant; any increase in the proportion of self-employed individuals in the workforce will expand the overall size of the economy, but at the same time reduce the productivity of capital and labor. In the eastern economic zone, under the established industrial structure, any increase in the proportion of the employees of mixed ownership enterprises in the workforce will expand the overall size of the economy.

From the analysis of the influence of the economic structure of the central economic zone on the economy, it can be seen that in the current economic structure, reducing the share of the primary or tertiary sector in the industrial structure, and at the same time increasing the proportion of the employees of mixed ownership enterprises and self-employed individuals in the workforce can deepen specialization and division of labor in society in the central economic zone, thus greatly expanding the overall size of the economy. However, in the central region, under the current factor ownership structure, any increase in the share of the primary or tertiary sector in the industrial structure will improve the productivity of capital and labor, and thus increase income derived from capital and labor. Under the current industrial structure, any increase in the proportion of self-employed individuals in the workforce will improve the productivity of capital, but at the same time reduce the productivity of labor. In other words, it will increase income derived from capital and reduce income derived from labor. Therefore, under market-oriented conditions, if the economic structure is adjusted entirely by the profit-making behavior of the owners of capital and the owners of labor, there will be no economic structural adjustment in the central economic zone that can deepen specialization and division of labor in society, namely, reducing the share of the primary or tertiary sector in the industrial structure, and at the same time increasing the proportion of the employees of mixed ownership enterprises and self-employed individuals in the workforce. It is found that the economic structure of the central economic zone is actually distinctly characterized by deindustrialization, that is, it has not yet formed an economic structure whereby the economic zone can be industrialized through market regulation. The main reason for this is that under the current factor ownership structure, it is not yet possible to form an industrialization process that enables both the owners of capital and the owners of labor in the market to achieve a Pareto improvement. Under the current factor ownership structure, increasing the share of the secondary sector in the industrial structure will increase income derived from capital, but at the same time reduce income derived from labor.

3.3.3 *Influence of the Economic Structure of the Western Region on the Economy*

From a qualitative point of view, in the Western economic zone, under the established factor ownership structure, any increase in the share of the primary sector will reduce the overall size of the economy, but at the same time improve the productivity of capital and labor, only the impact on the productivity of labor is statistically insignificant; any increase in the share of the secondary sector will reduce the overall size of the economy and improve the productivity of capital and labor, only the impact on the overall size of the economy and the productivity of capital is statistically insignificant; any increase in the share of the tertiary sector will increase the overall size of the economy and improve the productivity of capital, but will reduce the productivity of labor, only the impact on the overall size of the economy is statistically insignificant. In the western region, under the established industrial structure, any increase in the proportion of the employees of state-owned enterprises in the workforce will reduce the overall size of the economy and reduce the productivity of labor, but will improve the productivity of capital, only the impact on the productivity of labor is statistically insignificant; any increase in the proportion of the employees of private enterprises in the workforce will reduce the overall size of the economy, but will improve the productivity of capital and labor, only the impact on the productivity of labor is statistically insignificant; any increase in the proportion of self-employed individuals in the workforce will expand the overall size of the economy, reduce the productivity of capital and improve the productivity of labor. As in the eastern and central economic zones, in the Western economic zone, under the established industrial structure, any increase in the share of the employees of mixed ownership enterprises in the workforce will also expand the overall size of the economy.

From the analysis of the economic structure of the Western economic zone, it can be seen that in the current economic structure, lowering the share of the primary sector in the industrial structure, and at the same time reducing the proportion of the employees of state-owned enterprises and private enterprises and increasing the proportion of the employees of mixed ownership enterprises and self-employed individuals in the workforce can deepen specialization and division of labor in society in the Western economic zone, thus greatly expanding the overall size of the economy. However, in the western region, under the current factor ownership structure, any increase in the share of the primary sector in the industrial structure will improve the productivity of capital and labor, and thus increase income derived from capital and labor, only the impact on income derived from labor is statistically insignificant. In the western region, under the current industrial structure, reducing the proportion of the employees of state-owned enterprises and private enterprises in the workforce will have no significant impact on the productivity of labor, but will significantly reduce the productivity of capital, and thus reduce income derived from capital. Any increase in the proportion of self-employed individuals in the workforce will improve the productivity of labor, but at the same time reduce the productivity of capital. In other words, it will increase income derived from labor and reduce income derived from capital. Therefore, under market-oriented conditions, if the economic structure is adjusted entirely by the profit-making behavior of the owners of capital and the owners of labor, there will be no economic structural adjustment in the central economic zone that can deepen specialization and division of labor in society, namely, lowering the share of the primary sector in the industrial structure, and at the same time reducing the proportion of the employees of state-owned enterprises and private enterprises and increasing the proportion of the employees of mixed ownership enterprises and self-employed individuals in the workforce.

It is found that the economic structure of the Western economic zone is actually distinctly characterized by agriculturalization, that is, it has not yet formed an economic structure whereby the economic zone can be de-agriculturalized through market regulation. The main reason for this is that under the current factor ownership structure, it is not yet possible to form an de-agriculturalization process that enables both the owners of capital and the owners of labor in the market to achieve a Pareto improvement. Under the current factor ownership structure, in the process of de-agriculturalization in the western region, namely, increasing the share of the secondary and tertiary sectors in the industrial structure, the economic significance of increasing the share of the secondary sector is different from that of increasing the share of the tertiary sector. From the point of view of the size of the economy, neither has a significant impact on the size of the economy, but the potential impact of the secondary sector on the size of the economy is negative, while the impact of the tertiary sector is positive, so from the point of view of expanding the size of the economy, the process of de-agriculturalization in the western region should focus on increasing the share of the tertiary sector. From the point of view of the efficiency of factors, increasing the share of the secondary sector seems to improve the productivity of both capital and labor in the western region, and thus increase income derived from both factors, giving rise to a market-oriented process that represents a Pareto improvement in the western region. This is one of the important reasons why people naturally associate Great Western Development with the development of industry in the western region. But the efficiency improvement is quantitatively minimal, with no obvious impact on capital. The impact on labor is also very small quantitatively. However, increasing the share of the tertiary sector in the industrial structure has a very obvious impact on the factors, only the impact on the productivity of capital is positive, and the impact on the productivity of labor is negative. This negative impact arises from an increase in inputs of labor and will become positive if inputs of labor decrease. Therefore, as long as there is labor migration in the western region, increasing the share of the tertiary sector will significantly improve the productivity of capital and labor, and thus increase income derived from capital and labor, giving rise to a market-oriented economic structural adjustment that represents a Pareto improvement in the western region.

3.4 Research Implications

Through the analysis of the economic structure of the eastern, central and Western economic zones of China, we find that in the process of transition to a market economy that began with the start of reform and opening-up, in the existing economic structure that enables the eastern economic zone, the leader in China's modernization, to participate in high-level international competition, raising the share of the tertiary sector in the industrial structure, and at the same time increasing the proportion of the employees of mixed ownership enterprises and self-employed individuals will greatly expand the overall size of the economy, but such economic structural adjustment cannot be achieved through market behavior alone. Moreover, in the economic structure of the eastern region, privatization will increase the production elasticity of capital and labor, and thus attract large amounts of capital and labor inputs into the eastern region through the market, and increase income derived from capital and labor to promote economic growth. However, such privatization is not conducive to specialization and division of labor in society, that is, instead of expanding the overall size of the economy, it will hinder the progression of the market system to a higher level.

In the current economic structure of the central economic zone, reducing the share of the primary or the tertiary sector in the industrial structure, and at the same time increasing the proportion of the employees of mixed ownership enterprises and self-employed individuals in the workforce will greatly expand the overall size of the economy. But such economic structural adjustment cannot be achieved in the central economic zone through market regulation alone. Moreover, the economic structure of the central economic zone is actually distinctly characterized by de-agriculturalization, that is, deindustrialization enables the owners of capital and the owners of labor to achieve a Pareto improvement through the market, while industrialization only increases income derived from capital, and reduces income derived from labor.

In the current economic structure of the Western economic zone, lowering the share of the primary sector in the industrial structure, and at the same time reducing the proportion of the employees of state-owned enterprises and private enterprises and increasing the proportion of the employees of mixed ownership enterprises and self-employed individuals in the workforce can greatly expand the overall size of the economy, but such economic structural adjustment cannot be carried out through the market alone. Moreover, the economic structure of the Western economic zone is actually distinctly characterized by agriculturalization, that is, under the current economic structure, if the economy is regulated by the market alone, the economy will be agriculturalized to form a typical agricultural economy.

The above analysis shows that the economic structures of China's eastern, central and Western economic zones are quite different, as mainly reflected in the fact that a primary market economic structure capable of absorbing capital and labor in large amounts has taken shape in the eastern economic zone, the economic structure of the central economic zone is distinctly characterized by deindustrialization, and the Western economic zone is characterized by an agriculturalized economic structure. However, the characteristics of the economic structures of the economic zones are not conducive to the expansion of the overall size of the economies of the regions, that is, they are not conducive to the deepening of specialization and division of labor in society in the regions, as well as the formation of a high-level market economic system. Therefore, balanced economic development between regions cannot be achieved by relying on the regulatory power of the market alone, and market regulation will promote changes to the economic structure that are unfavorable for the further development of the economies of the regions. For this reason, the government's guiding intervention plays a key role in coordinating the economic development of the regions. In guiding the economic structural adjustment of various regions, the government should emphasize the development of a mixed ownership economy and individual economy, and in the eastern region, it should emphasize the development of tertiary industries, especially commercial and financial tertiary industries; in the central region, it should emphasize the development of secondary industries, especially industrialization; and in the western region, it should emphasize the development of tertiary industries, especially tertiary industries related to environmental protection, tourism, culture, technology, and defense. Moreover, such economic structural adjustment must also be accompanied by a planned transfer of labor from the Western economic zone to the eastern economic zone and the central economic zone.

4 Problems and Challenges in China's Economic Transformation

Since 1978, thanks to the demographic and reform dividends, China's economy has maintained high-speed growth. However, as China comes near the end of the middle-income stage, its original extensive mode of economic growth is no longer sustainable, and its economic development and transformation are faced with many challenges.

4.1 Imbalances in the Economic Structure

Generally speaking, the current structural contradictions in China's economy are mainly manifested in the following aspects.

First, the demand structure is unbalanced. The first is the imbalance between domestic and external demand. Although export dependence has declined since the financial crisis, as of 2016, the ratio was still as high as 19.6%, 3 percentage points higher than that of Japan and 7 percentage points higher than that of the United States. The second is the imbalance between investment and consumption. In recent years, with the decline of export-led growth, the contribution of investment and consumption to economic growth has increased. But the contribution of investment has grown even more: from 2007 to 2015, final consumption expenditure as a share of GDP rose by 1.81 percentage points, and gross capital formation as a share of GDP rose by 3.9 percentage points. The contradiction between investment and consumption that has existed for many years hasn't been resolved yet and is still growing.

Second, the industrial structure is unbalanced. In 2016, the ratio of the value added of the primary sector to that of the secondary sector to that of the tertiary sector in China was 8.56:39.81:51.63, which is in line with the current stage of China's development. But the contradictions in China's industrial structure mainly exist in the secondary and tertiary sectors. In the secondary sector, structural contradictions are manifested in the fact that there is serious overcapacity in energy-intensive and highly polluting industries such as heavy and chemical industries, the manufacturing industry is large but not strong, is still at the middle and lower end of the global value chain as a whole, and has difficulty adapting to changes in international and domestic demand, products are of low quality and uncompetitive, and there is a lack of influential brands and products. In the tertiary industry, structural contradictions are manifested in the fact that the overall competitiveness is not strong, the modern service industry is underdeveloped, weaknesses in the field of people's livelihood are prominent, and the support for the primary and secondary sectors is inadequate. China runs a trade surplus in goods, which reached \$512.7 billion in 2016, but it runs a trade deficit in goods, which reached \$242.2 billion in 2016. This reflects the fact that the overall competitiveness of China's service industry is not strong.

Third, the market competition structure is unbalanced. At present, the development quality of SMEs, which are the main participants in market competition in most industries in China, are not high, and their competitiveness is not strong; there are low-level competition, insufficient concentration and a lack of internationally competitive and influential multinational companies in the Chinese market.

In general, although economic imbalances are multifaceted and the influencing factors are complex, unbalanced distribution of income is the crux of the problem. Widening income inequality leads to a decline in the overall consumption-to-GDP ratio, a rise in the savings rate, and high levels of investment and exports. As a result, the industrial structure is biased toward industry and manufacturing, and the service industries, which are closely linked to consumption, are lagging behind in development. An industrial structure that is inclined toward industry creates a relatively high demand for resources, putting a lot of pressure on the environment.

4.2 *Disappearance of the Demographic Dividend*

In recent years, China's working-age population has declined continuously, and the pace of decline is accelerating significantly. People at home and abroad are very concerned about this development. According to the sixth census in 2010, the total number of working-age people aged 15–59 reached a peak of 940 million in 2010. The working-age population is projected to fall by 30 million to 910 million by 2020, and the decline will accelerate during this period. Accordingly, the percentage of the population that is of working-age has decreased from 70.1 to 66.0%. Due to a slight increase in the labor force participation rate in recent years, the economically active population is expected to grow at a slower pace and peak in 2017. Correspondingly, in the labor market, the number of new entrants to the workforce peaked in 2013 and since then has been growing at a negative rate of about 2% per year; the annual growth rate of the number of new entrants to the migrant workforce dropped significantly from an average of 4% in 2005–2010 to 1.3% in 2014.

Man is the most active factor of production. Changes in the size and structure of the population will pose serious challenges to the sustainable development of China's economy under the new normal.

First, labor shortages and rapidly rising wages will weaken the comparative advantage and international competitiveness of China's manufacturing sector. For example, from 2008 to 2016, real wages for migrant workers grew at an average annual rate of 11.8%. In addition, real wages for workers employed in manufacturing, construction, and agriculture have been growing by double digits annually on average. According to the Conference Board, the average annual growth rate of China's overall labor productivity was 9.5% in 2007–2012, slowed down to 7.3% in 2013, and fell to 7% in 2014. Rate at which wages are rising has exceeded the rate at which labor productivity is increasing, thus weakening the comparative advantage and competitiveness of China's manufacturing sector.

Second, because the average education level of new entrants to the workforce is much higher than that of people who have been in the workforce, the decrease in the number of new entrants to the workforce has slowed down the improvement of human capital.

Finally, a growing working-age population and an increasing percentage of the population that is of working-age are an important condition for sustaining a high savings rate and rate of return on investments. Conversely, a declining working-age population and a decreasing percentage of the population that is of working-age mean that this source of growth has been weakened, significantly dampening the momentum of economic growth.

4.3 Resource and Environmental Constraints

Under the traditional mode of economic development, China's economic growth is largely dependent on large amounts of factor inputs, consuming a lot of energy resources. China has become the world's largest energy producer and consumer, and the share of its consumption of major resource products in total global consumption is significantly larger than the share of its GDP in the global economy. According to statistics, at present, the average intensity of the consumption of the five major resources of fresh water, primary energy, steel, cement and common non-ferrous metals in China is about 90% higher than the world average, and China's energy consumption per unit of GDP is roughly 2.9 times that of the United States, 4.9 times that of Japan, 4.3 times that of the European Union and 2.3 times that of the world average, making China one of the countries with the highest energy consumption per unit of GDP in the world.

Meanwhile, China is not rich in resources. It is precisely because of extensive use of energy resources and insufficient reserves of energy resources that China's dependence on foreign sources of energy continues to increase. China's dependence on foreign sources of crude oil, iron ore, copper concentrate, bauxite, chrome ore, nickel ore, potassium ore, and other critical minerals has exceeded 50%, putting China under growing pressure to increase imports. Haze events have occurred frequently in China in recent years, incidents such as water pollution and heavy metal pollution occur from time to time, and the ecological environment as a whole has been deteriorating. If we continue down the path of extensive growth characterized by high inputs, high consumption, and high emissions, the energy resource and environmental constraints will be further intensified, which will inevitably have a serious impact on China's sustainable development.

Take oil as an example. China has been a net importer of crude oil since 1993, and its dependence on foreign oil reached 65.4% in 2016. First, domestic oil resources are insufficient, and crude oil production has entered a stage of minimal growth. Judging by the reserves-to-production ratio for fossil energy, China's energy supply prospects don't look good. Except for coal production that can still meet the needs of economic development, the production of oil, natural gas, and other resources has been tapering off. According to BP's 2014 statistics on proven reserves, as of the end of 2013, China's proven oil reserves were 2.5 billion tons, accounting for only 1.1% of the world's total proven reserves, with a reserves-to-production ratio of only 11.9 years; China's proven natural gas reserves were 3.3 trillion cubic meters, accounting for only 1.5% of the world's total proven reserves, with a reserves-to-production ratio of 28 years. Oil and gas resources are extremely limited. Due to resource constraints, China's crude oil production has generally grown at a slow rate within the range of 1%-2% in recent years. In 2014, China's crude oil production was 210.1 million tons, up only 0.56% year-on-year. In 2016, China's crude oil production was 199.7 million tons, down 6.9% year-on-year, the first decline since 2012. At present, most of China's major oil fields are in the middle and late stages of development, exploration and development costs keep on rising, and the production growth potential of major mature oil fields is limited. Daqing Oil Field, for example, saw a decrease of 1.83 million tons in production in 2016, and will reduce its annual production to 32 million tons by 2020, representing an annual decrease of more than 1.3 million tons. Overall, there will be less and less conventional oil and gas resources available for development and utilization in the future. China's crude oil production has entered a stage of minimal growth. It is estimated that the average annual growth of China's crude oil production will be only around 0.7% from 2015 to 2020.

Second, China's dependence on foreign oil continues to rise, and oil supply is controlled by foreign countries. There is a negative correlation between oil security and oil import dependence. The greater the dependence, the higher the supply risk is. Due to the shortage of domestic resources, since China became a net importer of oil in 1993, its dependence on foreign oil has risen year by year, and oil supply risk has gradually increased. In 2016, China's dependence on foreign crude oil climbed to 66%, making it the largest oil importer. There is a huge contrast between China and the United States in energy security. Since 2011, China's dependence on foreign crude oil has surpassed that of the United States, ranking first in the world. Thanks to the shale revolution, the United States has dramatically increased its own energy supply capacity and is now the world's largest producer of crude oil, surpassing Saudi Arabia and Russia. As China's resource bottleneck has not yet been broken, its crude oil production growth has been significantly slower than its demand growth, and its dependence on foreign oil will continue to rise in the future. Given China's high dependence on foreign oil, a guarantee of stable and long-term international oil supply will be the principal factor underpinning China's energy security.

China's environmental problems are mainly water pollution, air pollution, solid waste, and environmental emergencies. As has been the case with many developed countries, China's environmental problems are getting worse with the advancement of industrialization. According to the 2016 Report on the State of the Environment in China published by the Ministry of Ecology and Environment, of the 338 cities at or above the prefecture level where air quality is monitored according to the new standards across the country, 84 cities met the annual average standards for concentrations of air pollutants and 254 cities exceeded the limits on annual average concentrations of air pollutants. Precipitation monitoring was carried out in 474 cities (districts and counties) across the country, of which 19.8% were affected by acid rain. The average frequency of acid rain was 12.7%. Water quality monitoring was carried out in 1940 surface water monitoring sections (points) under the national monitoring program across the country. Sections with water quality rated as Grade I, Grade II, Grade III, Grade IV, Grade V, and inferior to Grade V accounted for 2.4, 37.5, 27.9, 16.8, 6.9, and 8.6%, respectively. The main pollution indicators were the chemical oxygen demand (COD), total phosphorus (TP) and BOD5. Of the 6124 groundwater monitoring points across the country, monitoring points with excellent water quality accounted for 10.1%, monitoring points with good water quality accounted for 25.4%, monitoring points with fairly good water quality accounted for 4.4%, monitoring points with fairly poor water quality accounted for 45.4%, and monitoring points with very poor water quality accounted for 14.7%. Of the 417 monitoring points in the country's coastal waters, monitoring points with water quality rated as Grade I, Grade II, Grade III, Grade IV, and inferior to Grade V accounted for 32.4, 41.0, 10.3, 3.1, and 13.2%, respectively. The main pollution indicators were inorganic nitrogen and reactive phosphate. The old way of pollution first and treatment later is the cause of

China's current worsening environmental problems. In the trend toward economic globalization, China has gradually become the world's factory, with a large number of highly polluting and energy-intensive industries moved to China. In the current situation of increasing pollution and rapid resource consumption, all kinds of ecological and environmental crises are lurking. Dwindling resources, the increasing scarcity of strategic resources, the aggravation of environmental problems and potential environmental threats will restrict the long-term sustainable development of China's economy.

4.4 *Lack of Technological Innovation*

China is lagging considerably behind developed countries in indigenous innovation capability, and there are many obstacles to the development of technological innovation in terms of systems and mechanisms.

First, its indigenous innovation capability is still not strong enough. According to the Global Competitiveness Report 2016 released by the World Economic Forum, China's competitiveness ranks 28th out of 138 major countries in the world. The ranking is at a moderate-to-high level and does not match China's status as a major economic power.

In terms of innovation and resource utilization efficiency, there is a significant gap between China and developed countries. The number of R&D personnel per 10,000 people in China is less than 1/4 of the average level of developed countries. China owns a very small share of the invention patents in the world. In particular, China's self-sufficiency rate for key technologies is low, and many key and core technologies have to be purchased. China's dependence on foreign technology has reached 50%. Due to the lack of core technologies and independent intellectual property rights, China is at the lower end in international specialization, and can only rely on the massive energy consumption to maintain economic growth. Although the contribution of technological advances to China's economic growth is increasing year by year, and the goal of 60% has been clearly spelt out in the 13th Five Year Plan (2016–2020), there is still a big gap compared with the level of over 70% in the United States, Japan and other developed countries.

Secondly, the problem of treating technology and economy as "two separate pieces of skin" has not been fundamentally resolved. At present, the combination of production, study, research and application in China is not close enough, the proportion of scientific and technological achievements converted to economic benefits is low, the position of enterprises as the dominant force in technological innovation hasn't been truly established, the original scientific and technological achievements of enterprises are few, the overall efficiency of the innovation system needs to be improved urgently, and technological innovation is fairly limited in its support for economic development. For example, the number of scientific and technological achievements has been growing rapidly, but there are not many breakthrough and original achievements; there are many application-oriented scientific and technological achievements, but the overall conversion rate is very low; the number of invention patents has been growing rapidly, but few have been industrialized; many scientific and technological awards have been presented, but the problem of scientific and technological achievements being idled and scientific and technological resources being wasted is serious; to some extent, scientific and technological personnel do scientific research with a view to earning titles and awards rather than achieving practical application. In 2013, for example, investment in R&D in China reached about 1.2 trillion Yuan, of which the government expenditure on science and technology was 500 billion Yuan, ranking first in the world. However, according to Zhang Xiaoqiang, former vice chairman of the National Development and Reform Commission, the conversion rate of scientific and technological achievements in China is only 10%, far below the 40% in developed countries.

Finally, systems and mechanisms related to science and technology do not meet the needs of economic and social development and international competition. China's scientific research management system is still not perfect, the allocation of scientific and technological resources involves too much red tape and is decentralized and repetitive; "Nine dragons regulating one water source" in the scientific research system makes scientific and technological activities "fragmented" and "difficult to focus"; in the case of scientific research projects, there are also serious waste caused by repetition and the phenomenon of "sprinkling pepper"; the management of scientific and technological projects and funds is not very reasonable; scientific research evaluation and scientific and technological reward mechanisms are not reasonable enough; investment in scientific research is more inclined toward equipment than people, and incentives are insufficient; efforts to build integrity in scientific research and foster a culture of innovation are weak; the enthusiasm and creativity of scientific and technological personnel have not been fully tapped.

4.5 *Lack of Effective Consumer Demand*

For a long time, there has been a lack of demand, especially effective consumer demand in China. Domestic demand mainly depends on investment. The mixture of a high investment-to-GDP ratio and a low consumption-to-GDP ratio has had a significant impact on the sustained and healthy development of the economy, the optimization and upgrading of the industrial structure, the improvement of people's quality of life and the promotion of national competitiveness. The average investment-to-GDP ratio in countries around the world is around 22%, and the average consumption-to-GDP ratio is around 78%. The average investment-to-GDP ratio in high-income countries is 20%, and the average consumption-to-GDP ratio is 80%; the average investment-to-GDP ratio in upper-middle-income countries is 22%, and the average consumption-to-GDP ratio is 75%; the average investment-to-GDP ratio in lower-middle-income countries is 31%, and the average consumption-to-GDP ratio is 66%; the average investment-to-GDP ratio in low-income countries is 29%, and the average consumption-to-GDP ratio is 75%. China's investment-to-GDP ratio is about 20 percentage points higher than the world average, and its consumption-to-GDP ratio is more than 20 percentage points lower than the world average.

At present, there are some prominent problems in China's consumer sector.

First, the cost of social consumption is high. First, the current consumer tax burden is higher than normal. For example, the tax rates on consumer goods such as cosmetics are still higher than normal, and taxes are still levied on consumer goods that should no longer be taxed. In addition, the rates charged in China's sectors such as highways and telecommunications are relatively high, which is not conducive to the growth of consumption in related fields. Second, consumer interest rates are higher than normal. As China is a large consumer market, interest rates on credit cards, auto loans, home loans, and other consumer loans in China are significantly higher than those in developed countries. Third, the prices of the same products are higher than in overseas markets. For example, the prices of luxury goods and some consumer goods in China is more than two times higher than those sold under the same brands in overseas markets, with some products 8–10 times more expensive, leading to serious consumption outflows. According to statistics, China's consumption abroad grew by an average of 25% every year from

2005 to 2015, twice the growth rate of China's domestic retail sales of consumer goods; cross-border consumption totals about 1.2 trillion Yuan and will continue to grow in the future. With the rise of middle- and high-income groups in China, demand for imported goods is strong, and categories are shifting from mass consumer goods to luxury goods. Large-scale consumption abroad and "grey cross-border online shopping" lead to the loss of tax revenue and corporate earnings, and exacerbate the loss of domestic purchasing power.

Second, it is difficult to cultivate emerging consumer markets, and the construction of the market system is lagging behind. In recent years, the process of diversification of the consumer psychology, consumer preferences and consumer demand of urban and rural residents in China has accelerated, but the corresponding market supply has not kept pace in terms of total amount, structure and quality assurance (such as consumer rights and interests, a social environment that promotes honesty and integrity, etc.). More significantly, development is lagging behind in fields such as elderly care, health care, tourism and leisure, sports and culture, and information consumption, which hinders the rapid expansion of consumption and the process of transformation and upgrading. Take tourism as an example. In 2015, China's GDP per capita was $8069, and vacation should be the main form of tourism consumption, but vacation spending as a percentage of income was much lower than in countries at the same stage of development. Due to the lack of vacation products, at present domestic tourism is focused on sightseeing. As a result, tourists stay for short periods of time and spend little money. This is at odds with the development of the tourism market which is going in the direction of "personalized, leisure and fashion." In addition, admission prices for tourist attractions are abnormally high, and supporting services are lacking. In some cases, outbound tourism offers better value than domestic tourism for the same money.

Third, the rates charged for information consumption are relatively high. Higher-than-normal telecom charges have become a major obstacle to the rapid popularization and application of the Internet, inhibiting the rapid growth of information consumption and affecting the implementation of the "Internet +" strategy. In 2016, China Mobile's monthly ARPU (Average revenue per user) was 55.5 Yuan, equivalent to 3.6% of the per capita disposable income of urban households and 7.4% of the per capita disposable income of rural households. This percentage is generally below 1% in developed countries (this is the upper limit of the basic requirements for achieving universal telecommunications services). High rates for telecommunications services in China not only put an unbearable burden on users, but also squeeze low-income groups out of the sphere of information consumption and inhibit-related consumption such as entertainment, shopping, and education. Meanwhile, on top of high rates, issues such as smaller-than-advertised bandwidths and slow Internet speeds are having a negative impact.

Fourth, the consumption environment is unsatisfactory. Environmental constraints affecting the release of consumption potential still exist. First, infrastructure construction in the consumer sector is lagging behind, with rural broadband networks, urban rail transit, and parking lots still in short supply. Second, the development of logistics, warehousing and other industries supporting the circulation of consumer goods is not in step with consumption upgrading, resulting in the circulation cost of consumer goods being much higher than in developed countries. Third, support for consumption in terms of fiscal, tax, financial, and credit policies is inadequate, resulting in a lack of willingness to spend on the part of the public, and large-scale consumption outflows erode earnings in the domestic consumer market. Fourth, the system of consumer market supervision and regulation measures is unsound, and issues such as food safety and counterfeit and shoddy products are cropping up here and there.

At a deeper level, because people on high-income have a lower marginal propensity to consume, and people on low income have a higher marginal propensity to consume, widening income inequality will diminish the average propensity to consume in the household sector. In a mature market economy, the government regulates the distribution of income through taxation. China's taxation system is comprised mainly of turnover taxes (including value-added tax, business tax, consumption tax, and customs duty). Turnover taxes are levied on turnover and are essentially consumption taxes, which are regressive in nature. The tax burden on people on low income is heavy as consumer spending takes up a big chunk of their income. In addition, the individual income tax is levied mainly on wages, while other incomes, such as rent and capital gains, are not taxed, resulting in the tax burden mainly falling on the working class, and differences in family burden are not taken into account. All of these make taxation fail to play an effective role in regulating income distribution in China.

Another reason for the low overall consumption-to-GDP ratio is a squeeze that enterprises put on household incomes. Because of the financial market is underdeveloped, residents have few financial instruments to invest in, and their financial assets are mainly bank deposits, which coupled with interest rate controls and low interest rates for bank deposits allows financial businesses and non-financial businesses that have access to loans to use the funds of the household sector "cheaply." Interest rates on household deposits are lower than the shadow price of funds, which pushes disposable household income down and thus inhibits consumption. In addition, compared with other markets, the dividend payout ratios of Chinese listed companies are significantly lower. These factors lead to an increase in corporate savings and the investment-to-GDP ratio, and residents are unable to effectively share in the increase in investment income that should be brought about by the growth of corporate earnings.

The government's squeeze on the household sector is another reason for the low overall consumption-to-GDP ratio. The Chinese government's expenditure structure emphasizes investment over public services and transfer payments, which prevents fiscal policy from effectively regulating income distribution, reduces disposable income and social security benefits for low-income groups, and drives down household consumption. In addition, the transformation of social security has transferred the relevant expenses previously borne by enterprises and the government to the household sector, which pushes up household savings and inhibits household consumption.

4.6 *Constraints of the Investment and Financing System*

At present, the basic contradictions in China's investment and financing landscape are as follows: on the one hand, accelerating the transformation of the mode of economic development, promoting economic structural adjustment, ensuring and improving people's livelihood, coordinating urban–rural and regional development, and raising the level of "going out" and opening-up all urgently need centralized, large-scale and long-term financing support; on the other hand, huge amounts of national savings and private funds cannot be converted into long-term construction funds, hot money is flooding in, speculation is running rampant, and investment projects are strapped for capital. Therefore, it is urgent that the building of a medium- and long-term financing system be accelerated.

First, the current investment and financing system has difficulty meeting the massive demand for medium- and long-term capital and project capital for the acceleration of urbanization and rapid economic development. It is difficult to cover such a huge demand for medium- and long-term capital and project capital by relying solely on government finances, commercial banks, and capital markets.

Second, there is a maturity mismatch between the long-term use of short-term loans granted by commercial banks and medium- and long-term financing needs. Considering the fact that commercial banks focus on short-term retail banking, and the maturities of their deposits and loans are poorly matched, operational risk will increase once infrastructure investment entities fail to repay their loans as scheduled or default on loans.

Third, the fiscal budget has difficulty meeting the growing financing needs of medium - and long-term projects. After the 1980s, the state's fiscal policy of "delegating powers and surrendering part of the profits" and "reducing taxes and ceding benefits" caused significant changes in the pattern of the distribution of national income. The transformation of the distribution structure of national income indicates that the economic surplus is gradually transformed from centralized control by the State to decentralized ownership by the people. The financing system in which the State plays a dominant role in fiscal allocation can no longer meet the needs of economic development, which objectively requires a new financing system arrangement to convert huge amounts of scattered and idle household savings into centralized, large-scale and long-term construction capital.

[Column 31]

China's economy faces a dilemma between deleveraging and deleveraging.

The "high leverage" normal will be part of the development of the Chinese economy for some time to come. The rapid expansion of China's leverage ratio started in 2009. Before that, China's debt grew relatively modestly. According to an aggregate calculation, China's leverage ratio has been rising at an average annual rate of 10 percentage points, and the overall leverage ratio stood at 257% at the end of 2016. According to the internationally accepted "530 rule," if a country's leverage ratio rises by more than 30% within five years, the country will be at risk of a crisis. Typical examples include the Japanese economy during the period 1985–1989, the European economy during the period 2006–2010, and the US economy during the period 2003–2007. This shows that a high level of leverage does not mean high risk, and what really affect risk are rapid changes in the leverage ratio over a certain period of time.

Let's examine the level of leverage in various sectors of China's economy. First, the leverage ratio in the government sector is generally manageable. According to the 2016 central final account report and budget & audit report made by the Ministry of Finance and the National Audit Office to the National People's Congress on June 23, 2017, at the end of 2016, the outstanding debt of China's central government and local governments was 27.3 trillion Yuan, and the government debt-to-GDP ratio was 39.6%, far below the international warning level of 60%. China's government debt-to-GDP ratio as calculated by the Bank for International Settlements for the same period was slightly higher, but it was only 46.4%. More than 60% of China's government debt is used to finance investments in municipal construction, transportation, indemnificatory housing, and land purchasing and reserving. Most of the investments have resulted in good assets that will generate a respectable amount of operating income for quite a long period of time.

While the central government debt remains basically stable and relatively low, local government debt has become a major risk point. This is mainly reflected in the fact that local government debt has been growing too fast, and risks in some regions are too concentrated; local governments have issued a lot of short-term debt, so there is a certain level of liquidity risk; repayment relies heavily on revenues from land sales.

Second, leverage risk for non-financial businesses lies primarily in the downward pressure on economic growth. According to the Bank for International Settlements, China's outstanding corporate debt in 2016 was $17.8 trillion, accounting for 166.3% of its GDP. Over the same period, US corporate debt accounted for 72.5% of its GDP. That figure was 104.2% for the Eurozone and 95.5% for Japan.

Third, household debt consists mainly of housing loans. Although the leverage ratio in China's household sector is rising faster than other countries in the world, it is generally low. In 2016, China's outstanding household debt was $4.7 trillion.

Fourth, the leverage ratio of financial institutions. Due to the particularity of financial businesses, in order to avoid double counting, the leverage ratio is calculated only based on the various types of bonds issued. At the end of 2016, the total debt of financial institutions was about 16.3 trillion Yuan, with a leverage ratio of 23.7%. The risks of financial institutions stem mainly from changes in credit asset quality caused by an economic slowdown. Meanwhile, the rapid expansion of the shadow banking sector, with its complexity, secrecy, and contagiousness, can easily lead to systemic risks.

At present, China's economy faces a dilemma between deleveraging and deleveraging. First, the pressure to maintain steady growth is huge, and it is necessary to increase leverage to hedge against an economic downturn; second, China's economy is in a catch-up phase characterized by rapid development, and the development of industrial enterprises requires a large amount of capital in the early stage, so high corporate debt and leverage are inevitable; third, state-owned enterprises also undertake some national economy and people's livelihood projects, and the high corporate leverage is to some extent the result of the transfer of government debt; Fourth, forced deleveraging is likely to lead to a "balance sheet recession," causing systemic risks.

5 Problems and Challenges in China's Social Transformation

While the economy is shifting gears, some social problems accumulated over a long period of time are becoming more and more prominent, and the original social structure and system are facing the challenges of transformation.

China is not only a country in transition with a socialist tradition, but also a developing country with multiple historical processes, and a large country with a population of 1.3 billion. Since the start of reform and opening-up, China has experienced the three processes of industrialization, urbanization, and globalization, and also faced the core challenges of these three historical processes. Even in cosmopolitan cities like Beijing, the characteristics of a traditional society, an industrial society, and a post-industrial society can be seen. Meanwhile, problems peculiar to various social classes have arisen.[19] These problems appeared at the same time and overlap each other, leading to multiple challenges for China's economic and social transformation as it crosses the middle-income trap.

[19] Sun Liping. *Fracture: Chinese Society since 1990s*. Beijing: Social Sciences Academic Press, 2003.

On the whole, to overcome the middle-income trap, China needs to start on three fronts: society, economy, and governance structures and approaches. On the social front, as developed countries have done, China should shift from the current "inverted T-shaped" social structure[20] to an olive-shaped social structure with a middle class of a certain size as soon as possible, and provide universal and effective welfare coverage so as to form stable and sustainable domestic demand expectations. On the economic front, China should, like other developing countries, modernize its economy as soon as possible, encourage technological innovation and institutional innovation, upgrade and transform its industries, and make the transition from "labor-intensive" to "capital-intensive" and "technology-intensive." On the institutional front, China should, like other countries in transition, strive to promote institutional breakthroughs and reforms, and while decentralizing and devolving power, overcome and eliminate various outmoded conventions and undesirable customs in institutions, so as to provide a good institutional environment for economic growth toward the high-income stage.

5.1 *Widening Gap Between Rich and Poor*

At present, the gap between rich and poor is large and social inequality is significant in Chinese society, forming a ruptured social fabric specific to the transitional period. The causes of this situation are complex and diverse, posing serious challenges for future social and economic development.

Nearly 40 years have elapsed since the start of China's reform and opening-up, which has had a profound and extensive impact on China's society and economy. In this process, the income distribution pattern of the whole country has also changed tremendously. On the whole, against the backdrop of a comprehensive and substantial increase in the income of residents, income inequality has been expanding. After nearly 40 years of development, China has moved from a country with relatively equal income distribution to a country with relatively unequal income distribution.

[20] Li Qiang. "T-shaped" Social Structure and "Structural Tension". *Sociological Studies*, 2005 (2).

5.1.1 *Trends in Income Inequality*

Since the start of reform and opening-up, income inequality among Chinese residents has been expanding. In 1981, at the beginning of reform and opening-up, the Gini coefficient for urban residents in China was below 0.20, the Gini coefficient for rural residents was slightly higher, with most estimates putting it between 0.21 and 0.24, and the Gini coefficient for residents in the whole country was 0.29.

China's Gini coefficient has been rising rapidly. China's Gini coefficient stood at 0.479 in 2003, 0.473 in 2004, 0.485 in 2005, 0.487 in 2006, 0.484 in 2007, 0.491 in 2008, 0.490 in 2009, 0.481 in 2010, 0.477 in 2011, 0.474 in 2012, 0.473 in 2013, 0.469 in 2014, 0.462 in 2015, and 0.465 in 2016.

It is clear that income inequality among Chinese residents has reached a fairly serious level. This can be illustrated by a simple international comparison. Income inequality among Chinese residents is not only higher than in most Asian countries, but also higher than in all former Eastern European and Soviet countries that that began market transition in the twentieth century.

Meanwhile, income inequality among Chinese residents was accomplished in just over a decade. The urban reforms that began in the mid-1980s accelerated the widening of income disparity among residents. By the mid-to-late 1990s, income inequality among Chinese residents had reached a considerably high level, second only to that in some African and Latin American countries.

5.1.2 *Institutional Causes of the Gap Between Rich and Poor*

On the whole, reform and opening-up have benefited the residents of the whole country, and the income of almost all the residents has increased substantially. The widening income gap shows that different groups of people have benefited from reform and opening-up to different degrees. More specifically, in the process of general income growth, the income of low-income groups grew much slower than that of high-income groups. The causes of this situation are also diverse.

Studies have shown[21] that since the start of reform and opening-up, the distribution of national income has changed continuously. At the

[21] Bai Chong'en, Qian Zhenjie. Who Is Squeezing Residents' Income—Analysis of the Pattern of the Distribution of National Income in China. *Social Sciences in China*, 2009 (5).

beginning of the reform, the labor share increased, while the capital share decreased. Since the mid-1980s, the labor share has been declining, while the capital share has been rising. Indirect taxes, which represent government revenue, remained unchanged until the mid-1990s and have been rising since then. Of capital income, which has grown the most as a share of national income, the part allocated to the business or government sector is generally on the rise, while the part allocated to the household sector is declining (see Table 3). Estimates of disposable income including regular transfer payments show that the share of the disposable income of the household sector dropped from 69.00% in 1996 to 60.65% in 2014, while the share of the disposable income of the business sector rose from 16.40 to 20.50%, and the share of the disposable income of the government sector rose from 16.40 to 18.85%.

Table 3 Sectoral Distribution of National Income from 1992 to 2014 (%)

Year	*Households*	*Businesses*	*Governments*
1992	68.70	13.40	17.90
1993	64.70	18.10	17.20
1994	66.90	18.60	14.50
1995	66.20	19.70	14.10
1996	69.00	16.40	14.60
1997	68.00	17.70	14.30
1998	68.30	17.50	14.20
1999	66.70	19.20	14.10
2000	66.10	19.40	14.50
2001	64.40	20.60	15.00
2002	62.60	21.10	16.30
2003	62.00	21.90	16.10
2004	59.10	24.30	16.60
2005	58.90	23.70	17.40
2006	58.40	23.70	17.90
2007	57.30	23.90	18.80
2008	57.20	24.50	18.30
2009	58.70	23.80	17.50
2010	58.40	23.60	18.00
2011	59.30	21.90	18.80
2012	60.20	20.60	19.20
2013	61.30	19.80	18.90
2014	60.65	20.50	18.85

Source National Bureau of Statistics

According to data released by the National Bureau of Statistics, China's per capita disposable income was 23,821 Yuan in 2016, an increase of 8.4% over 2015 in nominal terms.

Obviously, the income growth brought about by economic growth is not evenly distributed among different sectors of the national economy. The relatively slow growth of wages shows that the wage-earning haven't enjoyed the fruits of rapid economic development brought about by reform and opening-up. When other classes can obtain income by other means, their income grows much faster than that of the wage-earning class.

The current tax system makes it difficult for the government to use individual income tax to regulate income redistribution. First, because of the diversity of the sources of personal income, it is difficult for the government to monitor residents' income in a practical way; second, the way individual income tax is levied is not reasonable and the individual income tax exemption limit is too low, imposing the tax on middle-income earners instead of high-income earners; finally, individual income tax revenue as a percentage of GDP is low, so it is difficult to regulate income inequality through individual income tax.

Studies have shown[22] that while narrowing income inequality in cities and towns, current transfer payments widen income inequality in rural areas and between urban and rural areas. The reason for this is that transfer payments from the central government are more used more for investment and government consumption than for direct poverty alleviation; the majority of the transfer payments go to cities, and in the countryside, transfer payments are limited to only a few areas and projects. Therefore, such transfer payments can promote urban employment through investment and reduce income inequality in urban areas, but they also inevitably widen the urban–rural income gap. Table 4 shows the impact of China's fiscal policy on income inequality in 2002–2008.

China's current social security system is not perfect. Unemployment insurance reduces income inequality in urban areas (but at the same time widens the urban–rural income gap), while the popularization of basic endowment insurance and medical insurance has widened income inequality in urban areas to a certain extent. This is because high-income

[22] Li Jixiong. Analysis of the Effects of the Fiscal Redistribution of Residents' Income in China—Measurement based on the Severity of Poverty and the Gini Coefficient. *On Economic Problems*, 2010 (12).

Table 4 Impact of China's Fiscal Policy on Income Inequality in 2002–2008. (billion US$)

Year	*2002*	*2003*	*2004*	*2005*	*2006*	*2007*	*2008*
Urban residents							
GNI per capita	0.3179	0.3286	0.3368	0.342	0.3383	0.3332	0.3409
Per capita disposable income	0.3158	0.3261	0.3338	0.339	0.3356	0.3315	0.3393
Rural residents							
GNI per capita	0.3235	0.3303	0.3269	0.3239	0.3246	0.3326	0.3284
Cash income per capita	0.3788	0.3837	0.3854	0.37	0.3664	0.3746	0.3713
NNI per capita	0.3714	0.3812	0.3693	0.3758	0.3732	0.3736	0.3773

Source Li Jixiong (2010)

earners benefit more from the implementation of the latter two than low-income earners. Many low-income earners are not eligible for endowment insurance and medical insurance at all. The difference of social security coverage between urban and rural areas makes such a security system widen the urban–rural income gap.

Table 4 shows that after adjustment by China's fiscal policy, the income gap between urban residents has been reduced only to a negligible extent, while the income gap between rural residents has been widened, indicating that many of the government's redistribution programs have failed to fully deliver the intended outcomes.

5.1.3 *From an Income Gap to a Wealth Chasm*

A phenomenon worthy of special attention is that after nearly 40 years of reform and development, Chinese residents have accumulated a certain amount of family wealth, but the process of household wealth accumulation has laid bare the yawning gap between rich and poor caused by social inequality.

Generally speaking, the three ways to accumulate wealth are savings, inheritance, and asset appreciation. Among the three ways, savings are most important to Chinese households. Before reform and opening-up, Chinese urban residents had almost no accumulation of family property, so intergenerational inheritance is not the main way to accumulate wealth. Asset appreciation is premised on the ownership of assets. For Chinese residents, who had almost no family property, the original accumulation of assets undoubtedly came more from savings. Therefore, at the initial stage of wealth accumulation, savings which reflect the difference between income and consumption became the most important means of wealth accumulation.

The wealth accumulation of Chinese households began after reform and opening-up. Before that, Chinese households had almost no private assets. A number of reasons had contributed to the lack of wealth accumulation in Chinese households. First, China's socialist revolution had reduced family property to a minimum. Socialist transformation not only nationalized private assets to complete the process of "reverse stratification" aimed at eliminating class differences, but also made household wealth accumulation politically and legally impossible. Second, the development strategy of suppressing consumption and the low-wage system under the planned economic system in the following decades made the vast majority of households live a hand-to-mouth existence, and the accumulation of wealth by individual households became an unattainable goal. In addition, the whole market was controlled by the State, and individuals were disqualified from making profits in the market. This economically deprived individual households of the chance to accumulate wealth. The only thing that could be counted as family property was welfare housing, which was allocated by work units and could be passed on to the next generation. However, before the housing reform, such welfare housing was nominally owned by the State and could not appreciate in value or be converted into cash in the market. Finally, under the planned economy, the government provided relatively comprehensive social welfare benefits, so that residents needed not worry about education, health care, pensions, and other social amenities that were usually secured by savings or wealth accumulation. Therefore, it is fair to say that before reform and opening-up, the level of wealth inequality between households in China was relatively low - almost no one had private property.

After the launch of reform and opening-up, such wealth equality between households was gradually broken. Beginning in 1981, the government actively encouraged and supported the development of urban and rural self-employed households. Individuals gradually entered the market. They not only profited from market operations, but also began to hold private property. The opening-up of investment opportunities for individuals led to the rapid development of self-employed households and private enterprises. With the opening of the capital market in the

1990s, people could make a profit in the capital market. The commercialization of housing made it wealth accumulation by urban households a real possibility and an urgent need. Government-owned properties were sold to occupants at a low price, giving these people possession of family wealth. Since the beginning of the twenty-first century, driven by the ownership of private housing and the improvement of living conditions, buying property has become one of the important means for urban residents to accumulate family wealth. Another important reason why urban residents are eager to accumulate wealth is that, since the start of reform and opening-up, various social security measures provided by the government have been gradually replaced by market-oriented mechanisms, under which individuals have gradually assumed responsibilities for education, health care, unemployment insurance, and pensions. Wealth accumulation among urban residents has become an important security strategy.

The wealth accumulation process reflects an array of inequalities. First, the power factor is visible in the wealth accumulation process, and institutional imperfections in the transformation process make rent-seeking and profit-seeking by using power possible. Second, another inequality in the wealth accumulation process is the huge difference in the pace of wealth accumulation among different social classes. The rich accumulate wealth much more capably and quickly than the non-rich. This is because the "threshold effect" of wealth accumulation and the "amplification effect" of asset appreciation, once started, quickly become a process of self-expansion and amplification, inevitably accelerating the widening of the wealth gap. As the cycle continues, the wealth gap between the two groups grows. Therefore, asset appreciation has become an amplifier of wealth inequality among social classes. Third, the intergenerational transmission of capital has also changed. Assets and wealth can be directly transferred between generations, while the intergenerational transformation of human capital is more indirect and complex. On the one hand, the transmission of human capital may become insignificant, wages received in exchange for labor have become insignificant for classes that possess assets and wealth, and a rentier class that does not need to work may arise; on the other hand, the children of wealthy families have relative advantages in both physical capital and human capital, and the intergenerational transmission of such advantages allows the existing social class structure to be reproduced and passed on to form the so-called persistent social inequality. Fourth, because of the threshold effect of assets and the rapid appreciation of assets, the gap among the social classes of cities is widening, and social mobility across class boundaries is becoming increasingly rare and difficult. The haves accumulate wealth through assets, while the have-nots can only accumulate wealth through unspent wages. The threshold of assets excludes the poor from the propertied classes, and the process of asset appreciation is that the rich get richer and the poor remain poor. The path to upward mobility for members of the lower class is becoming increasingly inaccessible, and opportunities are becoming increasingly scarce.

5.2 *Ruptured Social Fabric*

The widening gap between rich and poor has led to a ruptured social fabric and tensions between interests. A large number of empirical studies have shown that the overall structure of the Chinese society is an unbalanced shape which is large at the bottom, relatively weak in the middle and small at the top—hence the term inverted T-shaped social structure. Such a structure has a tendency of "rupturing" in terms of both social mobility and intergroup relations: class boundaries are gradually rigidified, intergenerational social mobility is decreasing, the relationship between different interest groups is increasingly tense, and social consensus is difficult to form.

5.2.1 *Increasingly Rigidified Social Stratification*

A representative and wide-ranging study divides the Chinese society into ten social strata based on the four main mechanisms driving stratification, namely, the occupational division of labor, the hierarchy of authority, the possession of means of production and institutional segmentation, as well as the three kinds of resources by which society is stratified, namely, organizational resources, economical resources, and cultural (technological) resources, as shown in Table 5. On the basis of dividing society into ten social strata, this book groups the ten social strata into five social levels.[23]

The study found that the "state and social managers" stratum has grown slightly, with its proportion remaining unchanged at 2.3% in recent years; compared with 2001, the proportion of the "managerial workers" stratum increased by 1.1% in 2010; the "private business owners" stratum started from scratch, growing nearly 400% between 1999 and 2010; since

[23] Lu Xueyi, et al. *Analysis and Prediction of China's Social Situation in 2013*. Beijing: Social Sciences Academic Press (China), 2013.

Table 5 Comparison of Changes in the Ten Social Strata in Contemporary China (1978–2010) (%)

Ten social strata	*Year*				
	1978	*1999*	*2001*	*2006*	*2010*
State and social managers	0.98	2.1	2.1	2.3	2.3
Managerial workers	0.23	1.5	1.6	2.6	2.7
Private business owners	0.00	0.6	1.0	1.3	2.2
Professional and technical personnel	3.48	5.1	4.6	6.3	6.4
Clerks	1.29	4.8	7.2	7.0	7.3
Self-employed individuals	0.03	4.2	7.1	9.5	10.1
Commercial and service staff	2.15	12.0	11.2	10.1	11.3
Industrial workers	19.83	22.6	17.5	14.7	22.7
Agricultural workers	67.48	44.0	42.9	40.3	30.4
Unemployed and semi-unemployed	4.60	3.1	4.8	5.9	4.6

Source Lu Xueyi, et al. *Analysis and Prediction of China's Social Situation in 2013*. Beijing: Social Sciences Academic Press (China), 2013

the beginning of the twenty-first century, the "professional and technical personnel" stratum, the "clerks" stratum, and the "business and service personnel" stratum have been growing steadily, but at a slower pace than the "private business owners" stratum and the "self-employed individuals" stratum, whose proportions exceeded 10% in 2010; the "industrial workers" stratum has fluctuated over time, but increased rapidly in recent years, with its proportion reaching an all-time high of 22.7% in 2010, which represented a net increase of 46.61 million people over 2001, most of whom were migrant workers; the "agricultural workers" stratum has been shrinking, down 12.5% from 2001 to 2010, which represented a decrease of more than 80 million agricultural workers over a decade; the "unemployed and semi-unemployed" stratum has remained relatively stable, and its proportion has declined somewhat in recent years.

Therefore, the study holds that, in 2010, a distinct change in China's social class structure was that "the class which should be small continues to shrink, and the class which should be big continues to grow," as opposed to the finding in the 2002 Report on the Study of Social Strata in Contemporary China that "the class which should be big hasn't grown big, and the class which should be small hasn't become small." Specifically, in 2001, the middle class accounted for about 16% (i.e., "hasn't grown big"), and the "agricultural workers" stratum accounted for 42.9%

Table 6 Occupational Stratification in Urban and Rural China (2000–2010) (%)

	Urban areas			*Rural areas*		
	2000	*2010*	*Changes*	*2000*	*2010*	*Changes*
Upper-class jobs	12.98	12.67	−0.31	3.00	2.93	−0.07
Middle-class jobs	30.1	38.44	8.29	7.54	11.75	4.21
Lower class jobs	56.87	48.89	−7.98	89.47	85.32	−4.15
Total	100.00	100.00		100.00	100.00	

Source Li Qiang, Wang Hao (2014)

(i.e., "hasn't become small"). Ten years later, in 2010, the "agricultural workers" stratum fell by 12.5%, accounting for about 30.4%, while the middle class increased by 10%, accounting for about 26%. Although the pattern of "the class which should be big hasn't grown big, and the class which should be small hasn't become small" has not been fundamentally reversed, changes in the ten social strata since the beginning of the twenty-first century show that China's social class structure is slowly evolving toward the "olive-shaped" structure of modern society.

By measuring occupational prestige and the proportions of groups, some scholars have found that China's social structure is inverted T-shaped. After the rapid development in the first decade of the twenty-first century, inertia remains a stubborn feature of China's social structure: the proportion of upper-class jobs has hardly changed, the proportion of middle-class jobs has grown slowly, and the proportion of lower class jobs has not changed much.[24]

It should be noted that of the above-mentioned middle-class jobs (Table 6), commercial and service staff such as sales staff and sales promotion and exhibition staff account for the largest proportion. In addition, middle-class jobs also include tailoring and sewing staff, shoe and hat makers and administrative staff. These jobs offer relatively low wages, far below the so-called "middle-class" standard. Therefore, most of the middle-class jobs in urban and rural areas as shown in Table 6 should be

[24] Li Qiang, Wang Hao. The Four Worlds of China's Social Hierarchy. *Social Science Front*, 2014 (9); Li Qiang. A Social Structure Shaped Like the Chinese Character "土" is forming in China. *Beijing Daily*, 2015-05-25.

reclassified as lower class jobs. The lower class in China's social structure as shown in the above table is huge.

The current shape of China's social structure is an unbalanced shape which is huge at the bottom and weak in the middle, no matter from what perspective you look at it. Meanwhile, during the course of rapid development over the past 30 years, this structure has remained relatively stable, changing at an extremely slow pace. Data show that low-income earners, who account for 20% of urban households, take up 11.4% of the higher education resources; lower-middle-income earners, who account for 20%, take up 10.1% of the higher education resources; middle- and upper-middle-income earners, who account for 40%, take up 25.7% of the higher education resources; high-income earners, who account for 20%, take up 51.9% of the higher education resources. The children of high-income parents have access to better education resources and employment opportunities, thus becoming a new generation of high-income earners. The children of high-income parents, on the other hand, can only become a new generation of low-income earners as they lack access to high-quality education and employment resources. Channels of upward mobility, such as education and employment, have become increasingly blocked, resulting in increasingly visible class divisions.

5.2.2 *Increasing Tensions Between Interest Groups*

In any modern society, with the diversification and differentiation of interests, different interest groups will gradually form. Members of each interest group have similar social status and interests, and may, under certain conditions, safeguard common interests through collective participation. There are often conflicts of interest between different interest groups. How these interest groups resolve conflicts and form consensus often has a bearing on the basic order of a society.

Some studies have pointed out that the interest group model is more suitable for analyzing China's social hierarchy. On the one hand, "class" or "stratum" means a group whose interest differentiation has been completed and whose material interests have been relatively stable, but China's interest pattern is changing rapidly, and various social interest groups are being divided, dissolved and reconciled, so using the concept of a class or stratum which is relatively stable in status is not in line with China's actual situation. On the other hand, interest groups are more realistic actors, the period of social transformation in China is precisely the period in which the adjustment of relations among different interests in society is the most drastic, while some groups gain, others are bound to lose, and many contradictions and conflicts in real society are mostly directly or indirectly related to the adjustment of relations among different interests in society.[25] Therefore, the use of interest group model to analyze China's social hierarchy in the transformation period can better illustrate relationships among interest groups and the contradictions and conflicts arising therefrom.

According to a survey, two-thirds of Chinese residents think they have benefited a lot and their living standards have improved in recent years, with more than one-eighth of them thinking their living standards have improved a lot; one fifth feel that their living standards have not changed; one eighth think their interests have been damaged and their living standards have fallen. The results of the survey also show that different social groups have benefited to different degrees. Those from better-off families, who are younger, who are better educated or who earn a higher income feel they have benefited more in recent years.[26] See Fig. 1 for details.

Such changes in and perceptions of the interest pattern will inevitably bring about changes in relations among different interests and groups in society, which will inevitably lead to social conflicts arising in connection with the distribution of interests. The above studies also show groups who gain respond to social conflicts differently from groups who lose: groups who gain from changes in the interest pattern are more inclined to resolve social conflicts through institutions; those who lose have lost confidence in institutions, and once involved in conflicts, they are more likely to resort to measures other than institutions, or even more drastic means to resolve social conflicts.

In fact, any reform is the adjustment of relations among different interests, which will result in the gain and loss of material interests, and the gain and loss of interests are logically different aspects of the same process. Therefore, from the perspective of relations among different interests, we can more clearly observe the interests, demands, and expressions of various groups. From the reality of China's reform and transformation at the present stage, we find that between the state and society, urban

[25] Li Qiang. Four Interest Groups Have Emerged in China. *Review of Economic Research*, 2001 (23).

[26] Li Peilin, et al. *Analysis and Prediction of China's Social Situation in 2005*. Beijing: Social Sciences Academic Press (China), 2005.

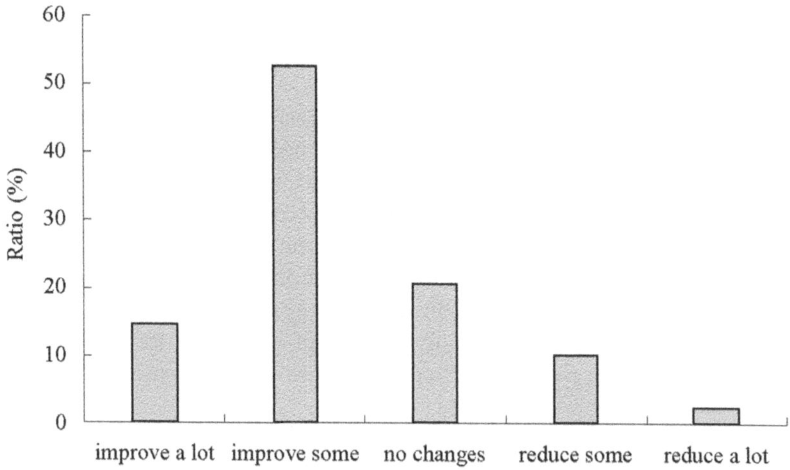

Fig. 1 Urban residents' evaluation of changes in their living standards in recent years (*Source* Li Peilin, et al. *Analysis and Prediction of China's Social Situation in 2005*. Beijing: Social Sciences Academic Press [China], 2005)

and rural areas, and the capitalist class and the working class are the most important interest relationship models, which are embodied in the relationship between officials and common people, right relations, and labor relations. These basic interest relationship models also lay the foundation for the presentation of interest-related demands and the articulation of interests by different groups, and also involve mechanisms driving stratification based on power, rights, and markets. Changes in the interest pattern have led to the differentiation of social groups and the aggravation of social conflicts related to interests, thereby increasing social risks. In dealing with conflicts of interest, any omission or error in coping strategies will further exacerbate social conflicts and lead to more serious social threats.

5.3 *Lack of Equity and Justice and Moral Decline*

In any society, equity, justice, and ethics are the basic conditions for keeping society functioning and ensuring social order. China's entry into the middle-income stage coincided with a lack of equity and justice and a moral decline.

5.3.1 *Lack of Equity and Justice*

Social equity and justice specifically means that the basic institutions of a society can treat every member of society fairly and equally, and can safeguard the basic social justice, such as distinguishing good from evil, being strict and fair in meting out rewards and punishments, helping the weak and relieving the poor and needy. Equity and justice have become a core value of modern society, and China is no exception. In a national survey on what makes a good society, 50.96% of the respondents said "equality" was the most important, ranking first among all options. Meanwhile, 43.2% of the respondents thought that "equity and justice" was the most important, ranking fourth among all the options.[27] It can be seen that the Chinese people also regard "equity and justice" as the most important social value.

At present, a considerable proportion of members of the Chinese society identify themselves as lower class and even disadvantaged. This tendency to identify oneself as lower class underscores one's disadvantaged position, conveys a feeling of being treated unjustly and unfairly, and indicates a strong sense of relative deprivation. Not only those recognized as disadvantaged groups, but also those who are usually admired, such as civil servants, police, teachers, private entrepreneurs and even leading cadres, generally feel disadvantaged, believing that they have been wronged in one way or another. At a time when China's economy is developing at such a high speed, this general feeling of being disadvantaged is very alarming. This phenomenon, at least in part, shows that in a society where equity and justice are not upheld, the members of every group are living in discomfort. Therefore, promoting social equity and justice is the most pressing issue in Chinese society today.

5.3.2 *Moral Decline*

As a kind of behavioral norms, morality, based on a complete value system, relies on certain moral forces and public opinion to ensure its implementation, has a significant impact on people's behavior, and can effectively control interpersonal interaction and maintain the basic social order. In a certain sense, morality is the basis of social order. Morality plays an

[27] Wang Junxiu. *The Characteristics of Current Social Values and the Reconstruction of Society's Shared Values—2014 Research Report on Social Psychology in China Research Report on Social Psychology in China (2014)*. Beijing: Social Sciences Academic Press (China), 2014.

important role in personal life and social stability. Based on Confucianism, Chinese traditional society which spanned thousands of years formed a set of moral norms centered on "denying self and returning to propriety" and "benevolence as the utmost virtue," which have been gradually internalized in the psychological basis of people's behavior, shaping people's personality and character. Fei Xiaotong[28] believed that the maintenance of order was not dependent on state power, but on edification by elders based on traditional norms. Village elders were the interpreters and defenders of moral norms and made people consciously observe etiquette through all kinds of edification.

In modern society, due to group differentiation and cultural diversity, the value and social foundation of traditional morality are gradually disintegrating day by day, and the effect of morality on controlling society is being weakened accordingly. Traditional morality is facing the impact of modern society, which is a common phenomenon in all countries around the world. This is particularly the case in China. In China, which has experienced nearly 40 years of rapid growth and transformation, traditional morality is facing great challenges, and there has been a sharp decline in morality. As the role of morality in regulating individual behavior weakens, utilitarianism, and opportunism may flourish, resulting in a bad situation where rules are disobeyed and everyone feels insecure. Not only do people not revere and observe morality, but they also mock, trample and play with it, and even violate it. Non-observance of morality and violation of morality have become acts that cost nothing and for which there's no price to pay, while observance of morality comes at a high cost and price.

Moral decline has caused social order to lose its foundation for existence. The basic trust among members of society has vanished, replaced by suspicion and resentment. The social trust system is on the brink of collapse. Surveys on social trust among urban residents in recent years show that social trust in China has been hovering around the minimum passing score line of "low trust," and once fell to "distrust." A 2010 survey on social trust among residents in Beijing, Shanghai, and Guangzhou shows that the overall social trust score was 62.9, which is

[28] Fei Xiaotong. *From the Soil: The Foundations of Chinese Society: The Institutions for Reproduction*. Beijing: Peking University Press, 1998.

the lower limit of low trust.[29] In 2011, the survey expanded to seven major cities in China, covering the eastern, central, and western regions of China. The results showed that the overall social trust score was 59.7 points, below the minimum passing score line.[30] According to the Report on the 2016 Survey on Social Trust Among Members of the Public in Beijing, 44% of the respondents said they would adhere to principles when faced with integrity issues; 45% said they would basically adhere to principles as necessary; only 8% said they would put their own interests first.

The above survey shows that social trust in China is low, trust has been seriously eroded, and the social trust system is on the verge of collapse. Some scholars believe that there is a serious social trust crisis in China, which is "unprecedented in depth and breadth and profoundly harmful".[31] The current trust crisis in China is mainly reflected in people's distrust of government and public power, distrust between stakeholders in markets and an interpersonal trust crisis among ordinary members of society.

5.4 *Growing Social Mentality Crises*

In a nutshell, social mentality is public perceptions of and public attitudes toward social reality that are formed in daily life. Social mentality is a collection of the feelings, value choices, and behavioral tendencies of members of society, which is dispersed in a society for a period of time and has an impact on the actions of members of society and the development of society as a whole. Generally speaking, social mentality involves different dimensions, including social satisfaction, perceptions of social justice, social trust, and social emotions. Social mentality not only reflects the public's basic perceptions and evaluations of social institutions, social

[29] Du Junfeng. *An analysis of Social Trust among Urban Residents in 2010—Based on a Survey Conducted in Beijing, Shanghai and Guangzhou. Annual Report on Social Mentality of China (2011).* Beijing: Social Sciences Academic Press (China), 2011.

[30] Rao Yinsha, et al. *Report on the Survey on Social Trust among Urban Residents.* Beijing: Social Sciences Academic Press (China), 2013.

[31] Yang Yiyin, et al. *A Study on Social Mentality in Contemporary China.* Beijing: Social Sciences Academic Press (China), 2013.

changes, and social life, but also reveals the values and behavioral orientations of members of society, and their confidence in and expectations about social development.

In the process of economic transformation of developed countries in Europe and America, developing countries in East Asia and Latin America, and countries in transition in Central and Eastern Europe, there have been social mentality crises such as general dissatisfaction and a collapse in trust. These different types of countries have tried to solve social problems through economic growth in the course of development. However, focusing on economic growth can cover up social contradictions, but it cannot solve these contradictions and the problems they cause. In the process of economic development, a lack of progress in social and political reform will lead to the accumulation of social contradictions and social problems, which will lead to social mentality crises. Social mentality crises will affect people's behavior and even lead to extreme social tendencies. It should be noted that social mentality is not simply the result of economic development and social structural changes, but has a certain degree of independence. Failure to solve social mentality crises may lead to a country experiencing various difficulties in the process of economic transformation and even sinking deeper and deeper into the middle-income trap. Therefore, in order to achieve economic transformation and social development, it is necessary to deal with social mentality crises cautiously.

From the experience of developed countries, developing countries and countries in transition, it can be seen that different strategies to deal with social mentality crises have led to different countries embarking on different development paths after becoming middle-income countries, with very different social consequences. Social dilemmas brought about by economic development were already a topic of discussion among Western scholars more than a century ago. They analyzed the inability to distinguish right from wrong, the lack of faith, and even the disintegration of the trust structure and value norm system that would arise in the development of modern society.[32] Developed countries in Europe and America also experienced serious social mentality crises in the process of economic development, especially during the time of economic hardship. During the two world wars and the Great Depression of the 1930s,

[32] [French] Emile Durkheim. *Suicide*, translated by Feng Yunwen. Beijing: The Commercial Press, 1996.

there was widespread discontent in both European and American societies, and people were skeptical and even pessimistic about their countries economic, political and social systems. Such discontent and suspicion prompted reflection on institutions. The public promoted institutional building through active social participation, with a focus on equity and justice, in an effort to solve social crises and economic difficulties. It should be noted that the rise and even spread of Nazism in Europe and America, especially in Germany in the 1930s and 1940s can also be seen as a response to social mentality crises at a time of economic hardship in European and American societies. Studies[33] have shown that Nazism claimed to want to maintain the superiority of the Germanic race, displaying a disregard for social equity and justice. This promise brought together most of the German people who were going through a difficult transition at that time, but resulted in a worldwide catastrophe. Like developed countries, developing countries also have to face social mentality crises in the process of economic development. In fact, one of the reasons why East Asia have been able to overcome the middle-income trap, while Latin America and ASEAN have been stuck in the middle-income trap for a long time is because of their ability to cope with social psychological crises. Before and after World War II, as Western countries made rapid advances in modernization, East Asian countries had to face social mentality problems such as the argument that Oriental civilization was in decline. However, it was precisely because of the active promotion of the improvement of social institutions and the development of non-governmental actors on the basis of emphasizing equity and justice that East Asian countries have built consensus and overcome the trap. In comparison, because vested interests control national decision-making and ignore the demands of people at the bottom, populism is rising, society-wide consensus is elusive, and hopes for a fair and just society have been extinguished, Latin American countries have been unable to resolve social mentality crises and complete economic and social transformation. Like Western developed countries and developing East Asian, Latin American and ASEAN countries, countries in transition in Central and Eastern Europe also face social mentality crises in the process of economic development. Before economic transformation, most of these countries faced a value vacuum and even an ideological crisis. Countries that straightened

[33] [British] Dahrendorf. *Conflict in Modern Society*. Translated by Lin RongYuan. Beijing: China Social Sciences Press (China), 2000.

out relations between different social strata and fostered social consensus on the basis of equity and justice have solved social mentality crises to successfully achieve transformation. Countries that still focus on special interest groups, because of the lack of consensus, have been unable to solve economic and social crisis, which may even lead to ethnic divisions and wars.

From the experience of these different types of countries, it can be seen that economic system reform alone cannot solve the social problems that a country face after it becomes a middle-income country. Only by facing up to the dual challenges of economic and social transformation, facing up to social mentality crises, building social consensus, strengthening social trust, and rebuilding the basic values and basic ethics shared by society, can we successfully achieve economic and social transformation.

5.5 *Challenges to Reform*

Promoting structural adjustment and achieving industrial upgrading and transformation through institutional changes so as to complete economic and social transformation is the basic thinking behind China's efforts to get out of the middle-income trap. However, when it comes to advancing the next phase of economic and social transformation, there are three conflicting trends that deserve our close attention.

First, institutional problems are becoming more and more prominent, but the impetus for institutional change is getting weaker. China's reform and opening-up, which started nearly 40 years ago, have entered the deep-water zone and a critical stage. Reforms that do not touch on institutions have long been completed. The hot spots and difficulties that reform currently faces are inextricably linked to current institutions at the root, which shows that China's institutional reform is far from complete. However, a number of special interest groups have formed in the reform process, and only under current institutions can they gain the maximum benefits. With China entering the middle-income stage, the extensive mode of growth adopted at the time of economic take-off is becoming less effective, so there is an urgent to reform the social structure and the interest pattern at the institutional level. However, as institutional reform becomes more and more urgent, the impetus for reform from within the system is getting weaker.

Second, the problems that were not solved in the early days of reform became more and more difficult to solve later. Since China pursues progressive reform, the determination of what to put on the reform agenda often follows the principle of little resistance and big returns. For example, rural areas where the cost of reform was smaller rather than cities where the cost of reform was bigger were chosen as the starting point of reform. One consequence of progressive reform is that reform for "hard bones" are difficult to gnaw is delayed as long as possible. In the end, the most difficult areas of reform come together to form a complex situation where any slight change will trigger a huge reaction. As a result, many complicated problems have arisen, which coupled with contentment with small achievements make reform difficult to start. For problems that were not solved in the early stages of reform, the cost of reform will not decrease with time, but may increase, and eventually the situation becomes unmanageable.

6 The Weak Links in the Rule of Law That China Faces in Overcoming the Middle-Income Trap

"When those who uphold the law are strong, the state is strong. When they are weak, the state is weak." Since the start of reform and opening-up nearly 40 years ago, China has achieved unprecedented economic development established and made great progress in building democracy and the rule of law, and a socialist legal system with Chinese characteristics has been basically established. However, we cannot shy away from the objective existence of many weak links in the rule of law that are incompatible with economic development. At present, China is at a critical stage of reform and development where the pressure on development is great and social contradictions are prominent. To successfully overcome the middle-income trap, we must follow the path of good law and sound governance, comprehensively deepen reform, perfect and develop the socialist system with Chinese characteristics, improve the Party's ability to govern and art of governance, uphold the rule of law, and unswervingly follow the path of socialist rule of law with Chinese characteristics. How to drive forward sustained, healthy economic and social development, promote the rule of law, and successfully overcome the middle-income trap concerns the building of a moderately prosperous society in all respects and the realization of the Chinese dream, and is one of the important challenges facing China at present.

6.1 *The Rule of Law Component of the Modernization of National Governance Still Needs to Be Improved*

The rule of law is at the core of the modernization of China's system and capacity for governance, and also an essential requirement and important safeguard for comprehensively deepening reform. After nearly 40 years of reform and opening-up, China's economic and social development has entered a new normal. To overcome the middle-income trap, we must shift from extensive development to scientific development and overcome the tendency of short-termism and utilitarianism; we must push reform across the deep-water zone, and explore ways to carry out reform in a balanced, transparent, fair, standardized and orderly manner; we must promote steady social transformation and resolve various complex and deep-seated social contradictions. There remains a lack of sound institutional arrangements and standardized legal support for public governance, market governance, and social governance; the efficiency of the national governance system in maintaining social stability and social order still needs to be improved.

6.2 *The Rule of Law Foundation of the Market Economic System Needs to Be Strengthened Urgently*

A market economy requires market entities to regard laws governing the market economy as a legally binding norms, requires the use of law to protect equal competition in markets so as to achieve Pareto efficiency, requires the use of legal means to deal with various contradictions and conflicts in the process of market operation, requires strict protection of the property rights of market entities from infringement, and so on. The rule of law cannot only guarantee free competition and efficiency, but also help to ensure and coordinate social distribution, manage conflicts of interest, and achieve the necessary social equity. A mature market economic system goes hand in hand with a sound legal system, so a market economy is essentially an economy founded on the rule of law. The economic history of world also shows that the few countries that have successfully overcome the middle-income trap in the past 100-plus years have implemented the rule of law, which empirically confirms the fundamental role of the rule of law in overcoming the trap. The most important precondition for markets to play a decisive role in resource allocation is that the rights and behaviors of market entities are bound and protected by law. Since the start of reform and opening-up, China's market economy system and legal system have been improved day by day, but there are still many gaps in the rule of law to be filled and weak links to be perfected. For example, the market rules, regulatory system, and price mechanism are not yet perfect; the property rights protection system and the state-owned asset management system need to be continuously improved; the rule of law guarantee for accelerating the transformation of government functions needs to be strengthened urgently; there is a long way to go in legislation for deepening reform of the fiscal, taxation and financial systems.

6.3 The Legal Environment for the Innovation-Driven Strategy Needs to Be Optimized

Creation and innovation are not so much the invention, discovery, and efficient application of technologies, but rather institutional arrangements for innovation, that is, "institutions are more important than technologies." Through the protection of intellectual property rights and the improvement of institutional systems that are conducive to and encourage innovation, the rule of law provides scope for technology talent and innovative enterprises to display their abilities and a supporting environment for the technological innovation-driven strategy. In other words, the rule of law is the foundation of innovation. Implementing an innovation-driven development strategy through technological and institutional innovation is the key to achieving economic transformation and upgrading and overcoming the middle-income trap. The experience of foreign countries also shows that, in order to overcome the middle-income trap, it is necessary to achieve a boost and leap in competitiveness at the present stage, foster internal growth momentum, and achieve a shift in the mode of growth from "imitation" to indigenous innovation. China's still has a lot of work to do in terms of the legal environment and the level of legal protection in order to meet the urgent need to implement an innovation-driven strategy. In terms of promoting technological innovation, China lacks the relevant national innovation system and the legal environment for indigenous innovation by enterprises; especially it lacks special regulations on technological innovation and technological advances by SMEs. In terms of promoting institutional innovation, laws and regulations are imperfect and disconnected, and the supervision system is flawed and very poorly implemented.

6.4 *A Belief in the Socialist Rule of Law with Chinese Characteristics Is yet to Be Established*

The socialist rule of law is a lofty ideal and belief shared by the whole society. Without a firm belief in the socialist rule of law, when faced with the "four tests" and "four dangers",[34] we will feel unsure about the future, spiritually bewildered and at a loss. To adhere to the road of socialism with Chinese characteristics, we must establish a belief in the rule of law, cultivate the habit of thinking based on the rule of law, promote the concept of the rule of law, and carry forward the spirit of the rule of law. The effective regulation of the market economy and social life by law is conditioned on loyalty to and faith in the law on the part of social actors. At present, the phenomenon of the law "hanging in the air" and "performing practically no function" due to a lack of faith in the law on the part of social actors is objectively present in the Chinese economy. As a result, many economic laws and regulations formulated and promulgated by the State have been shelved and exist in name only, making it difficult to realize their function and value in regulating and standardizing the market economy. In reality, there is still a market for the erroneous ideas of "the law must take second place to economic development," "only by constantly overstepping legal boundaries can we develop the economy better" and "the law is not as important as claimed and can be put on the back burner in favor of urgent priorities." In addition, integrity is the humanistic spirit element of building a country ruled by law and the cornerstone of the sound operation of the rule of law project. What is worrying is that integrity has been woefully lacking in the development of the market economy. Some business operators flout the law by seeking gains at the expense of others. Economic fraud poses a serious problem, debt evasion is quite common, and illegal and criminal activities such as financial fraud, evading foreign exchange controls, obtaining foreign currency under false pretenses and getting export tax rebates through fraudulent means are rampant; counterfeit and shoddy goods are causing growing concerns, damaging the interests of consumers and endangering

[34] The "four tests" are the test in exercising governance, the test in carrying out reform and opening-up, the test in developing the market economy and the test from the external environment; the "four dangers" are the danger of lacking in drive, the danger of incompetence, the danger of being out of touch with the people and the danger of passive corruption.

the physical and mental health of the people; local protectionism, barriers between localities, and departmental monopolies still exist, preventing the creation of a unified market.

7 Summary

Since the start of reform and opening-up, China's economy has maintained rapid development for nearly 40 years thanks to the demographic and reform dividends. However, with the demographic dividend disappearing, resources and the environment coming under strain, and reform becoming more difficult, China's existing mode of economic growth is facing many challenges and has become unsustainable. While China's economy has been growing rapidly over the past few decades, some accumulated social contradictions, such as environmental pollution and income disparity, have become increasingly prominent and caused social problems. Therefore, China urgently needs to carry out in-depth economic and social system reforms to promote the successful transformation of the mode of economic growth and social governance. Economic and social transformation needs to be maintained and safeguarded by a robust rule of law. At present, there are still many weak links in the rule of law in China that are not compatible with economic development and need to be further improved.

CHAPTER 4

Overcoming the Middle-Income Trap Requires Improving the Economic Governance Capability

General Secretary Xi Jinping pointed out in his report to the 19th CPC National Congress: "As socialism with Chinese characteristics has entered a new era, the principal contradiction facing Chinese society has evolved. What we now face is the contradiction between unbalanced and inadequate development and the people's ever-growing needs for a better life." To overcome unbalanced and inadequate development, we need to improve our economic governance capability. The modernization of the economic governance capability is an important part of the modernization of China's system and capacity for governance. The economic governance system is understood as the institutional system whereby the government and the market regulate economic agents; the economic governance capability is defined as the ability of the government and the market to regulate economic agents. In order to do a good job in economic governance through institutional design and institutional enforcement, it is necessary to properly handle the relationship between the government and the market.[1]

[1] Liu Chengli. Modernization of the Economic Governance System and Capability: From the Dual Perspectives of the Government and the Market. *The Economist*, 2015, 5(5): 28–34.

Z. Zheng, *Middle-Income Trap*,
https://doi.org/10.1007/978-981-15-7401-6_4

Earlier in this book, we analyzed national economic governance. Developed countries, particularly Europe and the United States, improved their economic governance capability in the process of overcoming the middle-income trap. For example, historical experience shows that the "crisis-change" model is the normal state of the existence and operation of the American economic governance model. A solid institutional core, periodic institutional adjustments, and a pendulum-like movement between free markets and government intervention ensure the vitality of the American economic governance model. The "end of the American model" view that prevailed during the economic crisis is one-sided. From the perspective of actual performance, economic recession is a process of eliminating bubbles and rebuilding confidence and does not mean a decline in production capacity, nor does a temporary increase in dependence on external markets indicate a decline in the international economic status of the United States. The fact that in the global economic crisis there is an opportunity for the reconstruction of the world economy and the rise of emerging countries makes it all the more important to objectively look at and rationally learn from the American model.[2]

In terms of economic governance, the British government plays a key role in macro-control. Macro-control is an important part of the economic governance capability.[3] The United Kingdom has established a macro-control system with the Treasury as the core. The Treasury is the most important Cabinet department. It wields great power and plays a pivotal role in macro-control in the United Kingdom. Reducing inflation, maintaining a good momentum of economic development, improving service quality, and maintaining a high standard of living for the people are the economic goals that the British government is committed to. To this end, the British government wants to reduce tax rates as much as possible, believing that low tax rates play a decisive role in the stability of financial markets.

After World War II, France promulgated the National Statistics and Public Accounting Law, accurately and timely grasped the national conditions, implemented economic policies based on indicative planning and

[2] An Ran, Wang Gezhong. The Vitality of the "American Model" from the Perspective of Economic Crisis and Institutional Change. *Expanding Horizons*, 2010 (4): 83–85.

[3] Qu Yanjia. The Role of the British Government in Macro-Control. *Economic Perspectives*, 1996 (7).

increased investment in scientific research and education, and technological advances made outstanding contributions to its economic growth. France is one of the most active countries in Europe to advocate and promote regional economic integration.[4]

The main feature of Germany's economic governance is to combine the government's regulatory role with market-oriented operations to create an incentive-based national model. Germany's economic governance has long been known for its prudence and soundness, not only as a departure from other European countries, but also as a key to Germany's rapid overcoming the consequences of the financial and economic crisis. It is not only what distinguishes Germany from other European countries, but also the key to Germany's ability to quickly overcome the consequences of financial and economic crises. Germany is the birthplace and testing ground of the "social market economy" theory, so its economic governance policy is distinctly characteristic of a social market economy.[5]

The economic governance of the United States, the United Kingdom, France, Germany, and most other developed countries has gone through the process of "spontaneous clustering-factor driven-market driven-innovation driven," and there are many successful experiences that we can learn from.

Meanwhile, this book also analyzes the experience of countries that have failed to overcome the middle-income trap and lessons learnt therefrom, such as Indonesia, the Philippines, and other Southeast Asian countries, Latin American countries, the Soviet Union, and east European countries in transition, which generally fell into the middle-income trap in the middle-income stage, and the lessons learnt therefrom. Among them, Indonesia still has some major problems in its economic development, including severe unemployment and poverty, regional imbalance in development, incomplete market-oriented reforms of the financial system, and an unreasonable economic structure. The Philippines' problems are long-standing economic, political, and institutional structural contradictions that severely constrain its economic development. The experience of Latin American countries in the middle-income stage and the lessons

[4] Li Mingye. Interpretation of the Current French Planning Concepts and Methods in the Context of the La Défense Renewal Plan. *International Urban Planning*, 2012 (5).

[5] Xue Yanping. Germany's Economic Governance in Retrospect and Prospect—The Impact of the Social Market Economy Model. *Contemporary World*, 2014 (9): 54–57.

learnt therefrom show that Latin America has been largely in the "growth in the trap" stage for the past half-century. They are mired in all kinds of social and economic problems. That's not to say that they have stopped growing, but they have grown so slowly as to fall far behind fast-growing regions.

1 International Experience in Overcoming the Middle-Income Trap and Lessons Learnt Therefrom

The fundamental reason why a country could shatter the bonds of poverty and achieve a takeoff, but fell into the middle-income trap is that the development mechanism needed for a country to make the jump from middle-income to high-income status is fundamentally different from the mechanism for achieving a takeoff. In other words, a country can continue to grow from a low-income economy to a middle-income economy following the original development strategy and mechanism, but it is difficult to make the leap from middle income to high income relying on the same strategy and mechanism. To continue to develop economically and socially and continue to improve their per capita income, middle-income countries must make fundamental changes to their original modes of growth and growth mechanisms, so as to thoroughly transform their modes of economic and social development. Only by doing so can they lay the foundation for continuous progress toward high-income status.

Historically, few economies have been able to successfully navigate through the complex technological, social, and political challenges that arose at this stage. Many countries have been able to reach the middle-income level very quickly, but few have managed to get out of the middle-income trap.

1.1 Lessons from Latin American Countries Falling into the Middle-Income Trap

1.1.1 Main Lessons from Latin American Countries Falling into the Middle-Income Trap

Failure to Change the Mode of Economic Development in Time According to the Different Stages and Characteristics of Economic Development

Most Latin American countries have vast fertile land and abundant mineral resources. With these favorable conditions, these countries once achieved a short period of high-speed growth, especially the "Latin American miracle" created after "World War II." But in the late 1970s, industrialization in these countries ran into difficulties. The reason was that they had long pursued the "import substitution" strategy and a model whereby big companies wielded monopolistic power. Import substitution had been pursued for general consumer goods, consumer durable goods, and capital goods. They had not changed their modes of development and implemented an opening-up and export-oriented strategy in time, and had been out of touch with the mainstream of global technological changes. Even when they were trapped in debt after the oil crisis in the early 1970s, they still financed their growth with debt. They continued the "import substitution" strategy for half a century.

Lack of Impetus for Technological Development and Innovation

After a country's economy enters the middle-income stage, it will gradually lose its low-cost advantage and therefore have difficulty competing with low-income countries in low-end markets; in middle and high-end markets, constrained by limited R&D capabilities and human capital conditions, it will have difficulty competing with high-income countries. In such an environment where it is squeezed at both ends, it can easily lose growth momentum and slip into economic stagnation. In order to overcome this challenge, it is necessary to improve R&D capabilities, attach importance to human capital, upgrade industries, and cultivate new competitive advantages. Latin American countries have been implementing import substitution strategies for a long time and lack the impetus for technological innovation. In the 1980s, influenced by Western neoliberalism, Latin American countries slashed public budgets, resulting in a sharp decline in R&D investment, thus missing the great opportunities brought by a new round of technological revolution.

Failure to Effectively Balance Government Regulation and Market Mechanisms

After the 1980s, influenced by the neoliberal trend spawned by the "Washington consensus," Latin American countries gave free rein to market mechanisms. Macro-control was extremely weakened and macroeconomic policies lacked stability, which coupled with high government debts and obstinate problems such as inflation and disequilibrium in the balance of payments led to the frequent occurrence of economic crisis, resulting in large fluctuations in the economy.

Woeful Lack of Progress in Institutional Adjustment and Change

In Latin American countries, obstructed by interest groups, institutional adjustment and reform are seriously lagging behind economic development. The "modern traditionalism" advocated by the elite places undue emphasis on economic growth and wealth accumulation, and opposes change in such areas as social structure, values, and power distribution, or minimizes such change. The excessive concentration of economic wealth and the powerful influence of interest groups have resulted in the spread of rent-seeking, speculation, and corruption, and seriously distorted the market's function of allocating resources.

Unequal Distribution of Income

The unequal distribution of income has seriously affected the economic growth of Latin American countries. First, the unequal distribution of income has led to sluggish domestic demand. The middle and lower classes in Latin America have been marginalized in the process of economic development, which directly limits the expansion of consumption and weakens domestic demand, creating a vicious circle of slow growth and insufficient domestic demand. Secondly, the unequal distribution of income limits the expansion of investment. Low savings rates and capital flight have led to inadequate capital formation in Latin America, and production investment has to rely on external funds, exposing macroeconomic operations to risks in the international environment. Finally, income inequality indirectly affects the accumulation of human capital in Latin American countries, leaving Latin America's economy with no basis for sustained growth. A lack of government investment in primary education has led to the poor quality of education in Latin America, which affects the improvement of human capital.

1.1.2 Common Reasons for Latin American and Southeast Asian Countries Falling into the Middle-Income Trap

Why have many Latin American and Southeast Asian countries fallen into the middle-income trap? The following reasons cannot be ignored.

Stalled Development

The essence of the middle-income trap is about growth. In an economy capable of sustained growth, various social contradictions can be gradually resolved through incremental adjustment, while a stagnant economy has to make stock adjustments, pushing itself into a vicious circle of "stagnant growth - social unrest - economic disorder - weak recovery." An economy must keep growing or it will fall into the middle-income trap. Across Latin America, the economy grew at an average annual rate of 1.2% in the 1980s, with GDP per capita growing only −1.9%. Argentina experienced 16 years of negative growth from 1963 to 2008.

Structural Imbalances

Brazil, Mexico, Argentina, Malaysia, and Thailand have long had structural imbalances. First, the industrial structure is out of balance. Countries such as Brazil, Argentina, and Mexico have labor-intensive industries in which they have a comparative advantage in favor of capital-intensive heavy and chemical industries such as steel and shipbuilding, resulting in an imbalance in the ratio between light and heavy industries and between industry and agriculture. Second, human capital and indigenous innovation are out of balance. The lack of high-end talents and low R&D capabilities seriously restricts the upgrading and transformation of the economic structure. In 2009, Japan and South Korea spent more than 2% of their GDP on R&D, while Chile spent only 0.7% of its GDP on R&D. In 2009, South Korea was granted 9566 patents, compared with 181 in Malaysia. Third, urban–rural development is out of balance. Industrialization is falling way behind urbanization which is developing too fast, resulting in a large influx of landless people into cities. Difficulties in employment, housing, income, and social security have caused serious social problems. Brazil's urbanization rate soared from 41.4% in

1950 to 85% in 2013, reaching or even surpassing the level of developed countries. Thailand has a total population of more than 60 million, and the capital Bangkok alone has a population of more than 10 million. Fourth, the social security mechanism is out of balance. The weakening of investment in employment, health care, and education has a huge impact on economic and social stability. Fifth, environmental development is out of balance. In Brazil, vast areas of the Amazon rainforest are being felled to make way for the planting of cash crops on an industrial scale; in Argentina, pastures have been overgrazed; Thailand's forest resources have been basically destroyed; in Manila and Jakarta, large amounts of garbage are being dumped directly into the sea.

Capital Drain

Countries with fragile financial systems lack independent financial systems, and their economies are severely constrained by the capital of developed countries. In particular, the phenomenon of borrowing short and lending long is common. In addition, because of the premature and excessive liberalization of capital controls, once the withdrawal of foreign capital leads to a capital drain, businesses will collapse or be on the verge of bankruptcy. Brazil, for example, was once the pride of South America, but it was heavily dependent on foreign capital in the latter stages, and the 1999 financial crisis shattered its already fragile financial system, resulting in a huge capital drain and sending its economy into a nosedive. For countries such as Mexico and Argentina, the story is similar.

Panic

Many countries that have fallen into the middle-income trap panicked when confronted with major difficulties or economic crises. As a result, difficulties evolved into crises, and small crises into big ones. First, some Latin American countries stubbornly adhered to the strategy of "financing growth with debt." Shortly after the oil crisis in the early 1970s, many Latin American countries continued to maintain the development strategy of "financing growth with debt," while European and American countries adopted austerity policies one after another, which greatly increased the debt burden of Latin American countries. Second, the economic policy of "fundamentalist market determinism" was implemented. In the 1980s, Latin American countries, still mired in stagnant economic growth, saw the "invisible hand" as a life-saving straw, preventing the "visible hand" of the government from coming to the rescue. Instead of eliminating the root cause of the debt crisis, the rescue plan in the absence of economic monitoring led to a worsening of the balance of payments. Third, many Latin American countries copied the Western high welfare system without regard to their own finances. From 1987 to 1988, Argentina and Uruguay, which established social insurance systems earlier in Latin America, had social security tax rates as high as 34–45 and 54–57%, respectively, close to those of European countries; social security tax rates in many Latin American countries were 20–30%, higher than Canada and the United States. A "welfare catch-up" distorted the market price signal, resulting in misallocation of resources and high levels of debt in macro-public finance. Fourth, after the Asian financial crisis, Malaysia and other Southeast Asian countries failed to adjust the economic model driven by low-cost trade in time, and failed to find new areas of economic growth.

1.2 *The Main Performance of South Korea and Japan in Overcoming the Middle-Income Trap*

In the early 1960s, more than 100 countries joined the ranks of middle-income countries, but so far only a few dozen have joined the ranks of high-income countries, and most of them are small countries. China has joined the ranks of middle-income countries. Some people believe that China is likely to fall into the middle-income trap. "Stones from other hills may serve to polish the Jade of this one." Analyzing the successful experiences of countries that have overcome the trap and lessons from countries that have fallen into the trap is very important to China's future development.

South Korea and Japan are typical examples of countries that successfully changed their modes of economic development through the transformation of mechanisms driving their growth and the reform of their economic development systems and then became high-income countries, and are of great significance in terms of providing precedents for China to learn from. Overall, judging from the experience of Japan and South Korea, crossing the trap is actually about a boost and leap in competitiveness at the present stage. At the core of Japan and South Korea's ability to sustain growth is to foster internal growth momentum, and the key is to make the shift from "imitation" to indigenous innovation. Their main experience is as follows.

1.2.1 *Adjusting the Mode of Economic Development*

From the early 1950s to the 1980s, Japan transformed and upgraded from light industry to heavy industry to the tertiary sector in time, and completed the shift from "founding the nation on trade" to "founding the nation on technology" to "founding the nation on culture." After the 1980s, Western countries pursued trade protectionism, which greatly impacted South Korea's export-oriented economy. South Korea put forward the policy goal of "upgrading the industrial structure," accelerated the shift from an extensive development strategy relying on increasing capital inputs and maintaining cheap labor to relying mainly on increasing R&D investment and improving the technological content of industries to enhance competitiveness. South Korea vigorously developed technology- and knowledge-intensive industries with a focus on the electronic industry, and reorganized low value-added industries such as light textile, fiber, and dyeing; gradually outsourced manufacturing processes in the automotive, shipbuilding and machinery industries, and focused on front-end processes such as R&D and design, and high value-added back-end processes such as marketing and after-sales service. This has laid an important foundation for South Korea to take the lead in global industrial structural adjustment and achieve sustainable development.

1.2.2 *Founding the Nation on Technological Innovation*

When in the middle-income stage, all high-income economies adopted various strategies and measures to improve their capacity for technological innovation, so as to secure an advantageous position in international competition. In 1982, South Korea officially put forward the strategy of "founding the nation on science and technology," and made it clear that its main goal was to use advanced technology to transform existing industries. In the 1990s, in order to reduce its technological dependence on developed countries, South Korea further implemented the strategy of "founding the nation on science and technology" by developing its high-tech industries. Similarly, since the 1980s, Japan has established the strategy of "founding the nation on innovation" and regarded it as the basic national policy for economic development in the new era.

1.2.3 *Increasing Total Factor Productivity*

In the 1970s, a remarkable feature of South Korea's mode of economic development was that capital inputs grew very fast, the contribution of total factor productivity to economic growth was negative, and economic growth replied on factor inputs. But by the 1980s, the contribution of total factor productivity to the South Korean economy had reached 28.94%. Total factor productivity surpassed labor inputs in terms of contribution to economic growth to become the second largest development driver after capital. From 1998 to 2011, total factor productivity contributed 44.87% of South Korea's economic growth, becoming the leading driver of economic growth. South Korea has truly achieved an economic transformation into an innovative economic development model that relies on total factor productivity for development. Japan experienced a period of rapid growth from 1951 to 1974, a period of steady growth from 1975 to 1993, and a lost decade from 1994 to 2005. One of the most important signs of each period was a corresponding increase or decrease in total factor productivity.

1.2.4 *Adjusting the Income Distribution Pattern*

The South Korean government adjusted the pattern of primary distribution through tax policy, and adjusted the pattern of redistribution through social security measures. Since the 1980s, its Gini coefficient decreased significantly and income distribution has become equalized. In 1991, the Gini coefficient of South Korea decreased from 0.39 in 1980 to 0.26, and the income gap between the high- and low-income groups was significantly narrowed.

1.2.5 *Striking a Balance Between Urban and Rural Development*

In the 1960s, the income gap between urban and rural South Korea gradually widened in the process of industrialization. In 1970, the South Korean government launched the "New Village Movement" aimed at narrowing the gap between urban and rural areas and coordinating the development of industry and agriculture. According to South Korea's Annual Statistical Report on Agriculture and Forestry, the rural population accounted for 44.7% of the country's population in 1970, and that proportion dropped to 6% in 2005. With a large number of farmers working in non-agricultural sectors, the urban–rural income ratio had changed significantly. By the early 1990s, the per capita income of rural residents in South Korea had reached 95% of that of urban residents, and the urban–rural income gap had basically disappeared. After World War II, with the development of industrialization and urbanization, the gap between urban and rural areas in Japan widened dramatically, leading to a series of problems such as overpopulation in big cities, underpopulation in rural areas, and a declining rural economy. The Japanese government formulated three comprehensive development plans in 1961, 1969, and 1977, respectively, continuously adjusted the agricultural and rural policy, improved the integrated urban–rural elderly care, health care, and education systems by strengthening the building of socialized service systems in rural areas, and brought uniformity between urban and rural areas in legal status, residents' political rights, social security, and governance model, thus effectively reassuring farmers who intended to move to cities or urban residents who planned to move to the countryside. After decades of development, Japan has become a country with a relatively small urban–rural gap in the world.

1.3 Summary of the Experience of Major Economies in Overcoming the Middle-Income Trap

From what discussed earlier in this book, it can be seen that due to different national conditions and different stages of development in overcoming the middle-income trap, countries have their own characteristics when it comes to market economic mechanisms, concepts, and consciousness, which makes their development paths different. There is no perfect development path in the world. We divide the development paths of high-income countries into three categories, namely, the development paths of "liberal capitalism," "social market economy," and "government-led capitalism" as represented by the United States, Germany, and Japan, respectively.

In the development stage where the United States and the United Kingdom overcame the middle-income trap, the development path they pursued was typical "liberal capitalism," with little government intervention in the economy, the tremendous development of the commodity economy, and high investment efficiency, which was conducive to productivity and economic development. This development path pays too much attention to efficiency and not enough to social equity. According to famous British economist David Coates, the main feature of this development path for overcoming the middle-income trap is that "the power to decide on accumulation rests with private companies, which are free to pursue short-term profit targets to the maximum extent and obtain capital through financial markets; workers can only enjoy limited labor and social rights as stipulated by law; people's general understanding of social politics and morality is individualism and liberalism." Its main advantages: highly flexible labor and product markets, low taxes, fierce competition and shareholder capitalism—shareholders exert pressure on managers to maximize their profits. Its main disadvantages: huge income disparity, low welfare benefits, poor quality of "public goods" such as primary and secondary education, disproportion between public services and social wealth, low investment-to-GDP ratio, and very low savings rate.

The main feature of the development path through which "social market economies" represented by Germany overcame the middle-income trap is that the relationship between banks and companies is close, and banks supervise companies as both shareholders and lenders. It is hoped that, through this development path, a balance between efficiency and equity can be struck by achieving the goal of creating high profits, a balanced distribution of benefits and a higher income level. According to David Coates, the main feature of a social market economy is that "there may be relatively little direct intervention by the state in the accumulation of capital, but the political system has strictly established a set of labor rights and welfare measures, so that organized workers have a quite influential market and the ability to directly participate in labor negotiations; the mainstream culture is social democracy and Christian democracy." Its main advantages: excellent education and training; low wage inequality and a high welfare system for residents contribute to the harmony of the whole society; the close relationship between companies and banks encourages high investment. Its main disadvantages: the labor market and product market are subject to many restrictions; trade unions that are too powerful, high tax rates, overly generous unemployment benefits, and extensive restrictions on the labor market and product market will lead to high unemployment. France's development path is close to this.

Japan and South Korea are latecomers among high-income countries. The two countries achieved remarkable rapid economic development in the 1960s and 1970s and the 1970s and 1970s, respectively. Their development path can be called "government-led capitalism," which enabled them to achieve the success of "catch-up modernization."

The main feature of this development path: first, become a heavily industrialized country through the "late-mover advantage" and by adopting the strategy of "catching up" with Europe and the United States; second, make technological advances mainly by introducing and absorbing a large number of advanced technologies; third, "found the nation on trade" with exports taking the lead; fourth, the government has long-term economic and industrial structure development plans and intervenes a lot in the economy, companies and the government work closely together, and banks and companies own stock in each other; fifth, implement financial control. According to David Coates, this development path "relies on private companies for making decisions about accumulation, but the final adoption of decisions must be determined in close consultation with public institutions, and government departments and banks play an indirect role in the decision-making process; it favors weakening the political and social power of workers, but leaves room for the form of labor relations, and advocates harmonizing relations between workers and private companies through corporate welfare measures; the mainstream culture seems to be conservative and nationalistic in content." Its main advantages: the lifetime employment system promotes employees' loyalty to companies and a high level of technical proficiency; the quality of public services (especially education) is high; there are close relationships between banks and other industrial and commercial enterprises; cross holding protects managers from impatient shareholders, so that they can focus more on long-term investments. Its main disadvantages: companies that are protected and not fully exposed to market forces are under little pressure to make efficient use of capital.

The relationship between the government and the market is one of the eternal topics in economics. This relationship varies depending on the development path for overcoming the middle-income trap. In a market economy, companies are the main demanders and suppliers in the market, and the level of their development can be used as a measure of the country's economic development. The development path of the United States emphasizes individual success and short-term financial benefits, and its market model is free and open. The US government's intervention in the market is mainly indirect regulation through the use of fiscal and monetary policies. The government only plays a very limited role in determining the way capital and labor interact: the task of the government is to create a good currency, and prevent monopolies from distorting factor and product markets and endangering free and open trade, thus ensuring and facilitating the full functioning of the market; in addition, the economic behavior of the government also includes the provision of public products (such as defense and social infrastructure); the government's policy on consumer goods manufacturing is heavily influenced by liberalism, and has long been and will continue, to a limited extent, focusing on shaping the market.

The development path through which Germany and Japan overcame the middle-income trap puts more emphasis on collective success and long-term interests, with more government intervention in the economy than in the United States. Germany is essentially a market economy regulated by the state. The government adjusts deviations in market operations through direct intervention (price control, various policies and regulations, participation in corporate investment, etc.) and indirect intervention. Germany was industrialized later than the United Kingdom and the United States, and the German government has acted as an implementer of economic modernization: the German government "played an important role in promoting labor laws for class cooperation, and implemented active labor market and welfare policies; the German government directly affected the local industrial accumulation rate in a number of crucial ways." But the German government's intervention in and guidance on the economy were not as extensive as the Japanese government. Japan's postwar economic growth owed much to the developmental role of state planning and guidance. The Japanese economy was built on the close cooperation and meticulous cooperation between state bureaucrats and private companies and industrial sectors, and was a "state-guided high-speed growth system." Japan's Ministry of International Trade and Industry and its role were a distinctive feature and initiative of Japan's development path. The government guided economic activities through industrial policies and economic plans, especially through strong intervention in and guidance on corporate decision-making, relied on fiscal, financial, tax, and other economic levers for indirect and effective macro-control of economic activities, and carried out micro-management at the corporate level.

In overcoming the middle-income trap, China should assimilate the experience and lessons of the three different development paths represented by the United States, Germany, and Japan, and fully study the impact of different national conditions and different development stages on the choice of development path.

2 Challenges Facing China's Economy in Overcoming the Middle-Income Trap and Measures to Be Taken

The problems faced by China in the present stage of economic development and the corresponding challenges include: challenges brought by a further rise in uncertainty about and the instability of the recovery of the world economy; challenges brought by continued in-depth adjustments to the global industrial structure and international specialization, and major changes in the economic landscape; challenges brought by the "simultaneous occurrence of three periods" in China's economy; challenges brought by China's current economic structure; challenges brought by rising production costs and inadequate innovation capability; challenges brought by overcapacity and resource and environmental constraints; challenges brought by increased fiscal and financial risks; challenges brought by the reform of the exchange rate system; challenges brought by globalization and deglobalization; challenges brought by complex and frequent social contradictions.

2.1 Major Challenges Facing the Economy in Overcoming the Middle-Income Trap

First, challenges brought by a further rise in uncertainty about and the instability of the recovery of the world economy. The profound impact of the international financial crisis continues to be present; external demand has not improved significantly; the structural problems of developed economies, such as the economic structural problem of the hollowing out of industries and the over-development of the service sector, especially the financial services sector, the economic model problem of low savings rates and high welfare spending, the fiscal structural problem of high deficits and high government debt, and the financial structural problem of over-leveraging cannot be solved overnight. In order to get out of the crisis and reverse the state of "high unemployment, high debt and low growth," developed countries, without exception, have adopted large-scale unconventional quantitative easing measures. On the one hand, quantitative easing can drive down government bond yields and lower the cost of debt in the short term, which helps boost market confidence to some extent; on the other hand, quantitative easing may trigger large-scale cross-border flows of international capital, which will exacerbate exchange rate fluctuations and affect the stability of international financial markets. Therefore, in the short term, the international economic environment is unlikely to improve significantly. Not only that, the downward pressure and potential risks facing the world economy may increase. A further rise in uncertainty about and the instability of the recovery of the world economy has caused a slowdown in global economic activity, and the expansion of demand in international markets is slow, further dimming the prospects for world trade.

Second, challenges brought by continued in-depth adjustments to the global industrial structure and international specialization, and major changes in the economic landscape. The challenges are mainly reflected in: First, the global industrial structure is "softening." The proportion of labor-intensive industries is gradually decreasing, while the proportion of knowledge-intensive and technology-intensive industries is increasing; high and new technologies as information technology are widely used in traditional industries; modern service industries such as finance, information, and consulting services have gradually become the leading industries driving economic growth, starting a new trend toward the upgrading of the industrial structure and the industrialization of high and new technologies. Second, the shift from traditional manufacturing to advanced manufacturing has accelerated. In recent years, major industrialized countries have formulated various development plans to promote a shift from traditional manufacturing to advanced manufacturing. The development of advanced manufacturing not only optimizes the internal industrial structure of manufacturing industry, but also provides a solid foundation for the technological progress and systematic structural optimization of the whole economy. Third, international specialization may be partially adjusted in the post-crisis era. First, the "re-industrialization" policies of developed countries may bring back some manufacturing industries, leading to a partial adjustment of the pattern of international specialization. Second, there may be some adjustments in the division of labor within emerging economies. Due to differences in factor endowments, technological levels, etc., the development of emerging economies will be differentiated to some extent. Meanwhile, the global financial crisis has seriously undermined the strength of traditional developed countries such as the United States, Europe, and Japan, and the Western world's role in the international system in the traditional sense has declined. Although emerging economies, especially China, have also been deeply affected, they have suffered relatively little impact compared with other countries and regions. They have played a leading role in world economic growth and recovery, and their role in the international system has been growing. They have begun to participate in the process of "setting rules and regulations" for the international system relatively equally and to varying degrees, changing the structure of the world economy and the global pattern of interests. The international community has called on China to "take greater responsibility" for major issues such as the trading system, climate change, and sustainable development. Therefore, how to enhance China's role in international specialization, correctly define China's role on the world stage, and assume international responsibility commensurate with its ability is undoubtedly a new challenge for a rising China.

Third, challenges brought by the "simultaneous occurrence of three periods" in China's economy. First, economic growth has entered a period of "downshifting." After years of high-speed economic growth since the start of reform and opening-up, we have to face the reality of a decline in the potential growth rate at the present stage. According to a forecast by the Development Research Center of the State Council, the average annual growth rate of China's GDP is likely to fall to around 7–8% during the 13th Five-Year Plan period, and by 2020–2030, China's GDP growth rate may drop further to around 5–6%. In other words, either because of the increase in the base and the transformation of the development mode, or because of the influence of other factors at home and abroad, China's economic growth may maintain a "new normal" of low growth in the future. Of course, a slowdown in economic growth is not all bad, because it can to some extent mitigate the damage to resources and the environment caused by high-speed growth in the past. But it is undeniable that, as mentioned earlier, China's current national conditions, such as a grim employment situation, the standard of living for low- and middle-income groups, the loss of social elites and livelihood issues, all require us to maintain a high economic growth rate. If we do not face up to the reality of slowing economic growth, we are likely to enact wrong policies, which will put the stable operation of the economy and economic and social stability in great peril. Second, the "period of pain" in economic structural adjustment. The contradiction between economic development and resources and the environment is becoming increasingly acute. It is imperative to accelerate the transformation of the mode of economic development and the adjustment of the economic structure.

The transformation of China's economic structure generally consists of: shifting from relying mainly on external demand to relying mainly on domestic demand, from relying mainly on investment to relying mainly on consumption, from relying mainly on government investment to relying mainly on social investment, and from relying mainly on ordinary factor inputs to relying mainly on advanced factor inputs.

But structural transformation is not a free lunch. In order to resolve excess capacity and optimize the industrial structure, some industries will inevitably be hit hard, and some companies will even withdraw from the market, which has to pay the price of "pain" in the structural adjustment. The price that has to be paid is the "pain" in structural adjustment. Third, the "digestion period" of earlier stimulus measures. The 2008 international financial crisis hit China's economy hard. In order to reverse the adverse effects of a rapid decline in growth, the government came up with a package of timely stimulus measures such as those for stimulating domestic demand and revitalizing industry to promote the rapid and stable recovery of economic growth, but the cumulative and spillover effects of these measures are still at work and continue to have a profound impact on economic growth. This constrains macro policy choices in the current period, greatly reducing the room for regulation and control.

Fourth, challenges brought by China's current economic structure. As things stand now, first, China has completed the transition from light industry to heavy industry, and the secondary sector is still the leading sector; second, the service sector as a share of GDP is low and is dominated by consumer services, and the development of the modern service industry is lagging behind; third, there is imbalance between consumption and investment, and processing trade accounts for half of exports; fourth, income inequality is gradually expanding, and asset price inflation has worsened wealth inequality; fifth, the financial structure is dominated by banks and there is financial repression. Trends in the evolution and development of China's economic structure in the next 20 years are as follows: first, there is a large space for urbanization in China in the future, and effective investment is still the main driving force for economic growth. China does not necessarily need to undergo "de-industrialization," but it needs to improve the core competitiveness of the manufacturing industry; the focus of corporate investment will gradually shift to technology-intensive areas such as equipment and software, and the focus of government investment will gradually shift from large-scale infrastructure to intangible assets such as technology research and development. The role of consumption will continue to strengthen and eventually surpass investment. Demand for manufactured goods will decline relatively, while demand for services will rise relatively. The modern service industry will become a major growth point. Foreign trade will enter a period of steady growth, in which exports are will face adjustment and quality improvement, and the share of exports in the demand structure will decline continuously. Second, due to slow changes in the demand structure and production structure, income inequality is likely to remain high and volatile (similar to the United States from 1890 to the early twentieth century), and wealth inequality is likely to continue to expand. Third, with in-depth financial disintermediation and the accelerated development of the securities market, the proportion of direct financing will increase significantly, but banking will still dominate China's financial sector and the economy will remain highly monetized.

Fifth, challenges brought by rising production costs and inadequate innovation capability. High costs include the high costs of land, housing, raw materials, energy, environmental protection, talent, ordinary labor, capital, intellectual property, logistics, taxes, and fees and transactions. As China enters a new stage of development, companies are faced with huge operational pressures caused by rapidly rising costs, resource, and environmental bottlenecks and constraints such as those on land and mineral resources are increasingly strengthened, and factor prices are rising, so it is becoming more and more difficult to support economic growth by massively increasing factor inputs and overtaxing resources and the environment. In response to the erosion of profits by high costs, most economists have prescribed "prescriptions" that emphasize innovation, but with rising production costs at home, the problem of inadequate innovation capability on the part of companies has become increasingly prominent. In the face of new trends in global industrial transformation centered on the digitalization and intelligentization of manufacturing, if we do not speed up the improvement of R&D capabilities and accelerate advances in industrial technology, some of the existing technological routes and production capacity will face the risk of being eliminated.

Sixth, challenges brought by overcapacity and resource and environmental constraints. Overcapacity has been a chronic problem in China's industrial development in recent years. In recent years, China's manufacturing capacity has expanded rapidly. While meeting domestic demand, China's manufacturing capacity is, to a great extent, released by expanding exports. But after the financial crisis, as international market expansion slowed down and China's economic growth decelerated, the contradiction of overcapacity became prominent. Not only is there serious overcapacity in traditional industries, but emerging industries such as wind power equipment and photovoltaics are also facing considerable pressure from overcapacity. Overcapacity is the biggest challenge in the new government's macro-control. The development of overcapacity will lead to a decline in corporate investment expectations, a decrease in net interest rates, and an increase in liabilities. An increase in accounts receivable in turn will lead to an increase in banks' non-performing assets and thus pass the risks to the banking industry. Reducing production capacity definitely requires the consolidation and closure of some factories, which will also lead to job losses and hit household income and consumer expectations, putting increasing downward pressure on economic growth. Not only that, the expansion of production capacity will also lead to the massive consumption of energy and resources, as well as the corresponding environmental pollution. Taking the low-carbon economy as an example, we can see this problem clearly. Nowadays, with global warming, China is facing increasing international pressure to cut carbon emissions. The Chinese government has promised to reduce carbon emissions per unit of GDP by 40–45% by 2020 compared with 2005. But China is in the mid-to-late stage of industrialization and urbanization, namely the stage of high carbon emissions; moreover, China's resource endowment is dominated by carbon; meanwhile, China is at the lower end of processing and manufacturing in international specialization; and so on. This poses great challenges to the low carbonization of future economic development.

Seventh, challenges brought by increased fiscal and financial risks. Under a mode of growth where benefits are realized at high speed, a slowdown in economic growth will inevitably bring a sharp drop in the growth of fiscal revenue and corporate profits, posing a severe challenge to meeting the necessary fiscal expenditures and ensuring the normal production and operation of companies. However, because the mode of economic growth driven by investment has not been fundamentally changed, in order to speed up economic growth, some regions will blindly expand investment and launch new projects regardless of the conditions. In the period of high-speed growth, expanding the scale of debt and credit, especially the large-scale lending by local government financing platforms, has led to the formation of implicit fiscal debt. Against the background of a slowdown in growth and an apparent decline in corporate profits, industries that rely on high debt and high investment to rapidly expand production capacity have seen a deterioration in their financial situation, which will lead to increased financial risk. At present in China, local financing platforms, real estate, overcapacity, and the overexpansion of shadow banking are interconnected to form a self-sustaining system. Adjustment in the real estate and financial sectors is likely to set off a chain reaction and result in passive tightening across the board.

Eighth, challenges brought by the reform of the exchange rate system. The exchange rate is one of the most important core variables in an open economy. Under the conditions of an open economy, the status of various economic variables will eventually be reflected in different degrees and forms in the exchange rate. Adjustments and changes in exchange rates will also have a wide-ranging impact on the external and internal aspects, the micro and macro aspects, and the real and financial sectors of a country's economy. Because adjustments and changes in a country's exchange rate behavior are closely related to the country's exchange rate system, the exchange rate system plays an important role in the economic policy, economic stability, and balanced development of a country. The exchange rate system not only directly affects the economic choices of various micro agents and the welfare consequences thereof, but also has a bearing on the macroeconomic and financial stability of a country, and thus affects the long-term growth and long-term development of the country's economy. Therefore, choosing a reasonable exchange rate system is an important issue faced by all countries in the process of economic development, and must be carefully considered when formulating long-term financial strategies, especially opening-up strategies.

Ninth, challenges brought by globalization and deglobalization. Globalization promotes the flow of factors of production and the further occurrence of effective allocation. Some developed countries, which strongly advocated economic globalization when it was beneficial to them, and even sanctioned countries that did not participate in globalization, are turning against globalization after they have reaped the dividends of globalization. There is no denying that globalization has caused some problems. The globalization pie is not easy to grow and may even shrink, especially during an economic downturn. The contradictions between growth and distribution, labor and capital, and efficiency and equity have become more prominent. Both developed and developing countries are under pressure. But we should not reject economic globalization just because there are problems. Instead, we should adapt to and guide economic globalization, eliminate the negative effects of economic globalization, and make it better benefit every country and every nation. The new economic model characterized by the Internet, big data, artificial intelligence, and the Internet of things has linked the world economy together. Technological innovation and progress have enabled the Internet to turn the world into a global village. Therefore, globalization is a major historical trend that cannot be reversed.

Tenth, challenges brought by complex and frequent social contradictions. Income inequality remains high, and conflicts of interests between different groups have increased. Public service facilities in urban and rural communities are still weak, essential public services vary greatly between urban and rural areas, regions, and groups, and the levels of essential public services enjoyed by low-income groups and rural people who have moved to cities are low. Mass disturbances caused by environmental pollution, land expropriation and demolition, illegal fund-raising, and group interest demands occur from time to time.

2.2 *Main Measures to Be Taken for the Economy to Overcome the Middle-Income Trap*

The middle-income trap is essentially about sustainable economic and social development in the middle-income stage. To solve the various problems that arise at this stage, China clearly needs a combination of measures, such as optimizing the investment, import and export, and consumption structures, achieving coordinated regional development through industrial transfer, promoting technological innovation, and focusing on improving China's total factor productivity. In addition, the following measures are also very important.

First, give full play to the strategic guiding role of the government. To overcome the middle-income trap, we must not ignore the role of the government. In Asia, for example, most of the countries that have successfully crossed the trap are countries where the government plays a strong role and economic decision-making is highly centralized, while countries that have abandoned the due role of the government have fallen into the trap. Since the 1930s, the Philippines had developed rapidly. 30 years later, its modernization level was second only to that of Japan. But starting in the mid-1960s, the Philippines copied the political and economic systems of the United States, and became heavily dependent on foreign forces such as the International Monetary Fund (IMF) and the World Bank for funding and policy. The weak role of the Philippine government and the lack of a clear and long-term economic development strategy have led to a protracted recession and social unrest, causing the Philippines to go from the "model of Asia" to the "sick man of Asia." After World War II, Japan positioned itself as a government-led market economy in which industry, government, and academia were combined, and banks and companies penetrate each other. In just two or three decades, its economic strength quickly surpassed that of Britain, France, and Germany. In the early 1960s, the South Korean government developed an economic decision-making model characterized by a high degree of centralization. Singapore is still a relatively authoritarian state by Western standards. China's national conditions and the development experience of these countries have proved that we must remain confident in the socialist path, theories and system with Chinese characteristics in order to maintain our own characteristics and cross the development trap.

Second, promote the reform of the urban–rural dual market. The dual structure of "urban-rural division" in China is mainly manifested in urban–rural division in terms of the land system, the provision of public goods, the public administration system, household registration management, and related systems. Successful urbanization is not simply an increase in the proportion of urban population and the expansion of urban areas. What's more important is to achieve a series of changes from "rural" to "urban," such as changes in the industrial structure, employment patterns, the living environment, people's quality, social security, and supporting policies. We should comprehensively promote the reform of systems and mechanisms in important areas and key links such as people, land, and money; we should make breakthroughs in urban and rural household registration, rural land property rights, urban and rural social security, and government fiscal and taxation systems, so as to coordinate urban and rural development, and overcome the middle-income trap in the process of deep urbanization. We should gradually break down the urban–rural dual structure and the dual structure within cities, and focus on shantytown redevelopment.

Third, deepen the reform of the income distribution system. To shift the mode of economic development from "production-driven" to "consumption-driven," we must reduce income inequality and increase household income. Efforts should be made to increase households' share of national income, and the share of labor compensation in primary distribution; efforts should be made to align increases in household income with economic development, and increases in labor compensation with the improvement of labor productivity, so as to create positive interactions between economic growth, equitable distribution, and social harmony. We should deepen the reform of the income distribution system and accelerate the formation of an "olive-shaped" distribution pattern dominated by the middle class. We should improve equality of social opportunity by starting with poverty reduction, essential public services, human capital construction, employment, and entrepreneurship. We should accelerate the establishment of an individual income tax system that combines comprehensive taxation and scheduler taxation, reasonably determine the scope of pretax deductions and adjust progressive tax rates, reduce the tax burden on low- and middle-income groups, and increase income adjustment for high-income groups.

Fourth, make "reform-driven" as the keynote of all measures. The financial crisis has prompted a profound adjustment in the global economic order. In order to seize the strategic commanding heights in the future, great powers have entered an unprecedented era of intensive innovation and industrial transformation. We should firmly grasp the strategic opportunities brought about by a new round of world scientific and technological revolution, hammer home the idea that economic growth should be "reform-driven" and "efficiency-driven," align reform with opening-up and with rules and mechanisms for globalization, enhance the competitiveness of "Made in China" and the influence of the "China model," and push China's economic and social development onto the track of endogenous growth.

Fifth, improve the existing investment and consumption structure. Although China's investment-to-GDP ratio is high, the issue must be approached from two angles: on the one hand, we should limit overcapacity, and extensive and inefficient investment; on the other hand, we should actively encourage high-quality, efficient, and innovative investment, vigorously promote private investment, and moderately increase effective supply. In terms of consumption, first, we should establish a reasonable income distribution and social security system, and promote social equity, so as to fundamentally change factors restricting China's household consumption. Second, expand consumer demand, improve the quality of consumption, adjust the consumption structure, promote consumption transformation, and foster new areas of growth in consumption. Third, upgrade China's consumption structure: reduce the proportion of food consumption in the overall consumption structure, increase the proportion of service consumption, and pay attention to food safety and improve the quality of consumer goods to make consumers feel reassured. Meanwhile, we should oppose excessive consumption, overspending and extravagance, and encourage rational consumption.

Sixth, accelerate the formation of a "new normal" economic structure dominated by the service sector. China should speed up its entry into a new era for the development of the service sector and form an economic structure dominated by the service sector. First, significantly increase the proportion of service consumption by expanding the scale of consumption and upgrading the consumption structure; second, inject impetus into the development of productive services through industrial transformation and upgrading; third, provide an important carrier for the development of consumer services through population urbanization, and accelerate the formation of a "new normal" economic structure dominated by the service sector.

Seventh, actively adjust the industrial structure. Actively support the development of modern agriculture, wean agriculture from overdependence on human labor by raising the level of mechanization, and improve the efficiency of agricultural production; actively support industrial structural adjustment, vigorously support the development of high-end manufacturing, encourage companies to improve their indigenous innovation capability, enhance the ability to transform scientific and technological achievements, and raise the overall technological level of industries; encourage and support the development of industries such as energy conservation and environmental protection, new energy and new materials; support industries that are conducive to promoting consumption and expanding domestic demand, and promote the accelerated development of companies in the service sector.

Eighth, solve the consumption dilemma in the transformation process. Consumption is not a simple economic issue. Apart from economic factors, social institutions, governance, income, and consumption policy also play a role in consumption. To boost domestic demand, we need to push forward reforms in relevant areas. From international experience, it can be seen that the formation of effective demand can create positive conditions for successfully overcoming the middle-income trap.

Although the "consumer revolution" and its impact take on different forms in different types of countries, judging by the positive and negative experiences of different types of countries in the middle-income stage, the transformation of the consumption structure has played a vital role. Consumption-led economic growth is the common direction of economic development in all countries.[6] According to empirical research in the United States, Japan, Australia and other countries, the GNI (gross national income) per capita corresponding to the first stage of economic growth in various countries is between $1000 and $3000, and within this range, investment and export play a significant role in promoting economic growth and are even on par with consumption in this regard; when GNI per capita reaches $3000, the impact of investment and exports on GDP begins to decline, the leading role of consumption in driving GDP growth is established or strengthened, and consumption becomes the undisputed main driver of economic growth.[7]

Of course, this change does not come naturally. Historical experience shows that, in the face of a cyclical economic crisis, the formation of a global market partially solves the problem of overproduction in developed countries, but the formation of internal markets is more important. Developed countries generally experienced a shift in the consumption structure from "daily necessities" to "consumer durable goods" when they entered the middle-income stage, namely a structural shift in consumption from large quantities of goods that have low unit prices and low elasticities to small quantities of goods that have high unit prices and high elasticities. The production of consumer durable goods in large quantities and the entry of the whole society into the stage of mass consumption are premised on at least three social conditions: first, a fairly high degree of urbanization; second, a general increase in the wages and income of urban

[6] A cross-country comparative study by Chenery shows that the consumption-to-GDP ratio is the highest (77.9%) when GNP (Gross National Product) per capita is less than $100 (US$ 1964), a phenomenon known as "high consumption while in poverty." As GNP per capita grows, the consumption-to-GDP ratio falls to 16.2%. But when GNP per capita crosses the threshold of $1000, the consumption-to-GDP ratio rises, reaching an average of 62.4% (*Chenery Patterns of Development [1950–1970]*. Beijing: Economic Science Press, 1988: 31).

[7] Guo Qiyou, Lu Lijing. A Change of Driver of Sustainable Economic Growth—International Experience in Consumption-Led Growth and Lessons Learnt Therefrom. *Journal of Sun Yat-sen University* (Social Science Edition), 2009 (2).

workers; third, relatively perfect social security measures and a relatively perfect consumer credit system.[8]

After decades of reform and opening-up, China's economy has emerged from the "shortage economy" situation. In some areas, such as steel, coal, cement, and shipbuilding, there is even serious overcapacity. However, at present, China still pursues an investment-led model, and a prominent problem in economic development is the lack of domestic demand.

The key to solving the problem of insufficient domestic demand lies in reforming income distribution, including primary distribution and redistribution, promoting structural tax reduction, increasing the consumption-to-GDP ratio, adjusting the income structure, and addressing income disparities. Meanwhile, we should release consumption capacity by increasing the provision of public services, promote the equalization of basic services, and enhance people's willingness to spend.

2.3 Accelerate Industrial Structural Adjustment to Help Economic Transformation

The experience of developed countries in overcoming the middle-income trap is inseparable from the successful transformation of the mode of economic development and the upgrading of the industrial structure. If China wants to successfully overcome the middle-income trap, it should make the perfection of industrial policy and the adjustment and upgrading of the industrial structure a top priority.

2.3.1 Eliminate or Limit Backward Production Capacity

China's rapid economic growth is largely dependent on the extensive input of factors of production including capital, labor, and natural resources in 2015, China's energy consumption per unit of output value exceeded three times the global average, and its energy consumption accounted for 25% of the global total. To change the extensive mode of economic development, we should focus on doing the following work well: first, increasing efforts to eliminate backward production capacity by taking a series of comprehensive measures such as economic, legal, technical, and necessary administrative means; second, raising barriers

[8] Sun Liping. Sociological Analysis of Insufficient Domestic Demand. *Journal of China Youth University of Political Studies*, 2000 (6).

to entry into key industries, especially by assigning more weight to the environmental indicator when designing indicators; third, strengthening "ecological GDP construction" to improve the quality of GDP. The production and service quality of China is not high. Backward production capacity limits the effectiveness of GDP. In "ecological GDP construction," we should increase investment in environmental as a percentage of GDP.

With regard to traditional industries with comparative advantages, we should actively expand the vast international markets of Asia, Africa, and Latin America, and strengthen economic and trade cooperation with relevant countries through the Belt and Road Initiative, bilateral (or multilateral) free trade zones and other strategies, so as to promote the transfer and export of relevant production capacity in China. Meanwhile, traditional industries can also be transformed and upgraded through technological innovation or technology introduction. On the one hand, this can make their production efficient and environmentally friendly; on the other hand, this can bring products to a higher level and make products more competitive to meet higher levels of consumer demand.

2.3.2 Support High-Tech Industries

High-tech industries play a fundamental and bridging role in international competition. To overcome the middle-income trap and narrow the gap with developed countries, China must actively support high-tech industries.

First of all, we should actively support high-tech industries and drive the development of other industries through high-tech industries. We must keep up with the forefront of the world's scientific and technological development. National decision-making should be inclined toward areas with broad prospects for industrialization, so as to establish a number of high-tech enterprises with advantages. We should build our own high-tech industries and strive to make breakthroughs in key areas, so as to make a good start for Chinese brands.

Second, we should give full play to the role of colleges and universities in scientific research, and strengthen collaboration between enterprises and colleges and universities in innovation. We should encourage the transformation of scientific research achievements into productive forces. Funds for scientific research in colleges and universities can be provided by market-oriented enterprises. We should allocate resources through the market and encourage the transformation of laboratory findings into actual products.

Finally, in order to encourage independent R&D by enterprises, we can refer to the model of developed countries. The government and enterprises sign an agreement under which the government delegates R&D projects to enterprises, and enterprises can do R&D better with funds and policy support from the government. As a result, the independent R&D capabilities of enterprises are strengthened.

At the international level, we should build the international image of China's high-tech industries. The high-tech industries will become the main driver of economic growth. We should cultivate a number of high-tech industries with international brands as the strong backing for the development of China's comprehensive national strength. The government should safeguard the image and interests of China's high-tech industries, and provide good policy and diplomatic support for high-tech enterprises to open up markets.

2.3.3 Encourage Strategic Emerging Industries

Strategic emerging industries are technology-intensive industries that are based on major technological breakthroughs and major development needs, play a major role in guiding and driving the overall and long-term development of the economy and society, consume few material resources, show great potential for growth, and deliver good comprehensive benefits. They are an important force for social development and have become a major strategy for major countries in the world to seize the commanding heights in the new round of economic and technological development.

On the basis of consolidating the contribution of China's basic industries to the real economy, we should vigorously support emerging industries as a new driver of economic growth. To cultivate strategic emerging industries, we should adhere to innovative development, accelerate the cultivation of strategic emerging industries into leading and pillar industries, and increase the proportion of strategic emerging industries in the industrial structure. Meanwhile, policywise, we should actively cultivate markets to encourage the development of strategic emerging industries. The focus of cultivating strategic emerging industries is to achieve technological breakthroughs in key areas, for example, by encouraging the new-generation information technology industry and the development and industrialization of the next generation of core Internet equipment and intelligent terminals; vigorously developing bioindustries, and improving the level and industrialization of biopharmaceuticals; promoting high-end equipment manufacturing, strengthening basic supporting capabilities, and strengthening China's manufacturing capabilities; developing the new energy industry, developing and utilizing biomass energy according to local conditions, and achieving sustainable development; developing the new materials industry and exploring alternative energy sources; striving to make breakthroughs in the new energy vehicle industry, conserving energy and protecting the environment, and vigorously promoting the development of energy-efficient and low-emission vehicles.

In addition, the development of strategic emerging industries is impossible without international cooperation. We should actively explore new modes of international technological cooperation, introduce and assimilate key and core technologies as soon as possible and at the lowest cost possible, and carry out re-innovation.

2.3.4 Accelerate Economic and Industrial Structural Adjustment

First, the upgrading of the industrial structure is an objective need for China's economic development. The fact that China's industrial structure is not high-end enough and its industrial competitiveness is at the lower end in the global value chain is still one of the most prominent manifestations of China's economic structural contradictions. Improving the innovation capability and technological level of industries, and changing the situation of low value added, overcapacity, and a shortage of high-end products through the transformation and upgrading of the industrial structure, and combining the promotion of ecological progress with industrial structural adjustment and developing resource-saving and environmentally friendly industries so as to break environmental and resource constraints and achieve a high-end and eco-friendly industrial structure is also one of the inherent requirements for turning China into an economic powerhouse.

Second, the low level of the industrial structure has resulted in a low industrial value-added rate. China's industry is dominated by low value-added heavy and chemical industries, most of which are at the lower end of international specialization, so the industrial value-added rate in China is far lower than in the United States, Japan, and other developed countries. China's industries are big but not strong. This is reflected most pointedly in a low industrial value-added rate. The quality and benefits of industrial development are reflected in industrial value added. Although there are more than 500 kinds of industrial products in China, high-grade, high-tech, and high value-added products account for only a small proportion, resulting in low industrial value added. This puts China in a disadvantageous position in competition in international markets. Thus it can be seen that China needs to increase the industrial value-added rate by upgrading its industries and elevating its position in international specialization. The basic barometer for whether the transformation of the mode of industrial development is successful is a significant increase in the industrial value-added rate, which is the fundamental way to solve the structural and quality problems of China's industry, and also an important guiding principle for promoting industrial transformation and upgrading.

Third, conditions for promoting industrial upgrading. Industrial transformation and upgrading, from low-end to high-end development, requires core technologies with independent intellectual property rights and technical personnel at all levels, as well as sound business operations based on the modern enterprise system, and must allow technologies and personnel to obtain reasonable benefits in the course of business operations.

Fourth, improve the mechanism for technological innovation. To speed up industrial transformation and upgrading, we must make breakthroughs in a number of core technologies with independent intellectual property rights, accelerate the cultivation of globally competitive independent brands, and obtain higher value added through innovation, quality, and brands. We should actively guide innovative elements and resources toward enterprises, help enterprises accelerate their efforts to become investors and actors in technology R&D and industrial transformation, guide enterprises in implement the strategy of independent intellectual property rights and independent brands, and strive to improve our indigenous innovation capability and brand development.

2.4 *Help Economic Structural Adjustment Through Development Finance*

Since 2013, the new Chinese administration has attached great importance to the transformation of the development mode and economic structural adjustment, actively slowed down growth, and constantly enhanced the vitality for the sustained and healthy development of China's economy in the medium and long term. But there are some downside risks for the economy at present. It is very necessary to adopt appropriate policies to stabilize growth in time to prevent the rate of growth of final demand growth rate from further declining and maintain stable economic growth. As a development finance institution, the China Development Bank (CDB) actively exerts the "blood-supplying" and "blood-making" functions of development finance, which relies on national credit, serves national strategies and utilizes capital in a way that preserves capital while making a small profit, takes the initiative to build a bridge between the government and the market, guides the flow of private capital, and vigorously supports the steady growth of China's economy and the "Belt and Road" Initiative.

2.4.1 *There Are Some Downside Risks for China's Economy*

China's economy is shifting gears, and the potential growth rate is on the decline. In terms of changes in the industrial structure, more and more manpower and resources are transferred from manufacturing to services, and the overall labor productivity is decreasing, resulting in a decline in economic growth. In terms of factors of production, the rate of growth of labor and capital inputs is declining, and technological advancements are slow. From the second quarter of 2012 to the third quarter of 2017, China's economy grew at a rate of less than 8% for 22 consecutive quarters. Overall, China's economy is still at the bottom of the post-2008 financial crisis economic cycle.

At present, there are some downside risks for China's economy, mainly as follows: First, the endogenous growth momentum of the economy is insufficient. It is mainly reflected in the fact that there is serious overcapacity in some industries, inefficient enterprises take up a lot of resources, economy-wide debt is accumulating rapidly, drivers of economic growth such as external demand and real estate are weakening, and resource and environmental constraints are becoming more apparent. Second, the three "horses"—consumption, exports, and investment—are weak.

In the current economic situation, maintaining stable economic growth is of great significance. First, stable growth creates effective space and conditions for structural adjustment. Once an economic slowdown is not effectively contained, key links such as employment, household income, and fiscal revenue will be affected. Pessimism in the market coupled with badmouthing with ulterior motives may discredit the market as a whole and intensify various social contradictions. If steady and rapid economic development cannot be maintained, there will be no effective space and conditions for structural adjustment. Second, steady growth is needed to create new jobs. If the economy slows down, and corporate earnings fall or losses increase, job growth is bound to slow, unemployment is bound to increase, and the pressure on social security will increase. Third, steady growth plays an important role in maintaining financial stability. If the economy stalls, and corporate earnings fall or losses increase, the NPL ratio at commercial banks is bound to rise, on-time payment will be difficult for more trust products, the debt chains of private financing markets will rupture one after another, and the risk of the financial system will rise significantly. Fourth, steady growth helps the government better perform its functions. An economic slowdown will slow fiscal revenue growth, which will not only increase local debt risk, but also affect the government's functions such as the provision of public goods and the ability to make countercyclical adjustments to economic operations.

2.4.2 *Development Finance Helps Steady Economic Growth*

Development finance is a financial form and method. Aiming at serving national strategies, with medium- and long-term investment and financing as the means, relying on national credit, through market-oriented operations, it eases bottlenecks in economic and social development, maintains national financial stability, and enhances economic competitiveness. CDB is an important pioneer and practitioner of development finance. Since its inception, with a view to achieving goals at different stages of national economic and social development, it has exerted the functions of medium- and long-term investment and financing in stabilizing fluctuations in the economic cycle, and provided strong financial support for the realization of national strategies and government intentions. The brilliant achievements of more than 20 years' development have proved that development finance plays an irreplaceable role in economic and social development and has been widely recognized by the central leadership and all sectors of society. The Third Plenary Session of the 18th CPC Central Committee put forward the proposition of "development finance institutions" at the level of the plenary session of the CPC Central Committee for the first time. The 13th Five-Year Plan defined development finance as an important part of China's financial system. Leading comrades of the CPC Central Committee have made it clear on various occasions that China does not lack large commercial Banks, but it needs development finance institutions like CDB, which is expected to play a bigger role in realizing national strategies.

According to needs for macroeconomic policy adjustment in different stages and cycles of China's economic development, CDB, by tapping fully into the countercyclical feature of medium- and long-term investment and financing, stays invisible in the market in favorable circumstances and props up the market in adverse circumstances. When the economy is in a period of rapid growth, CDB often stays invisible in the market, and controls the credit scale of the whole financial system by creating market outlets for projects and making more space for commercial finance; When the economy is in a downward cycle, it takes the lead in injecting funds into the key areas of the country's development to boost market confidence, and injects strong impetus for steady and fast economic growth by increasing efforts to support and stimulate bottleneck areas that restrict economic development.

From 1998 to 2003, in line with the requirements of the State for coping with the impact of the Asian financial crisis and expanding domestic demand, CDB provided nearly 80% of the credit funds for key national construction projects and over 30% of the supporting loans for national debt projects. From the second half of 2003 to 2008, CDB adhered to the principle of taking different approaches to different situations and encouraging the growth of some sectors while discouraging the expansion of others, ensured an uninterrupted capital chain for key projects related to the overall development of the country and various regions, actively adjusted the structure and use of loans, and increased support for areas such as people's livelihood and "Go Out." Since the end of 2008, CDB has put three-quarters of its new loans into indemnificatory housing projects, rural infrastructure, major infrastructure, medical, health, cultural and educational undertakings, ecological environment construction, indigenous innovation, post-earthquake reconstruction, and other key areas, thus playing a positive role in promoting China's economic stabilization and recovery and accelerating the transformation of the mode of economic development. In the face of the current complex economic situation at home and abroad, CDB will continue to exert "blood-supplying" function of development finance, and carry out targeted work to support steady economic growth in accordance with the overall requirements for macro-control.

First, CDB will serve new-type urbanization with a focus on shantytown redevelopment. Shantytown redevelopment is an important part of China's new-type urbanization. On the one hand, it can effectively improve people's livelihood; on the other hand, it can give a strong boost to investment and consumption. Shantytown redevelopment requires large sums of investment, has a long payback period and needs to be supported by relatively cheap and stable sources of finance. This requires development finance to play a unique role. At the executive meeting of the State Council on April 2, 2014, it was stressed that in order to promote shantytown redevelopment on a larger scale, we must "lead the ox by its halter" by focusing on funding, and effectively combine policy support with market mechanisms; in particular, we should tap into the "blood-supplying" function of development finance, which relies on national credit, serves national strategies and utilizes capital in a way that preserves capital while making a small profit, to provide lawful, compliant, easy to operate, appropriately priced and stable sources of finance for the acceleration of shantytown redevelopment and ensure funding for shantytown redevelopment, and strive to reduce the cost of capital. In order to implement the spirit of the executive meeting of the State Council, CDB has held several meetings to make comprehensive arrangements for work on shantytown redevelopment, set up a special organization for the construction of indemnificatory housing projects such as shantytown redevelopment—the housing finance division, done a good job in connecting with relevant ministries and commissions and local governments, promoted the development of a provincial-level unified lending platform, and speeded up development review and loan issuance for shantytown redevelopment projects. By the end of December 2016, CDB had issued a total of 2.5275 trillion Yuan of shantytown redevelopment loans, of which 972.5 billion Yuan were issued in that year, providing strong support for the construction of 18 million housing units in shantytown areas in China.

Second, CDB will continue to support key projects in the fields of infrastructure, basic industries, and pillar industries with a focus on railway construction. Since its inception, CDB has supported the construction of a large number of major projects related to the national economy and people's livelihood. At the executive meeting of the State Council, it was pointed out that in the present situation, speeding up the construction of railways, especially in the central and western regions, could not only expand effective investment and drive the development of related industries, but also promote new-type urbanization, improve the development environment of underdeveloped areas and help millions of people out of poverty. CDB will further increase support for railway construction, especially in the central and western regions, develop new types of railway construction bonds and new ways to issue them, do a good job in bond underwriting, guide private capital toward the construction of intercity railways, urban/suburban railways and resource development railways.

Finally, CDB will optimize the use of credit funds and support the deepening of supply-side structural reform. CDB will work hard to revitalize the real economy, with its efforts targeted at the five tasks of cutting overcapacity, destocking, deleveraging, reducing costs, and strengthening weak links; in line with the "four-region strategy" and "three grand strategies," CDB will push regions to cooperate with other and complement each other's advantages, increase support for regions such as northeast China, Tibet, and Xinjiang; CDB will facilitate the implementation of major projects, and make infrastructure connectivity, capacity cooperation, and economic, trade and industrial cooperation zones the focal point of its efforts to serve the Belt and Road Initiative.

In addition, CDB develops financial inclusion to safeguard and improve people's livelihood. Shouldering the mission of "strengthening national strength and improving people's livelihood," CDB attaches great importance to financial inclusion and actively advocates equal access to finance. By the end of March 2017, CDB had issued a total of 110.8 billion Yuan in student loans, of which 22.9 billion Yuan were issued in 2016, accounting for more than 90% of all student loans throughout the country, covering 26 provinces, 2094 counties and 2711 colleges and universities, and helping 8.98 million poor students realize their college or university dreams. In the future, CDB will, as always, continue to support the development of agriculture, rural areas and farmers, water conservancy, small and micro businesses, as well as social undertakings such as education and health and elderly care to safeguard and improve people's livelihood and promote steady economic growth.

2.5 *Promote National Strategies Through Development Finance*

As an important financial tool serving national economic security and diplomatic strategies, CDB actively gives full play to the advantages of developmental finance in China's foreign policy, and plays an important role in China's opening-up strategy. In order to adapt to the arrangements and requirements of China's Go Out policy, CDB has applied development finance methods and experience to international cooperation, made useful explorations in terms of cooperating with international financial institutions, helping domestic enterprises invest abroad, safeguarding national energy and resource security, and providing foreign financial services, and enhanced the implementability of China's foreign policy, thereby laying a solid foundation for Chinese enterprises to go abroad.

In the great practice of China's continuous opening-up, CDB firmly grasps the internal needs of the long-term development of industrialization, urbanization, and internationalization in China and the historical opportunity of the great development, adjustment, and change of the world economy, discovers, establishes, and expresses resource demand at the national strategic level, constructs the "global-regional-national-corporate entity" planning model, and vigorously develops international cooperation. Since 2016, CDB has earnestly implemented the central spirit and national macro policies. Guided by the five development ideas, adhering to the general work guideline of making progress while maintaining stability, and grasping the overall requirements for innovation and development, CDB has strengthened operation management and risk control, carried out the "Two Studies, One Action" campaign in a deep-going way, and made new progress in various work. In the course of operation and development, CDB insists on centering its work around supply-side structural reform and conscientiously performs the five tasks of cutting overcapacity, destocking, deleveraging, reducing costs, and strengthening weak links. In terms of cutting overcapacity, the outstanding balance of loans to the steel industry at the end of the third quarter was 147.4 billion Yuan, down 5.3 billion Yuan from the beginning of the year; in terms of destocking, CDB issued 389 billion Yuan of loans for monetized resettlement in shantytown redevelopment, reducing commodity housing inventory by 520,000 units or 48.35 million square meters; in terms of deleveraging, CDB used special funds and other investment tools to focus on supporting key areas such as shantytown redevelopment, railways, rail transit, and highways; in terms of reducing costs, CDB issued 343.2 billion Yuan of bonds to targeted investors under plan a debt-for-bond swap program from January to September, more than the total for 2015, and the average rate on RMB loans fell further; in terms of strengthening weak links, CDB increased support for weak links such as poverty alleviation, shantytown redevelopment, technological innovation, environmental protection and infrastructure. As of the end of September, the total assets were 13.69 trillion Yuan, the outstanding balance of loans was 9.34 trillion Yuan, the net profit was 88.9 billion Yuan, the capital adequacy ratio was 11.82%, and the NPL ratio was 0.86%, which had been kept within 1% for 46 consecutive quarters. CDB's work is focused on the following areas.

First, pool resources and take measures to support the steady and healthy development of the economy. Take strong and effective measures to put financial resources into key areas and weak links.

Second, pool wisdom and strength and take targeted and pragmatic measures to deliver tangible results in poverty alleviation. Conscientiously study and implement the important speech made by General Secretary Xi Jinping at the forum on poverty alleviation through east–west cooperation, and Premier Li Keqiang and Vice Premier Wang Yang's important instructions for work on alleviating poverty through relocation, make supporting poverty alleviation a major political task, a major development task, and a major task of improving people's livelihood, and make every effort to achieve results.

Third, work tirelessly to make good progress in shantytown redevelopment. Work harder and strengthen refined management, with a view to accomplishing objectives and tasks in shantytown redevelopment.

Fourth, strengthen management, ensure quality, and make solid progress in work on special funds. According to the overall thinking of "preventing and controlling risks, consolidating the foundation and steadily advancing," do a good job in work on special funds.

Fifth, vigorously promote international cooperation by serving strategies and defining priorities. We should overcome difficulties and make unremitting efforts to continue to play an important role in serving the country's economic and diplomatic strategies and supporting enterprises in "going out."

Sixth, continuously improve operations management by refining management and paying attention to quality and efficiency. Increase economic returns by improving management, and enhance the ability of operations management to support and safeguard business development.

Seventh, coordinate efforts and keep the bottom line to guard against risks.

Over the years, the practice of CDB in serving national strategies and social and economic development has fully proved that its function as the leading bank in the field of medium- and long-term investment and financing in China's overall social and economic development, its development finance idea and method of promoting market building, credit system development and institutional improvement with financing, its role in helping macro-control as a national macro-control tool, undertaking social responsibility, and promoting people's livelihood and harmonious social development, and its unique advantages in serving the country's economic, diplomatic, and energy strategies are irreplaceable. In the process of changing the mode of economic development, promoting the balanced growth of China's economy and causing finance to serve the needs of the real economy, highlighting the irreplaceable position and role of CDB in overall social and economic development is an inherent requirement for CDB to serve national strategies and its own development.

2.5.1 Help China Attain Its Foreign Policy Goals

China's unbalanced economic growth is not only manifested as an internal imbalance, but also as an external imbalance. Therefore, in the process of rebalancing the economy, in order to adjust the external imbalance, in addition to solving the internal imbalance, we must implement a more proactive opening-up strategy, further intensify the implementation of the Go Out policy, and strengthen cooperation with energy and resources powers in Asia, Africa, and Latin America through the Go Out policy to ensure the supply of energy and resources for economic development. Meanwhile, we should drive China's exports of major equipment and the transfer of excess capacity, gain the initiative and advantages in fierce international competition, create favorable conditions for economic structural adjustment and industrial upgrading, and improve our ability to safely and efficiently utilize both domestic and international markets and resources. The practice of development finance in countries around the world shows that development finance has advantages that are irreplaceable by commercial and policy-based finance in serving national security and foreign trade development strategy, including the advantage in medium-

and long-term project operations involving international M&As with the help of national credit, the advantage of being a development institution that complies with international rules and is recognized by international conventions, and the first-mover advantage of cooperating in national energy and resource areas that are difficult for commercial finance to access.

It is precisely because development finance is a market entity based on national credit that takes responsibility for implementing national economic policies in daily business activities, and aligns its credit policy with national goals that it can consciously increase or decrease the scale of lending and adjust the credit structure according to the needs of government macro-control. Development finance loans mainly go to infrastructure, basic industries, national pillar industries, high-tech industries, the construction of supporting projects, as well as SMEs. These areas are basic and source industries, which are at the top end of the industrial chain and can produce a strong domino effect. The multiplier effect of development finance is very significant because it can penetrate and influence all areas of the economy and society and fully amplify the contribution of capital accumulation through effective linkages between industries. Meanwhile, development finance can continuously promote credit system development, market building, institutional improvement, and so on through the financial innovation process, so it has significant economic externalities. To a large extent, development finance can significantly increase the output produced by factor inputs, so that the aggregate production function exhibits very strong increasing returns to scale. The basic path of its action on economic growth fully demonstrates that development finance can continuously influence economic growth more deeply and extensively in the long term, guide social resource allocation, and improve the targetedness and effectiveness of social resource allocation, so it plays an irreplaceable role in balancing the growth of China's economy.

With factors such as resources, energy, technology, and market being constrained by a series of objective conditions at home and abroad, in order to realize the transformation of the mode of economic development and enhance the potential of China's economy for sustainable development, we must implement a more active open-up strategy and further strengthen the implementation of the Go Out policy.

Therefore, in the process of promoting balanced economic growth, CDB should give full play to its advantages as a tool for implementing China's economic security and foreign policy, continue to strengthen international cooperation, especially cooperation with Asian, African, and Latin American countries, bearing in mind the overall situation of national security and development, and ease bottlenecks on resources, energy, and markets in the process of economic development with the cooperation mode of development finance, so as to make room for the transformation of the development mode. By establishing bilateral or multilateral development funds, carrying out equity investment, and providing large foreign currency loans, CDB helps strong financial institutions and enterprises "go out" and expands channels for the use of foreign exchange reserves. Meanwhile, by expanding RMB settlement in key areas such as currency swaps, offshore RMB loans and resources and energy, advancing RMB internationalization, and promoting the building of an international system centered on China and serving China's economic development, CDB enables China to seize the initiative and have a say in the reconstruction of the international financial system.

2.5.2 *Building a New International Economic Order Requires the Support of Development Finance*

Since the global financial crisis of 2007, changing the global economic governance structure dominated by developed countries led by the United States, increasing the voice of developing countries, including China, in global economic governance, safeguarding the interests of developing countries in global economic and trade exchanges, and building a global economic order with solidarity and win-win cooperation at its core has become necessary to cope with financial crises and promote global economic recovery.

The experience of economic development in developed countries shows that in the process of building a new international economic order, in order to ensure the economic security of a country, it is necessary to have a strong financial institution as a powerful tool to implement the country's foreign policy. The practice of development finance in countries around the world shows that development finance has advantages in serving national security and foreign development strategies that cannot be replaced by commercial and policy-based finance, including the medium- and long-term project operation advantage of using national credit for international mergers and acquisitions, the advantage of development institutions that follow international rules and are recognized by international conventions, and the project first-mover advantage of cooperating in the national energy and resource sector which is difficult to access for commercial finance.

Therefore, in the process of building a new international economic order, in order to ensure China's economic and diplomatic security, it is necessary to further tap into the unique advantages and functions of CDB as a powerful tool for implementing China's foreign policy, and increase comprehensive planning indicators for economic and social development to reduce China's investment risk.

2.6 Space for Economic Transformation and Upgrading in Key Areas in China

Since China became a middle-income country, dividends contributing to China's economic growth have gradually disappeared, and economic growth has gradually slowed down. It is necessary to gain new economic growth momentum through transformation and upgrading to promote steady economic growth. As far as China's economic development at the present stage is concerned, there are still large regional disparities and urban–rural disparities; the level of household income and consumption still needs to be improved; there is big room for industrial upgrading; the health and elderly care industry needs development, etc. These are the spaces and key areas for China's economic growth in the future. To make full use of these growth spaces and turn them into effective drivers of economic growth, China needs to further release market vitality, optimize the structure, deepen the reform of the economic system, and successfully realize the economic transformation from a mode of growth based on factor inputs to a mode of growth based on total factor productivity growth.

2.6.1 Space for Urbanization Development and Upgrading

China lags far behind developed countries with regard to the level of urbanization. As shown in Fig. 1, in 2016, China's urbanization rate reached 57.36% as calculated based on the permanent urban population, including farmers who have lived in cities and towns for more than half a year, but have not yet fully integrated into modern urban life.[9]

[9] If calculated by the registered urban population, the current urbanization rate is only about 35%.

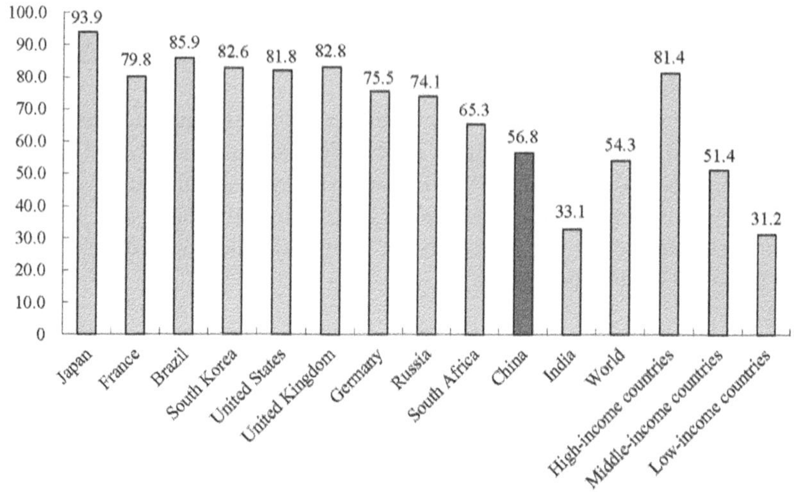

Fig. 1 Urbanization rates in the major countries of the world in 2016 (%) (*Data source* World Bank, World Development Indicators [http://databank.shihang.org/data/reports.aspx?source=%e4%b8%96%e7%95%8c%e5%8f%91%e5%b1%95%e6%8c%87%e6%a0%87])

This urbanization rate is in line with the world average, slightly higher than the level of 50% in middle-income countries, but about 30% lower than the average level in developed countries. At the current rate, it will take 20–25 years to achieve the 80% urbanization rate in high-income countries.

Urbanization is the greatest potential for expanding domestic demand as it can unleash enormous economic energy and drive sustained economic growth. Every 1% increase in the urbanization rate will lead more than 10 million rural people to live, study, and work in cities and towns, which will not only narrow the gap between urban and rural areas, but also increase the income of farmers, stimulate the growth of consumption and strengthen the growth momentum of the economy. The quality of China's urbanization is not high, the construction of urban infrastructure and the development of social undertakings cannot keep up with demand, and many public goods or quasi-public goods are still in critically short supply. These offer great potential for China's economic development. China has upgraded from general urbanization to new-type urbanization.

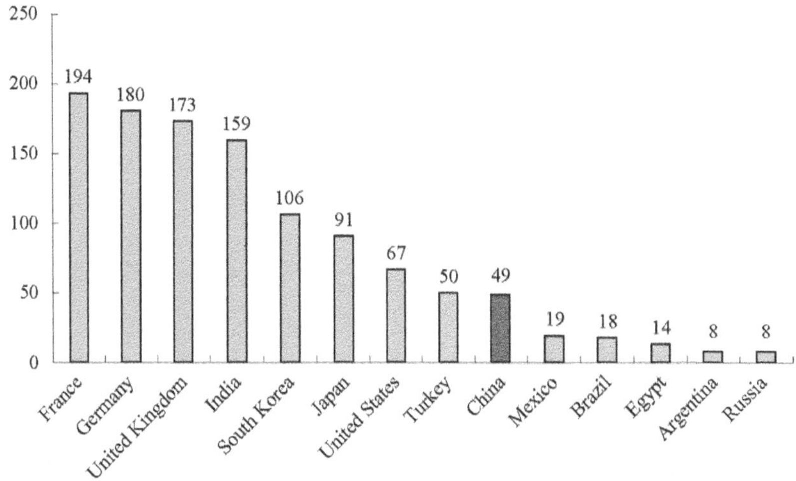

Fig. 2 Density of highway networks in the major countries of the world in 2016 (km/100 km^2) (*Source* International Statistical Yearbook 2016)

2.6.2 Space for Infrastructure Upgrading

Infrastructure plays a decisive role in economic growth, and infrastructure construction is an important guarantee for sustained and rapid economic development.

The Quality of Transport Infrastructure Still Needs to Be Improved

China has an extensive network of transport infrastructure, but its transport infrastructure is still at a low level in per capita terms. This is even more apparent when compared with developed countries. As shown in Figs. 2 and 3, the density of China's highway network in 2016 was 48.9 km/100 km^2, higher than that in middle-income countries, but only 1/4 of that in France; the density of its railway network was 1.29 km/100 km^2, far lower than that in the world's major developed countries, 1/4 of that in the European Union and 1/2 of that in the United States.

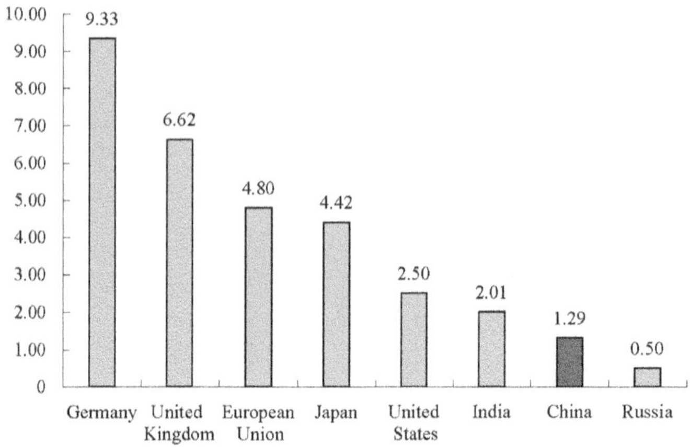

Fig. 3 Density of railway networks in the major countries of the world in 2016 (the length of double-track railways not doubled; km/100 km^2) (*Data source* World Bank, World Development Indicators [http://databank.shihang.org/data/reports.aspx?source=%e4%b8%96%e7%95%8c%e5%8f%91%e5%b1%95%e6%8c%87%e6%a0%87])

There Is Still Room for Further Development of Communication Infrastructure

In terms of communication, as shown in Figs. 4 and 5, the Internet penetration rate in China was 53.2% in 2016, a far cry from the level of about 80% in developed countries; the number of fixed broadband Internet users per 100 people was 20, on par with the global average. In 2015, the number of mobile phones per 100 people in China was 93, close to the level of 100 or more in developed countries.

Over the past decades, China has made brilliant achievements in infrastructure construction. China is already leading the world in terms of infrastructure stock, but it is still lagging behind on a global scale in terms of density and per capita level, which suggests that there is still huge space for the development and upgrading of China's infrastructure in the future. If the relevant policies for infrastructure development are adjusted in time, a new space for growth will be opened up.

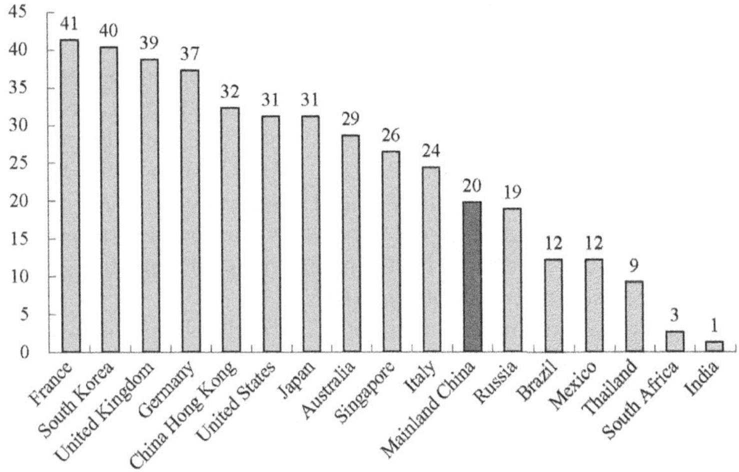

Fig. 4 Number of fixed broadband internet users per 100 people in the major countries and regions of the world in 2015 (*Source* CDB Research Institute Inspiration Drawn from A Comparison of China's Development with that of Other Major Economies in 2013 and Policy Suggestions)

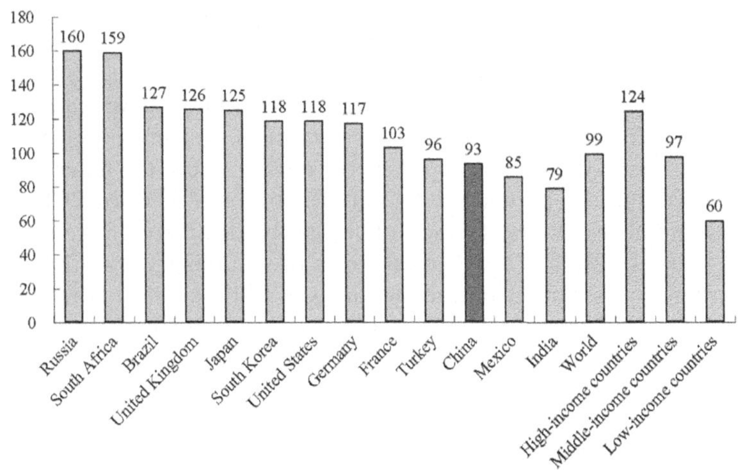

Fig. 5 Number of mobile phones per 100 people in the major countries of the world in 2015 (*Source* International Statistical Yearbook 2016)

2.6.3 *Space for the Development of Education and Scientific Research*

Since the start of reform and opening-up, China's compulsory education and higher education have developed rapidly. According to the relevant data of the Ministry of Education, the enrollment rate for primary school-age children was 84.7% in 1965, 93% in 1980, 97.8% in 1990, 99.1% in 2000, 99.9% in 2012, and 99.88% in 2015. Basically all school-age children have been enrolled in school. The gross enrolment ratio for junior middle schools was 66.7% in 1990, increased to 90% in 2002, reached 97% in 2006, and exceeded 100% in 2015.

The gross enrollment ratio for senior high schools in China reached 86.0% in 2013 and exceeded 87.0% in 2015. The gross enrollment ratio in higher education was only 1.55% in 1978, reached 3.7% in 1988, and increased to 9.76% in 1998. In 1999, the policy of expanding enrollment in higher education was implemented, leading to a surge in the gross enrollment ratio in higher education, which reached a historic high of 15% in 2002. According to international practice, China's higher education has begun to transition from elite education to mass education. The gross enrollment ratio in higher education in China reached 30.0% in 2012 and exceeded 40.0% in 2015 (see Fig. 6).

In terms of education attainment, China's mean years of schooling was only 5.2 years in 1982, and was 6.26 years in 1990, 6.72 years in 1995, and 7.62 years in 2000. According to data released by the Ministry of education, in 2009, China's mean years of schooling was 8.5 years, and the average number of years of education for newly added labor force was over 10, both above the world average levels; the illiteracy rate among young and middle-aged adults fell below 3.58%. In 2015, the average number of years of education for newly added labor force reached 13.3 years. In 2015, China's mean years of schooling were 9.28 years. According to the Survey on the Dynamics of China's Labor Force issued by Sun Yat-sen University in 2015, as of 2014, most of China's labor force had a secondary education, and the average number of years of education received by them was 9.28.

Since the start of reform and opening-up, China has made great achievements in educational development. However, compared with developed countries, China's education is still lagging behind.

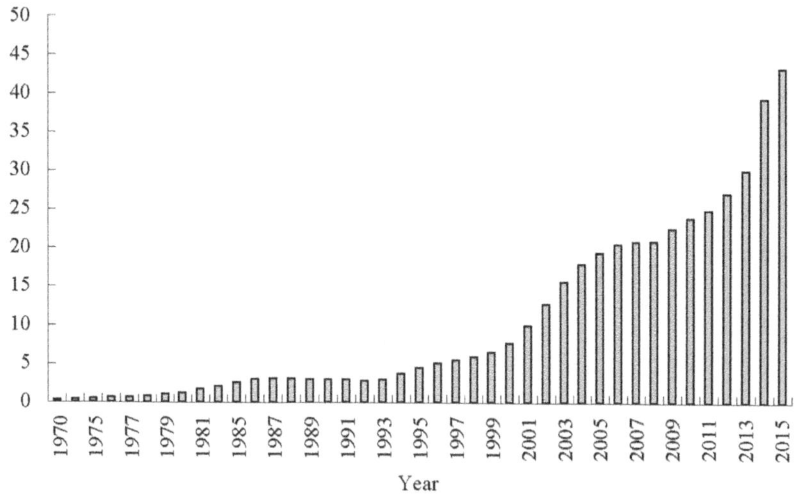

Fig. 6 Enrollment rate in higher education in China (1970–2015, %) (*Source* World Bank website)

First, there is a big gap between China and developed countries in terms of the percentage of the population with higher education. In terms of the enrollment rate in higher education alone, according to data for 2015, almost all developed countries have reached a level of more than 60%, and South Korea, which has the highest enrollment rate in higher education, has reached a level of 97%, while in China the number stands at a much lower level of only 43%. Even compared with India and South Africa, which are both emerging countries, China's advantage is not significant (see Fig. 7).

In 2015, the percentage of China's population with higher education was 40%, higher than the global average, but considerably lower than that in the major countries of the world. Among the major countries, Russia ranked first with 54% of its population having a higher education, Japan, the United States, and South Korea had a relatively high percentage of their population with higher education, and European countries had a slightly lower percentage of their population with higher education. Overall, an average of 26% of the population in G20 (an international economic cooperation forum) countries, and an average of 31% of the population in OECD (Organization for Economic Cooperation

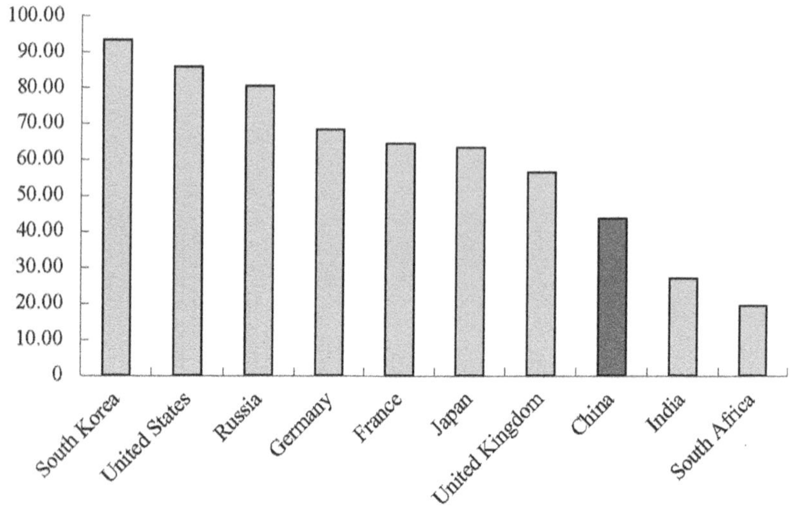

Fig. 7 Enrollment rates in higher education in China and some developed and emerging countries in 2015 (%) (*Source* World Bank website)

and Development) countries had a higher education, and China still had a lot of catching up to do (see Fig. 8).

In China's labor force, individuals with junior secondary education account for the highest proportion (46.97%), followed by—in descending order—individuals with primary education, individuals with regular senior secondary education, individuals with specialized secondary education, individuals with junior college education and individuals with regular college education or above. 2.93% of the labor force has not received any school education. The average length of schooling for women in the labor force is 0.7 years lower than that for men. There are large differences in educational attainment between urban and rural labor forces and labor forces in different regions. Members of the labor force with non-agricultural hukou status or resident hukou status outperform members with agricultural hukou in terms of the proportion of people with junior college education or above and years of schooling. Meanwhile, few members of the labor force have received professional or technical training. According to a report of Sun Yat-sen University, since July 2012,

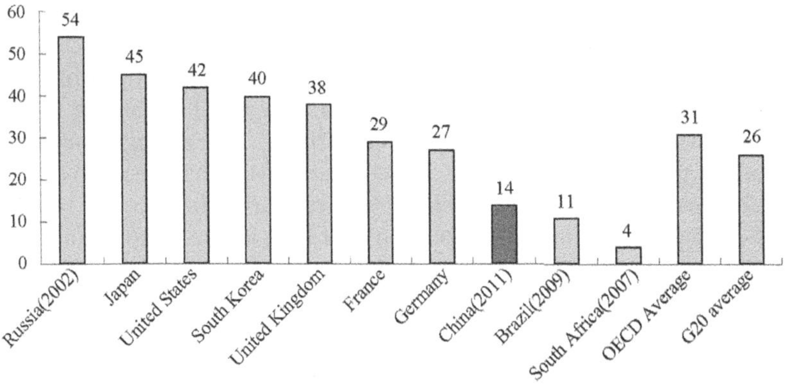

Fig. 8 Percentage of the population aged 25–64 with higher education in the major countries of the world in 2010 (%) (*Source* CDB Research Institute Inspiration Drawn from A Comparison of China's Development with that of Other Major Economies in 2013 and Policy Suggestions)

only 9.13% of China's labor force has participated in professional or technical training for at least five days, and only 11.75% of the labor force has obtained professional or technical qualification certificates.

Second, the total input in R&D and innovation and the total output are large, but significantly lower than developed countries in per capita terms. In 2015, China's R&D expenditure accounted for 2.10% of its GDP, reaching 1.4 trillion Yuan. Translated at the current exchange rate, China's R&D expenditure surpassed Germany in 2010 and Japan in 2013. China has become the world's second largest spender on R&D after the United States. But the expenditure on R&D per capita is only $158, far behind developed countries. In 2011, China already ranked No. 1 in the world for the absolute number of researchers (in full-time equivalent), but the number of researchers (in full-time equivalent) per 10,000 inhabitants was only 21.1, significantly lower than that in developed countries (only 1/5 of that in Denmark and 1/3 of that in Japan and South Korea).

Although the number of Chinese scientific papers published in international journals has grown rapidly in recent years, the quality still needs to be improved. According to the statistics on Chinese scientific papers published by the Institute of Scientific and Technical Information of China, from 2005 to 2015 (as of September 2015), Chinese scientists and technicians published a total of 1.5811 million international papers, which were cited 12.876 million times; compared with 2014, the number increased by 24.2%, with China ranking fourth in the world for the second year in a row. In terms of citation counts, China is still lagging behind the United States (60.417 million times), Germany (14.174 million times), and the United Kingdom (14.043 million times). The average number of citations per Chinese paper is 8.14, compared with the world average of 11.29, indicating that the quality of Chinese papers has not yet reached the average level on the whole. In 2014, Science, Nature and Cell published a total of 2126 papers. China ranked fifth in the world for the second year in a row with 177 papers, considerably fewer than the United States, which ranked first (1577 papers).

In recent years, the number of patent applications in China has grown rapidly, and the structure has been increasingly optimized, reflecting an improvement in China's ability to deliver scientific and technological outputs and the level and efficiency of such delivery. In 2015, the number of patent applications accepted in China was 2.799 million, an increase of 36.5% over 2012; the number of applications for utility patents exceeded one million for the first time, reaching 1.102 million, an increase of 68.8% over 2012; the number of applications for utility patents accepted was the highest in the world for the fifth year in a row. In 2015, 1,718,000 patents were granted in China, an increase of 36.9% over 2012, including 359,000 utility patents, an increase of 65.5% over 2012. Utility patents accounted for 20.9% of the patents granted, an increase of 3.6% over 2012. By the end of 2015, China had 5.478 million valid patents and 1.472 million valid utility patents, an increase of 1.969 million and 597,000 over 2012, respectively. In 2015, China accepted 30,548 international patent applications under the Patent Cooperation Treaty (PCT), ranking third in the world for two consecutive years since 2013. But the number of utility patents per 10,000 people in China currently stands at 6.3, about a quarter of that in Japan.

In 2015, China's R&D expenditure accounted for 2.10% of its GDP, a significant increase compared with 0.9% in 2000, and the highest among BRICS countries, but still lower than in developed countries. Israel ranked first in the world with 4.39%. Even the level of 2.5% that China is expected to reach by 2020 according to the 13th Five-Year Plan is far lower than the current ratio of R&D expenditure to GDP in South Korea and Japan (see Fig. 9).

In terms of the expenditure on R&D per capita, the gap between China and major developed countries has further widened. In 2012,

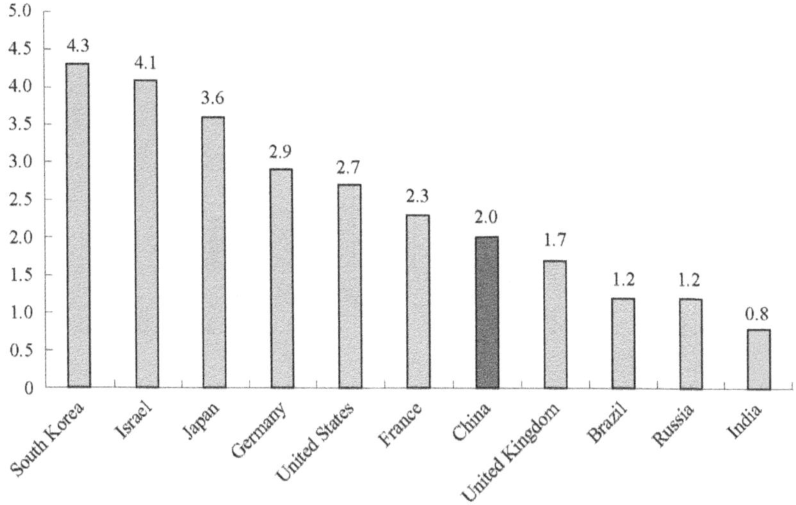

Fig. 9 R&D expenditure as a percentage of gdp in the major countries of the world in 2014 (%) (*Source* International Statistical Yearbook 2016)

China's expenditure on R&D per capita was $182 (at purchasing power parity), about 1/8 of that of Finland, the world's highest per capita spender on R&D; Japan and South Korea were far ahead of China (see Fig. 10). Although China's R&D expenditure in 2015 was as high as 1.4 trillion Yuan, translated at the USD/CNY exchange rate of 6.5, its expenditure on R&D per capita was only $158.

In terms of scientific research output, the total number of utility patents originated in China in 2015 reached 359,000, surpassing the United States and Japan, ranking first in the world, but the number of utility patents per 10,000 people was only 2.6, well behind Japan and the United States. In 2015, China's high-tech exports amounted to $655.3 billion, ranking first in the world, but on a per capita basis, its high-tech exports stood at only $475, far behind South Korea and Japan. According to 2014 data, in terms of royalties received on intellectual property (in current US dollars), the gap between China and developed countries was also quite large. The United States received about $130.3 billion, Japan about $36.8 billion, South Korea about $5.1 billion, and China only $680 million (see Fig. 11).

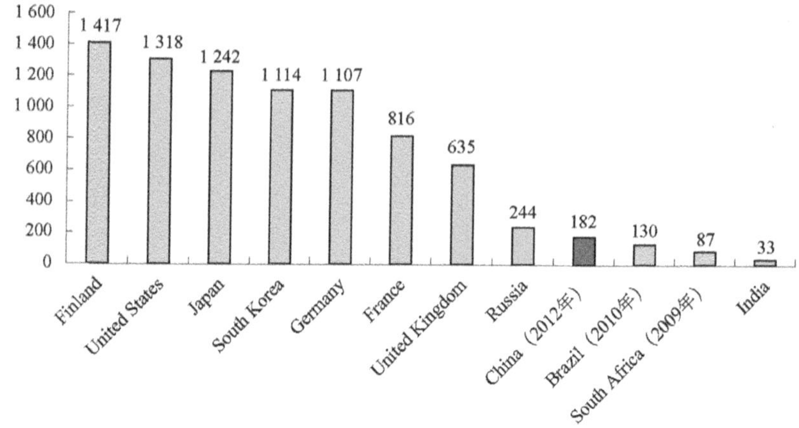

Fig. 10 Expenditure on R&D per capita in the major countries of the world in 2011 (US$) (*Source* CDB Research Institute Inspiration Drawn from A Comparison of China's Development with that of Other Major Economies in 2013 and Policy Suggestions)

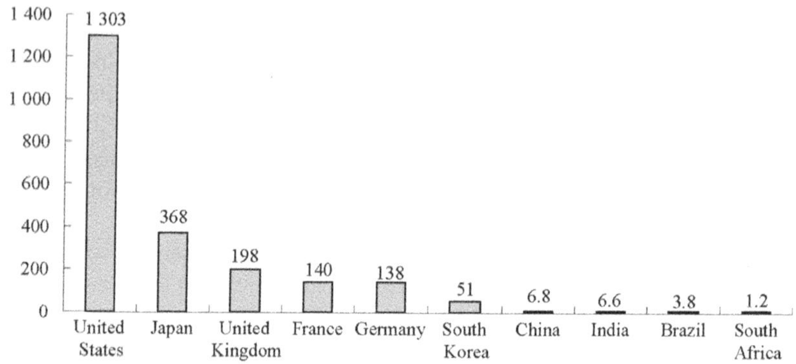

Fig. 11 Comparison of royalties received on intellectual property by China and some developed and emerging countries in 2014 (US$100 million) (*Source* World Bank website)

2.6.4 Space for the Upgrading of the Service Sector

The service sector contributes less to economic growth in China than in developed countries, and there is considerable room for further improvement. Despite China's rapid economic growth, China's service sector remains a weak link in economic and social development. In terms of composition by sector, in 2015, the primary sector accounted for 8.9% of GDP, the secondary sector 40.9%, and the tertiary sector 50.5%. Although the contribution of the service sector to economic growth in China has increased significantly, it is well below the share of about 70% in developed countries and about 10 percentage points lower than in developing countries with the same income level. Even among BRICS countries, the share of China's service sector is still the lowest (see Fig. 12).

China's service industry has broad space for development. Vigorously developing the service sector is of great significance for China to promote strategic adjustments to its economic structure, deepen reform and opening-up, and expand international cooperation. The service sector is becoming not only a new engine and new direction for promoting the recovery of the world economy and leading transformation and

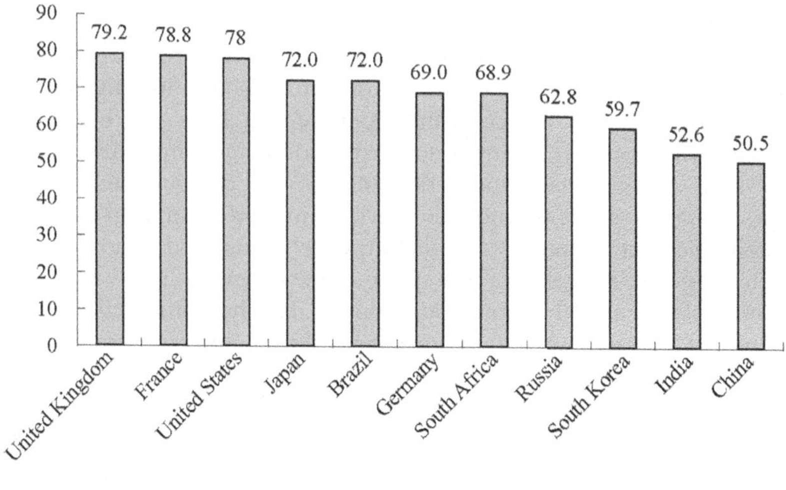

Fig. 12 Service sector as a percentage of gdp in the major countries of the world in 2015 (%) (*Source* International Statistical Yearbook 2016)

development, but also a new engine and new driver for the long-term sustained and healthy development, optimization, and upgrading of China's economy.

2.6.5 *Space for Agricultural Modernization*

At present, there is a tight balance between China's agricultural output and consumption, and the tight balance between grain supply and demand will likely be around for a long time to come. China's grain demand will grow inexorably. China's food demand will continue to grow in the long run due to population growth, urbanization, and the upgrading of its food consumption structure, as well as diversification of food use and increased industrial use of grains.

Since the 1980s, world agriculture, represented by developed countries, has gained new development space on the basis of existing achievements in modernization. First, high-tech agriculture. Since the 1990s, with continuous breakthroughs in and the application of high and new technologies—mainly biotechnology and information technology, new technologies including biotechnology, information technology, farming technology, water-saving irrigation technology, and other new and high agricultural technologies have become the pioneer and driver of modern agriculture, Secondly, informationized agriculture. Information and knowledge have increasingly become a basic resource and a driving force in modern agricultural production activities, and information and intellectual activities are contributing more and more to the growth of modern agriculture. Informationized modern agriculture involves the universal and systematic application of not only computer technology, but also many other technologies such as microelectronics technology, communication technology, photoelectric technology and remote sensing technology in agriculture. The goal is to achieve a high degree of sharing of agricultural information resources. Finally, multifunctional agriculture. Compared with traditional agriculture, modern agriculture is expanding in the direction of sightseeing, leisure, and landscaping. New forms of agriculture such as holiday agriculture, leisure agriculture, sightseeing agriculture, and tourism agriculture have rapidly developed into important industries that are neck and neck with product-producing agriculture. The space for the development of modern agriculture formed by combining with science and technology, information, etc. is huge.

2.6.6 *Space for the Development of the Environmental Protection Industry*

China's environmental protection industry has developed rapidly in recent years, but on the whole, the level of development is still relatively low, and there is still a long way to go before demand is met. This is mainly manifested as follows.

First, innovation capability is weak. The energy-saving and environmental protection technology innovation system led by enterprises is not perfect, the combination of production, education, and research is not tight enough, and investment in technology development is insufficient. Some core technologies have not been fully mastered, some key equipment still needs to be imported, and the performance and efficiency of some energy-saving and environmental protection equipment that can be independently produced need to be improved.

Second, the policy mechanism is not perfect, and investment in environmental protection still needs to be increased. China's system of regulations and standards on energy conservation and environmental protection is not perfect, resource product pricing reform and environmental protection charging policy have not yet been put in place, and fiscal, taxation, and financial policies need to be further improved. Although fiscal expenditures on environmental protection have increased year by year in recent years, investment in environmental protection as a percentage of GDP is still low. In view of the situation in developed countries, China's investment in environmental protection as a percentage of its GDP should be at least 2–3%. Much more needs to be done to achieve this target (see Fig. 13).

Third, the original economic structure of the environmental protection industry can no longer meet the development needs of the market economy. The current structure of the environmental protection industry is unreasonable, there are only a few types of products, economies of scale have not yet been achieved, and enterprises are generally small and scattered. Enterprises' technology and equipment are backward, the level of integration, serialization, standardization, and localization for environmental protection equipment is low, and the problem of low-level duplicate construction is serious.

The energy conservation and environmental protection industry involves energy-saving and environmental protection technology, equipment, products, and services. It has a long industrial chain, a high degree of relevance and a strong ability to create jobs, and therefore plays a

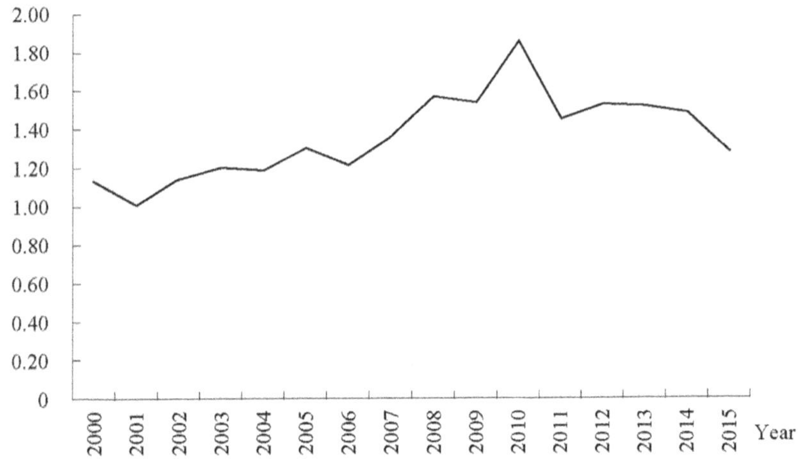

Fig. 13 China's total investment in environmental pollution control as a percentage of GDP (%) (*Source* Ministry of Environmental Protection)

significant role in driving economic growth. Accelerating the development of the energy conservation and environmental protection industry is an inherent requirement for adjusting the economic structure and changing the mode of economic development, and a strategic option for promoting energy conservation and emission reduction, developing a green economy and circular economy, building a resource-saving and environment-friendly society, actively coping with climate change, and seizing the commanding heights of future competition.

In recent years, China has enacted a slew of environmental protection laws and regulations in quick succession, such as the Law on the Prevention and Control of Environmental Pollution by Solid Waste enacted in 2004, the Law on the Prevention and Control of Water Pollution enacted in 2008, and the Comprehensive Work Plan for Energy Conservation and Emission Reduction During the 12th Five-Year Plan Period and the National 12th Five-Year Plan for Environmental Protection issued by the State Council in 2011. In 2010, the Decision of the State Council on Accelerating the Cultivation and Development of Strategic Emerging Industries identified energy conservation and environmental protection industry as one of the seven strategic emerging industries, underscoring the importance attached to environmental protection. A combination of environmental protection laws and policies has turned the environmental protection industry into a new growth point for the next round of economic development, starting a new journey for China's environmental protection industry. In 2016, the Central Environmental Protection Inspection Group was set up under the leadership of the Ministry of Environmental Protection. It is comprised of the relevant leaders of the Central Commission for Discipline Inspection and the Organization Department of the CPC Central Committee, and performs environmental protection inspection on party committees and governments in provinces (autonomous regions and municipalities directly under the Central Government) and their relevant departments on behalf of the CPC Central Committee and the State Council.

2.6.7 *Space for Industrial Modernization and Upgrading*

China's industry is dominated by low value-added heavy and chemical industries, most of which are at the low end of international specialization, and the industrial added value rate is far lower than that of the United States, Japan, and other developed countries. China's industries are big but not strong. This is reflected most pointedly in a low industrial value-added rate. Although there are more than 500 kinds of industrial products in China, high-grade, high-tech, and high value-added products account for only a small proportion, resulting in low industrial value added. This puts China in a disadvantageous position in competition in international markets. China needs to increase the industrial value-added rate by upgrading its industries and elevating its position in international specialization. The basic barometer for whether the transformation of the mode of industrial development is successful is a significant increase in the industrial value-added rate, which is the fundamental way to solve the structural and quality problems of China's industry, and also an important guiding principle for promoting industrial transformation and upgrading.

"Made in China 2025" is the first 10-year action plan of the Chinese government designed to transform China into a manufacturing power. "Made in China 2025" proposes to adhere to the guiding principles of "to have manufacturing be innovation-driven, emphasize quality over quantity, achieve green development, optimize the structure, and nurture human talent," adhere to the basic principles of "to have manufacturing be market-oriented, guided by the government, planned on both a short-term and long-term basis, pushed forward as a whole, focused on breakthroughs in key areas, independent in development, and open for cooperation," and achieve the strategic goal of turning China into a manufacturing power by following "three steps": First step—by 2025, China will become a manufacturing power; second step—By 2035, Chinese manufacturing will reach an intermediate level among world manufacturing powers; third step—by the centenary of the founding of the People's Republic of China, China will become the leader among the world's manufacturing powers.

2.6.8 *Space for the Development of the Health and Elderly Care Industry*

With China's gradual entry into an aging society, a huge elderly care market has been formed, but the development of the elderly care industry is relatively lagging behind. At present, China's elderly care institutions can accommodate only 0.8% of the aging population, far behind the 3% in developed countries. At the end of 2016, there were 126,773 elderly care institutions with 7.166 million beds in China, an increase of 6.0% over the previous year; there were 31 beds for every 1000 elderly people, an increase of 14.8% over the previous year. As there is still a large gap between supply and demand in China's elderly care industry, the industry has broad prospects for development and is undoubtedly a sunrise industry. The size of the industry is expected to reach 3.3 trillion Yuan in 2020 and 8.6 trillion Yuan in 2030.

In 2016, 887.77 million people in China were covered by basic endowment insurance, including 379.3 million covered by endowment insurance for employees and 508.47 million covered by endowment insurance for residents. The revenues of basic endowment insurance funds for the year totaled 3.7991 trillion Yuan, an increase of 18% over the previous year; of this amount, 2.75 trillion Yuan had been collected, an increase of 16% over the previous year. The expenditures of basic endowment insurance funds for the year were 3.4004 trillion Yuan, an increase of 21.8% over the previous year. The cumulative balance of basic endowment insurance funds at the end of the year was 4.3965 trillion Yuan. China's urban and rural basic endowment insurance system has been fully established; the basic endowment insurance system for enterprise employees has been gradually improved, and the basic institutional mode of combining social pooling and personal accounts has been established and consolidated; the supplementary pension system has been further developed, advancing the building of a multilevel endowment insurance system; a plan for basic endowment insurance for residents that unifies urban and rural areas has been basically formed.

The acceleration of the aging process has created a huge demand for elderly care facilities, but the corresponding supply of elderly care facilities is woefully inadequate. As the main part of elderly care facilities, senior housing real estate is scarce, and the investment value of the industry is increasingly prominent. In recent years, various institutions, mostly traditional real estate developers, industrial investors, insurance companies, governments, and foreign investment institutions, have been actively involved in the fields of senior housing real estate investment, development, and operation. The senior housing real estate market is expected to grow to 13 trillion Yuan by 2030, so there is enormous space for its development. Generally speaking, the health and elderly care industry is a strategic industry in an aging society, and also a new growth engine for China's economic development in the future.

3 Vigorously Promote Market-Oriented Reforms to Unleash the Vitality of the Economy

Deepening reform is the key to speeding up the transformation of the mode of economic development. The core of economic system reform is to "handle the relationship between the government and the market well." Throughout China's economic development, the relationship between the government and the market has marked nearly 40 years of reform in China. On the one hand, economic takeoff is impossible without the decisive role played by the market in allocating resources; on the other hand, how to promote the further development of China's economy and overcome the middle-income trap, vigorously promote market-oriented reforms and unleash the vitality of the economy is the focus of the transformation of the mode of economic development.

3.1 Deepen Economic System Reform and Transform Government Functions

Economic system reform is the key to comprehensively deepening reforms. The core issue is to handle the relationship between the government and the market well, so that the market can play a decisive role in resource allocation and the government can better play its role. The main responsibilities and functions of the government are to maintain macroeconomic stability, strengthen and optimize public services, ensure fair competition, strengthen market regulation, maintain market order, pursue sustainable development, promote common prosperity, and make up for market failures. The relationship between the government and the market is more complicated since China's economy has evolved from a planned economy.

The relationship between the government and the market is more complicated since China's economy has evolved from a planned economy. Although China has continuously promoted market-oriented reforms, on the whole, the vitality of the market mechanism has not been fully unleashed. To transform government functions, we need to streamline administration and delegate power, and make full use of the "invisible hand." For things that the market can manage well, we should delegate power to the market to improve the efficiency of resource allocation, so that the government can extricate itself from these trivial and complicated micro areas to do its own job well. We should combine transforming government functions with incorporating innovations into management practices. We should adhere to the direction of reform of the socialist market economic system, coordinate the stimulation of market vitality with the strengthening of market regulation, simplify and optimize administrative examination and approval, strengthen and innovate market regulation, and accelerate the building of a new market management system where the market is open, fair, standardized, and orderly, enterprises make decisions independently and compete equally, government powers and responsibilities are well-defined, and regulation is enforced with rigor. We should further separate government functions from enterprise management, the government's function of managing public affairs from the government's responsibilities as managers and owners of state-owned assets, administrative units from public institutions, and government administration from social organizations, delegate management power to enterprises, and reduce administrative examination and approval authority. Meanwhile, the government should give full play to its public service and management functions, focus on macro functions, and organically combine planning and the market to safeguard the market economy.

In order to enable the government to exercise public functions more effectively, the new public management, multicenter governance, and new public service theories which emerged in the mid-to-late 1980s all emphasize the reshaping of the public governance structure. According to the analytical framework of the new public management theory, the government is no longer a bureaucracy above society, but a responsible entrepreneur, and citizens are its customers or consumers. The relationship between the government and the public has evolved into an interactive relationship between a supplier and its customers on the basis of marketization and customer orientation. Accordingly, in the modern governance structure, the role of the government should be changed from "rowing" to "steering," and the role of the non-governmental sector should be changed from "passive exclusion" to "active participation." According to the research thinking behind the multicenter governance theory, with the continuous development and progress of society, people's expectations for the government are getting higher and higher, and becoming more and more diversified and fragmented. The traditional "single-center governance" model characterized by government monopoly is inefficient and unresponsive in the face of huge demand, and the multicenter governance structure characterized by "the decentralization of power, the overlapping of management and shared governance involving the government, the market and society" has become an ideal model to meet the needs of the public and improve the quality and efficiency of public services. As for the new public service theory, it emphasizes the public governance thinking of "taking public services as the core, democratic participation as the means and whether public interest is realized as the evaluation criterion." According to the theory, the most important responsibility of the government is to help citizens articulate their common interests clearly, and to use collective efforts and collaborative processes based on common values to enable the effective and responsible implementation of policies and projects that meet the needs of the public.

3.2 Expand Market Openness and Eliminate Market Barriers

Due to historical reasons, the Chinese government and enterprises have long been linked. Although a system of separation of government functions from enterprise management has been implemented, in the early stages of the establishing and perfecting the market economic system, the separation of government functions from enterprise management is not complete enough, the operational mechanism and management philosophy of enterprises have not yet been completely transformed, access to some industries has not yet been liberalized, and the pricing of key resources is still controlled by the government, which hinders economic efficiency; some enterprises, especially large state-owned enterprises, are keen to rely on the government and are accustomed to obeying the government's command and arrangements. Meanwhile, in order to increase taxes and ensure employment, local governments often have a strong impulse to rely on investment to drive the economy, thus supporting and protecting some inefficient large enterprises in terms of credit and policy. Local governments, acting out of self-interest, often use administrative orders to restrict, exclude, or hinder non-local similar enterprises from participating in competition, so as to pursue local or departmental interests, resulting in local protectionism and market barriers.

3.2.1 The Administrative Monopoly Suppresses the Innovation Drive and Operational Vitality of Market Entities

The administrative monopoly undermines the order of fair competition in the market, hinders technological progress and the development of productive forces, blocks and restricts market access over a long period of time, and prevents the market regulation mechanism from functioning normally, resulting in inefficient allocation of resources, which adversely affects business efficiency and industrial structural upgrading and even the healthy development of the whole national economy. The administrative monopoly causes distortions in resource allocation, and tilts the allocation of factor resources in favor of inefficient sectors, resulting in the loss of social welfare and jeopardizing the healthy and sustainable development of the whole national economy.

First, the excessive profits brought by the administrative monopoly disincentivize monopolistic enterprises from changing the mode of production and improving productivity, and hinder the R&D investment and management innovation. The reform of Chinese enterprises, especially state-owned enterprises, is not thorough, no scientific and reasonable modern enterprise management mechanism has been established, the sense of responsibility for investment and investment risk awareness are not strong, the phenomenon of high input and low output is very prominent, and investment efficiency is generally low.

Second, the administrative monopoly seriously hinders the optimization and upgrading of the industrial structure, and widens income and distributional inequality. In the secondary sector, monopolistic state-owned enterprises hold a dominant position, which is a prominent problem in China's industrial structure. In addition, private enterprises and SMEs are lagging behind due to various discriminatory policies and systems, while monopolistic state-owned enterprises are reaping huge monopoly profits through their monopoly over the prices of important resources.

Third, the administrative monopoly leads to rent-seeking, undermines the order of fair competition in the market, and hinders technological progress and the development of productive forces. Due to the lack of effective supervision and restriction on administrative power, administrative personnel take advantage of sectoral or departmental interests to privatize or personalize public power, resulting in rampant rent-seeking and corruption. The huge economic losses caused by the administrative monopoly in China have become an important part of the economic losses caused by corruption.

3.2.2 *We Need to Further Open Up the Market and Break Down Market Barriers*

At present, China's economy is undergoing transformation and upgrading, and there is still huge space for economic growth. However, valid investment opportunities are subject to numerous market access limitations, and markets are off limits to a lot of private capital, which affects the vitality and efficiency of the market. Therefore, we need to further open up markets, break down barriers, leverage the decisive role of markets in resource allocation, and create a level playing field for private capital, thus unleashing huge investment potential.

First, comprehensively implement a negative list system for market access both internally and externally upon the principle that "whatever is not prohibited by law should be allowed." A negative list generally refers to the scope of areas that a country, by making a list of them, explicitly prohibits or restricts foreign investment from entering. The Opinions on the Implementation of A Negative List System for Market Access, considered and adopted by the State Council in October 2015, for the first time made it clear that China would officially implement a nationally unified negative list system for market access starting in 2018. The central government's top-level design for the implementation of a negative list system for market access across the country means that this access system will be expanded from foreign investment to all investments including domestic investment, which is a major change in China's economic management system.

Second, focus on the development of key border areas, such as opening-up pilot zones, border state-level ports, border cities, and border and cross-border economic cooperation zones. These areas are an important platform for China to deepen cooperation with neighboring countries and regions, and an important support for the economic and social development of border areas. With a view to bringing stability, peace, and prosperity to border areas, we should comprehensively consider the needs of economic development, border stability, national unity, and peace and tranquility in surrounding areas, further advance the Program to Revitalize Border Areas and Enrich Local Residents, increase fiscal and tax support, implement differentiated support policies, deepen the reform of systems and mechanisms, and leverage the role of key areas along the border in influencing and driving the development of border areas. We should promote opening-up in border areas with reform and innovation, allow border areas to try first, boldly explore and innovate new models of cross-border economic cooperation, promote new mechanisms for the development of border areas, and find new ways to revitalize border areas and enrich local residents.

Third, improve the price formation mechanism in key areas and basically liberalize prices in competitive areas and links. We should improve the government pricing system, make a list of items that are priced by the government, and make government pricing open and transparent. The scope of government pricing should be mainly limited to important public utilities, public welfare services, network-based natural monopolies, and a scientific, standardized, and transparent price supervision system and anti-monopoly law enforcement system should be established. We should let the market determine prices whenever possible, combine delegating power with strengthening regulation, strengthen regulation both during and after the event concerned, and improve regulatory efficiency.

3.3 Promote the Reform of the Urban–Rural Dual System and Allocate Resources in a Balanced Way

At present, China's urban and rural development is not coordinated, which is manifested in three aspects: First, agricultural modernization is obviously lagging behind, and the level of development of agriculture is far behind that of industry. The agricultural foundation is still weak, and the ability to resist natural disasters such as droughts, floods, and epidemics needs to be strengthened. Second, rural development is still lagging behind. For a long time, we have not invested enough in rural infrastructure, leading to relative slowness in the construction of water, electricity, roads, gas, housing, and sanitation in rural areas; conditions at rural primary and secondary schools are poor, basic medical and health care conditions are backward, public cultural facilities are inadequate, the social security system is imperfect, and the urban–rural gap remains big. Third, the income gap between urban and rural households is still large.

3.3.1 *The Urban–Rural Dual Structure Distorts Resource Allocation and Hinders Urbanization*

The urban–rural dual structure greatly restricts the equal exchange of urban and rural factors and distorts the allocation of public resources. First, it leads to the distorted allocation of land resources in that urban land comes with different rights and prices than rural land of the same nature; second, it leads to the division of the labor market in that a large number of migrant workers are paid differently than urban residents for doing the same work; third, it leads to the uneven allocation of public resources between urban and rural areas in that the supply of public resources and services in urban areas far exceeds that in rural areas.

At present, the level and quality of China's urbanization development is not high, and does not match the development stage. The level of urbanization cannot provide more effective assistance and support for China's industrialization, agricultural modernization, and informatization. This is mainly manifested in the following four aspects.

First, a large number of rural people who have moved to cities have difficulty integrating into urban society, retarding progress in transforming them into urban citizens. The more than 200 million migrant workers who have been included in the urban population and their families have not had equal access to essential public services for urban residents in education, employment, health care, elderly care, and indemnificatory housing. New dual structural contradictions in cities and towns restrict the role of urbanization in promoting the expansion of domestic demand and structural upgrading, and may give rise to potential social risks.

Secondly, the spatial distribution of cities and towns does not match the resource and environmental carrying capacity, and the scale and structure of cities and towns are unreasonable. Some city-and-town concentrated areas in eastern China are facing increasingly severe resource and environmental constraints, and the urbanization potential of the areas with strong resource and environmental carrying capacity in central and western China has yet to be tapped. The layout of city clusters is not reasonable, the division of labor and cooperation within city clusters are inadequate, and the efficiency of city clusters is low; the population pressure in the main urban areas of some megacities is too high, and the contradiction between the population pressure and the comprehensive carrying capacity is increasing; the industry- and population-concentrating function of small- and medium-sized cities are insufficient, and their potential has not yet been fully exploited; small towns are large in number, small in scale, and weak in service functions. The unreasonable spatial distribution, scale, and structure of cities and towns increase the economic, social, and environmental costs.

Third, the problem of "urban diseases" has become increasingly prominent, and urban service management is poor. In some cities, the development of space is unregulated, population is over-concentrated, economic development is prioritized over environmental protection, urban construction is prioritized over management services, traffic congestion is serious, public safety incidents involving food and medicine occur frequently, air, water, soil, and other environmental pollution are worsening, urban management and operation are inefficient, public service supply capacity is insufficient, and the living environment in urban villages in cities, urban–rural fringes and other areas heavily populated by migrants is poor.

Fourth, systems and mechanisms are not perfect, which hinders the healthy development of urbanization. The current household registration management, land management, social security, fiscal, taxation, financial, and administrative systems have, to a certain extent, solidified the existing imbalance between urban and rural interests, hindering the transformation of rural people who have moved to cities into urban citizens and the integration of urban and rural development.

Successful urbanization is not the urbanization of land, but the urbanization of population, so we need to achieve the transformation of rural labor force into urban residents. Urbanization is not simply an increase in the proportion of the population living in urban areas and the expansion of urban area, but a series of changes from "rural" to "urban," such as changes in the industrial structure, employment patterns, the living environment, social security, and supporting policies. To gradually break down the urban–rural dual structure and the dual structure within cities, we should comprehensively promote the reform of systems and mechanisms in important areas and key links such as people, land, and money; we should make breakthroughs in urban and rural household registration, rural land property rights, urban and rural social security, and government fiscal and taxation systems, so as to coordinate urban and rural development, and overcome the middle-income trap in the process of deep urbanization.

3.3.2 *Priorities for Promoting the Reform of the Urban–Rural Dual Structure*

First, build a new agricultural operation system. Encourage the development of cooperative economy in rural areas, support the development of large-scale, specialized, and modernized operations, encourage and lead industrial and commercial capital to develop modern farming suitable for enterprise-style operations in rural areas, and bring modern factors of production and business models to agriculture.

Second, give farmers more property rights. Protect the rights of members of farmers' collective economic organizations, actively develop farmers' joint-stock partnerships, and give farmers the right to possess, profit from, withdraw in exchange for compensation, pledge as security or collateral, and inherit the shares of collective assets. Protect the usufruct of farmers' homesteads, reform and improve the rural homestead system, advance the pledging as security or collateral and the transfer of farmers' housing property rights, and explore ways for farmers to increase their property income.

Third, promote the equal exchange of urban and rural factors and the balanced allocation of public resources. Safeguard the rights and interests of farmers in factors of production, ensure equal pay for migrant workers, and ensure that farmers receive a fair share of land value-added income. Encourage private capital to invest in rural construction, and allow enterprises and social organizations to set up various undertakings in rural areas. Coordinate urban and rural infrastructure and community building, and promote the equalization of essential public services in urban and rural areas.

Fourth, promote the transformation of rural people who have moved to cities into urban citizens. Innovate population management, speed up the reform of the household registration system, and gradually convert qualified rural people who have moved to cities into urban citizens. Steadily extend urban essential public services to all permanent residents, include all farmers who have settled in cities into the urban housing and social security system, and integrate the endowment insurance and medical insurance they took out when living in rural areas into the urban social security system.

3.3.3 *Take the Road of Urban Intensification and Increase the Rate of Urbanization*

Urbanization is an inevitable trend in economic and social development, and also an important symbol of industrialization and modernization. Actively yet prudently advancing China's urbanization is one of the basic approaches and major strategies for building a moderately prosperous society in all respects, solving the Three Rural Issues which are unique to China, and developing the cause of socialism with Chinese characteristics. Promoting the transfer of surplus rural labor to non-agricultural sectors is a common challenge faced by developing countries in the process of urbanization.

The core of China's urbanization development is how to modernize the rural traditional economic and social structures in a relatively short period of time. This requires attaching great importance to the high correlation of human, material, and financial resources between large, medium-sized and small cities, small towns, and rural areas. While continuously strengthening the structural mutualistic effect of urbanization, we should form a system of towns and cities led by central cities, dominated by medium-sized cities and based on small cities and central towns, and continuously improve the agglomeration effect of urbanization.

Improving the agglomeration effect of urbanization has two meanings: first, industrial agglomeration and formation of leading cities and central towns. Urbanization should be based on industrial development. Without industry and employment, towns and cities cannot develop. Without the development of leading cities and central towns in a region, it is impossible to form a driving force and radiating power that can drive urban and rural economic and social development in the region. Second, the combination of the agglomeration of cities and the agglomeration of towns. The agglomeration of towns and cities is the guarantee and foundation of urbanization. Only by achieving the agglomeration of large and medium-sized cities, central towns and small towns in a certain region, can a high level of industrial integration between large and medium-sized cities and small towns be possible; only by giving full play to the radiating power and influence of cities and central towns over rural areas, can we modernize the economic and social structures of China's rural areas.

Prioritize the development of central cities and central towns, vigorously develop medium-sized cities in an effort to build a county-centric urban growth core led by central cities, prosper county economies, develop counties into small cities with a population of 100,000 to 200,000, form an urban network based on central towns, with medium-sized cities and small county-level cities as the satellite cities of regional central cities, and continuously increase the radiation and diffusion of the system of towns and cities toward rural areas, so as to promote the modernization of the rural economic and social structures.

Urbanization is not simply an increase in the size of towns and cities, but involves improvement in the quality of urbanization. A simple spatial expansion of towns and cities without improving the quality of urban industries and strengthening urban influence on rural areas is not real urbanization. A simple "make a big pie"-style extensive increase in the size of towns and cities is contrary to the inherent requirements for urbanization. In order to achieve the short-term, medium-term, and long-term goals of urbanization, we should attach great importance to technological innovation and environment protection for urban and rural industries on the basis of increasing the structural mutualistic effect, opening-up effect and agglomeration effect of urbanization, and increase the structural upgrading effect of urbanization.

Improvement in the quality of urbanization is mainly reflected in the following aspects: First, the capacity for technological innovation of urban industries is enhanced, and technological upgrading is accelerated; second, the transformation and integration of rural industries by technologically advanced urban industries is accelerated, the level of technology of rural industries is improved, and cooperation between rural and urban industries in technological innovation is continuously strengthened; third, with the integration of urban and rural industries, institutional barriers in education, employment, social security, and household registration between urban and rural areas are gradually eliminated, allowing resources to be shared between urban and rural areas; fourth, urban and rural lifestyles are gradually integrated; with the integration of urban and rural economy and culture, the phenomenon of "deruralization" among farmers is further intensified; traditional farmers are transformed into modern farmers, and farmers truly become part of the industrial workforce; fifth, the environment in urban and rural areas is improving, and people and nature are developing harmoniously.

At present, there are about 200–300 million semi-urbanized residents (migrant workers) in China, which is a resource with great potential in terms of consumption. Accelerating the transformation of migrant workers into urban residents will also greatly promote growth in consumer demand. To speed up the process of transforming farmers into urban residents, we should do the following: First, promote the rationalization of urban housing prices. There will be no urbanization if housing prices are high. The current housing price level in China is significantly higher than normal compared with the income level. Reducing housing prices will unleash huge demand for housing, and correspondingly speed up the urbanization process. Second, implement large-scale housing projects for migrant workers, which mainly involve the use of government power to build indemnificatory housing for migrant workers. Third, encourage the transfer of coastal labor-intensive industries to the central and western regions, and promote the urbanization of the central and western regions.

Maintaining the stability of farmers' land contracting management rights to enable farmers to move in both directions between urban and rural areas is crucial to the healthy development of urbanization. Lessons from India and Brazil remind us that the healthy development of urbanization has a lot to do with the rural land system. China's basic national conditions determine that for a long time to come, land will still be the most basic livelihood guarantee for farmers. For migrant workers, most of whom are in a state of instability, having a piece of land in their hometown remains their last line of defense. Before farmers settle down in towns or cities and achieve stable employment and income security, keeping their land contracting management rights to enable them to move in both directions between urban and rural areas will help prevent a large number of landless farmers from concentrating in cities, leading to the formation of slums. In the process of expanding the scale of agricultural land and promoting agricultural industrialization, we must not "pull up seedlings to help them grow," deprive farmers of their land contracting management rights, and create landless farmers. Adjust the thinking behind urban construction, and consider the needs of migrant workers in urban planning, housing construction, public services, and community management. The situation in India and Brazil shows that in addition to employment, another major issue for rural migrants is housing. There is a big difference between the employment of Chinese farmers in cities and that of landless farmers in India and Brazil. Some of the farmers can go back when they are out of work, but a considerable number of them will work and live with their families in cities for a long time. Cities should treat them as permanent residents, and incorporate the needs of the migrant population for housing, schooling, medical care, and other amenities into urban construction planning. When it comes to fiscal expenditure and public services, cities should not only consider the needs of the urban registered population, but also serve the whole society effectively.

3.3.4 "13th Five-Year" Plan: Promote New-Type Urbanization

The Outline of the 13th Five-year Plan for National Economic and Social Development (Draft) (hereinafter referred to as the "Outline") proposes that in pursuit of people-centered urbanization based on city clusters, supported by the comprehensive carrying capacity of cities, and safeguarded by system and mechanism innovation, we should speed up the pace of new-type urbanization, make further progress in building a new socialist countryside, strive to bridge the gap between urban and rural development, and facilitate the integration of urban and rural development.[10]

The Outline proposes: First, we should speed up the transformation of rural people who have moved to cities into urban citizens, comprehensively promote the reform of the household registration system and the equalization of essential public services, and improve the incentive mechanism for the transformation of long-term residents into urban citizens to promote the integration of more people into towns and cities; we should deepen the reform of the household registration system, implement the residence permit system, and improve the mechanism for promoting the transformation of rural people who have moved to cities into urban citizens. Second, we should optimize the layout and form of urbanization, and work faster in pursuit of an urbanization strategy which stresses the reasonable distribution and coordinated development of cities of all sizes and small towns and combines two horizontal axes—land bridges and the Yangtze River—and three vertical axes—China's coastline, the Beijing–Harbin and Beijing–Guangzhou railways, and the

[10] "13th Five-Year" Plan: Promote New-Type Urbanization \[EB/OL\]. *Xinhua News Agency*, 2016-03-05. http://news.xinhuanet.com/2016-03/05/c_1118243516.htm.

Baotou–Kunming Railway; we should accelerate the construction and development of city clusters, enhance the radiating and driving functions of central cities, and speed up the development of small- and medium-sized cities and towns with distinctive characteristics. Third, we should build harmonious and livable cities, change the mode of urban development, improve urban governance capability, intensify efforts to prevent and control "urban diseases," continuously improve the environmental quality, the quality of life of the residents and the competitiveness of cities, and strive to build harmonious, livable, vibrant, and distinctive cities; we should speed up the construction of new-type cities, strengthen the construction of urban infrastructure, accelerate the renovation of shanty-towns and dilapidated houses, and improve urban governance. Fourth, we should improve the housing supply system, build a housing supply system where the government mainly provides basic security and the market mainly meets different levels of demand, optimize the housing supply and demand structure, steadily improve housing standards for residents, and better ensure that people have a roof over their heads; we should improve the housing system that supports buying and renting simultaneously, promote the healthy development of the real estate market, and improve housing security. Fifth, we should promote the coordinated development of urban and rural areas, promote the coordinated development of new-type urbanization and the building of a new socialist countryside, enhance county economies' ability to support and radiate, facilitate a balanced allocation of public resources between urban and rural areas, and expand the space for rural development to form a new pattern of common development between urban and rural areas; we should develop county economies with distinctive characteristics, accelerate the development of beautiful and livable villages, and facilitate a balanced allocation of public resources between urban and rural areas.

3.4 *Implement Mixed Ownership Reform and Introduce Market Vitality*

In the past few decades of reform and opening-up, SOE reform has been an inescapable part of the process of China's transition to a modern market economy. The key to SOE reform is ownership reform. There is no panacea for reform. We must respect the basic economic laws, set reform goals in light of the economic situation, and make strategic advances on this basis, which is the prerequisite for the success of SOE reform.

3.4.1 *Key Points of SOE Reform*

First, we should improve regulation targeted on the basis of a clear definition of functions. The Report on the Work of the Government 2015 stated: "We will push forward with targeted reform of state-owned enterprises on the basis of having clearly defined their functions." Different types of state-owned enterprises play different roles in the market economy due to different attributes and objectives. The idea of reform targeted on the basis of a clear definition of functions not only emphasizes the profit-making nature of state-owned enterprises, but also takes into account the public nature of state-owned enterprises. Regulation targeted on the basis of a clear definition of functions is not only conducive to further strengthening the pertinence and effectiveness of state-owned assets regulation, but also beneficial to the development of the state-owned sector of the economy and improvement in national welfare.

Only after the functions of state-owned enterprises have been clearly defined, can mixed ownership reform be carried out according to different functions. Non-profit state-owned monopolistic enterprises are tasked with accomplishing mandatory social and public objectives, and operate not for profit, and providing high-quality public products and services to the public is the basis for evaluating their performance, with the focus on cost control and service quality; moderately for-profit state-owned monopolistic enterprises, including natural monopolistic state-owned enterprises and some state-owned enterprises with a monopoly over resources, focus more on social and public objectives than economic objectives, and the evaluation of their performance is focused on the ability to control risk and integrate market resources; competitive state-owned enterprises have profit maximization as their chief aim and have more autonomy.

Second, we should optimize the regulatory model. In terms of establishing channels, we should systematically set up state-owned capital operating companies between state-owned assets regulatory bodies and for-profit state-owned enterprises, and establish state-owned capital investment companies specialized in the operation and management of state-owned capital through restructuring. We should separate the functions of the regulator and the investor between state-owned assets regulatory bodies and state-owned capital investment and operation companies, and separate the functions of the investor and the enterprise between state-owned capital investment and operation companies and for-profit state-owned enterprises. Through two-level separation, a three-tier state-owned assets management structure comprised of state-owned assets regulatory bodies, state-owned capital investment and operation companies, and for-profit state-owned enterprises will be formed. Meanwhile, by withdrawing from, or having a non-controlling or controlling interest in various types of enterprises in key industries according to the strategy for regulating state-owned enterprises on the basis of having clearly defined their functions, restructured and newly established state-owned capital investment and operation companies enlarge the control and influence of state-owned capital.

We should reform the way the government regulates state-owned enterprises. First, we should de-administrate the way investors perform their duties, explore the use of a list of items managed by investors, and optimize the way state-owned assets regulatory bodies perform their duties. The core is to reduce enterprise-related items subject to examination and approval by state-owned assets regulatory bodies, and gradually confine the functions and powers of state-owned assets regulatory bodies to the scope of functions and powers granted by the Company Law to shareholders and shareholder committees. Second, we should return more management power to enterprises. For example, we should return the power to appoint and manage executives to competitive level enterprises, and only require them to report the appointment of executives to state-owned assets regulators for the record, establish standardized boards of directors dominated by outside directors, delegate decision-making power over investment plans, large guarantees, major property transfers, and other matters involving funds up to a certain amount to boards of directors, and explore a fully market-oriented approach to the management of mixed enterprises in which the state holds a stake of less than 50%. Third, we should actively promote the securitization of state-owned assets and overall listings of state-owned enterprises, inject more high-quality state-owned assets into listed companies through private placement, capital injection into holding listed companies, the divestment of non-core assets, and achieve overall listings of more competitive level enterprises, so as to achieve the goal of "multi-in-one" market-oriented regulation. Fourth, we should further optimize the distribution of state-owned resources, steadily promote M&As and restructurings with the help of capital market forces, and achieve the effective allocation of state-owned enterprise resources.

3.4.2 *Push Chinese Enterprises to "Go Out"*

Since the start of reform and opening-up, especially in recent years, Chinese enterprises have continuously expanded their investment abroad, and made remarkable achievements in "going out." To expand foreign investment by enterprises and individuals, we need to step up efforts to push Chinese enterprises to "go out." According to the 2015 Statistical Bulletin of China's Outward Foreign Direct Investment jointly issued by the Ministry of Commerce, the National Bureau of statistics and the State Administration of Foreign Exchange, in 2015, China's outward foreign direct investment scaled a new height and registered rapid growth for the 13th consecutive year, hitting an all-time high of $145.67 billion, which accounted for 9.9% of the global total, represented a year-on-year increase of 18.3%, was second only to the United States ($299.96 billion), put China in second place in the world for the first time (Japan ranked third with $128.65 billion), and exceeded the amount of foreign capital actually used by China over the same period ($135.6 billion), resulting in a net outflow of capital.

Strategic Arrangements for Chinese Enterprises to "Go Out" in Terms of Strategy

Strategic arrangements for foreign investment by Chinese enterprises are mainly reflected in the following six aspects.

First, arrangements regarding outward investors for Chinese enterprises to "go out." First, it should be clear that enterprises are implementers of the Go Out policy. The Decision on Some Major Issues Concerning Comprehensively Deepening the Reform (the "Decision") proposes to "establish the primacy of enterprises and individuals in outbound investment." In terms of the nature of outward investors, China's first outward investors were mainly state-owned enterprises. With the balanced development of various forms of ownership in the process of China's economic system reform, private enterprises have become increasingly involved in overseas investment. In terms of arrangements regarding outward investors, while continuing to promote foreign investment by state-owned enterprises, we need to further increase policy and financial support for the "going out" of private enterprises, reduce barriers to the "going out" of private enterprises, and create conditions for them to carry out greenfield investments, M&A investments, securities investments, joint investments, and project and labor service cooperation abroad. In terms of the regional distribution of outward investors, at present, the number and scale of enterprises "going out" in central and western China are still far behind those in eastern coastal areas, so it is necessary to further increase support for foreign investment by enterprises in central and western China to promote balanced regional development.

Second, spatial arrangements for Chinese enterprises to "go out." China's foreign investment has been expanding geographically, spreading all over Asia, Europe, Latin America, North America, Africa, and Oceania and diversifying into different markets. According to the latest data from the Ministry of Commerce, in 2016, Chinese domestic investors made non-financial direct investment in 7961 overseas enterprises in 164 countries and regions, with a total investment of $170.11 billion (1.12992 trillion Yuan), up 44.1% year-on-year. On the basis of consolidating existing markets for outward foreign direct investment by Chinese enterprises, we need to further expand overseas markets, especially to consolidate the foundation of China's cooperation with regions such as Latin America and Africa, and continuously expand investment cooperation with developing countries to achieve diversification for "going out."

Third, cooperation with countries along the Belt and Road has become a bright spot. In 2016, Chinese enterprises made $14.53 billion of direct investment in countries along the Belt and Road, and signed $126.03 billion worth of new contracts for foreign contracted projects, accounting for 51.6% of the total worth of new contracts signed by China in the same period. By the end of 2016, Chinese enterprises had established 56 cooperation zones of some size in countries along the Belt and Road, with a total investment of $18.55 billion; 1082 enterprises had moved into these zones, a total output value of $50.69 billion had been generated, 1.07 billion US dollars in taxes had been paid to host countries and 177,000 local jobs had been created.

Fourth, industrial arrangements for Chinese enterprises to "go out." The industrial structure of foreign investment has been further optimized, with the real economy and emerging industries being given special attention. In 2016, Chinese enterprises invested $31.06 billion in manufacturing, $20.36 billion in information transmission, software and information technology services, and $4.95 billion in scientific research and technology services. Chinese enterprises need to accelerate the pace of "going out" in the field of services. For service trade enterprises with strong competitiveness and management capabilities, we need to encourage and lead them to carry out overseas investment, promote the development of business cooperation models, and acquire overseas marketing networks and brand patents. For industries such as construction, transportation, and distribution, we should focus on supporting enterprises in making direct investment and localizing their operations in developing countries. In the fields of finance, education, culture and art, radio, film and television, press and publication, and tourism, we should promote overseas business selectively according to the characteristics of each country's market. For animation, online games, and other emerging industries, we should increase support for enterprises to "go out." For industries with Chinese characteristics such as traditional Chinese medicine and Chinese food, we should make full use of the brand effect of "time-honored brands" to expand overseas. In terms of providing high-end consulting services for enterprises to "go out," we should accelerate the establishment of local intermediaries and credit rating agencies. In addition, while realizing the international operations of enterprises, we should promote the "going out" of Chinese technology and standards.

Fifth, arrangements regarding the way to invest for Chinese enterprises to "go out." In terms of the way to invest, cross-border M&A has become an important way for Chinese enterprises to make foreign direct investments. The position and role of M&A have come to the fore, and areas selected for supporting structural adjustment, transformation and upgrading have become hot spots. In 2016, Chinese enterprises made a total of 742 overseas M&As, with an actual transaction amount of $107.2 billion, involving 18 industry categories in 73 countries and regions. Among them, 197 and 109 M&As were made in manufacturing, and information transmission, software and information technology services, respectively, accounting for 26.6 and 14.7% of the total number of overseas M&As made by China. Local enterprises play a leading role in foreign investment, and provinces and cities along the Yangtze River economic belt have been active in this regard. The Go Out policy for Chinese enterprises requires more diversified investments, including greenfield investments, M&A investments, securities investments, joint investments, foreign project contracting, and labor service cooperation, so as to realize the all-round "going out" of brick-and-mortar companies, financial institutions, the RMB, capital, marketing networks, and channels. In terms of equity investment, while increasing investment, we should note that equity participation as a kind of medium- and long-term strategic investment requires in-depth cooperation rather than short-term speculation. Meanwhile, we should cooperate with other countries to establish overseas cooperation zones, so as to give better play to the cluster effect.

Sixth, industrial chain arrangements for Chinese enterprises to "go out." The "going out" of Chinese enterprises can better integrate China into the global value chain, and elevate China's position in the division of labor in the value chain. First, the "going out" of Chinese enterprises can develop the overseas processing trade system. For a long time, processing trade has accounted for a large proportion of China's trade. With rising labor costs in China, we should upgrade China's position in international specialization from the low end, comprised mostly of the assembly link to higher value-added links in the front end of the value chain, and extend low-end links in international specialization outside of China through the Go Out policy for enterprises to create a processing trade production system led by Chinese enterprises. Second, ascend in the value chain through the "going out" of enterprises. The "going out" of Chinese enterprises can absorb foreign advanced technology and R&D resources, improve capacity for the production of high value-added intermediate products, and elevate China's position in the global value chain.

Problems that Chinese Enterprises Should Pay Attention to in "Going Out"

First, guard against the risks of "going out." We should resist and guard against the risks of "going out." On the macro level, in "going out," enterprises will face risks including global financial, exchange rate and commodity price risks. Domestic adjustments such as the adoption of a flexible RMB exchange rate regime, the opening-up of capital projects, and the opening-up of financial and capital markets may bring unexpected risks, which need to be prevented and resolved. On the microlevel, in "going out," enterprises need to enhance their capability at managing risks, including investment risk, market risk, and environmental risk in greenfield investment and cross-border M&As. Developed countries require the reporting or proactive reviews of overseas M&As involving key technologies and sensitive industries, including national security reviews, restrictions for specific industries, technology embargoes, and antitrust reviews. In particular, the special restrictions imposed by United States and other developed countries on M&As by state-owned enterprises have a great impact on China. In addition, in "going out," Chinese enterprises also face non-economic risks such as the "China threat theory" in the international community, so it is necessary to strengthen the "soft power" of enterprises to eliminate these effects.

Second, raise awareness for intellectual property protection. In recent years, intellectual property disputes encountered by Chinese enterprises in the process of "going out" have been on the rise, and have been growing in both scale and scope. This is due to the fact that the use of intellectual property rights to contain opponents has become increasingly valued by developed countries and has become a common method for consolidating their advantages in the field of innovation. As the economic strength of emerging market countries grows, multilateral and bilateral cooperation in the field of law and technology are getting closer and closer, and the global intellectual property landscape is also changing. In recent years, China has played an increasingly important role in international intellectual property cooperation. In the process of "going out," Chinese enterprises need to further raise their awareness on intellectual property rights, strengthen the development, application, and protection of intellectual property rights, and seize the initiative in competition in a complex international environment.

Third, attach importance to fulfilling social responsibility. With the increasing interaction and integration of Chinese enterprises with local communities in "going out," social responsibility has become an issue that cannot be ignored in the internationalization process of enterprises. To localize their operations, enterprises need to pay attention to fulfilling their social responsibility in the following areas: First, participate in public welfare undertakings that can help improve local people's livelihood. In international operations, enterprises can help improve backward local conditions in areas such as infrastructure, education and medical care. Thus, host countries can benefit from the "going out" of Chinese enterprises, which will help Chinese enterprises further expand business opportunities in host countries. Second, attach importance to the protection of the local environment and the conservation of local resources. During project construction and operation activities in "going out," enterprises need to design scientifically and construct reasonably, and achieve energy conservation and emission reduction through effective management, so as to minimize environmental pollution. Third, promote localized operations and develop together with local enterprises. "Going-out" enterprises need to cooperate more closely with local enterprises. By sourcing raw materials and hiring locally, "going-out" enterprises can increase their common interests with local enterprises, so as to provide opportunities for each other and achieve win-win development. Fourth, pay attention to the protection of the rights and interests of local employees. In the process of "going out," Chinese enterprises need to adopt the principle of equal pay for equal work for local employees, safeguard their legitimate rights and interests, and improve their professional skills through training.

Fourth, properly handle cooperative and competitive relations with other major powers in the world. In recent years, emerging economies have risen en masse. With the enhancement of China's economic strength and international status, developed economies such as the United States and Europe are adjusting their strategies toward China. For example, China is required to undertake greater adjustment tasks for rebalancing the global economy and take on more international responsibility. All this has intensified strategic competition between China and the world's major developed countries. New trends in regional economic cooperation after the financial crisis and the negotiation of high-standard international trade and investment agreements such as TPP, TTIP, TISA, and BIT led by developed countries have also increased the uncertainty of the Go Out policy for Chinese enterprises. Meanwhile, while optimizing the investment environment, China should ask other countries to reciprocate by opening their markets and lifting restrictions on the "going out" of Chinese enterprises.

3.5 Comprehensively Raise the Level of Export-Driven Economic Development and Integrate into and Lead the Globalization

China has entered the decisive stage of building a moderately prosperous society in all respects. Profound changes are taking place in the internal and external economic environment, with opportunities and challenges coexisting. To achieve the grand goal of building a moderately prosperous society in all respects and successfully overcoming the middle-income trap, we need to further expand opening-up, constantly improve the open economic system, and give full play to the powerful driving force of opening-up.

Internationally, for some time to come, the world economy could face a prolonged slump, weak external demand could become the norm, various forms of protectionism will be on the rise, and economic and trade frictions will peak. Competition among countries in market, resources, talents, technology, rules, and standards has become more intense. China's traditional advantageous industries have become more competitive with developing countries, and its mid- to high-end industries have become more competitive with developed countries. China's development is facing a more complex external environment.

Domestically, since China's accession to the World Trade Organization more than a decade ago, China has seen great improvement in social productivity, comprehensive national strength and people's living standards, formed a relatively complete industrial system, and has become more capable of participating in international competition and cooperation, so the foundation and conditions for further expanding and upgrading opening-up are already in place. The international community also has higher expectations of China's role in assuming international responsibility. Meanwhile, China's existing mode of economic development is extensive, resource and environment constraints have intensified, traditional advantages have been weakened, new advantages have not yet been established, the task of changing the development mode and optimizing the structure is arduous, there are still many structural and institutional obstacles to the development of an open economy, opening-up is facing increasing risks, and the level, standard, and efficiency of opening-up need to be improved.

In order to comprehensively improve the standard of China's opening-up in the future, we need to make breakthroughs in the following three aspects.

3.5.1 Strive to Change the Mode of Growth of Foreign Trade

1. Change the mode of export that mainly depends on low cost and quantity, change the extensive and quantity-oriented mode of economic growth, and diversify the forms of exporters and trade. Work hard to create exports of goods and services with our own intellectual property rights and brands, control the production and export of resource-intensive, energy-intensive and highly polluting products, and expand exports of new technologies, new products, and high value-added products. Improve the level of processing trade, change the current situation where the volume of product trade is increasing but the value added of trade is low, accelerate the upgrading of products, and shift export trade from quantitative expansion to quality improvement.
2. Adjust the product and market structures of imports, prioritize imports of high-tech products, high-tech equipment, high and new

technologies, and strategic resources that are necessary for domestic development, important and in short supply, diversify sources of imports of strategic materials and ways to import strategic materials, and stabilize channels for importing strategic materials.

3. Develop trade in green products, adapt to international trends in environmental protection, and strictly control trade in energy-intensive and highly polluting products, so as to form a trade structure conducive to resource conservation and environmental protection.

3.5.2 *Strive to Improve the Quality and Level of Foreign Capital Utilization*

1. Combine the introduction of foreign capital with the upgrading of the domestic industrial structure and technological level, with the promotion of coordinated regional development and the enhancement of enterprises' indigenous innovation capability. Reform, enrich, and improve existing enterprises through the introduction of foreign capital, achieve economies of scale through the optimization and upgrading of technology, and strive to increase the benefits of structural optimization, economies of scale, and the regional division of labor. Switch from relying mainly on increasing the amount of capital input to relying mainly on improving the quality of factors of production, and increase the contribution of total factor productivity to economic growth.
2. Make rational use of foreign capital, develop an open economy, change the situation of unreasonable structures, poor product quality and low value added in the economy, accelerate the progress of China's industrial structure by introducing a batch of high value-added and high-tech products, and do a good job transforming, assimilating, and incorporating innovation into introduced technology.
3. Improve the quality of foreign capital utilization, strengthen efforts to steer foreign capital into specific industries and regions, seize the opportunity of international industrial transfer to expand the scale of foreign direct investment, and get foreign investors to participate in capital construction projects encouraged by the State, including comprehensive agricultural development and construction projects involving energy, transportation, and important raw

materials, technological upgrading projects that possess advanced technology and can improve product performance, save energy, reduce consumption, and improve the economic efficiency of enterprises, technology projects that can prevent environmental pollution through the comprehensive use of energy, etc.

3.5.3 *Work Hard to Implement the Go Out Policy for Chinese Enterprises*

The implementation of the Go Out policy is an important measure for opening-up in the new stage and a necessary requirement for implementing a sustainable development strategy. We should encourage and support foreign investment by enterprises under various forms of ownership that have comparative advantages, promote the export of goods and services, and form a group of powerful multinational enterprises and famous brands. First, we should better optimize the allocation of resources around the world, seek survival and development in international markets, make full use of foreign natural resources, scientific and technological resources and human resources, implement strategic overseas investment, and create our own world-class brand-name products; second, we should take our technology, equipment and products out of China, give full play to our comparative advantages, actively carry out foreign economic cooperation, promote the development of the national economy in a mutually beneficial and win-win manner, promote the export of goods, technology, and services, increase the share of our goods in international markets, and enhance our ability to capture international markets in international specialization and cooperation; third, we should participate in international economic competition and cooperation, carry out transnational operations and investment, cultivate China's transnational companies, and make investment abroad mainly through enterprises, guided by the market and with a view to improving economic efficiency and enhancing international competitiveness. Investment should be focused on energy, raw materials, and high technology.

4 Promote the Innovation Drive and Stimulate Greater Vitality

Through years of hard work, China has become the world's second largest economy and made historical achievements in the development of various undertakings. But China ranks 72nd in terms of GDP per capita and 28th in the Global Competitiveness Index, the overall level of social productivity is still low, the problems of unbalanced, uncoordinated, and unsustainable development are very prominent, and structural problems in the economy have become a fundamental and overarching issue. There is a very urgent need to change the mode and adjust the structure. China's economy has entered a "new normal" and moved to a phase of medium- to high-speed growth. The driving force of economic development needs to be transformed, the economic structure must be adjusted, and industrial development is facing upgrading. The fundamental solution to these problems lies in institutional improvement and innovation. Structural problems in the economy are closely related to capacity for and the structure of technological innovation, and the level and structure of the workforce. China is under pressure to sustain a huge population and achieve sustainable development with few resources per capita and a fragile ecological environment, and facing severe challenges such as energy conservation, emission reduction, and climate change. The resources, environment, and other favorable conditions that developed countries once possessed are not available to China at present. The fundamental way out for China lies in technological innovation, product innovation, industrial innovation, business model innovation, and brand innovation. Technological innovation is the core and has a mission to develop itself and drive innovation in other areas. Without a substantial improvement in innovation capability, especially capacity for technological innovation, it will be difficult to complete economic structural adjustment and the transformation of the development mode.

After China enters the middle-income stage, the low-cost advantage of the economy will be gradually lost. We must improve R&D capabilities, attach importance to human capital, carry out industrial upgrading, and foster new competitive advantages. The 1978 energy crisis had a great impact on South Korea, depriving the country of its comparative advantage in labor-intensive industries. But South Korea actively sought change. It promoted industrial upgrading by implementing the strategy of "founding the nation on science and technology," and finally completed the transition from light industry to technology-intensive heavy industry and from "technological imitation" to indigenous innovation. Its spending in scientific research continued to grow at a high rate, accounting for 3.47% of GDP in 2007, surpassing the United States and Japan. Technological innovation contributes up to 70% to South Korea's economic growth.

Although China has made great achievements in science and technology and education since the start of reform and opening-up, its mode of economic growth has not been fundamentally changed and still relies mainly on cheap factors of production and large-scale investment. China's economic development is evidently characterized by high investment, high energy consumption, and high emissions. Technological advances and innovation contribute significantly less to economic growth in China than in developed countries and some emerging economies. The development path of China is very similar to that of the Soviet Union and Russia. The main reasons for this are as follows: First, practical reasons, i.e., comparative advantages in resources and labor force; second, at the decision-making level of choosing the development path, we excessively pursue the speed of economic growth, focus on rapid quantitative expansion while ignoring improvement in economic efficiency and quality; third, long-term, heavy dependence on the development path makes it difficult to reverse the mode of economic development in a short period of the term.

To change the mode of economic development by relying on technological advances and improving capacity for technological innovation, we need to start from the following two aspects: First, increase investment in education and scientific research, improve the quality of education, cultivate excellent technological innovation talents and teams, and accumulate a solid foundation for scientific research and innovation; second, reform the education and scientific management system, and innovate new ways and methods to encourage scientific research. On the one hand, provide a good and relaxed research environment for researchers; on the other hand, shift from the government-led scientific research management system into a market-driven enterprise spontaneous innovation mechanism, vigorously develop higher vocational and technical education based on market demand, strengthen communication and interaction between institutions of higher learning, scientific research institutes and enterprises in R&D, and improve the efficiency of the popularization of research findings.

To encourage indigenous technological innovation is mainly to reduce excessive incentives for areas other than indigenous innovation. As long as there are more incentives than those for indigenous innovation (such as excessive incentives for foreign investment and real estate), investment in indigenous innovation will not increase, but instead will decrease. This also includes a government crackdown on unproductive "entrepreneurship" (rent-seeking activities) as suggested by William Baumol. Therefore, the government should make great efforts to improve the overall incentive environment or direction, and change policy on incentives for indigenous innovation.

First, reduce excessive incentives for real estate, eliminate exorbitant profits in the real estate market, and prevent an excessive inflow of private funds into the real estate market. Throughout history, real estate has been not only a people's livelihood and development project, but also a very risky area. For China to develop, we should strictly limit incentives for foreign capital, abolish general preferential treatment, and grant equal national treatment to domestic capital.

Second, reduce the proportion of state-owned capital in strategic competitive industries, and give full play to the important role of private capital in industrial upgrading. Promoting the full development and internationalization of private capital will put Chinese enterprises in a more favorable position to participate in global competition. Therefore, private capital must be included in the development of strategic industries.

Third, use capital markets to promote indigenous innovation. Funnel large amounts of surplus private capital into capital markets, so that they are combined with industrial upgrading to promote the competitiveness of heavy and chemical industries. For example, formulate industry-differentiated policies for seeking financing and refinancing by listing on the stock market, principally with a view to significantly relaxing the conditions for upgraded heavy and chemical industry enterprises to seek financing and refinancing by listing on the stock market, and promoting the capital expansion and competitiveness of heavy and chemical industries; set up a number of industrial investment funds (equity-type and debt-type) to support the development of upgraded heavy and chemical industries; formulate targeted preferential policies to support the merger and reorganization of the upgraded heavy and chemical industries.

Fourth, establish the correct orientation for encouraging indigenous innovation. Mainly encourage enterprises to carry out indigenous innovation around conserving energy and saving money, adhere to the "compact" orientation for indigenous product innovation. The focus of industrial policy is to encourage compact product innovation, such as encouraging the purchases and production of economical cars, encouraging the purchases and production of compact housing (less than 90 square meters), and encouraging the construction of compact cities.

4.1 *Innovate Institutional Building and Protect Intellectual Property Rights*

China should steadily advance the building of intellectual property laws and regulations, cause enterprises to respect intellectual property awareness, resist Shanzhai culture which is based on imitation and plagiarism, advocate and protect indigenous innovation, change the practice of relying too much on foreign technology, protect intellectual property in terms of value assessment, guarantee objects, equity calculation, etc. The government should lower the threshold for enterprises to use intellectual property for indigenous innovation and entrepreneurship, and encourage enterprises to maintain and use intellectual property rights in the fiscal, financial, and taxation systems. At the enterprise level, we should be willing to invest in intellectual property such as patents and trademarks, and be good at self-protection.

4.2 *Optimize the Institutional Environment and Serve Innovation and Entrepreneurship*

First, promote industrial upgrading through technological innovation, and take innovation and entrepreneurship as the new engine of China's economic development. We need to create an enabling environment for innovation and entrepreneurship, and make improvements and efforts in education, the legal system, values, research policies, and capital markets.

Second, promote a fair, open, and tolerant environment for innovation. The restrictions of the household registration system, the unfair distribution of educational resources, a huge gap in wealth and income, and housing prices which are high relative to wage levels have largely inhibited the realization of the innovation and entrepreneurship potential of the whole society. We should create conditions to ensure that everyone enjoys equal opportunities in innovation and entrepreneurship and is not subject to systematic discrimination and exclusion. An open mind and social environment are conducive to learning and absorbing the creations, innovations, and achievements of civilizations shared by all mankind, and to the two-way communication between China and the outside world. We should use a tolerant social environment to encourage innovation and entrepreneurship. We should encourage people to make bold attempts and keep exploring, and promote the exchange and collision of different opinions and thoughts so as to draw on each other's strengths and seek common ground while shelving differences.

Third, establish a fair and equitable research funding allocation system and a scientific and rational research evaluation system. If the research funding is tilted toward researchers with certain administrative positions, it will lead to research elites scrambling for administrative positions. Under the existing distribution system, young scholars who are most energetic and most in need of support are often the least likely to get research funding. The control and domination of research funding by administrative forces not only strengthens the notion that official positions are the sole measure of social status in academic circles but also causes a huge waste of academic talents. A large number of excellent scholars are willing to take up administrative positions in order to ensure adequate research funding. We should end the situation where research funds are managed and allocated by administrative departments, set up a national research foundation led by the academic community, and ensure the fairness, openness, and transparency of the academic evaluation system. Meanwhile, we should optimize the structure of research funding, gradually reduce the proportion of government funding in R&D funds, and encourage enterprises to play a greater role in research investment and research activities.

Fourth, build an efficient and sound capital market, and establish a market feedback mechanism that promotes innovation and entrepreneurship. A sound innovation system needs the support of the capital market. Angel investment, venture capital, private equity, and other financial industries, as well as a sound M&A and stock market can greatly promote technological innovation. They not only provide initial financial support for innovation and entrepreneurship, but also provide channels for the development and growth (including successful exits) of start-ups. Only with a sound and developed local financial market can we avoid a future in which BAT (Baidu, Alibaba, and Tencent) is still controlled by foreign capital. Although finding out which country an enterprise belongs to has become less and less meaningful in the era of globalization, we at least hope that more of the wealth created in the Chinese market will remain on Chinese soil to be shared by more Chinese investors.

4.3 *Encourage Technological Innovation and Build an "Innovation-Oriented Nation"*

China is significantly behind developed countries in terms of R&D spending per capita. In 2015, China spent a total of 1.42 trillion Yuan in R&D, accounting for over 2.07% of its GDP, and the R&D spending per capita was only 377,000 Yuan. In 2012, but the number of researchers (in full-time equivalent) per 10,000 inhabitants in China was only 24, only 1/4 of that in Denmark and 1/3 of that in Japan and South Korea. In 2012, the total number of utility patents originated in China reached 152,000, ranking the third in the world, but the number per capita was only 1.13, 1/24 of that in Japan. In the first half of 2016, the total number of utility patents granted in China reached 164,000, an increase of 41% year-on-year; in 2012, China's high-tech exports reached $505.6 billion, ranking first in the world, but the value per capita was only $374, only 15% of that of South Korea. In 2016, China's high-tech exports reached $603.9 billion, down 7.8% year-on-year.

Therefore, we should change the mode of economic development by relying on technological advances and improving capacity for technological innovation.

To encourage indigenous technological innovation is mainly to reduce excessive incentives for areas other than indigenous innovation. Therefore, the government should improve the incentive environment or direction. First, we should reduce the proportion of state-owned capital in strategic competitive industries, and give full play to the important role of private capital in industrial upgrading; second, use capital markets to promote indigenous innovation. Funnel surplus private capital into the stock market, so that they are combined with industrial upgrading to promote industrial competitiveness.

4.4 *Promote a Shift from "Factor-Driven" to "Innovation-Driven"*

The 2008 financial crisis once plunged the world into the predicament of losing growth momentum. Accelerating structural reform has become the consensus of all parties. The crisis also made people start to pursue technological development and breakthroughs again, and work hard to seek new growth drivers.

We must further implement the strategy of innovation-driven development, deepen the reform of the science and technology management system, and speed up the process of building an "innovation-oriented" country. First, emphasize the important position of technological innovation in national prosperity and rejuvenation; second, emphasize unswervingly following the path of indigenous innovation; third, fully recognize the existing achievements and enhance confidence in our innovation capability; fourth, see deficiencies in current technological development and remain sober-minded; fifth, emphasize the innovation-driven development strategy; sixth, emphasize the integration of science and technology with the economy and deepen the reform of the science and technology management system; seventh, strengthen the building of the talent team and the protection of intellectual property rights; eighth, grasp new trends in science and technology in the world, and plan for and promote innovation from a global perspective.

There are five tasks in implementing the innovation-driven development strategy: First, make great efforts to integrate technological innovation closely with economic and social development. The key is to properly handle the relationship between the government and the market, further open up the channel between science and technology and economic and social development through deepening reform, and let the market truly become the force behind the allocation of innovation resources and enterprises truly become technological innovators. The government should play an active role in areas related to the national economy, people's livelihood, and the lifeline of industries, strengthen support and coordination, determine the overall technological direction and roadmap, make good use of national science and technology major projects, key projects, and other instruments, and concentrate on seizing the commanding heights. Second, make great efforts to strengthen our capacity for indigenous innovation. The key is to substantially improve our capacity for indigenous innovation and strive to master key and core technologies. It is imperative to improve the incentive mechanism, perfect the policy environment, stimulate enthusiasm and readiness for technological innovation both material and spiritually, adhere to the orientation of science and technology toward economic and social development, deploy the innovation chain around the industrial chain, improve the capital chain around the innovation chain, break down barriers to the transfer and diffusion of scientific and technological achievements, and improve the overall efficiency of the national innovation system. Third, make great efforts to improve the talent development mechanism. We should make good and creative use of talent, put in place a more flexible talent management mechanism, remove obstacles to the flow, use, and functioning of talent in terms of systems and mechanisms, and give maximum support and help to scientific and technological personnel in innovation and entrepreneurship. Fourth, make great efforts to create a good policy environment. We should increase government investment in science and technology, lead enterprises and society to increase R&D investment, improve tax policies that promote technological innovation by enterprises, and increase the support of capital markets for technology-based enterprises. Fifth, make great efforts to expand opening-up and cooperation in science and technology. We should deepen international exchanges and cooperation, make full use of global innovation resources, promote indigenous innovation at a higher starting point, and work with the international scientific and technological community to make our due contributions to addressing common challenges in the world.

4.5 *Promote Industrial Upgrading and Investment Abroad Through Innovation*

The key task for China to overcome the middle-income trap under the new normal is to transform and upgrade its economic structure by transforming its mode of economic growth from extensive and investment-driven growth to innovation- and consumption-driven growth, and vigorously promote extensive indigenous innovation, intensive industrial upgrading and win-win cooperation in investment abroad.

4.5.1 Promote Extensive Economic Growth Through Innovation

At present, China is badly in need of extensive innovation. "China needs indigenous innovation on a massive scale to help avert the middle-income trap," said Edmund Phelps, a professor at Columbia University who won the 2006 Nobel Prize in Economics. Phelps noted that when countries like the United States, Britain, and Germany encountered bottlenecks in income growth, they innovated at all levels of society and in most industries, and prompted other European countries to compete with and emulate them while avoiding the middle-income trap. Positive and negative experiences in developing countries have proved that strengthening indigenous innovation is an important determinant of whether a country can overcome the middle-income trap. Among countries with successful "middle-income transitions," Latin American countries such as Brazil, Argentina, and Peru have been hovering at the middle-income level, while Japan, South Korea, and Chile have joined the ranks of high-income countries. Technological innovation is one of the important factors that cannot be ignored. Drawing on international experience, we put forward the following suggestions for promoting extensive economic growth through innovation.

First, avoid overreliance on "import substitution" policies, which will cause industries to become excessively fragmented and lack international competitiveness. The government should not make significant cuts in the public budget and R&D investment. The State should develop and cultivate local R&D institutions. Meanwhile, we should take the issue of multinational corporations acquiring and reorganizing local enterprises in an attempt to occupy the high-end product market seriously. We should have independent policies on science, technology, industry, and innovation.

Second, at a time when labor-intensive industries are losing their comparative advantages, we should realize that only by developing science and technology and significantly enhancing our capacity for indigenous innovation can we promote the transformation of the development mode and structural transformation, and achieve steady and rapid economic growth. Establish the strategy of "founding the nation on science and technology, and invigorating the nation through innovation," and use advanced technology to transform existing industries. Shift from "introduction-based and imitative" innovation to "creative and indigenous" innovation. The government should give full play to the role of enterprises as technology R&D entities. In particular, the government should fully mobilize the enthusiasm of private enterprises for technological R&D.

Third, science and technology policy must shift the focus from introducing, assimilating, and utilizing to promoting through basic sciences. Japan set the goal of "producing 30 or so Nobel Laureates in 50 years" in 2000. By 2016, 28 people had made their way to the list. China can initiate a similar program to encourage and emphasize generating new knowledge, promoting original R&D, producing original results, and further strengthening basic research.

Fourth, develop a national strategy for cultivating capacity for indigenous innovation at home, support non-governmental R&D activities in terms of policy measures, platform building, etc., strongly support the building of indigenous innovation platforms, and effectively improve the rate of transformation of technological achievements.

Fifth, enhance the capacity for technological innovation and capacity for application and transformation of colleges, universities and research institutes, provide system support for technological innovation through institutional reform in multiple areas including education and research, and build a national innovation system that is dominated by enterprises and guided by the market, and combines production, education, and research.

Sixth, in terms of promoting innovation and entrepreneurship, ruling the country according to law emphasizes clarifying the boundary between the state and the market, limiting the role of the government in the possession and allocation of resources, protecting private property rights, and providing start-up owners and entrepreneurs with stable expectations and a stable business environment. Urge enterprises to increase investment in R&D, respect intellectual property rights, and prompt Chinese enterprises to truly embark on the path of sustainable development that relies on indigenous innovation, so as to lay a solid foundation for Chinese enterprises to "go out" and become respected world-class enterprises.

Seventh, the State should make innovation and entrepreneurship a goal that more people can choose and pursue through the regulating action of levers such as income tax, property tax and inheritance tax. The State should avoid competing with the people. Excessive taxation and high housing prices will inevitably squeeze the accumulation of capital that individuals and families could otherwise have used for education, entrepreneurship, and innovation, hinder investment in human capital, and reduce the likelihood of mass entrepreneurship.

Eighth, supporting innovation and entrepreneurship is not limited to building more industrial parks and business incubators, or providing seed funds for innovative enterprises, but also includes providing a stable business environment, equal social security, and public services for startup owners.

4.5.2 *Promote the Upgrading of Intensive Industries Through Innovation*

In recent years, China's capital-output ratio has been declining steadily, with an average annual decline of 3.3% since 2000. The demographic dividend window is about to close, and issues such as environmental pollution, ecological damage, public health, and food safety are prominent. Drawing on international experience, we should promote the upgrading of intensive industries through innovation.

First, continuously foster new areas of economic growth. With a push from the government, vigorously develop the tertiary sector, and gradually turn cultural creativity, tourism, health, and sports into leading industries.

Second, optimize the industrial development environment through policy interventions, and elevate the industrial and trade structures to a higher level. Attach importance to and fund the R&D activities of private enterprises. Strengthen industrial competitiveness through indigenous technological innovation. Provide preferential tax policies to the introduction, assimilation, and re-innovation of technology. Actively carry out cooperative innovation between enterprises, universities, and research institutes; support enterprises in co-building laboratories with research institutes or universities to tackle key problems.

Third, specifically formulate industrial policies to promote industrial upgrading, supported by specifically formulated financial, fiscal, and tax policies. Make strides toward seeking breakthroughs in economic development according to the law of economic development and the experience of other countries. For existing medium- and low-end industries, we should promote their upgrading in the direction of energy and resource conservation, increasing added value and indigenous innovation. Only by promoting a shift of the mode of economic growth from extensive growth to intensive growth can we start a new economic growth cycle.

Fourth, the direction of industrial upgrading and innovation should be to supply goods and services matching the upgrading of consumer demand through market-oriented forces. On the one hand, consolidate the foundation of industrial manufacturing by improving technological strength; on the other hand, orient industrial upgrading toward market demand, strengthen technological innovation, break through the shackles of imitation, and tap the potential consumer market through refined, personalized and differentiated supply and management. Make full use of the favorable conditions of China's massive population and big market. Even the "niche products" described in the Long Tail theory may create huge profits and commercial scales as long as we attach importance to consumer experience, and grasp and solve the "pain points" of consumers.

4.5.3 Promote Cooperative and Win-Win Investment Through Innovation

In 2016, China's direct investment abroad achieved a historic breakthrough, crossing the one trillion Yuan mark for the first time, with tens of thousands of overseas enterprises in nearly 200 countries and regions around the world receiving Chinese investment. Promoting cooperative and win-win investment abroad will play a dual role in putting the huge stockpile of foreign exchange reserves to work and adjusting the economic structure, thereby helping China overcome the middle-income trap.

First, investment abroad is conducive to more efficient allocation and use of China's massive foreign exchange reserves. According to data from the State Administration of Foreign Exchange, at the end of 2016, China's foreign exchange reserves were $3.010517 trillion.[11] The rate of return on China's huge foreign exchange reserves has been the focus of public attention. At present, the central bank invests its foreign exchange reserves mostly in US Treasury bonds. Data show that the average rate of return on US direct investment in China over the past 10 years was 15–20%, while the rate of return on Chinese investment in US Treasury bonds was only around 3% (Wu Song 2014). In order to find more ways out for China's foreign exchange reserves, we can buy strategic assets such as mines, energy and port terminals, or acquire high-tech enterprises overseas.

Second, to improve China's "soft power," we need to further adjust and upgrade the investment structure. Chinese enterprises have a strong ability to "go out" to acquire energy resources, but the level of their investment in high-tech enterprises is relatively low. As of the end of 2013, China's total foreign investment in energy resources reached $308.4 billion (including direct investment abroad and reinvestment through enterprises abroad), accounting for 46.7% of total outward investment. Even in the case of Japan, where natural resources are extremely scarce, investment in energy and mineral resources accounts for only about

[11] Data released at the press conference of the State Council Information Office on January 17, 2017.

10% of total outward investment. With the optimization and upgrading of China's economic structure, "going out" should not only acquire resources, but also bring tangible benefits and development to local people, so as to achieve a win-win situation.

Third, as the world's largest manufacturer, China should increase its investment in manufacturing. As of the end of 2015, manufacturing accounted for only 8.4% of the stock of China's outward investment. In the case of developed countries such as the United States and Japan, manufacturing accounts for more than 30% of outward investment. In recent years, China's power, telecommunications, aerospace, rail transit, marine engineering, and other equipment manufacturing industries have accelerated their pace of "going out," but at the same time, problems in the operation management and technical services of Chinese enterprises have become increasingly prominent (Shen Danyang, Wang Hongxia 2015). With manufacturing becoming increasingly servitized, manufacturing needs to be accompanied by services in "going out." Only by doing a good job in "Chinese services," can "Made in China" really go out and gain a firm footing.

Finally, cooperative and win-win investment is an important way to build the Belt and Road. In 2013, President Xi Jinping put forward the strategic visions of "jointly building a Silk Road economic belt with an innovative mode of cooperation" and "Building the 21st Century Maritime Silk Road," which received great attention and positive response from the international community. With the gradual rise of China's status as an economic power, China needs to assume more responsibilities commensurate with its level of development in world economic development and global governance, and make contributions to promoting trade and investment cooperation and infrastructure connectivity under the Belt and Road Initiative. For example, we should work with other countries to set up financial instruments such as the Asian Infrastructure Investment Bank and the Silk Road Fund to provide necessary financial support for the building of intra-regional connectivity; we should promote imports from Belt and Road-related countries to meet our own production and consumption needs, while providing a huge market for goods and services for other members.

5 Guard Against Debt Crises and Control Financing Risks

At present, China is in the middle-income stage. To overcome the middle-income trap, we need to avoid a financial crisis, which is one of the important issues. The key to guarding against financial crises is to prevent imprudent financial liberalization and the mishandling of corporate debt. Therefore, we must guard against debt crises and control financing risks, and raise awareness about the importance of financial governance. Throughout the world, countries in the process of developing from the middle-income stage to the high-income stage will face the enormous challenges of economic and social transformation, and the importance of financial governance plays a decisive role at this stage. The middle-income trap stems from the economic instability of middle-income economies, which in turn stems mainly from the prospect of a financial crisis. Financial crises in middle-income economies are due to a series of structural problems caused by their economic and social transformation. Avoiding the middle-income trap is crucial to guarding against financial crises: politically, we must establish strong institutions to support reform and prudential regulation; on the policy front, we must advance fiscal and financial reforms in a timely and prudent manner; technically, we must implement macro-prudential regulation, maintain financial stability, and establish effective mechanisms to deal with crises and accelerate recovery from crises.

With a structural slowdown in China's economy and mounting downward pressure, concerns about rising debt risks are growing. To assess China's government debt risks, we must first grasp the overall situation, and then analyze from the perspective of international comparison and the asset to liability ratio: China's government debt risks are generally controllable.[12]

[12] Zheng Zhijie. A Study of Sovereign Debt Crises and Financing Risks: Thinking Based on China and Other Major Economies of the World. *Frontiers*, 2018 (2) Next Issue.

5.1 *China's Government Debt from the Perspective of International Comparison and the Asset to Liability Ratio: The Risks Are Generally Controllable*

To assess China's government debt risks, we must first grasp the overall situation. To this end, we select an international reference standard and targets for comparison, and introduce the framework for balance sheet analysis for discussion.

5.1.1 *The Level of the Government Debt-to-GDP Ratio Is Relatively Safe*

An important measure of government debt risks is the debt-to-GDP ratio, which is the ratio of government debt outstanding at the end of the year to the GDP of the year. It reflects the ability of an economy's economic aggregate to carry government debt. By adding up the above-mentioned debt-to-GDP ratios of the central government and local governments, we get a debt-to-GDP ratio of 38.8%[13] for China's government sector at the end of 2016. Internationally, the 60% warning level set out in the Maastricht treaty is usually used as a reference standard, so China's government debt risk is at an acceptable level. Moreover, from the perspective of international comparison, the debt-to-GDP ratio of China's government sector is also lower than that of major market economies and some emerging market economies. Figure 14 compares the debt-to-GDP ratios of the central government and local governments of relevant countries with those of China. It can be seen that China's government debt-to-GDP ratio is the lowest among all the countries, 52.97 percentage points lower than the average of OECD countries; in particular, the central government debt-to-GDP ratio is significantly lower, 62.68 percentage points lower than the average of OECD countries. Relatively speaking, the local government debt-to-GDP ratio is generally at a medium-to-high

[13]According to the latest data disclosed by Minister of Finance Xiao Jie at the press conference on "Financial Work and Financial and Tax Reform" at the fifth session of the 12th National People's Congress on March 7, 2017, the outstanding debt of China's central government and local governments at the end of 2016 was approximately 27.33 trillion Yuan, with a debt-to-GDP ratio of about 36.7%. Our estimate differs slightly from this figure, possibly because of the lack of data or a tendency to overestimate. Especially the maximum value is taken for the amount of the existing debt of local governments to be replaced. It should be noted that as there is no further structural information in the latest data from the Ministry of Finance, it is not possible to calibrate our estimate at the present stage.

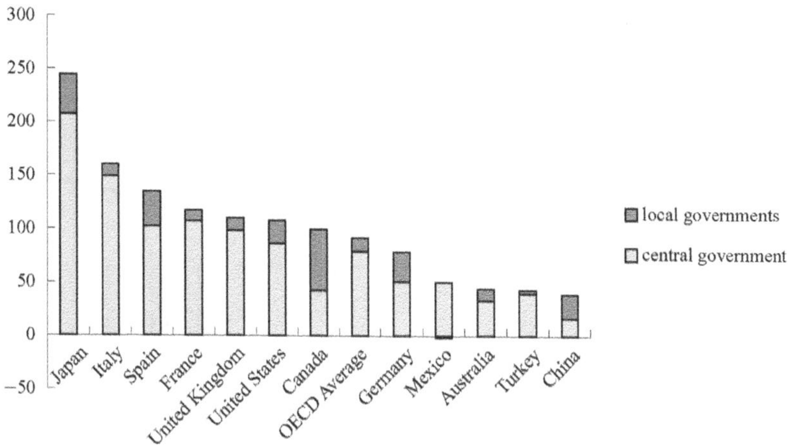

Fig. 14 Comparison of the government debt-to-gdp ratios of countries (%) (*Note* 2016 data for China, 2014 data for Japan and Mexico, and 2015 data for the rest of the countries. *Source* OECD database)

level, 9.71 percentage points higher than the average of OECD countries. Overall, China's government debt risks are manageable. Even if the aforementioned implicit quasi-fiscal debt is taken into account, the debt risk should be within the safe zone.

5.1.2 *The Sovereign Balance Sheet Is Relatively Robust*

In our opinion, to judge the debt risk, especially the debt risk of the government sector which bears the responsibility of the lender of last resort in a debt crisis, we should not only analyze from the perspective of debt expansion but also see whether there is a sufficient debt service guarantee, namely whether the government has enough resources to provide a bailout in the event of a debt crisis. This is actually the balance sheet perspective.

Based on our continuous tracking of China's sovereign balance sheets in recent years, we can find that in the past few years since the 2008 global financial crisis, although the leverage in China's public sector has risen, resulting in a considerable increase in sovereign debt, sovereign assets have also expanded. As a result, the Chinese government has a substantial net worth (see Fig. 15). In 2015, for example, calculated on a broad-scope basis, China's sovereign debt totaled 241.4 trillion Yuan,

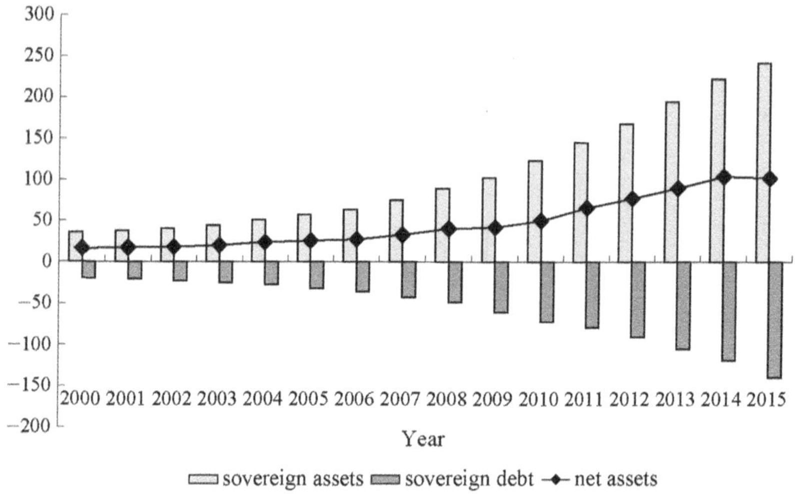

Fig. 15 China's sovereign assets and debt and net worth of the Chinese government (in trillion Yuan)

its sovereign debt 139.6 trillion Yuan, and its net assets 101.8 trillion Yuan. Given the limited liquidity of the state-owned assets of administrative units and public institutions and the fact that the right to use land and other resource assets cannot be completely transferred, China's sovereign assets should be calculated on a narrow-scope basis, i.e., after deducting the 16.2 trillion Yuan worth of state-owned assets in administrative units and public institutions, and substituting the 3.1 trillion Yuan of land transfer fees in 2015 for 68.5 trillion Yuan of state-owned assets, so that sovereign assets will be reduced from 241.4 trillion Yuan to 159.8 trillion Yuan. Thus, China's net sovereign assets calculated on a narrow-scope basis stood at 20.2 trillion Yuan. Whether calculated on a narrow-scope or broad-scope basis, China's net sovereign assets were positive.

Among the assets owned or controlled by the government sector, state-owned operating assets and some realizable resource assets are important guarantees of debt repayment. Even if the government has difficulty servicing its debt, it can opt to use these assets for debt service by securitizing or selling them. The Chinese government has enough sovereign assets to cover its sovereign debt, and there is virtually no "solvency risk," so the likelihood of a sovereign debt crisis will be extremely low for some time to come.

It should be added that in the existing estimation process, assets may be underestimated and liabilities may be overestimated.

Scenarios where assets may be underestimated include: (1) We estimate the equity of state-owned enterprises primarily on a historical cost basis. If the market-based valuation approach or fair value approach is used, the solvency and net assets of the government sector may be further improved. (2) Land and other resource assets, when converted into net land output, may also be underestimated, because as urbanization progresses, the uses and value of some land will change. (3) The value of some special assets is not sufficiently accounted for. In particular, the measurement of some public infrastructure assets is currently based primarily on acquisition or construction costs, and there is a lack of valid market transaction prices, making it impossible to use the market-based valuation approach to fairly reflect the value of assets. For some public infrastructure assets built in the early days, there are only quantity records and no value records, resulting in a greater underestimation.

An underestimation of public infrastructure assets is also reflected in the fact that their public attributes may mutate. In the future, some infrastructure will experience a shift from pure public goods to quasi-public goods. This is because of: (1) An increase in demand. With the development of the economy, there is a strong demand for infrastructure. When demand expands beyond a certain limit, public goods begin to become "crowded," which means that they are competed for, so that the marginal supply cost of adding additional users is no longer zero. At this point, it is necessary to charge consumers a certain royalty to exclude private consumption. (2) The development of technology. The emergence of technology for the quantification of exclusiveness has partially changed the non-competitive and non-exclusive nature of public goods, making it possible to exclude private consumption to a certain extent, so that users can be charged for benefiting from their use according to the Beneficiary Pays Principle.

When a price formation and charging system becomes necessary and possible, some infrastructure assets that were once not market-oriented begin to become "profitable," thus creating conditions for the generation of sustained cash flows. As a result, on the one hand, the value of assets is significantly increased; on the other hand, the liquidity of assets is also significantly enhanced. Under the combined effect, the government's solvency will be improved accordingly.

A possible overestimation of liabilities is mainly reflected in: (1) It is controversial to simply add actual liabilities and contingent liabilities up to get total liabilities. The amount of contingent liabilities becoming explicit varies depending on the value selected for the probability of the risk of contingent liabilities evolving into actual liabilities occurring. Therefore, how to determine the appropriate probability value is also a question worth considering. Our estimate was arrived at by directly adding up without considering the probability, so the liabilities may be overestimated. (2) Among non-performing loans (with the exception of loans classified as loss) which are contingent liabilities, subprime and doubtful loans can be recovered to a certain extent, so the actual scale of non-performing assets is smaller.

Given the above, the actual value of net sovereign assets may be higher. We believe that the high net worth of the Chinese government is a unique aspect that differentiates China from other countries. According to our rough estimate, the household sector accounts for slightly more than 1/3 of China's total net assets (including non-financial assets and net foreign investment positions), the non-state-owned sector accounts for almost 1/3, and the government sector (including state-owned enterprises) accounts for almost 1/3. This is significantly different from the national net asset structure of major developed countries. In these countries, the proportion of net assets in the household sector usually reaches 70–80%, while the proportion of net assets in the government sector is negligible or even negative. Because a very high proportion of remnant assets (including other available resources) are owned or controlled by the Chinese government, the risk of a debt crisis is significantly lower.

5.2 *International Experience in the Accumulation and Resolution of Government Debt: The United Kingdom, the United States, and Japan*

Sovereign debt has a long history, and most of them are linked to war. In a modern economy, due to the increasing role of the government, the accumulation and resolution of public debt has become an important economic issue, which always attracts the attention of the public and the media.

5.2.1 *British Experience*

As the oldest developed country, the United Kingdom has relatively complete long-term government debt data. Judging by these figures, Britain is probably the most successful country in the world in dealing with its government debt (see Fig. 16). The origins of the British national debt can be found during the reign of William III, who engaged a syndicate of City traders and merchants to offer for sale an issue of government debt. This syndicate later evolved into the Bank of England. Since then, the British government had financed the wars it was involved in, backed by the Bank of England and a developed financial market, and its debt had grown steadily. After the Napoleonic Wars, British government debt as a percentage of GDP rose to a staggering 260%. However, over the course of the next century, the British government started the process of deleveraging, reducing this percentage to 25% by 1914. The outbreak of World War I caused British government debt to expand rapidly again, soon surpassing 150% of GDP. World War II, which broke out soon after, brought British government debt to a new high, reaching 238% of GDP in 1947. In the decades that followed, the British government again succeeded in deleveraging. By 1991, the debt-to-GDP ratio was again reduced to 25%, and this low level was maintained until 2007. The

Fig. 16 British government debt/GDP (1692–2016) (*Source* www.ukpublicspending.co.uk)

global financial crisis that began in 2007 pushed British government debt up for the third time, to 85% of GDP in 2016.

The United Kingdom has been hailed as the most successful country in the world in resolving government debt. This is due to the fact that the United Kingdom has not defaulted on its government debt since the eighteenth century, in addition to the two long periods of deleveraging shown in Fig. 16. In other words, since the founding of the Bank of England, the British government has always honored its debt obligations, and every time it deleverages, it always uses economic means instead of defaulting. There are two main reasons for debt accumulation: economic crisis and war, both of which have always left governments deep in debt, and the United Kingdom is no exception. The ideal environment for deleveraging is relative peace and economic prosperity. The first period of deleveraging in the United Kingdom coincided with the Victorian era. During this period, the United Kingdom rose to the top of the world and became a global hegemon. Its territory reached 36 million square kilometers, its economy accounted for nearly 70% of the world's total, its exports were several times more than the rest of the world combined, and the wealth of the colonies flowed in continuously. The second period of deleveraging in the United Kingdom occurred during the great boom of global capitalism after World War II. During this period, despite the lingering shadow of the Cold War, a relatively peaceful environment enabled the global economy to achieve good growth. In Europe, the Marshall Plan helped fuel years of postwar prosperity that ultimately revolutionized the global economic and political landscape. After the 2008 financial crisis, British government debt rose rapidly again, and its future development deserves further attention.

5.2.2 *American Experience*

Besides the United Kingdom, the United States is another model for resolving government debt. As shown in Fig. 17, the United States has seen two peaks in government debt since the Great Depression of 1929. The first occurred in 1946, after World War II, with government debt reaching 118% of GDP. The second occurred after the 2008 financial crisis, with federal government debt reaching 108% of GDP in 2016. Although deleveraging has begun in the US household and corporate sectors, the growth of government debt has not been effectively curbed.

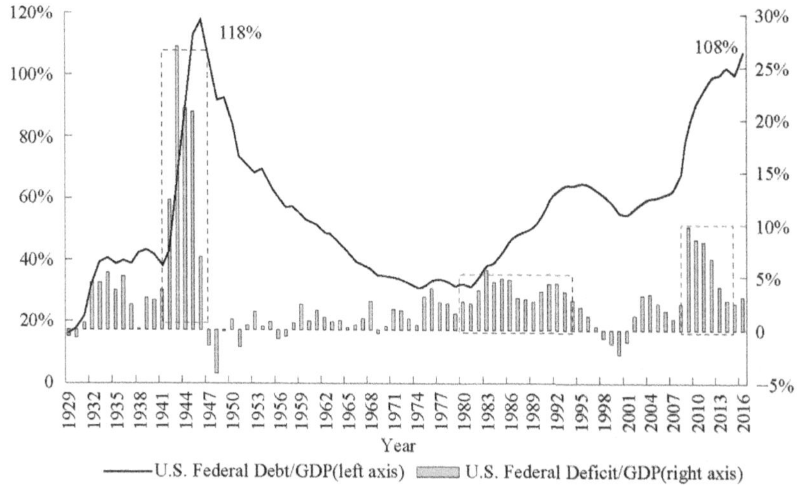

Fig. 17 US federal debt/GDP and deficit/GDP (1929–2016) (*Source* WIND, Congressional Budget Office)

Figure 17 also shows the US federal deficit as a percentage of GDP. Through comparison, you can get a clearer picture of the reasons for debt growth. The first debt peak came in two stages. The first stage was to deal with the Great Depression. The Great Depression broke out in 1929, and the federal government began to run a significant deficit in 1932, and by 1937, government debt was eventually pushed from 20 to 40% of GDP. The second stage began with the outbreak of World War II. It can be seen that the federal deficit ballooned, and its debt rose sharply to 118% of GDP. The second debt peak also came in two stages. The first stage was during the Reagan and the Bush administrations, from the Star Wars program to the Gulf War, when persistent deficits pushed debt as a percentage of GDP from about 30% to about 60%. The second stage began after the global financial crisis of 2008, with bailouts and stimulus packages pushing debt as a percentage of GDP to more than 100%.

Figure 17 shows another key indicator, the difference between the growth rates of the US economy and Treasury yields. In the long run, its value is significant. The first period of deleveraging in the United States coincided with the second in the United Kingdom. A feature of this period was that the rates of economic growth were consistently higher than Treasury yields. To put it simply, economic growth and inflation made debt "depreciated" faster than debt interest accumulated. This is almost a prerequisite for successful deleveraging. This, of course, is a condition for reducing debt in the medium and long term, provided that deficits are under control. During short periods of high deficits and ballooning debt, its role is relatively limited. As shown in Figs. 17 and 18, after the Great Depression and during World War II, there were once very favorable conditions for deleveraging, but high deficits quickly raised the debt level. Continuous quantitative easing (QE) and zero interest rate policy in the United States in recent years have also created relatively favorable conditions for deleveraging, but huge short-term deficits have pushed up debt as a percentage of GDP. The success or failure of the new round of deleveraging by the US government depends on both short-term and long-term factors. In the short term, it depends on whether deficits can be brought under control; in the long term, it depends on whether there is a new, long-lasting boom.

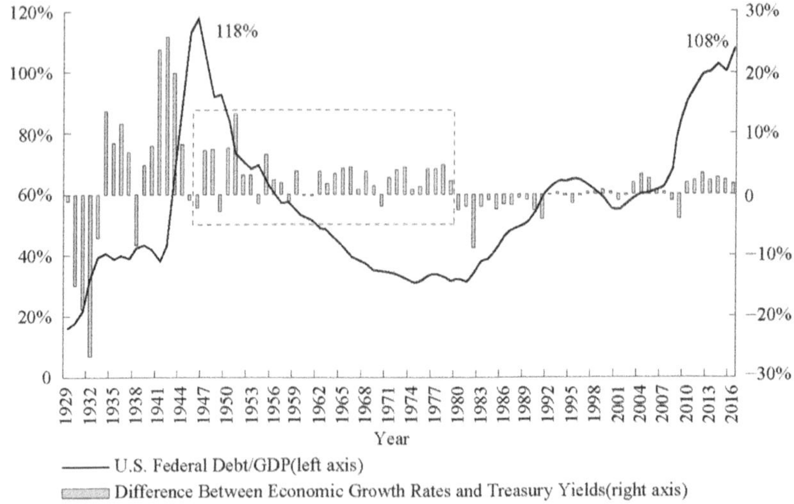

Fig. 18 US federal debt/GDP and difference between economic growth rates and treasury yields (1929–2016) (*Source* WIND, Homer and Sylla 2010)

5.2.3 *Japanese Experience*

If the United Kingdom and the United States are "model students" in resolving government debt, then Japan is notable for its debt tolerance. As can be seen from Figs. 19 and 20, the accumulation of Japanese government debt has gone through three stages. The year 1973 was a turning point for the Japanese economy. In the previous two decades, the Japanese economy grew at a rate of over 9%, creating an economic miracle. In the following two decades, the Japanese economy plummeted to an average growth rate of 3.5%. In an era of rapid economic growth, Japan's government finances were in good shape, and the difference between nominal growth rates and government bond yields often exceeded 10%, so government debt as a percentage of GDP remained in single digits for a long time. The two oil crises led to a rapid decline in Japan's economic growth, and government debt as a percentage of GDP reached 50% for the first time in 1985. The second stage of debt accumulation took place in the so-called "lost twenty years" after the bubble economy burst. From 1993 to 2012, Japan's economy grew by less than 1% a year on average. Under the triple pressure of fiscal deficits,

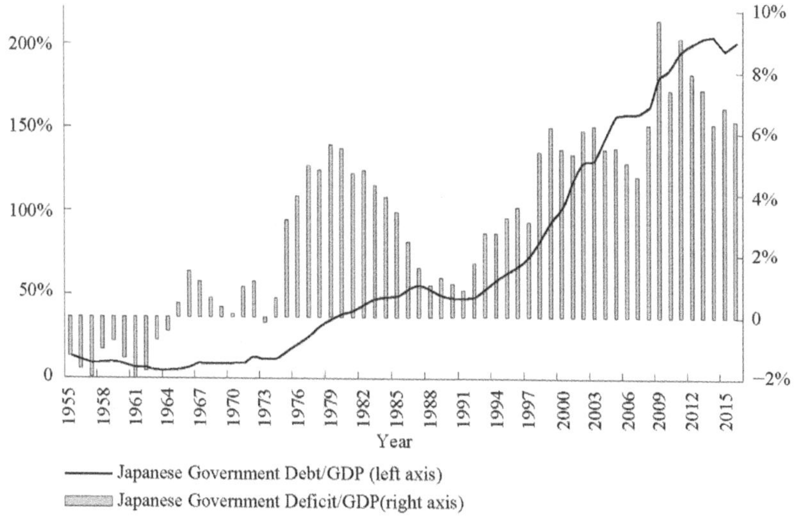

Fig. 19 Japanese government debt/GDP and deficit/GDP (1955–2016) (*Source* Ministry of Finance, Japan)

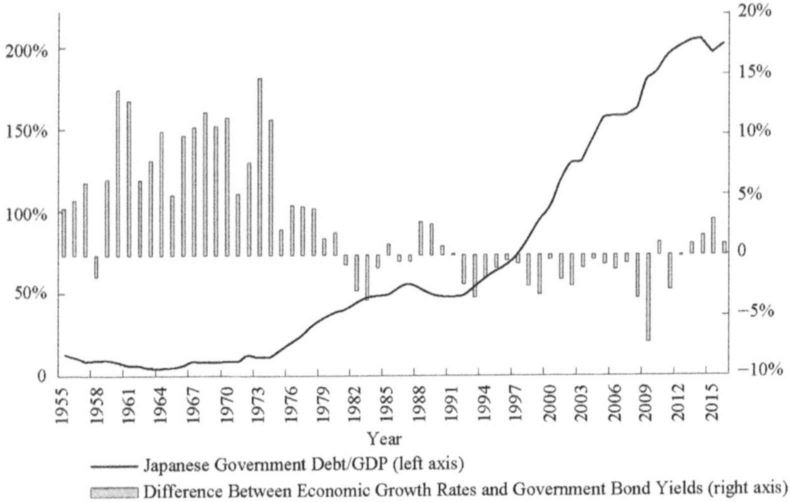

Fig. 20 Japanese government debt/GDP and difference between economic growth rates and government bond yields (1955–2016) (*Source* Ministry of finance, Japan, Homer and Sylla 2010)

economic downturns and deflation, Japan's government debt as a share of GDP exceeded 150% for the first time in 2005. The third stage of debt accumulation occurred after the global financial crisis of 2008. Japan's government debt as a share of GDP exceeded 200% for the first time in 2012 and has remained roughly at this high level in recent years.

At a time when the European debt crisis is in full swing and the government debt of the PIIGS (Portugal, Ireland, Italy, Greece, and Spain) hangs in the balance, Japan has come under the spotlight as a magical existence. Why does Japan seem comfortable with its government debt-to-GDP ratio far higher than the five countries mentioned above? Why didn't Japan become Greece? First, unlike many countries that have a "double deficit," Japan has been running a current account surplus for a long time despite its chronic fiscal deficit. According to the national income accounting identity, this indicates that there is a positive savings-investment gap. These excess savings have become a potential source of support for the government bond market. Second, Japan's current account surplus comes from two sources, one is trade surplus, and the other is income from overseas assets. Japan accumulated a lot of overseas assets before its bubble economy burst. These assets, on the one hand, provide a sustained flow of capital, contributing to Japan's robust current account surplus and, on the other hand, serve as an endorsement of government credit to some extent in that they can be sold to bail out the country in the event of insolvency. Third, Japanese households and corporations have very high savings rates and have a strong preference for investing in Japanese government bonds. In other words, Japanese households and corporations are willing and able to lend to the government. Finally, Japanese government bonds are mainly held by domestic entities. About 90% of Japan's medium- and long-term government bonds are held by domestic institutions and individuals, and about 70% of short-term government bonds are held domestically. All of these conditions have contributed to the Japanese government's particularly high debt tolerance.

However, with the continuous loss of these favorable conditions, Japan's government debt problem has become increasingly prominent. Debt eventually needs to be repaid, and high leverage cannot be sustained for long. When it comes to deleveraging, all countries are the same. In the short term, government finances must be improved and deficits must be brought under control. In the long run, there must be sustained economic growth. This is undoubtedly a daunting task for Japan today.

5.3 *A Comparison of the Debt Problems of China and the United States and the Inspirations Drawn Therefrom*

In recent years, China's debt problem has been growing, attracting a lot of attention at home and abroad. The international consensus is that China's regional and systemic financial risks brought about by high debt have seriously affected economic growth. Moody's and other international rating agencies have even downgraded China's sovereign credit rating outlook, the domestic real economy also lacks confidence to invest. In fact, compared with the United States and other Western countries, China's leverage ratio is not too high, and there are obvious differences in the debt structure and debt nature between China and Western countries. Comparing the debt problems of China and Western countries, especially the United States, is of great significance for having a deep understanding of the real situation of China's debt, helping the supply-side reform of "cutting overcapacity, destocking, deleveraging, reducing costs, and strengthening weak links," and unleashing the vitality of the real economy.[14]

5.3.1 *China's Overall Leverage Ratio Is Roughly Equal to That of the United States*

According to the BIS Statistical Bulletin, in the second quarter of 2016, China's overall leverage ratio was 254.9%, and that of the United States was 254.7%. China was only 0.2 percentage points higher than the United States. During the same period, the overall leverage ratio of Europe was 271.2%, and that of developed economies was as high as 281.4%, both much higher than that of China. The overall leverage ratio of G20 countries was 249.2%, slightly lower than that of China; the overall leverage ratio of emerging market countries was relatively low, at 188.1%.

China's overall leverage ratio has grown relatively fast. China's overall leverage ratio was 180.5% at the end of 2011 and grew 74.4 percentage points from then on until the second quarter of 2016, with an average annual increase of 16.5 percentage points. The United States remained roughly around 250% over the same period, and China only surpassed the United States for the first time in the second quarter of 2016. In the same period, the overall leverage ratio of Europe, developed economies, G20 countries, and emerging market countries grew by 18.6, 19.1, 29.7, and 57.2 percentage points, respectively, with an average annual increase of 4.1, 4.2, 6.6, and 12.7 percentage points, respectively.

5.3.2 *There Are Great Differences in Debt Structure Between China and the United States*

According to the BIS Statistical Bulletin, in the second quarter of 2016, the leverage ratio of China's government sector was 45.6%, that of the household sector was 41.8%, and that of the corporate sector was 167.6%. The leverage ratios of the government, household, and corporate sectors, respectively, accounted for 17.88, 16.39, and 65.73% of the overall leverage ratio. The leverage ratio of the US government sector was 103.5%, that of the household sector was 78.8%, and that of the corporate sector was 72.4%. The leverage ratios of the government, household, and corporate sectors, respectively, accounted for 40.64, 30.94, and 28.43% of the overall leverage ratio. The leverage ratios of China's government

[14] Zheng Zhijie, A Comparison of the Debt Problems of China and the United States and the Inspirations Drawn Therefrom. *China State Finance*, 2017 (12).

and resident sectors were much lower than those of the United States, only 44.06 and 53.05% of those of the United States, respectively, while the leverage ratio of the corporate sector was much higher than that of the United States, 2.31 times that of the United States.

China's debt structure is characterized by "two lows and one high." The leverage ratios of the government and household sectors are low, and leverage ratio of the enterprise sector is high. The leverage ratio of the corporate sector is 3.68 times and 4.01 times that of the government and the household sectors, respectively. The US debt structure is relatively balanced. The leverage ratio of the government sector is slightly higher, and there is little difference between the leverage ratios of the household and corporate sectors. The ratio between the leverage ratios of the government, household, and corporate sectors is 1.43:1.09:1.

From 2011 to the second quarter of 2016, the leverage ratios of the Chinese government, household and corporate sectors all increased, with the corporate sector growing the fastest with an increase of 47.7 percentage points, representing an average annual increase of 10.6 percentage points. The government and household sectors grew relatively slowly, by 12.6 and 14.1 percentage points, respectively, with an average annual increase of 2.8 and 3.1 percentage points, respectively.

In the United States, due to orderly deleveraging in the financial, real estate, corporate, private, and other sectors after the financial crisis, the leverage ratio of the household sector declined instead of rising, falling by 7.0 percentage points over the same period, with an average annual decrease of 1.6 percentage points. The leverage ratio of the corporate sector was also relatively stable, growing by only 6.1 percentage points, with an average annual decrease of only 1.4 percentage points. Due to an increase in leverage, the leverage ratio of the government sector grew relatively quickly, with an average annual increase of 2.6 percentage points.

The leverage ratio of the Chinese corporate sector is growing too fast, significantly faster than the government and household sectors, and also significantly faster than the three sectors in the United States, putting heavy pressure on the sustainable development of Chinese enterprises.

5.3.3 *Chinese Debt and US Debt Are Significantly Different in Nature*

China's Debt Is Mainly Domestic Debt, While a Large Proportion of the Debt of United States and Other Western Countries Is External Debt

According to data from the Bank for International Settlements and the National Bureau of Statistics, in 2015, China's external debt accounted for only 3.33% of government debt, 1.48% of GDP, and 6.58% of fiscal revenue. For domestic debt, whether it is the debt of the central government and local governments, or the debt of financial institutions, enterprises, financing platforms, etc., they are owed to essentially the same creditor. China has the ability, policy, time, and space to resolve these debt problems in a stable and orderly manner on its own, independent of the international environment. In the debt of the United States and other Western countries, external debt accounts for a large proportion. In 2015, the external debt of the United States and Japan accounted for 39.56 and 29.52% of government debt, respectively. In 2009, when Greece's debt crisis began, its external debt accounted for 97.64%. In countries with a high proportion of external debt, when there is an economic or financial crisis, foreign creditors will generally lose no time in seeking the repayment of their debts. High debt repayment pressure and the possible resulting regional and systemic fiscal and financial risks accelerate the economic collapse.

China's Debt Is Mainly a Short-Term Liquidity Problem, While the Debt of the United States and Other Western Countries Is Mainly a Credit Problem

The essence of debt is the intertemporal allocation of funds in the development process: if the debtor's return on investment can cover the project's capital needs well, even moderate borrowing will only cause a short-term liquidity problem; otherwise, it will cause a serious credit problem. At present, although China's economy has shifted gears from high-speed growth to medium- to high-speed growth, remarkable results have been achieved in economic transformation and upgrading, and significant progress has been made in supply-side structural reform. Even though some projects are unlikely to generate high returns in the short term and therefore erode the liquidity of funds, in the long term, sustained economic growth will provide a buffer against credit risk. The United States and other Western countries are in a difficult period of economic recovery. The uncertainty of the Trump era, Brexit, the refugee crisis, terrorist attacks, and other destabilizing factors have placed a heavy burden on them. With Western countries in an unrelenting economic recession and protracted social unrest, Western creditors fear that they will have difficulty recovering their debts, and the credit ratings of these countries have begun to decline, which in turn lead to credit problems.

China's Debt Is Mainly Investment and Constructive Debt, Which Corresponds to Good Assets, While the Debt of Western Countries Is Mainly Consumer and Supportive Debt, Which Is Mainly Used to Serve the People's Livelihood
The results of a national government debt audit show that more than 60% of China's government debt is used to finance investments in municipal construction, transportation, indemnificatory housing, and land purchasing and reserving. These projects mainly focus on reinforcing the provision of public goods, and have a significant positive spillover effect on upgrading infrastructure, improving the market environment and driving social investment. Most of the debt used to finance investments in urban rail transit, water, heat, electricity, gas, and other municipal construction, and highway, railway, airport, and other transportation facilities have resulted in good assets that will generate a respectable amount of operating income for quite a long period of time. Government debt repayment is guaranteed by a stable cash flow, and debt risk tends to decrease. The debt of the United States and other Western countries is mainly used in areas such as social welfare and the maintenance of social order. For example, the top five components of US government debt are education, national defense, military industry, pension, and environmental governance. These areas lack cash flows matching future debt repayment, and debt risk tends to spread. In the event of an economic or financial risk, even if the debt is small, a debt problem may arise. Greece's debt crisis has a lot to do with its high level of welfare.

Measured by the statistics of the Bank for International Settlements, China's overall leverage ratio is basically the same as that of the United States. Considering the nature of debt and the use of funds, if net debt is calculated according to assets and liabilities, China's debt level of China will be further reduced. From this point of view, China's government and household sectors still have a lot of room for borrowing. There are a basis and conditions for a phased increase in leverage. We should support deleveraging in the corporate sector, expand effective investment, and create a favorable market and policy environment for supply-side structural reform.

5.3.4 *Resolving China's Debt in the Course of Development, Innovation, Market Reform, and Opening-Up*

To Solve the Debt Problem Is Essentially to Achieve Stable Economic Growth

The debt problem is actually an economic development problem. To resolve debt, we need to unleash economic vitality and creativity, and solve the debt problem in the course of economic growth. On the basis of unswervingly advancing supply-side structural reform, we can achieve sustainable economic development and improve the profitability of the market. By creating a good macro environment, we can moderately expand aggregate demand and improve the return on investment in projects. We should move forward in an orderly manner with "cutting overcapacity, destocking, deleveraging, reducing costs, and strengthening weak links," gradually reduce outdated production capacity, activate traditional production capacity, foster new production capacity, and create new poles of growth for the economy. We should effectively control the total amount of debt, gradually optimize the debt structure, and comprehensively solve China's debt problem in terms of both quantity and quality.

Innovate Systems and Mechanisms to Enhance the Deleveraging Capacity of Chinese Enterprises

We should comprehensively promote capital market reform, improve the multitiered equity financing market, and build a modern financial market system in which direct financing and indirect financing are coordinated. We should actively promote mixed ownership reform in enterprises, optimize their governance structure, and enhance their profitability. We should learn from the successful experience of local governments in debt swapping, and explore debt swapping for strategic, key and fundamental enterprises that have high leverage but involve national security, the lifeline of the national economy or major livelihood issues. We should pursue pilot programs on debt-for-equity swaps to effectively resolve corporate debt in a market-oriented manner while adhering to the rule of law. We should give full play to the role of asset management companies, etc., and set up a special debt disposal fund to professionally dispose of corporate debt. We should strengthen the supervision of highly leverage enterprises such as real estate enterprises, optimize the allocation of financial resources in real estate enterprises, and guard against systemic risks.

Resolve China's Government Debt in a Market-Oriented Way

We should strengthen cooperation with policy-oriented, development-oriented, social security, insurance, and other medium- and long-term, large-value funds, accurately design financing models and debt-servicing mechanisms, and expand market-oriented financing channels for governments. Actively explore and standardize the development of PPP, industrial funds, asset securitization, and other new investment and financing models, increase the market liquidity of government projects, and encourage market capital to participate in the development of public goods. We should improve the local government debt financing mechanism, increase government deficit to issue bonds in compliance with laws and regulations, optimize the government debt structure, and guard against fiscal and financial risks. We should increase the scale of local government debt swaps, and improve the capacity of local economies for sustainable development by reducing local governments' principal and interest burden. We should prepare the balance sheets of local governments and enterprises, and liquidize remnant assets in line with the transformation of government functions and reform aimed at "strengthening and slimming down" state-owned enterprises. We should speed up the transformation of financing platforms into market-oriented state-owned enterprises, remove implicit debt that should not be borne by the government, and clarify the debt boundary between the government and the market.

Strengthen International Communication, Coordination, and Publicity Concerning China's Debt Problem

We should treat China's debt problems scientifically and objectively, and we should not get overly bearish or incite malicious hype. We should vigorously present China's economic prospects in a positive light, stabilize expectations about China's economy at home and abroad, and strengthen the confidence of the international market in China's economy. We should actively publicize China's measures and initiatives to solve the debt problem, and communicate and coordinate effectively with the outside world on a timely and regular basis to prevent over-interpretation or even misinterpretation by international media. We should strengthen international exchanges and cooperation in debt resolution and research, work with international organizations, governments, and research institutions to develop more accurate debt evaluation standards, and try to calculate the net debt of various countries.

6 Improve China's Economic Governance Capability

6.1 Improve Economic Governance Capability

The essence of overcoming the middle-income trap is not only about quantity, but also about the quality of governance. As long as the national governance structure and capacity for social governance are not modernized, there will be development traps in the red line stage of income. Although some countries have entered the high-income stage, they have seen a widening of the gap between rich and poor, which has further aggravated social contradictions and makes it difficult to ensure sustainable development. Therefore, at a critical time when China is trying to overcome the middle-income trap, it is necessary to analyze the successes and failures of countries around the world in overcoming the middle-income trap, improve economic governance capability, create a better synergy between China's fiscal policy and monetary policy, comprehensively build a rule of law mechanism and implementation path for national economic governance, and advance national governance along the track of the rule of law.

6.1.1 Improve Governance Capability for Coordination Between the Government and the Market

To overcome the middle-income trap, we should properly handle the relationship between the government and the market in all aspects. In China, the new-type urbanization process is the key to overcoming the middle-income trap. Let's take the handling of the relationship between the government and the market in urbanization as an example. According to the relationship between the government and the market, urbanization in the world can be classified into four models: market-led urbanization under the control of the government represented by Western Europe and Japan; laissez faire urbanization represented by the United States; urbanization in developing countries subject to colonial economic constraints represented by some Latin American and African countries; government-led urbanization under the planned economic system represented by the Soviet Union. Both successes and failures are closely related to whether the relationship between the government and the market can be handled properly. As a large developing country with a vast population, China cannot simply copy the urbanization model of any country. Especially at the important stage of overcoming the middle-income trap, we need to properly handle the relationship between the government and the market in the process of new-type urbanization, and blaze a path for new-type urbanization that suits our actual situation.

Behavior Mode and Functional Positioning that Limit the Government's Role in New-Type Urbanization

The development of new-type urbanization requires the "invisible hand" of the market and the "visible hand" of the government to work together as an organic whole in a way that makes full use of their advantages and avoids their disadvantages and divides responsibility between them reasonably. Government intervention is intended to make up for market failure, catalyze and enhance the power and efficiency of the market, and eliminate market failure. Where the market mechanism fails, the government must be active and do a good job managing affairs that are its responsibility; where the market mechanism can play a fundamental role in resource allocation, the government must step aside and completely let go of powers that should be delegated.

We should scientifically position government functions to create institutional impetus for new-type urbanization. In the process of new-type urbanization, it is necessary to scientifically position government functions. The most important thing is that the government should respect the law of market operation and clarify its position in the market economy. China is in a critical period for economic and social development and transformation. New-type urbanization is a process of institutional change. The government must take on the important historical task of tackling difficult issues in reform in the process of institutional change. To give full play to the limited functions of the government, the government first must shatter the shackles of the old system that hinders the development of new-type urbanization with the courage of a "brave man who severs his wrist that has received a bite from a venomous snake with promptitude and resolution" and create a policy environment and market conditions that are fair and equitable. In the process of advancing new-type urbanization, we not only need to completely get rid of the traditional mindset that the government should play a leading role in everything, but also guard against the illusion that the market can do everything.

Give Full Play to the Leading Role of the Market Mechanism and Tap into the Source of Vitality for the Development of New-Type Urbanization

A market economy is the most efficient way to allocate resources that human society has discovered so far, which should be the consensus of the economic circles. Respecting the law of the market is the basic principle underlying new-type urbanization. The practice of urbanization at all times and in all countries has proved that only when cities and towns are developed according to the law of the market can they flourish. The market is the source of vitality for the development of new-type urbanization. High-quality new-type urbanization can only be accomplished by further deepening market-oriented reform. Letting the market mechanism play a fundamental role in resource allocation and improving the efficiency of the allocation of economic and social resources in cities and towns through market competition is a necessary condition for promoting the sustainable development of new-type urbanization.

The relationship between the government and the market is an old and eternal topic in economics. The choice of the boundary between the government and the market in the process of new-type urbanization is dynamically and constantly adjusted. It cannot be done once and for all, and must keep pace with the times. Therefore, we must use the government's economic authority and comparative advantages to adjust and change the role of the government in a timely manner according to the stage of new-type urbanization and the environment we face, give full play to the limited and effective leading role of the government and the decisive role of the market mechanism in the resource allocation, and promote the sustainable and stable development of new-type urbanization. In new-type urbanization, the government must let go of powers that should be delegated, showing the determination of a "brave man who severs his wrist that has received a bite from a venomous snake with promptitude and resolution"; manage affairs that fall within its responsibility well to project itself as a government for the people. This is a basic principle for straightening out the relationship between the government and the market.

6.1.2 *Improve Governance Capability for Coordination Between Fiscal Policy and Monetary Policy*

In the critical stage of overcoming the middle-income trap, in order to ensure the effectiveness of fiscal policy and monetary policy, it is necessary to analyze the transformation mechanism of fiscal policy and monetary policy from the perspective of the economic structure. The analysis is different from the previous analysis of the transmission mechanism of fiscal policy and monetary policy in that it studies the transmission mechanism with a focus on the influence of the economic structure on the transmission effect, and then puts forward more targeted suggestions on the choice of fiscal and monetary policy tools.

Improving people's livelihood is the focus of increasing fiscal expenditure. The operation of active fiscal policy always has two working threads: increasing expenditure and reducing taxes. One of the most important reasons why the main carrier of fiscal expansion has changed from "increasing expenditure" to "reducing taxes" is that we must seek a balance between the two goals of maintaining steady growth and making structural adjustments.

In view of the fact that stabilizing the overall price level is still an important task for us, and more importantly the two goals of maintaining steady growth and making structural adjustments must be compatible, we can no longer follow the old path of maintaining growth at the expense of structural adjustments. That is to say, the focus of increasing expenditure should be shifted from investment to stimulating consumer demand in due time.

Specifically, in addition to continuing to focus on optimizing the investment structure, the most important task for the arrangement of "increasing expenditure" is to stimulate consumer demand through a series of spending programs that are mainly aimed at improving people's livelihood and increases in their scale. Among them, important ones are: implement the minimum wage system, and increase the labor compensation of low-income earners; increase of farmers' income; basically achieve the full coverage of new social endowment insurance for rural residents and social endowment insurance for urban residents, and raise subsistence allowances for urban and rural residents, benefits for people who are entitled to special care by the government and basic pension for enterprise retirees; support the establishment of a mechanism for guaranteeing the normal growth and payment of enterprise employees' wages; increase the size of government subsidies, raise the income of urban and rural residents, especially low- and middle-income earners, and reduce the burden of people in straitened circumstances in education, health care, housing, etc.; vigorously support the construction of government-subsidized housing, etc.

It can be expected that a series of operations to increase expenditure focused on structural tax reduction supplemented by the improvement of people's livelihood will have the two wings of revenue and expenditure coordinated with and responsive to each other. The future operation of active fiscal policy is likely to be in line with the current economic situation at home and abroad and coordinated with the overall macroeconomic policy.

To increase demand, we should adjust the financial system. At present, the real challenge facing the Chinese economy lies in the imbalance and unsustainability of economic growth. The important reason is that, on the one hand, demand is obviously insufficient, on the other hand, supply-side reform is inadequate. Before the global financial crisis, China's rapid economic growth was due in part to strong external demand from the United States and Europe, which is now dwindling. China's investment-to-GDP ratio will continue to decline. The first step in addressing issues concerning expanded demand and sustained growth in the Chinese economy should be to adjust China's fiscal system, which will help make up for slowing investment growth and weakening exports. The irrationality of China's fiscal budget lies in its limited size and the inconsistent distribution of revenue and expenditure between the central government and local governments. Socialist economies are characterized by the ability to possess and control all key resources and dominate all major strategic activities. China's total fiscal budget accounts for only 28% of GDP, which is quite small compared with other similar countries. This proportion is 35% in upper-middle-income countries and 40–45% in most OECD economies. According to the World Bank's China 2030 Report, compared with other similar countries, the social services and other consumer demand provided by China's fiscal budget as a percentage of GDP are the third lowest. This explains why China's overall consumption-to-income ratio (household and government) is 10–15% lower than other similar countries. If fiscal reform is implemented, it could increase government spending as a share of GDP by an additional 4–5%. In this way, we can ensure that China has sufficient demand to sustain its annual economic growth rate of 6–7%.

The orientation of and thinking behind monetary policy. The central bank will continue to implement a prudent monetary policy. Meanwhile, it will properly handle the relationship between stable economic development, structural adjustment, and inflation expectation management, and make every effort to maintain a balance between economic growth, price stability, and risk prevention. The main thinking behind this is as follows.

First, promote the establishment of standardized financial markets and vigorously deepen the reform of financial institutions. Continue to deepen the reform of large commercial banks, constantly improve all aspects of corporate management, gradually implement the modern financial enterprise system, continue to deepen internal management and risk prevention management, and improve innovation capability and international competitiveness.

Second, improve the allocation efficiency of the financial system, perfect the financial regulation mechanism, and steadily push forward the reform of interest rate liberalization and the reform of the RMB exchange rate formation mechanism. Speed up the establishment of a market-driven benchmark interest rate system, strive to improve the central bank's regulation of market interest rates, correctly and efficiently guide financial institutions in risk-based pricing, be good at using interest rate floating and pricing power for reasonable pricing, strengthen active liability management and cost constraints, scientifically assess interest rate risk, reasonably improve the pricing mechanism, consciously maintain the pricing order, and eventually promote coordinated economic and financial development.

Continue to deepen the reform of and innovations in the RMB exchange rate formation mechanism, enhance the two-way floating elasticity of RMB exchange rates, and allow the law of market supply and demand to play a greater role in the formation of exchange rates, so as to keep RMB exchange rates basically stable at a reasonable and balanced level. Meanwhile, accelerate the development of the foreign exchange market, promote innovations in exchange rate risk management tools, closely monitor the impact of changes in the international situation on capital flows, and strengthen the effective monitoring of international capital. Coordinate the use of the RMB in international trade and investment, and actively expand channels for the outflow and recycling of the RMB.

Third, fully support the adjustment of the economic structure and continuously optimize the allocation of credit resources so as to better serve the development of the real economy. Correctly guide financial institutions in strengthening management and product innovation, explore appropriate credit management models, increase financial support for energy conservation, emission reduction and low-carbon economic development, actively cultivate a multitiered, diversified and healthily competitive rural financial service system, provide more financial support for promoting agricultural production, growth in farmers' income and rural development, and strive to break new grounds in financial support for employment, poverty alleviation, student aid and other livelihood projects; increase financial support for SMEs, especially small and micro enterprises; increase support for major projects that affect the overall situation and provide a strong driving force and key areas of national economy such as science and technology, cultural industries, tourism, and strategic emerging industries; continue to do a good job in financial support and services for coordinated regional economic development in line with national policies for regional economic development. Strengthen structural adjustment for remnant credit assets. Resolutely implement differentiated housing credit policies, strengthen supervision over the construction of indemnificatory housing, and ordinary small- and medium-sized commodity housing units, and purchases of first owner-occupied ordinary commodity housing units, and resolutely curb speculative and investment purchases of housing.

Fourth, guide the steady and healthy growth of monetary credit and social financing in an all-round way, deepen the macro-prudential policy framework, make full use of various monetary policy tools, and maintain reasonable market liquidity. Continue to leverage the role of macro-prudential policy in countercyclical regulation, make appropriate adjustments to relevant parameters based on changes in the economic climate, the soundness of financial institutions and the implementation of credit policies, and guide financial institutions in supporting the development of the real economy in a targeted and flexible manner. According to the international macroeconomic situation and the relationship between comprehensive monetary income and expenses and liquidity supply and demand, use various liquidity management tools such as central bank bills, the reserve requirement, reverse repos, and repos to comprehensively adjust liquidity in the banking system and guide the stable floating of market interest rates.

Fifth, effectively maintain the stability of the financial system and guard closely against systemic financial risks. Consolidate and improve the early warning and assessment system for systemic financial risks, strengthen the monitoring and assessment of financial risks in different industries and markets as well as international financial risks, and prevent the transmission of risks in the real economy and informal finance from some regions, industries, and enterprises to the financial system. Create risk early warning and response plans, and promote the building of a deposit insurance system. Take comprehensive measures to maintain financial stability and do everything possible to nip disaster in the bud. Deepen the reform of macro-prudential policy, guide financial institutions in operating prudently, conduct in-depth research on policies and measures to strengthen the supervision of systemically important financial institutions, dare to innovate, and put forward practical measures. Urge financial institutions to strengthen internal control and risk management, and continue to strengthen risk assessment, monitoring, and management for off-balance sheet activities of financial institutions, loans to local government financing platforms and the real estate sector.

6.1.3 *Improve Debt Management Capacity*

China is a developing country in the primary stage of socialism, and is currently in the new normal period of economic transformation and upgrading, and a critical period for supply-side structural reform, while the United States and other Western countries are developed capitalist countries which have basically completed industrialization or are in the post-industrial society. The two have fundamental differences in terms of debt nature, debt risk, debt-servicing capacity, and financial market development. For example, China's debt is mainly domestic debt, while a large proportion of the debt of United States and other Western countries is external debt; China's debt is mainly a short-term liquidity problem, while the debt of the United States and other Western countries is mainly a credit problem; China's debt is mainly investment and constructive debt, which corresponds to good assets, while the debt of Western countries is mainly consumer and supportive debt, which is mainly used to serve the people's livelihood; and so on.

To improve debt management capacity, first, we need to achieve stable economic growth. To resolve debt, we need to unleash economic vitality and creativity and solve the debt problem in the course of economic growth. On the basis of unswervingly advancing supply-side structural reform, we can achieve sustainable economic development and improve the profitability of the market. By creating a good macro environment, we can moderately expand aggregate demand and improve the return on investment in projects. We should move forward in an orderly manner with "cutting overcapacity, destocking, deleveraging, reducing costs, and strengthening weak links," gradually reduce outdated production capacity, activate traditional production capacity, foster new production capacity, and create new poles of growth for the economy. We should effectively control the total amount of debt, gradually optimize the debt structure, and comprehensively solve China's debt problem in terms of both quantity and quality.

Second, we need to innovate systems and mechanisms to enhance the deleveraging capacity of Chinese enterprises. We should comprehensively promote capital market reform, improve the multitiered equity financing market, and build a modern financial market system in which direct financing and indirect financing are coordinated. We should actively promote mixed ownership reform in enterprises, optimize their governance structure, and enhance their profitability. We should learn from the successful experience of local governments in debt swapping, and explore debt swapping for strategic, key, and fundamental enterprises that have high leverage but involve national security, the lifeline of the national economy or major livelihood issues. We should pursue pilot programs on debt-for-equity swaps to effectively resolve corporate debt in a market-oriented manner while adhering to the rule of law. We should give full play to the role of asset management companies, etc., and set up a special debt disposal fund to professionally dispose of corporate debt. We should strengthen the supervision of highly leverage enterprises such as real estate enterprises, optimize the allocation of financial resources in real estate enterprises, and guard against systemic risks.

Third, we need to resolve China's government debt in a market-oriented way. We should strengthen cooperation with policy-oriented, development-oriented, social security, insurance, and other medium- and long-term, large-value funds, accurately design financing models and debt-servicing mechanisms, and expand market-oriented financing channels for governments. Actively explore and standardize the development of PPP, industrial funds, asset securitization, and other new investment and financing models, increase the market liquidity of government projects, and encourage market capital to participate in the development of public goods. We should improve the local government debt financing mechanism, increase government deficit to issue bonds in compliance with laws and regulations, optimize the government debt structure, and guard against fiscal and financial risks. We should increase the scale of local government debt swaps, and improve the capacity of local economies for sustainable development by reducing local governments' principal and interest burden. We should prepare the balance sheets of local governments and enterprises, and liquidize remnant assets in line with the transformation of government functions and reform aimed at "strengthening and slimming down" state-owned enterprises. We should speed up the transformation of financing platforms into market-oriented state-owned enterprises, remove implicit debt that should not be borne by the government, and clarify the debt boundary between the government and the market.

Fourth, we need to strengthen international communication and coordination concerning China's debt problem. We should treat China's debt problems scientifically and objectively, and we should not get overly bearish or incite malicious hype. We should vigorously present China's economic prospects in a positive light, stabilize expectations about China's economy at home and abroad, and strengthen the confidence of the international market in China's economy. We should actively publicize China's measures and initiatives to solve the debt problem, and communicate and coordinate effectively with the outside world on a timely and regular basis to prevent over-interpretation or even misinterpretation by international media. We should strengthen international exchanges and cooperation in debt resolution and research, work with international organizations, governments, and research institutions to develop more accurate debt evaluation standards, and try to calculate the net debt of various countries.

6.1.4 *Main Tasks Related to Accelerating the Transformation of the Mode of Economic Development*

Effectively Expand Domestic Demand, Especially Consumer Demand, and Promote Final Consumption as the Leading Force Driving Economic Growth

Since the beginning of the twenty-first century, China's industrialization and urbanization have accelerated, and its production capacity has expanded rapidly, put to use through external demand. In the process of rapid economic growth, the problems of imbalance between internal and external demand and inconsistency between investment and consumption have gradually emerged. In 2010, China's consumption-to-GDP ratio dropped to 47.4%, with the consumption-to-GDP ratio falling to

33.8%, and the contribution of final consumption to economic growth was only 36.8%. As can be seen from an international comparison, China's consumption-to-GDP ratio is low, even after accounting for statistical underestimates. With the slowdown in the global economy and the acceleration of global economic rebalancing, external demand has been declining, greatly reducing the space for providing an outlet for excess production capacity through international markets, which coupled with the disappearance of the "demographic dividend" and a decline in the savings rate makes economic growth that is highly dependent on exports and investment unsustainable, so there is an urgent to strengthen the role of consumer demand in driving economic growth and gradually increase household purchasing power and the consumption-to-GDP ratio. To this end, we should make expanding consumer demand the strategic focus of expanding domestic demand and build a long-term mechanism for expanding consumer demand. Actively yet prudently promote urbanization, and create more opportunities for employment and entrepreneurship; accelerate the reform of the income distribution system, adjust distribution between the government, corporate and household sectors, improve the income level and purchasing power of urban and rural residents, especially low- and middle-income residents, and expand the middle-income consumer base; significantly increase the proportion of expenditure on public services in financial expenditure, expand the coverage of the social security system, increase people's willingness to spend, and reduce precautionary savings; effectively expand the overall size of the domestic market and play a more active role in rebalancing the global economy.

Accelerate the Development of Modern Service Industries and Strategic Emerging Industries, and Foster New Areas of Economic Growth

The impact of the international financial crisis has made deep-seated contradictions and problems in China's industrial structure more acute. The proportion of industry is too high, the value added of industry is low, and the development of service industries is lagging behind; there is an over-reliance on processing and manufacturing, and the development of high value-added productive services is lagging behind; the proportion of high-tech industries is increasing rapidly, but they are basically concentrated at the lower end (processing, assembly, and production) of the value chain. With the shrinking of external demand, production capacity that has been and is being formed in China is facing new pressure to adjust. The high degree of dependence of economic growth on low-end processing and assembly and a lack of independent technologies and brands have created an unsustainable situation. There is an urgent need to accelerate a new round of industrial transformation and upgrading, and create new development space in the field of emerging industries while enhancing the competitive advantage of traditional industries. Shift structural adjustment from focusing on adjusting the proportion between industries to focusing on breaking through key links that restrict industrial transformation and upgrading, accelerate the development of productive services such as R&D, design, standards, logistics, marketing, brands and supply chain management, and improve the value added of good products in the industrial value chain. Adapt to new changes in the international industrial competition landscape, accelerate the cultivation and development of seven strategic emerging industries identified by the State Council, including energy conservation and environmental protection, next-generation information technology, biology, high-end equipment manufacturing, new energy, new materials and new energy vehicles, promote technological innovation and business model innovation, improve the innovation incentive mechanism and risk-sharing mechanism, and create a sound environment for the development of strategic emerging industries.

Choosing and developing strategic emerging industries is also an inevitable choice for China to transform its mode of economic development. The State has proposed to take the pursuit of development in a scientific way as the underlying guideline, accelerating the transformation of the mode of economic development as a major task, and important adjustments to the economic structure as the main direction of strategic development. Specifically, first, we should shift from relying too much on exports and investment to paying more attention to domestic demand, especially consumer demand, so as to create a situation where development is coordinated; second, we should shift from relying mainly on industrial growth to developing modern agriculture and vigorously developing service industries, especially promoting modern service industries, the structural optimization and upgrading of industry, and the coordinated development of strategic emerging industries; third, we should shift from relying mainly on resource and energy consumption to relying on technological innovation, management innovation, and making fuller use of advantages in manpower.

According to the characteristics of strategic emerging industries, and based on China's national conditions and technological and industrial foundations, the Decision of the State Council on Accelerating the Cultivation and Development of Strategic Emerging Industries identifies seven areas as strategic emerging industries. These seven areas include energy conservation and environmental protection, next-generation information technology, biology, high-end equipment manufacturing, new energy, new materials, and new energy vehicles. But the development goals of these seven areas are different. By 2020, energy conservation and environmental protection, next-generation information technology, biology, and high-end equipment manufacturing will become the pillar industries of the national economy, and new energy, new materials, and new energy vehicles will become the forerunner industries of the national economy. Pillar industries, also known as leading industries, refer to industries that account for a large proportion of output value, deliver high comprehensive benefits, and act as pillars of the national economy. Forerunner industries refer to industries that do not account for a high proportion at present, but have favorable conditions for development and a good development momentum, and are expected to be upgraded to leading industries in the future through support and cultivation.

Accelerate the Cultivation of New Competitive Advantages Based on Technological Innovation and Human Capital, and Enhance the Role of Innovation in Driving Economic Growth

With the weakening of China's low-cost advantage in labor and other factors of production, the high degree of dependence of economic growth on traditional comparative advantages has created an unsustainable situation. There is an urgent to cultivate and establish new competitive advantages based on technological innovation and human capital. To this end, it is necessary to establish the position of enterprises as the dominant force in technological innovation, encourage enterprises to increase R&D investment and talent reserves, support the development of innovative SMEs, and greatly enhance enterprises' innovation capability. Meanwhile, take human resources development and human capital investment as the strategic focus, take prioritizing the development of education and training as an important way to improve human capital, take cultivating innovative talent as an important goal of educational development and reform, organize the implementation of programs for the recruiting top talent, promote the flow of talent to enterprises, create and foster a "new demographic dividend" formed by improvement in the quality of workers, and increase the contribution of human capital to economic growth.

Reduce Energy and Resource Consumption and Emission Intensity, and Build Resource-Efficient and Environmentally Friendly Modes of Production and Consumption
As the international community's call for China to assume binding emission reduction obligations grows louder, the hard energy, resource, and environmental constraints faced by domestic economic development have further strengthened. Rapid economic growth through the consumption of massive amounts of non-renewable resources cannot be sustained. There is an urgent need to transform the process easing pressure on resources and the environment into the process of technological progress and industrial upgrading, and to maximize the efficiency of resource utilization.

Meanwhile, we should implement a more proactive opening-up strategy. A more proactive opening-up strategy means that China's central and western regions will continue to implement the comparative advantage strategy and leverage their comparative advantage in factor endowment; the eastern region will begin to implement the absolute advantage strategy and create an absolute advantage in technology.

For China, if it wants to adjust its trade structure and achieve sustainable growth in foreign trade, it should actively cultivate and create an absolute advantage in technology. The central and western regions still have an advantage in labor cost and should continue to capitalize on the comparative advantage. But the eastern region's advantage in labor cost is gradually weakening, and capital is no longer in short supply, so the conditions for it to cultivate and create an absolute advantage in technology are mature. Therefore, the eastern region should start to implement the absolute advantage strategy and promote the transformation of the trade structure.

The ultimate goal of China's foreign trade and economic development should be to achieve an absolute advantage in technology. Comparative advantage is based on the current situation, any country can find its own comparative advantage. But comparative advantage is not sustainable and will change over time. When a country (especially a big country) has reached a certain stage of economic development, its comparative advantage in labor is weakening, and its comparative advantage in capital has not yet been established, making it vulnerable to the middle-income trap. Before falling into the middle-income trap, we should actively cultivate an absolute advantage in technology. Absolute advantage is more sustainable. Absolute advantage means strong competitiveness worldwide.

6.1.5 *Optimizing the Financial Structure Can Help Transform the Mode of Economic Development*

From both theoretical analysis and empirical research, we can conclude that optimizing the financial structure promotes economic development. Due to differences in political and economic systems and historical reasons, countries around the world have respectively formed bank-based and market-based financial systems, which constitutes an important direction of research on financial structures and economic development. Allen and Gale (2000), Allen (2006), and Demirguc Kunt and Levine (2001), respectively, established corresponding theoretical models to study the different roles of these two different types of financial systems in resource allocation and risk resolution. The operational efficiency of financial institutions has a bearing on the efficiency of capital circulation in the whole market, innovation in financial products will bring more investment, but economic and financial risks will also expand with innovation in financial products. As a result, financial entities play a role in different ways in different types of financial structures, which affects the efficiency of capital allocation and risk control and thus has an impact on the development of a country's economy as a whole. Their comparative study shows that market-based financial systems are more efficient in allocating resources, while bank-based financial systems have a better ability to guard against internal short-term risks. Meanwhile, because savings funds are channeled into enterprises through banks, thus completing the conversion of savings into investment, banks have a clear advantage in eliminating information asymmetry under normal conditions. However, in a non-standard state and an uncertain market environment, market-based financial systems have a better ability to process information such as financial innovation.

According to the model established by Boot and Thakor (2000), the potential closeness between banks and enterprises in bank-led financial systems is higher than in market-based financial systems, but it also depends on economic development. Due to information asymmetry in financial markets, adverse selection, principal–agent problems, and so on will inevitably affect the corporate governance structure of financial institutions, thus affecting the efficiency of resource allocation of financial institutions. However, whether it is in a market-based or bank-based financial structure, the participation of financial institutions can mitigate or control such agency problems to a certain extent. Studies have shown that the promotion of economic development by financial intermediaries comes from the extreme importance of information throughout the financing process of financial markets, especially their significant impact on capital allocation. Through external financing, financial intermediaries can reduce information asymmetry and optimize capital allocation. Meanwhile, taking monitoring costs into account, financial intermediaries will drive capital flows to areas with the lowest monitoring costs, even if these areas have far more capital than other areas or markets with higher monitoring costs. Investors know that financial intermediaries with good monitoring can bring higher returns, while financial intermediaries with poor monitoring can only have suboptimal capital allocation. In addition, through financial innovation, financial institutions can reduce information asymmetry in financing markets, which in turn has a positive effect on economic growth and ensures stable economic development. Relevant studies have found that in the basic model of financing, debt contracts, and economic growth, debt contracts can reduce the free cash flow to enterprises, which can correspondingly reduce management's idleness and increase the proportion of business managers using new technologies. Another conclusion that can be drawn from studies in this field is that compared with developed countries, the financial markets of developing countries are more suitable for bank-based financial systems, and that this type of financial structure is more conducive to the economic development and market stability of developing countries.

Lin Yifu et al. (2009) believed that optimizing the financial structure could promote economic development.[15] An effective financial structure must reflect the needs of the real economy. Fundamentally, factor endowments (labor, capital, and natural resources) determine the industrial structure, which in turn requires the support of a specific financial structure. A country has different combinations of factor endowments at different stages of development. This combination determines factor prices, which in turn determines the most suitable industry structure, the

[15] Lin Yifu, Sun Xifang, Jiang Ye. A Preliminary Study on the Theory of Optimal Financial Structure in Economic Development. *Economic Research Journal*, 2009 (8).

relevant risk characteristics, and the size and distribution of enterprises (Lin Yifu 2008).[16] As enterprises in different industries have different scales of operation, risks, and financing needs, the real economy's needs regarding the financial structure will vary with the stage of development. When the characteristics and advantages of the financial structure are in line with the economy's current needs regarding the industrial structure, the financial system can perform its basic functions most effectively, thereby contributing to sustainable and inclusive development. Therefore, at every stage of development of the economy, a financial structure that matches it is needed.

Thus, a particular financial structure corresponding to a certain stage of development may be able to raise and allocate funds more efficiently. In other words, at a certain stage of economic development, an appropriate financial structure can allocate resources most effectively with given factor endowments. For developing countries, banks (especially small ones) often play a greater role in their financial structures than financial markets. For developed countries, the opposite may be true. Different financial structures have different effects on economic development.

An empirical study by Rousseau and Wachtel (2005) analyzed the level of financial development, and the health and structure of the banking industry in various countries, and their effects on economic development, including the 1997 Asian financial crisis. They found that if the banking industry was overdeveloped and generated too many bubbles, it would affect the stable development of the macroeconomy. Mayer Foulkes (2005) improved the general model to study the relationship between low levels of financial development and economic growth in low-income countries. The empirical results show that the economic development of these countries can be promoted more quickly by improving the financial structure and strengthening financial development. However, such growth is not necessarily stable. In a comparative study of financial markets around the world (2008), the World Bank pointed out that the multilevel and multi-structured development and improvement of financial markets would promote macroeconomic growth.

La Porta et al. (2001, 2006) used data on the equity or ownership of banks in various countries to verify the impact of the degree of nationalization of bank equity on the economic development of a country, and

[16] Lin Yifu. *Economic Development and Transition: Thought, Strategy, and Viability*. Beijing: Peking University Press, 2008.

found that banks with a high degree of nationalization were of low utility in relation to information asymmetry issues such as corporate governance structure, market information disclosure, risk control, and transaction cost reduction. They concluded that highly nationalized state-owned banks directly led to the low-level development of the banking industry; highly nationalized state-owned banks would restrict and affect the economic development of a country.

Loayza and Ranciere (2002, 2005) used panel data to analyze the long-run and short-run relationships between financial institutions and economic development in several countries (with the exception of Latin American countries). The study pointed out that bank lending is an important indicator of financial crisis and economic stagnation in the short term. Guiso et al. (2002) used data on regional housing finance and services in Italy to study the effect of regional financial development in a country on local enterprises and economic development, and found that regional financial development could improve entrepreneurial opportunities, increase industrial competition and promote enterprise development. Meanwhile, they also found that the effect of regional finance on large enterprises was much weaker, which was related to the amount of financing available to large enterprises. Beck and Levine (2003, 2005) used dynamic panel data to test the relationship between the stock market, the banking industry, and economic growth and found out the effect of financial factors on economic development. Christopoulos and Tsionas (2003) used a panel unit root and panel cointegration approach to study the relationship between financial development and economic growth in 10 developing countries. At first, they used a large amount of time series data and found that the deviation of the results yielded was due to short time spans of typical data sets.

Therefore, they combined the increase in sample size with a panel approach to analyze the time series data yielded. They found that the hypothesis of a correlation between long-run financial development and economic growth was true, but it was not interactive. Meanwhile, they also used unit cointegration factors to analyze the long-run relationship between economic and financial development.

Demirguc Kunt et al. (2011) used large-scale cross-border sample data to provide substantial evidence for the relationship between financial structures and economic development.[17] They used data from 72 countries between 1980 and 2008 to assess the role of financial structures in economic development. They found that deviating from the optimal financial structure has a great impact on the economy: a one-standard deviation will reduce economic out by 6%.

6.1.6 *Requirements of Accelerating the Transformation of the Mode of Economic Development for the Upgrading of the Financial Structure*

The tasks of accelerating the transformation of the mode of economic development include urbanization, the development of modern service industries and strategic emerging industries, the implementation of an innovation strategy, and energy conservation and consumption reduction. All these require increasing the proportion of direct finance, private finance, small- and medium-sized financial institutions, and financial institutions in the central and western regions in the financial structure. This is the direction of China's future financial restructuring.

The problem of local government debt has been the focus of much attention at home and abroad. Previously, local governments financed urbanization mainly through debt. However, in view of local governments' debt risk, developing direct finance, private finance, and small- and medium-sized financial institutions for the financing of urbanization has become a realistic option. In addition, as the central and western regions are economically backward and urgently need substantial financial support, it is essential to focus on the development of financial institutions in the central and western regions.

Developing service industries and strategic emerging industries means adjusting the existing financial structure. Service industries need the support of a large number of SMEs, and small- and medium-sized financial institutions are the most important source of financing to these SMEs. Over the past few years, overcapacity and a lack of innovation in strategic emerging industries which are supported by local governments have led to trade sanctions against China's emerging industries. In the next few years, the key to the development of strategic emerging industries will lie in encouraging SMEs to enter, grow through innovation and create

[17] Demiguc Kunt, Asli, Erik Feyen, and Ross Levin. Optimal Financial Structures and Development: The Evolving Importance of Banks and Markets, *Mimeo*, World Bank, 2011.

a competitive edge in technology. These enterprises also need to develop through direct finance and SME finance.

The implementation of an innovation strategy requires government support on the one hand, and the continuous pursuit of R&D by a large number of SMEs on the other. The implementation of energy conservation and consumption reduction also requires SMEs' R&D support for low-carbon technologies. New energy development needs not only to be led by the market but also to be guided by the government. These need to be supported by the development of direct finance and SME finance.

Changing the opening-up strategy also requires optimizing the financial structure. By using enterprise-level data, many scholars have found that financing constraints significantly affect the export of Chinese enterprises. Therefore, only by removing the financing constraints on enterprises can we further optimize China's foreign trade structure.

6.1.7 Development Finance Is Urgently Needed to Forge an Upgraded Version of the Economic System

Premier Li Keqiang has put forward the concept of "forging an upgraded version of the Chinese economy." Forging an upgraded version of the Chinese economy is an inevitable choice for China's economy to make further progress after more than 30 years of rapid growth, and also an important path to realize the Chinese Dream. With risks lurking in economic growth and contradictions interwoven with achievements, it will be difficult to move forward without transformation and upgrading. To forge an upgraded version of the Chinese economy is to change the extensive mode of economic development, adjust the unreasonable economic structure, and make new and substantial improvements in the quality and efficiency of the economy, employment and income, environmental protection, and resource conservation. The implications for our times of forging an upgraded version of the Chinese economy are mainly reflected in the following aspects.

First, an upgraded version of the Chinese economy is a close combination of speed and quality. To forge an upgraded version of the Chinese economy, we must have a precise grasp of the "degree" of "stability" and "progress." On the one hand, we must maintain sustained economic growth, prevent inflation and control potential risks; on the other hand, we must focus on making progress while maintaining stability, and strive to achieve qualitative improvement while maintaining "quantity."

Second, the new driver of China's economic upgrading comes from innovation, domestic demand, and reform. The key to upgrading is to promote economic transformation. To promote transformation, we need to combine the dividends of reform, the potential of domestic demand, and the vitality of innovation to create a new driver. Therefore, we should further strengthen the innovation-driven development strategy, and significantly increase the contribution of technological advances to economic growth in an effort to become an innovation-oriented nation. We should focus on promoting a high degree of integration of industrialization and informatization, accelerating the popularization and application of information technology and other high and new technologies, strengthening advanced manufacturing and strategic emerging industries from a high starting point, driving the upgrading of traditional industries, and elevating China's position in the global industrial and value chains. We should further promote reform and opening-up, and adhere to the direction of market-oriented and law-based reform; we should build an pro-innovation government, clarify the boundary between the government and the market, let the market play a decisive role in the allocation of resources, further delegate power to society and enterprises, unleash the vitality of society, and make the dividends of reform benefit the people even more. We should further firmly grasp the strategic basis of expanding domestic demand, accelerate the establishment of a long-term mechanism for expanding consumer demand, and expand the domestic market. At present, the focus is to tap the huge potential of domestic demand contained in urbanization, and make urbanization truly the largest source of domestic demand in China through reforming the household registration, land, fiscal, and taxation systems, strengthening the building of public service delivery capacity, and accelerating the reform of the income distribution system.

Third, the development of development finance is urgently needed in order to forge an upgraded version of the economic system. China's economy has achieved miraculous achievements in the past 30 years, but there remain concerns about "unbalanced, uncoordinated and unsustainable" development. Standing on a higher platform, how can we continue to maintain long-term stable economic growth, resolve potential systemic risks, make household income increase in step with the economy, and relieve growing pressures on resources and the environment? The only way out is to speed up the shift of the development mode from "factor-driven" to "innovation-driven and consumption-driven," and achieve economic transformation and upgrading. Development finance is national finance, and its purpose is to make up for backward systems and market failures, and to achieve the government's development goals. Development finance promotes project construction, institutional improvement and market building in covered areas through finance: It is based on national credit, supported by market performance, and revolved around credit system development; it combines the advantages of finance with governments' advantages in coordination and organization; it achieves the break-even point through the combination of government agency bonds and financial asset management.

Finally, the upgraded version of the Chinese economy is an organic unity of improving people's livelihood and promoting social equity. We should improve people's livelihood, allow people to breathe clean air, drink safe water and eat safe food, and weave a safety net covering education, health care, endowment insurance and housing that ensures the basic well-being of the whole people, which put forward specific requirements and objectives for China's economic transformation and upgrading. Promoting social justice and creating opportunities at the institutional level for all people and enterprises to compete and develop fairly will help promote private investment and entrepreneurship, expand employment, improve corporate competitiveness, and stimulate economic and social vitality, which is of great significance for promoting economic transformation and upgrading. In this sense, economic upgrading, improving people's livelihood, and social equity are mutually reinforcing and interconnected. Improving people's livelihood and providing social equity are the "humanistic attributes" of the upgraded version of the Chinese economy.

6.2 Improve Financial Governance Capability

China's participation in international macroeconomic policy coordination has two objectives: first, to create a stable international economic and financial environment for economic transformation and development; second, to promote global financial governance and create conditions for the stable development of the global economy. This study holds that whether in the important stage of overcoming the middle-income trap or in participating in the coordination of international financial governance, China should firstly serve its own development agenda, and secondly, increase its voice and influence. Serving China's own development agenda as the core objective is China's top priority.

First, strengthen the top-level design of the international coordination mechanism. The international macro policy coordination mechanism should have a package of strategic design, which will prop up China's overall development strategy and be coordinated with other strategies. In particular, international macroeconomic policy coordination should be focused on the provision of public goods closely related to a community of shared future for mankind. Meanwhile, China and the United States should take the lead in forming a macro policy coordination mechanism on some major issues, so as to benefit both China and the United States and create a new world order. Huang Wei believed that participation in international macro policy coordination requires top-level design, and if we have any vision for the future global monetary system and global trade and investment system, we should put forward clear ideas. Mei Xinyu said that in participating in international coordination, China should make it clear that it is a beneficiary and reformer of the existing international economic governance system, not a disruptor.

Second, we should focus on the use of the Eastern concept of coordination. China's concept should be different from the traditional concept of macroeconomic policy coordination mechanism. The traditional concept is centered on the West, pursues short-term results, makes other countries bear the responsibility and cost, and emphasizes the promotion of ideology, is the product of the Western political and economic system and reflects a hegemonic mindset. We should emphasize the integration of the Eastern and Western concepts of policy coordination.

Third, we should plan as a whole and make overall arrangements at multiple levels. China should make overall arrangements at three levels: First, coordination between China and the United States. This is the most important part of international coordination. China and the United States should establish a permanent coordination mechanism. The existing China–US economic and strategic dialogue mechanism can be further enhanced. Second, coordination between China and neighboring countries. We should further strengthen cooperation mechanisms such as "ASEAN 10 + 3," "ASEAN 10 + 1," the Shanghai Cooperation Organization, China–Japan–South Korea, and China–India. Finally, coordination between China and emerging countries. In addition to BRICS, we can also coordinate with countries such as Turkey and Nigeria. In practice, we can coordinate on a bilateral basis first and then on a multilateral basis, coordinate with countries in the same organizations as China first and then with countries that are loosely connected with China, coordinate with countries that agree with us first and then with other countries, and coordinate with neighboring strategic pivot countries first and then gradually expand to other countries.

Fourth, enhance transparency in policy and internal and external coordination. We should be transparent about our opinions regarding international coordination, and these opinions must be accessible, predictable, and stable. As China's influence grows, this could backfire if not handled properly. Meanwhile, we should pay attention to the ability of rules to resist attacks. Global rules are essentially an extension of the domestic rules of the United States, so we should learn from the American experience. When pursuing economic and financial governance reforms at home, we should plan for the next step of international coordination as a whole.

6.2.1 Deepen Our Understanding of Global Financial Governance and Improve Our Ability to Participate in Global Financial Governance

Countries and regions across the globe that have overcome the middle-income trap, especially at the critical moment when the 2008 financial crisis was raging. For the United States, the most important thing in the short term is to solve its financial credit problem and debt problem; in the long term, it needs to solve problems concerning the international monetary system. President Xi has proposed to build a community with a shared future for mankind. The establishment of a global financial governance system is conducive to preventing financial risks in China and other countries. Therefore, it is necessary to explore and study international experience models for conduct regulation, study the experience of countries that have "overcome the middle-income trap" and the lessons learnt therefrom, ask questions and find problems, and on this basis, determine a reform trend and target model for conduct regulation that is compatible with the development level of China's financial sector.

Crisis as a Driver of Improvements in Rules

Rules and regulations will only be truly taken seriously and designed when they encounter practical problems, so the post-crisis period is often the golden period for institutional improvement. Finance belongs to the

Table 1 Main financial regulators and their main responsibilities

Name	*Area of responsibility*
Federal Reserve Board	Regulate all Federal Reserve member banks, including financial holding companies
Office of the Comptroller of Currency (OCC)	Regulate federally chartered commercial banks
Federal Deposit Insurance Corporation (FDIC)	Regulate insured commercial banks, mutual savings banks, and savings and loan associations
Office of Thrift Supervision (OTS)	Regulate federally chartered financial institutions
Securities and Exchange Commission (SEC)	Regulate organized exchanges and financial markets
Commodity Futures Trading Commission (CFTC)	Regulate futures trading
National Credit Union Administration (NCUA)	Regulate federally chartered credit unions
Office of Federal Housing Enterprise Oversight (OFHEO)	Regulate financial institutions in the real estate sector
Foreign Transactions Commission	Regulate sovereign wealth funds

service category. Lax financial regulation may lead to a build-up of financial bubbles and give rise to a financial crisis. Because financial products have the attributes of public goods to some extent, and financial crisis is often linked to economic crisis, so crisis is often an important driver of institutional improvement, as evidenced by a series of financial laws and regulations enacted in the United States in 1933 and 2010. See Table 1 for details.

The 2008 financial crisis prompted the United States to strengthen financial regulation and introduce the Dodd–Frank Act. But the US financial sector still has a series of problems: First, there are significant moral hazard problems in the financial sector that are difficult to eradicate. From 2000 to 2008, some CEOs and a few employees of the top 14 financial institutions in the United States earned more than $2 billion. After the outbreak of the crisis, more than 8 million people lost their jobs. Total public debt increased by about $730 million (about 78% of the total debt in 2007) and net debt increased by $630 million (about 94% of that in 2007). Second, large financial enterprises enjoy "too-big-to-fail" advantage and government endorsement. In 1995, the total assets of the six major US banks (Morgan Stanley, Goldman Sachs, JPMorgan Chase, Bank of America, Citibank, and Wells Fargo) accounted for 17% of US GDP. This proportion was 55% in 2006 and rose to 62.5% in 2011. Compared with small- and medium-sized financial institutions, these banks tend to raise funds more cheaply. Third, non-bank financial companies of global importance and large transnational financial institutions have been inadequately regulated, and there are still loopholes that practitioners can exploit. Citibank, for example, has about $1.8 trillion in assets and 550 clearing and settlement systems in 17 countries, so liquidating it is easier said than done.

The Underdevelopment of China's Financial Structure Restricts Macroeconomic Policy Choices

First, the impact of changes in China's financial structure on the concept of macro-financial governance. Over the past 60 years, the Chinese government's governance of the financial sector has been basically guided by market-oriented reforms. Perfecting the market structure, expanding markets, and deregulating markets are the basic path choice. On the one hand, this is in line with China's basic national conditions; on the other hand, this is also necessary for China's gradual integration into the international economic and trade system. In the government work reports of the past decade, economic structural adjustment and economic system reform, raising the level and quality of opening-up, and national rejuvenation through science and education and sustainable development are the three most frequently mentioned topics.

Second, the underdevelopment of the financial structure restricts macroeconomic policy choices. A sound financial system can effectively mobilize social savings, boost investment, improve the efficiency of capital allocation, and promote the upgrading of the industrial structure and economic development. With the total amount of capital remaining unchanged, the more active financial activities are and the more intense the competition among financial institutions is, the more capital will go to industries and regions with low risk, short payback periods and high levels of profitability, thereby increasing the efficiency of capital use and improving the interindustrial structure. Economic development can increase the demand for finance and stimulate further improvements in the financial structure. As shown in Section 3 of this chapter, in 2012, China's financing instruments were still dominated by bank credit (more than 50%), and financing activities depended heavily on the banking industry. In 1999, only 35% of the financing instruments in the United States were bank credit, and the financing methods were more diverse and flexible, which helped to lower financing costs and improve the efficiency of capital supply. For most SMEs, the funding that commercial banks can provide is relatively limited.

Active underground financing channels have become the main source of funds for the development of enterprises in China's eastern coastal areas. Although the efficiency of underground finance is high, its borrowing rates are relatively high, ranging from 20 to 100%. The underground banking boom reflects a dearth of money for Chinese enterprises. There is a cap between capital supply and demand.

Third, similarities and differences in the development of the financial structure between China and the United States and their impact. The macro-governance thought determines the development direction of the financial structure. Meanwhile, the evolution of the financial structure is subject to the current level of financial development and the internal and external economic environment. In terms of the development of the financial structure, there are several important similarities and differences between China and the United States. China and the United States are similar in that both countries are in a period of mixed operation and have a fragmented regulatory regime. The main differences between the Chinese and American financial structures are as follows. First, their operating mechanisms are different: The Chinese financial structure is bank-based, while the American financial structure is market-based. Second, they are at different stages of development: China is still in the period of financial cultivation and practices financial repression, while the United States has established a full range of financial markets and is experiencing excessive financialization. Third, their degrees of openness are different: China's financial sector is relatively closed because capital markets are not yet fully open, while US financial markets are fully open and have pricing power and influence on a global scale.

The adjustment of a country's economic structure starts with the commercialization and industrialization of high-tech achievements, and the optimization of the economic, social, and industrial structures is facilitated through the effective allocation and utilization of capital and resources. High-tech startups tend to have more pressing needs for capital, but they also have less access to bank credit. In addition, improvement in incentive and restraint mechanisms in the form of equity, debt, etc. can promote the growth of "entrepreneurs." In short, from a financial structure perspective, China still needs to deepen market-oriented reform, improve competition among financial institutions, and provide more financing instruments.

China's Financial Structure Still Has Much Room for Improvement

China is still in the heavy industry stage, and there is high volatility in its macro economy. Due to an imperfect personal income tax system and the limited role of automatic stabilizers, discretionary fiscal policy is very important for macro-control. Moreover, China's current fiscal spending is tilted toward material resources and hardware. An industrial structure dominated by manufacturing industry and a mode of growth based on factor inputs have contributed to a strong upstream and downstream price transmission mechanism in China. The authorities have always been vigilant against inflation, and no specific employment targets have been set in monetary policy.

The characteristics of China's demand structure determine that fiscal policy plays a more prominent role and is predominant among anti-crisis stimulus policies. Many instruments that look more like monetary policy, such as bank loans, actually support the implementation of fiscal policy. Meanwhile, financial markets and financial instruments are underdeveloped, and the degree of interest rate liberalization is not high, so the role of monetary policy is not obvious, especially for large state-owned enterprises and listed companies. Therefore, monetary policy also focuses on quantity control, and the frequency of use of price-based instruments is not high.

Inequality in China reduces the effect of monetary policy, and the effect of monetary policy on easing inequality is minimal or even negative. The government has long held a strong position in income distribution, resulting in monetary policy mainly serving the government's development programs. The beneficiaries are mainly state-owned enterprises, state-owned banks, and the state finance. This will undoubtedly increase inequality between the non-state-owned sector and the state-owned sector. Financial market imperfections have exacerbated the deterioration of inequality. On the whole, the government, which has long held a strong position in macro distribution, dominates the formulation of monetary policy. Financial market imperfections have aggravated the uneven distribution of the growth effect of monetary policy and worsened inequality. Monetary policy should be combined with credit policy to tackle income and wealth inequality by mitigating the unequal distribution of financial resources. Tackling inequality requires coordination between direct and effective fiscal policy and monetary policy whose effects are evenly distributed, but China has little experience in coordinating fiscal and monetary policy to tackle income inequality.

The areas of fiscal policy most closely related to financial structure are sovereign bonds and non-sovereign bonds. Local governments use local financing platforms as a bridge for credit and bond financing, 85% of project financing funds rely on bank loans, while other parts rely on corporate loans and financial products. 85% of project funding needs are met by bank loans, and the rest by corporate loans and wealth management products. With the gradual decline of the dominant position of large state-owned banks in China, new banking financial institutions, such as joint-stock commercial banks and urban commercial banks, have gradually grown up, providing financing channels for "urban construction investment bonds" issued by local governments. The growing bond market has become the main market in which corporate bonds in the "urban construction investment bonds" category are traded.

China's financial structure is highly dependent on the banking industry, which has resulted in a high degree of monetization (M2/GDP). With the maturation of China's financial structure, such as the perfection of financial institutions and an increase in the types of financial products, China has experienced extensive financial disintermediation. China is an open market economy led by the government. Imperfections in the financial structure further weaken the resource allocation and price discovery functions, and inhibit the self-improvement function of the industrial structure. Under the basic thought of reasonable regulation and moderate relaxation, China's financial structure still has much room for improvement, which creates conditions for China to coordinate macro policies and promote spontaneous and healthy adjustments to its industrial structure in the future.

Deepen Our Understanding of Global Financial Governance

In the period of global financial change after the financial crisis, we must reflect deeply on our performance in the crisis in terms of global financial concepts, models, and patterns. In the long run, further changes are needed to provide a solid foundation for sustainable economic development.

First, the scale and operating mode of global finance will change dramatically. As a consequence of the financial crisis, the nominal value of these financial assets has shrunk sharply, and the scale of bank assets will also shrink rapidly. Financial derivatives trading, bond trading, leverage financing, and other off-balance sheet activities will gradually decrease. With the separation of Citigroup into Citicorp and Citi Holdings, the universal banking model aggressively pursued by traditional banks has also been called into question.

Second, the global financial market will undergo structural changes, and the trend toward diversification of international finance is inevitable. The United States United States was hit hard by the financial crisis, with a large number of enterprises going bankrupt, unemployment rising, and its economic strength declining significantly. In response to the crisis, the Eurozone adopted expansionary fiscal and monetary policies, which to some extent contributed to the overall recovery of the region's economy. But the rise of the euro has yet to be further tested by time, as weak economic growth and rising fiscal deficits have pushed Eurozone countries such as Iceland and Greece into sovereign debt crisis. After years of efforts, Asia is emerging as the world's center of economic growth, in sharp contrast to declining growth rates in the United States, Europe, and Japan. Meanwhile, Asia's position in the international financial market is gradually rising. Its huge amount of official foreign exchange reserves plays a pivotal role in the global financial market, and the responsible attitude of major countries such as China in several crises has been fully recognized and praised by the international community. Therefore, as the world redefines the structure of financial markets, Asia will receive more attention. Major cities such as Tokyo, China, Hong Kong, and Shanghai will usher in new development opportunities, and diversification of the global financial landscape has become an inevitable trend.

Third, sovereign funds are emerging as a new force in the international financial market. For a long time, the international financial market has been the stage for Western private financial capital. As a consequence of the financial crisis, the strength of these private financial institutions has been greatly weakened in the process of deleveraging and nationalization. After the outbreak of the 2007 financial crisis, major financial institutions in Western developed countries sought capital injections from sovereign funds. Non-Western sovereign wealth funds, including the Abu Dhabi Investment Council, the Kuwait Investment Board, China Investment Corporation, and Government of Singapore Investment Corporation successively acquired stakes in financial giants such as Citigroup and Goldman Sachs, with investments amounting to tens of billions of dollars, greatly stabilizing the international financial market.

Fourth, the global financial regulatory framework urgently needs to be rebuilt. The crisis has fully exposed the weaknesses and loopholes of the original Basel Accords, making all countries realize the importance of consolidated regulation, unified regulation, and global regulation. At present, almost all financial stock institutions, financial markets, and financial instruments will be properly regulated, a thought that has been reflected and implemented in the financial regulatory reform programs issued by the United States and the European Union. In addition, in response to the rapid and large-scale flow of capital, international consultation and coordination on regulation will be unprecedentedly close, and bilateral and multilateral financial cooperation will become an important form of international finance.

Of course, the development of the global financial landscape in the above four dimensions will be a complex process of competition, cooperation, and dynamic game among economic, financial, political, military, and other forces, involving core and sensitive issues such as the world's standard currency, international reserves and balance of payments. This requires countries to constantly seek cooperation amid competition, seek common ground while shelving differences, and work together to prevent another global financial crisis and promote the sustainable development of the world economy, and also requires major developed and developing countries to assume their responsibilities and fulfill their obligations in relation to promoting consultation and establishing a new international financial order.

Fifth, establish a global alliance of central banks. With the deepening of globalization, one country's monetary policy will inevitably affect other countries. At this point, there should be a more diversified portfolio of international reserve currencies. In the context of the financial crisis, it is necessary and imperative to establish a global alliance of central banks as a lender of last resort to important financial institutions in the world. The global alliance of central banks performs the functions of correctly guiding the global macroeconomy, monitoring financial transaction data and regulating financial institutions, conducts financial innovation through global financial governance, and is responsible for overall organization and coordination.

6.2.2 *Improve Our Ability to Participate in Global Financial Governance*

The Financial Structure Needs to Be Further Optimized

At present, China's financial structure is still dominated by banks, which is mainly reflected in the following aspects: bank assets make up for the bulk of all financial assets; although the development of capital markets has increased the proportion of direct financing, the dominant position of indirect finance has not been fundamentally changed; the development of insurance, trust, and financial leasing is slow; social financing risks are highly concentrated in the banking industry. An excess supply of monetary assets will undoubtedly squeeze the paths and space for social finance, reduce the ability and motivation to innovate in finance, and contribute to high levels of corporate debt, which is not conducive to the optimization of the financial structure and the development of the real economy. Resources are allocated largely to state-owned enterprises and large enterprises, thus excluding most SMEs and private enterprises from organized financial markets. This has objectively spawned various forms of private financial markets, and increased the difficulty of financial regulation while exacerbating the instability of the financial system.

China's Urban–Rural Dual Financial Structure Needs to Be Reduced

On the one hand, due to a low degree of industrialization, insignificant economic returns, high information costs and a lack of sufficient collateral and alternative means to prevent risks, financial institutions are often reluctant to conduct business in these rural and underdeveloped areas, resulting in "market failure"; on the other hand, due to reasons such as adverse selection and moral hazard, funds injected through government subsidies and donations from non-profit organizations are used inefficiently in practice, and defaults occur from time to time, which affects the recycling of funds and lowers the overall credit status of rural and underdeveloped areas, resulting in "government failure." These two "failures," in turn, will produce a significant siphon effect, causing the reverse flow of funds from rural areas to cities and from the west to the east, and further hindering local economic development and the formation of a reasonable and balanced financial structure.

Therefore, if China's finance is to play an important role in overcoming the middle-income trap and achieve its strategic rise after the international financial crisis, it must first focus on solving its own structural problems, constantly optimize the internal structure of the financial sector, establish a unified national financial market, and promote the healthy development of the financial system.

To Meet the SDR Challenge and Strengthen the Position of the Renminbi

The inclusion of the renminbi in the International Monetary Fund (IMF)'s Special Drawing Rights (SDR) basket marks the transformation of the global financial system, which is an important milestone in the integration of China's economy into the global financial system, as well as recognition for the progress China has made in monetary and financial system reform since the start of its reform and opening-up nearly four decades ago. But we must be soberly aware that this move is still largely symbolic. It will take time for the renminbi to truly become an important international currency. In the long term, the attractiveness of RMB assets will largely depend on the strength of China's economy. In the short term, the main challenge for the renminbi to join the SDR basket is to maintain a certain degree of exchange rate stability while allowing market forces to play a role.

6.2.3 Characteristics of the Development and Evolution of the International Monetary System and Financial Structures

Judging by the experience of various countries in overcoming the middle-income trap and the lessons learnt therefrom as discussed earlier in this book, the characteristics of the development and evolution of the structure of the international financial system and the financial structures and economies of various countries are worth learning from. To overcome the middle-income trap and expand the middle-income group, China needs to adopt various policies and measures. The core position of finance in a modern economy is determined by its special nature and role. Finance is an important lever for macroeconomic regulation and control in a modern economy. In modern economic life, monetary funds, as important economic resources and wealth, have become the lifeblood and medium that knit together the economic life of the whole society. In the important stage of overcoming the middle-income trap, China needs to accelerate the reform of the financial system. Building a more perfect financial system is of great significance for the rational allocation of resources, the promotion of economic growth, the maintenance of social equity and even the eventual overcoming of the middle-income trap.

An Analysis of Structural Change in and the Reform of the International Monetary System

In July 1944, delegates from major Western countries established the system at the United Nations Monetary and Financial Conference. In order to rebuild the international monetary order after World War II, the international community led by the United States and Britain established the Bretton Woods system through multilateral agreements. The main contents of the Bretton Woods system included: (1) the creation of the International Monetary Fund (IMF), the coordination of international monetary relations, especially the supervision of the exchange rate policies of various countries; (2) the implementation of an adjustable pegged exchange rate system based on gold and centered on the dollar; (3) when member countries found themselves in balance of payments difficulties, the IMF could provide short-term credit to supplement their international liquidity.

The Bretton Woods system was a gold exchange standard based on the dollar and gold. Its essence was to establish an international monetary system centered on the dollar. Its basic contents included the pegging of the dollar to gold, the pegging of other countries' currencies to the dollar, and the implementation of a fixed exchange rate system. The Bretton Woods system was actually an international gold exchange standard, also known as the gold-dollar standard, that is, the operation of the Bretton Woods system was closely related to the reputation and status of the dollar. It put the dollar at the center of the postwar international monetary system, the dollar became the "equivalent" of gold, the United States assumed the obligation to exchange for gold at the official rate, and the currencies of other countries could only relate to gold through the dollar to serve as world currencies. Since then, the US dollar has become a means of payment in international settlement and the world's primary reserve currency.

After the United States stopped redeeming dollars from foreign governments in the early 1970s, many countries unpegged their currencies from the dollar, and implemented to a floating exchange rate system, bringing the Bretton Woods system to the brink of collapse. In 1976, at the initiative and under the auspices of the IMF, the international community reached the Jamaica Agreement, announcing the non-monetization of gold, and recognized the legalization of the floating exchange rate systems implemented by various countries, which marked that the international financial system once again entered a turbulent era, not bound by global multilateral agreements. Because the Bretton Woods system was based on the convertibility of the dollar into gold, and required other countries to abandon the independence of their monetary policies, when the US balance of payments deficit kept widening and the convertibility of the dollar into gold could not be maintained, its continued existence was significantly challenged. Since the Jamaica Agreement was concluded in 1976, the international monetary system as a whole has not changed fundamentally. With the continuous improvement of international economic and financial integration, especially the rapid development of economic regionalization, some local changes have taken place in the system, mainly as follows.

First, the international exchange rate system is basically characterized by the coexistence of multiple exchange rate regimes dominated by floating exchange rate regimes. At present, there are three kinds of basic exchange rate regimes in the world: The first is independent floating exchange rate regimes, which are implemented by the United States, the European Union, Japan, and some emerging market economies; the second is fixed exchange rate regimes, which are implemented by countries with currency boards and traditional pegged exchange rate regimes, and countries that have abandoned their currencies (e.g., countries within the European Union and dollarized countries); the third is "middle way" regimes, that is, regimes between floating and fixed exchange rates, such as crawling pegs, bands, and managed floats, which are mainly implemented by developing economies that are strongly outward oriented or suffer from severe inflation.

As the United States, Europe, and Japan play an important role in the global economy, their floating regimes determine the nature of the international exchange rate system. For individual countries, the benefits of a floating exchange rate regime are mainly reflected in the ability to maintain the independence of monetary policy and correct to some extent balance of payments disequilibria via automatic adjustments. However, from the perspective of international financial stability, it has at least two defects: first, frequent fluctuations in exchange rates will adversely affect normal international trade and investment activities by greatly increasing the exchange costs and risks of global economic activities; second, it is likely to cause exchange rate policy conflicts in that the country will seek trade expansion by devaluing its currency so as to advance its own interests at the expense of other countries.

Second, the international financial market plays a significant role in balance of payments adjustment. In the era of the Bretton Woods system, due to the strict financial control implemented by various countries, the role of the international financial market in balance of payments adjustment was relatively limited, adjustment for current account deficits in many countries mainly depended on fiscal and monetary policies. In the event of a serious deficit, exchange rate policy could be used to a limited extent and a certain amount of short-term credit could be obtained from the IMF. However, since the 1970s, with the rapid development of the international financial market, countries have been able to easily make up their current account deficits through international commercial financing, thus avoiding adjustment measures such as fiscal tightening that could affect domestic economic stability. As a market-based arrangement, the international financial market provides abundant international liquidity, thus greatly reducing the cost of balance of payments adjustment. But on the other hand, it also creates new uncertainties. Chief among them is that it allows some countries to relax internal constraints, abuse fiscal expansionary policies, and delay necessary domestic economic reforms and adjustments. The result is that not only do their current account deficits eventually become unmanageable, but they are often burdened with heavy external debt and even become a source of financial instability.

Third, the lack of effective regulation of international capital flows has become a major source of international financial instability. Since the 1980s, with the continuous relaxation of capital controls in various countries, international capital flows have expanded rapidly. The daily trading volume in international capital markets has exceeded $1.5 trillion. Countries to which capital flows, especially developing countries, often suffer from the "overeating-starvation syndrome," that is, when the prospects for economic growth in some countries are good, international capital will flood into these countries; when these countries show signs of crisis due to excessive capital inflows, international capital will leave quickly. This often causes internal and external imbalances in the economy of these countries, and ultimately leads to monetary and financial turmoil. In addition, before and after a crisis, due to the lack of effective regulation, a surge of speculative and/or short-term capital inflows deepens the crisis in relevant countries, and plays a central role in the international transmission of the crisis.

Fourth, global monetary and financial cooperation has achieved little success, while regional monetary integration has made remarkable progress. The main channel for global monetary and financial cooperation is the G7 summit. In general, this coordination mechanism is often a mere formality and empty talk, with little substance. In recent years, the IMF and BIS have tried to play a more active role, but with little success, as they have no real binding authority over member countries. In contrast, regional monetary cooperation has made remarkable progress. After decades of hard work, the euro was successfully launched in 1999, and a unified central bank and monetary policy framework has been established within the Eurozone. It is worth noting that the birth of the euro had a significant demonstration effect. In recent years, in regions such as Latin America and Central and Eastern Europe, some countries have begun to adopt dollarization and a currency board, or to implement a fixed exchange rate regime. Although the financial crisis two years ago forced Argentina to abandon its monetary board, it seems that this trend has not changed.

Fifth, the financial hegemony of the dollar remains largely intact, but it is being challenged. International economic transactions have always relied on the currencies of a few sovereign states as means of international payment and reserve assets. The dollar is the most important of these currencies. Since the creation of the Bretton Woods system, the dollar has achieved global financial hegemony. Although the dollar's share of international reserves has declined over the past half-century or more, it is still around 60%.

Since the 2008 financial crisis, reform of the international monetary system has been on the agenda. Frequent fluctuations and continuous decline in the real value of the US dollar are an inherent defect of the current international monetary system based on the dollar, and also a major cause of global economic and financial imbalances. The 2008 financial crisis has completely exposed this major defect. The euro could have challenged the dollar's position, but the European debt crisis has severely dented the attractiveness of the euro. In view of the fact that the European and US Debt Crises have caused great fluctuations in the global financial market, confidence in the euro and the dollar, the two major reserve currencies, has been called into question, and the international community has not been able to find a replacement currency, many analysts have suggested expanding the SDR basket and its use as the direction of the reform of the international monetary system, so as to improve the representativeness, fairness, and stability of the global monetary system. China, India, Russia, Brazil, and South Africa believe that, given the need for a more balanced representation of the current world economic landscape by the current international monetary system, the inclusion of emerging market currencies in the SDR basket is a general trend.

Major countries and international organizations, while questioning the defects of the existing international monetary system, have put forward some constructive reform plans. The first is to move toward a more diversified international monetary system, give greater play to the role of currencies other than the dollar, and impose stricter discipline on international currencies; the second is to establish an international monetary system based on SDR; the third is to introduce a super-sovereign currency, which requires countries to surrender monetary sovereignty. The latter two plans require a high degree of international coordination and are less likely to be implemented.

In the future, the international monetary reserve system may be structured as "one supreme and four strong," with the dollar remaining the global reserve currency, the euro, and the pound being the two largest reserve currencies in Europe, and the renminbi and the yen being the two largest reserve currencies in Asia.

Looking ahead at the reform and development of the international monetary system, in the near future (2020), it will be difficult to shift the center of gravity for the international monetary system away from the dollar, but the international monetary system is in a period of preparation for drastic changes, which has a significant impact on the structural development of China's monetary and financial system. In the medium-to-long term (2050), with the continuous development of economic globalization, (2050), with the continuous development of economic globalization, economic ties between countries will be closer and deeper. Especially with China becoming the largest economy around 2026, it is expected that China's voice in the reform and development of the national monetary system will be substantially increased. How to build an international monetary system adapted to global economic integration and informatization has become a key decision-making issue for currency and financial strategists and central governments in various countries.

Basic Characteristics of the Development and Evolution of the Financial Structures and Economies of Various Countries

The financial structure theory describes and analyzes the process and law of financial development. It was one of the earliest and most influential theories of financial development. Its founder and main representative was Raymond W. Goldsmith, whose masterwork was Financial Structure and Development published in 1969.

After comparing the financial history and data of 35 countries for a period of more 100 years, Goldsmith creatively proposed the stock and flow indexes to measure the financial structure and development level of a country; he conducted the first-ever quantitative and comparative study of differences in financial development among countries; he studied and revealed the internal path and law of financial deepening; he showed that there was a significant relationship between financial development and economic growth and proposed the research direction. He opined that different financial interrelations ratios in a free enterprise economy produced radically different types of financial structures. He summarized various financial phenomena into three basic aspects: financial instruments, financial institutions, and financial structure. He defined "financial instruments" as evidences of claims against other economic units or ownership in them, "financial institutions" as financial intermediaries whose assets and liabilities are mainly composed of financial instruments, and "financial structure" as the institutional and instrument composition of an economy's financial sector. He opined that the essence of financial development was change in the financial structure, and studying financial development was to study of the change process and trend of the financial structure. Through comparative analysis, Goldsmith came to the conclusion: There exists only one major path of financial development, a path marked by certain regularities in change in the financial structure; a path on which different countries have started at different dates and along which they have traveled at different speed; and a path from which they have deviated only to a minor extent, deviations being primarily connected with war finance and with inflation. In terms of research methodology and the basic structure, the financial structure theory has had a profound influence on the study of finance and financial development.

Goldsmith reduced the theoretical discussion of the effect of financial superstructure on economic development into a judgment, that is, the financial superstructure, in the form of both primary and secondary securities, facilitates the migration of funds to the best users, i.e., to the place where funds will yield the highest social return. In this sense, financial superstructure accelerates economic growth and improves economic performance.

Financial development plays an active role in economic development. The emergence of financial instruments and the establishment of financial institutions have expanded the scope of financial assets, resulting in the separation of savings and investment. The separation of savings and investment can improve investment returns and increase the ratio of capital formation to GDP; meanwhile, financial activities through the two channels of savings and investment can boost economic growth. The emergence of financial instruments has separated savings and investment into two independent functions. This special division of labor overcomes the contradiction of imbalance between revenue and expenditure in funds movement. On the one hand, this allows a unit to have a level of investment greater or smaller than its savings, so as not to be bound by the limits of its ability to save; on the other hand, this brings added value to savers in that savings are not only a store of wealth, but also increase income. For this reason, both savers and investors can accept the social division of labor brought by financial activities. Analysis from this perspective is mainly applicable to primary financial instruments such as bonds and stocks issued by non-financial economic units such as industrial and commercial enterprises, national statistical departments and governments. The optimization of resource allocation and the growth-inducing effects of financial institutions on the economy stem from the rearrangement of the capital supply and demand of savers and investors.

The promotion of economic growth by developed financial institutions is achieved through the two channels of increasing savings and the overall level of investment and allocating funds effectively. The more developed the financial structure, and the more choices and opportunities provided by financial instruments and financial institutions, the stronger people's desire to engage in financial activities, and the faster savings growth. With a certain amount of capital, the more active financial activities are, the more efficient the use of capital will be. Therefore, the more developed finance is, the stronger the penetration of financial activities into the economy, and the faster economic growth and economic development. Attaching importance to the supply of financial instruments and emphasizing the normal operation of the financial mechanism are the core of the financial structure theory, and also the key to the development of finance and the promotion of economic growth. This view was inherited by the later financial development theory.

6.2.4 *China's Financial Structure Is Presented with Historical Opportunities for Transformation and Upgrading*

Overall Situation of China's Financial Size and Financial Structure

Since the start of reform and opening-up, China's total financial assets have increased rapidly. In 1978, China's total financial assets were only 325.74 billion Yuan, accounting for 88.55% of its GDP. In 2016, China's total financial assets reached 230.3756 trillion Yuan, accounting for 309.59% of the year's GDP, about 707 times those in 1978. In terms of the relative quantity measured by the financial interrelations ratio (FIR), China's financial size has also been increasing. The so-called financial interrelations ratio refers to the ratio of total financial assets to national wealth at a certain point in time. It reflects the relationship between a country's financial superstructure and its economic infrastructure. Table 2 lists China's financial interrelations ratio for the relevant years from 1978 to 2016. As can be seen from Table 2, China's financial interrelations ratio increased from 0.9 in 1978 to 2.77 in 2006, then gradually declined, began to recover in 2013, and rose to 3.09 in 2016.

However, growth in the size of China's financial assets is mainly due to a simple expansion in the number of financial assets within the framework of the original financial structure and financial system. Although China's financial size has grown rapidly, China's financial structure has not improved accordingly and is unreasonable in many ways.

The Organizational Function Structure of the Financial System Needs to Be Upgraded

The organizational function structure of the financial system means the forms of the financial sector, including banking, insurance, trust, securities, and leasing. Since the start of reform and opening-up, China's financial sector has developed from a banking industry into a complete financial sector system covering banking, securities, insurance, trust, and leasing. But the structure of China's financial sector is very uncoordinated. Specifically, the banking industry is dominant, and the proportion of other industries within the financial sector is lower than normal. In particular, the development of the trust industry and leasing industry

Table 2 China's financial interrelations ratio (FIR) from 1978 to 2016

Year	*1978*	*1997*	*1998*	*2006*	*2009*	*2010*	*2011*	*2012*	*2013*	*2014*	*2015*	*2016*
Balance of finance assets	326	18379	21432	60000	78800	95300	113300	133622	151355	172336	199345	230376
GDP	362	7446	7940	21631	34090	40151	47288	53912	59042	64479	68264	74413
FIR	0.90	2.47	2.70	2.77	2.31	2.37	2.40	2.48	2.56	2.67	2.92	3.09

Note Both the balance of financial assets and GDP are measured in billions of Renminbi
Source China Statistical Yearbook, China Financial Yearbook

is slow, coordination between industries is inadequate, and the overall quality of industries is low.

Because the banking industry provides indirect finance and the securities industry provides direct finance, the dominance of the banking industry has caused a serious imbalance between direct finance and indirect finance in China. The composition of financial assets is very unreasonable. In 2016, loans and promissory notes accounted for 76.18% of total social financing, while equity and bond financing accounted for only 23.82%. The balance of bank loans and promissory notes accounted for 85.67% of the existing funds for social financing at the end of 2016, while the market value of corporate stocks and bond balance accounted for only 14.33%, which was far lower than in the United States and the United Kingdom (73 and 62%, respectively) where direct finance was dominant, and also lower than in Germany and Japan (39 and 44%, respectively) where indirect finance was dominant. From the perspective of household investment in financial assets, bank deposits account for 64% of the total, while stocks, bonds and funds, and other investments account for less than 14%. Among household investment in financial assets in the United States, stocks, funds, and pension money invested into capital markets together account for nearly 70%.

The Organizational Scale and Structure of China's Financial System Need to Be Optimized

The concentration of financial institutions in China is significantly higher than normal. The proportion of large financial institutions is too high, while small- and medium-sized financial institutions are small in number and lagging behind in development. With the deepening of economic reform, China's SMEs have made great progress, accounting for 99% of the total number of enterprises in the country and contributing up to 50% of the development of the national economy. With the development of these SMEs, a large number of small- and medium-sized financial institutions are urgently needed to finance them. However, at present, China's financial institutions are still mainly large state-owned financial institutions, and financial business is highly concentrated in these large state-owned financial institutions. The proportion of state-owned financial institutions is higher than normal, market concentration is higher than normal, the proportion of local small- and medium-sized financial institutions is rising slowly, and non-bank financial institutions need further development.

The Shareholding Structure of China's Microfinance Enterprises Needs to Be Optimized

China's financial property rights structure is very unreasonable, and state-owned financial institutions are predominant. China's financial system reform is carried out by gradually introducing additional participants into the system without undermining existing vested interests in the system. We should not touch the interests of state-owned banks that play a leading role in the financial structure. Instead, we should gradually relax market access conditions for emerging commercial banks, and even loosen restrictions on the proportion of foreign ownership, so as to gradually expand the number and size of market-oriented financial institutions, and allow market competition within a certain scope. Meanwhile, we should gradually deepen the reform of the property rights system of state-owned banks and improve the corporate governance structure. In the whole financial property rights structure, state-owned financial institutions have an absolute monopoly.

From the perspective of the development of the national economy as a whole, the result of China's gradual reform is that the proportion of state-owned enterprises in the national economy continues has been declining, while the proportion of collective economy, private economy, and other economic components has been rising. In order to win in the competition of the market economy, the non-state-owned economy represented by the private economy is increasingly pursuing technological progress in its production process, and urgently needs large amounts of money to support its R&D efforts. However, financial institutions dominated by state ownership still mainly provide financial support to large and medium-sized state-owned enterprises. Corporate bond issuance and stock listing policies are generally favorable to large enterprises, especially state-owned enterprises. A significant asymmetry exists between the financial supply structure and demand structure. The financing difficulties of China's non-state-owned economy greatly diminish its prospects for further rapid growth, thus affecting the sustained, rapid, and healthy development of the whole national economy.

The Structure of China's Financial Markets Is in Need of Strategic Adjustments

Financial markets, also known as "capital markets," are markets for financing where funds are allocated between capital suppliers and demanders through credit instruments, including money markets and capital markets. According to international experience in financial market development, money markets are generally developed earlier than capital markets, and finally a situation where "both money markets and capital markets are strong" is created. However, for China, although the development of money markets started earlier than capital markets, they have developed much slower than capital markets, and the development of the two is separated. Capital markets are stronger than money markets in terms of both trading volume and policy orientation. The inadequate development of money markets not only weakens the basic operation of money markets and affects macro-control by the central bank and the functions of interest rates, but also has many negative effects on the financial order and undermines the foundation for the coordinated development of money markets and capital markets. In the past two years, although China has emphasized the development of money markets and achieved some results, the overall pattern of money markets lagging behind capital markets has not changed.

The Spatial Layout of China's Financial System Urgently Needs to Be Optimized

China's financial spatial structure is unreasonable, which is mainly reflected in the fact that national financial are geographically scattered, regional financial centers are divided by non-market forces, especially financial development in urban and rural areas is not coordinated, and financial development in the eastern, central and western regions is also not coordinated. Meanwhile, the development of Internet mobile payment and urbanization has accelerated financial liquidity. From the perspective of urban and rural financial development, similar to the dual structure of the Chinese economy, China's financial structure has two very different parts in that urban and rural financial development is extremely and increasingly uncoordinated. Rural finance has been subject to very severe constraints, which is mainly manifested as follows: (1) The closure and consolidation of a large number of county-level financial institutions have led to the shrinkage and even "hollowing-out" of the county-level financial system, and in many places rural credit cooperatives are the only financial institutions. (2) The amount of bank credit funds committed is insufficient, and there has been a massive outflow of funds from rural areas. Since 2004, agricultural loans have been mainly issued by rural credit cooperatives, and the amount of funds used by state-owned commercial banks for agricultural loans has been very small. Because state-owned commercial banks have taken the authority to approve loans away from their county-level branches, most of the deposits held by their county-level branches have gone to cities, resulting in the striking "de-agriculturalization" of rural funds. The massive outflow of funds from rural areas where funds are already in short supply has further widened the supply–demand gap for rural credit funds and exacerbated the supply–demand imbalance for rural funds. (3) The functions of rural finance have been weakened, financial products are few, financial services are lacking in variety, there is basically only traditional deposit and loan business, and there is only a very limited selection of intermediate and foreign exchange business. (4) Rural capital markets have not yet developed. At present, securities companies only have securities service departments in a few economically developed county-level cities, and the conditions necessary for farmers to participate in securities investment are virtually nonexistent. Due to high barriers to entry into the Main Board, a large number of SMEs in rural areas have difficulty gaining access to capital markets to obtain finance, and thus difficulty finding long-term capital support.

From the perspective of the regional distribution of the financial structure, financial development in the eastern, central, and western regions is extremely uncoordinated. On the one hand, under China's state-owned property rights-based financial system, the establishment of financial institutions is mainly based on administrative divisions, resulting in the structural convergence of financial institutions in economically developed regions and economically poor regions. For example, the establishment of the four major state-owned commercial banks is based on an administrative hierarchy that makes no distinction between the eastern, central, and western regions, which inevitably leads to the waste of financial resources. On the other hand, because the eastern region is more economically developed, capital is overly biased toward the eastern coastal areas, while only a small portion of the capital goes to the central and western regions where growth is slow and even declining, which is not conducive to the development of the western region and the reduction of regional disparities.

The Maturity Structure and Risk Structure of China's Finance Urgently Need to Be Optimized

China is in a critical period for economic structural upgrading. A lot of large-scale infrastructure and information system infrastructure urgently need the support of long-term funds, which in turn need the support of a financial market environment with stable returns but low risks. China's social security funds and insurance funds are long-term funds, but because of system and mechanism constraints, they have difficulty meeting the needs of long-term construction. China's banking system raises short-term funds such as household deposits, but it invests heavily in long-term construction because of land mortgages, government credit guarantees, etc. On the whole, the maturity structure of China's finance needs to be optimized to reduce systemic risk in finance.

6.3 Uniqueness and Advantages of Development Finance

Over the years, through the practice of serving national strategies, CDB has discovered a new form of development finance that links the government and the market, and makes up for the defects of commercial finance and policy-based finance, and established its unique position in China's financial arrangement. This highlights its indispensability and irreplaceability in China's financial arrangement and overcoming the middle-income trap. Specifically, the uniqueness of CDB in China's financial arrangement is mainly reflected in the following aspects.

6.3.1 Uniqueness of Development Finance in China's Financial Arrangement

Policy-Serving Nature of Business Objectives

The policy-serving nature of development finance is specifically embodied in areas covered by development finance. Internally, it supports the development of the national economy and the upgrading of the industrial structure, improves and cultivates market systems, alleviates and resolves contradictions in economic development, and improves the welfare of the whole people; externally, it supports international economic cooperation and promotes the implementation of China's economic security and diplomatic strategies. Development finance is a tool to serve national policy, so it is inevitable that it is distinctly "political" in nature.

The most basic reason for the existence of development finance is to help achieve the government's strategic goals as a vehicle for the government's will. With the help of development finance, the government acts on gaps or weak links that are not covered by the market mechanism, and achieves the effective transfer and allocation of funds from a national strategic height, so as to enable construction in social bottleneck areas. Specifically, development finance implements national policy objectives, supports industries and project construction that have a significant impact on national economic development and are encouraged by policies internally, and actively supports international economic cooperation externally. In the process of supporting economic development, development finance makes overall arrangements for financing, adjusts business strategies and directions in time, and always uses loans in a manner that responds to the requirements of national industrial policies and structural adjustments, so as to better serve China's economic development and ultimately improve the living standards of the whole people.

As a tool to implement the government's policy objectives, development finance depends primarily on whether the government's policies for promoting economic development are clear, and whether the policy objectives set for development finance institutions are correct. Only when policies are clear and policy objectives are appropriate, can we ensure that development finance institutions play a positive role in promoting the economy. According to development economics, in order to achieve an economic takeoff and complete industrialization and modernization in a relatively short period of time, and catch up with or even overtake developed countries, latecomer countries must strongly intervene in economic activities and consciously guide economic development. A very important means is to formulate industrial policies and guide the rationalization and rapid upgrading of the industrial structure through policies, instead of letting let the market run its course and the economy develop freely. The investment orientation of development finance shows not only the regulatory tools currently used by the government but also the government's judgment on future industrial development planning and economic trends. Successful development finance institutions are, in a manner of speaking, pioneers in implementing government intentions and plans through financial means.

A Targeted Choice of Business Areas

Development finance is "policy-oriented," and its choice of business areas generally does not follow commercial principles and is highly targeted. In developed countries, the government limits the scope of business of development finance institutions through independent legislation. With the development and change of economic conditions, the business areas of development finance institutions may be adjusted, but the adjustment is based on the change of the strategic objectives of national development. In this case, the law will also be adjusted accordingly.

According to international practice, development finance generally does not go directly into highly mature business areas, but starts from immature markets. It builds markets in places where there are no markets, makes full use of and improves markets in places where there are markets, and uses financing as a lever to channel private capital to areas prioritized for support by the State, so as to effectively fill gaps in financial markets in weak links and backward areas. In both developing and developed countries, as long as there are bottleneck areas and the allocation of resources by the market mechanism is flawed, development finance will be needed to accomplish tasks that cannot be accomplished solely by relying on the market and commercial finance, achieve government objectives, and promote coordinated economic and social development.

In the early stages of economic development, the market foundation is not sound. In order to implement the "catch-up strategy," the government must concentrate part of its financial resources on the basic areas of the economy, and guide the development of the economy. In the early stages of economic development in developing countries, there is a vicious circle, that is, due to economic backwardness, developing countries have low national income, which leads to low savings, which further leads to low investment, which in turn leads to low income. In order to break the vicious circle of economic backwardness, backward countries must concentrate limited financial resources on supporting the development of basic industries and key industries, and basically pursue the "heavy industry first" strategy in the early stages of industrialization. Basic industries and heavy industry are characterized by large investments, long payback periods, and huge positive externalities. An enormous amount of long-term funds is the fundamental guarantee for the implementation of this strategy. However, in a financial environment where funds are extremely scarce, the use of funds by general commercial financial institutions tends to be short term and exploitative. It is therefore necessary for development finance institutions to implement national policies to provide long-term loans in these areas to promote economic development.

While providing strong credit support for social bottleneck areas and promoting healthy and coordinated economic and social development, development finance constantly promotes institutional improvement and innovation, the perfection of the market system, and the betterment of the economic environment, and strives to create a virtuous circle between the activities of development finance and market building, mechanism transformation, and institutional reform.

Marketization of Business Practices

In today's world, the market mechanism is the main way of allocating economic resources. Despite the possibility of failure, the market mechanism is the most efficient way of allocating social resources. An important reason for the success of development financial institutions is that they respect the market and make up for market failure, rather than trying to replace or interfere with the market. As mentioned above, development finance institutions have dual business objectives. While striving to achieve policy objectives, they make a small profit to ensure their sustainable operation. But development finance institutions always adhere to the principles of complementarity, neutrality, and no loss, which is an important guarantee for their effective functioning.

The policy-serving nature of development finance determines that they follow different financing principles than commercial finance institutions. Development finance is legally entitled to sovereign-level national credit, and national credit is the basis for the market-oriented operation of development finance. The sovereign-level credit of development finance is applied to capital markets and the bond markets to ensure the issuance of low-risk bonds that are easily accepted by the market in capital markets, so as to raise long-term stable and low-cost funds to provide financing assistance to key areas of national development, and to play a role in guiding funds in the process of market building by attracting commercial funds. Viewed from this angle, development finance plays an important role in that it builds a bridge between immature areas and future mature markets with national credit as the fulcrum. Development finance can also make national credit play a positive role through organization credit enhancement. National and government organization credit enhancement is a way of cooperation between development finance institutions and governments. Based on national credit, the two sides jointly build a new platform for resource allocation. The platform combines the organizational advantage of governments with the financing advantage of development finance, and relies on the reintegration of the credit system to control risks and losses, so as to achieve the specific economic and social development goals of governments.

Since the main mission of development finance is to fulfill policy intentions, provide financing and intellectual assistance in social bottleneck areas, and provide loans that are more reasonable than commercial finance, the primary purpose of development finance is not to make a profit. However, not intending to earn a profit does not mean that development finance institutions ignore profit or simply do not care about making a profit (this is a common misunderstanding regarding the operation of policy-based finance institutions). Development finance must maintain and enhance the national credit in actual operation. Therefore, only with excellent market performance, good asset quality, and sound management can we gain market trust and improve national credit ratings. Excellent market performance is also an important guarantee for maintaining and enhancing national credit, and is an important and basic means for achieving the sustainable development of development finance. In fact, in order not to burden the State's finances and also to expand their business, many development finance institutions attach importance to improving their profitability. Profitability improves the day-to-day operations of development finance institutions, and expands their scale and influence, so that they can better implement policy-related business and serve national strategic objectives.

Inductive Effect of Business Philosophy

Because the main mission of development finance is to implement national policy intentions and strategic objectives, act on market bottleneck areas, make up for institutional deficiencies, and support key areas and weak links, the investment orientation of development finance institutions indicates the country's long-term development goals. Commercial finance institutions believe that the financing of development finance institutions is supported by government policies and have privileged access to policy information. Therefore, the financing of development finance institutions can induce commercial finance institutions to extend loans. Backed by strong support from the State, commercial finance institutions will lower the threshold for the approval of projects in bottleneck areas and increase the supply of credit in these areas. Development finance can indirectly induce commercial finance institutions to lend to key industries in line with policy intentions or strategic objectives for the country's long-term development. Meanwhile, in some cases, if a project passes financing review by development finance institutions, commercial finance institutions will "take a free ride" by following suit, resulting in coordinated financing. This also shows an inductive effect. Development finance institutions first make inductive investments, and commercial finance institutions follow suit. Development finance institutions then shift their investments and start another cycle.

Meanwhile, development finance institutions make use of their advantages in macro industries to select excellent enterprises and improve the reputation of enterprises in the financing market, thus creating a mechanism whereby development finance has an inductive effect on the investment orientation of commercial finance. Although credit funds provided by development finance are incomparable with those provided by general commercial finance institutions in amount, they can guide the flow of social funds as a whole, thus playing a key role in adjusting the industrial structure, developing the important areas of the economy, and establishing social and public welfare undertakings.

6.3.2 Unique Advantages of Development Finance in Promoting the Balanced Growth of China's Economy

In view of the aggregate and structural imbalances in China's economic rebalancing, development finance has an irreplaceable advantage in China's economic rebalancing because it combines national credit with market operation, and advanced development finance concepts with China's national conditions.

Ease "Bottleneck" Constraints on Economic and Social Development, and Promote the Formation of Private Capital

As mentioned above, development finance is based on national credit, serves national economic development strategies and objectives, and uses various modern financial instruments to raise funds at home abroad and channel these funds to projects of a public nature such as infrastructure and basic industries. Development finance also guides the flow of commercial capital and private capital, and promotes the formation of private capital, thus becoming an important tool to break through bottleneck constraints on social and economic development. Meanwhile, development finance adheres to a market-oriented approach to using funds, forms a "hard budget constraint" on local governments and enterprises, and improves the investment efficiency of private capital. Furthermore, development finance can make full use of the financing and organizational advantages of national credit, accelerate the transformation of fiscal funds and private capital into construction capital, and promote the expansion of and improvement in the quality of private capital. As can be seen from CDB's development finance practice, under circumstances where limited public financial resources are available, the investment and financing functions of development finance can be used to make up for the shortfall in the government's public finances, alleviate "bottleneck" constraints on economic development, and promote the formation of private capital.

Promote Market Building and Institutional Improvement

To achieve balanced economic growth and promote the transformation of the mode of economic growth, we must properly handle the relationship between market regulation and government intervention in the allocation of social and economic resources. In economic development, the government and the market are not mutually substitutable and completely separated, but complement and penetrate each other. While ensuring that the market plays a fundamental role in resource allocation, we should complement market operation with moderate government intervention, so as to realize the optimal combination of market regulation and government intervention. For a long time, in addition to market failure, prominent problems facing China's economic development were gaps in and the defects and backwardness of the market system. Especially in the field of financial markets, due to the backwardness of micro institutions and financial infrastructure, the lack of qualified market entities, and the imperfection of basic credit institutions, a large amount of social savings cannot be turned into investment, and economic balance can only be achieved by expanding external demand. In order to solve these problems, we must resort to active institutional improvement instead of relying solely on spontaneous market regulation. Through financing, development finance combines the government, the market, and finance to create a joint force for improving micro institutions and financial infrastructure. The government credit characteristic of development finance determines that it does not enter highly mature markets to compete with commercial finance, but starts from immature markets. That is to say, it enters areas of investment and finance that have market defects and institutional defects such as legal person system defects but are promising, and actively uses and relies on national credit to cultivate markets, improve market conditions and the market environment, and carry out project construction, corporate governance structure development, market system development, institutional improvement, and credit system development. By participating in and cultivating sound market entities and perfect markets, development finance plays a role in "paving the way" and "bridging" for commercial finance, and promotes the conversion of savings into investment.

In terms of positive externalities, development finance is more inclined to pursue overall social benefits, and provides financing support to gaps or weak links where the "market fails," including providing leadership in the creation and improvement of financing service systems for SMEs and financing platforms for high-tech industries, and effectively serving the government's objectives, so it is a public good that has greater positive externalities. In terms of negative externalities, because the funds of commercial finance institutions are borrowed directly from households, they are likely to experience a bank run in the event of a crisis or loss, which may lead to economic instability and social unrest. By way of contrast, development finance institutions raise funds mainly through the issuance of financial bonds, creditors have a high tolerance for risk and are highly professional, so the scope and chain of crisis spread are much smaller than for commercial finance.

Improve the Efficiency of Resource Allocation

To achieve balanced economic growth and promote the transformation of the mode of economic growth, we must solve the problems of urban–rural imbalance, regional imbalance, and imbalance in industrial structure in the allocation of economic and financial resources, and improve the efficiency of resource allocation. The solutions to these problems include fiscal finance, commercial finance, and development finance. Financial finance is constrained by fiscal revenue and budget size; commercial finance, driven by a profit motive, may further exacerbate the imbalance in resource allocation. In comparison, development finance is conducive to achieving balanced resource allocation in terms of the goals, functions, and efficiency of resource allocation. First, development finance always look at things from the perspective of national strategies and the overall situation, aims at implementing national strategies rather than making a profit, and invests funds in areas of economic development where resources are scarce, such as supporting urbanization, promoting economic development in backward regions, and supporting high-tech pillar industries. Second, development finance not only promotes market building and project construction with government credit financing, but also embodies and enhances government credit with excellent market performance and support for economic and social development. Meanwhile, development finance can combine government credit and governments' ability to organize and coordinate with the strength of enterprises and markets, and effectively use and enlarge the functions of government credit in market building, so as to provide sustained financial support for the balanced and coordinated development of urban and rural areas, regions, and industrial structures.

Development finance can also effectively serve national economic strategic objectives and promote the soundness of microfinance institutions and the stability of the macrofinance system. According to international experience, due to the advantages in information, transaction costs, and other aspects that are unmatched by commercial finance, development finance can make up for the gap caused by the shortage of commercial finance. Especially in the presence of financial repression such as interest rate control and access restrictions, the ability and incentive of commercial finance to screen borrowers and shield risks through credit contracts are limited. Meanwhile, because of the homogenization of commercial finance risks under a unified regulatory system, risks are prone to "resonance," posing the danger of risks erupting. Development finance can make up for this regulatory deficiency and play a corrective role.

Smooth Out the Economic Cycle

In recent years, in the process of economic development, uncertainty about economic growth has increased, and the cyclical nature of economic growth has become increasingly obvious. Economic fluctuations are characterized by grossly "unbalanced" growth, that is, in each economic cycle, the expansion of the economic aggregate is accompanied by structural differentiation; conversely, the imbalance in economic development shrinks as the economy recedes. The financial crisis also shows that all kinds of financial organizations, including capital markets, commercial banks, etc., have behaved procyclically. Therefore, building a countercyclical macro-prudential policy framework has become a top priority for all countries in the world. Traditional tools for countercyclical macroeconomic regulation and micro intervention measures, which are mainly fiscal policy, monetary policy, and financial supervision, are subject to great uncertainty because they are targeted primarily at government departments and their effects are affected by many factors. Because development finance is oriented toward credit policy rather than profitability, it can flexibly increase or decrease the scale of lending and adjust the credit structure according to the needs of government macro-control. It has the directness and covertness of countercyclical regulation and can better accommodate the need to fine-tune credit supply. Meanwhile, development finance has different characteristics and requirements from commercial finance in terms of externalities, resource allocation, and crisis relief, and can accommodate the need to actively regulate the economic cycle, so it plays an important and unique complementary role in countercyclical regulation. Meanwhile, the financing mechanism of development finance whereby "the government selects the project entrance, and development finance incubates and realizes a market exit" has a demonstration effect in countercyclical regulation. When the economy is in a downturn or depression, and commercial finance adopts a tight credit policy because of its procyclical nature, development finance institutions can, in accordance with the needs of government macro-control, provide credit support to enterprises and areas that urgently need support from the government, ease financing constraints on enterprises, and help them normalize their investment and production activities, which in turn has a demonstration effect on the credit supply of commercial finance, and leads commercial finance institutions to increase loans to such enterprises. It can be seen that the directness, timeliness, and demonstration effect of development finance as a direct micro market entity in countercyclical regulation effectively compensate for the shortcomings of indirect regulation and control by government departments, making development finance a supplement to government macro-control.

Help the Country Achieve Its Foreign Policy Objectives

The above research shows that China's unbalanced economic growth is manifested not only as an internal imbalance, but also as an external imbalance. Therefore, in the process of rebalancing the economy, in order to adjust the external imbalance, in addition to solving the internal imbalance, we must implement a more proactive opening-up strategy, further intensify the implementation of the Go Out policy, and strengthen cooperation with energy and resources powers in Asia, Africa, and Latin America through the Go Out policy to ensure the supply of energy and resources for economic development. Meanwhile, we should drive China's exports of major equipment and the transfer of excess capacity, gain the initiative and advantages in fierce international competition, create favorable conditions for economic structural adjustment and industrial upgrading, and improve our ability to safely and efficiently utilize both domestic and international markets and resources. The practice of development finance in countries around the world shows that development finance has advantages that are irreplaceable by commercial and policy-based finance in serving national security and foreign trade development strategy, including the advantage in medium- and long-term project operations involving international M&As with the help of national credit, the advantage of being a development institution that complies with international rules and is recognized by international conventions, and the first-mover advantage of cooperating in national energy and resource areas that are difficult for commercial finance to access.

In summary, it is precisely because development finance is a market entity based on national credit that takes responsibility for implementing national economic policies in daily business activities, and aligns its credit policy with national goals that it can consciously increase or decrease the scale of lending and adjust the credit structure according to the needs of government macro-control. Development finance loans mainly go to infrastructure, basic industries, national pillar industries, high-tech industries, the construction of supporting projects, as well as SMEs. These areas are basic and source industries, which are at the top end of the industrial chain and can produce a strong domino effect. The multiplier effect of development finance is very significant because it can penetrate and influence all areas of the economy and society and fully amplify the contribution of capital accumulation through effective linkages between industries. Meanwhile, development finance can continuously promote credit system development, market building, institutional improvement, and so on through the financial innovation process, so it has significant economic externalities. To a large extent, development finance can significantly increase the output produced by factor inputs, so that the aggregate production function exhibits very strong increasing returns to scale. The basic path of its action on economic growth fully demonstrates that development finance can continuously influence economic growth more deeply and extensively in the long term, guide social resource allocation, and improve the targetedness and effectiveness of social resource allocation, so it plays an irreplaceable role in balancing the growth of China's economy and overcoming the middle-income trap.

6.3.3 *Accelerate the Building of Medium- and Long-Term Financing Systems for Development Finance*

Chen Yuan, vice chairman of the CPPCC National Committee and former chairman of CDB, pointed out that development finance institutions played an irreplaceable role in serving national development strategies, and that the design of China's financial industry system should not only conform to modern financial principles and the law of the market, but more importantly serve the purpose of governing and rejuvenating the country.

With China gradually becoming an important influencing factor in the international political and economic landscape, development finance has become an important means to serve national development strategies. In the important stages of China's urbanization, industrialization, and internationalization, development finance has formed the strategic goal of "an important means of national development strategy, an important medium of RMB internationalization, an important tool of national financial diplomacy, and an important force of global resource integration." Therefore, accelerating the building of a medium- and long-term financing system is of great significance for policy banks and development finance institutions to better serve national development strategies and participate in global resource allocation and economic governance. Throughout the course of global economic development, as important policy tools to compensate for market failure, policy-based and development finance institutions have long been present in many Western developed economies. No matter in developing or developed countries, and no matter in the stage of stable economic development or in the stage of coping with financial crisis, policy-based and development banks, as the mainstay of medium- and long-term investment and financing, are an indispensable part of the financial system and play an important role in moving the market. The task of national politics is to correct "market failure" by adopting certain intervention measures when the market is unable to generate social demand. In line with this, the task of policy-based and development finance is to solve the maturity mismatch risk that is common for development loans by issuing medium- and long-term bonds for direct finance, and provide long-term stable, sustained, and rapid financing support for infrastructure construction and other areas. As a developing country, China is still at the development stage economically developed countries such as the United States, Europe, and Japan were at 30–50 years ago. Its per capita income is only one-tenth of that of developed countries, and there are a lot of policy- and development-related areas. What's more, development finance faces not only market failure, but also market gaps and defects, which requires it to build from scratch and develop by leaps and bounds. This determines that policy-based and development finance institutions have longer term and broader development space in China. The basic national conditions in the primary stage of socialism determine that China needs to start with "construction" in developing its economy and improving people's livelihood. "Construction" is the main contradiction and characteristic of China's current economic and social development. The construction phase will last for decades or even centuries. During the development period of the 13th Five-Year Plan (2016–2020), first, development finance should focus on the needs of China's urbanization, industrialization, and internationalization, and continue to increase support for infrastructure, basic industries, and pillar industries; second, it should increase support for grassroots finance and people's livelihood, promote social construction and development, constantly summarize, improve and promote good practices with a view to serving the overall development of the country and easing financing bottlenecks on economic and social development, and establish a sustainable business support model; third, it should serve China's energy and resources strategy and diplomatic strategy, and further expand international cooperation. These prescriptive and developmental factors determine that in the building of China's medium- and long-term financing system, national financial policymakers and development finance institutions must, in accordance with the requirements of national development strategic planning, drive "savings funds" and "private funds" to the building of medium- and long-term financing systems while making fiscal or bond-type development finance inputs into medium- and long-term projects, so as to effectively coordinate domestic and international overall situations and markets.

6.3.4 *The Role and Advantages of Developmental Finance in Promoting Balanced Economic Growth in China*

Under the conditions of a market economy, balanced economic growth can be achieved through the spontaneous behavioral adjustment of economic agents and the reallocation of resources under market regulation. However, under the conditions of China's transition economy, economic development and growth are more policy-oriented. Coordination between the government and the market is the institutional basis for the long-term, rapid and stable development of China's economy. Since its inception in 1994, CDB, as a means of combining the government and the market, has played a unique role in breaking through "bottleneck" constraints, promoting the formation of private capital, smoothing out the economic cycle, and serving people's livelihood, and has played an important role in the balanced development of China's economy for a long time. One of the deep-seated reasons why China's social and economic development since the start of reform and opening-up has led to China's current economic development model, which is dominated by investment and external demand, is that the foundation of economic development is weak, there is a serious shortage of private capital, and there are many "bottleneck" areas that restrict economic development. For example, infrastructure and basic industries that can promote the effective formation of private capital are weak, there is a lack of pillar industries, and the development of agriculture, rural areas, and farmers is slow. Obviously, to ease such "bottleneck" constraints on social and economic development and promote the large-scale formation of private capital, we should rely mainly on the support of public finance. However, in the primary stage of China's economic development, the foundation of economic development is weak, and the public financial resources are limited, so it is impossible to increase the total amount and efficiency in order to meet the needs of rapid economic development. As can be seen from the practice of economic development in countries around the world, especially developing countries, under circumstances where limited public financial resources are available, the investment and financing functions of development finance can be used to make up for the shortfall in the government's public finances, alleviate "bottleneck" constraints on economic development, and promote the formation of private capital. Since 1998, CDB, on the basis of national credit, and with a view to serving national strategic objectives, has adapted to the needs of the allocation of financial resources at different stages of China's economic and social development by continuously reforming and adjusting its function of serving China's social and economic development, contributing to the realization of national strategic objectives at different stages. Over the years, CDB, making full use of the unique advantages given by the State to medium- and long-term bond wholesale banks, and combining national credit with market-oriented operation, has raised a large amount of social funds for the implementation of national strategic objectives at different stages through the issuance of medium- and long-term financial bonds in domestic and foreign markets, effectively mitigating and reducing the fiscal pressure and burden on governments in economic development. In view of the aggregate and structural imbalances in China's economic rebalancing, development finance has an irreplaceable advantage in China's economic rebalancing because it combines national credit with market operation, and advanced development finance concepts with China's national conditions. Development finance is based on national credit, serves national economic development strategies and objectives, and uses various modern financial instruments to raise funds at home abroad and channel these funds to projects of a public nature such as infrastructure and basic industries. Development finance also guides the flow of commercial capital and private capital, and promotes the formation of private capital, thus becoming an important tool to break through bottleneck constraints on social and economic development. Meanwhile, development finance adheres to a market-oriented approach to using funds, forms a "hard budget constraint" on local governments and enterprises, and improves the investment efficiency of private capital. Furthermore, development finance can make full use of the financing and organizational advantages of national credit, accelerate the transformation of fiscal funds and private capital into construction capital, and promote the expansion of and improvement in the quality of private capital.

6.4 Promote Financial Reform and Guard Against Risks

Historically, countries caught in the middle-income trap were often faced with serious inflation and an economic slowdown during their most difficult times, with their financial systems on the verge of collapse. Therefore, in order to achieve a successful economic transformation, we must accelerate the reform of the financial system and mechanism, encourage the development of diversified finance, manage and control systematic risks, and better serve the real economy. Meanwhile, we must guard against economic crisis caused by housing bubbles and high debt.

6.4.1 Encourage Financial Diversification and Serve the Real Economy

China should constantly optimize the system of diversified finance, and eliminate the causes of crisis that may trigger or cause major financial risks to safeguard the long-term healthy development of the real economy. First, we should establish a diversified financial development cooperation system and form a multitiered, diversified, and comprehensively coordinated pattern of financial reform and opening-up. Second, we should strengthen the building of the risk prevention and control mechanism, should not rely too much on the indirect finance system, especially the banking industry, and should establish a sound risk diversification mechanism through a diversified financial pattern. Undoubtedly, the development and reform of China's financial system shows that the indirect finance system has been associated with China's social and cultural development over a long period of time, and banks play a central guiding role in the credit system of the whole society. However, from the perspective of preventing and controlling systemic financial risks, a diversified financial development cooperation system itself requires the creation of an intermarket and intersectoral risk diversification system to address the causes of inflation crisis that may trigger a descent into the middle-income trap. Although China is facing a risk of inflation, the risk is mainly due to economic structural adjustment at the present stage, a relatively complex external environment and weak demand, and is not a long-term risk. But on the other hand, if a successful transition from the short-term policy of stimulating the economy by increasing the money supply is not achieved, and an effective channel for guiding the monetary policy is not found, factors that cause inflation may arise in the future. For example, the current development dilemma faced by Japan is related to its relatively underdeveloped direct finance system, with companies unable to achieve "deleveraging" for a long time, and a low interest rate policy leading to relatively slow economic growth in the context of a steep aging trend. One of the key solutions to this problem is to speed up the building of a direct finance system, strengthen the capital replenishment mechanism for indirect finance as much as possible, and accelerate the development of a diverse range of direct finance instruments. Instead of confining ourselves to the stock market, we should find new ways from the perspectives of asset securitization, equity markets at different levels, convertible capital instruments, long-term bond market innovation, Internet finance, etc. to gradually form a sustainable operation mode of "deleveraging" with Chinese characteristics. Finally, the contradictions between economic transformation and social transformation should be solved through a diversified financial development system to prevent systemic financial crisis. At present, the main contradictions between economic transformation and social transformation are reflected in the widening gap between rich and poor, a lack of new impetus and advantages for economic development, the failure of industries to complete effective upgrading, the failure to achieve the fair and effective distribution of social wealth, and the failure of the social security system to effectively keep up. To this end, we should form a multitiered capital market structure, and effectively reduce the "leverage ratio" of the real economy. Meanwhile, we should always strengthen the contribution of a diversified financial development system to raising employment rates, reducing capital costs, and optimizing output efficiency. Through the Belt and Road, Beijing–Tianjin–Hebei coordinated development and the Yangtze River Economic Belt and other national strategies, we can achieve a rational distribution of industrial value chains in China's eastern, central and western regions, and form a cross-regional financial cooperation network that connects China and the rest of the world. For example, we should consider setting up a wholesale-style Internet finance cooperation platform for development finance in the Shanghai Free-Trade Zone, accelerate the building of international economic, trade and investment partnerships in new industries with countries along the Belt and Road by relying on the FTZ cooperation mechanism, create new drivers and new advantages for economic development, strengthen the foundation of the real economy that supports the social security system, effectively enhance the value content of the renminbi around the globe, gradually wean ourselves away from excessive dependence on the dollar, find and establish new channels for putting base money into circulation, strengthen the dynamic monitoring of money supply during the implementation of strategies for steady growth, and effectively guard against potential systemic inflation crisis.

6.4.2 *Improve Financial Regulation and Guard Against Financial Risks*

With the development of China's financial markets, the enhancement of financial innovation, the diversification of financial products, and an increase in competitive pressure, especially a rise in the debt-to-GDP ratio due to an economic slowdown after China's economic development entered the middle-income stage, China's financial regulation has become more difficult, and financial risks have risen. Therefore, it is urgent to improve financial regulation and guard against financial risks.

Characteristics of Financial Risks

Financial risk is complex, including systemic and global risks at the macro level, financial business risks at the meso level, and conduct and operational risks incurred by specific institutions or individuals at the microlevel. Financial risk is exogenous or endogenous. Financial risk is distinguished from other industry risks by complexity, high leverage, contagiousness, and great harm. First, complexity. Compared with other industries, the financial industry has a large market size, complex financial products, and a wide range of participating institutions and personnel, and has penetrated almost all professions and trades. Although financial theory has been continuously improved, the frequency of financial crises has increased with the development of the world economy, which indicates that the complexity of financial risks is also increasing. Second, high leverage. Financial enterprises have high debt ratios and high financial leverage, resulting in large negative externalities. In addition, financial instrument innovation and derivative financial instruments are also accompanied by high financial risks. The 2008 financial crisis started as the US subprime mortgage crisis and then spread globally through international financial markets. Finally, great harm. The financial industry is the lifeblood of the economy. Compared with other industries, it has huge externalities. Once financial risk evolves into financial crisis, it will not only lead to economic recession but also social crisis and even political crisis. Most typically, in the 1990s, Latin America was over-liberalized, with excessive external debt triggering a financial crisis that eventually led to a severe economic crisis and social unrest.

Financial Risks Faced by China

The national financial work conference held on July 14, 2017 conveyed an important policy signal, that is, the importance of financial work had greatly increased compared with the past. In his speech, General Secretary Xi Jinping clearly put forward "three important's": The first "important" is that finance is an important part of the nation's core competitiveness, a notion that hasn't been mentioned before; the second "important" is that financial security is an important part of national security, and financial security and national security are inextricably linked; the third "important" is that the financial system is an important basic system for the country's economic and social development. The three important's, e.g., an important part of the nation's core competitiveness, an important part of national security and an important basic system for the country's economic and social development, have greatly increased the importance of China's financial work and financial industry. The third aspect of our understanding of importance is that there are still some outstanding problems in the financial industry, and that these problems need to be resolved in order for the financial industry to bear three important responsibilities. So, what are the problems in China's financial industry? There are certain risks in the financial industry, and the existence of risks is a prominent problem in the development of our financial industry. This meeting focused on the overall arrangement of the meeting. One of the basic points in the overall arrangement of the meeting was to strengthen the regulation of the financial industry and financial activities. Why should we strengthen regulation? It's about guarding against risk. The risks in China's financial industry should, of course, be understood in a broad sense. There are many risk points, and the risks are relatively high. But on the whole, China's current financial risks are still controllable, and haven't reached the point where they are exposed or manifested. But we must take precautions, so we need to understand the increased importance of the financial industry and the three important's from the perspective of the development and competitiveness of the financial industry. In this way, the development of China's financial industry can be aligned with the development requirements of the Party and the State.

With decades of rapid economic development in China, great achievements have been made in the reform and development of the financial industry. By the end of 2016, the total assets of China's banking financial institutions had exceeded 230 trillion Yuan, and the balance of broad money supply (M2) had reached 155 trillion Yuan. In terms of financial institutions, we have established a complete and diversified system dominated by banks and comprised of insurance, securities, trust, leasing, small loans, funds, Internet finance, etc. In terms of financial markets, we have established a complete and varied range of markets such as interbank markets, foreign exchange markets, securities markets, commodity futures markets, and equity markets, and these markets have been expanding. In terms of financial products, with the development and opening-up of the financial industry, the portfolio of financial products has become increasingly diversified, and complex financial derivatives in developed international markets have been appearing in the Chinese market. But as the financial industry booms, risks are piling up.

At the macro level, for a period of more than ten years during which China's economy developed rapidly, China's M2 grew at a high speed, and now its M2 has exceeded 160 trillion Yuan. According to data from the Bank for International Settlements, at the end of 2016, China's total debt was $27.49 trillion, accounting for 257.0% of GDP, compared to 181.1% in 2011. The rapid rise in China's leverage is a definite fact and requires great vigilance. Until 2008, the leverage ratio of China's non-financial enterprises had been stable at about 100%. After the global financial crisis, the leverage ratio rose significantly, with the debt of non-financial enterprises as a share of GDP rising from 97.4% in 2008 to 166.3% in 2016. The leverage ratio of China's non-financial enterprises is relatively high, and the risk implications are worthy of attention. As the economic growth rate declines, the debt risk we face will increase.

At the meso level, China's securities market, bond market, futures market, real estate market, and other financial markets have been volatile in recent years. Since 2014, the non-performing loan ratio of the banking industry has generally risen. The aftermath of stock market crash of 2015 is still being felt. The real estate market has been overheated since 2016. The bond market took a sharp downward turn in the second half of the year. In the insurance industry, "barbarians" have taken advantage of universal insurance to carry out hostile takeovers. The securities industry has seen the Sealand Securities "Radish Seal" incident. The Internet finance industry has seen the collapse of a large number of P2P platforms such as Ezubao and Zhongjin Asset Management.

At the microlevel, risks are also increasing. 2016 saw a slew of incidents related to financing secured by negotiable instruments, with a number of banks exposed to risks associated with negotiable instruments and more than 10 billion Yuan at risk, exposing a series of problems such as regulatory loopholes, the lax internal control of banks, and the rule-breaking operations of negotiable instrument intermediaries. A large number of real estate agents have provided "zero down payment" products in violation of the regulations.

At present, China's financial risks are growing, not only because of an economic slowdown and the increasing complexity of financial markets but also due to the imperfection of the regulatory system. This also explains the internal defects of the financial regulation system and departmental coordination mechanism, and reflects the deficiencies in research on and the regulation of financial institutions in China. There is an urgent need to make up for these defects and deficiencies in the future reform of the financial regulation system.

Financial Regulation in China

Since the 2008 global financial crisis, the progress of China's financial regulatory reform has been mainly reflected in the dynamic adjustment of differentiated reserve requirements of the People's Bank of China (the central bank) and the four major regulatory tools of the CBRC.

First, in 2011, the central bank introduced the dynamic adjustment of differentiated reserve requirements based on the concept of macro-prudential regulation and liquidity management needs. The goal is to guide the steady and moderate growth of monetary credit and improve the ability of the financial system to guard against risks. The principle is to guide and motivate banks to maintain robustness and adjust credit supply based on the extent to which bank credit deviates from economic growth plus the price index, with the impact of each bank on the overall deviation as well as the importance and robustness of their respective systems taken into account. Under the scheme of dynamic adjustment of differentiated reserve requirements, banks with smaller credit deviation and a higher level of robustness can correspondingly hold less reserves and lend more; otherwise, they need to hold more reserves and lend less. When banks hold more reserves than required, they can decrease their reserves as appropriate. The dynamic adjustment of differentiated reserve requirements is one of the core tasks of the central bank in constructing the framework of the countercyclical macro-prudential management system. The dynamic adjustment of differentiated reserve requirements has two main characteristics of macro-prudential instruments, namely, adjusting upward when credit supply is too fast and regulating systemic importance financial institutions more stringently.

Second, in recent years, the China Banking Regulatory Commission (CBRC) has successively issued the Guiding Opinions on the Implementation of New Regulatory Standards in China's Banking Industry, the Measures for the Administration of the Leverage Ratios of Commercial Banks, the Measures for the Administration of the Capital of Commercial Banks and the Measures for the Administration of the Liquidity Risk of Commercial Banks (for Trial Implementation). These measures are in line with the spirit of Basel III, which was agreed in 2010, in that liquidity risk regulation was introduced in addition to capital adequacy regulation, and macro-prudential regulation was introduced in addition to micro-prudential regulation. They provide for slightly stricter regulation than Basel III and were implemented earlier.

In addition, other regulatory reforms include: the CBRC strengthened the regulation of China's unique shadow banking system which is comprised of off-balance sheet lending, trust financing, etc.; the CBRC strengthened the regulation of loans to local governments' financing platforms, and loans for the construction of major infrastructure such as railways, highways, airports, and water conservancy works; departments related to the protection of financial consumers were set up in "One Bank, Three Commissions"; the central bank was put in charge of regulating the rating industry; the responsibilities of the CBRC, the CSRC, and local governments for Internet finance regulation were clarified.

In general, China's financial industry is dominated by the banking industry, and the banking industry is dominated by traditional credit business, which has an undiversified product mix and few high-risk and complex derivatives and securitized products; before the financial crisis, the capital adequacy ratio was relatively high, the quality of capital was relatively high, subordinated debt, preferred stock, and hybrid capital instruments were not widely used, and high leverage was not used; international business accounted for a small percentage of China's banking industry and was small in size, so the financial crisis had less impact on China's banking industry than on the European and American banking industries. Accordingly, China's financial regulatory reform after the financial crisis was not as deep and broad as in Europe and the United States.

At the technical level of regulation, China is converging with international standards. We have adopted market-oriented regulatory measures for off-balance sheet lending, trust financing, as well as China's unique risk points such as loans to local governments' financing platforms, and loans for the construction of major infrastructure such as railways, highways, airports, and water conservancy works. The dynamic adjustment of differentiated reserve requirements is of innovative significance in countercyclical regulation. All these are worthy of recognition. But there are also several deficiencies.

The first deficiency is that in the context of increased demand for regulatory coordination, the approach to and intensity of financial regulation are inadequate. After the financial crisis, countries actively strengthened their financial regulatory coordination mechanisms and set up substantive and institutionalized regulatory coordination bodies. For example, the United States set up the interagency the Financial Stability Oversight Council, and the United Kingdom merged the FSA's regulatory functions into the Bank of England. China has formed the "One Bank, Three Commissions" pattern for separate financial regulation, but "One Bank, Three Commissions" work in isolation, which impedes the flow of information and makes management difficult to coordinate. The implementation of macro-prudential regulation requires effective coordination between three regulatory authorities: banking, securities, and insurance, as well as between the central bank and the three regulatory authorities.

The second deficiency is that China's conduct regulation system for "proactive intervention-style" early monitoring is not sound enough. Prudential regulation focuses on compliance with regulatory indicators and requirements for prudential operations (e.g., capital adequacy ratio, asset liquidity, and risk concentration), while conduct regulation focuses on "proactive intervention-style" early monitoring, product and business analysis, and correcting financial consumers' deviations from established norms of conduct. Both are indispensable. Since the 2008 international financial crisis, conduct regulation has been widely practiced around the world. In recent years, the World Bank, the International Monetary Fund, Consumers International, the G20, and the Financial Stability Board have issued guidelines and investigation reports on strengthening conduct regulation and financial consumer protection, such as the World Bank's Good Practices for Financial Consumer Protection and the G20's High-Level Principles on Financial Consumer Protection.

Suggestions on Strengthening Financial Regulation

The financial regulatory system is a worldwide challenge. From the perspective of reforms after the financial crisis, the financial regulatory system is mainly affected by two key issues.

The first issue is how to design a macro-prudential regulatory framework, including coordinating financial regulation and monetary policy in dealing with procyclicality and countercyclicality, and central banks, fiscal authorities, regulatory authorities, and deposit insurance institutions in dealing with systemically important financial institutions. Especially coordination between monetary policy and financial regulation should be strengthened. The IMF evaluated the practices of various countries and found that some countries had set up specialized agencies and some have set up coordination committees, and there were pros and cons in every model. Based on this, we offer the following suggestions: First, the central bank should play an important role in macro-prudential regulation; second, a complex and fragmented regulatory system is not conducive to the effective management of systemic risks; third, systemic risk prevention and crisis management are different functions and should be institutionally separated. At the end of 2015, the central bank announced that it would upgrade the mechanism for dynamic adjustment of differentiated reserve requirements and consensual loan management to a macro-prudential assessment (MPA) system beginning in 2016. The main components of the MPA system include: capital and leverage, assets and liabilities, liquidity, pricing behavior, asset quality, external debt risk, and credit policy implementation, with the capital adequacy ratio being the core of the evaluation system. The MPA system focuses on broad credit, and includes bond investment, equity and other investment, buybacks, etc., in order to steer financial institutions away from the practice of circumventing credit regulation by transferring assets to other uses. Meanwhile, interest rate pricing behavior is considered an important aspect to be examined in order to check irrational pricing behavior.

The second issue is the relationship between prudential regulation and financial consumer protection. A growing number of countries have adopted a model of separation of prudential and conduct regulation, and set up full-time departments responsible for conduct regulation. For example, under the Dodd–Frank Wall Street reform and Consumer Protection Act, the United States merged the financial consumer protection functions of multiple departments to create the Consumer Financial Protection Bureau (CFPB); under the Financial Services Act 2012, the United Kingdom thoroughly reformed its financial regulatory system, and created the Financial Conduct Authority (FCA), which is responsible for the conduct of all financial institutions, including banking financial institutions. In 2011, the Hong Kong Monetary Authority (HKMA) of China adjusted and reorganized its departments in 2011, creating a banking conduct department with a focus on stiffening penalties for violations of laws and regulations.

We offer the following suggestions for rationalizing the financial regulatory system.

First, adhere to the mode of decentralized operation and regulation, and prudently conduct pilot programs for integrated operation. Commercial banks and investment banks are essentially different in terms of commercial profit model, source of funds, risk taking, and culture. The financial crisis has exposed two prominent problems in the mixed operation model: First, under the deposit insurance system, banks can use low-cost deposits as a source of funds for high-risk, highly leveraged investment banking operations, which is equivalent to subsidizing investment banking operations with deposit insurance and poses a moral hazard; second, once problems in investment banking endanger deposits, remittances, payment and settlement and other basic commercial banking operations, the foundation of the financial system may be shaken. In the United States, the Volcker Rule restricts banks from investing in hedge funds and private funds and engaging in proprietary trading. In the United Kingdom, the Independent Commission on Banking recommended the separation of retail and investment banking. Both moves are intended to partially restore the Glass–Steagall Act and correct excessive mixed operation.

Second, in order to promote regulatory coordination under the mode of separate operation and regulation, the National Financial Work Conference held on July 14, 2017 announced the creation of the Financial Stability and Development Committee under the State Council, and decided to reinforce the responsibilities of the People's Bank of China for macro-prudential management and systematic risk prevention, lay out the responsibilities of financial regulatory authorities, and strengthen accountability. At the meeting, General Secretary Xi Jinping said that the strengthening of regulation was a major decision made in the new international and domestic economic situations and was of great significance. The development of the financial industry is not possible without strong regulation, so it is necessary to strengthen regulation. The strengthening of regulation should in principle be market-oriented. Strengthening regulation in the development of the financial industry does not mean that we manage through administrative means. The explicit mention of market orientation implies that the development of the financial industry should still adhere to the important principle that the market plays a decisive role, that is, we should remain committed to building a socialist market economy, and continue to make the market play a decisive role in the allocation of financial resources. The role of the government is to strengthen top-level design, strengthen institutional design, strengthen regulation, and strengthen capacity for execution. For the principle of market orientation, getting back to basics is paramount. Getting back to basics, optimizing the structure, strengthening regulation, and market orientation are the meeting's overall arrangements for the development of the financial industry. The goal is to achieve a virtuous circle and the healthy development of economy and finance; the bottom line is to ensure that no systemic financial risks occur; the three major tasks are to serve the real economy, prevent financial risks and deepen financial reform; the four areas are getting back to basics, optimizing the structure, strengthening regulation, and market orientation. This is the general spirit of the financial conference.

In its 2011 Financial System Stability Assessment on China, the IMF made similar recommendations regarding the regulatory system: a permanent Financial Stability Committee should be established, with the PBC as its secretariat. It should be chaired by a very senior official and have a clear mandate and authority to identify and monitor the emergence of systemic risks and to make recommendations to address them. Members would include the PBC, the three supervisory commissions, the MOF, and other relevant ministries or agencies.

Third, strengthen the central bank's role in macro-prudential regulation and the prevention of systemic financial risks. The central bank has the ability to analyze the macroeconomy, determines important monetary policy variables such as interest rates and total loans, participates in and understands the capital and insurance markets, serves as the lender of last resort, and oversees payment and payment systems, so it should be the leader of the macro-prudential regulation system. This is a general trend worldwide.

Fourth, draw on the Dodd–Frank Act which created the Office of Financial Research, and set up a similar body within the central bank to systematically collect and organize data and information on China's financial system to provide analytical support for systemic risk monitoring. The Office of Financial Research operates within the Department of the Treasury, and aims to provide policymakers with high-quality data and in-depth analysis of the financial system. It has two main operating centers. The first is the Data Center, which is responsible for standardizing, validating, and maintaining data that helps regulators identify vulnerabilities in the financial system. The second is the Research and Analysis Center, which is responsible for implementing, coordinating, and funding research projects that help improve financial institutions and market regulation. Data and analytical reports from the Office of Financial Research are provided to policymakers and regulators, including the US Congress and the Financial Services Oversight Council, and are also available to the public in some form, thereby contributing to the promotion of financial stability and market discipline.

6.4.3 *Promote RMB Internationalization Under the Belt and Road Initiative*

With the comprehensive advancement of China's Go Out policy and the Belt and Road Initiative, RMB internationalization in the Eurasian region has ushered in new historical opportunities. The building of an RMB trade settlement system and RMB investment and financing system is the focus of RMB internationalization in the Eurasian region. While building a policy coordination mechanism, we should actively promote the building of a cooperation platform and pursue innovation in the cooperation model for RMB internationalization.

Guided by Planning, Build a Policy Coordination Mechanism for RMB Internationalization

According to the characteristics and needs of international and regional financial markets, and the requirements of the Belt and Road Initiative for the opening-up of and cooperation in China's financial industry, combine Eurasian financial cooperation with the advancement of RMB internationalization, formulate medium- and long-term plans for Eurasian financial cooperation under the Belt and Road Initiative with a focus on RMB internationalization, and build an Eurasian information sharing system for RMB internationalization Improve the regular meeting and consultation mechanism of the SCO Financial Cooperation Committee, deepen communication and information exchange among financial institutions, establish an Eurasian credit rating mechanism and investment and financing guarantee mechanism, and strengthen communication and coordination on policies, institutions, cooperation projects, and cooperation mechanisms. Encourage and support Chinese financial institutions in setting up branches in Eurasian countries along the Belt and Road, promote the establishment and improvement of the Cross-Border Interbank Payment System (CIPS), expand RMB settlement for cross-border trade and investment, and to achieve full coverage of the regional financial services network. Comprehensively advance work on RMB financing in the Eurasian region, increase the amount of RMB loans, and expand the scale of RMB-foreign currency swaps.

Comprehensively Expand the Scope of RMB Credit Cooperation and Pursue Innovation in the Cooperation Model for RMB Internationalization

From the perspective of implementing the medium- and long-term development goals of RMB internationalization, there are broad prospects for credit cooperation in the Eurasian region under the Belt and Road Initiative with RMB as the main funding currency. In the future, we should gradually shift the focus of RMB financing support from traditional areas such as energy resources to infrastructure, high and new technologies, new energy and other non-resource areas, the green economy, and people's livelihood. We should step up RMB financing support in key areas of cooperation, use cross-border infrastructure connectivity and regional industrial cooperation as a lever to encourage countries in the region to draw on each other's strengths through capacity cooperation, and strengthen matching for industries and projects. Aggressively pursue innovation in the RMB credit cooperation model, build a RMB investment and financing system, combine RMB cross-border investment and financing with national economic and diplomatic strategies, combine foreign aid funds with loan funds, integrate various forms of financial cooperation such as project financing, bank credit and syndicated loans, and promote the securitization of RMB loans and credit assets, accelerate the development of the offshore RMB market, carry out offshore RMB business, support companies and financial institutions with high credit ratings in countries such as Russia and Kazakhstan in issuing RMB bonds in China, and seek financing by listing in Hong Kong, Shanghai, and Shenzhen.

Orderly and Smooth Cooperation in Financial Markets

In terms of opening-up the interbank bond market, it has become more convenient for foreign institutions to issue RMB bonds in China, and the central banks of Mongolia, Malaysia, Singapore, Thailand, Indonesia and other countries along the Belt and Road have been approved to invest in the interbank bond market. In terms of promoting the opening-up of the Asian bond market, the People's Bank of China has actively participated in the issuance and management of the Asian Bond Fund under the EMEAP (Executives' Meeting of East Asia and Pacific Central Banks) mechanism, taken part in the Asian Bond Markets Initiative under the "10+3" Financial Cooperation Mechanism, and co-launched the regional credit guarantee and investment fund, which provides guarantees for the issuance of local currency bonds rated investment grade or above by companies in "10 + 3" countries to promote the development of the local currency corporate bond market. In addition, discussions are underway over issues such as the establishment of a multicurrency bond issuance framework and regional bond clearing intermediaries. The Shanghai-Hong Kong Stock Connect was successfully launched, further simplifying the administration of foreign exchange under capital accounts.

In addition, the RMB has been trading against the Malaysian ringgit and the Russian ruble in the national interbank foreign exchange market. The trading of the RMB against the Thai baht in the interbank market has been allowed in Yunnan Province, and the direct trading of RMB against the currencies of neighboring countries such as South Korea won, Vietnamese Dong, Laos Kip, and Kazakhstan tenge has been allowed in places such as Shandong, Jilin, Guangxi, and Xinjiang.

China's Capital Markets Are also Accelerating Integration with Countries Along the Belt and Road

In August 2015, the China Securities Regulatory Commission said it would further open up the securities industry to foreign companies, noting that it would continue to actively promote market opening through cross-border trading and connectivity, encourage exchanges to integrate market resources, and support cooperation with overseas exchanges in cross-shareholdings, cross-listings, and interoperability among market entities.

The Regional Financial Cooperation Mechanism Has Been Continuously Enriched and Improved

China has actively carried out multifaceted cooperation with countries along the Belt and Road and co-organized regional financial cooperation platforms such as the China-India Financial Dialogue, the Bangladesh–China–India–Myanmar Forum for Regional Cooperation, the China-ASEAN Expo, the China-South Asia Expo, the China-Asia-Europe Expo, the China-Arab States Expo, Central Asia Regional Economic Cooperation, the Boao Forum for Asia, the China-ASEAN Credit Research Center, and China-Pakistan Investment Co., Ltd.

In addition, local governments in some provinces and regions of China are also actively building platforms for financial cooperation with countries along the Belt and Road to promote regional financial cooperation. For example, cross-border RMB business innovation was launched through the establishment of the China-Kazakhstan Horgos International Border Cooperation Center in Xinjiang. China and Laos have also signed the General Plan for the Construction of the China-Laos Mohan-Boten Economic Cooperation Zone and the General Plan for the Joint Development of the China-Laos Mohan-Boten Economic Cooperation Zone to build the China-Laos Mohan-Boten Cross-Border Economic Cooperation Zone in China's Yunnan Province and Laos' Luang Namtha province.

7 Summary

China's economy is in a critical period where China has to deal simultaneously with the slowdown in economic growth, making difficult structural adjustments, and absorbing the effects of previous economic stimulus policies. The period is also a critical period for promoting economic transformation and overcoming the middle-income trap. Despite the need for adjustment and a slowdown in growth, China's economy still has a high potential growth rate, and there is a lot of room for economic transformation and upgrading. We need to deepen the reform of the economic system, further release the reform dividend and stimulate market vitality in order to seize the opportunity.

The focus of China's economic transformation is to make the market play a decisive role in the allocation of resources through reform, and at the same time give better play to the role of the government. We should actively transform government functions. On the one hand, we should streamline administration and delegate power, and remove market barriers; on the other hand, we should actively create a good foundation and environment for economic transformation. For example, we should eliminate investment barriers in monopoly industries and push ahead with the reform of the urban–rural dual system. Meanwhile, we should strengthen investment in education and further improve the talent cultivation model, so as to promote technological innovation through talent. We should strengthen the protection of intellectual property rights and create a fair and just environment for entrepreneurship. In a complicated international situation, China should continue to open up, actively participate in the reshaping of the new international economic order, and create a favorable environment for China to explore the international market. Internally, we should guard against real estate bubbles and debt risks.

Achieving economic transformation is the only way for China to overcome the middle-income trap. Only by comprehensively and deeply advancing the reform of the economic system can we remove all obstacles and achieve successful transformation.

This study holds that at an important stage where China is overcoming the middle-income trap and in a new situation where China is participating in the coordination of international economic and financial governance, the key is how to build a new mechanism for China's participation in international macroeconomic policy coordination and further expand to areas such as structural reform. International macroeconomic policy coordination is divided into three levels: the first level is the coordination of exchange rate relations, the second level is the coordination of monetary and fiscal policies, and the deepest level is related to the need for structural reform (systems, mechanisms and basic institutions in a broad sense). The main recommendations of this book are as follows.

First, set up a mechanism for more frequent communication among major economies. Under the G20 framework, major economies (the EU, the US, etc.) should establish a communication mechanism, assume responsibility for sharing information, and communicate more frequently (e.g., once a month) over issues such as international capital flows, and inflation, prosperity, or recession in major economies. On this basis, they should establish a crisis early warning mechanism.

Second, create a global crisis response fund. In view of growing risks and uncertainties in the global economy, it is suggested that the Chiang Mai Initiative be globalized. Under the globalized Chiang Mai Initiative, the world's major economies inject (or commit) a certain amount of foreign exchange reserves into the "common foreign exchange reserve fund," so that when a country faces a shortage of foreign exchange reserves, other countries will help it mitigate the crisis. China can seize the initiative by first proposing the idea.

Third, broaden the use of SDR. The promotion of the SDR as a "super-sovereign" currency in international payments will help reduce the risk of the international monetary system and increase the IMF's financial resources. These include: revising the SDR-related institutions and establishing settlement relationships with other currencies; expanding the use of the SDR in the balance of payments and crisis relief for members of the IMF; expanding the use of the SDR as a pricing unit in international trade and investment; the IMF provides SDR loans to member central banks and other multilateral development banks to promote the use of the SDR in investment in major global infrastructure projects.

Fourth, promote the creation of a multilevel reserve currency system. Establish an international monetary management committee dedicated to international monetary coordination, maintain the exchange rate within a band of ±10–15% under a target zone regime, and levy a unified 0.5% Tobin tax on a global scale (or in Asia first).

Fifth, build a "5 + 1" global macroeconomic policy coordination mechanism. The coordination mechanism, comprising the central banks behind the five currencies that make up the SDR, and the IMF, can operate in the form of regular meetings focusing on their respective macroeconomic policies, including fiscal, monetary, foreign exchange, trade, and structural reforms, with the aim of expanding the positive spillover effects of the macroeconomic policies of the five major economies and reducing negative spillover effects.

Sixth, form an international economic union. A coalition should be formed with Brazil, India, and other countries that are highly related to China's economy, and countries that are remotely or negatively related to the US economy to counteract the negative spillover effects of the economic policies of dominant countries.

CHAPTER 5

Overcoming the Middle-Income Trap Requires Improvement in Capacity for Social Governance

Overcoming the middle-income trap requires both economic transformation and social transformation. Economic transformation cannot be accomplished without the modernization of economic governance; social transformation cannot be accomplished without the modernization of social governance.

Social governance is regulating the behavior of social actors, coordinating social relations, solving social problems, resolving social conflicts, eliminating social conflicts, and preventing social risks based on social values, legal rules, and other social norms. From social management to social governance, the difference is not only a change of concept, but also the sublimation of the concept of reform. The modernization of social governance embodies the comprehensive upgrading of the concept and methods of social management, and is an important part of the modernization of national governance.

The essence of the middle-income trap is that the relationship between development and governance is not properly handled, resulting in government failure, market failure, and anomie coexisting and intertwining with each other, hindering the successful transformation and further development of the economy and society. Studies of Latin America, South Asia, the Soviet Union and the socialist countries of Eastern Europe show that these countries fell into the middle-income trap not only because of inadequate innovation and poor economic transformation, but also

Z. Zheng, *Middle-Income Trap*,
https://doi.org/10.1007/978-981-15-7401-6_5

due to deep-rooted social reasons such as a malformed social structure, income inequality, the unbalanced representation of interests and a lack of progress in building the rule of law. On the other hand, Western developed countries, Japan and South Korea, despite their different paths and strategies for entering the high-income stage, have handled the relationship between development and governance well and achieved successful economic and social transformation under the framework of the rule of law.

Since the start of reform and opening-up, China's economy has become the second largest in the world, and its social development has entered a period of profound adjustment. The interests of different classes are becoming increasingly divergent, conflicts of interest among different groups are becoming increasingly prominent, social concepts and social values have been diversified, and many deep-seated problems accumulated over a long period of time in social development are gradually emerging, interwoven with new situations and new problems, posing severe challenges to traditional social management concepts and management models.

"A halo around the moon indicates the rising of wind; the damp on a plinth is a sign of approaching rain." Since the 18th CPC National Congress, the CPC Central Committee, with Comrade Xi Jinping at its core, on the basis of grasping the stage-specific characteristics of and historical changes in China's economic and social development in a timely manner, and scientifically analyzing the opportunities and challenges faced by the Party and the State, has put forward the strategic vision of coordinating efforts to advance the building of a moderately prosperous society in all respects, deepen reform in an all-round way, comprehensively govern the country in accordance with the law, and comprehensively enforce strict Party discipline, and mapped out a realistic path to achieving the Chinese Dream of the great rejuvenation of the Chinese nation. Meanwhile, from the perspective of advancing the modernization of China's system and capacity for governance the CPC Central Committee has scientifically put forward top-level design for innovating social governance, improving the mode of social governance, and enhancing capacity for social governance.

In November 2013, the Third Plenary Session of the 18th CPC Central Committee decided to "innovate in the social governance system," and put forward principled requirements in four aspects:

improving social governance, stimulating the vitality of social organizations, innovating systems for effectively preventing and resolving social contradictions, and improving the public security system. In October 2014, the Fourth Plenary Session of the 18th CPC Central Committee proposed to adhere to systematic governance, governance according to law, comprehensive governance, and governance at the source, and raise the level of the rule of law in social governance. In November 2015, the Fifth Plenary Session of the 18th CPC Central Committee proposed to strengthen and innovate social governance, improve the "law-based social governance system under which Party committees exercise leadership, governments take the lead, non-governmental actors provide assistance, and the public get involved," promote the refinement of social governance, and build a social governance model based on collaboration among all people and the common interests of all people. Our Party's theoretical research on social governance is getting deeper and deeper, its thinking on governance is becoming increasingly clear, and the intension, extension, and focus of social governance are becoming increasingly definite, laying a good foundation for the realization of scientific and modern social governance.[1]

Comrade Xi Jinping has pointed out that the "middle-income trap" will surely be overcome, but the key question is when to overcome it and how to achieve better development after overcoming it.[2] The historical experience of the past 30 years and more shows that only by persisting in reform, emancipating the mind, being confident, seizing the opportunity, and making overall arrangements from the perspective of top-level design can China successfully cope with this challenge.

To overcome the middle-income trap, we need to promote social transformation, improve capacity for social governance, and advance the modernization of social governance. Follow the top-level design of "improving the law-based social governance system under which Party committees exercise leadership, governments take the lead, non-governmental actors provide assistance, and the public get involved,"

[1] Xie Zhiqiang. Innovate Social Governance: What to Govern, Who to Govern and How to Govern—Problems and Challenges That China Faces in Strengthening and Innovating Social Governance and Countermeasures. *Guangming Daily*, 2016-07-13.

[2] The above is an excerpt from the speech by President Xi Jinping at the Dialogue between Asia-Pacific Economic Cooperation (APEC) Leaders and APEC Business Advisory Council (ABAC) Representatives held in Beijing on November 10, 2014.

gradually transform the functions of the government under the leadership of the Party, and stimulate the vitality of diverse social actors; gradually narrow the gap between rich and poor, optimize the social structure, and expand the size of the middle class as soon as possible; promote equal access to essential public services, improve the social security system, and weave a strong safety net to ensure people's well-being; strengthen the rule of law, blaze a trail to good law and sound governance that suits China's national conditions, achieve lasting peace and stability, and build a new social governance model based on collaboration among all people and the common interests of all people.

1 Improve Capacity for Social Governance to Help Overcome the Middle-Income Trap

1.1 The Relationship Between Overcoming the Middle-Income Trap and Improving Capacity for Social Governance

Although the middle-income trap is mainly measured by quantitative indicators of economic growth and economic development, it is essentially a dilemma in institutional transformation, that is, the internal logical relationship between development and governance is not properly handled, resulting in government failure, market distortion/failure, and social anomie coexisting and intertwining with each other with the result that the process of transformation is held up.[3] Therefore, the middle-income trap is an economic problem on the surface, but at a deeper level it is a social problem.

1.1.1 Improving Capacity for Social Governance Is an Inherent Requirement for Overcoming the Middle-Income Trap

The basic principles of Marxism tell us that the economic base determines the superstructure, and the superstructure reacts on the economic base, and must be constantly adjusted to adapt to the development of the economic base. As the economy grows, people's income increases, and interests are increasingly diversified, the social structure and form

[3]Tian Guoqiang, Chen Xudong. How Can China Overcome the "Middle-Income Trap"—Based on the Perspective of Institutional Transformation and National Governance. *Academic Monthly*, 2015 (5): 18.

will change. If the issue of social transformation is not handled properly and social inequality is not effectively curbed, social contradictions will tend to crop up frequently, thus restricting economic development. Therefore, in a sense, the middle-income trap is also an issue concerning social transformation and the modernization of social governance.[4]

Internationally, an important reason for the failure of countries that have fallen into the middle-income trap to transform was that they failed to solve a series of social problems in the process of an economic catch-up, such as the uncoordinated development of urban and rural areas, widening income inequality, social polarization, imbalances in social security, political unrest, and an improper welfare catch-up, resulting in social development becoming severely disconnected from and lagging far behind economic development. In Latin America countries, where transformation failed from the 1970s to the 1990s, for example, the "modern traditionalism" advocated by the dominant elite places undue emphasis economic growth and wealth accumulation, and opposes change in such areas as social structure, values, and power distribution, or minimizes such change, resulting in social development seriously lagging behind economic development. Severe social disparities led to violent social unrest and even regime change, which seriously hindered the transformation and upgrading of their economies to a higher level, eventually leading to a descent into the middle-income trap of economic and social development. On the other hand, developed countries in Europe, the United States, Japan, and South Korea, despite their different paths and strategies for entering the high-income stage, have overcome the middle-income trap by changing their governance ideas and models in a timely manner, properly solving or mitigating social contradictions in the process of economic transformation, and successfully achieving economic and social transformation.

Therefore, to overcome the middle-income trap, we need not only to improve our capacity for economic governance and adapt to the requirements of economic development, but also to improve our capacity for social governance and properly solve and deal with social contradictions that are prominent in the middle-income stage and sensitive issues that emerge during the process; we need not only to clearly define the governance boundary between the government and the market, but more

[4] Zheng Zhijie. Good Law and Sound Governance Help Overcome the "Middle-Income Trap". *Study Times*, 2014-12-08.

importantly, to clarify the governance boundary between the government and society. Only by improving our capacity for social governance and achieving the modernization of social governance, can we pave the way for overcoming the middle-income trap.

1.1.2 *Improving Capacity for Social Governance Is a Necessary Guarantee for Overcoming the Middle-Income Trap*

Economic development is the basis of and a prerequisite for social development, social development is the starting point and ultimate goal of economic development, and the two complement each other.[5] The middle-income stage is a period when various economic variables are changing most drastically, and also a period when the social structure is undergoing rapid changes and recombination. The economic development pursued at this stage is not simply an increase in the speed of economic development and structural adjustment, but also the coordinated development of economic development and social progress, which is benign, high-quality and sustainable development.

In the process of their economic transformation, developed countries in Europe, the United States, and Japan, South Korea and other East Asian countries that have successfully overcome the middle-income trap all provided a good institutional guarantee and created a stable social environment and social class foundation for industrial upgrading and economic transformation through such means of social governance as improving the welfare system, adjusting the social structure, and balancing political rights, thereby creating the social conditions for rapid economic growth. For example, the United States gave full play to the role of government system adjustment and comprehensive social construction; Germany and France attached importance to the establishment of a social security system and social welfare system; the United Kingdom matched the social security system with the actual level of economic development; Japan implemented the Income Doubling Plan, leading to the formation of a modern middle-class society; South Korea carried out the New Village Movement to narrow the gap between urban and rural areas; Japan and South Korea attached importance to social governance reforms and innovations such as adjusting social psychology with Confucian culture. Although different countries have

[5] Deng Weizhi. Economic Development and Social Development. *Social Sciences in Nanjing*, 1995 (8): 31.

adopted different measures, the role of social governance in ensuring rapid and steady economic development is obvious.

Therefore, improving capacity for social governance is a prerequisite for economic development, and economic development requires social governance to win more space for it. Through social governance, we can create a harmonious and stable social environment, which is conducive to ensuring the steady development of the economy; only through social governance and institutional building can we provide an institutional guarantee for innovation and stimulate the vitality of innovation; through social governance, we can optimize the social structure, narrow the gap between rich and poor, stimulate consumption, boost domestic demand, and provide a source of power for economic development; through social governance, we can build consensus among diverse social actors, reduce the resistance to economic transformation, and further economic development. Capacity for and the level of social governance are arguably the "shortest stave" that determines the water level in the barrel of economic development. A high level of social governance will accelerate the speed of economic development in the future. If the level of social governance cannot keep up, future economic development will be limited.

1.2 In Order to Overcome the Middle-Income Trap, It Is Imperative to Improve Capacity for Social Governance

Since the start of reform and opening-up, China's society has undergone a series of profound changes, the most prominent of which is the transition of the economic system from a planned economy to a market economy. China has also transitioned form a traditional society to a modern society. New situations and problems are emerging one after another in the social sphere, creating an urgent need to adjust and innovate in the traditional mode social management. This presents higher requirements for improving capacity for social governance.

1.2.1 China's Social Transformation Is Facing Challenges

Rapid economic and social transformation has accelerated social mobility. According to statistics, in the past, "unit person" accounted for more than 95% of the total urban employed population, and this proportion has now dropped to about 30%.[6] From 2010 to 2016, China's floating population remained above 200 million, and a large number of "unit persons" changed to "social persons." The scale of social mobility is increasing, cross-regional mobility has become the norm, and more and more members of the floating population have chosen to settle down with their families for the long haul, creating some difficulties for social public services.

Economic and social transformation are intertwined, which strengthens the differences between different classes and social groups. The social structure has become more polarized, and stakeholders and their demands have become more diverse, posing a serious challenge to the traditional model of social governance. As the development of social productivity continues to meet the demands of diverse stakeholders, the benefit gap among different classes, groups, and individuals has widened further, which, coupled with the fact that some institutions cannot meet the needs of the coordination of interests in the period of social transformation, has further complicated social contradictions. Years of market-oriented reform has fostered diverse market entities. How to coordinate the demands of different classes and different interest groups, how to strike a proper balance among their interests, and how to set up an sound benefit distribution mechanism adapted to the socialist market economic system are issues that must be resolved through effective social governance after entering the middle-income stage.

Public awareness of rights is rising rapidly, and expectations and demand for equity and justice are becoming more urgent. Rights awareness is people's perception and understanding of and attitude toward all rights, and a psychological reflection of people's choice of ways to realize their rights, and what remedies to take when their rights are compromised. In a middle-income society, the market mechanism has been established and gradually perfected, people's level of income and education has increased significantly, people have higher expectations for equality of opportunity, the fairness of rules, and distributive justice, individuals' rights awareness has been further heightened, and people are more aware of and concerned about their own rights and interests, and

[6] Xie Zhiqiang. Innovate Social Governance: What to Govern, Who to Govern and How to Govern—Problems and Challenges That China Faces in Strengthening and Innovating Social Governance and Countermeasures. *Guangming Daily*, 2016-07-13.

will take all kinds of actions to safeguard their rights more actively and consciously.

1.2.2 *Limitations of the Traditional Social Management Model*

Social management refers to the intervention, coordination, adjustment, and control of social life by the state through its power organs or authorized departments according to certain rules, and is the government's management behavior aimed at adjusting social relations, standardizing social behavior, and maintaining social order. After China has entered the middle-income stage, the social sphere is facing many new challenges. The original social management model can no longer meet the new needs in the new situation, and changes are urgently needed.

A lack of diversity in management entities is not in line does not accord with the trend of diversification in social development. In the past, China's social structure was relatively simple, social management mainly depended on the government, not enough attention was paid to the diversification and individualization of demand, a strong emphasis was put on control. In some areas, such a control-centered management model would also lead to the waste of administrative resources and a reversal of previous gains in management, producing a negative impact on social construction. In the face of information dispersion and complex social affairs in the process of transformation, we can no longer meet the objective needs of social governance by relying solely on the power of the government, and need to give full play to the role of multiple parties. Various types of social organizations are rising rapidly, and the vitality of many areas of the private sphere has been effectively unleashed, contributing to economic and social prosperity and progress. But on the whole, the autonomy of social organizations is still fragile, the government still dominates everything, and communication channels between the government and social organizations and the public, and the consensus-based governance mechanism still need to be further improved.

The top-down control-centered management approach is unable to adapt to growing social rights awareness. Social management is inseparable from the government's control and regulation of society, but when the diversity of social actors is becoming increasingly prominent, the simple continuation of traditional practices is likely to lead to conflicts between the government's intentions and the will of society, between government power and social rights, and between the government's management approach and methods by which social choices are made, and cause a series of social problems, such as a lack of flexibility in management, the limited effectiveness of management, emphasis on management over services, the unreasonable allocation of resources, and a mismatch between the provision of and demand for public services.

A lack of diversity in administrative means is not conducive to dealing with a complex web of interests. Some government departments have long been accustomed to using directive and mandatory administrative means to manage public affairs, only emphasizing the obedience and cooperation of social organizations and members of society, and not paying enough attention to their rights. The "one-size-fits-all" management approach is unable to meet the different demands of diverse stakeholders. Moreover, most of the administrative means are short-term and campaign-styled, unable to fundamentally solve the problems of inadequate top-level design and lack of a long-term mechanism. Often social problems are dealt with and remedied only after they have accumulated to a certain extent, which is likely to lead to a situation where tightening regulation "kills" and relaxing regulation means chaos.[7]

Some of the above problems are caused by structural conflicts, institutional frictions, normative gaps and conflicts of departmental interests in the transformation of social structure, and some are caused by inadequate ideological understanding and improper management methods. All these need to be solved gradually by changing the way of social governance and improving capacity for social governance.

1.2.3 *Promote the Transformation from Social Management to Social Governance*

In order to better cope with challenges in the course of social transformation and successfully overcome the middle-income trap, we must push for a transition from traditional social management to modern social governance in terms of value orientation, participants and means, and promote positive interaction between the government and society. In terms of value orientation, we should no longer simply emphasize the responsibilities, obligations, obedience, and cooperation of members of society, but adopt such concepts as putting people first, equity and justice, and make it our primary goal to realize, safeguard and develop the fundamental interests of the people. In terms of participants, we should not only adhere

[7] Wang Mingji. Transformation of Social Management Practices: Key Issues and Path Choices. *China Economic and Trade Herald Journal*, 2013 (13): 50–51.

to the dominant position of the government in social governance, but also advocate participatory governance by giving full play to the role of diverse actors such as enterprises, institutions, social organizations and citizens in cooperation and negotiation, and allowing members of society the right to participate and voice their opinions in relevant decisions, so as to achieve the organic combination of government governance and social autonomy. In terms of means, we should use a combination of legal, administrative, and ethical means to regulate the behavior of members of society and to organize, coordinate, serve, supervise, and control public affairs.

1.3 Improve Capacity for Social Governance and Advance the Modernization of Social Governance

Improving capacity for social governance and proactively responding to various social contradictions and problems faced in the new stage of social development in China is a necessary requirement for socialist modernization with Chinese characteristics, and also an important part of advancing the modernization of social governance in China. The modernization of social governance is to institutionalize, scientize, standardize, proceduralize, and refine the system of social governance, enable social administrators to govern society with law-based thinking and approaches, and legal institutions, and turn the institutional advantages of socialism with Chinese characteristics in all aspects into the effectiveness of social governance.[8] Overcoming the middle-income trap and achieving the grand goal of building a moderately prosperous society in all respects are impossible without the modernization of social governance. At present, we should follow the central government's top-level design for the modernization of social governance and push for standardized, diversified, and law-based social governance.

1.3.1 Push for Standardized Social Governance and Improve the Social Governance Mechanism

The social governance mechanism is the systematic process in which different governance actors cooperate and interact positively with each other in different areas of governance. Improving the social governance

[8] Xu Meng. The Scientific Connotations, Value Orientation and Path to the Realization of the Modernization of Social Governance. *Academic Research*, 2014 (5): 15.

mechanism is a necessary requirement for the standardization of social governance, as well as the gradual transformation of government functions and the modernization of capacity for social governance. We must strive to adapt to the overall process of national modernization and the new situation in the era of industrial upgrading and new media, organically integrate reform of the social governance system with social innovation, and adapt to changes in the economic system, the social system, cultural concepts, and the administrative governance model.

First, improve institutional building and promote the institutionalization, standardization, and proceduralization of the governance of various social affairs. Social governance is a huge and complex systematic project. Its complexity, wholeness and collaborative nature require us to adhere to the combination of governance at the source, comprehensive governance and treating both symptoms and root causes, and carry out institutional building and mechanism innovation in areas such as the opinion expression mechanism, the interest coordination mechanism, the social security mechanism, the public security mechanism, the emergency management mechanism and the grass-roots governance mechanism, so as to reflect and coordinate the demands of various stakeholders in all aspects and at all levels in a timely manner.

Second, improve the ability of state institutions to perform their duties, provide public services through law-based, scientific, and diversified means of governance, and take care of the interests of different groups. This also provides an effective way to maintain social stability and ensure social equity and justice, so as to avoid the further aggravation and escalation of social contradictions, and enable social problems to be properly solved through rational consultation.

Third, through the equalization of essential public services, ensure that the fruits of development can benefit the whole people more profoundly and equitably. Gradually narrow the gap between rich and poor, optimize the social structure, strengthen safeguards for people's livelihood, resolve social contradictions, promote social harmony, reflect social equity, and establish a comprehensive social security system covering urban and rural residents.

1.3.2 *Promote the Diversification of Social Governance Actors and Stimulate the Vitality of Multi-actor Co-governance*

In the current situation of social diversification and complicated interests, the government alone can no longer integrate the interests of different groups and classes for effective management. This requires improving the working capabilities of Party and State organs, enterprises and institutions, people's organizations, and social organizations as soon as possible, so that the national governance system can function more effectively.[9] In order to achieve innovation in the social governance system, governance must be shifted from the government taking care of everything to non-governmental actors providing support and the government taking the lead. We should not only leverage the leading role of the government, but also actively encourage and support participation by non-governmental actors, so as to achieve a positive interaction between government governance and self-regulation by non-governmental actors and self-governance by residents.

First, the government should play a leading role in promoting the building of a law-based and service-oriented government, let the market play a decisive role in the allocation of resources, guarantee the rights and interests of the people in all aspects through reasonable institutional arrangements, and truly serve society and the masses; improve the way of social governance, and govern society with law-based thinking and approaches, so that all kinds of social activities are conducted within the framework of law and order.

Second, we need to ensure that social organizations clearly define their rights and responsibilities, exercise self-governance in accordance with the law, and play their roles; services that can be properly provided by and issues that can be properly resolved by social organizations should be handed over to social organizations; we should improve social organizations' capacity and skills for the exercise of self-management and self-governance according to law.

Third, cultivate and develop social organizations such as industry associations, public charities, community services, and technological innovation, strengthen the management of social groups and non-governmental organizations, and guide them in carrying out activities according to law.

[9] Xi Jinping, *Xi Jinping: The Governance of China*. Beijing: Foreign Language Press, 2014: 105.

Fourth, optimize the social structure, expand the size of the middle class, give full play to their positive roles in economics, culture, political ecology, etc., improve people's ability to participate in the management of state affairs, economic, social and cultural affairs, and their own affairs in accordance with the law, and form a social environment where order and vitality are united, so as to achieve a positive interaction between government governance and self-regulation by non-governmental actors and self-governance by residents.

1.3.3 Push for Law-Based Social Governance and Safeguard Social Equity and Justice

The report to the 19th CPC National Congress pointed out that "comprehensively implementing the rule of law is an essential requirement and key guarantee for socialism with Chinese characteristics." To push for law-based social governance, we must highlight the fundamental role of good law and sound governance.[10] Our Party's understanding of the important role of the rule of law in national and social governance is in line with the theoretical and practical requirements for modern state building worldwide. The organic integration of good law and sound governance will further promote the perfection of China's socialist market economic system and the sustained and healthy development of the economy and society, and is the foundation and guarantee for overcoming the middle-income trap and realizing the Chinese dream of the great rejuvenation of the Chinese nation.

The rule of law is fundamental to the modernization of social governance. The rule of law can construct a rational public domain for the social community through a large number of procedural rules and substantive institutions, so that people can deal with complex and changing relations and conflicts in daily life in a standardized and rational way. We should build social consensus during the transition period by capitalizing on the advantages of the rule of law such as predictability, operability and redressability, so that different stakeholders can seek common ground while shelving differences, and pursue and maximize their own interests in accordance with the law. We should form a scientific and effective mechanism for restricting and coordinating power to confine power to an institutional cage. We should uphold the legal authority of

[10] Zheng Zhijie. Good Law and Sound Governance Help Overcome the "Middle-Income Trap". *Study Times*, 2014-12-08.

the Constitution, speed up the building of a socialist legal system that is fair, just, efficient and authoritative, and safeguard the rights and interests of the people. We should work hard to create a sound legal environment in which people conduct their business according to the law, turn to the law when they require assistance, use the law to solve problems, and rely on the law to resolve contradictions. We should carry out all kinds of work on the track of the rule of law, treat people's demands fairly according to law, and make people feel equity and justice in good law and sound governance.

2 Transform Government Functions and Innovate Social Governance

Throughout the history of social development in various countries, although the government's political power has been rapidly diverted internally and externally in the era of globalization, and more and more social groups and organizations have begun to share the power that originally belonged to the government, the government's dominant position in social governance is unshakable. Whether it is in terms of economic growth, political development, cultural innovation, and the overall coordination of social progress or ultimate concerns such as efficiency and equity, democracy and the rule of law, development and stability, and harmony between man and nature, the government is the only dominant force, with a unique position and strong appeal that other social actors cannot replace. The government implements a unified ideology, enacts policies conforming to the law of social development and formulates reasonable social institutions through the various state machineries and organizations at its disposal.

So far as China's situation is concerned, adhering to the dominant position of the government in social governance is in line with the realistic needs of China's social development. On the one hand, there has always been a tradition of strong government governance in China. In the practice of social governance, the market and society rely on and obey the government, and local governments rely on and obey the central government.[11] On the other hand, the degree of Chinese people's participation in social governance is still relatively low compared with developed countries, and they lack the initiative to participate in the governance of public affairs. Meanwhile, there are some deficiencies in the present situation and capacity of social organizations with respect to participation in social governance. Therefore, giving full play to the leading role of the government in social governance is the key to achieving the goal of social governance.

Since the start of reform and opening-up, in addition to creating an economic miracle, China has begun to transform from a socialist planned economy to a socialist market economy, from an agricultural society to an industrial society, and from a relatively closed society to an open society. In this process, China's social governance is facing an extremely complex social background and new problems, new contradictions and new risks, such as the growing gap between urban and rural areas, between regions, and between industries, inadequate reforms in education, employment, health care, social security and income distribution, and difficulties faced by the floating population and the poor; stakeholders and their demands are becoming more and more diverse, leading to increasingly complex social contradictions; the double-edged sword effects of informatization and networking on social governance are gradually becoming visible. According to the experience of Western developed countries, like the United States, Britain, France, and Germany, in economic and social transformation, they have made great efforts to innovate social governance, and have overcome the middle-income trap after successfully completing economic and social transformation. Therefore, in the important stage of overcoming the middle-income trap in China, it is of great significance to transform government functions, innovate social governance and give full play to the leading role of the government in social governance.

2.1 *Change the Concept of Government Governance*

Thought is a precursor to action. A change of concept is a prerequisite for the transformation of government functions, and a correct concept of government governance is essential to the transformation of government

[11] Ma Baobin. *Theory and Practice of Public Governance*. Beijing: Social Sciences Academic Press, 2013: 77.

functions. To promote the transformation of government functions, we should first adopt the concept of putting people first, and the concepts of a limited government, a service-oriented government, and a law-based government.

2.1.1 Adopt the Concept of Putting People First

With the development of the economy and society, and the improvement of people's living standards, people's awareness of rights, democracy and the rule of law has been growing as they partake of the fruits of development, and there have been increased demands for quality of life, self-development, and the realization of interests, rights protection, and government governance. China is a socialist country under the people's democratic dictatorship led by the proletariat. Serving the people wholeheartedly is the fundamental purpose of the party, as well as the starting point and objective of government governance. First, "putting people first" requires the government to protect human rights. "People" refers not only to collectives and the public in the sense of social groups, but also to citizens with independent personality. The government should seek a balance between the interests of the people and the interests of individuals, focus on the fundamental interests and common interests of the people, and at the same time respect and protect the legitimate rights and interests of individuals. Second, "putting people first" requires that the government's public decision-making and public management activities should conform to public opinion, constantly realize, develop and safeguard the fundamental interests of the vast majority of the people, so that the government's public management activities are truly implemented to meet public needs, realize public interests and improve people's living standards. To this end, the government needs to give citizens sufficient autonomy, respect the primacy of citizens, constantly broaden channels for citizens to articulate their interests and participate in politics, and build a responsive and efficient interest articulation mechanism, so that the government's public decision-making and public management activities can respond promptly to public opinion and reflect the interests of the broad masses of the people. In addition, "putting people first" should also break the dominance of the government in social governance, so that people can play a major role in social governance, and ultimately achieve self-governance.[12] Only in this way can we mobilize the enthusiasm, initiative, and creativity of the vast majority of the people for participating in the socialist cause, and achieve the sustained and healthy development of society and the economy and the all-round development of people.

2.1.2 Adopt the Concept of a Limited Government

To shift the government governance model from an omnipotent government to a limited and effective government, and public management from taking care of everything to acting according to one's ability has become an inevitable choice and trend for governments in the new era. *Limited* implies that: first, the government's power is limited—the government's power comes from the Constitution and the will of all citizens, so the government must be limited by legislative and judicial power, and open to public supervision, instead of exercising power arbitrarily; second, the government's functions are limited—the government should limit itself to important and essential public affairs, and try not to get involved in detailed and specific public affairs; the government is not allowed to interfere in citizens' private affairs; third, the size of the government is limited—the government should be moderately sized and efficient. Adopt the concept of a limited government, do what we are allowed to do and avoid doing what we aren't allowed to do; do a good job managing things that we should manage, and do not meddle in what's not our business. Specifically, the government should reduce micro intervention and administrative examination and approval items, relax market access, introduce a competitive mechanism, separate government administration from self-government by social organizations, cultivate social organizations, and shift government functions to creating a good development environment, providing high-quality public services, and safeguarding social equity and justice.

2.1.3 Adopt the Concept of a Service-Oriented Government

Since the late 1970s, Western developed countries have carried out government reform, and the new public management theory and model have gradually emerged. It is customer-oriented and upholds the idea of putting customers first. It has changed the relationship between the

[12] Zheng Zhijie. Overcoming the Middle-Income Trap Urgently Needs Improved Economic Governance. *Study Times*, 2016-08-11.

government and the public under the traditional model. The government is no longer an authoritative bureaucracy that issues orders, but a public service provider. At the 2011 Workshop on Social Management and Innovation attended by major provincial and ministerial leaders, Comrade Hu Jintao said that social management was, in the final analysis, managing and serving people. At the closing ceremony of the workshop, General Secretary Xi Jinping stressed that all social management departments were departments that serve the masses. We should have a correct view of the relationship between management and services correctly, embed management in services, embody services in management, and realize management in services. We should let go of the concept formed under the planned economic system that "only the government can manage public affairs well" and "official positions are the sole measure of social status." The relationship between the government as the manager and the managed is no longer about control and obedience; the government should not monopolize all resources, take charge of everything, and get too much involved in micro-managing economic and social affairs. Instead, we should adopt the concept of a service-oriented government, elevate the public service function to the main function of the government, make the public service department the main department of the government, and make public service expenditure the main expenditure of the government. By optimizing the government structure, innovating government mechanisms, standardizing government behavior, and improving government efficiency, we can meet people's growing demand for public services.

2.1.4 Adopt the Concept of a Law-Based Government

The so-called "law-based government" means that the government is formed in accordance with the law, the government is controlled by the law, the government governs well in accordance with the law and serves the people, the government is answerable to the law, and the government and citizens are equal in legal status.[13] Throughout the history of human society, countries that strictly adhere to the rule of law have enjoyed relatively stable economic and social development, so that their people can live and work in peace and contentment. The rule of law has become an important measure of the progress of modern civilization. The report

[13] Yang Haikun, Zhang ZhiYuan. *A Study of the Government Rule of Law Theory with Chinese Characteristics*. Beijing: Law Press, 2008: 137, 140.

to the 18th CPC National Congress stresses that an important sign of China finishing building a moderately prosperous society in all respects by 2020 is that a law-based government is basically in place. Meanwhile, we should promote law-based administration, conduct law enforcement in a strict and civilized way according to due procedures, and realize the rule of law in all work of the State by making laws in a scientific way, enforcing them strictly, administering justice impartially, and ensuring that everyone abides by the law. The adoption of the concept of a law-based government lies not in the number of laws, but in a change in the manager awareness. Speaking at a gathering marking the 30th anniversary of the current edition of the Constitution, General Secretary Xi Jinping pointed out that "officials at all levels should improve their ability to deepen reform, promote development, resolve conflicts and maintain stability by using the law-based thinking and approaches." According to this requirement, government managers should respect and revere the law, take the lead in abiding by the law, govern according to the law, consciously maintain the dignity and authority of the law, and shall not have the privilege of transcending the law, nor shall they substitute their words for the law, suppress the law with power, or bend the law for personal gain.

2.2 *Leverage the Leading Role of the Government*

2.2.1 *The Leading Role of the Government in the Multi-actor Social Governance System*

In her book *Collaborative Governance and the New Administrative Law*, Jody Freeman, an American sociologist, argues that in the model of collaborative social governance, administrative organs are: the setters of the minimum standards; the conveners and enablers of multi-party consultations who propose goals, standards, and test methods to determine whether the foregoing goals and standards have been met; the builders of institutional capacity who enable relevant institutions to form partnerships in co-regulation.[14] According to this theory, the leading role of the government in the multi-actor social governance system is reflected in the following aspects: First, the government should become the setter of minimum standards for social governance and make draw a clear bottom line on various social governance matters. Second, the

[14] Jiang Bixin. Promote the Modernization of China's Governance System and Governance Capability. *Guangming Daily*, 2013-11-15.

government should be the convener and facilitator of consultation and cooperation among governance actors. The government should formulate policies and establish mechanisms to promote broad social participation and the formation of consensus, but the government should not be the determiner of the final governance plan or outcome. Third, the government should be an enabler of participation for governance actors. The government can support and encourage the participation of social organizations by providing funding or technical expertise, and promote the formation of partnerships among relevant governance actors in collaborative governance. Fourth, the law can give the government the responsibility as the ultimate regulator of social governance. The government supervises and manages behavior and effects in the process of social governance according to the powers conferred by law.

2.2.2 *The Path for the Government to Play a Leading Role in Social Governance*

The Decision of the CPC Central Committee on A Number of Major Issues Concerning Comprehensively Deepening Reform adopted at the Third Plenary Session of the 18th CPC Central Committee states: "we should strengthen the leadership of Party committees, leverage the leading role of the government, encourage and support the participation of all sectors of society, and achieve a positive interaction between government governance and social self-regulation and residents' autonomy." Under such an arrangement for social governance actors, the government, as the leader in social governance, should pay attention to strengthening the top-level design of public affairs governance, focus on solving outstanding problems at the level of systems and mechanisms, and draw on the cohesiveness of goals and its ability to integrate resources and control responsibility to act as an important organizer, promoter, participant and server in public affairs governance. Specifically: First, the government should strengthen its responsibility as the primary supplier of essential public services, and act as the "promoter" and "provider" of public services; second, the government should separate government administration from self-government by social organizations, truly release social organizations from direct management, support the development of social organizations by promoting the formulation of laws and regulations, and at the same time actively cooperate with other non-governmental forces; third, in the process of guiding civil society in exercising autonomy, the government should actively and consciously provide the institutional environment for the autonomy of civil society, create political, economic, and cultural conditions for citizens to participate in politics and realize their rights, and actively guide, organize and support citizens in participating in politics and civil society in exercising autonomy, so as to promote social justice and progress; fourth, the government should play a key role in ensuring public safety and national security, and the leading role of the government, especially in the areas of food and drug safety, work safety, network information security and national security, which are of greatest concern to citizens, should be strengthened.

2.3 *Clarify the Boundary of Government Functions*

Since the Third Plenary Session of the 11th CPC Central Committee, the State Council has undergone several rounds of institutional reform, and government functions have been adapted to the requirements of the socialist market economic system. This is reflected in the following aspects: continued progress was made in reform of the administrative examination and approval system; greater efforts were made to streamline administration and delegate power; direct management and micro intervention were gradually reduced; the macro-control system was improved; solid progress was made in law-based administration; and the focus of government functions was further shifted to social governance and public services. While acknowledging the achievements, we should pay more attention to the problem of the government "overstepping its functions (monopolizing)," "misplacing its functions," and "failing to perform its functions adequately" in governance, and put forward improvement measures.

2.3.1 *Streamline Administration and Delegate Power, and Take Back the Government's "Overstepping" Hand*

At present, the government "overstepping" its functions mainly refers to that the government directly undertakes public goods and services that could have been provided by the market or non-governmental public organizations. This is mainly reflected in the following aspects: First, the government controls social organizations. The government directly intervenes in the internal management and affairs of various associations, societies, residents' autonomous organizations, and villagers' autonomous organizations through supervision and guidance, directly or indirectly turning these social organizations into government affiliates, curbing the development and autonomy of social organizations, and greatly constraining the role of social organizations in social governance. Second, the government has taken over the development of institutions. The "big government" model formed in the history of our country has caused the establishment and functions of the government and public institutions to be intertwined. There are not only administrative organs that use the establishment of public institutions, but also public institutions that use the establishment of administrative organs. Some public institutions undertake the administrative functions of the government, and are actually an extension of administrative departments. To solve the above-mentioned problem of the government overstepping its functions, we need to further streamline administration and delegate power, and take back the "overstepping" hand as soon as possible. Following the principles of "market first" and "social autonomy first," the government should no longer intervene in matters that the market can regulate and that citizens, legal persons, and other economic organizations can decide on their own initiative and at their own risk and manage through self-discipline; for all matters for which management objectives can be achieved through regulation during and after the event concerned, prior government approval shall be canceled; for matters that can be resolved by legal and economic means, no administrative means shall be used; economic and social matters that are directly related to grass-roots levels, numerous in number and extensive in coverage, and can be more conveniently and effectively managed at local levels shall all be delegated to local and grass-roots levels. By taking back the "overstepping" hand, the government can truly "slim down" and become "strong," so that the government can fundamentally shift its functions to creating a good development environment, providing high-quality public services, and maintaining social equity and justice to become a law-based and service-oriented government.

2.3.2 *Concede Appropriately, and Take Back the Government's "Monopolizing" Hand*

To transition from an omnipotent government to limited government, we should rationalize the relationship between the government and social organizations, optimize the operation mechanism of non-governmental social organizations, shift the role of the government from "monopolizing" to "assisting," and create a good social environment for the rational positioning and independent operation of social organizations. First, we should make social organizations take up the micro-management and certain service functions transferred out during the transformation of government functions to become the bridge between the government and enterprises, and the link between the government and the market, so that the government can further free itself from the shackles of specific affairs and improve its macro-management capacity; second, we should give full play to the advantages of social organizations such as their close relations with grass-roots levels, low operating costs, and high service efficiency to better solve issues concerning social welfare, community services, environmental protection, etc., so as to help the government share its burden and solve difficulties; Finally, we should make social organizations play a greater role in expanding employment channels, the improving social security system, etc., so as to reduce the burden of the government and enterprises.

2.3.3 Do a Good Job at Providing Services to Bring Back the Government's "Missing Hand"

Since the start of reform and opening-up, economic development has been our most important task. The government is basically an "economic development-oriented" government, and most of its energy is devoted to participating or intervening in microeconomic activities rather than providing public services. Although the central government has clearly stated that the functions of the government are economic regulation, market regulation, social management, and public services, the tradition of prioritizing development over everything else still persists. The government functions in some areas and sectors have not yet been shifted to public services, resulting in the government failing to perform its functions adequately in some public spheres, as follows: First, the government fails to live up to its responsibility for the management of public crisis such as social security crisis, work safety crisis, and food and drug safety crisis; second, the construction of water conservancy facilities, environmental infrastructure and other necessary infrastructure is still not adequate enough to fully meet the needs of the people; third, the provision of social security services is insufficient, and medical, elderly care, unemployment, relief and other social security services still fall short of people's expectations; fourth, there is a shortage of public services, and public education services, public health services, and urban public utilities services that should be provided by governments at various levels still cannot meet the needs of the public. The 19th CPC National Congress called for deepening reform of institutions and the administrative system, transforming government functions, further streamlining administration and delegating power, innovating regulatory methods, strengthening government credibility and capacity for execution, building a service-oriented government that the people are satisfied with, and deepening reform of public institutions to see that they focus on serving public interests, relieving them of government functions, keeping them away from business activities, and letting them run their own day-to-day operations while maintaining supervision over them.

Therefore, the government should increase efforts to make up for the "shortest stave" of public services. On the issue of strengthening the government's public service function, we should proceed from the reality, adjust measures to local conditions, and avoid pursuing a one-size-fits-all approach; we should make full use of existing resources, make rational use of social funds, and avoid haphazard investment and redundant construction; we should strengthen infrastructure construction, the development of public welfare undertakings, and the construction of public utilities while improving their operating mechanisms; we should learn from the advanced experience of Western advanced countries in enterprise-style government management and the socialization of services, and continuously improve capacity for public service governance. Specific measures include: establishing and improving the public financial system, and increasing the government's investment in public services; establishing a wide-ranging and moderately advanced public service model with Chinese characteristics that takes into account both fairness and efficiency based on China's national conditions, and expanding the coverage of public services on the basis of ensuring a minimum standard of living, primary health care, and compulsory education and with a focus on protecting the poor and disadvantaged, so as to achieve the goal of universal access to essential public services; intensifying the development of public services in rural areas and effectively solving the problem of urban–rural imbalances; strengthening China's weak public health system, and giving all people equal access to essential public health services. The 19th CPC National Congress proposed that everyone should perform their duties and share in the benefits, basic needs should be met, key areas should be prioritized, institutions should be improved, public expectations should be guided, and the public service system should be improved.

2.4 *Innovate Means of Social Governance*

According to the requirement of "establishing a social governance model based on collaboration, participation, and common interests" set forth in the report to the 19th CPC National Congress, the government should make efforts to improve multiple means of governance. In addition to using traditional administrative means, the government should adjust measures to local conditions in the process of social governance. According to the particularity and complexity of governance matters, the government should comprehensively use legal, economic, market-based, moral, and other non-administrative means. When necessary, measures such as psychological counseling, ideological guidance, and emotional incentives should be strengthened.

2.4.1 *Strengthen the Use of Market-Based Means*

In order to solve the problems of insufficient investment, low efficiency and waste of resources that the government is facing in the field of public services, we should use the market mechanism to adjust the provision of and demand for public services through bidding, contracting, franchising and other market-based means, and give full play to the decisive role of the market in resource allocation, so as to achieve the purpose of reducing costs and improving efficiency. Therefore, we should further promote and standardize the government purchase of services, that is, through the market mechanism, some of the public services directly provided by the government and the services required for the performance of the government's duties are entrusted to qualified non-governmental entities and public institutions in certain ways and according to certain procedures, and the government pays them according to the contract. The government purchase of services should follow the following requirements: First, put in place a sound mechanism for the government purchase of services from non-governmental entities in accordance with the principles of openness, equity and justice, timely and fully publish information such as the service items to be purchased by the government, the contents of such service items, and the requirements and performance evaluation criteria for service providers, and put in place sound standardized processes for project filing, budget preparation, organizational buying, project supervision, and performance evaluation. Second, the buyer shall sign a contract with the service provider in accordance with the contract management requirements, clarifying the range of services to be purchased, the subject matter, and the quantity and quality requirements, as well as the service period, the method of payment, rights and obligations, and liability for breach of contract, pay according to the contract, and strengthen the supervision of the whole process of service provision and the inspection and acceptance of service results. The service provider shall strictly perform its contractual obligations, complete tasks under the service project on time, and ensure that services are delivered as per the specified quantity, quality and effect. Third, the purchase shall be conducted in accordance with the relevant provisions of the Government Procurement Law; the service provider shall be determined by means of open bidding, an invitation to tender, competitive negotiation, single sourcing, or an inquiry; subcontracting is strictly prohibited. Fourth, put in place a sound comprehensive evaluation mechanism composed of the buyer, service recipients, and third parties, evaluate the purchased service items in terms of quantity, quality and the use of funds, and publicize the evaluation results.

2.4.2 Comprehensively Use Ideological and Emotional Guidance and Public Opinion Guidance

Throughout the world, problems such as moral chaos, civilization degradation, and psychological crisis are common to countries that have fallen into the middle-income trap. In China's social transformation, there are also social and cultural problems such as lack of social integrity, moral decline, and spiritual weakness. If these problems are not solved, they will adversely affect China's efforts to overcome the middle-income trap. In solving the above-mentioned social, spiritual, and cultural problems, the government should focus on the use of multiple means of governance such as ideological guidance, psychological counseling, and public opinion guidance. In terms of ideological guidance, the government should strengthen ideological and moral education for the whole people, strengthen education in social morality, professional ethics, family virtue, and personal morality, cultivate a positive social mentality characterized by self-esteem, self-confidence, rationality and peace, guide citizens in consciously abiding by the law, fulfilling social and family responsibility, and maintaining social order. In terms of psychological counseling, the government should establish a psychological intervention mechanism, widely publicize and popularize personal mental health knowledge, and set up a psychological crisis intervention and early warning mechanism to prevent and reduce social risks. In terms of public opinion guidance, the government should correctly guide public opinion and improve its ability to guide public opinion. The government should make the Internet and other new media an important means and part of social governance, and use them to publicize the Party's lines, guidelines and policies, understand social conditions and public opinion, and harmonize social emotions. In accordance with the principles of active utilization, scientific development, management according to law and ensuring security, the government should intensify efforts to manage the Internet according to law, accelerate the improvement of the Internet management leadership system, ensure national network and information security, and make the Internet an important medium for correctly guiding public opinion.

2.5 *Stimulate the Vitality of Diverse Social Actors*

In the period of China's social transformation, government services, and the authoritative governance model are far from enough to meet the need for taking into account the interests of multiple stakeholders, and dealing with complex social problems and contradictions. Building a government-led social governance community and tapping into the ability of diverse social actors to cooperate is the fundamental way to resolve social problems, resolve social contradictions, and ensure the normal operation of society. As the leader in social governance, the government should actively cultivate and develop diverse actors such as social organizations that recognize each other politically, trust each other ethically, have clearly defined powers and responsibilities, and harmonize with each other in terms of interests, so as to form a multi-actor governance model under which the government and the social governance community cooperate on an equal footing and respect each other.

2.5.1 *Promote the Healthy Development of Social Organizations*

The Third Plenary Session of the 18th CPC Central Committee called for stimulating the vitality of social organizations, properly handling the relationship between the government and society, accelerating the separation of government administration from social organizations, and pushing social organizations to clarify their powers and responsibilities, exercise autonomy in accordance with the law, and play their role. Public services that can be properly provided by and issues that can be properly resolved by social organizations should be handed over to social organizations. But at present, social organizations in China are not sufficiently capable of autonomy, and lack autonomy, willingness and organization due to reasons such as limited growth space and a strong orientation toward administration, which will inevitably affect the ability of social organizations to play their due role in the social governance community. Therefore, the government should actively promote the healthy development of social organizations. First, we should speed up reform of the social organization system, speed up the process of their "de-administration" and "de-monopolization," cut off the chain of interests between government departments and social organizations, and restore the non-governmental attributes of social organizations. Second, the government should emancipate the mind, fully recognize the role of social organizations in China's current economic and social development, bring into play social organizations' primary function of providing services for society, invite bids from social organizations for some livelihood projects, entrust new public service functions to social organizations through the government purchase of services, return functions that originally belonged to social organizations, and transfer functions that social organizations can perform more effectively to social organizations. Third, the government should actively cultivate social organizations, conduct scientific regulation, make reasonable arrangements, and optimize the structure according to the fields of activity and functions of social organizations, formulate targeted incentive policies, make overall plans and take all factors into consideration, proceed in a step-by-step fashion, highlight priorities, make advances under separate categories, and build a system for the scientific, stable and orderly development of social organizations. Fourth, the government should improve relevant laws and regulations to regulate the behavior of social organizations; strengthen supervision and management and beef up law enforcement to ensure that social organizations carry out activities in accordance with the law and promote the healthy development of social organizations. Fifth, strengthen the self-development of social organizations and the building of talent teams for social organizations to improve their ability to serve society and their credibility. Social organizations win recognition from society and the public through credibility, and improve their visibility and expand their influence by serving society. Only with professional service capabilities can social organizations actively and effectively participate in social governance and public services.

2.5.2 *Strengthen the Cultivation of "Active Citizenship"*

The concept of "active citizenship" is an important part of the "view of citizenship" of Hannah Arendt, a German political theorist in the twentieth century. According to Arendt, "active citizens" are citizens who possess thoughts, judgment and sensus communis, and they advocate active action and care about public life. According to Arendt's theory, citizens who uphold the public spirit, care about the public sphere, and actively participate in social and political life critical to the success or failure of the social governance community.[15]

With the deepening of reform and opening-up and the development of democracy and the rule of law, Chinese citizens' awareness of political participation has gradually increased, and their political participation has gradually expanded and has become increasingly active. But overall, the level of Chinese citizens' political participation is still very low. This is mainly reflected in the fact that they are generally not enthusiastic about participation; their political participation is evidently motivated by self-interest, and in most cases their participation is motivated by a desire to safeguard their rights; their participation is apparently marked by irrationality and a tendency toward disorder, and is poorly systematized. These problems have restricted the level of citizens' participation in social management to a certain extent, thus affecting the development of multi-actor social governance. Therefore, the cultivation of "active citizenship" should be made an important task in the building of a social governance community. On the one hand, the government should foster the concept of citizens' participation in public affairs. The concept encompasses not only citizens' belief in and commitment to public interest, but also citizens' belief in and commitment to the "publicness." It means that citizens' respect for and adherence, responsibilities, and obligations to "publicness" can encourage every individual citizen to participate actively in public affairs as a citizen. Only by comprehensively raising citizens' subjective awareness, awareness of publicness, awareness of responsibility, and awareness of participation can their enthusiasm and capacity for autonomy be enhanced. On the other hand, the government should also put in place a sound citizen participation mechanism. In order to promote full exchange, communication, consultation, and cooperation among citizens, the government should put in place a sound interest

[15] Wang Hui, Chen Yangu. *Culture and Publicness*. Beijing: SDX Joint Publishing Company, 2005: 7.

communication mechanism and interest coordination mechanism, give citizens the opportunity to express their will, and guide citizens in articulating their interests and resolving conflicts of interests reasonably and legally, thereby increasing citizens' participation in social co-governance.

3 Narrow the Gap Between Rich and Poor, and Optimize the Social Structure

Excessive income inequality, disparities between rich and poor, and even polarization are the most prominent and common problems in all countries that have fallen into the middle-income trap. After entering the middle-income stage of development, many countries have seen an explosion of social problems, an intensification of social contradictions, and even social unrest due to growing income inequality, which has become a major drag on economic growth. The most prominent reason why some Latin American countries have fallen into the middle-income trap is a drastic widening of income disparities and severe social divisions. This reflects the fact that many institutional arrangements related to income distribution cannot meet the needs of economic development. In such a situation, the basic conditions for stable social and economic development will be lost. Therefore, improving the relevant institutions, narrowing the gap between rich and poor, and optimizing the social structure is an important task to accomplish in order for China to overcome the middle-income trap.

3.1 Expand the Size of the Middle Class and Build a Stable Social Structure

The formation of a social structure dominated by the middle class is a key step toward successful economic and social transformation in every country. As long as a country can form an "olive-shaped" social structure in which high- and low-income groups make up a low proportion of the population, and middle-income groups make up more than half or even more than 70% of the population, it can overcome the middle-income trap relatively smoothly. A middle class of a certain size plays an important stabilizing role in the economic, cultural and political fields, and constitutes the cornerstone of the normal order of modern society. Economically, the middle-class stimulates, drives and guides social consumption, and is the main provider of domestic market demand

and an important force behind social and economic growth; culturally, the middle class has a good sense of civic responsibility and is morally and culturally refined, and is the most important carrier of the mainstream culture of society and the spiritual pillar that maintains social stability; politically, the middle class generally shows a strong tendency to support the existing political system or is moderate when it comes to political reform, and is the most important structural force for effectively preventing and mitigating social contradictions and maintaining social stability. When the middle-class reaches a certain size, it will play an economically, culturally, and politically positive role, become a social stabilizer, and constitute the main force behind economic and social transformation.

China's current social structure is far from satisfactory due to various historical and institutional reasons. Studies at the turn of the century found that from the perspective of economic and social status, China's social structure was an inverted T-shaped structure: two-thirds of the population made up the huge and flat bottom of the social hierarchy, and the proportion of middle-income groups was relatively low. Follow-up studies in recent years have found that after more than a decade of development, the "inverted T-shaped" structure has evolved into a "±-shaped" structure: People at the bottom of society are still large in number, accounting for more than half of the total population; some segments of the middle class have expanded, but the overall social structure has not fundamentally improved, and the middle class is still a small part of society. From the perspective of economic and social transformation, the "±-shaped" social structure still cannot provide sufficient impetus for overcoming the middle-income trap in the economic, cultural, and political fields. This requires us to expand the size of the middle class as soon as possible, form a relatively stable "olive-shaped" social structure dominated by the middle class, so that most members of society can partake of rich social resources, fair development opportunities, and the fruits of reform and opening-up in economic and social development, which is an inevitable choice for building a moderately prosperous society in all respects and achieving stable, scientific and sustainable development. Cultivating and strengthening the middle class and building an "olive-shaped" modern social structure cannot be accomplished overnight, and requires concerted, multi-pronged, step-by-step, and coordinated efforts.

3.1.1 *Adjust the Structure and Change the Mode to Consolidate the Economic Foundation*

An "olive-shaped" social structure must be built on a reasonable industrial structure, a scientific mode of development, and abundant social wealth. Only by speeding up industrial structural adjustment, changing the mode of development, promoting steady economic growth, increasing total social wealth, and making the "cake" big enough, can every individual get a greater share, and can we get rid of poverty, continuously improve living standards, prevent excessive polarization, and improve access to more equitable choices and public resources for most members of society. To this end, we must vigorously promote new-type urbanization and agricultural modernization, coordinate urban and rural development, and make every effort to narrow the income gap between urban and rural households; we must vigorously pursue new-type industrialization, build a modern industrial system with distinctive characteristics, constantly increase the size of the middle stratum of society, and raise the contribution of new-type industrialization to economic and social development and household income growth; we must vigorously promote the development of service industries with a focus on the development of tertiary industries including financial securities, modern logistics, information technology, and cultural industries, so as to make them major industries to absorb surplus labor and drive the transformation of the social structure.

3.1.2 *Strengthen Income Control and Improve Wealth Distribution*

While increasing total social wealth, we should actively rationalize social wealth relations, improve the current income distribution system, straighten out the relationship between economic agents belonging to different interest groups, and try to divide the "cake" well. The government should focus reform of the economic system on supporting the growth of the middle class, accelerate the transformation into a "welfare-oriented" and "people-enriching" government. We should always adhere to the principle of giving priority to efficiency with due consideration given to equity, strengthen the macro-control of income distribution, shift from distribution according to work to distribution according to factors, with labor, technology, assets, capital, and management all allowed to participate in income distribution; we should raise the minimum wage standard, ensure normal wage growth, establish a corporate wage determination mechanism of checks and balances, continue to improve the distribution mechanism for business operators, link growth in business operators' income with growth in employees' income, and ensure that employees' income grows in pace with growth in corporate profits; we should broaden and protect the property income of residents, help residents open up new sources of income, and speed up the formation of system of diversified income sources. In addition to improving capital markets at multiple levels, banking, life insurance, the stock market and the real estate market, we should establish and improve urban and rural banks, develop financial derivatives, improve the stock futures market, expand private equity (PE), venture capital (VC) and other large-scale legal financing channels, and further develop the insurance market, so as to open up a variety of investment channels for residents; we should comprehensively strengthen the stability of the financial system, build a healthy financial structure, hierarchy and system, avoid improperly pushing up prices in a single capital market by concentrating investment, prevent hot money from impacting domestic residents 'capital, and ensure that residents' property and capital income increases and social wealth expands; we should improve and standardize the securities market, and establish a set of scientific, systematic and perfect rules and regulations covering market access, listing, supervision, etc., according to the internal laws of the securities market, so as to ensure the legitimate rights and interests of investors and increase the capital income of residents; we should encourage laborers to turn their consumption surplus into assets while obtaining labor compensation by dint of their own labor, and recognize and protect their legitimate non-labor income.

3.1.3 *Coordinate the Demands of Stakeholders and Facilitate the Sharing of Fruits*

An "olive-shaped" social class structure means that members of society generally benefit from the process of modernization, the vast majority of them can obtain full employment and enjoy comprehensive social benefits, their demands are responded to, and they have a strong sense of social identity and well-being. To this end, based on the experience of France, Germany, and other countries, combined with China's national conditions, practical measures can be taken to further refine the legal system of the market economy and the social security system, comprehensively enhance people's livelihood, and improve quality and efficiency. These measures include attaching great importance to the interests of the middle class, establishing systems and mechanisms that match the diversity and complexity of the demands of the middle class in China, and giving them access to the relevant social resources and institutional arrangements so as to prevent their interests from being infringed; implementing a more proactive employment policy, creating more jobs, encouraging and supporting entrepreneurship, gradually removing institutional barriers in household registration, education, identity, etc., and promoting reasonable class mobility, so as to gradually expand the middle-income group; speeding up the creation of a social security system covering urban and rural areas, appropriately raising the urban and rural poverty lines and subsidies for poverty alleviation, ensuring the basic livelihood of low-income groups in society, perfecting mechanisms such as Urban Resident Basic Medical Insurance, New Rural Cooperative Medical Scheme, and New Rural Social Pension Insurance, and improving the interconnected social security system consisting of social insurance, social assistance, social welfare and charity.

3.2 *Reform the Income Distribution System and Pay More Attention to Distributive Equity*

Income distribution is usually divided into three levels: primary distribution, secondary distribution and tertiary distribution. Primary distribution is distribution according to the quantity and quality of the factors of production supplied by suppliers of factors of production under market regulation. Secondary distribution is the distribution formed after the adjustment of primary distribution through taxation and social welfare measures under government regulation. Tertiary distribution is based on the results of secondary distribution. It is a kind of redistribution of personal income guided by moral force. It does not have any elements of compulsion and is entirely voluntary. Examples include donations, poverty alleviation measures, public welfare funds, etc. The role of the government in this situation is to formulate sound and perfect laws, regulations, and rules, encourage voluntary donations by individuals, and prevent relevant units, institutions and personnel from embezzling charitable donations.[16]

[16] Li Yining. *Chinese Economy in Dual Transition*. Beijing: China Renmin University Press, 2013.

The report to the 18th CPC National Congress stated that household income as a share of national income and the proportion of labor compensation in primary distribution should be increased, and clarified the basic direction of deepening reform of the income distribution system. The report also stated that both efficiency and equity should be taken into account in primary distribution and redistribution, and more attention should be paid to equity in redistribution. The issue of income distribution is not only a prominent issue faced by China in the period of social transformation and high-speed economic growth, but also a key link in the process of breaking through the overall development dilemma, overcoming the middle-income trap, and striding forward toward the grand goal of building a moderately prosperous society in all respects. To shift the mode of economic development from "production-driven" to "consumption-driven," we must reduce income inequality and increase household income. Anxiety over economic slowdown should not be solved by "drinking poison to quench thirst" and re-stimulating the economy, but by promoting reform of the income distribution system and strengthening social welfare. In order to quickly and effectively arrest the trend toward polarization between rich and poor, we should adhere to a goal-oriented approach, make precise efforts, strengthen institutional building, and use institutions to ensure distributive equity.

3.2.1 Primary Distribution Should Be Based on Market Regulation and Take Equity into Consideration

Primary distribution mainly addresses the issue of the distribution of benefits between owners of capital and owners of labor. The main criterion for judging whether the primary distribution of national income is fair is the distribution rate, namely, the share of labor compensation in GDP. The higher the distribution rate, the fairer the primary distribution of national income.[17] But wages in China have been falling behind economic growth, and the labor and capital income structure is unreasonable with capital taking precedence over labor in distribution. At present, the market mechanism is still subject to many limitations when it comes to influencing the primary distribution of income in China, and cannot play a fundamental regulatory role. The current wage system smacks of a planned economy and does not match the market economy: the wage

[17] Li Baogeng. Some Thoughts on China's Income Distribution System. *Special Zone Economy*, 2011 (2).

growth mechanism is rigid and not institutionally guaranteed; the wage structure is unreasonable in that performance-related pay as a percentage of the annual payroll is too low to reflect reasonable wage differentials, and therefore provides no incentives and restraints; The minimum wage and wage payment in non-state-owned units in the labor market are not effectively guaranteed, the rights and interests of employees are violated, and the labor compensation of unskilled and non-technical workers is artificially suppressed.

To improve the primary distribution system, we must actively rationalize social wealth relations, always adhere to the principle of balancing efficiency and equity, and strengthen the macro-control of income distribution.

Improve the Minimum Wage Guarantee System

For low-income groups such as some front-line workers in enterprises and persons in flexible employment, the government should improve the wage guideline system and provide reference standards for collective wage bargaining in enterprises. We should improve the minimum wage guarantee system. On the basis of economic development and the improvement of corporate efficiency, we should make the minimum wage grow slightly faster than the average wage in society, and gradually raise the minimum wage to 40–60% of the average wage in society in line with international practice. We should use legal means to encourage enterprises to put in place a sound normal wage growth mechanism and a wage payment guarantee mechanism. The government should reduce taxes and fees for enterprises, so as to encourage enterprises to increase wages for workers and reduce the cost burden on enterprises.

Increase the Proportion of Labor Compensation

Labor compensation is the main source of income for low-income groups. We should adjust the national income distribution structure by increasing household income as a share of national income while reducing the proportion of corporate income and government revenue. We should increase the proportion of labor compensation in primary distribution, so that low-income people who can only earn income by selling their labor can get a bigger share of the fruits of economic development. We should ensure that growth in household income keeps in pace with economic development, and growth in labor compensation keeps in pace with increases in labor productivity.

Ensure Normal Wage Growth

We should establish a corporate wage determination mechanism of checks and balances, continue to improve the distribution mechanism for business operators, link growth in business operators' income with growth in employees' income, and ensure that employees' income grows in pace with growth in corporate profits; we should broaden and protect the property income of residents, help residents open up new sources of income, encourage laborers to turn their consumption surplus into assets while obtaining labor compensation by dint of their own labor, and recognize and protect their legitimate non-labor income.

Pay Attention to the Regulation of Government Behavior and Give Play to the Decisive Role of the Market in Resource Allocation

We should create a level playing field between suppliers and demanders of factors of production, and a level playing field between commodity producers as soon as possible, make institutional preparations for the adjustment of primary distribution, and reduce wealth inequality caused by "non-market" factors. We should give support to some entities in emerging industries, create the new situation of "mass entrepreneurship and innovation," enable more people to start businesses and find jobs, and allow every citizen to enter and exit the market freely, become market entities, and get a share of the dividends of the market economy.

3.2.2 More Attention Should Be Paid to Equity in Reform of Secondary Distribution

Primary distribution is mainly based on market regulation and puts a greater emphasis on efficiency, while secondary distribution is focused on delivering equity through the government's reasonable public policies.[18] Equity based on efficiency should be the value pursued by social governance under the conditions of China's socialist market economy. Although the market mechanism is an effective way of allocating resources, the market is no panacea. The allocation of resources by the market mechanism has an insurmountable flaw, namely, the so-called "market failure," and the widening gap between rich and poor is one of its main manifestations. Therefore, the government in a modern

[18] Cai Fang, Zhang Chewei, et al. *A Study on Income Distribution in China*. Beijing: China Social Sciences Press, 2016.

market economy should use public policies to influence and regulate redistribution.

We should establish a fair and reasonable tax burden mechanism, and use tax policies to adjust the social wealth structure so as to tilt the redistribution of national income toward underdeveloped areas, low-income people and disadvantaged social groups. We should further deepen the reform of the tax system, continue to pursue the standardization and transparency of personal income, improve the individual income tax system, and strengthen efforts to balance the opposite ends of the income spectrum through upward and downward adjustments. We should continue to increase redistribution spending, increase income subsidies and support for low-income groups, launch a mechanism of linkage between living allowances for low-income residents and the cost-of-living index for low-income residents in due course, further strengthen financial subsidies for rural and underdeveloped areas, and increase the proportion of transfer payments to rural and underdeveloped areas in total fiscal expenditure.

Improve the Top-Level Design of the Social Security System and Make It More Inclusive

The inadequate redistributive effect of China's social security system is also an important reason why the income gap is difficult to narrow. China's social security system is characterized by the need for individual contributions and an emphasis on linking benefits with contributions, but its function of regulating income distribution needs to be strengthened. To improve the social security system, we need to start with its top-level design, make it more inclusive and fairer, and leverage its role as a means of redistribution to adjust income distribution. To this end, we can consider implementing the old-age allowance system or establishing a unified non-contributory public pension system throughout the country, reforming the current endowment insurance system for urban employees, and further improve the occupational and enterprise annual pension system.

Strengthen Welfare Measures and Focus on Equal Treatment for Migrants

When it comes to public services, the greatest injustice is that people living in the same region or even the same city are treated differently based on their identity, with rural people who have been working and living in cities and towns for a long time bearing the brunt of unfair treatment. In order to speed up the equalization of public services, it is imperative to bring this part of the migrant population into the local public service system as soon as possible, which is required not only to narrow income inequality, but also to maintain social harmony and stability.

3.2.3 Attention Should Be Paid to Institutional Guarantees for Charity and Public Welfare Undertakings in Tertiary Distribution

Tertiary distribution means that people who have gotten rich first voluntarily surrender part of their wealth to help poor areas and disadvantaged groups improve their medical, cultural, educational, and living conditions through charity. In some developed countries, the total amount of tertiary distributions such as charity accounts for about 3–5% of GDP, while in China, it only accounts for 0.1% of GDP. This shows that we need to vigorously promote tertiary distribution, and encourage those who have gotten rich first to support disadvantaged groups according to their ability and on a voluntary basis, so as to achieve the goal of common prosperity.

China's "tertiary distribution" system is deficient. Private charities and public welfare undertakings are important components of income redistribution and social welfare development in mature market economy countries. However, at present, China still lacks the social mechanism to encourage and support non-governmental forces to embark on charity and public welfare undertakings, and it is still uncommon for enterprises and individuals to participate in charity. In light of this fact, first, the government should give positive guidance and offer policy support to provide a development platform for charity. Second, the government should strengthen the development of laws and regulations in relevant fields. The Charity Law of the People's Republic of China (hereinafter referred to as the "Charity Law") introduced in 2016 marked a big step forward in charity legislation, but in terms of access for charities, Internet fundraising, tax incentives, etc., public power still exerts strong administrative control over private entities involved in charity. On the other hand, the law provides for no correspondingly rigorous control over the exercise of public power, and many matters affecting the rights and interests of private entities are left to the discretion of administrative departments. In the implementation of the law, the relevant departments should also change their thinking, eliminate the space for power rent-seeking, put an end to monopolistic and discriminatory practices, and protect the rights of charitable organizations; implement the spirit of the Charity Law that encourages the development of charity, rectify parts of the law that are heavily power-oriented, switch from a mode of control to a mode of supervision, put emphasis on regulation after the event concerned, maintain basic trust in the market regulation mechanism on the basis of ensuring the openness, fairness and competitiveness of the public welfare market in line with the "right"-oriented original intention of the Charity Law, and complete the "Pareto" improvement of tertiary distribution to further promote social equity.

3.3 Strengthen the Protection of Farmers' Property Rights and Coordinate Urban and Rural Development

The report to the 19th CPC National Congress calls for the implementation of a "rural revitalization strategy." The process of China's economic and social development is distinctly characterized by an urban–rural dual structure. An important manifestation of this is the large income gap between urban and rural households. By the time reform and opening-up was initiated, China had pursued the strategy of giving priority to the development of heavy industry for a long time. Under the strategy, the process of industrialization was accelerated by absorbing agricultural surplus to provide capital accumulation for industry and subsidize cities, thereby tilting the distribution of income in favor of urban residents.[19]

After the start of reform and opening-up, China began to transform from a planned economy to a market economy. In this process, vague property rights, uncertain subjects of rights and unclear rights and responsibilities are the main obstacles to reform and also a huge drag on development. Therefore, property rights reform is a breakthrough point and a source of power. Under the current property rights system, although farmers can enter the market freely, their contracted land and homesteads, as well as houses built on their homesteads have no clear property rights, and therefore have been unpledgeable for a long time. The transfer of rural land is largely affected by non-market factors, and farmers cannot get reasonable compensation for being deprived of land. In addition, because farmers do not have clear property rights, and land

[19] Yu Guoan, Qu Yongyi, et al. *A Study on Income Distribution*. Beijing: Economic Science Press, 2008.

income is subject to many restrictions, they have no capital income and cannot become independent market entities. Under the land property rights system, farmers have no tangible rights, such as the right of control, the right of disposal, and the right to earn income.[20] As a result, farmers' land rights are not guaranteed, land has long been managed by individual households on a small scale and cannot be managed on a large scale through free trade. This inevitably leads to high costs, low efficiency, low land productivity, and the absence of scale economies.

The Third Plenary Session of the 11th CPC Central Committee proposed the creation of the "Separation of Three Rights" model (i.e., the separation of the land ownership right, land contract right and land management right), giving farmers the right to pledge as security or collateral the right to possess, use, earn income from and transfer, as well as the right to the contracted management of their contracted land. The Several Opinions on Comprehensively Deepening Rural Reform and Speeding Up Agricultural Modernization issued by the CPC Central Committee and the State Council in 2014 further clarified the institutional design of the "Separation of Three Rights," and made it clear that on the basis of implementing the collective ownership of rural land, farmers' contract right should be stabilized, control over the land management right should be loosened, and the right to the contracted management of land should be allowed to be pledged to financial institutions to raise financing. This reform policy has been further strengthened in relevant documents since then. The "Separation of Three Rights" model is an important innovation in China's agricultural management system. It solves the problem of land being broken up into small plots that had been present since the establishment of the right to the contracted management of rural land in the 1990s, facilitates the introduction of green agriculture and high-tech agriculture, effectively promotes the development of agricultural economy by creating economies of scale, and improves farmers' capital income.

In order to implement the requirement of "granting the right to pledge as security or collateral the right to the contracted management of rural land" put forward by the central government, the following work needs to be done.

[20] China Institute for Reform and Development (CIRD). *Solution to Challenges Facing Income Distribution Reform*. Beijing: China Economic Publishing House, 2012.

3.3.1 Expand the Scope of Confirmation of Rights for Rural Land

The biggest asset of farmers relative to urban residents is land. Under the current system of collectively owned farmland, farmers are unable to maximize the value of this asset. Once farmers' land is expropriated by the state, any increase in the value of the land will have nothing to do with them. Farmers will not only miss out on the benefits of increases in the value of land, but also see their interests compromised by urbanization. Therefore, there is an urgent need to clarify land ownership.[21] In order to put in place the usufruct of rural land, and give farmers more property rights, the No. 1 central document No. 1 issued on January 31, 2013 stated: "We should comprehensively carry out the confirmation of rights, registration and certification for rural land. We should improve the registration system for the right to the contracted management of rural land, and strengthen the protection of the right to the contracted management of rural land, such as farmland and woodland." Through application for land registration, cadastral surveying, certification of title, registration, land certification and other land registration procedures, the attribution of rights pertaining to each parcel of land is finally confirmed.

The confirmation of rights and certification for rural land will promote the transfer of land, with land gradually going into and concentrating in the hands of people who farm on a large scale and are expert at farming, which will help cultivate a batch of family farms run mainly by farmers and give birth to a batch of leading agricultural enterprises. The stability of ownership, the perfection of property rights protection, and the standardization of transactions in land transfer lower the risks of all parties involved in transfer, reduce opaque links in the transfer process, enhance the stability of transfer, and increase the coverage and scale of transfer. Practice has proved that, because of farmers' entitlement to property rights and property income, coupled with independent management and capital accumulation, farmers are highly motivated to expand production and improve productivity, greatly reducing the gap between per capita income in urban and rural areas.[22] These factors have contributed to a shift in primary distribution in favor of farmers.

[21] Shanghai Institute of Finance and Law. *Re-explain China's Worries and Its Way Out*. Shanghai: Shanghai Joint Publishing, 2013.

[22] Li Yining. *Chinese Economy in Dual Transition*. Beijing: China Renmin University Press, 2013.

3.3.2 *Implement the "Separation of Three Rights" for Rural Land*

The "Separation of Three Rights" means that under the basic rural management system, property rights in rural land are broken down into three kinds of rights: land ownership right, land contract right and land management right. Farmers who have the right to the contracted management of land can transfer their rural land by transferring their land management right while retaining the land contract right.

The "Separation of Three Rights" property rights structure clearly defines the "contract right" and "management right." On the one hand, acknowledging that the land contract right arises from farmers' membership of collective organizations is conducive to strengthening the protection of farmers' contract right; on the other hand, protecting the safety of the transfer of management right can stabilize operators' expectations and is conducive to improving land productivity. The "Separation of Three Rights" can achieve an effective unity of equity and efficiency by protecting the contract right to deliver equity and making flexible use of the management right to deliver efficiency.[23]

At present, the urgent issue is to endow the management right mentioned in the central document with the disposal function that comes with real rights by means of explicit legal provisions. Although the Real Right Law stipulates that holders of the right to the contracted management of land have the right to possess, use and earn income, it does not specify the way to dispose of these rights. In practice, the transfer of the land management right is generally done by the contractor allowing the holder of the management right to cultivate his or her contracted land in exchange for a consideration without changing the contract relationship with the collective, and the holder of the management right signing a lease contract with the collective economic organization or individual farmer. But the right is a claim and is subject to a 20-year maximum term under the Contract Law.[24] In general, it does not require real estate registration, or even notarization. Its legal circulation is insufficient, the legal protection for it is not rigorous enough, and its transfer is not secure enough. Only when it is established as a real right and endowed with the

[23] Gao Shengping. The Legal Logic of the Farmland Property Rights Structure under the New Agricultural Management System. *Chinese Journal of Law*, 2014 (4).

[24] The first paragraph of Article 214 of the Contract Law of the People's Republic of China stipulates: "The lease term shall not exceed 20 years. If the lease term exceeds 20 years, the excess part shall be invalid".

functions of possession, use, earning income and disposal, can it meet the requirements for being "transferable" and "pledgeable." In particular, the duration of the right should be allowed to exceed the maximum term of 20 years stipulated in the Contract Law, so as to meet the right holder' needs for long-term production and operation.[25] In addition, endowing the "management right" with the function of disposing according to law also strengthens the ability of the right to enter the market. As a real right in immovable property, it can be incorporated into immovable property registration in practice. After registration, whether the right is transferred or pledged, the legal operation will be very convenient, and the protection of the right will be strengthened.

3.3.3 Promote the Transfer of the Right to the Contracted Management of Land

In order to promote the transfer of the right to the contracted management of land, it is necessary to include the right to the contracted management of land among pledgeable property under the Real Right Law to bring the financial value of the right to the contracted management of land into play. For a long time, China's rural areas have been under severe financial constraints. Commercial finance characterized by secured loans has been struggling in rural areas, and farmers can hardly have as much access as urban residents to finance. It is found in practice that the lack of collateral is one of the important factors that make it difficult to obtain loans in rural areas. To some extent, collateral can ease the problem of information asymmetry between the two sides of credit, alleviate adverse selection on financial markets and reduce moral hazard. In China's rural areas, the most important property owned by farmers is the right to the contracted management of land. The financialization of the right to the contracted management of land has become an important path and breakthrough point for deepening rural land reform.

China's Real Rights Law classifies the right to the contracted management of land by the way in which it is acquired. The pledging of the right to the contracted management of land acquired by means of bidding, bidding, auction, public consultation, etc., is positioned as a way of transfer, and the right to the contracted management of land thus

[25] Sun Xianzhong. A Study on Legislation for Promoting the "Separation of Three Rights" Model for Farmland. *Social Sciences in China*, 2016 (7).

acquired can be "transferred, converted into shares, pledged or otherwise disposed of"; right to the contracted management of land acquired by way of household contracting, on the other hand, is limited in terms of pledging, and is confined to "subcontracting, swapping, transferring, etc."

The decision of the Third Plenary Session of the 18th CPC Central Committee pointed out that "the right to the contracted management of rural land should be allowed to be pledged as security or collateral"; the Several Opinions on Comprehensively Deepening Rural Reform and Speeding Up Agricultural Modernization issued by the CPC Central Committee and the State Council made it clear that the "right to the contracted management of land" could be pledged to financial institutions to raise financing. These understandings have strengthened the real right and property attributes of the right to the contracted management of land and improved the pledgeability of the right to the contracted management of land as security or collateral, providing an important way to promote the transfer and financialization of rural land and solve the financing problems of farmers.

At the present stage, we should gradually loosen restrictions on the marketization, of rural land, liquidize the land assets accumulated in the hands of farmers, fully realize the market value of rural land, and create conditions for credit supply for land management on an appropriate scale and intensive agricultural management. We should encourage finance institutions to carry out rural land finance business, reduce the cost of realizing the right to pledge rural land, and promote the transfer of rural land in accordance with the provisions of the Real Right Law.

In 2015, 232 county-level divisions, including Daxing District of Beijing, launched a pilot program on pledging the right to the contracted management of rural land as security for loans. Legal provisions incompatible with the pilot program will remain suspended in areas where the pilot program on pledging the right to the contracted management of land and farmers' housing property rights as security for loans is implemented for the duration of the pilot program. After the pilot program has proven successful, consideration may be given to amending the Real Right Law, the Guarantee Law and the Rural Land Contract Law to include the right to the contracted management of land among property that is pledgeable under the law.

3.3.4 *Reform and Improve the Rural Homestead System*

Granting farmers the right to dispose of their housing property rights and giving farmers more complete rights and interests in real estate that cover use value and exchange value through legal empowerment is an important channel to increase farmers' property income and also a way out of the predicament facing the development of rural commercial finance. We should reform and improve the rural homestead system, and explore ways for farmers to increase their property income. The 19th CPC National Congress called for efforts to consolidate and improve the basic management system for rural homesteads and deepen the reform of the rural land system. Farmers' housing property rights consist of housing ownership and the right to use the homestead, and are an important piece of property for the vast majority of farmers. The current law explicitly prohibits the pledging of the right to use the homestead, which to a large extent restricts the full realization of the financial value of this piece of property. The Decision of the CPC Central Committee on A Number of Major Issues Concerning Comprehensively Deepening Reform clearly states: "we should protect the usufruct of farmers' homesteads, reform and improve the rural homestead system, select a number of experimental units, prudently and steadily advance the pledging as security or collateral and the transfer of farmers' housing property rights, and explore ways for farmers to increase their property income." The pledging of farmers' housing property rights involves many subjects whose interests are entangled in a complex web, and touches on major theoretical, policy and legal issues. Therefore, it is extremely important and urgent that we carry out systematic research on the pledging of farmers' housing property rights, summarize practical experience in time, and study the scope and form of homestead disposal and the distribution of proceeds from homestead disposal in the realization of the right to pledge, as well as the prevention of risks related to pledging. Under the guidance of the policy of "protecting the usufruct of farmers' homesteads," farmers should be given the right to pledge property rights as soon as possible. Farmer's right to pledge their housing property rights cannot be created without registration, and be realized by means of a voluntary auction or sale, compulsory auction or sale, or enforcement. In the case of a disposal of a pledged property, the transferee does not necessarily have to be a member of the collective economic organization. But if the farmer's housing property rights are transferred to a person other than a member of the collective economic organization, the person can obtain the ownership of the house and at the same time acquire, on a leasehold basis, the right to use the homestead. In this way, the original pledger can receive proceeds from the lease of the right to use the homestead so as to guarantee his or her basic housing rights.

3.4 Improve the Transfer Payment System and Promote Coordinated Regional Development

The 19th CPC National Congress calls for "implementing the coordinated regional development strategy" The level of economic and social development varies greatly from region to region in China. There is not only a horizontal imbalance in development between the eastern, central and western regions, but also a vertical imbalance in development at the provincial, city and county levels. Under the unified fiscal system, tax revenue varies substantially by locality, which objectively increases the difficulty of equalizing essential public services. The report to the 19th CPC National Congress stated: "We will devote more energy to speeding up the development of old revolutionary base areas, areas with large ethnic minority populations, border areas, and poor areas. We will strengthen measures to reach a new stage in the large-scale development of the western region; deepen reform to accelerate the revitalization of old industrial bases in the northeast and other parts of the country; help the central region rise by tapping into local strengths; and support the eastern region in taking the lead in pursuing optimal development through innovation. To this end, we need to put in place new, effective mechanisms to ensure coordinated development of different regions." Therefore, it is necessary to reasonably increase local governments' financial resources, and at the same time, the central government should appropriately concentrate part of its financial resources on increasing transfer payments, so as to balance development across different regions.

The central government and local governments often have different preferences for transfer payments. Generally speaking, special transfer payments and general transfer payments have their own characteristics: the former reflect the central government's policy orientation, and are to easy to supervise and inspect; the latter can be used flexibly by local governments according to their overall plans. The central government is generally inclined to increase special transfer payments in order to strengthen guidance and implement the central government's major decisions and arrangements. Local governments generally want to increase the proportion of general transfer payments to order to make it easy to use government financial resources according to their overall plans. To make a reasonable overall plan for transfer payments proportionally, we must first reasonably plan for the responsibilities for handling essential public services and fiscal powers of the central government and local governments, and improve the transfer payment system that matches responsibilities for handling essential public services with fiscal powers.

3.4.1 Properly Divide Responsibilities for Handling Essential Public Services and Expenditure Responsibilities Between the Central Government and Local Governments

Clear responsibilities for handling essential public services and expenditure responsibilities are an important prerequisite for enhancing the scientificity of government decision-making, and improving the efficiency of government work and the efficiency of the use of government funds. On the basis of speeding up the transformation of government functions and clarifying the boundary between the roles of the government and the market, responsibilities for handling essential public services and expenditure responsibilities can be divided among governments according to principles such as legal provisions, the range of beneficiaries, cost efficiency, and giving priority to grass-roots levels.[26] The construction of major trans-regional infrastructure and other projects involving sustainable economic and social development shall be led or mainly undertaken by the central government; the central government shall increase spending on items that are closely related to people's immediate interests and of general public concern, such as spending on basic livelihood, to promote social equity and justice; other responsibilities for handling essential public services shall be reasonably divided among governments at and below the provincial level. The division of responsibilities for handling essential public services and expenditure responsibilities among governments involves the adjustment of the functions of governments at all levels and personnel of relevant institutions, requires speeding up legislative research and forming a list of administrative and expenditure responsibilities that is constantly refined in practice, and needs to be gradually

[26] Jia Kang. Reform of the Fiscal and Taxation Systems and Fiscal and Taxation Regulation That Are Carried Out with a View to Serving the Overall Interests of the Country. *Journal of Guangdong University of Business Studies*, 2012 (7).

stabilized and standardized in the form of legislation. After responsibilities for handling essential public services have been divided among governments and expenditure responsibilities have been clarified, transfer payments can be designed in an integrated way according to the nature of responsibilities for handling essential public services to ensure the fair and reasonable distribution and use of transfer payment funds. As different regions are unequal in terms of financial resources and revenue does not completely match expenditure, the focus should be on adjusting and perfecting the transfer payment system. Expenditures that fall under the responsibilities for handling essential public services of local governments shall, in principle, be supported by the central government through general transfer payments, so as to expand local governments' authority for using transfer payments according to their overall plans and strengthen their expenditure responsibilities.

3.4.2 *Appropriately Increase the Proportion of General Transfer Payments*

We should enhance governments' capacity for guaranteeing public services in poor areas by appropriately increasing the proportion of general transfer payments, especially the proportion of transfer payment subsidies, improve the transfer payment systems of resource-exhausted cities, and increase support for resource-exhausted cities. We should increase transfer payments to old revolutionary base areas, areas with large ethnic minority populations, and border areas, further support the large-scale development of the western region, the rise of the central region, and the revitalization of old industrial bases in the northeast and other parts of the country, and help these regions speed up their development. We should give priority to closing the gap between revenue and expenditure in areas where (ecological, agricultural, forest, etc.) exploitation is prohibited or restricted, and promote the development of functional zones. Meanwhile, we should study the possibility of integrating some financial resource-supplementing transfer payments and special transfer payments into general transfer payments according to the development of different regions in China at the present stage, taking full account of main objective factors such as population density and regional differences in natural environment endowments, so as to enhance the ability of grass-roots governments to make overall arrangements for financial resources and provide public services.[27]

3.4.3 Classify and Standardize Special Transfer Payment

First, we should integrate and standardize the special transfer payment system, and guide local governments and the central government in pooling their efforts to effectively support critical expenditures. For affairs that are jointly handled by the central government and local governments, the proportion of expenditures to be borne by the central government and local governments shall be clarified by law; for affairs entrusted by the central government, the expenditures needed shall be paid in full by the central government through special transfer payments. For local affairs that are in line with the central government's policy orientation, the central government shall provide guidance through special transfer payments, but the amount shall not be too large.

Second, we should scientifically define standards for special transfer payments, and comprehensively sort out, classify, clean up and merge existing special transfer payment programs according to the functions and objectives of special transfer payment programs. We should strictly control the establishment of new special transfer payment programs, and cancel, cut down and integrate existing special transfer payment programs. We should cancel programs with unclear policy intentions, and clean up and merge duplicate projects. Projects funded through special transfer payments should be projects that produce spillover benefits, or are unexpected, special or non-stationary, such as the management of large trans-regional rivers, the building of protective forest belts, responses to unexpected natural disasters or epidemics, poverty relief in poverty-stricken counties, and projects entrusted by the central government.

Third, we should standardize the central government's policy on grants to local governments, and allocate grants on a region-by-region basis with a view to alleviating the fiscal pressure on poor areas. Grants often come with a requirement for matching funds, which should differential treatment. In principle, a higher matching requirement should be imposed on rich areas, a lower matching requirement should be imposed on poor

[27] Chinese Academy of Fiscal Sciences. Strategic Orientation of China's Fiscal and Taxation System Reform: 2010–2020. *Reform*, 2010 (1).

areas, and destitute areas can be exempted from the matching requirement. In addition, projects funded through special transfer payments must undergo scientific appraisal and rigorous approval procedures. We should strengthen the supervision, inspection and performance evaluation of special transfer payment programs, prevent funds from being intercepted or misappropriated, and improve the efficiency of their use. We should improve the transparency of funding arrangements and put an end to the so-called phenomenon of "getting money by pulling some strings with people working in ministries and commissions". We should prevent projects that are unexpected, special or non-stationary from being standardized formalized and routinized, so as to ensure their operational efficiency. We should standardize the distribution, supervision, management and performance evaluation of special transfer payments, and give full play to the functions of competent departments in the formulation of relevant public service standards and policies, and in the supervision and management of the implementation process. We should further improve the predictability and standardization of special transfer payments, continue to improve legislation for transfer payments, and accelerate efforts to improve and standardize the legal basis for transfer payments.

4 Strengthen People's Livelihood Security and Promote Coordinated and Sustainable Economic and Social Development

In his report to the 19th CPC National Congress, General Secretary Xi Jinping pointed out that "the principal contradiction facing Chinese society has evolved into the contradiction between unbalanced and inadequate development and the people's ever-growing needs for a better life." People's livelihood is the foundation of people's happiness and social harmony. The 19th CPC National Congress stressed that to ensure and improve people's livelihood, we must address the most immediate and realistic interests of the people. Strengthening people's livelihood security and improving people's well-being is the basic function of a modern service-oriented government, and also a necessary requirement for achieving social transformation and overcoming the middle-income trap. The 19th CPC National Congress called for persistent efforts to ensure and improve people's livelihood through development, and strengthen institutional safeguards. For countries that have fallen into the middle-income trap, one of the common problems they face is an imbalance in the people's livelihood security mechanism, with investments in employment, health care, education, and social security not matching economic and social development, and a welfare policy which is caught between a rock and a hard place sapping economic momentum and even triggering violent social unrest. China has joined the ranks of upper-middle-income countries and is transitioning from a survival-oriented society to a development-oriented society. People are increasingly demanding people's livelihood security, and the contradiction between the provision of and demand for public services has become more apparent and has increasingly become a bottleneck restricting economic and social development. This requires us to continuously improve people's livelihood security, and promote social stability and sustainable economic development.

4.1 *Tighten the Safety Net for People's Livelihood and Achieve a Virtuous Circle Between Economic Development and the Improvement of People's Livelihood*

Economic development and the improvement of people's livelihood promote and complement each other. Economic development is the prerequisite. Talking about improving people's livelihood without economic development is like water without a source and a tree without roots. People's livelihood security is the "compass" that guides economic development. Only by continuously improving people's livelihood and weaving a robust safety net for people's livelihood can we maintain social stability, motivate people to develop production, unleash consumption potential, boost domestic demand, and provide a strong endogenous impetus for economic development, transformation and upgrading. Meanwhile, the practice of some Latin American countries has shown that if developing countries blindly seek to catch-up on welfare in the middle-income stage, resulting in over-welfareization, the sustainability of their economic development will be undermined, causing them to fall into the middle-income trap. Therefore, balancing people's livelihood security and economic development and achieving a virtuous circle between the two is critical to a country's development.

4.1.1 *Grasp New Requirements for Ensuring People's Livelihood in the New Era*

Since the founding of the People's Republic of China, reform concerning people's livelihood security in China has undergone at least two significant turning points. The first turning point occurred in the 1980s, a critical period of transition from the era of a traditional planned economy to the era of a modern market economy. Compared with the pre-transition period, the policy on people's livelihood security of this period advocated the limitedness of government responsibility and emphasized the responsibility of individuals and society. The second turning point occurred in the late 1990s. Especially since the beginning of the twenty-first century, the policy on people's livelihood security has seen the gradual establishment of a social security system covering urban and rural areas, as prominently marked by a moderate return of state responsibility.[28] The creation of a new rural cooperative medical care system in 2003 marked that the building of China's social security system had begun to cross the wall separating urban and rural areas, taking a groundbreaking step in the transition from special welfare to universal welfare. Since then, the rural minimum subsistence allowance system and the new rural endowment insurance system have been established successively, and the universalization of social security has been accelerated across the board. This change not only reflects the development of the Party and government's governing philosophy, but also shows the dynamic trade-offs between development and people's livelihood, and efficiency and equity at different stages of economic and social development.

Since the 18th CPC National Congress, the CPC Central Committee, adhering to a "people-oriented" and "human-centered" governing philosophy, has constantly improved the safety net for people's livelihood, and pushed forward the fight against poverty in an effort to increase people's sense of gain and make the fruits of reform and development benefit all the people more profoundly and equitably. The Fifth Plenary Session of the 18th CPC Central Committee focused on weak links in building a moderately prosperous society in all respects, put forward the concept of shared development, and set forth specific requirements for goals such as helping specific groups of people with special difficulties, striving to achieve full coverage of essential public services for permanent

[28] Zhang Yi. *Social Structure Change and Social Governance in Contemporary China*. Beijing: Economy & Management Publishing House, 2016: 369–370.

residents, and ensuring basic livelihood. In recent years, although China's economic growth has shifted from high speed to medium-to-high speed, the level of people's livelihood security has been constantly improved, and the growth rate of a number of expenditures related to people's livelihood has been higher than the overall growth rate of fiscal expenditures in the same period. According to statistics, in 2016, spending on people's livelihood accounted for more than two-thirds of total government spending in 31 provinces, with this figure exceeding 75% in 17 provinces. A large amount of financial resources are focused on people's livelihood, extending to grass-roots levels and covering rural areas. Both the intensity and scale of spending have continuously increased.

However, at present, China's people's livelihood security is still in the initial stage of improving the system, perfecting the mechanism and raising the level. The level of security is low, and the imbalance between regions, urban and rural areas and departments is prominent. Meanwhile, China is at the critical stage of deepening reform in an all-round way and in a deep-water zone. Livelihood issues such as health care, education, income distribution, social security and the ecological environment are becoming increasingly prominent, and new challenges have arisen. For example, an increase in the level of urbanization requires accelerating the equalization of essential public services between urban and rural areas, and strengthening the overall development of people's livelihood security; population aging requires strengthening the sustainability of institutional design; the new normal of medium-speed economic growth requires reasonably arranging fiscal spending on people's livelihood and improving the efficiency of the use of funds; the increasing demands of the public requires a reasonable determination of the range of social security benefits and a normal growth mechanism; the widening gap between rich and poor requires strengthening social security's function of providing the basic necessities of life, and so on. This objectively requires us to take a long-term view and stay current, to be both moderately visionary and realistic, to create and improve a safety net for people's livelihood with Chinese characteristics, to properly resolve social contradictions, to narrow the gap between rich and poor, to increase people's sense of gain, and to inject lasting impetus into sustainable development.

4.1.2 *Uphold the Concepts of Bottom-Line Equity and Moderate Inclusiveness*

In the process of building a moderately prosperous society in all respects, the key to improving the people's livelihood security system lies in choosing a welfare model suitable for China's national conditions. China is a developing country with a large population, and its per capita income is still low. This is a fundamental reality of people's livelihood security in China. It determines that China cannot repeat the past egalitarian low welfare model, nor can it copy the high welfare path of Western countries. Instead, we should start with guaranteeing the basic needs of members of society, and adhere to the principles of bottom-line equity and moderate inclusiveness.[29]

Bottom-line equity means that we should guarantee the basic needs of members of society, mainly including food and clothing (survival), basic education (development), and public health and health care (health). Bottom-line equity emphasizes that the government should hold the bottom line for equity, provide consistent guarantees for the basic needs of the people, and ensure that every citizen has equal access. As for social welfare above the bottom line, we should give full play to the role of the market mechanism, charity mechanism, mutual assistance mechanism and self-help mechanism, and meet the diversified and differentiated welfare needs of citizens through a variety of means. The bottom-line equity model is a flexible model that "combines inelasticity and elasticity." It combines the inelasticity and elasticity of social welfare, delimits the scope of government responsibility, limits inelasticity to a range, and leaves more room for the development of an elastic mechanism.

Moderate inclusiveness is to ensure that the public goods and services provided by the government and society can benefit as many people as possible based on the principles of equity and justice. It is between the "residual" and "universal" models and is a dynamic development process. It has the following characteristics: First, universal—it targets the most important aspects of the basic life of all citizens, and addresses the worries of all urban and rural residents; second, multi-tiered—it is based on social insurance, social assistance and social welfare, focuses on the basic endowment insurance, basic medical insurance and subsistence allowance systems, supplemented by charity and commercial insurance,

[29] Jing Tiankui, Bi Tianyun. On the Bottom-Line Equity Welfare Model. *Social Science Front*, 2011 (5): 161–177.

gradually expands the scope of protection, and continuously improves the quality of life and self-development vitality of members of society; third, moderate—it emphasizes that the level of welfare should guarantee bottom-line equity and commensurate with the level of economic development.[30]

4.1.3 Establish an All-Round People's Livelihood Security System That Is Balanced Both Internally and Externally

The principles of bottom-line equity and moderate inclusiveness focus on the internal and external balance of people's livelihood security, so as to achieve self-maintenance, self-regulation and self-balance. From an internal point of view, people's livelihood security is very broad in meaning, covering various institutional arrangements such as social insurance, social relief, social welfare, special care and placement, social charity, and poverty alleviation. Meanwhile, there are different types of systems in China, such as urban social security, rural social security, and social security for urban employees and non-employees. This requires us to have a systematic and global consciousness, plan as a whole, coordinate efforts, and strengthen the coordination and connection between various systems to form a complete system that has all the required functions and works well. From an external point of view, people's livelihood security is based on public welfare, but its market-orientedness and society-orientedness cannot be ignored and excluded. While ensuring that the government assumes primary responsibility, we should give full play to market and non-governmental forces, and make them work together to meet the multi-level and diversified needs of different groups. In view of China's current situation, we should focus on the following issues in the establishment and improvement of the people's livelihood security system.

First, in terms of functions, we should focus on meeting the basic needs of members of society and increase investment in basic education, public health, medical care, and social security. Different from the Western developed countries, China is still a developing country with a large economic aggregate but a low per capita income. Unlike Western developed countries, China is still a developing country with a large economic aggregate, but low per capita income. When it comes to improving people's livelihood, we need to keep in mind our national conditions and set policy

[30] Qi Hongfang, Zeng Ruiming. A Review of Research on Moderately Inclusive Social Welfare in Recent Years. *Social Security Studies*, 2011 (5): 9, 14.

goals and priorities accordingly. First, we need to clarify the government's responsibility for providing the basic necessities of life, build a robust safety net for social security, and provide basic livelihood security for disadvantaged groups. At present, the focus is on doing a good job in poverty alleviation, thoroughly implementing targeted poverty alleviation and elimination, and closing the "last-mile gap" in building a moderately prosperous society in all respects. Secondly, we need to improve the social security system, especially the endowment and medical insurance systems. Finally, we need to optimize the structure of people's livelihood security, highlight certain aspects of social security such as education and housing in response to key and major issues facing social development, and try to develop a relationship between economic growth and welfare in which the two positively encourage each other. Practice has proved that investing in education yields high economic returns and is of great significance for enhancing the "blood-forming function" of the welfare system. For example, the per capita national income of South Korea and Greece was basically the same in 1995, at $7660 and $7390, respectively. But South Korea's spending on education as a percentage of total government expenditure (16.8%) was about twice as much as Greece's (8.5%); Greece's spending on housing and social welfare as a percentage of total government expenditure was about twice as much as South Korea's, and its spending on health care as a percentage of total government expenditure was five times as much as South Korea's. Obviously, the welfare structures of the two countries were different. South Korea attached more importance to the direct effect of education on promoting economic development and improving the quality of its people, while Greece put more emphasis on the improvement of quality of life. At present, South Korea is significantly better than Greece in terms of international competitiveness and position in the industrial hierarchy.[31]

Second, in terms of coverage, we should ensure that people's livelihood is well covered at all levels by shifting from specific service targets and a small number of disadvantaged groups to all members of society. The basic characteristics of people's livelihood security in the modern sense are society-orientedness and public-orientedness. It is a public or social policy for all citizens, not a local, limited charity activity for a few people. After nearly 40 years of reform and opening-up, China is still faced with

[31] Zhang Yi. *Social Structure Change and Social Governance in Contemporary China*. Beijing: Economy & Management Publishing House, 2016: 351.

the phenomenon of group welfare brought about by urban–rural division and division between groups, and the negative effects brought about by it are increasingly apparent. Therefore, we need to build a people's livelihood security system that benefits the whole people and promote the realization of social equity and justice. In particular, China is still in the development stage of low-level welfare where people's livelihood security often means the bottom line for equity, inequality rather than want is the cause of trouble, and particular attention needs to be paid to equalization and equity. However, we should also note that spending on social welfare is highly inelastic in that once established, social welfare needs to be provided continuously, so the government must have enough financial resources to ensure long-term supply. Therefore, we should strengthen the top-level design of people's livelihood security to ensure that moderate inclusiveness is adhered to under the basic national conditions. Considering China's national conditions, overall planning for the development of social welfare should focus on breakthroughs in the following areas: increase support for rural areas in light of the urban–rural dual structure; increasing support for underdeveloped areas in light of regional differences; strengthen efforts to accurately identify disadvantaged groups, ensure that they receive at least minimum support, and provide them with the basic necessities of life; innovate mechanisms and bring in non-governmental forces to meet the sophisticated and personalized needs of some groups.

Third, in terms of providers, we should place primary responsibility on the government and clarify its primary responsibility for providing essential public services. Modern people's livelihood security is essentially a government-led public good, and its supply has always been the responsibility of the government rather than the market. According to the principle of bottom-line equity, the government's welfare responsibility is first and foremost bottom-line welfare responsibility. It is incumbent on the government to shoulder primary responsibility for meeting the bottom-line welfare needs of citizens. In recent years, public finances at all levels in China have gradually assumed responsibility for basic education, strengthened investment in public health and urban and rural grassroots medical institutions, and established a rural subsistence allowance system. These social policies embody the principle that "the government should bear primary responsibility." Of course, "the government bears primary responsibility" is not "the government bears full responsibility." The government should not and cannot bear all the welfare responsibility. Businesses, non-governmental organizations, families and individuals should assume corresponding responsibility when meeting the non-bottom-line welfare needs of members of society.

4.2 Increase the Provision of Public Services and Promote the Equalization of Essential Public Services

Increasing the provision of public services and promoting the equalization of essential public services is one of the main goals of China's 13th Five-Year Plan Period. According to international experience, after a country enters the middle-income stage, it will pay more attention to the rights of individuals and the all-round development of people, demand for public services will increase, and the contradiction between the provision of and demand for public services will get worse and become one of the bottlenecks restricting economic and social development. At present, essential public services in China are in short supply, low in quality and institutionally imperfect, and there are multiple standards and disparities between regions and between urban and rural areas, resulting in a significant level of "fragmentation".[32] We need to start with the management mechanism, pool the efforts of the central government and local governments, and further improve the system of standards and institutional guarantees for the provision of essential public services.

4.2.1 Make Innovations in the Mechanism for Providing Essential Public Services and Promote the Diversification of Providers

The provision of essential public services should embody the principle of equity, but the principle of efficiency should be considered when it comes to choosing a mode of provision. China's current system for the provision of essential public services relies too much on the government. Under such a mode of provision dominated by the government, the government's responsibility and pressure keep on increasing, and market entities and non-governmental actors are unable to enter smoothly and play their due role, resulting in the insufficient provision and uneven distribution of essential public services in China. Western countries have rich experience in this regard. Beginning in the 1970s, in the face of a severe "stagflation" crisis and mounting fiscal pressure, European countries pushed for the

[32] Zhao Yu. *Social Governance: New Thinking and New Practice*. Beijing: Social Sciences Academic Press (China), 2014: 452.

marketization and socialization of public services in an effort to improve the public service system and cope with challenges to the sustainable development of the public service system.

First, promote the diversification of providers. The government should play a leading role in the provision of essential public services. It has the ultimate responsibility for ensuring the provision of public services in the event of "market failure" or "social failure," and has advantages in providing administrative leadership and overall coordination. But market forces, the public and social organizations are also indispensable in the mechanism for the provision of public services. They have advantages in that they are efficient and flexible in form, and can adapt to huge and diversified demand for public services. On the one hand, we should adhere to the principle that the government should bear primary responsibility and provide the basic necessities of life, clarify the government's support for essential public services at the legal and policy levels, draw the bottom line of people's livelihood security to be delivered by essential public services, ensure that the boundary between the government and non-governmental actors in providing public services is reasonable, and their rights and responsibilities are clear, and prevent excessive marketization and socialization. On the other hand, we should integrate the comparative advantages of the government, the market and non-governmental actors, speed up the reform of social programs, and promote the formation of a reasonable division of labor in the provision of public services; we should actively support the investment of private capital in the production and provision of public goods and services under strict government regulation, and ensure that private non-profit organizations enjoy the same treatment as their public counterparts; we should promote the restructuring, reorganization and privatization of public service institutions, especially social welfare institutions, and accelerate the cultivation of social actors in the field of public services.

Second, promote the diversification of providers. We should properly introduce a competition mechanism. For public services that should preferably be provided by the market, we should adopt a market-oriented approach, invite competitive bids from private investors, and support non-governmental organizations or other non-governmental actors in undertaking these public services through the government purchase of services, cooperation between the government and private capital, franchising, etc. We should promote the government purchase of public services. Public services that can be provided by the government through purchase shall no longer be directly undertaken by the government, but shall be undertaken by qualified and reputable social organizations, social institutions, public institutions, and enterprises. For public services that can be provided through cooperation between the government and private capital, we should extensively solicit the participation of private capital. The government should give priority to supporting projects undertaken collaboratively by the government and private capital through investment subsidies, fund injection and other means. We should develop voluntary and charitable services, give full play to the important complementary role of charitable organizations and professional social work organizations in the provision of essential public services, and implement relevant preferential policies for charitable donations.

Third, promote the socialization of financing channels and expand the sources of funding for the provision of public services. Under the mode of provision dominated by government, the main source of funding for public services in China is fiscal inputs. This relatively limited source of funding has difficulty meeting the rapidly growing demand for public services, and also makes it difficult to effectively monitor the efficiency of fiscal inputs. Meanwhile, most of the funding for public services is provided by local governments at all levels, especially local governments at grass-roots levels. In circumstances where county and township governments are cash-strapped or the fiscal transfer payment system is unreasonable and imperfect, the development of public services will be restricted to some extent. We should further strengthen innovation in financing models, leverage the advantages of development finance and policy-based finance in providing large amounts of funding over a long period of time and offering financial guidance, combine the strengths of governments, markets, enterprises, finance, and society, mobilize the enthusiasm of all parties, and guide more private capital toward people's livelihood and social development.

4.2.2 Improve the Fiscal Input Mechanism for Essential Public Services

It is the responsibility of public finance to promote the building of an essential public service system, and the fiscal system is the core institutional guarantee for advancing the equalization of public services. In recent years, the publicness of fiscal expenditure in China has been continuously enhanced, and spending on people's livelihood security has been growing faster than fiscal revenue, but there are still problems such as insufficient and unreasonably structured fiscal expenditure. We need to further innovate ways and methods, improve the fiscal input mechanism, and identify areas that should be prioritized for receiving fiscal inputs, so as to meet the ever-growing demand for essential public services.

First, ensure that public finance increases inputs in essential public services. At present, China's investment in essential public services is still insufficient. According to statistics, in 2012, the central government spent 1.3848 trillion Yuan on education, health care, employment, housing and social security, of which 31.42% was spent on public services, but in many other countries that figure was as high as 60–70%. Compared with middle-income countries in the world, China's fiscal input in public services is still low.[33] While making the cake bigger, the government should also change the budget structure. Governments at all levels should gradually increase inputs in essential public services and at the same time reduce administrative expenditure. In particular, we should strengthen the supervision and restriction of people's congresses on fiscal budgets, scientize, rationalize and refine budgets, proceduralize and democratize budget reviews, and make budget implementation open and transparent.

Second, reasonably divide responsibilities between the central government and local governments, and ensure that responsibilities for handling public affairs and services match financial resources. We should put in place a sound mechanism for sharing essential public services among governments at all levels, and clarify the responsibilities of the central, provincial and local governments in providing essential public services. First, we should moderately centralize responsibilities for handling essential public services under the central government and provincial governments. Governments at a higher level should be responsible for essential public services that have strong externalities, span multiple regions and involve relatively simple information collection; local governments should be responsible for essential public services that are regional and subject to information asymmetry, so as to avoid the overlapping of responsibilities for handling essential public services. We should moderately centralize responsibilities for handling essential public services under the central government and provincial governments, and reduce responsibilities delegated to grass-roots governments. National management and handling

[33] Sun Xuning. The Building of a Rule of Law System for the Equalization of Essential Public Services and the Bottom-Line Guarantee for People's Livelihood. *Chinese Public Administration*, 2014 (8): 101–104.

agencies should be set up in necessary areas. Secondly, we should further clarify the expenditure responsibilities of governments at all levels by referring to the division of responsibilities for handling essential public services, so as to ensure that their responsibilities for handling essential public services are commensurate with their expenditure responsibilities. We should clarify the division of fiscal powers and public service responsibilities between the central government and local governments, and ensure that the main objective of the fiscal expenditure structure is the equalization of public services. Finally, we should increase the proportion of the central government and provincial governments' expenditure, and transfer resources to underdeveloped provinces, regions and rural areas through fiscal transfer payments and other measures; we should increase the proportion of general transfer payments and gradually reduce the scale of special transfer payments, so as to increase the autonomy and enthusiasm of local governments in providing essential public services, and better meet the essential public service needs of the public.

Third, strengthen expenditure management and improve the management and efficiency of the use of funds for the provision of essential public services. With China's economic growth entering a new normal, fiscal revenue growth has slowed down, while spending on essential public services has been increasing each year. Efforts should be made to improve the use of funds, so as to meet the growing spending needs of people's livelihood that "will not go down, but only go up." We should include the equalization of essential public services among the key points to be considered when assessing the performance of local governments, improve the incentive mechanism for local government governance, shift from being "economy" oriented to being "economy, society and efficiency"-oriented, and make essential public services an important measure of the government's capacity for social development. We should innovate systems and mechanisms, strengthen the participation of citizens and other social actors, actively mobilize market forces, non-governmental capital and private capital, and leverage fiscal funds in a manner that "produces a large force by exerting a small force." We should improve "budgets that cover all receipts and expenditures," strengthen hard budget constraints, continuously scientize and refine budget management. We should strengthen the supervision of fiscal expenditures, carry out performance evaluation that covers the entire process from budgeting to implementation, and improve the all-round financial supervision system that combines supervision before, during and after the event concerned. In addition, for essential public services, the improvement of the efficiency of the use of fiscal funds is not only reflected in the improvement of the direct benefits of some projects, but more importantly in an increase in comprehensive benefits and social benefits. We should further explore criteria for quantifying the benefits of the use of financial funds at the institutional, managerial and technical levels.

4.2.3 Promote the Effective Convergence of Essential Public Service Systems in Urban and Rural Areas and in Different Regions

In recent years, the widening of the urban–rural gap and regional inequality in essential public services has slowed down. But due to factors such as a long-standing lack of social development in rural areas, a regional imbalance in economic development and institutional policies, urban–rural inequality in essential public services remains very significant, which is mainly manifested as inequalities in investment, provision, quality and cost bearing. Therefore, advancing the equalization of public services is an arduous systematic project. Under the current framework of urban–rural dual and regional division, it will take some time to achieve the integration of systems, and the foundation for system integration is not yet solid. We should adopt a phased approach to gradually break down institutional barriers. At present, we should first promote the effective convergence of public service systems in urban and rural areas and in different regions.

First, promote the convergence of public service standards and systems. We should put in place a sound list system for essential public services, clarify the national essential public services that governments at all levels should provide and the assurance standards, gradually establish unified equalization standards, and strive to generally equalize essential public services between urban and rural areas and between regions. We should speed up the integrated design and implementation of compulsory education, social security, public health, and employment systems in urban and rural areas. We should push for the integration of planning, policies, investment and projects on a county-by-county (or county-level city-by-county-level city or district-by-district) basis in a step-by-step and phased manner, make overall plans for the construction of facilities and personnel arrangements, and promote the unification and convergence of content and standards for services in urban and rural areas.

Second, improve the level of intra-regional equalization of services. We should strengthen the overall planning function of provincial people's governments, increase support for areas with weak essential public services within provinces, and gradually narrow the service gap between county-level administrative divisions and between prefecture-level cities through measures such as dividing responsibilities for handling essential public services and standardizing transfer payments. We should strengthen cross-regional coordination and cooperation, and promote the convergence of service items and standards.

Third, speed up the transfer of social security between urban and rural areas and between regions. China's social security is somewhat "fragmented." There are multiple separate and distinct categories under the same security project, and each category is further divided between urban and rural areas and between regions. This has not only resulted in the application of different security systems to different groups, making it difficult to coordinate mechanism arrangements as a whole, but also caused conflicts between and gaps in systems. Therefore, the first step in improving China's social security system should be to establish a channel for transfer between different systems and achieve smooth transfer between urban and rural areas and between regions. Migrant workers are the most mobile group in China, so we should focus on solving issues related to the connection of their social insurance when they move between urban and rural areas or between regions.[34] We should treat urban and rural social security as an organic whole and carry out scientific and reasonable planning and design to facilitate an effective connection between urban and rural security systems. Considering the current imbalance between the urban and rural social security systems, limited economic strength and other constraints, we should gradually align the rural social security system with the relatively advanced and mature urban social security system, and try to avoid designing the basic components of the two differently, so as to lay the foundation for the unification of urban and rural social security in the future. Meanwhile, we should do the relevant basic work well, unify social security information management standards, achieve the national unification of information index systems and coding systems, and accelerate the construction of informatization projects.

[34] Zhao Yu. *Social Governance: New Thinking and New Practice*. Beijing: Social Sciences Academic Press (China), 2014: 460.

4.2.4 *Build a Rule of Law Foundation for the Equalization of Essential Public Services*

The equalization of essential public services is impossible without the foundational support of laws and regulations. Especially in countries with a mature market mechanism and a high level of economic development, social security and other essential public services are more dependent on laws. In the United States, for example, the Social Security Act was enacted as early as 1933, covering insurance for the aged, the disabled and survivors, health, unemployment and industrial injury insurance, and welfare, and the social security system was created with the act as its core. At present, there is a lack of basic laws on essential public services in China, and legislation in special areas is lagging behind and at a low level. The current legislation, such as the Social Insurance Law and the Compulsory Education Law, is scattered in different areas, making it difficult for them to play a role in top-level coordination. China should build a scientific rule of law system, a comprehensive institutional system that is founded on the constitution, based on basic laws and refined by special laws. In particular, China should strengthen the building of key legal systems. In the face of a complicated situation of fragmentation in the field of public services, we can consider introducing an Essential Public Service Law, so as to solve the problem of "fragmentation" in the field of public services by legal means, avoid the departmental interest orientation of administrative legislation, ensure the fairness and authority of the essential public service system, promote integration across regions and fields by top-level legislation, and establish a unified essential public service system.

4.3 *Improve the Social Security System and Consolidate Basic Guarantees for Social Equity*

Social security's function of providing the basic necessities of life is essential to overcoming the middle-income trap. A fair and sustainable social security system cannot only ensure basic security, provide the basic necessities of life, and maintain minimum bottom-line equity, but also provide strong support for resolving social conflicts and promoting social equity. China has established a social security system framework covering urban and rural residents. It consists of four categories: social insurance, social assistance, social welfare and social special care, and covers endowment insurance, medical insurance, work-related injury insurance, unemployment insurance and maternity insurance, of which endowment insurance and health care insurance are the most basic and important components in that they not only account for a relatively high proportion of the cost in the social security system, but also have a direct bearing on the vital interests of the majority of the people and constitute the core of people's livelihood security.

Old-age care and medical care have been the most pressing and debated issues worldwide. Population aging has become the biggest challenge to the sustainable development of welfare systems in all countries. China is the country with the largest and fastest growing aging population in the world where families' function of providing security has been weakening due to low fertility and aging, and it is facing the challenge of "getting old before getting rich." Whether China can effectively deal with old-age care and medical care issues brought about by aging has a direct bearing on whether it can achieve the healthy and sustainable development of the economy and society.

4.3.1 Improve the Endowment Insurance System and Actively Respond to the Challenges Posed by an Aging Population

After nearly 40 years of development since the start of reform and opening-up, China's endowment insurance exists in multiple forms and basically covers all urban and rural residents. But the problems have become increasingly prominent, such as the challenges posed by an aging population, high contribution rates, and the unbalanced distribution of endowment insurance benefits.[35] In addition, as aging occurs at a stage where the level of economic development is relatively low, to improve and reform endowment insurance, which is a compulsory institution, we need to establish a fairer and more sustainable endowment insurance system, while taking account of the contradiction between the level of social security and economic development and competitiveness.

First, further improve the basic endowment insurance system. We should promote the implementation of an universal coverage scheme, encourage and lead all kinds of units and qualified personnel to get and stay covered, focus on providing coverage to employees of some non-public economic organizations, persons in flexible employment in urban areas, migrant workers, and some rural residents, and basically

[35] Song Xiaowu. *A Study on Major Issues Concerning China's Social Security System during the 13th Five-Year Plan Period*. Beijing: China Labor and Social Security Publishing House, 2016: 23.

achieve coverage for all persons who are required to be covered under the law. We should push for the national coordination of endowment insurance, further improve the provincial coordination of basic pension funds, and promote the unification of institutions and policies, contribution rates, benefits and payment methods, fund uses, fund budgets, business procedures, etc. at the provincial level, so as to draw upon surplus funds to make up for deficiencies and fend off risks on a wider scale. We should improve the individual account system for endowment insurance for employees, strengthen the link between contributions by individuals and the level of benefits they receive, and improve the incentive mechanism where the more one pays, the more one gets, and the longer one stays subscribed, the more one gets. To adapt to an accelerating trend toward population and occupational mobility, we should establish a more convenient mechanism for social insurance transfer and succession.

Second, accelerate the building of a multi-layered endowment insurance system. At present, there is an imbalance in development between the three pillars of endowment insurance (i.e., basic endowment insurance, supplementary pensions, and individual commercial endowment insurance) is unbalanced. The second and third pillars of the endowment insurance system are lagging behind, accounting for a relatively low proportion and playing a weak role, which to some extent has aggravated the pressure on basic endowment insurance and created a social psychology of over-dependence on public pensions.[36] We should strengthen incentives for the development of occupational pensions, supplementary pensions and all kinds of commercial endowment insurance through preferential policies such as tax exemption and tax deferment. We should reduce social insurance rates in due course and appropriately to allow room for supplementary insurance. We should innovate and develop various forms of commercial endowment insurance products, develop commercial group endowment insurance and endowment insurance management, facilitate the connection of commercial endowment insurance with social insurance and supplementary insurance, and build a multi-layered endowment insurance system.

Third, strengthen the connection of the endowment insurance system with other social security systems. We should strengthen the connection of the endowment insurance system with the social welfare system

[36] Hu Yongtai, Lu Ming. *Overcome the "Middle-Income Trap"—Looking Forward to the Sustainability of China's Economic Growth*. Beijing: Truth & Wisdom Press, 2012: 95.

which is comprised of subsidies for economically disadvantaged elderly and disabled elderly, etc. with the social assistance system which is comprised of subsistence allowances, relief and support for people in extreme poverty, etc., and with rural poverty alleviation and development policies. We should gradually postpone the retirement age, and raise the age at which urban and rural residents can receive basic pensions in due course and appropriately. Efforts should be made to build a multi-layered old-age security system underpinned by social assistance, centered around social insurance, and supplemented by social charity, supplementary pensions and commercial insurance and in which all layers are connected with each other.

Fourth, strengthen investment management and supervision for social endowment insurance funds. We should strictly implement relevant laws and regulations, and actively and steadily promote the market-oriented and diversified investment operations of pension funds while ensuring the timely payment of pensions and the safety of pension funds, so as to maintain or increase the value of pension funds. We should improve the fund risk management and internal control systems, further refine the risk management process and measures, and strengthen the identification, measurement, evaluation and monitoring of and response to various risks in accordance with the principle of risk management that covers all aspects, the whole process and all people.

4.3.2 Deepen the Reform of the Medical Insurance System and Advance the Building of a Healthy China

As general secretary Xi Jinping said, "Prosperity for all is impossible without health for all." Health is not only a necessary requirement for promoting the all-round development of the people and a basic condition for economic and social development, but also a key mark of a prosperous nation and a strong country. Since the 18th CPC National Congress, the CPC Central Committee has elevated "healthy China" to the position of a national strategy. The world's largest basic health care network was established within a relatively short period of time; a multi-layered security framework centered around basic medical insurance has been preliminarily established; the medical insurance system that covers the whole population has been further improved. However, China is still facing new challenges brought by industrialization, urbanization, an aging population, an evolving ecological environment and changing lifestyles.

We need to take a holistic approach to solving major and long-term issues related to people's health.

First, we should fully implement the serious illness insurance system for urban and rural residents. Medical resources in China are unevenly distributed, and the difficulty of getting medical services and the difficulty of getting hospitalized have always been a "serious illness" that haunts people. The phenomena of poverty caused by illness and returning to poverty due to illness still exist in some areas. We should further improve the serious illness insurance system to cover all urban residents covered by medical insurance and the new rural cooperative medical care system, and link it closely with other systems such as medical assistance to combine their effects on protecting people at the bottom of society, so as to effectively prevent catastrophic health expenditure.

Second, we should integrate the basic medical insurance systems, rationalize the management system for medical insurance for residents and new rural cooperative medical care, and speed up the integration of the basic medical insurance systems for urban and rural residents. We should perfect the mechanism for stable and sustainable financing and reimbursement rate adjustment for medical insurance, and improve policies on paying for and subscribing to medical insurance. We should reform the way medical insurance is managed and paid for, properly control medical expenses, and achieve a sustainable balance for medical insurance funds. Improve individual accounts, and consolidate outpatient costs. Speed up the push for the settlement of the costs of medical treatment received by persons covered by basic medical insurance in places other than where their coverage is maintained, so that retirees who have moved their residence out of provinces where their coverage is maintained can directly settle their medical expenses in their places of residence. In view of the increasing cost and burden of long-term care for the elderly brought by population aging, we should explore the establishment of a long-term nursing insurance system and launch a pilot program for long-term care insurance.

Third, encourage the development of supplementary medical insurance and commercial health insurance. We should actively encourage the development of supplementary medical insurance paid for by jointly by employers and employees, and commercial health insurance paid for by individuals alone. On the basis of implementing preferential tax policies for basic medical insurance and supplementary medical insurance, we should improve preferential policies on pre-tax deductions for individuals purchasing commercial health insurance.

4.3.3 *Promote Targeted and In-Depth Poverty Alleviation and Shantytown Redevelopment to Improve the Well-Being of Urban and Rural Residents*

Poverty remains the most prominent "weak link" in China's economic and social development and is an important part of overcoming the middle-income trap, in which the role of the government is the key factor. Since the 18th CPC National Congress of the Communist Party of China, the CPC Central Committee has made poverty alleviation and development a big priority related to the political direction, fundamental institutions and development path of the Party and the State, and made it clear that by 2020 the rural poor must be lifted out of poverty by the current standards, and the battle against poverty must be won, sounding a clarion call for eradiating absolute poverty and securing a decisive victory in building a moderately prosperous society. For urban residents, in 2013, the executive meeting of the State Council put forward the goal of "improving more than 10 million housing units in shantytowns in the next five years." China will vigorously push forward shantytown redevelopment, with people's happiness and housing needs as the starting point and objective. From 2013 to 2016, the number of poor people in rural areas decreased by more than 10 million every year, with a total of 55.64 million people out of poverty; the poverty rate fell from 10.2% at the end of 2012 to 4.5% at the end of 2016, down 5.7 percentage points; the income of rural residents in poor areas has been growing faster than the national average, the living standards of poor people have improved significantly, and conditions in poor areas have improved markedly. We should enable the poor and disadvantaged to share in the fruits of reform and development so as to achieve common prosperity.

First, poverty alleviation and development is a task that must be accomplished in order to build a moderately prosperous society in an all respects and overcome the middle-income trap. A sizable portion of the population living in deep poverty remains a basic feature of China's poverty problem, and is also a prominent weakness that must be addressed in order for China to build a moderately prosperous society in all respects and overcome the middle-income trap. The key to poverty alleviation and development lies in precision. We should give full play to the leadership role of the government and the guiding role of the market, take precise and targeted measures, adjust measures to local conditions, and implement policies on a case-by-case basis to steadily improve the ability of the poor to increase their income and lift themselves out of poverty;

based on the resource endowment of poor areas, we should promote the transformation of poverty alleviation from "blood transfusion" to "blood making"; we should vigorously implement the relocation of people from inhospitable areas as part of poverty alleviation efforts, choose relocation and resettlement methods in light of local conditions, and take multiple measures to steadily increase the income of relocated people, and ensure that they can move out, settle down and get out of poverty. Meanwhile, we should further strengthen special poverty alleviation projects such lifting people out of poverty by transferring rural surplus labor to non-agricultural sectors, poverty alleviation through health care, and poverty alleviation through ecological protection.

Second, shantytown redevelopment is a major livelihood project that embodies a people-centered development philosophy, and is an important measure to promote new-type urbanization. In view of problems such as an increase in the difficulty of advancing shantytown redevelopment and a lack of progress in the construction of supporting infrastructure, it is necessary to implement various supporting policies and local responsibilities, strengthen supervision and inspection, manage and use special funds for shantytown redevelopment well, improve amenities such as water, electricity, gas, heating, roads, education and health care, improve the occupancy rate, and increase the proportion of cash compensation in lieu of rehousing in cities and counties with a large inventory of commercial housing units and sufficient homes on the market. We should increase central government subsidies and support in terms of finance, land use, etc., innovate and diversify financing channels, and promote the use of investment and financing models such as the government purchase of services and cooperation between the government and private capital to increase financing for shantytown redevelopment. Meanwhile, we should consider business promotion, social construction and livelihood development as a whole, combine shantytown redevelopment with the transformation of resource-exhausted cities, with promoting the employment and reemployment of residents displaced by shantytown redevelopment, with improving urban infrastructure construction and enhancing urban functions, and with improving the happiness index of residents in residential communities in place of shantytowns, so as to make shantytown redevelopment a heart-winning project that "moistens," warms and wins people's hearts, and deliver both social and economic benefits.

Third, give play to the role of the minimum living security system in providing the basic necessities of life. The minimum living security system is an important part of social assistance in China. It plays the role of a social "safety valve" by providing the most disadvantaged in society with the minimum living security. For those in poverty who are totally or partially incapacitated for work, we should provide subsistence allowances to lift them out of "absolute poverty." We should strengthen the institutional connection between subsistence allowances and poverty alleviation, do our best to lift people out of poverty and ensure that people who are eligible for subsistence allowances receive subsistence allowances, and develop a reasonable institutional arrangement whereby subsistence allowances and poverty alleviation work together to ensure that the poor can share in the fruits of reform and development, with the former maintaining a basic standard of living and the latter emphasizing ability improvement, so as to achieve common prosperity.

5 Strengthen the Rule of Law and Improve Social Governance

The rule of law is an important part of the superstructure. Any attempt to solve social contradictions in a fair and just way, and to scientifically regulate the behaviors of social actors must be backed up by the law as supported by the rule of law. History has proved time and again that "a country where the rule of law prevails will prosper, while a country where the rule of law is in decline will descend into chaos." Countries that have successfully overcome the middle-income trap have a relatively sound rule of law system, and a backward rule of law system is an important reason why countries have fallen into the middle-income trap. At present, China's is in a period where important strategic opportunities for development and prominent social contradictions coexist. Its economic development is experiencing the "simultaneous occurrence of three periods," its reform has entered a critical stage and the deep-water zone, stakeholders and their demands have been diversified, and injustice remains a major problem in some areas. Comprehensively advancing the rule of law is an inevitable choice for China's social transformation to enter a new normal.

The Fourth Plenary Session of the 18th CPC Central Committee sounded a clarion call for building a socialist country under the rule of law, providing a solid institutional framework and legal guarantee for building moderately prosperous society in all respects, comprehensively deepening reform, and achieving the great rejuvenation of the Chinese nation. The Decision of the CPC Central Committee on Several Major Issues Concerning Comprehensively Advancing the Rule of Law adopted at the plenary session proposed that efforts should be made to form a well-equipped system of legal standards, an effective system for implementing the rule of law, a rigorous system for overseeing the rule of law, a strong system for guaranteeing the rule of law, and a perfect system of party rules, pursue coordinated progress in the law-based governance of the country, the law-based exercise of state power, and law-based government administration, adopt an integrated approach to building a law-based country, government, and society, and modernize China's system and capacity for governance. These ideas embody the organic integration of good law and sound governance, and further promotes the sustainable and healthy development of China's economy and society, lays a solid rule of law foundation for safeguarding people's rights and interests, social equity and justice, and national security and stability in accordance with the law, and provides a strong rule of law guarantee for overcoming the middle-income trap.

5.1 The Rule of Law Is a Necessary Requirement for the Modernization of the Social Governance System and Governance Capability

Social governance is an organic unity of the social governance system and capacity for social governance. The social governance system is a set of closely connected and coordinated social governance institutions, which is the sum of systems, mechanisms and legal and regulatory arrangements in the field of social construction; capacity for social governance is the level and performance of using relevant institutions to manage social affairs, and reflects the quality of social governance. The modernization of social governance is a basic condition for overcoming the middle-income trap. The overall strategy of the CPC Central Committee for governing the country and managing government affairs makes it clear that the rule of law and reform as "two wheels" will drive progress toward the goal of building a moderately prosperous society in all respects and advance the modernization of China's system and capacity for governance. Improving the socialist system with Chinese characteristics and advancing the modernization of China's system and capacity for governance is impossible without the modernization of the rule of law.

5.1.1 "Good Law and Sound Governance" Is an Important Criterion for Measuring the Modernization of Social Governance

Modern social governance manifests itself in the fact that common values such as fairness, justice, democracy, human rights and order are highlighted in governance objectives, there has been a shift from the government serving as the sole social governance actor to multiple actors participating and the government taking the lead, and the governance rules and methods are transparent, stable and standardized. "Good law and sound governance" embodies a high degree of agreement between the spirit of the rule of law and consensus on social governance. The organic integration of the rule of law and social governance is an inherent requirement for modernizing the social governance system and governance capability and building the rule of law in China. "Good law" is a prerequisite for good governance, "good governance" is the bedrock on which good law is based, and the two promote and complement each other.[37]

Among them, "good law" focuses on the static goal of institutional building for social governance and emphasizes common values such as fairness, justice, democracy, human rights, order, and harmony, which are highly consistent with the internal attributes of the spirit of the rule of law. Although standards for "good law" are limited by many factors such as historical conditions, cultural traditions and political ideology, and are diverse, they always reflect the common progressive ethics of mankind. "Sound governance" focuses on the dynamic process of social governance, and emphasizes the improvement of capacity for social governance. Social governance involves the protection of social rights, the coordination of social interests, the resolution of social contradictions and the management of social conflicts. The most direct and effective way to solve these problems is to strengthen the rule of law in social governance. Only by substituting the rule of law thinking for the thinking of administrative orders, control, and stability maintenance, defining the boundary of the

[37] Zhang Wenxian. Modernization of Governance. *Law of China*, 2014 (4): 5.

rights of multiple actors by means of explicit legal provisions, ensuring law-based administration through the coercive power of the rule of law, and creating a good atmosphere in which all citizens respect and abide by the law with the belief in the rule of law can we achieve the best results of social governance.

5.1.2 The Rule of Law Is the Fundamental Guarantee for the Modernization of Social Governance

The essence of overcoming the middle-income trap is not only a matter of quantity (income), but also of quality (governance). In order to modernize the social governance system and capacity for social governance, we must advance social governance along the track of the rule of law. We should correct the phenomena of non-compliance with the law, lax law enforcement, and inaction against lawbreakers, rectify the problems of using power for personal gain, suppressing the law with power, and bending the law for personal gain, treat people's demands fairly in accordance with the law, make people feel equity and justice, and eliminate destabilizing factors in society that could lead to a descent into the middle-income trap.

The rule of law provides a stable institutional foundation for the modernization of social governance. During the period of social transformation, destabilizing factors are increasing, social contradictions are building up and occurring frequently, the focus of public attention is expanding from income and living standards to areas such as people's livelihood security and social welfare, and task of social construction is arduous. The rule of law pursues the common values of human society, such as popular sovereignty, equity and justice, and human rights protection, and is an extension of progressive social ethics in the institutional field. Through a series of specific, standardized and unified institutional arrangements, the rule of law restrains the power of the state and protects the rights of citizens, laying the institutional foundation for achieving social equity, justice, stability and harmony. The rule of law emphasizes the supremacy of the law and maintains the continuity, stability and authority of the ruling philosophy, ruling line and ruling guideline; the rule of law is implemented by the state's coercive power through open and transparent rules and procedures, so as to create reasonable expectations on the part of the public and maintain the credibility of social governance.

The rule of law is the most basic means of regulating social contradictions and maintaining social stability. For many countries, overcoming the middle-income trap is not only a structural and institutional change, but also a major change in the way of thinking and methods for dealing with social contradictions and conflicts. How to navigate this period which is riddled with contradictions smoothly and orderly, and how to complete the "dramatic leap" in the transformation process are the challenges that all countries that are trying to overcome the middle-income trap must face. Some new problems have emerged in China's social transformation. The diversification of stakeholders and their demands has further complicated social contradictions. The double-edged sword effect of informatization and networking on social governance has gradually appeared. These problems need to be solved through effective means. In fact, any social contradiction has its corresponding legal relation. The adjustment of social contradictions is the adjustment of legal rights and obligations. We must give full play to the role of the rule of law, judge and determine what is right and wrong, what is legal and illegal and what constitutes illegality and criminality, and assess responsibility and determine punishment according to law, and promote social stability and social harmony.[38]

5.2 *Promote the Modernization of the Social Governance System with the Rule of Law*

The social governance system includes a series of institutions and procedures to regulate social governance. To promote the modernization of the social governance system is to adapt to the changes of the times, which involves not only reforming systems, mechanisms, laws, and regulations that do not meet the requirements of practical development, but also continuously building new systems, mechanisms, laws, and regulations, so as make various institutions more scientific and perfect, and institutionalize, standardize and proceduralize the governance of social affairs. Legislation is the process of establishing and improving the legal system. It is the basis of the law-based exercise of state power, strict law enforcement, judicial justice, and all citizens abiding by the law, and plays a guiding and driving role in advancing the national governance system.

[38] Yu Keping. *The Country's Bottom Line: Fairness, Justice and the Law-Based Governance of the Country*. Beijing: Central Compilation & Translation Press, 2014.

At present, compared with the goal of modern governance, there are still some adaptation and coordination problems in China's legislation. The socialist legal system needs to be further improved. Some institutions fail to fully reflect objective laws and the will of the people, and are not targeted and operable. The legislative tendency of departmentalization and local protectionism still exists. Some legal norms conflict with each other, leaving law enforcers, law-abiders and persons who administer justice at a loss as what to do. Adhering to scientific and democratic legislation and improving the scientificity and impartiality of legislation is a prerequisite for the modernization of the governance system. Democratic legislation is the process of making laws through equal game, rational consultation and mutual compromise among various social actors under an open and fair institutional framework. Democratic legislation is a procedural requirement for scientific legislation, and scientific legislation is the fundamental guarantee for improving the quality of legislation.[39]

5.2.1 *Improve the Socialist Legal System with Chinese Characteristics with the Constitution at Its Core*

The challenges a country faces as it transitions from the middle-income stage to the high-income stage are different from the problems it faces before entering the middle-income stage. As internal and external reality evolves, the original institutional arrangements are not necessarily sustainable and effective, which may restrict economic and social development, so institutional transformation must be carried out in due course.

The law is an important instrument for governing a country, and good law is a prerequisite for sound governance. Building a complete socialist legal system with Chinese characteristics is a prerequisite and basis for breaking free from the middle-income trap. Faced with a new situation of reform and development, we should continue to improve the socialist legal system with Chinese characteristics which has the Constitution as the "commander-in-chief," the law as the backbone, and administrative and local regulations as an important part. We must give priority to legislation, give full play to the guiding and driving role of legislation, implement core socialist values, and ensure that every piece of legislation conforms to the spirit of the Constitution, reflects the will of the people, and is supported by the people. We should enact, reform, repeal, and interpret at the same

[39] Tang Huangfeng. Construct the Rule of Law Order: The Only Way to Modernize China's National Governance. *Journal of Xinjiang Normal University*, 2014 (4).

time, make laws and regulations more timely, systematic, targeted, and effective, and ensure that different branches of law and normative legal documents of different origins are well connected with each other, so as to better meet the needs of China's economic and social development.

We should improve the constitutional enforcement and supervision systems. The Constitution is the fundamental law of our country. It not only stipulates the basic rights and obligations of citizens, but also prescribes the fundamental systems and tasks of the state, and regulates the exercise of state power. It has supreme authority in the legal system. The whole society must take the Constitution as the fundamental criterion for its activities, and has a duty to safeguard the dignity of the Constitution and ensure its enforcement. We must uphold the principle that everyone is equal before the law. No organization or individual shall have the privilege of being placed above the Constitution and laws. Violations of the Constitution shall be investigated and corrected. In order to ensure the enforcement of the Constitution, we should improve the constitutional supervision system of the National People's Congress (NPC) and its Standing Committee, and perfect the procedure mechanism for the interpretation of the Constitution. We should strengthen the filing and review system and capacity building, bring all normative documents into the scope of filing and review, and revoke and correct normative documents that violate the Constitution and laws in accordance with the law.

5.2.2 Improve the Legislative System in Which Legislatures Take the Lead and Various Parties in Society Participate in an Orderly Manner

In order to ensure the quality of legislation and make legislation more scientific, we should further improve the staff composition of legislatures, perfect the legislative process and upgrade legislative techniques. In particular, we should keep the public opinion expression mechanism up and running through a variety of means, strengthen the connection between public opinion and legislation, and increase the level of democratic participation in legislation.

We should strengthen the self-development of legislatures and improve the legislative system. We should strengthen the Party's leadership over legislative work and improve the Party's procedures for making decisions on major issues in legislative work. We should give full play to the leading role of people's congresses and their standing committees in legislative work, and apply the principles of openness, equity and justice through the whole legislative process. The relevant special committees of the National People's Congress and the Legislative Affairs Commission of the NPC Standing Committee shall organize relevant departments to participate in the drafting of important draft laws that are comprehensive, of broad importance, or fundamental, and put in place a sound system whereby specialists are appointed as legislative advisors for special committees and working committees. We should strengthen the organization and coordination of the legislative work of people's congresses, improve the system for collecting and evaluating legislative items, enhance mechanisms for drafting, evaluating, coordinating, and deliberating legislation, perfect the mechanism for soliciting legislative opinions from lower-level people's congresses, establish a system for staying connected with local communities on legislative matters, and promote the refinement of legislation. We should clearly define the boundaries of legislative power, and employ systems, mechanisms, and procedures to prevent the enactment of laws that protect departmental interests or encourage local protectionism, strengthen the building of government legislative systems, and improve the procedures for the formulation of administrative rules and regulations. For important legislative matters that have caused major disputes among departments, we should introduce third-party assessment, fully listen to the views of all parties, and decide through coordination. For problems found in the application of laws, the interpretation of laws shall be done in a timely manner to clarify the meaning of laws and the basis for the application of laws.

We should innovate ways in which the public participates in legislation. We should widen channels for the public to participate in legislative work in an orderly manner through discussion, hearing, assessment and publicizing draft laws; actively address social concerns through inquiry, investigation of specific problems, and putting on record for examination. We should improve the mechanism for communication between legislatures and the public, carry out legislative consultation, give full play to the role of CPPCC members, democratic parties, federations of industry and commerce, public figures without party affiliation, people's organizations, and social organizations in legislative consultation, and explore the establishment of mechanism for relevant state organs, social organizations, experts and scholars to appraise and give advice on major interest adjustments involved in legislation. We should improve the mechanism for publicly soliciting opinions on draft laws and regulations and providing feedback on the adoption of public opinions, so as to build a broad public consensus. We should fully listen to and meet the value demands of all stakeholders, improve the responsiveness and adaptability of laws to social and economic issues, and give full play to the functions of the law in integrating and coordinating interests in a pluralistic society.

5.2.3 *Strengthening Legislation in Key Areas During the Transition Period*

We should protect citizens' rights in accordance with the law, accelerate the improvement of legal systems that embody equality of opportunity, the fairness of rules, and distributive justice, protect citizens' rights such as personal rights, property rights and basic political rights from infringement, ensure that citizens' economic, cultural and social rights are implemented, and ensure that citizens' rights are protected by the rule of law. We should raise the whole society's awareness of the need to respect and protect human rights, and improve channels and methods for providing remedies for infringement of citizens' rights.

We should improve the legal system of the socialist market economy, with the protection of property rights, the maintenance of contracts, a unified market, equal exchange, fair competition and effective regulation as the basic guide, so that the market will play a decisive role in the allocation of resources. We should improve the property rights protection system with fairness as its core principle, strengthen the protection of the property rights of economic entities under all forms of ownership and natural persons, clear up the provisions of laws and regulations that are contrary to the principle of fairness, form a modern market system in which enterprises operate and compete in accordance with the law. We should strengthen legal systems for markets and promote the free flow, fair trade and equal use of goods and factors of production. We should improve rule of law support for innovation-driven strategies, and perfect the intellectual property protection system that encourages innovation, and systems and mechanisms for promoting the transformation of scientific and technological achievements. We should speed up legislation on technological innovation, and encourage original, core, advanced and development-driving technological innovations. We should strengthen the application and protection of intellectual property rights, improve the incentive mechanism for technological innovation, form legal systems for technological innovation that support and coordinate with each other, stimulate the innovative vigor of various actors, and guarantee and promote comprehensive innovation. We should develop technology markets, improve technology transfer mechanisms, improve venture capital mechanisms, and promote the capitalization and industrialization of scientific and technological achievements. We should promote the application of the rule of law to supporting policies for technological advancement, the distribution of strategic emerging industries and indigenous innovation by enterprises. We should strengthen and improve macro-control and market supervision in accordance with the law, oppose monopoly, promote rational competition, and maintain a fair market order.

We should improve legal systems for social governance and promote innovation in social governance systems. We should strengthen the rule of law guarantee for social development and transformation, perfect the mechanism for citizens' orderly participation in social governance, keep interest articulation channels open, accurately grasp the social mentality, and safeguard the rights and interests of the masses, regulate social behavior, resolve social contradictions, and maintain social order in accordance with the law, so as to help China successfully overcome the middle-income trap. In terms of the mode of social governance, we should improve the relevant systems under which the government takes the lead, non-governmental actors provide support, and multiple parties participate. We should improve the Organic Law of the Local People's Congresses and Local People's Governments of the PRC, clarify the government's responsibilities for social governance, transfer the government's power for social governance in an orderly manner, and give full play to the government's leading role in social governance. We should strengthen legislation on social organizations, regulate and guide the healthy development of all kinds of social organizations, lower barriers to entry for social organizations, improve the constitutions, governing bodies and exit mechanisms of social organizations, and encourage social organizations to exercise autonomy in accordance with the law. In terms of narrowing the gap between rich and poor, we should put in place a sound modern property rights system and reform the income distribution system. In terms of ensuring and improving people's livelihood, we should strengthen and standardize public services in accordance with the law, and improve laws and regulations on education, employment, income distribution, social security, medical and health care, food safety, poverty alleviation, charity, social assistance and the protection of the legitimate rights and interests of women, children, the elderly and the disabled.

5.2.4 *Achieve an Effective Connection Between Legislation and Reform Decision-Making in the Transition Period*

Comprehensively deepening reform based on China's national conditions is a necessary requirement for overcoming the middle-income trap. The deeper reform goes, the more emphasis should be placed on the rule of law. We should guide the direction of reform, advance the reform process and safeguard the fruits of reform through legislation, so that all the people can share in the dividends of reform and the rule of law. In order to ensure that the process of building a rule of law system matches the comprehensive deepening of reform, we should properly handle the relationship between the variability of practice and the stability of law, and between the foresightedness and feasibility of laws. We should take the initiative to adapt legislation to the needs of reform and economic and social development, respect and reflect the objective laws of economic and social construction, actively respond to people's expectations, better coordinate interests, and make major reforms based on the law. When studying reform plans and measures, we should consider the legislative issues involved in reform, and put forward legislative needs and suggestions in a timely manner. Practice has proved that effective governance or reform measures should be elevated to the status of law in time; For reform measures that require preliminary trials as the conditions for practice are not yet ripe, the trials should be authorized in accordance with legal procedures; laws and regulations that do not meet the requirements of reform should be amended and repealed in time.

5.3 *Modernize Capacity for Social Governance with the Rule of Law*

Capacity for social governance refers to the ability to use relevant systems to manage social affairs, which involves the dynamic implementation and operation of legal systems, including law enforcement, the administration of justice, and the creation of a rule of law culture. The modernization of capacity for social governance requires that we should build a keen awareness of the need to act in accordance with rules and conduct affairs in accordance with the law, be good at using law to govern the country, translate institutional advantages into the efficiency of social governance, and enhance our capacity for scientific, democratic and law-based governance.

5.3.1 *Administer in Accordance with the Law, Strengthen Supervision Over the Exercise of Power, and Ensure That the Law Is Enforced*

Administering in accordance with the law is a necessary requirement for regulating the exercise of public power and guaranteeing the realization of private rights. The administrative acts of administrative organs directly affect the public's trust in the government and determine the effect of social governance. In recent years, with the transformation of the market economy and the adjustment of the pattern of social interests, new problems and new contradictions have increased, and mass disturbances have been on the rise. Unbridled administrative power is one of the reasons that cannot be ignored. Some departments and cadres are accustomed to using administrative orders or simple and blunt means to push forward work, which can easily lead to contradictions between cadres and the masses; some departments and cadres are divorced from reality, blindly pursuing so-called political achievements and carrying out "image projects" regardless of public opinion; some cadres overstep their authority, misplace their functions, violate the law and discipline, and are very bureaucratic in their styles, which has brought negative impact on social development. Effective measures must be taken to correct these undesirable tendencies.

Fully Perform Government Functions in Accordance with the Law

We should firmly establish the idea that power comes from the people and is conferred by law, adhere to the principle that functions and powers should be prescribed by law, improve legal systems for administrative organizations and procedures, promote the legalization of institutions, functions, authorities, procedures and responsibilities, and form an administrative system characterized by the integration of power and responsibility, a reasonable division of labor, scientific decision-making, smooth enforcement, and effective supervision. Administrative power shall be exercised along the track of the rule of law in accordance with the administrative principle that "duties prescribed by law must be performed, and matters not explicitly provided for in law shall be prohibited." We should correct nonfeasance and misconduct on the part of administrative organs, overcome lazy governance and lax governance, punish negligence and dereliction of duty, give full play to the government's statutory functions in economic regulation, market supervision, social management and public services, and actively respond to the needs and concerns of the public. Administrative organs are prohibited from establishing power outside the law, and must not detract from the legitimate rights and interests of citizens, legal persons, and other organizations or increase their obligations if no basis for doing so can be found in any law or regulation. We should introduce a list of government powers, eliminate the space for power rent-seeking, and promote the procedure- and law-based exercise of power by governments at all levels.

Improve Mechanisms for Law-Based Decision-Making

We should define public participation, expert argumentation, risk assessment, legality review, and collective discussion and decision-making as statutory procedures for major administrative decision-making, so as to ensure that the decision-making system is scientific, the procedures are proper, the process is open, and responsibilities are clear. We should establish internal mechanisms within administrative organs for reviewing the legality of major decisions, actively implement a government legal counsel system, ensure that legal counsels play an active role in making major administrative decisions and promoting law-based administration, and make sure that the contents of decisions are legal and compliant. We should establish a lifelong accountability system for major decisions and an accountability review mechanism.

Deepen the Reform of the Administrative Law Enforcement System

We should establish an authoritative and efficient administrative law enforcement system with the integration of power and responsibility, strengthen grass-roots law enforcement forces, integrate law enforcement bodies, support interdepartmental comprehensive law enforcement in areas where conditions permit, and do our best to resolve the problems of overlapping powers and responsibilities and duplicate law enforcement. We should reasonably allocate law enforcement forces according to the powers and functions of governments at different levels, and in accordance with the principle of reducing levels, integrating teams, and improving efficiency. We should strictly implement a certification and qualification management system for administrative law enforcement personnel. We should improve the mechanism that links up administrative law enforcement and criminal justice, establish a system for information sharing, case notification and case transfer among administrative law enforcement organs, public security organs, procuratorial organs, and judicial organs, overcome the problems of failing to transfer cases, having difficulty transferring cases, and substituting administrative punishments for criminal punishments, and create a seamless interface between administrative punishments and criminal punishments.

Adhere to Strict, Standardized, Impartial and Civilized Law Enforcement

We should punish all kinds of illegal acts in accordance with the law and intensify law enforcement in key areas that concern people's immediate interests. We should improve law enforcement procedures and establish a system for recording the entire process of law enforcement. We should clarify specific operational procedures and focus on standardizing law enforcement actions such as administrative licensing, administrative punishment, administrative coercion, administrative collection, the charging of administrative fees, and administrative inspections. We should strictly implement a legal review system for major law enforcement decisions. We should put in place a sound system of benchmarks for administrative discretion, specifying and quantifying the standards for administrative discretion as well as defining its scope, categories, and scale. We should strengthen informatization and information sharing for administrative law enforcement, and improve the efficiency and standardization of law enforcement. We should strengthen support for administrative law enforcement, and deal with illegal acts that hinder the normal working order of administrative organs or prevent administrative law enforcement personnel from performing their duties in accordance with the law. We should comprehensively implement a responsibility system for administrative law enforcement, strictly determine law enforcement responsibilities and accountability mechanisms for law enforcement personnel in different departments, agencies, and positions, strengthen law enforcement supervision, eliminate interference in law enforcement activities, overcome local and departmental protectionism, and punish corruption in law enforcement.

Strengthen the Restriction and Supervision of Administrative Power

We should put in place a scientific and effective system for restricting and supervising the exercise of power, strengthen the systems for intra-party supervision, supervision by people's congresses, democratic supervision, administrative supervision, judicial supervision, supervision through auditing, public supervision, and supervision by public opinion, and enhance the synergy and effectiveness of supervision. For departments and positions where power is concentrated, we should put in place an arrangement whereby power is exercised on a case-by-case basis, power is assigned to different positions, power is granted at different levels, and people change positions on a regular basis, strengthen internal process control, and prevent abuse of power. We should improve hierarchical and special supervision within governments, improve the supervision of lower-level organs by higher level organs, and set up a system of a regular supervision. We should improve the mechanism for error correction and accountability, improve the methods and procedures for holding people accountable, and deal with acts such as disobeying orders, defying prohibitions, administrative nonfeasance, negligence and dereliction of duty, and illegal administrative acts sternly in accordance with laws and regulations. We should improve the auditing system, audit every aspect of public funds, state-owned assets, state-owned resources and leading cadres' performance of economic responsibilities, strengthen the leadership of higher level audit organs over lower-level audit organs, explore the unified management of the personnel, property, and resources of local audit organs at or below the provincial level, and promote the professionalization of auditing.

Comprehensively Promote Transparent Government

Administrative organs should make the disclosure of government information an important part of law-based administration, adhere to the principle that disclosure is the norm and non-disclosure is the exception, and promote the openness of decision-making, implementation, management, services, and results, so that administrative power is exercised in a fair and transparent manner that enables the public to see, understand and supervise. Governments at all levels and their working departments shall, on the basis of the list of powers, fully disclose to the public matters such as government functions, legal bases for such functions, entities implementing such functions and their responsibilities and authority, management processes, and supervision methods. We should focus on promoting the disclosure of government information in areas such as fiscal budgets, the allocation of public resources, the approval and implementation of major construction projects, and the development of public welfare programs. Normative documents relating to the rights and obligations of citizens, legal persons, or other organizations shall be published in accordance with the requirements and procedures for the disclosure of government information. We should implement a publicity system for administrative law enforcement. We should give a greater role to IT in the disclosure of government information, and improve online government information services and online administrative services.

5.3.2 Ensure the Fair Administration of Justice and Improve Judicial Credibility

Judicature is the process by which the judicial organs of the state use law to deal with cases according to their statutory functions and powers and statutory procedures. The fair administration of justice is the last line of defense for settling disputes, resolving social contradictions, and ensuring equity and justice. At present, China's judicial environment is generally good, but there are still deficiencies in practice. The handling of some cases is interfered by external factors, some cases have been dragging on for a long time, judicial injustice and judicial corruption still occur, and the legitimate rights and interests of the parties concerned cannot be effectively protected. Especially after society enters the transition period, how to actively respond to the needs of society and how to make a ruling in the absence of the relevant legislation has become a new challenge facing the judiciary. Therefore, we must improve the judicial management system and the mechanism for the exercise of judicial power, regulate judicial behavior, strengthen supervision over judicial activities, and strive to make the people feel equity and justice in every judicial case.

Exercise Judicial and Procuratorial Powers Independently and Impartially in Accordance with the Law

We should put in place a sound mechanism for protecting judicial personnel in performing their statutory duties. We should strictly implement a system for recording instances of leading cadres interfering with judicial activities or meddling in the handling of specific cases, circulating a notice against them and holding them accountable for doing so. No Party or government organs or leading cadres shall allow judicial organs to do anything that violates their statutory duties or obstructs justice, and no judicial organ shall comply with the request of any Party or government organ or leading cadre for illegally interfering in judicial activities. Those who interfere with the handling of cases by judicial organs shall be investigated for responsibility according to law.

Optimize the Allocation of Judicial Functions and Powers

We should improve systems and mechanisms whereby public security organs, procuratorial organs, judicial organs, and judicial administrative organs to perform their respective functions, cooperate with each other and check each other. We should improve the judicial system and move forward with the pilot reform of the system that separates judicial power from executive power. We should improve regimes for enforcing criminal penalties and unify systems for enforcing criminal penalties. We should improve systems and mechanisms for administrative litigation, and effectively resolve the difficulties that administrative litigation faces in case filing, trial and enforcement. We should reform the system whereby courts accept cases. For cases that should be accepted according to law, we should make sure that every case is placed on file and every complaint is heard, and protect litigants' right of action. We should improve the system of judicial supervision over administrative coercive measures that touch upon citizens' rights and interests in their person or property. We should explore the establishment of a system whereby public interest litigation is initiated by procuratorial organs. We should improve the internal supervision and restriction mechanism of judicial organs, and establish a system for recording instances of personnel from within judicial organs intervening in cases and a system for holding personnel from within judicial organs accountable for intervening in cases. We should improve the case-handling responsibility systems for presiding judges, collegial panels, chief procurators, and lead investigators.

Promote the Rigorous Administration of Justice

With facts as the basis and the law as the criterion, we should improve legal institutions that make sure facts are ascertained in accordance with the objective truth, the results of case handling are in line with substantive justice, and the case-handling process is in line with procedural justice. We should unify norms and standards for adjudication, strengthen and standardize judicial interpretation and case guidance, and unify standards for the application of laws. We should advance the reform of the trial-centered litigation system, and ensure that factual evidence in cases investigated and prosecuted can stand the test of the law. We should fully implement the rules of evidence-based adjudication, improve the system for witnesses and appraisers to appear in court, and ensure that court trials play a decisive role in ascertaining facts, identifying evidence, protecting the right of action, and delivering impartial judgments. We should clarify the responsibilities, working procedures, and working standards of all kinds of judicial personnel, implement a system of lifelong responsibility for the quality of case handling and a system of accountability for misjudged cases, and ensure that cases can stand the test of the law and history.

Ensure That the People Can Participate in the Administration of Justice

We should rely on the people for the fair administration of justice and safeguard people's rights and interests through the fair administration of justice. The people's right to participate in judicial activities such as judicial mediation, judicial hearings, and litigation-related petitioning shall be guaranteed. We should improve the system of people's assessors, protect citizens' right to jury trials, expand the scope of their participation in trials, improve the random selection method, and further improve the credibility of the system of people's assessors. Gradually, the people's assessors will no longer vote on issues relating to the application of law during trials, and will only participate in the fact-finding phase of trials. We should establish a "sunshine" judicial mechanism that is open, dynamic, transparent, and accessible to the public, make trials, procuratorial work, police affairs, and prison affairs public, disclose the basis, procedures and processes for law enforcement and the administration of justice, the results of law enforcement and the administration of justice and legal documents that have become effective in connection with law enforcement and the administration of justice, and put an end to backroom dealings.

Strengthening Judicial Safeguards for Human Rights

We should strengthen institutional safeguards for the right of litigants and other participants in litigation to know, make representations, defend, debate, apply, and appeal. We should improve legal institutions for the implementation of legal principles such as legally prescribed punishment for a specified crime, no punishment in doubtful cases, and the exclusion of illegal evidence. We should improve judicial supervision over judicial measures and investigative measures that restrict personal freedom, and improve mechanisms for effectively preventing and promptly correcting wrongful convictions. We should effectively solve the difficulty of enforcement, enact a law on enforcement, and standardize the judicial procedures for sealing up, seizing, freezing and disposing of property in question. We should speed up the establishment of legal institutions for credit supervision, deterrence and punishment against dishonest persons subject to enforcement. We should ensure the timely realization of the rights and interests of winning parties in accordance with the law.

Strengthening Supervision Over Judicial Activities

We should improve legal institutions for the exercise of supervisory power by procuratorial organs, and strengthen legal supervision over criminal, civil, and administrative proceedings. We should improve the system of people's supervisors. Judicial organs should respond to social concerns in a timely manner, regulate media coverage of cases, and prevent justice from being swayed by public opinion. We should regulate judicial personnel's contact and interaction with parties concerned, lawyers, persons in a special relationship with them, and intermediary organizations according to law, and combat corruption in the judicial field. We should strictly prohibit acts that violate the law or discipline, and punish acts of judicial brokerage to prevent the illegal conveyance of benefits. We should resolutely eliminate all kinds of hidden rules and should not allow relationships, the moral obligation to maintain a relationship and money to influence case handling. We should oppose and overcome the idea that prerogatives and privileges go with position, the bureaucratic style of work and the overbearing style, and oppose and punish acts of rough and brutal law enforcement.

5.3.3 *Foster an Awareness Among the People of the Need to Abide by the Law, and Promote the Building of a Law-Based Society*

Modern social governance emphasizes "governments take the lead, non-governmental actors provide assistance, and the public get involved." Building the rule of law lies not only in the improvement of hardware conditions such as legal systems and legal institutions, but also in universal observance of and heartfelt belief in and support for the authority of the Constitution and the law across society. Citizens abiding by the law, knowing the law, understanding the law, and mastering basic legal skills is a prerequisite for effective participation in social governance and ensuring compliance with the law. Citizens' weak awareness of the rule of law, shaky belief in the rule of law, poor mastery of the application of laws, and insufficient awareness of the need to comply with the law when defending their rights will all have a negative impact on social governance. Improving the law education mechanism, raising the public's awareness of the rule of law, putting the spirit of the rule of law into people's minds and hearts, and creating a good atmosphere in which people consciously learn, respect, trust, abide by, use and protect the law is a necessary condition for the modernization of social governance.

Promote an Awareness of the Rule of Law Throughout Society
We should view efforts to promote universal understanding and observance of the law as long-term, foundation initiatives for implementing the rule of law, carry out in-depth publicity and education on the rule of law, and guide the whole people in consciously abiding by the law, turning to the law when they require assistance, and relying on the law to solve their problems. We should make leading officials taking the lead in studying the law and setting an example in abiding by the law as the key to building a sense of rule of law, improve the system for the study and use of the law by state functionaries, and incorporate education on the rule of law into the national education system. We should improve the mechanism for publicizing and educating people on the rule of law, innovate the specific forms of publicity and education on the rule of law, strive to cultivate modern citizens, and make the spirit of the rule of law and belief in the rule of law take root firmly in people's hearts. We should incorporate education on the rule of law into the promotion of cultural and ethical advancement, carry out mass activities on the rule of law as a culture, improve the system for public interest-oriented media campaigns to popularize basic knowledge of law, strengthen the application of new media and new technology in popularizing basic knowledge of law, and improve the effectiveness of efforts to popularize basic knowledge of law. We should combine education on the rule of law with moral education, strengthen efforts to improve civic morality, carry forward core socialist values and fine traditional Chinese culture, strengthen the moral foundation of the rule of law, strengthen the awareness of rules, advocate the spirit of contract, and promote public order and good customs. We should give full play to the role of the rule of law in solving outstanding problems in the field of morality, and guide

people in consciously fulfilling their statutory obligations, social responsibilities, and family responsibilities. We should strengthen social credibility building, refine mechanisms to reward people for good faith when they abide by the law and punish them for bad faith when they break it, establish a cross-regional, cross-departmental, and cross-sectoral joint reward and punishment mechanism through credit information sharing, and form a co-governance structure featuring coordination among government departments, self-regulation by industry organizations, the active participation of credit service agencies, and extensive supervision by public opinion.

Promote Law-Based Governance at Multiple Levels and in Multiple Areas

We should adhere to systematic governance, law-based governance, comprehensive governance, and governance at the source, and strengthen the role of the rule of law in social governance. We should carry out in-depth activities to establish the rule of law at different levels and in various forms, support the self-restraint and self-management of various social actors, and give full play to the role of social organizations in guiding the behavior of their members, constraining the behavior of their members by rules, and protecting the rights and interests of their members. We should give full play to the positive role of social norms in social governance, such as citizens' conventions, village regulations and folk conventions, industry rules, and charters of organizations. We should give full play to the positive role of people's organizations and social organizations in building a law-based society, and establish sound mechanisms and institutional channels for social organizations to participate in social affairs, safeguard the public interest, help people in need, help and educate special groups, and prevent crimes. We should strengthen the self-regulatory and professional service functions of social organizations such as trade associations and chambers of commerce, speed up the decoupling of trade associations and chambers of commerce from administrative organs, and make them truly become social actors with sound organizations, sound systems, clear rights, and responsibilities, and standardized operations. We should properly handle social issues involving ethnic and religious factors in accordance with the law and promote harmonious ethnic and religious relations.

Build a Complete Legal Service System

We should speed up the establishment of a sound public legal service system that conforms to national conditions, covers urban and rural areas, and benefits the whole people, integrate public legal service resources, expand the field of public legal services, improve capacity for and raise the level of public legal services, strengthen legal services in the field of people's livelihood, continuously meet people's demand for basic legal services, and promote social equity and justice. We should improve the legal aid system, expand the scope of assistance, and perfect the judicial aid system to ensure that people receive timely and effective legal assistance when they encounter legal problems or their rights are violated. We will coordinate legal service resources in urban and rural areas and different regions, and develop foreign-related legal services.

Improve Mechanisms for Safeguarding Rights and Resolving Disputes in Accordance with the Law

We should strengthen the authoritativeness of the law in safeguarding the rights and interests of the people and resolving social conflicts, guide and support people in rationally expressing their demands, and safeguarding their rights and interests in accordance with the law, and resolve issues people care about most and issues that concern their most realistic interests. We should establish institutions and systems that play a major role in safeguarding the interests of the people, put in place sound mechanisms for early warning of social contradictions, for the articulation of interests, for consultation and communication, and for relief and assistance, and keep legal channels for coordinating the interests of the people and safeguarding their rights and interests open. We should bring petitioning under the rule of law, ensure that reasonable and legitimate demands can be reasonably and legitimately satisfied in accordance with legal provisions and procedures, standardize the procedures for handling petitions, and keep channels for people to voice their demands, coordinate their interests, and protect their rights and interests open. We should improve mechanisms for preventing and resolving social conflicts and disputes, and perfect the diversified dispute resolution mechanism whereby mediation, arbitration, administrative adjudication, administrative reconsideration, and litigation are organically connected and coordinated. We should strengthen the building of industry-specific and specialized people's mediation organizations, and improve the work system for coordinating people's mediation, administrative mediation, and judicial mediation. We will improve the arbitration system and enhance the credibility of arbitration. We should improve the administrative adjudication system and strengthen the functions of administrative organs in resolving civil disputes closely related to administrative activities. We should push forward the comprehensive management of social security, perfect the multi-tiered prevention and control system for public security, and effectively prevent and resolve problems that affect social stability, so as to ensure the safety of people's lives and property. We should severely crack down on violent terrorism, crimes involving gangs, cults, pornography, gambling, drug abuse and other illegal and criminal activities, and strengthen efforts to tackle key issues such as endangering food and drug safety, compromising work safety, damaging the ecological environment, and undermining network security in accordance with the law.

5.4 *Combine the Rule of Law with the Rule of Virtue to Build a Harmonious Socialist Society*

"Ruling the country by law" and "ruling the country by virtue" are the ruling strategies put forward by the CPC central committee on the basis of drawing on and summarizing the historical experience of China and foreign countries and in the light of the reality of Chinese society. The "rule of law" and the "rule of virtue" have been a topic of discussion for thousands of years. But the combination of the two ruling strategies of ruling the country by law and ruling the country by virtue is a pioneering undertaking in Chinese governing theory, and the combination of the two is conducive to promoting the building of a harmonious socialist society and the long-term stability of the country. General Secretary Xi Jinping once said: "A country cannot prosper without virtue, and a man cannot succeed without virtue. We must raise the ideological and moral standards of the whole society, inspire people to develop good moral intentions and kind moral feelings, cultivate correct moral judgment and a sense of moral responsibility, enhance their abilities to practice virtue, especially their abilities to do so consciously, and lead people to pursue lives where moral standards are valued, respected and abided by, forming an upward force, a force of goodness. Our nation will be full of hope as long as the Chinese pursuit of a beautiful and lofty moral realm continues from generation to generation."

The rule of virtue belongs to the category of ideology, and the rule of law belongs to the category of politics. The two are different means and ways of governing the country. The rule of law is coercive and authoritative and involves the use of the coercive power of the state to ensure the orderly operation of society and protect the legitimate rights and interests of the people. It requires that no person or organization should go beyond the law or be above the law, powers should be exercised and obligations performed within the limits prescribed by law, all violations of law should be punished by law, and everyone should be equal before the law. The rule of virtue relies on invisible forces such as public opinion, value judgment, conscience and beliefs, guides people's behavior by persuading, exhorting, influencing, educating, etc., permeates and influences social life deeply, and achieves the purpose of social governance through inner guidance. Ruling the country by virtue is inner self-discipline.

5.4.1 *Dialectical Unity of the Rule of Law and the Rule of Virtue*

The rule of virtue is the moral basis of the rule of law. Virtue emerged earlier than law. The rule of virtue is the source of the rule of law. Most laws are derived from virtue. Law is a distillation of virtue. The rule of virtue provides a moral basis for the rule of law, which is reflected in all stages of the rule of law. First, in the legislative stage, virtue determines the direction and guiding ideology of legislation and provides a standard and starting point for the formulation of good laws. Second, in the process of law enforcement and the administration of justice, law enforcement and judicial personnel are required to have a sound moral compass, strictly abide by professional ethics, and exercise the powers conferred by the state in accordance with the requirements of the law. Meanwhile, the evaluation function of virtue provides supervision by public opinion for law enforcement and judicial work, which is conducive to ensuring a standard of rigor and impartiality in law enforcement and the administration of justice. Finally, in the law-abiding stage, virtue lays a good moral and ideological foundation for citizens to abide by the law, improves citizens' moral quality, and strengthens citizens' identification with and belief in the law, so that citizens are willing to observe the limits set by law from the bottom of their hearts and consciously abide by the law.

The rule of law provides a legal safeguard for the rule of virtue. It is impossible to maintain social stability, economic order, and cultural prosperity by relying on the rule of virtue alone. Especially for people who commit serious illegal acts and lack moral values, the coerciveness and authoritativeness of the rule of law is particularly necessary and crucial. As the saying goes, "the law is the last line of defense of virtue." The law cultivates citizens' habit of observing discipline and abiding by the law, improves citizens' ideological and moral quality, and ensures the smooth implementation of the rule of law by severely punishing those who seriously violate morality and touch the bottom line of law and safeguarding legitimate rights and interests.

The rule of virtue and the rule of law complement and promote each other. Laws have limitations and lag behind reality in that they cannot regulate all areas of social life, take time to make, and cannot adjust in time to new social problems. Virtue, on the other hand, exists everywhere and all the time, making up for gaps in laws. Meanwhile, due to the randomness and non-coerciveness of virtue, virtue cannot remedy itself when it is damaged, so virtue needs to be protected by the coerciveness and authoritativeness of the law. It can be seen that the rule of law and the rule of virtue complement each other, promote each other, and bring out the best in each other. The rule of law needs to be supplemented by the rule of virtue, and the rule of virtue needs to be guaranteed by the rule of law. Only by combining the rule of virtue closely with the rule of law can our country enjoy enduring peace and stability.

5.4.2 The Combination of Ruling the Country by Law and Ruling the Country by Virtue Is a Necessary Requirement for Building a Harmonious Socialist Society

In the process of establishing and developing the market economy, people's values have changed greatly, forming a diversified moral system. But the legal system needs to be further improved, so many aspects have not been included in the scope of legal adjustment. At this stage, it is very necessary to combine the rule of virtue with the rule of law to build a harmonious socialist society. This is determined by the basic national conditions of our country at the present stage.

Socialist Political Harmony Requires the Combination of the Rule of Virtue and the Rule of Law

The combination of the two provides a complete set of ruling strategies for the building of a harmonious society and lays the institutional foundation for political harmony. Political harmony first requires political democracy. The combination of the rule of virtue and the rule of law is an important guarantee for the realization of democratic politics. The rule of law provides a way for the realization of political democracy. The rule of virtue provides supervision, evaluation, and publicity for political harmony, so as to make democratic politics take root firmly in people's hearts. Meanwhile, the rule of virtue and the rule of law cultivate excellent leading cadres for the establishment of harmonious politics by improving their moral quality by virtue, and regulating their words and deeds by law.

Socialist Economic Harmony Requires the Combination of the Rule of Virtue and the Rule of Law

The socialist market economy is a rule-of-law economy as well as a moral economy. The development of the market economy needs legal protection and moral restriction. We need to combine the rule of virtue and the rule of law—regulating the development of the market economy and punishing irregularities by law, and purifying people's heart and improving people's moral standard by virtue to defend them against bad ideas in the development of the market economy, so as to build a fair, honest and harmonious socialist market economy system.

Socialist Cultural Harmony Requires the Combination of the Rule of Virtue and the Rule of Law

Cultural development has always been the focus of our party's work, and the building of a harmonious socialist society is impossible without a harmonious culture. Ideological and moral education is an important part of the building of a harmonious culture, which has to be achieved through the rule of virtue. Meanwhile, the building of a harmonious culture needs to be legally protected and institutionally supported by the rule of law. Only by combining the rule of virtue with the rule of law can the building of a harmonious culture dominated by the system of socialist core values be integrated into every sphere of social life, thereby significantly improving the quality of citizens which is comprised mainly of ideological and moral cultivation and the concepts of democracy and the rule of law.

Ecological Harmony Requires the Combination of the Rule of Virtue and the Rule of Law

Since the industrial revolution, countries have carried out the predatory exploitation of natural resources for development at the expense of the environment. Since the beginning of the twenty-first century, natural disasters have become a more frequent occurrence around the globe. Now environmental issues have become a common challenge for all countries around the world. Ecological harmony is essential to the realization of a harmonious socialist society in China. To achieve ecological harmony, first, the state needs to develop relevant legal institutions, bring ecological protection into the scope of legal adjustment, act within the reasonable scope prescribed by law, and investigate and prosecute persons and organizations who violate the law by damaging the ecological environment according to law; second, the government should develop policies that guide citizens in building ecological harmony and harmony between man and nature; finally, we should pay attention to education and publicity on ecological ethics and establish the notion of ecology among citizens to lay a good foundation for ecological harmony.

5.4.3 *Create a Law-Based Environment in Which the Rule of Law Is Promoted by the Rule of Virtue*

Problems such as moral chaos, lack of integrity and corruption are common to countries that have fallen into the "middle-income trap." Countries that value "virtue" tend to receive a boost to their efforts to overcome the "middle-income trap." Confucianism advocates reducing the need for punishment through moral education. Countries and regions that attach great importance to Confucianism, such as South Korea, Japan, Singapore, China Taiwan, and China Hong Kong, have all overcome the middle-income trap fairly quickly. Germany, Sweden, Finland and other countries that attach great importance to social civilization and norms can still maintain sustained and stable development after they have overcome the middle-income trap. According to a survey of 2757 courses offered by 623 US universities, 50% of them involve ethics or professional ethics. The "rule of law" is discipline by others, governing people by restricting their behavior; while the "rule of virtue" is self-discipline, restricting people's behavior by restricting their ideology.

"The law is written virtue, and virtue is the law in our hearts." The two are mutually reinforcing, and both are necessary and provide support for overcoming the middle-income trap. The purpose of good law is sound governance. Sound governance is not only inseparable from mandatory legal norms, and from various informal institutional arrangements accepted by people, including guidelines for the regulation of virtue. Sound governance is preconditioned on the rule of law, which keeps people's behavior within the limits of the country's law. The focus of sound governance is coordination. We must uphold both the rule of law and the rule of virtue. We must lay emphasis on the rule of law on the one hand, giving full play to the normative function of law, and embodying moral values and promoting moral development with the rule of law, and lay emphasis on the rule of virtue on the other, attaching importance to the educational function of virtue, and fostering the spirit of the rule of law and building a rule of law culture with virtue. By upholding both the rule of law and the rule of virtue, we can make law and virtue complement each other, and the rule of law and the rule of virtue bring out the best in each other. While emphasizing the rule of law, we should also emphasize strengthening moral education for citizens, reinforce the moral foundation of the rule of law, and promote public order and good morals. We should "combine the rule of law with the rule of virtue," for only laws guided by virtue are laws that are reasonable and serve the public. In the future, we should not only give play to the normative function of the rule of law and the regulating function of the rule of virtue, and reinforce the moral foundation of the rule of law. As a pair of "wings," the rule of law and the rule of virtue inject new impetus into economic and social development. In running our country and society, we need to lay emphasis on both the rule of law and the rule of virtue, not only highlighting the normative function of law, but also valuing the educational function of virtue, so that law and virtue complement each other and rule of law and rule of virtue bring out the best in each other.

6 Education Is the Key to Overcoming the Middle-Income Trap

The report to the 19th CPC National Congress pointed out that "building a strong country in education is fundamental to the great rejuvenation of the Chinese nation." There are many factors that influence whether a country can overcome the middle-income trap, such as politics, the economy, culture, the rule of law and resources, but education is the fundamental and long-term one. Education can directly enhance the quality of citizens and workers, optimize the structure of human resources, raise the efficiency of human resources, increase intellectual resources, ensure innovation-driven development, promote industrial upgrading, refine the structure of productive forces, improve production relations, promote economic and social progress, and ultimately optimize the economic foundation of society. Only through education can we shift from the traditional capital- and resource-driven growth to labor-driven growth. Although Germany had been devastated by wars, a perfect education system and advanced education concepts supplied a large number of all-round, high-quality professionals for its economic development, providing critical manpower support for its economic take-off. Japan is a resource-poor country and had also been ravaged by wars. Japan's education and the technology generated by education account for more than 60% of its economic development. Vigorously developing education is the very foundation of the State of Israel and its path to prosperity. The abundant human resources and high overall quality of citizens created by education ensure the continued rapid development of the Israeli economy. Among the four pillars of Britain's economy, trade, technology, education and tourism, education is not only an independent pillar of the economy, but also provides strong support for the other three pillars. The impetus that education provides for the development of science and technology is the fundamental driving force enabling many developed countries to become rich and powerful, and is the key to national economic development and social stability. The report to the 19th CPC National Congress of the communist party of China pointed out that building a strong country in education is fundamental to the great rejuvenation of the Chinese nation, and that we must give priority to education, further reform in education and speed up its modernization.

Among the five factors of production, labor, land, capital, entrepreneurship and information, three are determined directly by education. China, in particular, has been under enormous pressure in terms of resources, environment, labor force and capital efficiency after nearly 40 years of rapid growth, and the original development model is clearly unsustainable. Through education, we can tap and improve the potential of the factors of production of labor, entrepreneurship and information, and ease huge constraints and bottlenecks on resources and the environment. The most fundamental and overarching factors to overcoming the middle-income trap are economic transformation and social transformation. We believe that education is the source factor that profoundly influences these two factors. Therefore, education is irreplaceable as the source. Developing education is the key to overcoming the middle-income trap and the only way to overcome it.

6.1 The Key Role of Education in Overcoming the Middle-Income Trap

On a deeper level, the relationship between education and overcoming the middle-income trap is actually a manifestation of the relationship between education and the economy. As an organic part of the social system, education plays an increasingly important role. "Whoever wants to develop the economy must develop education first." This is a universally accepted law in contemporary people's understanding. Education is providing more and more intellectual and manpower support for economic development. Education directly changes the quality of workers in the structure of productive forces through the cultivation of talents. Workers are the most active factor in productivity. Through education and training of workers, the quality of workers can be greatly improved, thereby improving economic efficiency. Therefore, education can produce labor capacity. By changing the structure of productive forces, education changes the structure of productive forces, promotes changes in relations of production, and ultimately changes the economic foundation of society.

The fundamental purpose of education is to cultivate and bring up talents, so it is an important way to produce and reproduce labor force. The production of labor force includes not only the growth of natural life, but also education and learning. The latter forms the brainpower and intelligence of workers, thus realizing the production and reproduction of social labor force. According to the 2016 Research Report on the Quality of Employment among College Graduates, the employment rates for people who hold a junior college degree, people who hold a regular college degree, and people who hold a master's degree are the highest. Therefore, education plays a direct role in economic development. First, education shortens the necessary labor time in society and improves labor productivity, and is an important means to improve labor proficiency, production skills and techniques, and labor speed. Second, education is an important way to transform science into technology. Science and technology are primary productive forces. In order to turn science and technology into primary productive forces, we must give play to the role of education, which is the intermediate link that transforms science into production technology. Meanwhile, education is also the most effective way to reproduce scientific knowledge and transform science into production technology. Third, education can improve economic management.

By training economic managers, we can improve their decision-making and management skills, thus improving economic efficiency.

In the course of economic development and social reform and opening-up, education has gradually become a pioneer in coordinated economic and social development at home and abroad. Education spreads advanced thoughts, builds a positive cultural atmosphere, and produces new ideas. Some of the thoughts and ideas will become driving forces for economic and social development. Similarly, education also plays a leading role in overcoming the middle-income trap.

Although education does not directly produce products and promote economic development as enterprises do, it provides a lot of human capital for economic and social development through the cultivation of talents. The development and utilization of human capital play a huge role in economic growth and social development. Experience has proved that the accumulation of human capital brought about by education is one of the most important contributors to economic growth. Education and the accumulation of human capital generated by education are a key contributor to a country's wealth and economic growth. Educational progress can bring about rapid accumulation of human capital, which in turn will bring about rapid economic growth. Meanwhile, the knowledge accumulation and technological progress brought about by advances in education are also a fundamental prerequisite for economic transformation, industrial upgrading and successfully overcoming the middle-income trap.

Education permeates every nerve of the social system through the cultivation of talents. From family education to school education to social education, education affects people and the development of society through formal teaching and training, or imperceptibly influences the formation of people's values, thus affecting the process of social development. Therefore, in the process of overcoming the middle-income trap, education plays a role in improving the quality of the labor force.

In summary, education plays an important role in overcoming the middle-income trap by providing human capital, and the accumulation of human capital is a prerequisite for rapid economic growth. Education can facilitate the transformation of scientific knowledge into technology, and promote economic transformation and industrial upgrading, thereby creating conditions overcoming the middle-income trap. Education can also, to some extent, provide financial support for overcoming the middle-income trap. Therefore, we must continue to give full play to the fundamental, guiding, and global role of education in overcoming the middle-income trap, and always put education in a position of national strategic importance.

6.2 Increase Investment in Education and Overcome the Middle-Income Trap

The next 10–15 years will be an extremely important stage for China's economic, social and educational development. After over 30 years of rapid economic growth, China has entered a "new normal" and faces the historical task of building a moderately prosperous society in all respects and overcoming the middle-income trap.[40]

According to statistics, of the 101 middle-income economies in 1960, only 13 had become high-income economies by 2008, and of the rest of the countries and regions, some remained in the middle-income stage, and some even had fallen back into low-income status. In the practice of countries overcoming the middle-income trap, there are not only the successful experience of Japan and South Korea, but also lessons learnt from the failure of Latin American and Southeast Asian countries.

There are many successful experiences, but an important aspect is an emphasis on investment in education and the implementation of the strategy of "founding the nation on education" to transform the quantitative demographic dividend to a qualitative one. In order to develop education, we must increase the intensity and level of investment in education to provide strong support and lay a solid foundation for the development of education.

6.2.1 The Relationship Between Investment in Education and the Level of Economic Development

In terms of the overall level of investment in education, China's total investment in education accounted for 5.34% of GDP in 2013. This proportion was below that in high-income countries with a gross national income (GNI) per capita of less than $20,000, i.e., countries that have overcome the middle-income trap, and even lower than other high-income countries.

[40] Li Liguo, Huang Haijun. Higher Education Plays a Bigger Role in Overcoming the Middle-Income Trap. *Guangming Daily*, 2015-12-08.

According to the World Bank's country classifications by income level for August 2010, countries with a GNI per capita of less than $1005 were low-income countries, countries with a GNI per capita between $1006 and $3975 were lower-middle-income countries, countries with a GNI per capita between $3976 and $12,275 were upper-middle-income countries, and countries with a GNI per capita higher than $12,276 were high-income countries. An analysis of the relevant characteristics of educational investment in countries at different stages of economic development (middle-income countries, high-income countries with a GNI per capita of less than $20,000, i.e., countries that have recently overcome the middle-income trap, high-income countries with a GNI per capita of more than $20,000 but less than $50,000, and high-income countries with a GNI per capita of more than $50,000) shows that educational investment will gradually increase as the level of economic development increases.

Public expenditure on education as a share of GDP is 3.97% in middle-income countries, 4.60% in high-income countries with a "GNI per capita of less than $20,000," 5.12% in high-income countries with a GNI per capita of more than $20,000 but less than $50,000, 5.48% in high-income countries with a GNI per capita of more than $50,000, and 4.30% in China.

6.2.2 *Public Expenditure as a Share of GDP*

The level of public expenditure in China exceeds that in middle-income countries, but there is still a gap compared with "high-income countries with a GNI per capita of less than $20,000," i.e., countries that have overcome the middle-income trap. China's expenditure on education per student is lower than other countries except for secondary education on which China's expenditure per student is higher than middle-income countries. Take the specific data for 2013 as an example.

In 2013, China's expenditure on preschool education per student was $1025, 64.8% of that in middle-income countries, 28.6% of that in "high-income countries with a GNI per capita of less than $20,000," 16.9% of that in "countries with a GNI per capita of more than $20,000 but less than $50,000," and 11.6% of that in "high-income countries with a GNI per capita of more than $50,000."

In 2013, China's expenditure on primary education per student was $1323.99, 85.1% of that in middle-income countries, 35.3% of that in "high-income countries with a GNI per capita of less than $20,000,"

19.4% of that in "countries with a GNI per capita of more than $20,000 but less than $50,000," and 13.6% of that in "high-income countries with a GNI per capita of more than $50,000."

In 2013, China's expenditure on secondary education per student was $1882.03, 109.1% of that in middle-income countries, 45.8% of that in "high-income countries with a GNI per capita of less than $20,000," 22.8% of that in "countries with a GNI per capita of more than $20,000 but less than $50,000," and 16.2% of that in "high-income countries with a GNI per capita of more than $50,000."

In 2013, China's expenditure on post-secondary non-higher education per student was $2192.91, 47.1% of that in "high-income countries with a GNI per capita of less than $20,000," 30.6% of that in "countries with a GNI per capita of more than $20,000 but less than $50,000," and 29.2% of that in "high-income countries with a GNI per capita of more than $50,000."

In 2013, China's expenditure on higher education per student was $4008.47, 58.7% of that in middle-income countries, 62.8% of that in "high-income countries with a GNI per capita of less than $20,000," 34.8% of that in "countries with a GNI per capita of more than $20,000 but less than $50,000," and 21.3% of that in "high-income countries with a GNI per capita of more than $50,000."

6.2.3 A New System of Educational Investment That Combines a Variety of Sources of Investment with the Government as the Main Source of Investment

The lack of high-quality human capital helps explain why Malaysia and Thailand have become synonymous with the middle-income trap, according to New Evidence on the Middle-Income Trap, a study co-authored by Eichengreen and two Asian economists. By contrast, the rapid expansion of secondary and higher education helps explain the successful transition of South Korea from a middle-income country to a higher income country.

Whether China can avoid the middle-income trap will depend in part on whether it can develop an education system that successfully produces graduates with the skills needed by employers. Judging by the successful experience of Japan and the Four Asian Dragons in overcoming the middle-income trap and the failures of the Tiger Cub Economies (Malaysia, Indonesia, Thailand, and Philippines), it is necessary to invest heavily in education and human resources development and to increase investment in education in order to overcome the middle-income trap.

China has made great strides in educational investment in recent years, but it still needs to further expand investment. With a per capita income of about $8000, China is currently an upper-middle-income country. According to international experience and the current reality in China, we need to shift from the single-source structure dominated by government investment to a new system of educational investment that "combines a variety of sources of investment with the government as the main source of investment."

First, we should gradually raise the level of investment in education. In terms of total expenditure on education, among high-income countries with a GNI per capita of less than $20,000, Argentina spends 6.78% of its GDP on total expenditure on education, Chile 6.43%, Poland 5.71%, Estonia 5.43%, Hungary 5.04%, Russia 4.8%, the Czech Republic 4.75%, and Slovakia 4.4%, with an overall average of 5.42%. Considering that China will overcome the middle-income trap and join the ranks of high-income countries in the next ten years, we should strive to increase total expenditure on education to about 5.4% of GDP.

Second, in terms of public expenditure, the government should, in accordance with the requirements of the "three growths" stipulated in the Education Law, strive to increase public expenditure on education to about 4.6% of GDP in the next decade. According to international experience in public expenditure on education, among countries that have just overcome the middle-income trap, i.e., "high-income countries with a GNI per capita of less than $20,000, Argentina spends 5.83% of its GDP on public expenditure in education, Estonia 5.14%, Poland 5.08%, Hungary 4.85%, Russia 4.28%, the Czech Republic 4.15%, Slovakia 3.76%, and Chile 3.74%, with an overall average of 4.6%. In terms of expenditure structures at different stages of education, we should greatly increase public expenditure on preschool education. Spending on preschool education as a percentage of China's public expenditure on education is too low, only 3.52% in 2013, less than 1/3 of the 11.65% in "high-income countries with a GNI per capita of less than $20,000."

Third, the level of private expenditure, especially the level of household expenditure, can be moderately improved. Judging by changes at different stages of economic development, household expenditure will increase first and then decrease, that is, household expenditure will inevitably increase during a certain period of time as the country transitions from the middle-income stage to the high-income stage, and after the country enters the high-income stage, as private expenditure on education increases, household expenditure will gradually decline. According to the 2013 data for China, household expenditure accounted for 11.23%, which was higher than the 10% in "countries with a GNI per capita of more than $50,000," but lower than other high-income countries at different stages. Therefore, there is still some room for appropriately raising the proportion of household expenditure in total expenditure on education. Especially in the stage of higher education, a new system should be established, in which school runners provide the bulk of the funding, educatees pay a reasonable share of the costs of education, and colleges and universities raise funds through multiple channels.

Fourth, efforts should be made to increase spending per student at all levels of education. Compared with countries in different stages of economic development, spending per students at all levels of education in China is generally low. Worldwide, as countries progress toward higher levels of development, their spending per student at all levels of education will increase. Therefore, continuously increasing spending per student at all levels of education is of great significance.

6.2.4 *Guide the Modernization of Education with New Ideas*

According to the 13th Five-Year Plan for the Development of Education, since the start of the 12th Five-Year Plan period, especially since the 18th CPC National Congress, in accordance with the decisions and arrangements of the CPC Central Committee and the State Council, remarkable achievements have been made in China's educational reform and development, education on socialist core values has been further advanced, the fundamental task of fostering character and civic virtue has been effectively implemented, the ideological and moral qualities of students have continued to improve, and new progress has been made in the modernization of education, making important contributions to promoting economic development, social harmony and cultural prosperity.

China gained itself a position among "upper-middle bracket" countries in terms of the overall level of educational development. The nine-year compulsory education has been popularized in an all-round way and entered a new stage of balanced development; the 2020 target gross enrollment rate for three-year preschool education set in the Outline of the National Program for Medium- and Long-term Education Reform and Development has been achieved in advance; Senior high school education has been basically popularized; the basic public education service system and modern vocational education system have been basically established; the level of popularization of higher education has been significantly improved; continuing education has developed continuously; the trend of lifelong learning for all has taken shape. The quality of education has been steadily improved; Chinese students have performed well in the OECD's Programme for International Student Assessment; China has become a signatory to the Washington Accord maintained by International Engineering Alliance; a number of universities and disciplines have significantly improved their world ranking.

Significant progress has been made in education equity. The educational disparity between urban and rural areas and between different regions has been further narrowed; the "craze for good schools" in the compulsory education stage in large- and medium-sized cities has eased; the national student aid system has been improved; the Nutrition Improvement Plan for Rural Students in Compulsory Education has been implemented in depth; the physical health of students in poor areas has been improved; the right to education of children who live with migrant parents in cities, left-behind children in rural areas, and students with disabilities has been better protected; access to quality higher education for students in the central and western regions, especially those in rural areas, has increased significantly.

The ability to serve economic and social development has improved markedly. Every year, vocational schools supply nearly 10 million technical and skilled talents and provide training to hundreds of millions of people. Regular colleges and universities have supplied more than 20 million professionals. Colleges and universities have taken the lead in undertaking a large number of major national scientific research tasks and major engineering projects, produced a large number of landmark research findings with international influence that serve national strategies, and achieved significant results in technology transfer and the commercialization of research findings.

The ability to develop education has improved significantly. A historic breakthrough has been made in educational investment; in 2012, the goal of increasing the national expenditure on education as a percentage of GDP to 4% was achieved for the first time; a system for allocating funds on a per student basis has been gradually established; The operating conditions of all kinds of schools at all levels, especially schools in rural schools, have greatly improved; the quality of teachers has been further improved; comprehensive progress has been made in the application of information technology in education. The level of opening-up of China's education has increased significantly, and its international influence has grown steadily. Important progress has been made in the reform of the education system, with the reform of the personnel training system, the school running system, the management system, the evaluation system and the support system being comprehensively deepened, and breakthroughs being made in some key areas and links. Reform of the examination and enrollment system has been launched across the country, and the modern education supervision system has been further improved.

On the whole, the stage-specific goals set out in the Outline of the National Program for Medium- and Long-term Education Reform and Development have been achieved on time; the 12th Five-Year Plan for the development of education has come to a successful end; China's education has entered a new stage where we need to improve quality, optimize the structure and promote equity.

6.3 Deepen Education Reform and Promote Talent Cultivation

China still has a lot of catching up to do with developed countries on education. In 2016, China's gross enrolment rate for higher education was 42.7%, significantly lower than the 50% in Europe and the United States, and far below the 98.4% in South Korea. In 2012, expected years of schooling in China was 13 years, 2–4 years less than in developed countries. China's investment in education as a proportion of GDP is still lower than most developed countries. The United States spends more than 7% of its GDP on education, compared with 4% in China.[41]

China should rely on education which promotes indigenous innovation capability rather than on an excessive input of resources and capital. China's future development requires converting the demographic dividend into a talent dividend and further improving the quality of talents. This transformation requires the realization of high-quality universal

[41] Li Liguo, Huang Haijun. Higher Education Plays a Bigger Role in Overcoming the Middle-Income Trap. *Guangming Daily*, 2015-12-08.

education, modern education, traditional education, fair education, life-long education, innovative education, and competency-based education. We should create a learning-oriented society in an effort to join the ranks of human resource-rich countries.

6.4 *Improve Talent Cultivation Platforms*

To overcome the middle-income trap, we need all-round talents, innovative and creative talents, and open-minded, internationally competitive talents, including skilled workers in different industries and at different levels in the process of economic development. Education is an extremely important way to cultivate the above-mentioned talents. Take the United States as an example. At least half of the world's top ten universities are in the United States; the United States also enrolls hundreds of thousands of international students each year, accounting for about a quarter of the total number of international students worldwide. High-quality talents are core resources for China's industrial transformation and upgrading.

6.4.1 *Promote Equity in the Allocation of Educational Resources*

On the one hand, the excessive concentration of educational resources in cities and key schools deprives people in remote rural areas and disadvantaged groups in cities of equal educational opportunities; on the other hand, human resources in China are mainly in rural areas, so talent resources should also be mainly in rural areas. At present, the allocation of educational resources is tilted in favor of cities. We should change the status quo by strengthening education in rural areas so as to improve the quality and quantity of rural talents.

6.4.2 *Short-Term Talent Cultivation Objectives Should Be Coordinated with Medium- and Long-Term Talent Strategies*

China has released its first Outline of the National Program for Medium and Long-term Talent Development (the "Outline"), which sets out strategic objectives for talent development by 2020. Under the guidance of the Outline, short-term talent cultivation implementation plans should respond positively and relevant departments should see that these plans are fully implemented. In order to achieve short-term objectives, the government should provide talent cultivation funding to research organizations, educational institutions and private enterprises, and at the same time formulate a detailed evaluation programs to evaluate results delivered by funding recipients. Specific evaluation criteria can be quantified into a series of indicators.

6.4.3 Talent Cultivation Bases Rely on School Education and Existing Labor Force Platforms

As open talent cultivation bases, schools should focus on two areas: First, education is closely linked with the market, so higher education courses should be set according to industry development and market demand for talents, for example, by offering business courses for trade and engineering courses for specific projects; second, in the long run, we should have specific implementation measures for comprehensive education starting with primary education, offer research-based courses with a view to cultivating all-round innovative talents, enhance students' awareness about and ability to conduct basic research, and at the same integrate teaching staff, set up an auxiliary teacher system, encourage professionals in key fields to teach, and adopt a co-cultivation model. Workforce training as continuing education should be regarded as a supplement to school education. In terms of training providers, in addition to vocational technical schools and vocational skills training centers, employers can also act as training providers. The government shall set up corresponding talent cultivation platforms, qualified enterprises can apply for participation and cultivate talents, and the government shall provide certain funding and preferential policies. In specific projects, professionals in various fields should be recruited from different regions to provide technical guidance.

6.4.4 Attach Equal Importance to Actively Recruiting Talents and Preventing Brain Drain

On the one hand, China has formulated the "Thousand Talents Plan." By the first half of 2016, China had recruited more than 6000 high-caliber talents in various fields. In addition to attracting Chinese students studying abroad, expanding the number of foreign students studying in China can promote the recruitment of outstanding talents. In the future, China will continue to attract talented people from all over the world. We need to attract more technical talents, continue to strengthen the implementation of the "Thousand Talents Plan," and send foreigners with special talents or specialties to China's top technology companies and universities. We will bring an inflow of foreign capital by recruiting business elites. We will continue to recruit talents for key national innovation projects, disciplines and laboratories, central enterprises and state-owned commercial and financial institutions, as well as various parks, primarily high and new technology industrial development zones, and focus on supporting a group of strategic scientists and leading talents who can make breakthroughs in key technologies, develop high-tech industries, and drive emerging disciplines in innovating and starting their own businesses in China.

On the other hand, we should pay sufficient heed to the phenomenon of brain drain. At present, China is in a critical period for industrial upgrading, improving international competitiveness and building an open economic system. The loss of a large number of high-caliber talents will adversely affect China's economic transformation and development. To prevent the loss of high-caliber talents will help cultivate talents at home. Cooperation between high-caliber talents and training institutions and training bases is feasible. In order to retain talents as much as possible, we need to formulate a series of policies, such as improving college education, lowering college tuition, and treating local talents and returnees of the same overall quality alike in entrepreneurship, employment, etc.

6.4.5 *Build a Domestic Talent Development Platform*

The domestic talent development platform will be guided by the government, dominated by educational institutions such as schools, public research institutions and private research institutions, and supplemented by a constantly improving market environment. In terms of talent cultivation, talent attraction and talent utilization, various policies and measures should be adopted to strengthen basic research and improve the quality of education. Talent cultivation planning should start from policy-making, institutional operation, the market environment and so on.

6.4.6 *Formulate a Plan for China's Talent Competitiveness with an Emphasis on the Cultivation of Talents from a Young Age*

We should be willing to invest in training and recruiting high-quality teachers, improve moral education and the teaching of basic subjects, and encourage students to major in science, technology, physics, engineering and mathematics. Talent competitiveness planning should be holistic, comprehensive and open. "Holistic" means that talent policy is usually closely linked to policies on education, immigration, science and technology, etc.; "comprehensive" means that the talent cultivation under the talent strategy is multifaceted; "open" means that relevant policies are targeted at not only Chinese nationals, but also talents from other countries in the world.

6.5 Pursue Innovation in the Education Model and Strengthen Vocational Education

6.5.1 Try Out a Decentralized Two-Track Vocational Education Model

China's industrial structure determines that China needs a large number of professional talents. This requires the government to regulate and guide vocational education to lay a solid foundation for vocational education. We can draw on the experience of Germany to build an effective technical and business education system, so as to improve the literacy and expertise of workers at all levels. Guilds play an irreplaceable role in vocational education system. Guilds urge migrant workers in cities to actively participate in relevant vocational training, and learn the necessary skills related to their own occupations, so as to adapt to occupational changes and improve their social status in cities, and play a positive role in producing and supplying skilled workers. In addition, guilds foster an honest business attitude and business atmosphere, cause their members to adapt to the unprecedented high requirements of industrialization as soon as possible, and encourage their members to receive higher levels of education. Such a diversified education system provides a lot of development opportunities for citizens, promotes the technological advancement of industries, and helps to prevent the blind and ineffective pursuit of high academic qualifications. It also lays the groundwork for career diversification.

6.5.2 Give Full Attention to Strengthening Vocational and Practical Education

We can refer to the practices of developed countries: on-site job training, handicraft apprenticeship training, and closed training in corporate practice workshops and schools. Factory schools can also be set up. In addition to receiving practical training in apprenticeship workshops, apprentices also need to receive theoretical training in factory schools.

People who haven't undergone vocational education are not allowed to work.

7 Summary

In order to overcome the middle-income trap, China needs to accomplish both economic and social transformation. After entering the middle-income stage, China has the characteristics of both developing countries and transition countries, so it faces multiple challenges at the same time. China's road to social transformation is also extremely complicated. Therefore, in order to overcome the middle-income trap, we must emancipate our minds, seek truth from facts, keep pace with the times, be realistic and pragmatic, proceed from reality and national conditions, draw on the useful experience of foreign countries, and boldly promote innovation in theory and practice.

We need to adhere to the following four principles to successfully achieve social transformation.

7.1 Top-Level Design

The goal of social transformation is to construct and perfect institutions and social conditions that adapt to the high-income stage. These institutions and social conditions include a good relationship between interest groups, a balanced distribution pattern, a stable social structure, and effective governance capability. This involves the political, economic, cultural and other aspects of a country, and often affects the whole situation, so we must see the whole picture, look at the situation from all angles, and carry out top-level design.

First, establish the core objectives of social transformation and identify areas in urgent need of reform. The establishment of the core objectives requires drawing extensively on the experience of developed, transitional, and developing countries in social transformation and the lessons learnt therefrom, and giving full consideration to China's unique national conditions and stage of development. Neither can be neglected. The establishment of the core objectives of building consensus on reform, strengthening governance capability, adjusting the pattern of interests, and improving the social structure requires more detailed research and careful evaluation.

Second, clarify the main measures for social transformation. In each area of reform, we should identify policies and practices for achieving the core objectives: rebuild social consensus with promoting "equity and justice" as the core value and basic objective of reform; optimize the industrial structure, adjust the pattern of interests, expand the middle class and improve the social structure; rebuild trust, reshape morality, strengthen the government's governance capability, and deal with the crisis of moral decline in society; increase investment in people's livelihood, promote the rational distribution of public resources, and resolve potential social contradictions and conflicts.

Third, clarify the order in which social transformation is advanced, consider reform as a whole, determine the path of advancement, and establish the sequence of reforms. The areas covered by social transformation often overlap and influence each other. For example, the distribution pattern and the social structure interact with each other, and the social structure and the relationship between interest groups influence each other. The sequencing of reforms in these areas will affect not only the complexity of reform but also the ultimate success or failure of reform. Therefore, we must be cautious in determining the sequence of reforms in areas covered by social transformation.

7.2 The Rule of Law Leads the Way

Substituting the rule of law for the rule of man, giving full play to the role of the market in resource allocation, and creating a transparent, orderly, fair, and just market environment is a precondition for ensuring fairness and overcoming the middle-income trap. Comprehensively advancing the rule of law, deepening reforms with law-based thinking and law-based approaches, adjusting social relations in an orderly manner, and reasonably allocating social resources is not only a necessary requirement for social transformation and development in the new situation, but also the historical responsibility and the mission of the times for the development of the rule of law in China.

Building the rule of law lies not only in the establishment and improvement of hardware conditions such as legal systems and legal institutions, but also in universal respect for and obedience to and heartfelt belief in and support for the authority of the Constitution and the law across society. No aspect of the modernization of the national governance system can be separated from the track of the rule of law. We must gradually consolidate the rule of law basis for letting the market play a decisive role in resource allocation and enabling the government to better play its role, improve the modern property rights system, and form a modern market system in which enterprises operate and compete according to law. Comprehensively advancing the rule of law will greatly promote technological innovation and management innovation. Regulating social transformation must be guaranteed by and coordinated with a good rule of law. In order to deliver political integrity, social equity, a sense of stability, and lasting peace and stability, it is essential that we transform the government's management behavior by the rule of law.

7.3 The Government Gives Impetus

The experience of relevant countries in the world and the lessons learnt therefrom show that the government plays an increasingly important role in efforts to overcome the middle-income trap. Compared with the United States and Britain, which were the first countries to enter the high-income stage, the role of the government in the economic and social transformation of developed countries such as Germany and France was significantly enhanced. In the case of developing countries like Japan and South Korea, the government's active intervention and effective guidance were even more instrumental in enabling them to enter the high-income stage relatively smoothly. For countries that have been caught in the middle-income trap for a long time, a striking common feature is government incompetence and policy ineffectiveness. In Latin American countries, for example, incompetent governance has led to the polarization of society, putting the government in a difficult position as it often cannot strike a balance between development and equity, and is caught between a rock and a hard place when making policy choices, which may eventually lead to frequent change of government and political unrest. This shows incompetent governance by Latin American governments in a particular social structure: The government can neither completely side with the rich and powerful to become an oligarchy nor completely become a sustainable "populist" government. For China, which is a developing country, it is a matter of course that key role of the government in economic and social transformation cannot be replaced.

First, the government needs to be transcendent. In modern society, the state is autonomous and has independent interests and demands, and does not represent the interests of a specific class or group. One major lesson from Latin American countries is that the formulation and implementation of policies are controlled by special interest groups, and the government has essentially lost its autonomy and transcendence. In order to avoid falling into the middle-income trap as Latin American countries did, the government must take the initiative to separate itself from special interest groups, so as to fairly represent the interests of various social groups and interest groups.

Second, the government needs to be inclusive. This means how the government deals with the people. Only inclusive economic development can be effective and sustainable. Similarly, only inclusive social development can be effective and sustainable. Here, inclusiveness has two meanings: On the one hand, the government should seek the broadest possible consensus on reform and attract as many social groups as possible into the reform camp, so as to minimize the resistance to reform; on the other hand, the government should be confident, actively accommodate different interests, listen to different opinions, and provide more effective channels for ordinary people to express themselves.

Third, the government needs to be responsive. Responsiveness is an important attribute of responsible government. As an ideal model of government, responsible government is reflected in the fact that the government can respond to the needs of citizens and society quickly and effectively, and is well-equipped to provide public demand-oriented public services. The government's responsibility, responsiveness, and service-orientedness are closely linked. Responsiveness is the transmission mechanism of government responsibility. Through effective responses, the government carries out its responsibilities and achieves the ultimate goal of public services. For modern governments, the key to responsiveness lies not only in responding to the demands of the people, but also in taking positive and effective measures to solve problems. To this end, the government should establish a scientific and effective response mechanism and continuously improve the government's ability to respond, so that policies that reflect the needs of the public can be formulated in a relatively short period of time to meet the needs of the public at a lower cost. Meanwhile, as public awareness grows about rights, supervision, and democratic participation, the Chinese people are increasingly demanding democracy. We need to attach importance to the positive role of citizen participation in democratizing and opening-up government decision-making, establish a government that can be "seen, understood and trusted" by the masses, and continuously improve the credibility of the government.

7.4 Public Participation

Public participation and support are also essential to overcoming the middle-income trap. Lessons from some South American countries falling into the middle-income trap show that due to a lack of checks and balances, a lack of transparency on media, and ordinary people's lack of a right or ability to protect their own interests, marketization and privatization reforms often evolve into a process of plundering the wealth of society and the people. The experience of countries that have successfully overcome the middle-income trap shows that democratic supervision is essential, and that the institutionalization, standardization, and proceduralization of public participation in the administration and discussion of state affairs are crucial. Therefore, both economic and social transformation need the active participation and full cooperation of ordinary people.

First, carry out various forms of democratic consultation at the community level. We should promote the institutionalization of consultation at the community level, put in place a sound mechanism for supervision by residents and villagers, and encourage people to manage, serve, educate and supervise themselves in accordance with the law in urban and rural community governance, community-level public affairs and public welfare undertakings. We will strengthen the building of democratic mechanisms in social organizations and protect the democratic right of employees to participate in the management and supervision of various enterprises.

Second, stimulate the vitality of social organizations. We should properly handle the relationship between the government and society, accelerate the separation of government administration from self-government by social organizations, and push social organizations to clarify their powers and responsibilities, exercise autonomy according to law, and play their role. Public services that can be properly provided by and issues that can be properly resolved by social organizations should be handed over to social organizations. We should support and develop voluntary service organizations at all levels, actively cultivate and develop social organizations that engage in charity and urban and rural community services, and improve residents' ability to serve and manage themselves.

Third, innovate institutionalized channels and ways to prevent and resolve social conflicts. We should recognize and accommodate the legitimate demands of different interest groups, and improve the mechanism for assessing risks that major decisions pose to social stability, establish smooth and orderly mechanisms for the expression of demands, psychological intervention, conflict mediation and management, and rights and interests protection, so that people's problems can be reported, conflicts can be resolved, and rights and interests can be protected. In this way, we can address the root causes of conflicts and achieve lasting peace and stability.

CHAPTER 6

Participate in Globalization and Explore China's Development Path

1 Participate in Global Governance

The political and economic situation facing China at home and abroad is undergoing profound changes. Significant changes have taken place in forces that drive globalization. The rise of emerging economies has become the primary force driving change in the global economic and political landscape. New efforts are underway to intensively reconstruct global trade and investment rules, but the pace of reform of the global governance system is slow. China and other emerging economies have to work hard for a long time to achieve status commensurate with their economic strength. Objectively and rationally assessing changes in the domestic and international economic environment, and make scientific predictions about the international situation during the 13th Five-Year Plan (2016–2020) period is a prerequisite and the basis for formulating new, longer range objectives and policies in line with China's national conditions.

1.1 Trends in Global Economic Growth

During the 13th Five-Year Plan period, despite increasing instability and uncertainties in global economic growth, on the whole, there will be a period of relatively stable and slow development.

First, US recovery is picking up speed. Thanks to falling oil prices and continued monetary easing, the US economy is experiencing a modest

Z. Zheng, *Middle-Income Trap*,
https://doi.org/10.1007/978-981-15-7401-6_6

recovery. The labor market and business and consumer confidence are improving steadily. Conditions that stimulate the economy, including moderate inflation, loose fiscal policy, and an improving housing market, continue to exist. A stronger dollar suggests that the US economy remains resilient. This trend is likely to continue in the next five years. If a large amount of international capital flows back to the US market, it is likely to fundamentally reverse the dollar's decline that started in 2002, and break the consolidation pattern for the dollar formed in 2008, further buoying the dollar. However, US economic growth prospects do not look very good because of insufficient innovation and slowing productivity growth in addition to an aging population, and the impact on US exports from a stronger dollar will continue to be felt.[1]

Second, growth in the eurozone will remain slow. Despite being hit by the debt crisis, the eurozone is still a group of developed countries, with a population and economy that occupy an important position in the world, a relatively mature economic system, good infrastructure, abundant capital, and strong technological prowess. Recently, the eurozone economy has shown clear signs of improvement, with inflation easing, the unemployment rate gradually falling, and the economic sentiment index continuously rising. But the euro zone pays is more concerned about equity than efficiency in its choice of market economy model, and tends to maintain a higher level of social welfare, which is likely to bring about the malady of rigidity while protecting the rights and interests of workers. As a result, even if the debt crisis comes to an end and the current predicament is temporarily eased, it will be difficult for the eurozone to achieve relatively rapid growth.

Third, Japan's economic outlook remains bleak. "Abenomics" has indeed achieved some short-term success in helping Japan's economy recover. In particular, it has made remarkable achievements in boosting the stock market, stimulating the vitality of large export-oriented enterprises, increasing economic efficiency, and solving employment problems. However, due to many short-term risks, such as declining real income, a depreciating yen, weak external demand, and higher consumption tax rates, it is difficult to continuously improve the three "horses" of consumption, exports, and investment, which coupled with many structural problems, such as an accelerated decline in fertility, an increasingly

[1] Gao Lingyun. Basic Judgment on the International Economic Situation during the 13th Five-Year Plan. *Globalization*, 2015 (11).

aging population, a widening gap in social security funding, a worsening fiscal situation, difficulty in improving total factor productivity, and a decline in innovation capability makes it difficult to be optimistic about Japan's medium-to-long-term prospects.

Finally, growth in emerging economies will generally slow down. Developing countries, especially emerging economies, have maintained rapid economic growth for a long time, giving a strong boost to world economic development. But in the next five years or even longer, all emerging economies will face challenges to varying degrees, such as shrinking or changing external demand, insufficient momentum for internal demand growth, a relatively simple industrial structure, severe overcapacity, and a build-up of debt and financial risks. Overall, growth remains the mainstream of emerging economies.

1.2 Trends in International Specialization

International specialization represented by global value chains (GVCs) has become a major feature of trade and investment in today's world and an important driving force for globalization. The in-depth development of GVCs will further change the international industrial landscape and the patterns of trade, investment, and production between countries.

GVCs have achieved comprehensive development in today's world of economic globalization. For developed countries, GVCs are an important way to reap huge benefits. At present, developed countries dominate high-end links in value chains, occupying both ends of the "smile curve" and obtaining the greatest gains from trade and investment. For example, in the East Asian international production network, economically developed countries such as the United States, Japan, and South Korea control the R&D, design and marketing of products, while countries such as China, Malaysia, and Thailand serve as factories, making only a small profit. Developed countries and developing countries play different roles in the upstream and downstream parts of GVCs. The higher a country's level of economic development, the more upstream high-tech components it produces. Developing countries mainly produce downstream labor-intensive components and perform assembly tasks.

For developing countries, there may be different development paths for participating in GVCs, and this depends entirely on the trade and investment strategies adopted by developing countries. With regard to enhancing their position and participation in GVCs, developing countries can pursue development at different stages along the following paths according to their own conditions: First, engage in production activities in GVCs. Developing countries establish non-equity relationships with multinational companies and engage in processing trade by attracting FDI. Their exports contain a growing number of intermediate goods and services. They expand the extensive margin of participation in globalization through trade and investment activities under this non-equity production model. Second, seek upgrading in GVCs. Developing countries with a high degree of integration expand the intensive margin of participation in globalization by increasing exports of high value-added products and services. Third, dare to compete in GVCs. Some developing countries use domestic production capacity to compete in high value-added links and integrate domestic production enterprises into the global production system through cross-border M&As. Fourth, transform the GVC model. Developing countries can improve their import composition in processing trade based on their export composition. Their import composition and production capacity can change the GVC model. Fifth, make great strides in the development of GVCs. The export competitiveness of some countries has been enhanced by the rapid expansion of domestic production capacity. FDI plays a catalytic role in trade integration and domestic production capacity building.

Therefore, the position and structure of the above developed and developing countries in GVCs are not static. We judge that during the 13th Five-Year Plan period, there will be overlap between developed and developing countries in some links in GVCs, leading to increased competition in international markets. First, emerging economies will continue to grow significantly faster than developed economies, which will lead to more and more emerging economies "going out" and implementing cross-border investment strategies for overseas companies, as reflected in the fact that emerging economies as a whole will move from the downstream part to the mid-stream and upstream parts of GVCs. Second, due to differences in factor endowments and technological levels, some adjustments may be made to the division of labor within emerging economies, and some emerging economies (e.g., China) will enter the mid-stream and upstream parts of GVCs. Finally, the "re-industrialization" policies of developed countries may bring back some manufacturing industries. In response to persistently high unemployment rates after the financial crisis, developed countries, led by the United States, have put forward the "re-industrialization" goal of "reinvigorating manufacturing." If labor costs in emerging economies continue to rise rapidly, manufacturing, especially high-end manufacturing, may return.

1.3 Trends in Industrial Structural Adjustment

The 13th Five-Year Plan period and beyond will also be a period of major adjustments in the international industrial structure. These adjustments are first reflected in a "softening" trend. The so-called "softening" of the industrial structure is the process of transitioning from the traditional hardware industrial structure that is associated with material production in the era of the industrial economy to a software industry structure that is associated with technology and knowledge production. The "softening" of the industrial structure refers not only to the rising proportion of the tertiary sector during the evolution of the industrial structure, which has given rise to the so-called "economic serviceization" trend, but also the fact that the evolution of the entire industrial structure is more dependent on "soft factors" such as information, service sharing, new technology, and knowledge. This trend is mainly manifested as follows: First, the proportion of labor-intensive industries is gradually decreasing, while the proportion of knowledge- and technology-intensive industries is increasing, giving rise to the new trends of industrial structure supererogation and the industrialization of high and new technologies. Second, information technology and other high and new technologies are widely used in traditional industries, providing new opportunities and space for the development of traditional industries; meanwhile, information technology has accelerated the pace at which technologies blend into and penetrate each other, improved the level of informatization of industrial products and the level of digitalization and intelligentization of production tools, and greatly promoted the improvement of productivity and the transformation of the mode of production, becoming an important driving force for global industrial structural adjustment in the new era. Third, modern service industries such as finance, information, and consulting services have gradually become the leading industries driving economic growth, playing an increasingly prominent role in economic and social development.

Second, these adjustments are also reflected in a trend of going "advanced." "Advanced" here refers to forms of high-tech manufacturing that use advanced technology and equipment and modern management techniques. The development of advanced manufacturing plays a vital role in promoting the upgrading of the internal structure of the secondary sector. Driven by economic globalization and a revolution in information technology, the mode of production of international manufacturing is undergoing major changes. In recent years, major industrial countries have formulated development plans to promote a transition from traditional manufacturing to advanced manufacturing. Speeding up the development of advanced manufacturing has become an irreversible new trend in the development of manufacturing worldwide. The development of advanced manufacturing not only optimizes the internal industrial structure of manufacturing, but also provides a solid foundation for the technological progress and structural and system optimization of the whole economy.

Finally, these adjustments are also reflected in a trend of "greening" in industrial transformation. Climate change and environmental pollution caused by carbon emissions have had irreversible consequences for the global ecosystem. The global "low-carbon revolution" marked by "low energy consumption, low pollution and low emissions" will gradually deepen. From an economic point of view, "greening" requires the rational use of resources and energy, reducing production costs, and conforming to the requirements of sustainable economic development. This requires countries to pay more attention to the improvement and maintenance of the ecological environment while pursuing their own economic growth rate and quality targets. Therefore, greening and beautifying the environment, attaching importance to environmental protection, vigorously developing environmental protection industries, and green industries, and building a low-carbon, green, and eco-friendly modern industrial system will become an important trend in global economic development and industrial transformation.

1.4 Trends in Regional Economic Integration

Regional economic integration is a process whereby two or more countries or regions that are geographically close to one another or at similar levels of economic development, in pursuit of common interests, integrate their planning and arrangements, take a unified approach to specialized production, cooperate with each other based on the division of labor, eliminate trade barriers between each other, and gradually coordinate development and optimize the allocation of resources in the region according to the principle of regional economic integration by establishing a common coordinating body, breaking administrative boundaries, and formulating unified economic and trade policies, on condition that they adhere to the principle of equality and mutual benefit, voluntarily restrain their respective economic sovereignty, or even share or surrender part of their national sovereignty, so as to promote the development of economic and trade, and achieve industrial complementarity and common economic prosperity. During the "Thirteenth Five-Year Plan" period and beyond, there will be more regional trade integration arrangements with more new features.

1.4.1 The Number of Regional Trade Agreements (RTAs) Will Continue to Grow Rapidly

We judge that the number of RTAs will continue to grow rapidly during the 13th Five-Year Plan period. First, WTO-led global multilateral trade negotiations have been negotiations that are fraught with difficulties. As more countries join the WTO and the ranks of developing countries grow, there are not only serious conflicts of interest between developed and developing countries, but also many contradictions and differences within developed and developing countries, making it extremely difficult to coordinate and reach consensus. For this reason, the Doha Round, being bogged down repeatedly, has ended in failure. Many countries and regions have gradually lost confidence in multilateral trade negotiations under the WTO framework and turned their attention to the establishment of regional or bilateral free trade agreements (FTAs). Second, the advantages and flexibility of FTAs have been increasingly recognized and accepted. For FTAs, there are fewer participants, negotiations are more flexible and voluntary, and it is easier to reach a consensus. FTAs can also be signed with different counterparties at different times, so that the benefits of trade can be realized in a short period of time. In addition, the FTAs go beyond reducing tariffs and quantitative restrictions, expand into services, investment, and other fields, and can create a better trade and investment environment for contracting parties. Finally, there is a domino effect. Some countries, while reluctant to join regional trade agreements, will feel under enormous pressure on account of being separated from regional trading blocs. As a result, they must consider joining regional trade agreements, creating a domino effect.

1.4.2 Economic Integration Will Take on More New Features

RTAs around the globe and in major regions have taken on many new features in terms of the mode of cooperation, organizational structure, geographical focus, and areas of operation. Moreover, based on the creation of regional trade rules, supplemented by the development of plurilateral trade rules regulating a certain field, multilateral trade rules are gradually formed through the integration of rules on trade in goods, investment, intellectual property rights, and trade in services, which will definitely produce many new features and innovations at the institutional level.

First, the mode of regional economic integration and cooperation breaks the limits of traditional theories, homogeneity in organizations in terms of geography or the level of economic development has weakened as their memberships become increasingly diverse or hybrid, and North-South cooperation has become the new mainstream of development. According to the traditional theory of regional economic integration, the same social, economic, and political systems, similar levels of economic development, geographical proximity and common historical and cultural backgrounds are the basic conditions for the establishment of regional economic integration organizations, that is, it is easy for similar countries to integrate economically and carry out economic coordination and cooperation, as demonstrated by the EU before eastward enlargement and the United States–Canada Free Trade Area. However, with the development of production networks between developing and developed countries through the fragmentation of production, this trend has been basically changed by the development of RTAs in recent years, and more North-South regional economic integration organizations have been established. This shows that with the development and change of the international situation, ideology will become increasingly insignificant in regional economic cooperation and integration.

Second, the pattern of regional economic integration and cooperation is becoming increasingly complex, with economic integration organizations structured in multiple layers, featuring overlapping memberships, networked, and spanning continents. In the past, regional economic integration organizations were distinct entities that face the outside world with a united front, and there was more competition than cooperation and more confrontation than coordination between regional economic groups. The members of regional economic integration organizations are essentially geographically contiguous or adjacent to each other. One of the main motivations for the formation of trading blocs is to deal with other stronger trading blocs and ensure bargaining power in multilateral negotiations and import and export markets. But in recent years, this closed integrated development path has changed a lot. This shows that countries are not pursuing regional economic integration that is geographically and temporally limited. As long as conditions and opportunities are ripe, integration on a wider geographical scale is an inevitable choice.

Third, the Asia-Pacific region is the focus of the current and next round of regional integration. Since the end of 2009, regional economic cooperation in the Asia-Pacific region has become the focus of global attention. First, the United States' high-profile involvement and push have made the Trans-Pacific Strategic Economic Partnership Agreement (TPP) the biggest attention-grabber in Asia-Pacific regional cooperation today. On January 23, 2017, the United States officially announced its withdrawal from the TPP. There will be more uncertainty as to whether the other 11 countries participating in the negotiations of the TPP can reach a preliminary agreement without US participation. Second, on November 20, 2012, 10 ASEAN countries and the six countries with which ASEAN has free trade agreements—China, Japan, South Korea, India, Australia, and New Zealand, officially launched negotiations for the Regional Comprehensive Economic Partnership (RCEP) with a view to integrating and optimizing the free trade agreements that ASEAN has signed with six countries including China, Japan, and South Korea to build a high-quality free trade area. This has not only played an important role in furthering the economic relations between ASEAN and these six countries, enhancing the cohesion between them, and consolidating and developing the voice of ASEAN in Asia-Pacific regional cooperation, but also injected a strong impetus into East Asian economic integration. Third, after 10 years of hard work, new steps have been taken in building an East Asian free trade area. On the one hand, the creation of a free trade area between China, Japan, and South Korea will expand the regional market, promote the economic integration of the three countries and achieve mutual benefit and win-win for the three countries; on the other hand, it will have far-reaching significance in promoting the integration process of Northeast Asia and even exerting a great influence on global economic and trade patterns.

Fourth, regional economic integration and cooperation involve an increasingly wide range of fields, are growing in both depth and breadth and taking place at increasingly high levels, and will be the key to reshaping the basic rules of international economic cooperation. Changes in GVCs have brought countries closer to each other, with their interests intertwined. The integration of production requires the consistency of market rules and the compatibility of standards among countries. This requires more complex international trade rules to deal with the cross-border movement of goods and factors, and to expand the application of international trade rules from border barriers to behind-the-border barriers These behind-the-border rules mainly regulate a country's domestic policies, such as corporate behavior, intellectual property protection, labor, etc. The challenges posed by GVCs also include the need for global trade to be driven more by international direct investment (FDI) and the need to integrate trade and investment rules. The correlation between trade in goods and trade in services has been strengthened, and new fields such as transportation services, commercial flows, and information services have emerged. New trade rules are needed to coordinate the development of trade in services related to trade in goods. The movement of intermediate goods between countries caused by the fragmentation of production requires more detailed rules of origin.

Traditional RTAs focused on the liberalization of trade in goods, mainly through the elimination or reduction of tariffs and non-tariff barriers, and later extended to the liberalization of trade in services. New-generation RTAs, on the other hand, are increasingly wide-ranging, growing in both depth and breadth, in addition to being consistent with WTO rules. In addition to the above, they also cover trade and investment facilitation, trade and investment promotion, intellectual property protection standards, environmental protection standards, labor standards, rules of origin and trade dispute settlement mechanisms. In addition, some agreements also cover economic and technical cooperation and customs cooperation, and some have exceeded WTO requirements by containing "WTO-plus provisions" that impose WTO-plus commitments on members in certain respects. Such "WTO-plus provisions" in new-generation RTAs provide more free economic and trade space for partner countries on the basis of following the basic principles of the multilateral trading system, thereby achieving mutual benefit. It is worth noting, however, that in addition to seeking economic interests through cooperation agreements, developed countries are markedly more willing to influence the future international economic landscape through the making of internal rules for economic integration and cooperation. For example, the Trans-Pacific Partnership (TPP) and the Transatlantic Trade and Investment Partnership (TTIP) reflect a strategic intent on the part of developed countries that traditionally dominated the old international economic order, especially the United States, to retain the final say in global trade in the face of new economic challenges by cooperating, leading negotiations on trade and investment rules, and reshaping new rules of global trade, so as to maintain their dominance in the world economy, international trade, and global governance.

1.5 Trends in Trade Protectionism

Economic crises are often a breeding ground for trade protectionism. The world hasn't fully recovered from the US subprime mortgage crisis and the European debt crisis, so, during and after the 13th Five-Year Plan period, trade protectionism will remain a fast-growing trend. While focusing on possible changes in the means, methods, and contents of trade protection, we can be sure that China, on the one hand, China will still be the biggest victim of trade protectionism; on the other hand, China is also a country participating in global governance and leading globalization.

1.5.1 New Changes in Trade Protectionism

First, we need to be alert to the use of public assistance in trade protection. In order to get out of the crisis as soon as possible and accelerate the pace of domestic economic recovery, governments have adopted a series of economic stimulus policies, including government procurement and government bailouts. These economic policies shift the focus from restricting imports to expanding exports, and increase the international competitiveness of domestic products through the support of government economic policies, thus stimulating economic growth. Since November 2008, public assistance and government procurement have accounted for 26% of all trade protection measures, making them one of the most important means of protection. In the past, tariff and non-tariff measures were the most commonly used trade protection measures, and now they account for less than 1/5 of all trade protection measures. Therefore, economic policies introduced by various countries during the rise of the new wave of trade protectionism have replaced the previous trade restrictions and become a new means of trade protection.

Second, we need to be alert to the shift of trade protection to emerging industries and scarce resources. Information technology, biotechnology, energy conservation and environmental protection, new energy and other emerging industries are regarded as important engines that will pull the world economy out of the doldrums, so all major economies see emerging industries as new economic growth points, and are leveraging their advantages in funding and technology in an attempt to control key areas of emerging industries and seize the commanding heights of future industrial development. As scarce resources are widely used in high-tech industries and strategic emerging industries, developed countries pay special attention to controlling these strategic resources. In their early stages of economic development, developing countries, being technologically backward, had to export resource-based products in large quantities. Many resources that were once found in abundance have become extremely scarce as a result of extensive operations and large-scale exports over a long period of time, and some even need to be imported to meet domestic demand. As a result, governments around the world have resorted to export restrictions and other means of trade protection to protect resources in their countries, and trade frictions have gradually intensified over scarce resources.

Finally, we need to be alert to the possibility of global governance has become a new "protective umbrella" for trade protection measures. With the change of people's concepts of life, the international community is increasingly focused on issues such as climate change, low-carbon economy, food and food security, and energy and resource security. These issues are not only issues that have a direct bearing on human survival, but also major issues concerning economic development, and have come to the top of the agenda for building a new global governance mechanism. For this reason, many countries, especially developed countries, often camouflage "trade protectionism" by putting on the cloak of global governance. For example, some developed countries put forward concepts such as low-carbon economy and green economy under the slogan of energy conservation and emission reduction, safe in the knowledge that they have advantages in environmental protection technology. Subsequently, the "three carbons"—carbon tariffs, carbon labels, and carbon footprint verification came into being, and more and more countries are supporting the "three carbons."

1.5.2 China Will Remain the Primary Target of Trade Protectionism

According to the Global Trade Alert, between July 2008 and May 2013, China was subject to 877 discriminatory trade practices, or 41% of trade protection measures around the world. Among them, anti-dumping, countervailing, special safeguards and other trade remedies have become the main means of imposing trade restrictions against China, accounting for more than 20% of all measures implemented against China; the objects of trade protection against China have gradually expanded from labor-intensive industries with export competitiveness to new energy and high-tech industries, including solar panels, wind towers, steel and iron, and chemicals. In November 2011, the United States officially launched an anti-dumping and anti-subsidy probe into solar cells imported from China, opening the first US anti-dumping and anti-subsidy probe into Chinese clean energy products. Immediately afterwards, the United States launched an anti-dumping and anti-subsidy probe into crystalline silicon photovoltaic cells and utility scale wind towers from China. In 2012, France set up 11 committees to oversee some of its core industries, such as aerospace and renewable energy, so as to intervene in mergers and acquisitions by foreign companies when "necessary." In the same year, the European Union began an anti-dumping and anti-subsidy probe into photovoltaic cells from China and threatened to impose punitive tariffs.

It is particularly noteworthy that the international community's trade protection measures against China have become increasingly covert in recent years. Foreign countries often practice trade protectionism cloaked in the veil of national security, the rejection of M&As, investment review, etc. For example, the US government has repeatedly used "national security" as a pretext for preventing Chinese companies such as telecom equipment manufacturers Huawei and ZTE from making acquisitions or supplying equipment in the United States. The aim is to suppress foreign companies, protect American companies, and implement trade protection. For example, India banned domestic operators from buying telecom equipment from Huawei and ZTE on the grounds of national security, and it was not until Huawei and other companies accepted its harsh terms that India allowed them to re-enter the Indian market. With the further development of China's economy, China will face more and more trade frictions, encounter more and more resistance and interference in foreign investment, and face more and more strict restrictions on the import of technologies, especially high technologies, which will directly affect the further expansion and deepening of China's opening-up.

1.6 Trends in the Reform of the Global Economic Governance System

During and after the 13th Five-Year Plan period, with the end of the "old normal" characterized by great stability, the global economy will enter a "new normal" characterized by deep adjustment and rebalancing. The profound structural changes the global economy is undergoing and the increasingly frequent movement of factors have created an urgent need for a new international economic governance mechanism.

1.6.1 Direction of Reform of Global Economic Governance

The current global economic governance mechanism was formed under the leadership of the United States, Europe, and other developed countries after World War II. It is an economic governance model that takes the multilateral trading system and the international monetary and financial system as the core, adjusts international economic relations through the system of international treaties such as economic, trade and financial agreements, and consists of governance platforms and bodies. Among them, representative global economic governance platforms include the G8, the G20, the BRICs cooperation mechanism, and the Asia-Pacific Economic Cooperation (APEC); representative global economic governance bodies include the World Trade Organization (WTO), the International Monetary Fund (IMF) and the World Bank. In recent years, although new steps have been taken and some progress has been made in the reform of global economic governance through the concerted efforts of all parties, there are still some problems in the current global economic governance mechanism, such as the over-concentration of dominant power.

During the 13th Five-Year Plan period, the reform of the global economic governance mechanism will be reflected in four requirements. First, the global economic governance mechanism should truly reflect changes in the international economic landscape. In keeping with the trends of international political and economic power "rising in the east and falling in the west" and "rising in the south to the north," we should ensure that all countries participate on an equal footing in setting the agenda and making decisions on global economic governance, and the opinions and concerns of all parties are reflected in a balanced way, so that the final results are in the interests of all parties and win-win results are achieved. Second, considering the contradiction between representativeness and decision-making efficiency, the global economic governance mechanism should be an organic unity of representativeness, decision-making efficiency, and implementation effectiveness. Third, the global economic governance mechanism should include a mechanism for consensus-seeking consultation and a mechanism for the formulation of binding rules. Under the global economic governance mechanism, we should not only reach a consensus on policy objectives and orientations on a voluntary basis through consultation, but also formulate some binding rules and quantitative indicators, such as the "quantitative rules" in the international macroeconomic framework considered for the governance structure of the International Monetary Fund. Finally, the global economic governance mechanism should take into account both a short-term economic crisis emergency response mechanism and a long-term economic governance mechanism. As General Secretary Xi Jinping pointed out at the 2013 G20 St. Petersburg Summit, "All countries should take a long view, strive to shape a world economy, where all countries enjoy development and innovation, growth linkage, and interests integration, firmly maintain and develop an open world economy." At the 2017 G20 Hamburg Summit, General Secretary Xi Jinping stressed the need to stay committed to building an open global economy, foster new sources of growth for the global economy, achieve more inclusive global growth, improve global economic governance, promote interconnected growth for shared prosperity and build toward a global community with a shared future.

1.6.2 Reform of the Global Economic Governance Will Be Gradually Advanced

The outbreak of the international financial and debt crisis has exposed deficiencies in global economic governance. However, the reform of the global economic governance mechanism involves the redistribution and readjustment of the interests of all parties, as well as games and contests among major powers and groups. Specifically speaking, the interests of all countries, regardless of their size and level of economic development, should be respected, but the interests of other countries should also be considered and taken care of. On this basis, a governance model and rule system for realizing the common interests of all countries can be reached through full consultation and compromise. Each member is allowed to differ in the scope and size of responsibilities, and the manner in which and the time frame during which responsibilities are performed according to their own capabilities and characteristics, and the prevailing principles of international law. It would be against fairness and rationality to one-sidedly emphasize common responsibilities without differentiating responsibilities. Meanwhile, every member of the international community, big or small, strong or weak, must assume the responsibility of contributing to the resolution of global economic problems to the best of their ability. Without common responsibilities, differentiated responsibilities will lose their foundation like trees without roots. All of this means that the reform of the global governance system will be a gradual process.

1.7 Conclusion

In summary, during and after the 13th Five-Year Plan period, the global economy can basically maintain moderate growth. Meanwhile, under this overall trend, there will be significant overlaps between developed and developing countries in some links in value chains, which will intensify competition in international markets. Correspondingly, the international industrial structure will undergo major adjustments in the direction of "softening," going "advanced" and going "green." Regional economic integration will be greatly improved in both quantity and quality. In addition, trade protectionism will keep rising rapidly, and China will remain the country most affected by trade protectionism. Although these have put forward higher requirements for the reform of the global economic governance system, the reform of the global economic governance system at the institutional level will continue to be difficult.

Domestically, there are three changes that require special attention during the 13th Five-Year Plan period. First, under the "new normal," China's economy is facing many challenges brought by the "simultaneous occurrence of three periods," and the average annual GDP growth rate may fall to 7% or below. Secondly, corresponding to the economic slowdown, China's foreign trade will enter a period of low-speed growth. This is because, on the one hand, the world economy is still in a period of deep adjustment, and it is difficult for aggregate demand in international markets to return to sustained high-speed growth before the financial crisis; on the other hand, with the arrival of the "Lewis turning point," China's labor costs will continue to rise, and the resource, energy and ecological environment constraints on economic and trade development will intensify. Finally, China's position as a net capital exporter will be further strengthened. The growth rate of foreign investment in China has slowed down significantly, and China's outbound investment is still expected to grow rapidly at an annual rate of over 10% in the next 10 years.

Based on the situation at home and abroad, we suggest that the focus should be placed on following work during and after the 13th Five-Year Plan period: First, actively participate in a new round of trade and investment rule-making, and advance the global agenda for China's free trade areas in the Asia-Pacific, North America, Latin America, central and eastern Europe, the Eurasian Economic Union, Africa, Arab countries, and other countries and regions in a targeted manner; second, through the Belt and Road Initiative, accelerate infrastructure connectivity between countries along the Belt and Road and around the world, strengthen cooperation with countries along the Belt and Road in energy and resources development, strengthen people-to-people exchanges, and promote international cooperation in production capacity; third, while actively attracting high-end factors from around the world, improve the quality and comprehensive benefits of foreign capital utilization, vigorously promote outward foreign direct investment by Chinese enterprises and cultivate world-class multinational enterprises; fourth, actively participate in international and regional financial cooperation, steadily promote RMB internationalization and capital account liberalization, and establish a safe, efficient and open international financial system; fifth, financial security is an important part of national security, so financial security should be closely linked to national security.

2 Global Value Chains and the Direction of Industrial Structure Adjustment

Global value chains (GVCs) are a major feature of trade and investment in today's world, and also an important driving force for globalization. The in-depth development of GVCs has changed the world economic landscape, as well as the mode of trade, investment, and production among countries. In the past 20 years, GVCs and factors such as the current world-leading business and regulatory environment, new technologies, corporate concepts and strategies, and trade and investment liberalization have all contributed to the fragmentation of production. In the new international production system, international organizations and policymakers will bridge the gap between traditional rule-making and economic realities. The increasing fragmentation of production also has important policy implications, including emphasizing that countries participating in GVCs must have open and transparent trade and investment policies to attract foreign suppliers, international investors, and domestic producers if they want to obtain economic benefits.

2.1 New Developments in GVCs in a Changing World

The development and change of GVCs reflect the change of each country's position in GVCs or its economic structure. For a country, to raise its level of globalization, it should not only actively participate in GVCs, but also more importantly integrate GVCs into its national development strategy. Countries need to be clear about their position in GVCs, which is judged based on two factors: one is the level of participation of the country's economy in GVCs and the country's ability to create value; the other is the position and ability of the country's economy at the technical level in GVCs. A country's industries (or enterprises) generally go from resource-intensive activities to low-, medium-, and high-tech manufacturing service activities, and then to high value-added knowledge-based creative activities, which is reflected in the structural upgrading of production activities. Changes in GVCs are the process of participating in integration at different levels, with the entire value chain following a path of cascading development.

For countries that rely only on resource-based economies, their GVC development strategies are enhanced by increasing participation in the fragmentation of production within GVCs, expanding diversification, and increasing exports of intermediate goods and services. The above-mentioned production and exports are located at the ends of GVCs where the level of technological complexity is low and is realized by low-cost labor. Although this model is involved in multiple value chains, it is all low-end processing and manufacturing, so the domestic value added in exports is very low. For the development of resource-based countries in GVCs, they can develop their processing and manufacturing industries and gradually increase domestic value added by absorbing foreign investment, so as to make the leap from comparative advantages in resources to economies of scale.

Even countries possessing advanced technologies differ in their level of participation in GVCs. The key to these countries continuously moving up GVCs is to raise the level of products and processing, and improve productivity and the ability to create value added, so as to move toward more technologically advanced and complex links in GVCs. It can be seen that if a country wants to integrate into and move up GVCs, it must make use of its factor endowments and conditions to obtain a successful development path in GVCs. Participation in GVCs is not only a necessary choice for countries to achieve economic development, but also an important way to globalize trade and investment.

2.2 *Structural Reconstruction and Development Path of GVCs*

The structure of GVCs is undergoing changes in the process of economic globalization, and is also facing transformation and reconstruction. At the world level, more and more Chinese enterprises are "going out" to invest in overseas companies; the United States has announced efforts to "return to manufacturing" in the wake of the crisis; the real economy in Europe has been hit hard by the debt crisis, while emerging economies have risen as a new force leading post-crisis economic growth. New changes in the world economic landscape will have a strategic impact on the structure and development of GVCs.

Different countries have brought their comparative advantages to bear in GVCs, obtained the corresponding trade in tasks, fully participated in the global production system, and won more benefits. In this context, there may be different development paths for GVCs, depending entirely on the mode of countries' participation in GVCs, especially the trade and investment strategies adopted by developing countries. Developing countries can seek to enhance their position and participation in GVCs according to their own conditions along the following paths:

First, engage in production activities in GVCs: Developing countries establish non-equity relationships with multinational companies and engage in processing trade by attracting FDI. Their exports contain a growing number of intermediate goods and services. They expand the extensive margin of participation in globalization through trade and investment activities under this non-equity production model.

Second, seek upgrading in GVCs: Developing countries with a high degree of integration expand the intensive margin of participation in globalization by increasing exports of high value-added products and services.

Third, dare to compete in GVCs: Some developing countries use domestic production capacity to compete in high value-added links and integrate domestic production enterprises into the global production system through cross-border M&As.

Fourth, transform the GVC model: Developing countries can improve their import composition in processing trade based on their export composition. Their import composition and production capacity can change the GVC model.

Fifth, make great strides in the development of GVCs: The export competitiveness of some countries has been enhanced by the rapid expansion of domestic production capacity. FDI plays a catalytic role in trade integration and domestic production capacity building.

2.3 *Direction of International Industrial Structure Adjustment*

2.3.1 *The Direction of International Industrial Structure Adjustment Is Mainly Reflected in the Following Three Aspects*

First, the global industrial structure is "softening." The so-called "softening" of the industrial structure is the process of transitioning from the traditional hardware industrial structure that is associated with material production in the era of the industrial economy to a software industry structure that is associated with technology and knowledge production. The "softening" of the industrial structure refers not only to the rising proportion of the tertiary sector during the evolution of the industrial structure, which has given rise to the so-called "economic serviceization" trend, but also the fact that the evolution of the entire industrial structure is more dependent on "soft factors" such as information, service sharing, new technology and knowledge. This trend is mainly manifested as follows: First, the proportion of labor-intensive industries is gradually decreasing, while the proportion of knowledge- and technology-intensive industries is increasing, giving rise to the new trends of industrial structure supererogation and the industrialization of high and new technologies. Second, information technology and other high and new technologies are widely used in traditional industries, providing new opportunities and space for the development of traditional industries; meanwhile, information technology has accelerated the pace at which technologies blend into and penetrate each other, improved the level of informatization of industrial products and the level of digitalization and intelligentization of production tools, and greatly promoted the improvement of productivity and the transformation of the mode of production, becoming an important driving force for global industrial structural adjustment in the new era. Third, modern service industries such as finance, information, and consulting services have gradually become the leading industries driving economic growth, playing an increasingly prominent role in economic and social development.

Second, traditional manufacturing is transitioning toward advanced manufacturing at an accelerated pace. Advanced manufacturing refers to the forms of manufacturing that employ advanced technologies and equipment and modern management techniques and have a high technological content. The development of advanced manufacturing plays an important role in promoting the upgrading of the internal structure of the secondary sector. Driven by economic globalization and a revolution in information technology, the mode of production of international manufacturing is undergoing major changes. In recent years, major industrial countries have formulated development plans to promote a transition from traditional manufacturing to advanced manufacturing. Speeding up the development of advanced manufacturing has become an irreversible new trend in the development of manufacturing worldwide. The development of advanced manufacturing not only optimizes the internal industrial structure of manufacturing, but also provides a solid foundation for the technological progress and structural and system optimization of the whole economy. In developed countries such as the United States, and Japan, high-tech industries account for more than 60% of manufacturing. The continuous improvement of production efficiency is mainly driven by advanced manufacturing. The high growth rate of labor productivity in manufacturing, especially advanced manufacturing, has led to an overall improvement in labor productivity in the secondary sector.

Finally, international industrial specialization may be partially adjusted in the post-crisis era. The outbreak of the financial crisis has also affected the pattern of international industrial specialization at the present stage to a certain extent, which may lead to a partial adjustment of the pattern of international industrial specialization. First, the "re-industrialization" policies of developed countries may bring back some manufacturing industries. In response to persistently high unemployment rates after the financial crisis, developed countries, led by the United States, have put forward the "re-industrialization" goal of "reinvigorating manufacturing." If labor costs in emerging economies continue to rise rapidly, manufacturing, especially high-end manufacturing, may return, which may lead to a partial adjustment of the pattern of international specialization. Second, there may be some adjustments to the division of labor among emerging economies. Since the outbreak of the international financial crisis, emerging economies have grown significantly faster than developed economies. However, due to differences in factor endowments and technological levels, the development of emerging economies has also diverged to some extent. In a situation where developed countries are unable to relocate industries abroad on a large scale in a short period of time, different economic development prospects may lead to some adjustments to the existing system for the division of labor among emerging economies. Of course, this depends on the direction of policy adjustment and the economic development prospects of emerging economies.

3 Explore the Development Path of China in the New Era

Since the start of China's reform and opening-up, it has experienced nearly 40 years of rapid economic growth, creating an economic miracle of the world. China's overall productive forces have significantly improved and in many areas our production capacity leads the world. Statistics show that, in the 38 years from 1978 to 2016, China's GDP at constant prices grew by 32.3 times, with an average annual growth rate of 10%, far higher than the average annual growth rate of about 3% of the world economy in the same period; on the whole, the people have reached a well-off standard of living; the number of people living in absolute poverty in rural areas has fallen from 250 million to more than 10 million, and the incidence rate of absolute poverty has fallen from 30% to less than 1%; China is the only country in the world to fulfill the Millennium Development Goal of halving the number of people living in poverty ahead of schedule. Especially since the outbreak of the 2008 financial crisis, the global economy as a whole has slowed down across the board. China's economy is still growing at a medium-to-high speed and plays an increasingly important role in gradually pulling the world economy out of the trough. In 2016, China contributed about 30% to the world economy, more than the United States, the Eurozone, and Japan combined, ranking first in the world. The development path that China has long been committed to and its development experience have drawn more and more attention and interpretation from the international community. The development path can be used to summarize a country's development in the past, and also to describe the way a country plans to achieve a certain goal in the future (e.g., making the transition from a middle-income country to a high-income country). To study China's development path, we should first summarize China's experience, namely, the basic path, methods and institutional arrangements for developing from a low-income country to a middle-income or an upper-middle-income country; second, we should study a collection of methods, policies or institutions (or strategic choices) that enable China to successfully develop from the current development stage (upper-middle-income) into a high-income country.

3.1 The Basic Experience of China's Development Path

Although scholars and political leaders at home and abroad have expounded on the basic connotation, theoretical basis, main contents, practical significance, and historical limitations of China's development path from different perspectives, there are great differences in the interpretation and understanding of China's development path due to differences in standpoints and analytical perspectives. According to the report to the 19th CPC National Congress, in the past 40 years of modernization practice, China has creatively formed a socialist system with Chinese characteristics in economy, politics, society, culture, diplomacy and other aspects, as well as the basic path for the formation of these systems and institutions, which in a nutshell is China's development path. To put it simply, the essence of China's development path is: not blindly copy the development paths and models of foreign countries; explore a path of socialist development with Chinese characteristics based on China's national conditions and by drawing on the successful development experience of foreign countries.

In addition to large-scale factor inputs, technological progress and effective institutional innovation, China owes much of its ability to maintain high-speed growth over a long period of time to a unique path of reform, opening-up and development chosen based on its national conditions Although there are many developing countries in the world that are open to the outside world and have late-mover advantages, large developing countries like China which has a population of 1.3 billion and has maintained high-speed economic growth over a long period of time are rare. This is largely due to the reform mode and development path chosen by China. Its main experience can be summarized as the following three points.

First, political and social stability. In the course of more than 30 years of economic development, China has always pursued political ideologies and institutional guarantees with social stability as the first priority. Unlike many developing countries and countries in transition, China has a strong ruling party and strong governments under the leadership of the party, especially a powerful central government, which is an important political prerequisite for the success of China's reform and opening-up.

Second, induced institutional change and gradual reform. "Crossing the river by feeling the stones" is the most vivid depiction of China's reform strategies. Almost all of China's reform strategies are carried out in an "experimental" manner: First select several regions for "pilot projects," build special zones, development zones, and experimental zones, observe the specific effects, and then decide whether to roll out the specific measures of reform across the country. Such a reform path greatly eases social contradictions, avoids fierce collisions between the new system and the old system, and effectively ensures the smooth implementation of reform measures.

Third, government-led economic reform. The essence of China's economic reform and opening-up is to establish a perfect and efficient market economy, but the market economy that China needs to establish should always adhere to the reform direction of "market regulation supplemented by government intervention," and we should oppose and be alert to the reform direction for the market economy advocated by the market omnipotence theory, market fundamentalism and "neoliberalism." Although we can't deny that Western developed countries have created a high level of material and spiritual civilization under the conditions of a mature and perfect market economy, it's obviously unrealistic for China, a country with the basic national conditions of a large population, a poor foundation, a weak concept of the rule of law, and a history and culture that are essentially different from those of Western developed countries, to establish a market economy similar to those of Western developed countries to regulate the economy.

These three pieces of basic experience are unique experiences with Chinese characteristics which was not copied from the West and was formed in the process of exploring a path of socialist development in China, and will still provide important guidance for the continued exploration of China's development path for a long time to come.

3.2 New Challenges to China's Development in the New Era

During the takeoff period of economic growth (e.g., the early and middle stages of industrialization), China's economic growth depended mainly on large-scale factor endowments and investment in physical capital, such as abundant labor and natural resources, and large-scale investment expansion. As the economy develops to a higher stage, due to the existence of the objective economic law of "diminishing marginal returns," it is becoming increasingly unsustainable to rely solely on factor endowments and investment in physical capital to promote sustained economic growth. The transition from high-speed growth to medium high-speed growth, characterized by structural optimization and technological upgrading, and the transition from a middle-income country to a high-income country, will become the new normal of China's economy in the next 10 years.

As shown by the development history and experience of various countries, when a country (e.g., China) completes the early stage of industrialization, that is, when it is in the upper-middle-income stage of development (in the middle and late stages of industrialization, where the GDP per capita is \$4000–\$12,000), its economic development will face a critical transition period. It took the United States 13 years (1967–1980), Germany 13 years (1973–1986), France 12 years (1974–1986), the United Kingdom 12 years (1975–1987), and Japan 12 years (1974–1986) to cross this stage. The development of developed countries shows that when a country moves from the upper-middle-income stage to the high-income stage, its economic growth will slow down.

Among catch-up countries, there are not only countries whose development has significantly accelerated such as South Korea and Russia, but also countries whose economies have been stagnating for a long time such as Argentina and Brazil. Specifically, it took South Korea eight years (1988–1996), Russia seven years (2004–2011), Argentina 21 years (1990–2011), Brazil 16 years (1995–2011) to cross this stage. An important reason why middle-income countries are vulnerable to falling into the growth trap is that the industrial development of these countries is often between mature industries dominated by low-income countries and emerging high-tech industries dominated by high-income countries, and subject to a double squeeze from fierce market competition posed by low-income countries and the technological advantages of emerging industries in high-income countries. In other words, industrial upgrading is of great significance for middle-income countries to escape the middle-income trap, and if sustained high economic growth cannot bring about a steady increase in their industrial competitiveness and technological levels, they will inevitably fall into the middle-income trap.

For a long time, the two main drivers of China's rapid economic growth have come from investment and exports, and the marginal pull of these two engines has weakened significantly. On the one hand, relying on large-scale investment to drive economic growth is not sustainable. First, sustained high levels of investment will inevitably lead to a decrease in the marginal return on capital, and it is an objective economic law that the stimulating effect of investment on the economy will decrease progressively. Second, a large portion of China's investment over a period of time goes to real estate and related industries. The real estate industry is characterized by extensive development, which brings huge pressure on the environment, severely squeezes household consumption, and reduces the driving force for sustained economic growth. On the other hand, the mode of economic growth, which relies too much on trade expansion and massive foreign direct investment, has become increasingly difficult to sustain. First, the rapid expansion of China's foreign trade is based on cheap factors of production such as labor and land. In recent years, with a sharp rise in the prices of labor and other factors of production, the "demographic dividend" effect has gradually weakened, and there has been less and less room to compete solely on price in international markets. Second, since the outbreak of the 2008 financial crisis, the global economy has entered a period of difficult and slow recovery and adjustment. Countries have resorted to loose monetary policies and competitive devaluation, and China's exports, constrained by the external economic environment, can hardly achieve rapid expansion again. Finally, foreign direct investment has had many beneficial effects on economic development, but it is difficult for multinational companies to transfer core technologies, so foreign direct investment has only a limited effect on promoting domestic industrial upgrading.

In general, if China's current development path is not adjusted strategically, it will not be able to successfully upgrade its industries because of insufficient incentives for innovation and slow technological progress: On the one hand, labor-intensive industries will gradually lose competitiveness due to rising factor costs at home and competition from low-income countries; on the other hand, given competitive pressure from multinational corporations and the difficulty of establishing its own effective incentive mechanism, coupled with inadequate indigenous innovation capability in capital-intensive industries, and a lack of core technological advantages and competencies, it is difficult for China to develop a strong competitive edge in international markets.

3.3 How to Improve China's Development Path in the New Era

We must be soberly aware that the development path that China has been pursuing for more than 30 years is still fraught with troubles and challenges, and some social, economic, and political issues have not been fundamentally resolved because of rapid economic development. The key to improving China's development path under the new normal lies in achieving high-quality development. The basic idea is to shift from "two overdependence's" to "two reliance's," that is, we should rely mainly on the expansion of domestic demand for economic growth, expand and upgrade domestic demand mainly by expanding consumer demand, and rely mainly on indigenous innovation capability rather than an excessive input of resources and capital. This shift in growth dynamics requires major adjustments to the existing distribution structure and incentive mechanism, the establishment of a new distribution structure and incentive mechanism, and the acceleration of the reform of important economic systems that restrict the upgrading of industries and the expansion of domestic demand.

3.3.1 Deepen the Reform of the Economic System and Change the Functions of the Government

The report to the 19th CPC National Congress clearly pointed out that comprehensively deepening the reform of the economic system is the key to accelerating the transformation of the mode of economic development. The issue at the heart of the reform of the economic system is to properly handle the relationship between the government and the market. We must show more respect for the law of the market and give better play to the role of the government. The role of the government in a well-regulated and mature market economy is mainly reflected in the following aspects: adjusting income distribution; correcting market failures; safeguarding justice; restricting monopoly and encouraging competition; providing public goods and services; and carrying out macro-control. The government's failure to perform its functions adequately is mainly manifested in: the adjustment of income distribution is inadequate; the monitoring of market failures needs to be strengthened and made more efficient; the provision of public goods and services needs to be strengthened; a service-oriented government culture has yet to be established; fair market norms and rules need to be better maintained; a judicial system independent of administrative intervention has yet to be established. The government's overstepping of its functions is mainly manifested in: interfering too much in industries and resources that have no natural monopolistic attributes and do not involve national security.

Therefore, the first priority is to clarify the relationship between businesses and the government and the boundaries of its rights. The government needs to change its role from a multitasker to a provider of social services who maintains the smooth operation of the rules of fair play. The role of the government is mainly reflected in the following aspects: First, in areas not related to the national economy and people's livelihood, lower the threshold for market access and bring in diverse investors; second, provide public goods and services more effectively and control market failures; third, build community services and social governance with Chinese characteristics, and further improve the public management capability and model for mobilizing resources and organize emergency responses in times of crisis; fourth, guide the formation of a healthy culture and social atmosphere on the basis of respecting democracy; fifth, establish a sound legal and regulatory system and a more efficient and fair judicial system.

3.3.2 Narrow the Income Gap, Urban–Rural Gap, and Inter-Regional Gap

The three major gaps refer to the income gap between urban and rural residents, the inter-regional gap, and the wealth gap between urban and rural residents, which are "tigers" blocking the road to a moderately prosperous society in all respects. Since the 18th CPC National Congress, the CPC Central Committee with Comrade Xi Jinping as its core has adhered to a people-centered development philosophy and taken improving people's lives and improving their well-being as the starting point and objective. On March 8, 2017, NPC deputies and CPPCC members at the two sessions held a heated discussion on narrowing the "three gaps" and achieving common prosperity for all people as they contribute to and gain from development.

According to the Blue Book of China's Society: Society of China Analysis and Forecast (2017) published by the Chinese Academy of Social

Sciences, there has been a new trend in income growth among urban and rural residents. Overall, the income of urban and rural residents has been growing, but the year-on-year growth rate has dropped significantly. From January to September 2016, the per capita disposable income in China was 17,735 Yuan, up 8.4% year-on-year in nominal terms, and 6.3% in real terms after deducting price factors. In terms of per capita disposable income by permanent residence, the per capita disposable income of urban households was 25,337 Yuan, up 7.8% year-on-year in nominal terms and 5.7% in real terms after deducting price factors; the per capita disposable income of rural households was 8998 Yuan, up 8.4% year-on-year in nominal terms and 6.5% in real terms after deducting price factors; the income gap between urban and rural households continued to narrow. The per capita disposable income of urban households was 2.82 times that of rural households, 0.01 times smaller than the same period in 2015.

It should be noted that the income gap in Chinese society is not just reflected in the income gap between urban and rural households, but the income gap between industries, regions, and members of society also has an important impact on the overall income gap. Overall, the income gap in these respects has been narrowing in recent years. In addition, the state's transfer payments to low-income and poor people have been increasing year by year, and efforts have been made to narrow the gap in transfer income between different social classes and groups. As a result, the overall income gap in China has been narrowing since 2009, with the Gini coefficient decreasing from 0.491 in 2008 to 0.462 in 2015. From the perspective of the social class structure, the narrowing of the income gap means the expansion of the middle-income group.

How to define the middle-income group is an important theoretical and practical issue in the world. If income groups below 75%, between 75 and 125%, between 125 and 200%, and above 200% of the median per capita disposable income are defined as the low-income group, the lower-middle-income group, the upper-middle-income group, and the high-income group respectively, then according to the Chinese Social Survey 2015 (CSS 2015) conducted by the Institute of Sociology, Chinese Academy of Social Sciences, of all the surveyed households, excluding households that did not provide information on household income, 39.9% belonged to the low-income group, 18.9% the lower-middle-income group, 18.5% the upper-middle-income group, and 22.8% the high-income group in 2014. If the lower-middle-income group and the upper-middle-income group are combined into the middle-income group, then the middle-income group accounted for 37.4%.

Since the start of reform and opening-up, although rapid economic growth has covered up the huge negative impact of the three gaps on social development to some extent, but we believe that as China's gear of growth shifts from high speed to medium-to-high speed, these gaps will become a major obstacle to sustained economic growth. When the economy reaches a certain stage of development, the main growth momentum will come from technological progress and household consumption. Narrowing the gap can deliver a significant Pareto improvement, and narrowing the gap by one point has a greater growth-boosting effect than increasing investment by many points. If the income gap, urban–rural gap, and inter-regional gap remain unimproved for a long time, they will constitute a significant constraint on the expansion of consumption.

First, we can take the following policy measures to narrow the income gap and the urban–rural gap: First, eliminate inequality of opportunity, which is principally about accelerating the equalization of basic education and medical services, increasing the government's investment in on-the-job and off-the-job training, and establishing a social security, social health insurance, and unemployment insurance system that treats both urban and rural areas equally. Second, increase incentives for employment expansion, set up government financial services institutions to support the development of SMEs, and encourage the development of non-governmental intermediary service organizations. Third, promote the full development of the labor market, strictly implement the new labor law, raise the wages of employees, regulate the order of income distribution, and ban and crack down on illegal and gray income. Fourth, raise taxes on monopoly industries and some non-innovative profiteering industries, and increase efforts to redistribute income. Fifth, raise farmers' income, improve the land system and land circulation system, and increase subsidies for agriculture.

Second, we can narrow the inter-regional gap by fostering new regional growth points. With abundant resources, convenient transportation, a good industrial foundation, and a huge market potential, the central region is already in a favorable position to accelerate development, and the strategy for the rise of the central region can be upgraded to a national development strategy in the new era. An effective way to maintain the competitiveness of labor-intensive industries in China is to accelerate the transfer of labor-intensive industries to the central and western regions, especially to the adjacent central region, make them repeat the development process of the coastal areas in the 1980s and 1990s by using their abundant natural resources and labor, and at the same time promote industrial upgrading in coastal areas.

3.3.3 Encourage Technological Innovation, Improve Industrial Competitiveness, and Pursue Innovation-Driven Development

After China enters the middle-income stage, the low-cost advantage of the economy will be gradually lost. We must improve R&D capabilities, attach importance to human capital, carry out industrial upgrading, and foster new competitive advantages. The gap between South Korea and Brazil was not large in the 1980s. The 1978 energy crisis had a great impact on South Korea, depriving the country of its comparative advantage in labor-intensive industries. But South Korea actively sought change. It promoted industrial upgrading by implementing the strategy of "founding the nation on science and technology," and finally completed the transition from light industry to technology-intensive heavy industry and from "technological imitation" to indigenous innovation. Technological innovation now contributes up to 70% to South Korea's economic growth.

To change the mode of economic development by relying on technological advances and improving capacity for technological innovation, we need to start from the following two aspects: First, increase investment in education and scientific research, improve the quality of education, cultivate excellent technological innovation talents and teams, and accumulate a solid foundation for scientific research and innovation; second, reform the education and scientific management system, and innovate new ways and methods to encourage scientific research. On the one hand, provide a good and relaxed research environment for researchers; on the other hand, shift from the government-led scientific research management system into a market-driven enterprise spontaneous innovation mechanism, vigorously develop higher vocational and technical education based on market demand, strengthen communication and interaction between institutions of higher learning, scientific research institutes and enterprises in R&D, and improve the efficiency of the popularization of research findings.

To encourage indigenous technological innovation is mainly to reduce excessive incentives for areas other than indigenous innovation. As long as there are more incentives than those for indigenous innovation (such as excessive incentives for foreign investment and real estate), investment in indigenous innovation will not increase, but instead will decrease. Therefore, the government should improve the incentive environment or direction. First, reduce the proportion of state-owned capital in strategic competitive industries, and give full play to the important role of private capital in industrial upgrading. Second, use capital markets to promote indigenous innovation. Funnel surplus private capital into capital markets, so that they are combined with industrial upgrading to promote industrial competitiveness.

3.3.4 *Pursue New-Type Urbanization*

Urbanization and city clusters are an inevitable trend in economic and social development, and also an important symbol of industrialization and modernization. Actively yet prudently advancing China's urbanization is one of the basic approaches and major strategies for building a moderately prosperous society in all respects, solving the Three Rural Issues, and promoting the stable and sustainable growth of China's economy.

Urbanization is not simply an increase in the size of towns and cities, but involves improvement in the quality of urbanization Improvement in the quality of urbanization is mainly reflected in the following aspects: First, the agglomeration and capacity for technological innovation of urban industries are enhanced; second, cooperation between rural and urban industries in technological innovation is continuously strengthened, and integration is accelerated, leading to an improvement in the technological level of rural industries; third, with the integration of urban and rural industries, institutional barriers in education, employment, social security, and household registration between urban and rural areas are gradually eliminated, allowing resources to be shared between urban and rural areas; fourth, urban and rural lifestyles are gradually integrated, traditional farmers are transformed into modern farmers, and the phenomenon of "deruralization" becomes more apparent; fifth, the environment in urban and rural areas is improving, and people and nature are developing harmoniously. New-type urbanization involves the land system, urban management, regional development, agricultural modernization, and so on. It is a complex systematic project and demands greater scientific management capabilities in economy and society on the part of the government.

A major challenge in the process of urbanization is transfer of rural surplus labor to non-agricultural sectors. At present, there are about 200 million semi-urbanized residents (migrant workers) in China. They will make up the bulk of farmer-turned urban residents. To speed up the process of transforming them into urban residents, on the one hand, we can implement large-scale housing projects for migrant workers, and use government power to build indemnificatory housing for migrant workers; on the other hand, we can encourage the transfer of coastal labor-intensive industries to the central and western regions, and promote the urbanization of the central and western regions.

3.3.5 Comprehensively Improve the Level of Export-Oriented Economic Development

The practice of China's reform and opening-up has proved that reform and opening-up, as two fundamental driving forces for China's development, promote each other, and are inseparable. At present, China's reform has entered a critical stage and the deep-water zone. Faced with deep-seated contradictions and development bottlenecks, we need to further promote the reform of domestic systems through a higher level of opening-up, so as to create another opening-up dividend period for the sustainable development of China's economy. First, in the service sector, the level of China's opening-up is low, and there are still barriers to the movement of capital, labor, technology, and other factors. We need to promote the deep integration of international and domestic markets, let the market play a decisive role, integrate resources globally, optimize the allocation of sources at home and abroad, accelerate international economic cooperation and participate in international competition in key areas and crucial links, and cultivate new growth points. Second, in terms of introducing foreign capital, on the one hand, we should optimize the industrial and regional structure of investment; on the other hand, we should participate in the reconstruction of international investment rules through the negotiation of investment agreements, thereby "forcing" the reform of domestic supporting systems; in terms of outward investment, we should accelerate the building of a supporting system for outward investment, establish an information statistics and consulting service system, support the development of local overseas investment intermediaries, solve financing difficulties for enterprises in "going out" at multiple levels, and encourage enterprises with different types of ownership to jointly "go out." Third, in terms of foreign trade, we should improve the existing foreign trade management system, and establish a quality- and efficiency-oriented trade promotion system and a multi-directional opening-up pattern to adapt to the international high-standard system of trade rules, form a trade development strategy based on the value chain, and realize the role change from "participant" to "leader," and a shift from a big trading nation oriented toward quantitative expansion to a strong trading nation oriented toward quality improvement. Fourth, in terms of international finance, with the aim of diversifying our foreign currency holdings, improving our international voice in emerging markets and maintaining global financial stability, we should adhere to the three parallel foreign financial strategies of participating in the governance of international financial institutions, expanding regional monetary cooperation in East Asia and RMB internationalization. Meanwhile, we should strengthen the interaction and mutual promotion between domestic financial reform and international financial strategy to form a virtuous circle.

4 The Transformation of the Role of the Government Is the Key to Overcoming the Middle-Income Trap

Judging from the history of world economic development, Britain and the United States relied on massive government intervention instead of the free market to achieve rapid growth. The rise of Britain as the world's economic hegemon was marked by huge government borrowing and spending—mainly for the financing of wars started to build the world's largest empire. In 1763, British government debt accounted for more than 150% of GDP; in 1815, this proportion even exceeded 250%. During its rise to global hegemony, the United States used government intervention to establish one of the world's most protectionist tariff regimes. These high tariffs were designed to protect industrial development in the northern states of the United States.

Both lessons from Latin American and ASEAN countries and the experience of some East Asian countries show that the change of the government's systems and its political and economic policies play a decisive role. After the GDP per capita reaches a certain level, economic growth will slow down and the economy will be confronted with the need for transformation, which is a common problem in all countries of the world. How to deal with this inevitable situation? Although there are countermeasures and rationales to follow in economic theory and economic policy, such as industrial upgrading and technological innovation, whether a country can achieve upgrading, transformation and innovation, and even whether it can introduce and implement reasonable economic policies and elicit a response from the public is not an economic issue, but a typical political and social issue. Therefore, we need to take a close look at the role of the government.[2]

4.1 *China's Development Model and the Role of the Government*

Let's first review the basic development model that China has formed since the start of reform and opening-up and the leading role played by the government.

After the start of reform and opening-up, with the full implementation of the household responsibility system, the vitality of rural areas was unleashed, promoting the rapid development of rural industrialization and the adjustment of the national industrial structure. Township and village enterprises first emerged in the developed coastal regions, and flourished in the central and western regions of China in the late 1980s. The period from the mid-1980s to the mid-1990s saw the fastest growth in the proportion of industrial output, driven mainly by township and village enterprises. In addition to the advantages of township and village enterprises compared with state-owned enterprises in terms of industrial structure, property rights structure and governance structure, a strong push from local governments is also a remarkable fact. Some scholars pointed out that the "fiscal responsibility system" implemented by the central government and local governments in the mid-1980s provided incentives for the development of township and village enterprises in terms of government behavior. However, at this stage, the rapid development of industrialization was not in tune with the pace of urbanization. Prior to 1994, industry's contribution to GDP grew at an average annual rate of 3.7%, and the proportion of urban population grew at an average annual rate of only 0.6%, a sharp contrast to the

[2] Zheng Zhijie. Government-Led Economic Model and Transformation. *The Party School of the CPC Central Committee, Theoretical Trends*, 2015-06-20.

average annual growth rate of 1.3% after 1994 (China Monthly Economic Indicators, 2008). Industrialization based on township and village enterprises was industrialization where farmers "left the field and worked in factories without the need to leave their villages and enter cities." Farmers left agriculture, but did not leave the countryside. Although their employment and income situation had improved considerably, but not through urbanization, the urban–rural dual barrier had not been broken. From the perspective of government behavior, local state corporatism promoted by the fiscal responsibility system actually constructed a behavior mode of "local protectionism." By "running enterprises in a big way" and "running big enterprises," local governments sought a share of the excess revenue under the responsibility system. Under the "package" responsibility system, product tax and value-added tax made the bulk of local fiscal revenue, and the mode of industrialization driven mainly by the expansion of local investment fits exactly into the system. From another point of view, "local protectionism" is no other than "intergovernmental competition," and the "championship" among local governments on GDP and fiscal revenue is the result of "fiscal decentralization" brought about by the fiscal responsibility system. Although the effect of such regional competition on economic growth has been empirically proved, few scholars have discussed the relationship between fiscal decentralization, regional competition, and urbanization in a positive light.

Although the reform of the tax-sharing system in 1994 completely changed the pattern of fiscal revenue of the central government and local governments and also changed the relationship between local governments and enterprises by "decoupling" local governments from state-owned enterprises and township and village enterprises under them, it did not change the basic pattern of regional competition among local governments. Some scholars still attribute intergovernmental competition after the reform of the tax-sharing system to fiscal decentralization, because they only use the expenditure approach to measure decentralization. In fact, although the tax-sharing system has not changed the distribution of powers between the central government and local governments, it has completely upended the distribution of fiscal powers. Most scholars have acknowledged the financial difficulties at grass-roots levels caused by the concentration of fiscal powers and the resulting county and township financial crisis and burden on farmers. The relationship between the State and farmers has changed greatly. From the rapid closure and transformation of township and village enterprises in the mid-1990s, as well as the radical shareholding reform of state-owned enterprises, it can be seen that the tax-sharing system has also upended the relationship between local governments and enterprises. What the tax-sharing system hasn't changed are the proportion of public expenditure and the "promotion championship" personnel system of local governments. This helps us understand why regional competition between local governments has not changed since the reform of the tax-sharing system, but has intensified. But changes in the relationship between the State and farmers, and between governments and enterprises have far-reaching implications: The content and mode of regional competition among local governments have changed dramatically. If the previous regional competition was brought about by local governments promoting industrialization by running enterprises in a big way, then the subsequent regional competition was brought about by local government promoting urbanization by managing land commercially.

Under the current land system, local governments can obtain substantial fiscal revenue by monopolizing the process of land acquisition, development, and transfer, which is called "land finance" in academic circles. The shift of local governments to land finance after the reform of the tax-sharing system is not only in line with the empirical facts that we can directly observe, but also has been corroborated by financial and land data. This does not mean that there is a direct causal relationship between the tax-sharing system and land finance. From our above analysis, it can be seen that land finance is a new way for local governments to make money after the reform of the tax-sharing system. The content of land finance includes not only land transfer fees obtained by local governments through land transfer, but also construction industry business tax, which has been a major pillar of local fiscal revenue since the reform of the tax-sharing system. According to data released by the Ministry of Finance, in 2013, local governments collected 4.125 trillion Yuan in land transfer fees (revenue from the transfer of state-owned land use rights), an increase of 44.6% over 2012 and accounting for 1/1.68 of local fiscal revenue. These two major sources of income are closely related to the process of urban land acquisition, development, and transfer. Without urban expansion and large-scale construction, there will be no land finance. One may well say that "where there is land, there is wealth." Local governments gain fiscal revenue by building cities and managing land commercially, but land revenue is different from tax revenue generated by industrial enterprises and is exogenously unstable. Both land transfer fees and construction industry business tax are expected to grow steadily after being included in the budget. Both urban expansion and land acquisition require a lot of capital investment, and land transfer fees are far from meeting the needs of urban infrastructure construction. The "operation of cities" by local governments inevitably requires the involvement of financial capital.

Local governments cannot directly use loan funds for urban construction. Government agencies can neither borrow directly from financial institutions nor guarantee loans. In practice, local governments usually use fiscal funds as registered capital to set up state-owned urban construction investment companies, and use these companies for financing. These companies generally include urban construction investment companies, urban transportation companies, urban water groups, land reserve centers, etc., which are managed by the SASACs of local governments, operate as companies, and use state-owned construction land allocated by the government to secure loans from banks for urban construction. This mode of operation has been implemented in eastern coastal cities since the beginning of the twenty-first century. Chongqing's so-called "Eight Investment Companies" model was the earliest in the western region. These urban construction companies, collectively referred to as "local financing platforms," are commonly found in cities and counties all over the country. According to the Notice of the State Council on Strengthening the Management of Local Financing Platforms (Guo Fa [2010] No. 19), local financing platforms refer to "entities established by local governments and their departments and agencies through fiscal appropriations or the injection of land, equity and other assets, which undertake the function of financing government investment projects and have independent legal personality." These local financing platforms usually use state-owned land as collateral to secure loans at 70% of the appraised value of the land for the construction of urban infrastructure and public welfare projects. It should be noted that although local governments are not authorized to guarantee loans under the Guarantee Law of the People's Republic of China, according to the CSRC's 2010 inventory of local financing platforms, as of August 2010, nearly half of the 7.66 trillion Yuan (3.6 trillion Yuan) worth of outstanding loans to financing platforms were government-guaranteed loans.

Banks face relatively small risks for loans offered to local governments' financing platforms against land. In practice, banks can implement a dynamic mortgage rate and appraise the value of land dynamically in real time. In this way, once property prices fall, the borrower will be required to replenish the collateral. When property prices rise, the borrower can transfer or develop the original collateral by replacing it. Under this arrangement, most of the risks and extra income brought by changes in property prices are taken by the financing platform of the local government. In fact, land prices have been rising since the creation of financing platforms, and the potential risks involved have not materialized. Compared with other loans, loans secured by land are considered the highest quality loans by commercial institutions such as banks. Therefore, as long as financing platforms use state-owned land as collateral, they can obtain loans relatively smoothly.

In conclusion, we can see that there are strong supporting mechanisms in terms of land, finance, and banking behind urban expansion: On the one hand, local governments obtain state-owned construction land for urban construction through land acquisition, development and transfer; on the other hand, local governments earn a large amount of land revenue and, through the operation of local financing platforms, obtain loans from banks against land to support urban construction and pay the cost of newly acquired land. This constitutes a circular mechanism composed of three elements: land, finance, and banking. This mechanism continuously absorbs land and capital to create booming cities that change with each passing day. We can call it the new "three-in-one" urbanization model.

From the above analysis, we can see that the mainstream explanation is that China's sustained high-speed growth over the past nearly 40 years of reform and opening-up is inseparable from the role of the government. In the 1990s, the demographic dividend and comparative advantage theory was a more representative explanation, but it was soon replaced by the political economic explanation of "intergovernmental competition," which has almost become a consensus in academic circles at home and abroad regarding China's economic growth. We can summarize the role of the government as follows.

First, the corporatized or "corporatist" behavior of local governments. Local governments behave like "corporate headquarters" that exercise total control over their localities. With GDP and fiscal revenue growth as the fundamental objective, they compete in resource allocation and performance improvement.

Second, the relationship between the central government and local governments is an important factor in shaping the characteristics of local government behavior. Before the reform of the tax-sharing system in

1994, the local government took "running enterprises in a big way" and "running big enterprises" as their primary objectives, which was closely related to the "fiscal responsibility system" between the central government and local governments. After the reform of the tax-sharing system, the main content of intergovernmental competition became urbanization competition centered on land management and land financing, and this characteristic is closely related to the tax-sharing system.

Finally, the behavior of local governments, combined with industrialization and urbanization and using exports and land management, have delivered sustained high-speed local economic growth. Since the mid-1990s, with the reform of the land management system and China's accession to the World Trade Organization, a large number of cheap laborers have flocked from the central and western regions to eastern coastal cities, making China the manufacturing base for labor-intensive products in the world and creating huge wealth and foreign exchange reserves. This is also closely related to the land and urban management strategies of local governments. On the one hand, local governments use cheap industrial land to compete for investment; on the other hand, through the acquisition, development, and transfer of commercial and residential land, they drive a large number of land investment, they have achieved rapid urbanization. These two aspects complement each other. Industrialization drives urbanization, which, led by investment, in turn further increases GDP and fiscal revenue.

4.2 Problems and Challenges Encountered by the Government-Led Development Model

From the above explanations, we can sum up the driving force of economic growth over the past nearly 40 years of reform and opening-up as running on two parallel tracks. The growth of manufacturing brought by the demographic dividend and investment-driven growth brought by intergovernmental competition went hand in hand and drove each other, enabling China to grow from a poor and backward agricultural country to a middle-income country in a short period of time. However, in the face of the need to transform the economy and upgrade industries in order to overcome the middle-income trap, such driving force of economic growth has been tapering off, and problems accumulated over the years are gradually emerging.

In the new situation, past experience may become present problems. Macro conditions such as rising labor costs, the relocation of manufacturing operations, and poor government finances have prompted us to reflect on the role of the government in the past. From a big picture perspective, the main problems are as follows.

1. The government-led economic model is facing severe challenges, and the decline in manufacturing growth has led to a dilemma for investment-led growth.

Since the mid-1990s, local governments have managed cities on a land-centric basis through acquisition, development, transfer, and other government-monopolized privileges, leading to massive infrastructure investment. The basic medium of this economic model is land, and the core of its operation is land financing. By setting up local financing platforms, various localities use the oversupply of money from the central government intended to stimulate the economy for urban infrastructure construction, which on the one hand promotes the rapid growth of GDP, and on the other hand raises the price of urban land and real estate, indirectly increasing the cost of living in cities. The cost of this is that the floating population, numbering more than 200 million people and consisting mainly of industrial workers, is always on the move, and has difficulty settling down and living in cities. When the external demand is strong and the industrial economy is booming, this is not a big problem, but when the labor price is rising and industries are moving out, government finance and local finance will be seriously affected. This is mainly reflected in the sluggish growth of real estate in the second- and third-tier cities, empty properties that are found all over the place, and local governments' lack of confidence in further increasing infrastructure investment. What is worrying is that the decline of manufacturing and the relocation of industries are not a temporary phenomenon. With the disappearance of the demographic dividend and the growing attractiveness of Southeast Asian and South Asian countries to manufacturing, this will be a long-term phenomenon, which is also the main manifestation of the arrival of the middle-income trap. Therefore, the era where the government relies mainly on investment with land financing as the core to drive economic growth is coming to an end.

In this situation, the most pressing issue for the government is how to deal with the huge amount of local debt. The central government's use of an oversupply of money as a fiscal tool to stimulate investment over the past more than ten years was based on the sustained and rapid growth of China's foreign exchange reserves when it was the "world's factory." With a shrinking trade surplus and a gradual slowdown in the growth of foreign exchange reserves which are part of a long-term trend, financial risks accumulated by the debt problem are increasing.

2. From the perspective of the relationship between governments and enterprises, the cost of enterprise upgrading and transformation is very high.

Under the past development model, on the one hand, local governments attracted investment through cheap land; on the other hand, with the implementation of high tax policy, the manufacturing industry was generally faced with a high tax burden, which is one of the main reasons why manufacturing enterprises cannot bear the rise in labor prices. According to a report released by the Ministry of Finance in late July 2013, with taxes, government fund charges, social security payments, and other items taken into account, the tax burden on Chinese enterprises in 2012 reached about 40%, higher than the average level of OECD countries. At present, Chinese enterprises are faced with three major difficulties, namely, financing difficulties, high taxes and difficulty in hiring, and generally face double pressures from the government and labor force. Among them, financing difficulties and high taxes make enterprises generally lack capital accumulation, which constitutes a huge obstacle to enterprise transformation and industrial upgrading. The financial sector generally follows the practice of the past few decades, with local governments' financing platforms still being preferred recipients for receiving loans and enterprises struggling to get investment required for expansion or even normal operation, let alone funds for technological transformation.

3. From the perspective of the relationship between the central government and local governments, local governments' ability to transform is insufficient.

The relationship between the central government and local governments in China has been following the prefecture-county model, vacillating between "over-concentration of power in the central government" and "weak central government and largely autonomous local governments," which is mainly manifested in military matters, personnel matters and administration in a traditional society. Since the founding of the People's Republic of China, economic development has gradually become the main content of the relationship between the central government and local governments. In addition to military matters, personnel matters and administration, economic and financial policies often oscillate between "decentralization" and "centralization." For almost 40 years since the start of reform and opening-up, we have not fundamentally broken free from the "centralization-decentralization model." The fiscal responsibility system in the early stage of reform can be seen as a decentralization model adopted to stimulate local industrialization. After the reform of the tax-sharing system, most of the fiscal and financial authority was returned to the central government. The "project system" which has become popular in recent years is actually the result of the centralization of power. As a result of centralization, local governments are increasingly caught in a "championship" over economic growth, and the "trophy" is economic indicators centered on GDP and fiscal revenue. Of course, political and social indicators are also included in the government's target-oriented responsibility assessment, but these indicators are generally difficult to quantify and implement, so despite awareness of problems and dangers brought by such a "championship," so far no more reasonable institutional arrangements have emerged. The assessment and competition system is centered on economic indicators, which leads to a strange paradox in the relationship between the central government and local governments: economic growth is often associated with "edge ball," "rent-seeking" and corruption; emphasizing competing on indicators tends to breed corruption, and emphasizing combating corruption may harm economic growth. Of course, there are social system-related reasons for this, such as the lack of social supervision and judicial independence, imperfections in the rule of law, and other deep-rooted problems. Under this circumstance, even if the central government tries to promote the transformation of industrial institutions and encourage technological innovation, the actual effects will be compromised because of this centralized "championship" system.

4. Excessive income inequality reduces the space for government transformation, and a "rigidified" social structure makes it difficult to implement various policies.

China's rapid growth in the past 40 years has been accompanied by widening income inequality. According to official statistics, the Gini coefficient is 0.474, though unofficial estimates are higher. Such statistics are based on household or individual data. In fact, on the macro level, income inequality in China is also manifested as a gap between urban and rural areas, between regions, and between different occupational groups; structurally, it is manifested in the weakening of vertical mobility and the increasing separation between different income groups. On the whole, the vitality of social mobility has diminished. It is a common phenomenon that economic growth will widen income inequality, and the role and responsibility of the government is to regulate income inequality in the process of development and slow down the widening of income inequality. But China's past development model has been based in part on the widening of income inequality. Industrialization in coastal areas relies on low-wage industrial workers, but urban construction driven and home prices pushed up by urbanization have rapidly widened inequality between the "homeowning class" and the "non-homeowning class," and turned such inequality into a permanent feature: the government makes money from land, businessmen make money from real estate, and homeowners make money from their homes, which constitutes the basic pattern of income inequality in China. Meanwhile, the government and capital, especially real estate capital and real estate capital transformed from industrial capital, together form a monopolistic interest group. The combination of power and capital is not only one of the main driving forces of the past development model, but also one of the transformation difficulties facing China today. The formation of various interest groups has created huge obstacles for the government's regulatory functions and transformation policies.

5. The government is facing a renewed crisis of confidence, which has led to the rapid shrinking of space for transformation.

It's fair to say that the current crisis of widespread public distrust faced by the government was not caused by the current economic and social policies. In fact, the government's anti-corruption efforts are unprecedented, which is conducive to strengthening public trust in the central government. The crises of confidence in some local governments were gradually accumulated during past high-speed economic growth. Only in the context of economic growth, people generally have relatively strong positive expectations for the future, so these crises are often masked to some extent by economic growth. But masking crises does not mean eliminating them. Once economic growth slows down and people's expectations for the future decline, these accumulated crises are likely to be unleashed in a more extreme way, leading to the rapid shrinking of space for the government to design and implement policies.

Judging from the current situation, the above five problems are the main obstacles faced by the central government and local governments, and none of these obstacles can be solved through the adjustment of existing economic policies or the implementation of new economic policies. Simply relying on economic reforms may make these problems even worse, especially in the context of slowing economic growth. If these problems are not alleviated or resolved, the chances of China falling into the middle-income trap will be high.

4.3 *The Key to Changing the Mode of Development Lies in the Transformation of the Role of the Government*

Based on the experience of countries around the world and lessons learnt therefrom, we believe that the most urgent task at present is to adjust the role of the government in economic transformation, and to introduce policies that focus on mitigation and stability rather than simply stimulating economic growth. Efforts should be focused on the following areas.

1. Transformation of government's development strategy.

The past mode of development should be changed, that is, the "manufacturing + urban investment" mode of development should be replaced by a mode of economic growth dominated by high-tech, service, and cultural industries. This is a long-term and macro goal, which in the current situation cannot be achieved simply by the central government introducing a series of support and preferential policies. The key is to get rid of the mode of development whereby local governments rely too much on land finance and land financing, which requires adjustment of the fiscal and taxation systems of the central government and local governments. The history of the tax-sharing system shows that adjusting the fiscal and taxation systems of the central government and local governments has a significant effect on changing the behavior of local governments.

The role of the government should also be changed significantly in relation to local industrial enterprises. Emphasize the principle of market-based allocation supplemented by government regulation, give full play to the signaling function of market prices, reduce government intervention in the pricing of private goods, and ensure that enterprises have complete autonomy over their operations; meanwhile, strengthen and improve the legal system to ensure a sound soft environment for the operation of enterprises; strengthen fiscal and taxation policy support for enterprise transformation.

2. Adjust the relationship between the central government and local governments, and change the assessment method that accords too much importance to GDP and fiscal revenue.

We should focus on study the system of indicators for assessment, change the assessment method, make a point of strengthening the examination of the structure of GDP and fiscal revenue, and adjust and reform the fiscal and taxation systems in an effort to steer local governments in the direction of industrial upgrading and economic transformation. Specifically, the system of indicators for assessment should reflect the overall development of the economy, society, and people. In particular, mandatory indicators that are conducive to changing the mode of development such as energy conservation and emission reduction and industrial upgrading should be added.

3. Adjust the income structure and increase government spending on social welfare and social security.

The transformational experience of many countries in the world shows that a healthy income structure is key to supporting middle-income countries' transition into high-income countries. Anxiety over economic slowdown should not be solved by "drinking poison to quench thirst" and re-stimulating the economy, but by promoting the reform of the income distribution system and strengthening social welfare. At present, China's main income distribution is dominated by monopolistic interest groups. If this pattern is not changed, it will be difficult for China to avoid the danger of falling into the middle-income trap. To change this pattern, we should take advantage of the central government's anti-corruption drive. On the one hand, we should increase the wages of ordinary people; on the other hand, we should make social security and social welfare one of the government's spending priorities, so that ordinary people can have access to childcare, medical services, elderly care, and housing.

4. Vigorously strengthen investment in education, and focus on supporting technological innovation and cultural industries.

The successful transformation of East Asian countries is mostly due to the fact that East Asian culture emphasizes education and their governments invest heavily in running schools. The accumulation of human capital often plays a great role in promoting social stability and economic growth. As far as the current government investment in education is concerned, although the total scale is large, the emphasis is on quantity rather than quality and on skills rather than the foundation, and in colleges and universities, scientific research is prioritized over teaching. The tendency to seek quick success and instant benefits is too obvious. In terms of industrial policy, we should focus on learning from the experience of South Korea, focus on supporting private enterprises, and stimulate the innovative power of the whole society.

5. Strengthen the rule of law and promote the transformation of government behavior.

The crisis of confidence in the government is mostly manifested in widespread labor-management conflicts and conflicts between public officials and ordinary citizens, which are unavoidable during the transition period. The focus of the transformation of government behavior is to gradually bring conflicts between public officials and ordinary citizens and labor-management conflicts into the framework of the rule of law, and a precondition for doing so is to strengthen the rule of law and put the authority of the law above the government.

The middle-income trap is fundamentally a matter of a country's political and social structural transformation. What need to be avoided most in this process are widespread social and political crisis and the resulting social unrest and social chaos. To avoid this situation, we need to make the reform and transformation of the government itself the top priority, which is also the biggest difficulty.

5 Summary

Since the outbreak of 2008 financial crisis, the economies of the United States, Japan, and Europe have been in trouble, while the economic prospects of emerging economies and developing countries have been generally positive. There is a widespread concern among emerging economies and developing countries that the quantitative easing policies, expansionary fiscal policies, and protectionist structural adjustment policies adopted by the United States, Japan and Europe are in fact intended to shift their crises and contradictions to emerging economies and developing countries. When this shift brings an economic recovery to the United States, Japan, and Europe, and inflation and asset bubbles intensify social and economic contradictions in emerging economies, will there be another round of economic adjustment and crisis?

At the critical stage of overcoming the middle-income trap, does China want to be a responsible global power or a marginalized power in the future? Will China rise to the new challenges posed by high-standard rules, high-standard investment, and the liberalization of trade in services? Will China be able to gain the status of a big open country with pricing power over commodities around the globe, the power to make important rules, a sense of responsibility, and the ability to make countercyclical adjustments? From this point of view, the new situation of economic globalization will not only have a far-reaching impact on international economic governance, the multilateral trading system, and bilateral economic and trade cooperation, but also affect the building of China's open economic system through different channels. To this end, the Decision of the CPC Central Committee on A Number of Major Issues Concerning Comprehensively Deepening Reform adopted at the

Third Plenary Session of the 18th CPC Central Committee clearly states that a new system for an open economy should be built to adapt to the new situation of economic globalization. In his report to the 19th CPC National Congress, General Secretary Xi Jinping put forward a plan for applying a new vision of development and developing a modernized economy in a new era.

At the critical moment when China is overcoming the middle-income trap, new systems for developing an open economy should be built in response to the new situation of economic globalization. The specific work can be summarized into the following four aspects.

First, to build new systems for developing an open economy, we must give full play to the decisive role of the market in resource allocation. Under China's model for developing an open economy over the past 40 years, a huge manufacturing capacity and a cycle of massive imports and exports have been formed through the large-scale introduction of foreign capital under the leadership of local governments at all levels, with efforts focused on attracting investment and supported by development zones. The core of this model is that it caters to the fundamental impetus for international industrial transfer with low cost and satisfies the market demand constraint needed for economic takeoff, enabling China's economy to achieve and maintain high-speed development for a long period of time. However, the disadvantages brought about by this model, such as the misallocation of resources, price distortions, overcapacity, environmental degradation, etc., are becoming increasingly prominent.

To switch from a government-led open model that takes no account of costs to an enterprise-led open model that gives full play to the market allocation mechanism, we need to focus on work in the following three aspects: First, improve systems for developing an open economy, revise laws and regulations that impede the development of an open economy in time, and maintain stability over a long period of time; second, reduce policy-based regulation, strengthen institutional regulation, leave markets to regulate themselves according to demand and prices, and allow enterprises to decide on exports and imports based on the market situation and their own competitiveness; third, in terms of institutional setting and the performance of government functions, make sure that the government does not overstep its functions, performs its functions adequately, and does not misplace its functions. The government is mainly responsible for the implementation of rules and the maintenance of order.

Second, to build new systems for developing an open economy, we must actively promote domestic openness together with openness to the outside world. Domestic openness and openness to the outside world are essentially the same thing. The purpose of expanding domestic openness is to build a more dynamic and just economic and social system at home and achieve sustainable economic and social development. The purpose of expanding openness to the outside world is to make full use of external resources to serve China's economic and social development, and to improve China's position in international specialization and the distribution of benefits in international trade as soon as possible. Today, as China and the world become increasingly connected and their mutual influence deepens, China's reform and development, more than ever before, requires us to persist in and expand opening-up to the outside world. By promoting reform through opening-up, we can better understand the world, and enable the world to have a deeper understanding of China. We should further expand the convergence of interests with other parties, continuously expand areas of cooperation, and promote the orderly and free flow of international and domestic factors, the efficient allocation of resources, and the deep integration of markets.

To actively promote domestic openness together with openness to the outside world, we need to focus on work in the following four aspects: First, implement a unified market access system, further reduce pre-approval and accreditation items, encourage all kinds of capital to participate in banking, insurance, telecommunications and other industries in various ways, and expand cooperation between different regions of the country in trade and investment; second, speed up efforts to formulate policies and measures for further opening-up, implement supporting measures to meet specific requirements for further opening-up with a sense of urgency, unify laws and regulations on domestic and foreign investment, and promote orderly opening-up; third, at the beginning of reform and opening-up, only some coastal areas were opened up to the outside world, and now the whole country has been opened up to the outside world, so we need to accelerate the economic development of the central and western regions, especially to open them wider to the outside world; fourth, further open up inland and border areas, tap the opening-up potential of inland and border areas, and create a new pattern of regional opening-up featuring division of labor, cooperation, complementarity, balance and coordination.

Third, to build new systems for developing an open economy, we must speed up the construction of free trade areas (FTAs). FTAs are an important vehicle of international economic cooperation. In recent years, major economies in the world have made it a strategic priority to advance FTA negotiations, and free trade agreements have become an important tool for major powers in geopolitical and economic games. The United States and the European Union are actively promoting high-standard "next-generation free trade agreements," which not only require the opening-up of a large number of sectors and a high degree of opening-up, but also seek to formulate and form new rules in areas such as labor, government procurement, intellectual property, investment, human rights and environment, so as to set a new "benchmark" for future FTA negotiations around the world—hence the so-called "new issues for the 21st century."

To build new systems for developing an open economy, we must conform to this new trend and speed up the implementation of the FTA strategy. At present, we need to focus on work in the following four aspects: first, continue to improve the new pattern of opening-up, and with the China (Shanghai) Pilot Free Trade Zone as a new starting point, on the basis of advancing existing pilot projects, select a number of qualified regions to develop free trade parks (ports), so as to explore new ways and accumulate new experience for comprehensively deepening reform and opening wider to the outside world; second, reform management systems for customs supervision, inspection, and quarantine, and implement a "single window" system to further facilitate trade; third, fully rely on existing bilateral and multilateral mechanisms between China and relevant countries, take the Belt and Road Initiative as a new starting point for China's all-round opening-up, and inject new content and vitality into existing and proven regional cooperation platforms; fourth, actively promote FTA negotiations with other countries, speed up negotiations on new issues such as environmental protection, investment protection, government procurement, and e-commerce, and form a network of globally oriented high-standard FTAs. To be specific, at the bilateral level, we should pursue innovation in the mode of cooperation with developed countries, strengthen policy coordination and enhance openness and mutual trust; work with emerging markets and developing countries in a manner that makes our strengthens complement theirs and vice versa, and carve our own niche without competing against them, so as to safeguard common interests. At the multilateral level, we should maintain the status of the multilateral trading system as the main channel, oppose protectionism in any form, and reduce and eliminate trade and investment barriers; take an active part in the formulation of international economic and trade rules, and promote a more equitable and reasonable international economic order. At the regional level, we should accelerate the implementation of the FTA strategy with a focus on neighboring countries, actively participate in negotiations on new issues, and form a network of globally oriented high-standard FTAs. At the sub-regional level, we should deepen regional cooperation in the Greater Mekong River, the Pan-Beibu Gulf and the Great Tumen River to form a new geo-economic and geopolitical landscape that is favorable to China.

Fourth, to build new systems for developing an open economy, we must reform management systems for foreign capital utilization and outbound investment. Judging by international trends, the focus of trade policy is shifting from "first-generation trade policies" (e.g., tariffs, and permits) to "second-generation trade policies" (e.g., investment, competition policy, trade facilitation, deregulation, and environment). However, the use of foreign capital in China is still mainly managed based on project approval plus industry guidance catalogues. The advantage of this mode of management is that it is strongly industrial policy-oriented; the disadvantage is that there are many approval procedures, policy stability is insufficient, and both administrative and business costs are high. In the field of outbound investment, our focus over the years has been on "bring in." The current examination and approval system is likely to tie down the "hands and feet" of enterprises in overseas investment and M&As. While continuing to actively open up the domestic market and improve the quality of foreign capital utilization, we should uphold the principles of interest exchange and reciprocal opening-up, remove obstacles to China's outbound investment and Sino-foreign cooperation, promote the orderly and free flow of international and domestic factors, and continuously expand the space for China's economic development.

Raise the level of "bring in" and "go out." To reform management systems for foreign capital utilization and outbound investment, we need to focus on work in the following three aspects: First, reform management systems for foreign capital utilization and outbound investment with a negative list and pre-establishment national treatment as the starting point. Up to now, the management of foreign capital in China has been based on a positive list. The shift from "positive" to "negative" fully reflects the proactive opening-up strategy that facilitates investment and relaxes access restrictions on foreign investment, and is of groundbreaking significance. Second, continue to encourage investors from all over the world to invest and start businesses in China, effectively protect the legitimate rights and interests of investors, provide foreign companies with opportunities to compete fairly and share in China's development dividends, and hope that foreign investors will invest more in areas that are in line with China's industrial upgrading and in the central and western regions; promote the orderly opening-up of service industries such as finance, education, culture, and health care, and lift access restrictions on foreign investment in service industries such as child and elderly care, architectural design, accounting and auditing, commercial logistics, and e-commerce. Third, accelerate the implementation of the Go Out policy, relax restrictions on outbound investment in accordance with the principle that enterprises make decisions on their own in a market-oriented manner, implement the principle that "whoever invests shall make decisions, and whoever benefits shall take risks," establish the dominant position of enterprises and individuals in outbound investment, allow enterprises and individuals to capitalize on their advantages to carry out investment cooperation abroad, allow enterprises and individuals to freely undertake projects and labor cooperation projects in various countries and regions at their own risk, and allow enterprises and individuals to "go out" in innovative ways to make greenfield investments, M&A investments, securities investments, joint investments, etc.

Afterwords

Building a Common Civilization for All Mankind: China's Efforts

On the occasion of the publication of Middle-income Trap: An Analysis Based on Economic Transformations and Social Governance, I'd like to extend my gratitude to the professors of the research group at the School of Social Sciences at Tsinghua University and researchers from the Center for Research & Development and the Legal Department of China Development Bank, who did a great amount of research during the writing of this book. My gratitude also goes to John Thornton, Chairman of Brookings Institution for writing the Preface for the book and Prof. Li Yining from Peking University for writing the Introduction. I also want to express my appreciation for my fellow scholars whose work I have used as reference for this book. My thanks also go to Tsinghua University Press and its editors and proofreaders.

As the world's second largest economy, China's GDP per capita stands at 8123 dollars. In order to be responsible for itself and for the world, there's no room for failure for China to cross the middle-income trap. No one can ignore China's achievements since the Reform and Opening-up, including proposing the "Belt and Road Initiative" as a platform for world economic development, founding the Asian Infrastructure Investment Bank and cofounding the New Development Bank as supplements to the global financial system, pushing for more global cooperation in a number of areas and advocating a community of shared

Z. Zheng, *Middle-Income Trap*,
https://doi.org/10.1007/978-981-15-7401-6

future for all mankind. It's undeniable that China has striven to lead and reshape a common civilization for all mankind that encompasses economic development, institutional innovation, globalization, and human values. Therefore, China's development is closely in line with the world's development as a whole. And not only will China succeed in crossing the middle-income trap, it will be trusted to offer economic opportunities and security for the world as a high-income country in the future. This article is written as an afterword.

Mankind has only one earth in which to live, and countries have only one world to share. As globalization continues to develop in depth, the international community has become a community with a shared future and each country's growth and prosperity are closely interconnected. However, just as The Globalization Paradox points out, the fatal flaw of globalization is that there is one government for each country but only one market for the world. This fatal flaw has led to anti-globalization sentiment, leading to political tension and upheavals in the global economy. In recent years, the unprecedented wave of globalization taking form after the Second World War based on the UN Charter and the Bretton Woods System has constantly been under threat. As the current anti-globalization crisis goes beyond the wit of traditional globalization thinking dominated by Western experiences and concept, the international community urgently needs new values and an ideology to guide the future development of the world. China's President Xi Jinping has discussed on several occasions the need to establish a community of shared future for all mankind since the 18th National Conference of the Communist Party of China.

China's efforts to establish socialism with Chinese characteristics since its Reform and Opening-up have resulted in rich experiences and set up solid examples for exploring and building a common civilization. Ever since the Third Plenary Session of the 18th Central Committee of the CPC, the Party Central Committee with President Xi as its core has continued to hold high the banner of socialism with Chinese characteristics. In politics, it has shown its resolve and courage to "cut the wrist like brave warriors" to create an unwelcome environment for corruption, create an honest political setting, and build a clean government. Regarding the economy, the Party Central Committee drafted its strategic blueprint called "Belt and Road Initiative" that is opening up globalization even further despite the emergence of anti-globalization sentiment in the west. In terms of social development, the strategy of "targeted poverty alleviation" has been a success, with 70 million people leaving poverty behind. As for environmental protection, promoting ecological progress has been included into the "Five-in-one Strategy" in the pursuit of "Lucid waters and lush mountains" and "Clear skies and white clouds." In the report of 19th National Congress of CPC, President Xi Jinping put forward the idea of carrying out the new development, and the plan for the construction of modern economic system in the new era. All in all, the "Chinese Dream" is keeping up with the times and forging ahead and will definitely lead in the creation of a common civilization for all mankind.

Propose and Practice Peace and Development as Underlying Trends of Our Times

After the Second World War, with anticolonial campaigns in developing countries reaching a climax and competition in full swing between the two Cold War rivals, the Soviet Union and the United States, the postwar political and economic system of the world set up at the Yalta Conference was constantly brought to the verge of collapse by opposing ideologies. But China as the second largest socialist country at the time was not involved in this ideological combat. As early as the beginning of the 1980s, Deng Xiaoping, the general designer of China's Reform and Opening-up came up with the famous theory that "Peace and development are the main themes of the times" to replace the dated world view of "War and Revolution" dominated by current widespread ideology.

In response to the peace and development themes of our times, the Communist Party of China ended the ideological argument between capitalism and socialism and made the decisive move to Reform and Open-up. Since then, China has gradually established a market economy system with Chinese characteristics. China also joined the World Trade Organization as an active participant of the world trade system, global production and socialized division of labor. All those practices are evidence that China is a crucial participant, builder, contributor, and sharer of globalization. The rise of China's economy is the result of an international environment of peace and development, as well as the basic state policy of Reform and Opening-up. China's economic achievements have attracted global attention, setting up a good example for other countries to follow in their own development.

Sticking to the underlying theme of peace and development, the Communist Party of China successfully achieved the return of China Hong Kong and China Macao to the motherland and maintained continuous prosperity and stability of the two regions by wisely applying the principle of "one country, two systems." The policy is a great invention by China, offering a new approach for the international community to solve similar problems. It is a new contribution the Chinese nation has made toward world peace and embodies China's ancient wisdom of inclusiveness.

With the concept of peace and development in mind, the Chinese people led by the Communist Party of China have been upholding the Five Principles of Peaceful Coexistence: mutual respect for each other's sovereignty and territorial integrity, mutual nonaggression, mutual noninterference in each other's internal affairs, equality and mutual benefit, and peaceful coexistence. China has also been implementing its policy of "building friendships and partnerships with neighboring countries," in which China's neighbors benefit from its development. Through its actions, China has proven wrong the despicable "China Threat Theory," providing history with an honest example of a "peaceful rise."

Leading Globalization Through the Belt and Road Initiative

A globalization featuring international communication and open trade is a major driving force for building a community of shared future for the world. However, ever since the Global Financial Crisis, Western countries have been home to rather gloomy economies, with a widening wealth gap and emerging social contradictions along with the rise of populism rooted in anti-globalization sentiment. American President Donald Trump's trade protection and "America First" policies as well as "Brexit" are all challenges for globalization and steps backward for humanity. Therefore, it is imperative that nations abandon a zero-sum-game mentality when it comes to traditional theories of sovereignty and establish an economic community based on mutual benefits and rewards sharing, in order to balance globalization with national sovereignty and to set up a sustainable global governance framework.

Against this backdrop, the Chinese government created the "Belt and Road Initiative," showing its responsibility and ability to lead the world toward a new globalization. The "Belt and Road Initiative," taking a community of shared future for all mankind as its base principle, calls for countries to accommodate each other's legitimate concerns when pursuing their own individual interests, to promote common development for everyone as part of their overall development plans, to build up a new type of global development partnership that is more equitable and balanced, to stick together in times of difficulty and to share rights and shoulder obligations, all in a bid to boost the common interests of humankind. The Silk Road spirit is about peaceful cooperation, openness and tolerance, mutual learning, and mutual benefit. The "Belt and Road Initiative" aims to pave a road to peace, prosperity, and openness.

The "Belt and Road Initiative" is about creating a community of shared future for all mankind. It upholds the principle of achieving shared growth through discussion and collaboration to boost the development of all involved countries. The initiative has received positive responses, with support from more than 100 countries over the past four years; more than 40 countries and global organizations have also signed collaboration agreements with China. Chinese companies have already invested over 50 billion US dollars in countries involved in the initiative, translating into a series of major projects that promote economic development and create plenty of jobs.

In conclusion, the "Belt and Road Initiative" is China's effort to lead a more in-depth globalization and further promote the opening-up and development of all nations. It comes at a time of anti-globalization sentiment and emerging extremism in many countries. The initiative in a practical manner complements the theoretical system of creating a community of shared future for all mankind. As the initiative continues to deepen implementation, the theory of a community of shared future will be more widely accepted, and the road for peaceful development, cooperation, and mutual benefit will widen as well.

AIIB: Reshape the International Financial Order, Seek Common Development

The financial system represents the core of a modern economic system and national competitiveness, and plays an important role in shaping the global political and social order. The current global financial system is led by the World Bank, supported by regional development banks, such as the AIIB, with developed countries playing a guiding role, including the United States, some West European countries and Japan, to name a few. This entrenched framework has severely deprived the vast number of developing countries, including China, of their powers of discourse and interests in the system.

After the global financial crisis in 2008, the global financial system and economy underwent fundamental changes. The world economic recession posed great challenges to developing countries in getting the necessary funding to expand infrastructure, which is of great significance to a country's economic promise. As such, the international financial system requires immediate reform. Asia, for example, arguably the most dynamic and promising region globally, constitutes one-third of global GDP and has 60% of the world's population. However, the lack of capital limited its development of infrastructure, such as railways, roads, bridges, ports, airports, and communications facilities. Against this backdrop, during visits to countries in Southeast Asia, Chinese leaders decided to set up AIIB, aiming to support infrastructure expansion in Asia.

The international community extensively supports the AIIB. It conforms to the requirements of many countries, and thus they are willing to join it. As the founder of the AIIB, China has become for the first time a rule-maker in global economic management. So the initiative not only improves the discourse power of developing countries, but also highlights China's willingness to take responsibility and provide public services for the international community. The AIIB was jointly built through extensive consultation to meet the interests of all members, which complies with the trend of international cooperation and openness. Under the AIIB's framework, all countries, no matter big or small, shall follow the bank's relationship code featuring equality and mutual benefit, cooperation, and win-win. This represents the spiritual wealth left behind by China during its peaceful rise.

Targeted Poverty Alleviation: Let All People Live in a Well-Off Society, Improve People's Sense of Gain Through Reforms

For thousands of years, poverty has been the great enemy of humanity. Poverty alleviation and common prosperity rank top among all development issues. Statistics show that currently, there are 700 million people living in extreme poverty, among whom, half live in sub-Saharan Africa and one-third in the South Asia. After the September 11 attacks in the United States, some international institutions pointed to poverty as a hotbed of terrorism, arguing that poverty alleviation is important to safeguard world peace. In September 2015, Transforming Our World: the 2030 Agenda for Sustainable Development was passed by all state leaders at UN headquarters. To eliminate extreme poverty in all forms is the Agenda's top priority.

"Poverty isn't socialism"! Over the 40 years of reform and opening-up, the Chinese government has always put poverty relief and development on the top of its agenda and it continues to make progress in that regard. Until now, over 700 million people have shaken off poverty, a feat for which the Chinese government has been given due credit. The World Bank commented that China's great achievements in poverty relief helped to significantly reduce the population of the world's poor. "People's aspiration for a good life is what we are fighting for"! Since 2013, the Chinese government has adopted targeted poverty alleviation measures. Within four years from 2012 to 2016, China's rural poor population was reduced by 13.91 million, raising the total population that has shaken off poverty in rural areas to 55.64 million. In the same period, the poverty rate was reduced from 10.2 to 4.5%. At this pace, by 2020 the rural poor population in China will have completely shaken off poverty. By then, extreme poverty will have entered the annals of history, with China reaching the goals formulated in the Agenda ten years ahead of schedule. Such is truly a miracle in the history of poverty alleviation.

Since ancient times, poverty has been a chronic disease in human civilization, and to alleviate it is a task of global proportions. It will be an unprecedented feat for China, the largest developing county in the world to alleviate poverty. China has formulated its "Chinese Solution," an example for the world to effectively alleviate poverty. China will make a great contribution to the world by reducing poverty and shrinking the wealth gap by building a well-off society in an all-round way and internationalize its experience.

The Battle for Environmental Protection Aims to Bring Back a Beautiful Landscape and Witness Green Development

Green development is the foundation for sound and sustainable development and an ecological civilization. Modern Western civilization is built through a predatory development mode, namely, treatment following pollution, whose worldwide spread posed serious problems for the resources and environment of the world. In 2008, the United Nations proposed that all countries should implement the Green New Deal.

The Chinese government attaches great importance to green development. It made protecting the environment and saving resources as basic state policy, proposed to build a resource-saving and environment-friendly society, and pioneered a path to a civilized development featuring production growth, affluent living and a sound ecosystem with the aim of shaping a new pattern of modernization and harmonious development between humans and nature. In the 5th Plenary Session of the 18th CPC Central Committee, the Chinese government put green development into the Proposal on Formulating the Thirteenth Five-year Plan. On the first day of 2015, the government enacted and implemented the amended Environmental Protection Law of the People's Republic of China, in which harsh punishments, such as daily penalties, suspension of business and administrative detention, and restrictions on and suspension of production were imposed for environment pollution. The law is an effective measure for pollution control and is known as the severest law for environmental protection in history. With heavy penalties in hand, the Ministry of Environmental Protection of China strengthened environmental protection and held public interviews with mayors of more than 20 cities on the matter. This unprecedented battle for environmental protection fully presents the responsibility of the Chinese government to ensure China's future and the people's well-being as well as its deep reflection on the need to advance human civilization.

"Lucid waters and lush mountains are invaluable assets." In recent years, green development and environmental protection have become China's name card to the world. China is now exploring a new development mode with its own concepts and actions to contribute to the creation of a more environmentally sound world. For example, in 2016 the sales volume of new energy automobiles in China was 50% of the total global sales volume, and the growth of renewable energy sources accounted for more than 40% of the world's total. The total installed capacity of hydroelectricity, wind power and photovoltaic power generation ranked first in the world. The international community can see that China now has become the lead engine in the transformation of global energy.

China, with one-fifth of the global population, is the second largest economy and the largest manufacturing state in the world. Green development drives the country's growth and China's green urbanization strategy aims to boost the country's economy. Green development as part of China's industrial transformation will definitely provide models and blueprints for the world economy. The World Wildlife Fund said in one report that if everyone enjoyed a lifestyle in line with American standards, then 4.5 earths would be needed. China, with its 1.3 billion people, has taken a different, more sustainable approach. It has pioneered a path of green development, one that greatly contributes to humanity and social progress.

To boost a green, low-carbon and sustainable development of the world, China is now doing its part to help other developing countries. China's South-South Cooperation Fund on Climate Change was launched and the Chinese team has started cooperation with 27 developing countries to help them improve management ability and financing capacity with regard to green development. At this critical juncture when the United States and other countries have withdrawn from the Paris Agreement and global climate protection is under severe stress, the Chinese government has solemnly promised the world in 2015 that CO_2 emissions per unit of GDP will fall by 60–65% and that the ratio of non-fossil energy to primary energy consumption will reach 20% or so by 2030. This means we are closer to the climate change goals of the Paris Agreement. It illustrates China's responsibility and undertaking as a rising power in its belief of a global community of common destiny.

Conclusion: China's Progress Offers a New Approach for the World

To sum up, the historic and cultural background of China's inclusive development provides new values for global development, and an economic platform where the fruits of growth are shared with everyone. China's contribution to the world is not only embodied in its development mode but also in the values of human civilization. Under the "peace and development" theme of the times, the state policy of reform and opening-up laid an internal and external foundation for the rise of China's economy. The economic wonder and political civilization that China has created has played an increasingly important role in transforming global economic governance and exerts a subtle influence on the future direction of global civilization. At the moment, an inclusive political and economic system is being built with integrity at its core; under the guidance of the Belt and Road Initiative, globalization has deepened and consists of a more open global economic system defined by mutual benefits and win-win results. A moderately prosperous society in an all-round way is being built through targeted poverty alleviation to enhance people's sense of gain and happiness and to achieve coordinated and comprehensive development. China's transformation takes environmental protection as its driving force. The values behind these great practices of China's development are of great significance in the context of globalization. The values represent the direction of China's advanced culture and are themselves a massive contribution to humanity's own common values. Moreover, these values are ready for the whole world to sublimate and shape toward creating a new world.

Therefore, there has been an urgent need to complete a development mode with Chinese characteristics. Since the 3rd Plenary Session of the 18th CPC Central Committee, there has been a need by the CPC Central Committee to improve in particular new concepts and a strategic layout pertaining to political civilization, economic development, social construction and governance, and the creation of an ecological civilization. The reason is to ensure that a development mode with Chinese characteristics has influence in the international community, and that contemporary China's outlook on development and the environment can guide and shape the common civilization for all mankind.

In a word, the "peace and development" theme of the times practiced through socialism with Chinese characteristics and the remarkable achievements witnessed through China's reform and opening-up have made it clear to the world that the eastern civilization is of great significance and has made a huge contribution to reshaping the common civilization for all mankind. At the root of eastern civilization is the belief that peace is most precious. There is a need to seek common ground and reserve differences and strive for universal harmony. The efforts that China has made to reshape the common civilization include its efforts to revise the original mode of globalization based on Western values led by traditional Western ideology. The efforts that China has made for peaceful coexistence and its commitment to a peaceful rise have broken the spell of the Clash of Civilizations advocated by Western scholars. Carrying on the initiative of a new globalization, contributing China's wisdom and solution for global governance, China will guide the win-win efforts of all countries and create a new global common civilization.

Zheng Zhijie

References

Bai Luxun. *Views on Political Development*. Tianjin: Tianjin People's Publishing House, 2009.

Berend, Ivan. Transformation and Structural Change: Central and East Europe's Post-Communist Adjustment in Historical Perspective. In *The Emerging New Regional Order in Central and East Europe*, Tadayuki Hayashi (ed.). Slavic Research Center, Hokkaido University.

Bruce. *Socialist Politics and Economy*. Beijing: China Social Sciences Press, 1981.

Byrd, William A., Qingsong Lin (eds.). *China's Rural Industry: Structure, Development, and Reform*. London: Oxford University Press, 1990.

Cai Fang. Breakthrough of Reform Under the Negative Growth of Working Population. *Economic Guide*, 2014 (2): 82–84.

Cai Hongbin. The Key to Avoid Falling into the Middle-Income Trap Is to Increase Social Mobility. *Business Observer*, 2011 (3).

Cao Ying, et al. Research on Social Psychology in the Transition Period. *China Social Psychology Research Report (2012–2013)*. Beijing: Social Sciences Literature Press, 2013.

Chen Kang, A.L. Hillman, Gu Qingyang. Fiscal Centralization and Behavior Change of Local Government: From Aid Hand to Grab Hand. *Economics* (quarterly), 2002 (4).

Chen Peng. The Legal Rights Struggle of Urban Owners in Contemporary China—An Analysis Framework on the Activities of Owners' Rights Protection. *Sociological Research*, 2010 (1).

Chen Xiuying. Economic Statistics of Soviet Union and Eastern European Countries. *World Economy*, 1991 (5).

Z. Zheng, *Middle-Income Trap*,
https://doi.org/10.1007/978-981-15-7401-6

Chen Xiwen. *A Study on County and Township Finance and Farmers' Income Increase in China*. Taiyuan: Shanxi Economic Press, 2003.
Cheng Li. The End of CCP's Resilient Authoritarianism? A Tripartite Assessment of Shifting Power in China. *The China Quarterly*, 2012, 9(211): 595–623.
China Reform Journal. Interview with Wu Jinglian: The Most Important Issue in China's Current Reform *China Reform*, 2011, 12.
[British] Dahrendorf. *Conflict in Modern Society*. Translated by Lin RongYuan. Beijing: China Social Sciences Press (China), 2000.
Du JianZheng, et al. Just World Belief: Concept, Measurement and Research Hotspot. *Psychological Progress*, 2007 (2).
Du Junfeng. Analysis of Social Trust of Urban Residents in 2010 Based on the Survey of Beijing, Shanghai and Guangzhou//Wang Junxiu, Yang Yiyin. *Research Report on China's Social Psychology* (2011). Beijing: Social Sciences Literature Press, 2011.
Edited by China Economic Prosperity Monthly. Digital China 30 Years: Statistical Data Collection of 30 Years of Reform and Opening Up. *China Economic Prosperity Monthly Supplement*, 2008.
Fang Hao. Interest Groups and "Middle-Income Trap": Reflection on Latin American Model. *Economic System Reform*, 2011 (5).
[US] fitter, Reese. *American Economic History*. Shenyang: Liaoning People's Publishing House, 1981.
Gao Wenjun, et al. Satisfaction of Several Important Needs: An Analysis of Social Psychology Based on Internet Survey Data//Wang Junxiu, Yang Yiyin. *China Social Psychology Research Report* (2012–2013). Beijing: Social Sciences Literature Press, 2013.
Gao Yong. Mobility of Social Barriers: An Investigation of Intergenerational Mobility in the Context of Structural Change. *Sociological Research*, 2009 (6).
Guo Qiyou, Lu Lijing. Transformation of the Driving Force of Sustained Economic Growth: International Experience and Reference of Consumption Led Growth. *Journal of Zhongshan University* (Social Science Edition), 2009 (2).
He Lingnan, et al. Research Report on Intuition of Internet Users in Guangdong//Wang Junxiu, Yang Yiyin. *Research Report on China's Social Psychology* (2014). Beijing: Social Sciences Literature Press, 2014.
[US] hedric Smith. *Russian*. Shanghai: Shanghai People's Publishing House, 1977.
Huang an Nian. *20th Century American History*. Shijiazhuang: Hebei People's Publishing House, 1989.
Huntington, Samuel. *Political Order in Changing Societies*. New Haven: Yale University Press, 1968.

Huntington, Samuel. *The Third Wave: The Tide of Democratization in the Late Twentieth Century*. Translated by Liu Junning. Shanghai: Shanghai Sanlian bookstore, 1998.

Jiang Shixue. Social Problems in Latin American Countries. *International Studies*, 2011 (1).

Jin Jun. From Realistic Conflict to Unrealistic Conflict. Chazuo, *Sociologist*, 2009 (4).

Jin Yan. Achievements, Experiences and Lessons of Poland's Economic Transition. *International Economic Review*, 2003 (2): 20–29.

Jin Yan. Some Problems in the Transformation of "Eastern Europe" in the Past 20 Years. *Beijing Daily*, 2011-08-29 (20).

Jin Yan. *From "Eastern Europe" to "New Europe": A Review of the 20-Year Transition*. Beijing: Peking University Press, 2011.

Jin Yan, Qin Hui. Czech Republic: After Equal Starting Point. *Reform*, 2001 (2): 112–127.

Jin Yan, Qin Hui. *Economic Transition and Social Justice*. Zhengzhou: Henan People's Publishing House, 2002.

Jin Yan, Qin Hui. *Ten Years of Vicissitudes: Economic and Social Transition and Ideological Change in Eastern European Countries*. Shanghai: Shanghai Sanlian bookstore, 2004.

Kennedy, Paul. *The Rise and Fall of the Great Powers: Economic Change and Military Conflict from 1500 to 2000*. New York, NY: Vantage, 1989.

Kharas, Homi, Geoffrey Gertz. 2010. "The New Global Middle Class: A Cross Over from West to East". In *China's Emerging Middle Class: Beyond Economic Transformation*, Cheng Li (ed.), Chapter 2. Brookings Institution Press.

Knell, M., C. Rider. *Socialist Economies in Transition: Appraisals of the Market Mechanism*. Aldershot: Edward Elgar Publishing Limited, 1992.

[Hun] kolner. *Economics of Shortage*. Beijing: Economic Science Press, 1986.

[Hun] Kornai. *Socialist System—Communist Political Economy*. Beijing: Central Compilation and Translation Press, 2007.

Li Qiang. "T-Shaped" Social Structure and "Structural Tension". *Sociological Research*, 2005 (2).

Li Qiang. A Social Structure Shaped Like the Chinese Character "土" Is Forming in China. *Beijing Daily*, 2015-05-25.

Li Xin. Understanding of Two Economic Transformations in Russia. *Russian Journal*, 2014 (1): 34–47.

Li Zhenjing, et al. *Development Reform and Public Opinion Basis: A Survey of the Reflection of Urban Residents on Development Reform in China*. Beijing: China Finance and Economy Press, 2015.

Lin Justin Yifu, Liu Zhiqiang. Fiscal Decentralization and Economic Growth in China. *Economic Development and Cultural Change*, 2000 (49): 1–21.

Liu Xuan, et al. 2012 Analysis Report on Social Psychology of Internet Rights Protection Public Opinion Events//Wang Junxiu, Yang Yiyin. *China Social Psychology Research Report* (2012–2013). Beijing: Social Sciences Literature Press, 2013.

Liu Xuyi, Yang Shengmao. *The Third Volume of American General History: American Civil War and the Gilded Age*. Beijing: People's Publishing House, 2008.

Liu Xuyi, Yang Shengmao. *The Rise and Expansion of the Fourth Volume of General History of the United States*. Beijing: People's Publishing House, 2008.

Luo Zhiru, Li Yining. *British Economy in the 20th Century: A Study of British Diseases*. Shanghai: Commercial Press, 2013.

Maddison, Angus. *The World Economy: Historical Statistics*. Paris: OECD Publishing, 2003.

Mills, C. Wright. *The New Men of Power: America's Labor Leaders*. Urbana, IL: University of Illinois Press, 1948.

Oi, Jean C. Fiscal Reform and the Economic Foundations of Local State Corporatism in China. *World Politics*, 1992, 45(1) (Oct.): 99–126.

Oi, Jean C. *Rural China Takes Off: The Institutional Foundations of Economic Reform*. Berkeley, CA: University of California Press, 1999.

Olson, Mancur. *Rise and Fall of the State: Economic Growth, Stagflation and Social Rigidity*. Shanghai: Shanghai Century Publishing Group, 2007.

Peng Qinghua. Study on the Change Track of Consumption Rate Across the "Middle-Income Trap"—Based on the Inspiration of Some Countries (Regions) in East Asia and Latin America. *Journal of Lanzhou Business School*, 2014 (4).

Qian Nali. *Development Pattern (1950–1970)*. Beijing: Economic Science Press, 1988.

Qin Jia, Li Jianmin. Population Age Structure, Employment Level and the Middle-Income Trap: An Empirical Analysis Based on 29 Countries and Regions. *China Population Science*, 2014 (2).

Qu Jingdong. Possession, Management and Governance: A Triple Concept Analysis of Township Enterprise. *Society*, 2013 (1) (2).

Rao Yinsha, et al. Survey Report on Social Trust of Urban Residents. *China Social Psychology Research Report (2012–2013)*. Beijing: Social Sciences Literature Press, 2013.

Rao Yinsha, et al. 2013 Survey Report on Social Trust of Residents in Eight Major Cities in China//Wang Junxiu, Yang Yiyin. *Research Report on China's Social Psychology* (2014). Beijing: Social Sciences Literature Press, 2014.

Ren Jiantao. The Destiny of Socialist Country Reform. *21st Century*, 2012 (10).

Ru Xin, et al. *Analysis and Prediction of China's Social Situation in 2009*. Beijing: Social Sciences Literature Press, 2009.

Sun Liping. National Autonomy in the Process of Transition to Market Economy. *Strategy and Management*, 1996 (4).

Sun Liping. Sociological Analysis of Insufficient Domestic Demand. *Journal of China Youth Political College*, 2000 (6).

Sun Liping. *Fracture: Chinese Society Since 1990s*. Beijing: China Social Sciences Literature Press, 2003.

Sun Liping. How Roosevelt Solved the Great Depression in the 1930s. *China Reform*, 2009 (7).

Sun Liping. Talk About China's Entering the Era of Durable Consumer Goods Again. *Economic Observer*, 2010-07-19.

Sun Liping, et al. Institutionalization of Interest Expression for Long-Term Social Stability. *Leaders*, 2010 (4) (general issue 33).

Sun Liping, et al. "Middle-Income Trap" or "Transformation Trap"? *open era*, 2012 (3).

Sun Xiulin, Zhou Feizhou. Land Finance and Tax Sharing: An Empirical Explanation. *China Social Sciences*, 2013 (4).

Szelenyi, Ivan. Social Inequalities Under State Redistributive Economies. *International Journal of Comparative Sociology*, 1978 (1): 61–87.

Szelenyi, Ivan. Eastern Europe in an Epoch of Transition: Toward a Socialist Mixed Economy? In *Remaking the Economic Institutions of Socialism: China and Eastern Europe* (1989): 208–232.

Tian Chunsheng. "Insider Control" and Interest Groups: An Empirical Analysis of Corporate Governance Structure in China and Russia. *Comparison of Economic and Social Systems*, 2002 (5): 18–25.

Wang Chunlei. Decline of Income Share in the Residential Sector: Cause Analysis and Fiscal and Tax Policy Orientation—Analysis Based on the Physical Transaction Part of the Capital Flow Statement (1992–2009). *Tax Research*, 2013 (1).

Wang Junxiu. Pay Attention to People's Dignity and Happiness, Promote Social Justice and Harmony—2010–2011. *China Social Psychology Research Report*//Wang Junxiu, Yang Yiyin. *China Social Psychology Research Report* (2011). Beijing: Social Sciences Literature Press, 2011.

Wang Junxiu. Focusing on Social Emotions, Promoting Social Identity, and Building Social Consensus—2012–2013. *China Social Psychology Research Report*//Wang Junxiu, Yang Yiyin. *China Social Psychology Research Report* (2014). Beijing: Social Sciences Literature Press, 2013.

Wang Junxiu. Characteristics of Current Social Values and Reconstruction of Social Shared Values—2014. *China Social Psychology Research Report*//Wang Junxiu, Yang Yiyin. *China Social Psychology Research Report* (2014). Beijing: Social Sciences Literature Press, 2014.

Wang Xiaolu. Grey Income and National Income Distribution. *Comparison*, 2010, 48 (7).

Weitzman, Martin L., Xu Chenggang. Chinese Township Village Enterprises as Vaguely Defined Cooperatives. *Journal of Comparative Economics*, 1994, 18 (Apr.): 121–145.

Wen Zongyu. Fiscal and Tax Policies to Support Economic Transformation and Industrial Upgrading: From the Perspective of Low-Carbon Economy. *Local Finance Research*, 2010 (1).

[US] William Manchester. *Glory and Dream: A Record of the United States in the Twentieth Century*. Translated by Zhu Xie. Shanghai: Commercial Press, 1993.

Xie Yu, et al. *China's Livelihood Development Report 2014*. Beijing: Peking University Press, 2014.

Yan Kun, Zhang Licheng. Analysis of Financial Difficulties of Counties and Townships in China and Research on Countermeasures. *Reference for Economic Research*, 2003 (90).

Yang Ming, et al. Social Trust in Changing Society: Stock and Change—1990–2010. *Journal of Peking University* (Philosophy and Social Sciences Edition), 2011 (6).

Yang Yiyin, et al. *Research on Social Psychology in Contemporary China*. Beijing: Social Sciences Literature Press, 2013.

Yao Yang. Neutral Government: An Explanation of China's Economic Success in the Transition Period. *Economic Review*, 2009 (3).

Yu Hailong. The Gini Coefficient of National Resident Income in 2014 Is 0.469 [EB/OL]. Caixin.com, 2015-01-20.

Yueping. Industrial Structure Adjustment in the Region of Economic Transformation—An Investigation Report on Industrial Structure Adjustment in Germany and Hungary. *Macroeconomic Research*, 2000 (4): 59–63.

Zhai Xuewei. Trust and Risk Society: Western Theory and Chinese Issues. *Social Science Research*, 2008 (4).

Zhang Yan, Gong Liutang. Tax Sharing Reform, Fiscal Decentralization and China's Economic Growth. *Economics* (quarterly), 1998, 5 (1).

Zhang Yi. Chinese Social Status Acquisition, Class Inheritance and Intra Generational Mobility. *Sociological Research*, 2004 (4).

Zhang Youlun, Lu Jingsheng. *The History of American Workers' Movement*. Tianjin: Tianjin People's Publishing House, 1993.

Zhang Zhun, Zhou Mi, Zong Jianliang. Research on Corruption in the "Gilded Age" of the United States. *Productivity Research*, 2008 (15).

Zhao Deli. Investigation Report on the Social Justice Mentality of Residents in Heilongjiang Reclamation Area//Wang Junxiu, Yang Yiyin. *Research Report on China's Social Mentality* (2014). Beijing: Social Sciences Literature Press, 2014.

Zhao Zhaoxia. Research on Investment and Financing Mode of Chongqing Development. *Business Economy*, 2012 (5).

Zheng Hui, Li Lu. Intergenerational Transformation and Class Reproduction of Urban Elites in China. *Sociological Research*, 2009 (6).
Zheng Yongnian, et al. The Crisis of Social Trust in China. *Culture*, 2011 (2).
Zhou Feizhou. Ten Years of Tax Sharing System: System and Its Influence. *Chinese Social Sciences*, 2006 (6).
Zhou Feizhou. Making Money: Government and Farmers in Land Development and Transfer. *Sociological Research*, 2007.
Zhou Feizhou. Construction: Land Finance and Local Government Behavior. *Comparison of Economic and Social Systems*, 2010 (3): 77–89.
Zhou Feizhou. *Profit for Profit: Financial Relations and Local Government Behavior*. Shanghai: Shanghai Sanlian bookstore, 2012.
Zou Hengfu, Zhang Tao. Fiscal Decentralization, Public Spending, and Economic Growth in China. *Journal of Public Economics*, 1998 (67): 221–240.

The manufacturer's authorised representative in the EU is Springer Nature Customer Service Centre GmbH, Europaplatz 3, 69115 Heidelberg, Germany. If you have any concerns regarding our products, please contact ProductSafety@springernature.com

Printed and bound by CPI Group (UK) Ltd, Croydon, CR0 4YY
30/09/2026
02225327-0019